The *Iliad*

෨෨෨

The *Iliad*

Structure, Myth, and Meaning

BRUCE LOUDEN

THE JOHNS HOPKINS UNIVERSITY PRESS
Baltimore

·

© 2006 The Johns Hopkins University Press
All rights reserved. Published 2006
Printed in the United States of America on acid-free paper
2 4 6 8 9 7 5 3 1

The Johns Hopkins University Press
2715 North Charles Street
Baltimore, Maryland 21218-4363
www.press.jhu.edu

Library of Congress Cataloging-in-Publication Data
Louden, Bruce, 1954–
The Iliad : structure, myth, and meaning / Bruce Louden.
p. cm.
Includes bibliographical references and index.
ISBN 0-8018-8280-x (hardcover : alk. paper)
1. Homer. Iliad. 2. Epic poetry, Greek—History and criticism. 3. Achilles
(Greek mythology) in literature. 4. Trojan War—Literature and the war.
5. Rhetoric, Ancient. I. Title.
PA4037.L655 2006
884′.01—dc22
2005018075

A catalog record for this book is available from the British Library.

Contents

Acknowledgments

Sometime after having finished my previous study, *The Odyssey: Structure, Narration, and Meaning* (Baltimore: Johns Hopkins University Press, 1999), I was in the early stages of a book on Greek myth, when I realized that the techniques I had developed for analyzing the structure of the *Odyssey* could also be applied to the *Iliad*. Accordingly, the first four chapters of this book use the same notions and terms, a narrative pattern existing in three sequences (though one need not have read that book to follow the arguments in this study). But the last three chapters grew out of my exposure to Ugaritic myth, which came from reading Considine's "The Theme of Divine Wrath in Ancient East Mediterranean Literature" and M. L. West's *The East Face of Helicon: West Asiatic Elements in Greek Poetry and Myth*. From there I worked my way back to the studies of Cyrus Gordon, the dean of American Ugaritic scholars, and important works by Mark Smith and others on the interrelations of Ugaritic myth and the Old Testament.

In 2000, just as I began work on this book, I was fortunate to be a Summer Fellow at the Center for Hellenic Studies in Washington, D.C., where I wrote a draft of the third chapter. I thank the interim director Mary Depew, the incoming director Greg Nagy, and my colleagues there for their stimulating company and conversation. I paid a few visits to the Classics and Graduate libraries at the University of California at Berkeley, and thank those who helped facilitate my stays and my host on those occasions, Rob Dobbin, for his hospitality. Bruce Heiden and Greg Thalmann both read and commented on early drafts of the first two chapters. Robert Alter (who was also patient in fielding my questions about Old Testament narratives) did the same for an early draft of the fifth chapter. I thank these scholars for their help (though ask for their indulgence if I have retained any points with which they still disagree).

I gave earlier versions of parts of chapters 2, 3, 5, and 6 as papers at annual meetings of the Classical Association of the Middle West and South

(2000 in Knoxville, Tennessee; 2001 in Provo, Utah; 2002 in Austin, Texas; 2003 in Lexington, Kentucky; and 2005 in Madison, Wisconsin). I thank CAMWS for providing me with these valuable forums for testing my ideas, and the audiences for hearing me out and offering vital feedback. An earlier version of part of the third chapter appeared as an article, "Eurybates, Odysseus, and the Duals in Book 9 of the *Iliad*," in the *Colby Quarterly* 38 (2002): 62–76. I thank the editor, Hanna M. Roisman, for inviting me to be part of that all-Homer volume and for permission to repeat the argument here in revised form. I should also like to thank Allen Gleason for responding to my many Old Testament queries and Brian R. MacDonald for his great help as copy editor. Lastly, I wish to express my gratitude to the staff of the Inter-Library Loan Department of the University of Texas at El Paso, whose diligent efforts allowed me to pursue the unexpected turns my research sometimes took.

All translations of Homeric epic are my own. Translations of other ancient texts are as noted.

The *Iliad*

Introduction

Any analysis of structure in the *Iliad* is, at least in part, a study of repetition, since the epic exists almost entirely as a series of repetitive elements.[1] Words repeat as a group, lines repeat in groups and type-scenes recur; even interlocking sets of type-scenes and motifs repeat together. Such fundamental use of repetition in an ancient narrative suggests that the text descends from an oral tradition, in which repetitions are crucial for the comprehension of a listening audience as well as necessary techniques for a performing bard. Homeric criticism in much of the twentieth century attempted to demonstrate how the *Iliad* and *Odyssey* might be better understood as oral or oral-derived works (see Foley 1990: 5–8). The investigation of oral theory, however, led all too often to studies of very small units—a word or a phrase. Articles and chapters, even whole books have been written, and careers founded, on the study of a noun and adjective. Though pioneering early works such as Lord's *Singer of Tales* pointed the way to the study of much larger narrative units,[2] they largely proved the exception. Valuable studies have been made of type-scenes. Edwards and others, sometimes applying the insights of Arend, established the constituent elements of various type-scenes—arrivals, feasts, and the like. Reece uncovered all possible permutations of the Homeric hospitality scene. Fenik traced larger narrative strands, how one type-scene might interlock with another or, in some instances, with whole chains of motifs. The present study, influenced especially by the examples of Lord and Fenik (cf. Lowenstam 1993), pursues the larger interconnected narrative structures in the *Iliad*, arguing that a lengthy chain, an *extended narrative pattern*, which is repeated three times, in three *sequences*, underlies most of its plot.

There have been many previous studies of the *Iliad*'s structure, though none has proved completely persuasive (leaving more than enough room for this study). However, these previous studies have established a consensus that the poem has three movements, a conclusion with which I agree.

At least seven critics (Wade-Gery, Davison, Schadewalt, Taplin, Stanley, Heiden, and Schein) have presented arguments to this end.[3] But in spite of the consensus that the *Iliad* has three movements, there are significant differences of opinion on the beginning and ending of each movement,[4] and very different arguments underlying them. Some arguments are based on theories of performance, some on length of the three units, some on the form of the narrative. My analysis is not based on consideration of performance (though clearly performance factors must be responsible for helping to shape the current text), since our notions of performance are too conjectural to offer a sound basis for interpretation. Rather, I have carefully noted the text's larger series of repetitions, exploring how one part of the *Iliad* corresponds with another.

In determining which books constitute the three parts (1–7, 8–17, 18–24, which I refer to, respectively, as the initial, middle, and final sequences of the narrative pattern), my analysis confirms both Stanley's and Schein's, though my arguments for so doing are independent, being built on principles different from theirs. Significantly, three separate investigations have now arrived at the same divisions for the three parts. Schein (1997: 349) gives a quick overview of his understanding: "Generally speaking, the narrative of the *Iliad* consists of three parts or stages: Books 1–7, Books 8–17 . . . , and Books 18–24. These parts may correspond to or reflect units of oral performance/composition; structurally they are more important than the conventional division of the text into twenty-four books."

How does one part of the *Iliad* relate to another part? Why are there so many parallels between Diomedes' duels and various encounters in books 5–6 and those of Akhilleus in books 20–21? Central to the narrative pattern, in each of the three sequences, is an *aristeia* (see glossary) by the "best of the Akhaians" (see Nagy 1979: 26–41), a depiction of Hektor with his family, and a defeat of Hektor by the best of the Akhaians in a duel. The poem's hero, Akhilleus, is prominent at the beginning of each of the *Iliad*'s three sequences (books 1–2, 9–10, 18–19), but then, because of his quarrel with Agamemnon, he is largely offstage for much of the initial and middle sequences (books 4–7, and 8, 10–17). Instead, in all but the final sequence (books 18–24) he is replaced by a surrogate "best of the Akhaians," another champion who temporarily functions like Akhilleus, paralleling him in some ways. The initial sequence (books 1–7) first inserts Diomedes, who has an *aristeia* (books 4–6) that closely parallels the first parts of Akhilleus' eventual *aristeia* (books 20–22). But following the conclusion of Diomedes' *aristeia*, the initial sequence continues with Telamonian Aias as the best of the Akhaians (7.50, 2.768, 17.279–80, 13.324 ff) capable of defeating Hektor in a duel.

Why are there two heroes to replace Akhilleus in the initial sequence?

This is an example of bifurcation, a Homeric technique by which the functions of one key character are split into two separate figures who both parallel the key character.[5] Diomedes functions as the best of the Akhaians in terms of his *aristeia* and relations with the gods (with Athena in particular), but Aias functions as the best of the Akhaians who can defeat Hektor, the best of the Trojans. Akhilleus himself, in the final sequence, will participate in all twenty motifs composing the narrative pattern, whereas in the initial sequence, Diomedes will go through motifs 2–8, but Aias will then enact motifs 9–19.[6] The *Iliad* implies that both Diomedes and Aias should be seen as the best of the Akhaians in Akhilleus' absence (7.179), with the two together serving as a composite Akhilleus in the initial sequence. The middle sequence employs the same technique. Agamemnon and Patroklos together serve as a composite best of the Akhaians, but in rather different ways, for the middle sequence inverts the values that prevail in the initial and final sequences. In the middle sequence Hektor is triumphant and the Greeks are temporarily driven back. Consequently, the two *aristeiai*, Agamemnon's and Patroklos', both result in these best of the Akhaians being driven from battle, wounded. To a lesser extent, Menelaus also briefly serves as a best of the Akhaians, though his role is more symbolic and less martial (in his duel with Paris in book 3 and in the battle for Patroklos' body in book 17). The *Iliad* usually keeps these different "best of the Akhaians" separate, taking pains to keep Akhilleus apart from Diomedes and from Aias. The exceptions are the brothers Agamemnon and Menelaus and intimate friends Akhilleus and Patroklos; the latter are further bound because Patroklos' death, resulting from his attempt to be a best of the Akhaians, prompts Akhilleus to resume his own role as the same.

In its entirety, the narrative pattern is quite lengthy, making recognition of some of its parallels difficult. But because the *Iliad* itself implies a natural division of the narrative pattern into two parts, as noted above (with Akhilleus' prominence at the beginning of each sequence contrasting with his absence for much of the rest of the initial and middle sequences), I separate it into two sections. The first, which I call the *introductory pattern* (books 1–2, 9–10, and 18–19), focuses on Akhilleus' interactions with a problematic assembly. The second, which I call the *principal pattern*, depicts the best of the Akhaians in battle (books 4–7; 8, 11–17; 20–24). Chapter 1 analyzes the principal pattern that contains the more heroic motifs, *aristeia*, and duels. Chapter 2 analyzes book 3, which also serves as a natural division separating the introductory pattern (books 1–2) from the principal pattern (4–7). I argue that book 3 serves as an overture for the *Iliad*, introducing the key motifs of the narrative pattern. Chapter 3 then explores the middle sequence (books 8, 11–17), which functions as an inversion, or parody, of the heroic motifs seen in books 4–7 and 20–24. Chapter 4 concludes the first section by analyzing the introductory pattern (books 1–2, 9–10, 18–19), the problematic assembly.

Contemplating the narrative pattern is no mere exercise in formalism. Rather, once it is observed, the narrative pattern serves as a hermeneutic device for understanding and interpreting the *Iliad*. By virtue of its three parallel sequences, the narrative pattern supplies invaluable contexts for understanding problematic scenes and episodes. The parallels revealed by the narrative pattern offer significant evidence for considering such episodes as Helen on the wall (book 3), why the Greeks build their wall (book 7), the notoriously problematic dual forms (book 9), and why Hektor dies of a neck wound (book 22). The three sequences of the narrative pattern, through their repetitions, reveal that certain characters serve specific thematic functions, which the narrative pattern allows us to recover and delineate. Perhaps the clearest example of a character's thematic function is Telamonian Aias, who repeatedly serves as "the best of the Akhaians defeats Hektor." Similarly, Odysseus is closely involved with restoring order after a breach of discipline and serves this function thematically in the *Iliad*.

Through its three repetitions, the narrative pattern reveals a greater significance than is usually afforded to some relatively minor characters, such as the heralds, Eurybates and Talthybios, in the introductory pattern (books 1–2, 9–10, 18–19) and Idaios in the episodes when Priam leaves Troy (books 3, 7, 24). Comparative neglect of the roles played by heralds has hindered recognition of significant parallels, vital for addressing the problem of the duals in book 9, as discussed with the motifs in chapter 4 (5. *Agamemnon dispatches Odysseus to lead a delegation that includes two heralds to return a companion dear to Akhilleus 6. Akhilleus receives the delegation hospitably*). Among the Trojan characters, Antenor and Theano have suffered similar neglect.[7] Their roles become clearer through comparison with Priam and Hekabe.

The narrative pattern emphasizes the *Iliad*'s tendency to figure the Trojan side as comprising three elements: the Trojans themselves, the Dardanians, and the other allies, of whom the Lykians serve as the most prominent element.[8] The *Iliad* underscores this tripartite deployment in a recurring formula, "Trojans, and Lykians, and close-fighting Dardanians," Τρῶες καὶ Λύκιοι καὶ Δάρδανοι ἀγχιμαχηταί (8.173; 11.286; 13.150; 15.425, 486; 17.184), all instances in the middle sequence. Each group has a leader: Hektor for the Trojans, Aineias for the Dardanians, and Glaukos (or Sarpedon; cf. Asteropaios) for the Lykians. Consequently, in each sequence the narrative pattern systematically pits the best of the Akhaians against the leader of each of the three groups and is thus partly structured around this tripartite deployment of the Trojans.

The narrative pattern helps explain the presence of a particular detail that otherwise might seem out of place. Occasionally a motif works better, or makes more sense, in one sequence than in another, but it is present in all three sequences of the pattern because the composer has in mind the full narrative pattern, and the larger sweep and trajectory of the poem. The parallels between the three sequences also reveal the *Iliad*'s use of parody as a structural element. The middle sequence (books 8–17), for instance, tends to invert key motifs from the narrative pattern. Thus where the best of the Akhaians defeats Hektor in the initial and final sequences, near the end of the middle sequence Hektor slays Patroklos. Where the gods, but not Zeus, engage in violence with each other in the initial and final sequences, Hera defeats Zeus in the middle sequence. Paris, who has his greatest successes in the inverted middle sequence, is treated as a parodic figure throughout.

Why does the narrative pattern exist? It is the skeletal structure of the *Iliad*, a large-scale design that is the ultimate manifestation of epic's tendency toward thematic organization, or what Austin termed, "one vast and joyful paean to correspondence."[9] It is not, however, simply a static skeleton, but a vehicle that carries themes. The initial sequence states the central themes to be explored. The middle and final sequences restate these themes, though with variations, allowing the themes to gain strength through restatement and deeper significance through contrasts.[10] Such restatement is necessary and advantageous to both performer and audience. The existence of the narrative pattern supports the notion that the *Iliad* could have been performed by an oral poet.

A POEM AS RICH AND COMPLEX as the *Iliad* did not spring ex nihilo into the world, but must derive from, and have been strongly influenced by, preexisting traditions of myth, both the Greeks' own traditions and other peoples' with whom they had contact. Since we have no Greek myths earlier than Homeric epic,[11] we must turn to non-Greek traditions to establish earlier and contemporary contexts through which to interpret the *Iliad*.[12] I formerly believed that knowledge of comparative Indo-European materials was key to interpretation of Homeric epic,[13] and that Hittite and Indo-Iranian myths especially shed light on certain facets of the *Iliad* and the *Odyssey*. I am now convinced, and am supported by considerable scholarship,[14] that Homeric epic has far more in common with Near Eastern narrative traditions than with a putative inherited Indo-European tradition. Overemphasis on an assumed Indo-European background for Homeric epic has hindered recognition of how close the parallels are with Near Eastern myth, particularly with West Semitic cultures. Mondi (187) offers a reasoned assessment of the situation:

An overview of Greek myth in the light of the Orient strongly suggests that the world view that emerges from the earliest Greek literary monuments is already a blend of Indo-European mythic thought with elements subsequently derived from contact with the considerably more advanced cultures to the East and South. The result of this contact is a mythological system that, as Dumezil acknowledges, "escapes Indo-European categories" but lends itself well to interpretation in terms of the categories of Oriental myth.

Mondi is not talking specifically about Homeric epic but Greek myth in general, including Hesiod. In my view, when one turns specifically to Homeric epic the extent of parallels with Near Eastern myth is even greater. I argue, on the basis of the parallels adduced in chapters 5, 6, and 7, that Homeric epic learned its specific narrative vehicles from Near Eastern, especially West Semitic, cultures.

To establish why a Near Eastern context is relevant for the *Iliad*, we need first consider what an epic is, and how it could relate to older traditions of myth. Critical reception of the *Iliad* has oddly neglected to analyze or classify the subgenres of myth that compose its plot. Modern scholarship is typically content to classify the *Iliad* as "heroic myth" or—focusing on the very first word, *menos* (wrath)—to label it "a poem of wrath." I define epic *not* as a type of myth, such as "heroic myth," but rather as a *framework* that can contain within it almost any other kind of myth, but which emphasizes a heroic modality, a hero's close interaction with the gods, and explores mortality, what it means to have to die. The governing framework of the *Iliad* focuses on Akhilleus, his quarrel with Agamemnon and later his wrath against Hektor. But the *Iliad* has episodes of theomachy (gods fighting with each other), divine councils, even allusions to creation myth, all of which are standard motifs or mythic subgenres in earlier Near Eastern traditions. Other episodes feature assemblies, prophets, and heralds, again recurring figures in Near Eastern myth. The *Iliad* thus draws on types of myth that may have little or nothing to do with the designation "heroic" but are common in Near Eastern myth. In chapters 5 and 6, I classify the discrete types of myth that characterize the *Iliad*, defining fourteen specific subgenres of myth and adducing Near Eastern instances of each type. My classification does not aim at a complete accounting of every subgenre of myth in the *Iliad*. Rather, I have sought to balance two competing agendas, to explore subgenres that have a significant impact on the *Iliad*'s plot and that are clearly extant in Near Eastern myth.

Near Eastern parallels can establish a context for understanding the particular tendencies and rules of a given episode in the *Iliad*. Having determined through comparison with parallels in other myths what is typical or atypical in a given Iliadic scene, we have surer grounds for interpreting the significance of a given motif or subgenre of myth in the *Iliad*. Put another way, episodes, motifs, and themes in the *Iliad* become more intelligible when placed in a wider context of similar myths. A few episodes, regarded as problematic, are common subgenres of myth outside of the *Iliad*. Such episodes (e.g., Zeus' deceptive dream for Agamemnon in *Iliad* 2) become less problematic when considered in their broader context. Accordingly, in chapters 5–7, I break the *Iliad* down into more-specific components and place each of these in a Near Eastern context. *Gilgamesh*, the *Enuma Elish*, and other Mesopotamian texts, together with the less well-known Ugaritic myths, *Aqhat*, the *Baal Cycle*, and *Kirta*, and Old Testament (OT) myth, provide our context for interpreting the *Iliad*. The Ugaritic texts are crucial for two reasons. The Ugaritic divine economy offers the closest parallel to the *Iliad*'s divine economy (cf. Morris 1992: 79), with close counterparts for several figures, and instances of the same type-scenes featured in Homeric epic.

Ugaritic myths also provide an early glimpse (ca. 1400 B.C.E.) into the milieu out of which OT myth evolved. In the Old Testament, the Canaanites, and the Israelites themselves, are depicted worshiping the principal deities of Ugaritic myth, El, Asherah, Baal, and, implicitly, Anat. Because of its partial genesis from Ugaritic myth, and probably because of close contact with the Phoenicians (and Philistines), OT myth also offers surprisingly close comparanda for the same subgenres of myth found in the *Iliad* and *Odyssey*, particularly myths about prophets. I therefore turn with greatest frequency to these last two, Ugaritic and OT myth. In chapters 5 and 6, I adduce more parallels from OT myth than from any other Near Eastern tradition, and in chapter 7, I place the divine economy of the *Iliad* alongside that in Ugaritic myths. The selectivity the *Iliad* exercises in emphasizing one type of mythic vehicle over another is one of the best hermeneutic tools for eliciting meaning from it.

The Old Testament contains the same subgenres of myth that occur in both Homeric epics, but the OT does not frame and organize them all under a heroic rubric, as does Homeric epic.[15] Thus the *Odyssey*, for instance, largely revolves around theoxeny, the subgenre of myth in which a god, disguised as a traveler, tests the hospitality of mortals, the same subgenre that OT myth employs prominently in Genesis 18–19.[16] Theoxeny is not a heroic genre and, hence, not terribly suitable for epic. But the *Odyssey* makes theoxeny more heroic by having a mortal play the role normally assigned a god: Odysseus both tests hospitality and exacts the punishment on the impious who fail to be hospitable (see Louden 1999a: 22–23). When Menelaus wrestles a god and then receives a prophecy and blessing (*Od.* 4.388–570), he instantiates the same subgenre of myth as Jacob (Gen 32:24–30), who likewise wrestles God and receives a prophecy and blessing. But Homeric epic casts a warrior in this mythic subgenre, whereas the OT adapts the same type for a patriarch. In general, OT myth has less emphasis on heroic subgenres and more on patriarchal and prophetic mythic types, narratives centering on figures such as Abram, Jacob, Joseph, and Moses, on the one hand, and Elijah, Elishah, and Micaiah, on the other. But heroic myth does dominate several books of the OT, especially Joshua, Judges, 1 and 2 Samuel, and 1 and 2 Kings.

The *Iliad* has a sustained focus not only on various subgenres of heroic myth but especially on what might be thought of as the high style of heroic, *the great hero and his duels*, a style the Bible *does* use, though more sparingly than Homeric epic. In the OT duels are almost exclusively used of encounters with the Philistines (see de Vaux 127), the very people whom some think are related to Mycenaean Greeks.[17] In a further basic narrative difference, the OT presents most of its stories in a quick and simple style, what Lord would call unornamented form, whereas Homeric epic extends themes to greater length and depth, with fuller development. The two theoxenies in Genesis 18 and 19 are quite brief, whereas the *Odyssey* develops the same subgenre of myth to considerable length (see Louden 1999a: 95–99). Basic affinities have been overlooked between subgenres of myth in the *Iliad* and the OT. Examination of the parallels reveals not only that Greek myth shares specific subgenres of myth but that extended homologies exist between specific characters. For example, the *Iliad* has Agamemnon in the same subgenres of myth that the OT uses for Saul and Ahab, while the Homeric Athena is depicted in the same mythic subgenres as is the Ugaritic goddess Anat.

If I am correct that OT myth offers the most relevant comparanda for the *Iliad*, why has previous scholarship not engaged the two traditions more closely? Commentators have occasionally recognized some similarities between Greek and OT myth. Gordon (especially 1965b, 1967) particularly noted parallels between Homer, OT, and Ugaritic myth but rarely pursued them in detail. Burkert (1966: 103, n. 4) has commented on the exceptionally close parallels in sacrificial ritual: "It seems to be well established that . . . Semitic (Phoenician and Hebrew) sacrificial rites offer the closest parallel to Greek ritual. . . . It is one of the paradoxes of our profession that neither Nilsson nor Meuli, in their expositions of Greek sacrificial ritual, refer to the Old Testament, which contains the largest extant collection of ancient sacrificial rites."[18] J. P. Brown has issued his multivolume series, detailing all manner of specific parallels between ancient Greek and Israelite culture. But these are the exceptions.[19] Perhaps largely because of reasons of faith, a wall exists between the study of Greek and OT myth, resulting in almost complete segregation of the two disciplines. Since polytheistic Greek religion is no longer practiced, whereas Judaism and Christianity are dominant religions, the sacred narratives of the Bible are held to be "real" and to provide ethical models, whereas Greek myths are seen, by comparison, as false and even immoral. But however modern audiences may feel about them, Greek myths *are* sacred narratives, were thought to be the word of god, and were written in most of the same specific mythic subgenres as was the OT.

For the purposes of this book, I define myth as *a sacred, traditional narrative, which depicts the interrelations of mortals and gods, is especially concerned with defining what is moral behavior for a given culture, and passes on key information about that culture's institutions.*[20] By sacred I mean that myths are the "word of god" and invested with divine authority, as the *Iliad* signals in its first line, and as Hesiod demonstrates in the opening of the *Theogony*. By traditional I mean both that a myth probably has its genesis in an oral tradition and that it is not believed to be new, or original, but composed entirely out of commonly known, preexisting elements. I apply this same definition to all OT narratives discussed here as well—that they are myth, or sacred, traditional narratives. Thus, if a composer, such as an author of Ezekiel, describes a siege of a city that is known to have occurred but uses the techniques of myth to depict the siege, such as divine intervention or divine wrath, I classify the narrative as a myth. The OT regularly uses the techniques of myth to depict both historical figures, such as Sennacherib (whom we will see as a partial parallel for Agamemnon in chapter 5), and more mythical figures, such as Moses.

Myths are inherently concerned with moral instruction. I make the highly unfashionable argument that the *Iliad* is also intended as moral instruction. One reason modern audiences have difficulty seeing the *Iliad* or Greek myth as intended for moral instruction is the behavior of the gods. Van Erp Taalman Kip has written recently on the morality of the Homeric gods, and I take her position to represent a current consensus.[21] My own views, however, are virtually the exact opposite. In evaluating the Homeric gods she has no interest in placing them in an ancient context but analyzes them primarily according to late twentieth-century rhetoric. She seems unaware that the objections she raises could also be raised against Yahweh as he is depicted in OT myths. For instance, how could Athena, a god, lead, Pandaros on to his death (390–91)? This is immoral! Yet Yahweh does the same thing with Ahab in 1 Kings. I do not here defend the conduct of either Athena or Yahweh, but what might their parallel behavior tell us? Both cultures saw fit to depict their gods acting in such a manner. This suggests that Homeric and biblical depictions of divine behavior are not necessarily constructed to satisfy a late twentieth- or early twenty-first century moral perspective. To make sense of them, we need to consider what *was* regarded as acceptable divine behavior in the first millennium B.C.E.

Not only does Van Erp Taalman Kip gloss over the fact that moral standards shift, sometimes drastically, over millennia, but she does not take into account the thematic construction of the *Iliad*'s plot, that it gives a highly skewed presentation of the gods to mirror the strife among the mortals. Thus the verbal theomachy that opens book 4, the shocking threats to destroy cities, parallels the abuse Akhilleus and Agamemnon hurl at each other in the book 1 assembly. Do Akhilleus and Agamemnon kill each other, as they threaten to do so? No. Do Zeus and Hera swap the destruction of cities as they suggest? No. Van Erp Taalman Kip and other studies ignore the ancient perspective on the gods' sense of time. There is no indication, as she asserts, that Zeus ignores the claims Menelaus and Agamemnon make on punishing those who transgress hospitality because he does not immediately respond. The traditional ancient view of the gods' sense of time is stated by Agamemnon, when he remarks on the punishment that awaits Pandaros for violating the oaths:

> For if the Olympian has not immediately brought this to completion,
> eventually [ὀψὲ] he will, and they will pay a great price.
>
> (*Il.* 4.160–61)[22]

As Lefkowitz (151) notes, "Because the gods can take a longer view than short-lived mortals, they are content to wait to administer their justice and to postpone revenge even for several generations." In OT myth Yahweh often postpones punishment, as at 1 Kings 11:34 where Solomon participates in the worship of the goddess Ashtoreth. Yahweh decides to take the ten tribes of the kingdom away as punishment, but then waits until Solomon dies and takes them from his son, Rehoboam. Indeed, the whole notion of inherited guilt, central to OT myth, depends on divine punishment delayed much longer (e.g., Exod 20:5) than the *Iliad*'s gods take to cause the death of Pandaros, or Paris, or the destruction of Troy.

How are the gods *supposed* to behave in ancient myth? Clearly not according to human standards. Zeus is married to his sister. Does this legitimize incest among mortals? No, since the Greeks had a strong taboo against incest. Is it immoral that Zeus is married to his sister? Other than a few philosophers, most ancient Greeks apparently did not think so. What, then, does it show us? There is a separate morality for gods, both those of the *Iliad* and of OT myth. Mortals are to do as the gods say, not as they do. One is not supposed to try to be like Yahweh, which would be dangerous arrogance, but do what he commands. OT myths frequently depict Yahweh performing acts troubling by contemporary standards: he destroys the innocent along with the guilty (Gen 19), commands the Israelites to slaughter all the non-combatants in a city, including women and children (1 Sam 15:3), deceives Ahab to lead him to his death (1 Kings 22), notes the circumstances under which it is permissible for a father to sell his daughter into slavery (Exod 21:7), and demands the death even of a family member who would lead someone to practice a different religion (Deut 13). OT myths repeatedly depict owning slaves or a man having sex with his female slaves as acceptable behavior, even mandated by Yahweh. If not for such behavior on the part of Abram and others, there would be no OT. These examples (and many others like them) show both that the gods' behavior is not to be understood by human moral standards, whether the god is Yahweh or Zeus, and that what is regarded as acceptable in an ancient myth may be considerably at variance with more recent moral codes.

The *Iliad* emphasizes moral behavior in mortals in the thematic depiction of the Trojans' failings and in Akhilleus' behavior when not fighting (in books 1, 9, and 23–24). Four subgenres of myth, as defined in chapter 5, involve Akhilleus and focus on ethics: *2b. The hero intervenes to check the god-sent plague; 4. The king, who has offended god, quarrels with his greatest warrior (or eris); 6a. The hero's personal relationship with the deity;* and *7. The hero as the ethical man who has unjustly suffered wrongs.* The *Iliad* offers a sustained depiction of past and present misconduct and recklessness by various Trojans. From Laomedon, who committed wrongs against the gods, to Paris, who brought an alien woman and stolen goods among his people, to present wrongdoing in Pandaros, Dolon, and even Hektor, the *Iliad* depicts precisely the kinds of wrongdoing that provoke divine wrath and punishment in OT myths.

Although there is considerable overlap between Homeric and OT myth, key differences remain. One with significant ramifications for the *Iliad* is the autonomy that gods such as Athena and Hera have; in monotheistic myths deriving from earlier polytheistic cultures, such beings would be angels, barely, if at all, individuated, and performing the behests of the principal god rather than pursuing their own initiatives. The *Iliad* emphasizes this difference to an unusual degree (much more than the *Odyssey*) primarily because epics are constructed in highly thematic manner, another manifestation of their repetitive structure. Here the gods have strifes among themselves because they are paralleling the two great strifes around which the *Iliad* is constructed: the war between the Greeks and the Trojans, and the quarrel between Akhilleus and Agamemnon. Polytheism and monotheism are not, I suggest, the mutually exclusive opposites that they are usually thought to be, but rather occupy overlapping positions on a spectrum of possibilities. Polytheism virtually always has the seed of a possible monotheism at its core in a sky father figure who is quite similar in type to the Yahweh of OT monotheism. Monotheism, on the other hand, usually retains features from an earlier polytheistic tradition, including other immortal beings and divine councils (Job 1:6, 2:1).

For considerations of length (and the complexity of the problem), I do not detail a theory asserting *why* the *Iliad* has such close parallels with Near Eastern and especially OT myth. But I briefly sample a variety of views to illustrate how wide open the debate has become. Burkert's (1992: 1–8) theory of an orientalizing period in Greece is well known, that Greek culture from 750–650 B.C.E. was particularly receptive to influences from Near Eastern cultures. To support this view Burkert notes, among other evidence, close parallels between a passage in book 15 of the *Iliad* and the *Enuma Elish*,[23] and passages in book 14 of the *Iliad* and the *Atrahasis*.[24] Although the connections he draws are valuable, and the parallels adduced between the myths help us understand the *Iliad*, despite his assertions no direct contact can be demonstrated. Even close parallels, unless they are significantly more extensive than these, do not demonstrate the specific influence or allusion that Burkert claims. While they evidence contact between the Greeks and the Near East, they do not permit us to determine what kind it was.

Yadin (386–87) makes an opposite argument, that some parallels between the *Iliad* and OT myth exist because OT authors are aware of Greek myth and specifically allude to the *Iliad*. In a close analysis of correspondences between David's duel with Goliath and Hektor's with Aias in *Iliad* 7, Yadin sees Near Eastern allusion and response to Homeric epic: "The parallels to Homeric epic are no . . . evidence of the antiquity of these elements, but of the familiarity of the redactor with Greek culture and, more specifically, with its 'national' literature. Indeed the battle of David and Goliath is best read with the *Iliad* as its intertext." While I am intrigued by the argument, there are so many close parallels between the *Iliad* and the OT, not just these two contexts, that we need to be hesitant in forming a theory that focuses on only one set of correspondences. Yadin's arguments will not work as well for some of the parallels collected in this study, between Ahab and Agamemnon, for instance, or between Elijah and Kalkhas.

The interactions between the *Iliad* and Near Eastern myth must have been quite complex, and accordingly no one model that has so far been proposed fully accounts for the variety of different subgenres linking Greek and Near Eastern myth. It seems highly likely that some form of the people we think of as the Phoenicians may have served to mediate between Greek and Israelite culture, an intermediary possibly conveying myths and traditions in both directions. The possibility remains that some forms of contact may be quite ancient, as the archaeological data demonstrates (though text-based scholarship in both traditions, Homer and OT, is currently concerned with moving dates up to more recent times), and possibly involve the Philistines as a segment of Mycenaean Greek culture. If correct, this suggests the cultures could have had direct contact and could have exerted influence upon each other. David, who is probably the OT persona most like a character from Homeric epic, can be seen as a symbol of such contact.

At present I am inclined to agree with a middle position, something along the lines of what West (1997: 624) suggests: "The Greek poets' debts to Near Eastern tradition . . . presuppose situations in which Greeks and peoples of the East lived side by side for extended periods and communicated fluently in a shared language." Phoenician culture, whether on the mainland, on Cyprus, or even in Greece, seems the likeliest candidate. West notes times and places in which such contact could easily have occurred. The high Mycenaean period (1450–1200) "had commercial connections with Ugarit and Cyprus" (West 1997: 625). The subsequent period (1200–1050) saw substantial Greek colonization of Cyprus, site of the joint temple to Athena/Anat.

◈◈◈

CHAPTER ONE

The Principal Narrative Pattern

In analyzing the principal narrative pattern, the string of connected motifs that underlies books 4–7 and 20–24,[1] I especially note parallels between the *aristeiai* of Diomedes and Akhilleus, and Hektor's duels with Aias and Akhilleus. The precise order of the narrative pattern's motifs is not completely fixed in the different sequences—for example, Diomedes and Aias go through the motifs in slightly different order than does Akhilleus.[2] Such variance, or flexibility, highlights differences between the characters, conferring greater emphasis or drama on a specific occasion, and increasing the pathos or irony of the moment, by temporarily assigning higher priority to local considerations. The sequences vary in order largely because they have different heroes: while Diomedes and Aias closely parallel Akhilleus in some respects, in other respects Akhilleus is unique. For instance, the duel between Hektor and Akhilleus is largely built out of motifs found in the duel between Hektor and Aias; however, Akhilleus is superior to Aias, and the occasion is more pivotal and is marked by greater divine intervention. Perhaps the most significant difference between the initial and final sequences is Akhilleus' wrath, which prompts him to excessive measures; because Diomedes lacks such motivation, greater self-control characterizes his *aristeia*.

Diomedes serves as the fuller parallel. His *aristeia* closely resembles Akhilleus' but lacks a conflict with Hektor. Aias parallels Akhilleus in his combat with Hektor and his possession of an exceptional shield (and, outside of the *Iliad*, in dying at Troy); he is twice designated best of the Akhaians after Akhilleus (*Il.* 2.768–69; *Od.* 11.550–51).[3] Diomedes goes through motifs 1–8, Aias following with motifs 10–18. Akhilleus goes through all twenty. While Akhilleus is offstage, Aias is thematically "the Akhaian who defeats Hektor," defeating him repeatedly (7.312; 14.409 ff; 17.126 ff, 700 ff). This is his key thematic function in the *Iliad*. Even when Hektor briefly prevails, he is not able to wound Aias (16.101–24). Janko (1992: 330) notes, "Hektor's failure to harm Aias is telling, like his defeat by him while Zeus sleeps at

14.402ff." Homeric epic also displays this same tendency—the splitting up between two characters (Diomedes and Aias) functions elsewhere found in one (Akhilleus)—in the *Odyssey*'s bifurcation of functions between Nausikaa and Arete that are found singly in Penelope and Kirke (Louden 1999a: 7, 138 n. 7). Because of their tendency to parallel distinct functions of Akhilleus, Diomedes and Aias rarely appear together in the poem. In book 11, for instance, Diomedes is wounded early, while Aias remains active when Hektor becomes increasingly prominent. Aias continues as Hektor's principal antagonist during the middle sequence (books 8–17). But in the games in book 23, the poem diverges from its usual tendency of keeping them separate and has Diomedes meet Aias in the armed duel.

We proceed, then, to delineate the extended narrative pattern as it occurs in books 4–7 and 20–24 (chapter 2 deals with book 3; chapter 3, books 8, 11–16; and chapter 4, books 1–2, 9–10, and 18–19). The motifs we pursue are listed below. The list of motifs from books 4–7 and 20–24 is partial, including only acts that have strong counterparts in at least two of the three sequences (though many omitted motifs are discussed in chapters 5–7).

1. *When theomachian frictions surface at a divine council, Zeus dictates the permissible level of divine intervention.*
2. *The best of the Akhaians arms himself as prelude to his* aristeia.
3. *A god places* μένος, *"battle might," in him as he goes face the Trojans.*
4. *Thus inspired, he begins an* aristeia, *through which he will earn fame.*
5. *He encounters the second greatest warrior on the Trojan side, Aineias, leader of the Dardanians, in a duel.*
   a. *Aineias consults with an archer, "Lykaon."*
   b. *Aineias' descent from Aphrodite is emphasized, as well as his ancestors (Tros and Ganymede are mentioned only here) and his illustrious horses.*
   c. *A corresponding consultation takes place on the Greek side.*
   d. *Challenging speeches are the final prelude to combat.*
   e. *The duel includes the same* khermadion *("boulder") sequence.*
   f. *The duel is deprived of a climax when a deity intervenes through a pivotal contrafactual, carrying off Aineias.*
6. *The best of the Akhaians' exploits are accompanied by a Greek-partisan god's defeat of a Trojan-partisan god.*
7. *The best of the Akhaians three times attacks Apollo, while he protects a Trojan hero, but gives way on his fourth attempt.*
   a. *He is called* δαίμονι ἶσος *("like a god") only during his* aristeia *and, with one exception, only when he attacks a Trojan-partisan deity.*
   b. *The best of the Akhaians fights and wounds another Trojan-partisan god, causing the wounded deity to ask another god for help.*

8. The best of the Akhaians duels with and defeats a great Lykian warrior.

9. The greatest Trojan warrior, Hektor, meets his mother, sister-in-law, and his wife, Andromakhe, near the Skaian Gates, and the women, especially Andromakhe, who predicts his death and worries about their son, ask him not to return to battle.

a. Andromakhe and Helen refer to Hektor as their brother.

b. His fear of shame counters their attempts at persuasion.

10. As a result of the plotting of Apollo and Athena, the best of the Akhaians now encounters Hektor in a duel to decide the whole war.

a. Hektor is persuaded by his brother to battle the best of the Akhaians.

11. Panic seizes Hektor on first seeing the best of the Akhaians, prompting his retreat, which normally would be back into the army.

12. Hektor asks the best of the Akhaians to swear an oath to return the corpse of the defeated to his companions, undefiled, but deprived of its armor.

13. The best of the Akhaians has a unique shield.

14. When Hektor strikes the best of the Akhaians, his spear is driven back by the special shield.

15. Hektor's imminent defeat is emphasized by a pivotal contrafactual, which demonstrates his dependence on Apollo.

16. In the duel's climax, the best of the Akhaians wounds Hektor in the neck with his spear.

17. Hektor exchanges armor with the best of the Akhaians.

18. The best of the Akhaians is honored for his victory (by his commander in chief) at a feast.

19. Priam, disturbed over his son's mortal combat, drives out to the middle of the battlefield to propose a truce to care for the dead.

20. Both sides mourn their dead and construct a tomb.

1. *When theomachian frictions surface at a divine council, Zeus dictates the permissible level of divine intervention*

In heroic myth, such as the *Iliad*, theomachy often parallels, elevates, and serves as a fanfare for the momentous deeds to come on the mortal plane in the *aristeia* of the best of the Akhaians (Richardson 10, 52; Frazer 56). After Menelaos defeats Paris in their duel (3.373; analyzed in chapter 2), book 4 opens with a divine council. Zeus begins the council by intentionally provoking Hera:

> At once the son of Kronos tried to rile [ἐρεθιζέμεν] Hera
> speaking provocatively with taunting words.
>
> (4.5–6)

Slatkin (14) argues that the *Iliad* uses Zeus' epithet "the son of Kronos" to evoke his role in the ancient theomachy between the Olympians and the Titans. This council thus suggests potential theomachian conflicts already present, if only at the verbal level. Zeus here specifically provokes Athena and Hera against Aphrodite (4.7–12), a thematic parallel for Athena's later attack on Aphrodite (21.422 ff). After fractious exchanges with Hera, Zeus nonetheless adopts her suggestion of manipulating events so that the Trojans will break the truce sworn in book 3 (discussed in chapter 6). Because no Trojan-partisan deity speaks up here, the council presents only a pro-Greek perspective, dominated by Hera. The resultant breaking of the truce by Pandaros will quickly lead to Diomedes' *aristeia,* by way of Agamemnon's marshaling of the Akhaians (4.223–418), in which his stinging comments to Diomedes (4.365–400) provide impetus for Diomedes' explosive deeds.

Shortly before Diomedes' *aristeia,* the poem first introduces the motif of a problematic stripping of armor from a corpse. When Elephenor attempts to strip Ekhepolos' corpse, Agenor then slays Elephenor, too busy obtaining booty to defend himself (4.457–69). The poem subtly introduces the motif that will loom large in Akhilleus' return to battle: inappropriate seizure of a foe's armor. In an additional parallel between Diomedes and Akhilleus, in their motivations to fight immediately before their *aristeiai,* both have been verbally abused by Agamemnon; both enter battle shortly after the poem's first and last instances of problematic stripping of armor from a corpse.

The divine council in book 20, which, like that in *Iliad* 4, precedes the coming *aristeia,* has no verbal conflicts. The gods are more than ready to oppose each other because of earlier frictions, developed in book 5 and elsewhere. The council in book 20 is the biggest (in number of deities present, as enumerated in 20.7–9) in Homeric epic. In both *aristeiai,* the gods themselves intervene and fight alongside the mortal heroes. The *Iliad* uses the same vocabulary to articulate this at similar points in the two *aristeiai* (ἀρηγό-νες, 4.7; ἀρήγεθ᾽, 20.25). Among several theomachian encounters, the *Iliad* intends the combat between Athena and Ares as a specific parallel to the combat between the best of the Akhaians and his Trojan opponents, especially Hektor (discussed in chapter 6, subgenre 11c).

◈

2. The best of the Achaians arms himself as prelude to his aristeia

Diomedes' *aristeia* lacks a full arming scene, because it would be superfluous so soon after the entire army has been depicted in a general arming scene earlier the same day (2.382–85 ff). But considerable emphasis is placed on the gleam emanating from Diomedes' armor (5.4–7), which can be taken as a substitute (Edwards 1987: 79), or metonymy, for a fuller arming type-scene. The armor's gleam, as Krischer (1971: 13–89; cf. Schein 1985: 80) has shown, is particularly significant for indicating the subsequent success of a hero as he begins an *aristeia*. While Akhilleus is clearly the best of the Akhaians in terms of the overall myth of the Trojan War, Diomedes is explicitly so designated a number of times (Τυδεΐδης ὄχ' ἄριστος at 5.103, 414; cf. 5.839, 6.98, 23.357). The shared terminology helps designate his *aristeia* as thematically parallel to that of Akhilleus and implicitly delineates his status as a stand-in for the son of Thetis.[4]

Akhilleus' arming scene is uniquely developed beyond the usual instantiations of this typical motif.[5] The *Iliad* bifurcates the arming scene into Hephaistos' fashioning of the armor (18.478–616),[6] and, the more usual passage, Akhilleus' donning the armor (19.369–91). Here, unique attention is placed on the spear (19.387–91) with which he will slay Hektor (below, motif 16). This second passage comes after a general arming of the Greeks (19.351–52), which corresponds to that in books 2 and 4.

∽

3. A god places μένος, *"battle might," in him as he goes to face the Trojans*

The motif of a deity giving special force to the hero before combat is a traditional one in ancient Near Eastern myth.[7] Such proximity and aid to the hero signals his divine favor. While a number of such terms are used in the *Iliad* (cf. θάρσος, "daring," and κράτος, "power"), thematically *menos* appears to be the most significant. Athena is the deity whose aid secures success for the hero, her aid to Diomedes and Akhilleus being particularly key (Athena's relation to the hero is discussed in chapter 7). The motif had been prefigured shortly before in Agamemnon's account of the aid Athena gave to Diomedes' father, Tydeus (4.390), and is repeated soon after when Athena, to whom the wounded Diomedes prays for aid, reminds him that she has placed *menos* in him, just as she had done for his father (5.125). Athena's doing so in the first two lines of book 5 launches Diomedes' *aristeia* (Ἔνθ' αὖ Τυδεΐδη Διομήδεϊ Παλλὰς Ἀθήνη / δῶκε μένος καὶ θάρσος). Her aid will reach a climax when Diomedes successfully assaults two Olympian gods, Aphrodite and Ares (below, motif 6).

In a more complex presentation the motif is doubled to initiate Akhilleus' *aristeia*. First, Thetis places *menos* in her son after having delivered the new armor to him (19.37). Akhilleus subsequently refers to himself as full of *menos* (19.202). Athena, who in the poem's opening scenes prevents Akhilleus from acting on his *menos* (ἦλθον ἐγὼ παύσουσα τὸ σὸν μένος, 1.207), then comes to instill nectar and ambrosia into Akhilleus (19.347–54; cf. the angel appearing to Elijah, 1 Kings 19), forming a doublet with Thetis' earlier action. A third such scene is also hinted at with Poseidon at 20.121 (κράτος).

᠆

4. Thus inspired, he begins an aristeia, *through which he will earn fame*

The *Iliad* distinguishes the two *aristeiai* of Diomedes and Akhilleus through a formula used sparingly in the poem and absent from all other *aristeiai*. The narrator ascribes Athena's motivation in prompting Diomedes to greatness as "that he might . . . earn noble fame" (ἵν᾽ . . . κλέος ἐσθλὸν ἄροιτο, 5.2–3). Since a chief concern of the *Iliad* is the *kleos*, or fame of Akhilleus, the narrator in this exclusive use draws close parallels between the two characters. Diomedes repeats the formulation as he encourages Sthenelos in their pursuit of Aineias' horses, "we would earn noble fame" (ἀροίμεθά κε κλέος ἐσθλόν, 5.273). Akhilleus utters the same formula of himself, at that precise moment when he resolves to return to battle, "Now I would earn noble glory" (νῦν δὲ κλέος ἐσθλὸν ἀροίμην, 18.121). The formula (noun, "glory," adjective, "noble," both as object of the verb ἄρνυμαι, in the optative mood) is the same in all three passages. This appears to be Homeric epic's specific formula for a successful *aristeia,* as opposed to the less successful *aristeiai* of Agamemnon and Patroklos (discussed in chapter 3).

᠆

5. He encounters the second greatest warrior on the Trojan side, Aineias, leader of the Dardanians, in a duel

The importance of the encounters with Aineias is signaled by their considerable length, in accord with Austin's formulation, "Where the drama is most intense the digressions are the longest and the details the fullest" (Austin 1966: 306; cf. Edwards 1987: 4). Aineias' important scenes look ahead to his special role as the Trojan hero who will survive the war (discussed in chapter 6). Although some parallels between the two episodes have long been noted, others have escaped notice because of the slightly varied sequence in the two contexts and the lack of exact verbal correspondences.[8]

Two tendencies thematically distinguish Aineias' encounter with Akhilleus from that with Diomedes. In Akhilleus' sequence, the gods have a larger function, several times playing roles taken by mortals in Diomedes' sequence. Second, the rest of the Greeks refrain from taking part while Akhilleus is active, increasing the focus on the protagonist.[9] Consequently, Akhilleus has no consultation scenes with mortals, as does Diomedes, nor does his *aristeia* contain scenes of other Greeks involved in duels, as does Diomedes' (5.37–84). The first of the six principle correspondences is presented here in five parts:

Aineias consults with an archer, "Lykaon,"
which consultation contains the rhetorical expression "where now are . . . ,"
in which one Trojan bids the other to pray for success against the Akhaian hero and mentions a prior encounter,
complaining that a god always aids him.

a. Aineias consults with an archer, "Lykaon"

In book 20 the encounter with Aineias is the first episode of Akhilleus' *aristeia*, after the brief startup of the theomachy (20.4–75). Diomedes' *aristeia*, as the first in the poem, is burdened with a few additional responsibilities, which help establish the generic form of an *aristeia*. But after a few very brief scenes (the first of which is discussed below), including being wounded by Pandaros (5.95–130), the first substantial episode is his encounter with Aineias (5.166–317). Aineias begins each encounter by engaging in a lengthy dialogue with an archer, Pandaros, son of Lykaon (5.171–238), and Apollo, in the form of a different Lykaon, a son of Priam (20.81). Both discussions can be regarded as instances of Fenik's (1968: 24–26) "consultation pattern." Each of the two different "Lykaons" will soon be killed by the respective best of the Akhaians (5.296, 21.117). Some differences remain between the dynamics of the two discussions. In book 5 Aineias seeks out Pandaros and initiates the consultation, whereas in book 20 the disguised Apollo seeks out Aineias.

The consultation contains the rhetorical expression, "where now are your . . . ?"

To provoke the Trojan, whom they are trying to motivate against the best of the Akhaians, Aineias in book 5 and Apollo/Lykaon in book 20 both begin their speeches with the same rhetorical expression, "Where now are your . . . ?" (ποῦ τοι; 5.171, 20.83). This is not a common expression in Homeric poetry, as there are only four other collocations of the interrogative ποῦ with τοι in the *Iliad* (13.219, 770, 772; 15.440).

One Trojan bids the other to pray for success against the Akhaian hero

As Aineias witnesses Diomedes' successful *aristeia*, he bids Pandaros pray to Zeus for success in wounding him with an arrow (ἀλλ᾽ ἄγε . . . Διὶ χεῖρας ἀνασχών, 5.174). In book 20 Apollo goes on to suggest that Aineias pray for success against Akhilleus (ἀλλ᾽ ἄγε καὶ σὺ θεοῖς αἰειγενέτῃσιν / εὔχεο, 20. 104–5).

And mentions a prior encounter

In reply, Pandaros mentions an earlier encounter with Diomedes, in which he shot at him but was unable to hit or wound him (5.187 ff). In book 20 Aineias responds to the disguised Apollo, noting an earlier, unsuccessful encounter he had with Akhilleus (20.89–97).[10]

Complaining that a god always aids him

Pandaros in book 5 and Aineias in book 20 go on to complain that some god always appears to be protecting the best of the Akhaians, Diomedes (5.185–87) and Akhilleus (20.98; cf. 20.95).[11]

b. Aineias' descent from Aphrodite is emphasized, as well as his ancestors (Tros and Ganymede are mentioned only here) and his illustrious horses

In book 5 Sthenelos, in the Greek consultation scene, notes Aineias' descent from Aphrodite, attempting to persuade Diomedes not to face him (5.247–50). Apollo as Lykaon points out that Aineias is descended from a greater goddess than is Akhilleus (20.105–7). Much of Aineias' importance in the poem lies in his lengthy lineage, in both directions: his ancestry and future descendants. While his ancestors occasionally figure elsewhere in the poem, only here does the *Iliad* offer extended discussion of them, including the sole references to Tros and Ganymede (5.266, 20.230–32). Though the Trojans as a whole are thematically connected with fine horses throughout the *Iliad*, only in these passages are fabulous horses linked specifically with Aineias (5.222–24, 265–73; 20.220–29).

c. A corresponding consultation takes place on the Greek side

Each episode continues with a consultation scene on the Greek side. Diomedes plots strategy with Sthenelos (one of the Epigonoi, like Diomedes himself) to deal with Aineias' approach (5.241–73). In Akhilleus' sequence, gods, Hera and Poseidon, concerned by Aineias' approach, consult over how to reassure Akhilleus (20.112–50). As the *Iliad*'s climactic *aristeia*, Akhilleus' *aristeia*, though parallel to Diomedes', is at the same time elevated above it. Increasing the gods' presence in the pattern, assigning them roles elsewhere given to mortals, is one way the *Iliad* elevates Akhilleus' sequence.

Sthenelos and Diomedes' consultation begins with the former so concerned at Aineias' approach that he tries to persuade Diomedes to flee (5.243–50). Hera consults with Poseidon (with Athena and other gods in attendance) because she knows Apollo has inspired Aineias. Alarmed as Aineias approaches, she directs Poseidon to stand by Akhilleus, and to instill κράτος ("power") into him (20.115–31). Essentially, this is a further instantiation of an earlier motif, *3. A god places* μένος *in the best of the Akhaians as he goes to face the Trojans.*

d. Challenging speeches are the final prelude to combat

Diomedes replies to Sthenelos that it would be ignoble to flee and that they might earn glory if they can capture Aineias' horses, descended from those Zeus gave Tros as recompense for Ganymede (5.252–73). In book 20 Poseidon responds to Hera's concern by promising to intervene if Apollo or Ares intervenes, or if Akhilleus is threatened (20.133–43).

In the final prelude, both sides exchange challenging speeches, or flyting, a traditional element in heroic myth.[12] In book 5 Pandaros is first to speak, referring to an earlier encounter he had with Diomedes, hoping for greater success this time (5.277–79). In book 20 Akhilleus is first to speak, referring to an earlier encounter he had with Aineias and assuming he will have even greater success this time. He urges Aineias to retreat (20.178–98). In book 5, when Pandaros throws his spear at Diomedes and misses, the Greek responds (accurately) that either he (Pandaros) or Aineias will die today (5.287–89). In book 20 Aineias responds to Akhilleus' taunt by saying that one set of parents or the other will have to mourn for what happens today (20.209–11). In a further parallel, the same speech formula occurs, τὸν πρότερος προσέειπε, used of Diomedes as he addresses Lykaon (5.276), and of Akhilleus as he addresses Aineias (20.177).[13]

Homeric scholarship has failed to reach a sensible consensus to explain Aineias' prominence in these scenes, often focusing instead on ancillary, extratextual issues. But, as we note, the *Iliad* thematically depicts the Trojan side as consisting of three elements, the Trojans themselves, the Dardanoi, and the allies (Kirk 1985: 253). The poem consistently portrays a leader of each group, Hektor, Aineias, and Glaukos or Sarpedon. The narrative pattern is structured around this fact, and pits the best of the Akhaians against the leader of each group, Hektor, Aineias, and Glaukos/Sarpedon/Asteropaios (see motif 8 below). Part of Aineias' importance in the poem thus lies in his being leader of this second group, the Dardanoi.

But Aineias serves additional thematic functions, which heighten our understanding of the roles of Hektor, Akhilleus, and the people of Troy. Aineias is the Trojan warrior second only to Hektor. Unlike Hektor, however, he is not in line for the kingship, as Akhilleus pointedly reminds him (20.180–83). Further, Aineias is designated the war's key Trojan survivor (20.302; discussed in chapter 6), whereas Hektor personifies the fall of Troy. As a known survivor, with less at stake as a personification of Troy, Aineias serves as a foil for Hektor, and his presence increases Hektor's pathos.

Part of the reason Aineias survives is that his goddess mother, Aphrodite, secures him from harm in the encounter with Diomedes. Having an immortal mother who can intervene on his behalf aligns Aineias with Akhilleus, the special son of a goddess who can save him from harm. Akhilleus, though another version of such a figure, goes against the expected motif. Thus, when Aineias is rescued by his divine mother in book 5, the tragedy of Akhilleus is further increased because of our consciousness that he *could* conform to the same motif, but will not. The two mothers are further aligned in that, unlike goddesses such as Eos and Kalypso, who willingly take on mortal lovers, Thetis and Aphrodite unwillingly entered into relations with their mortal mates, Peleus and Anchises, compelled by Zeus. Aineias thus mediates between the poem's two principal heroes, Akhilleus and Hektor, functioning as partial parallel and partial foil for each.

Aineias also has no part in the thematic wrongdoing attributed to the Trojans (as Poseidon infers at 20.297), the ancestral guilt provoked by Laomedon. Frequent mention of Laomedon's wrongdoing implies a connection with the coming destruction of Troy. As Aineias is not descended from Laomedon,[14] he does not inherit this guilt (discussed in chapter 6). Aineias is an instance of the "one just man" who survives apocalyptic destruction, a prominent type in OT myth (Lot, Noah).[15]

e. The duel includes the same khermadion ("boulder") sequence

Preliminaries concluded, each duel proceeds according to a similar series of generic gestures: a Trojan makes the first move, throwing his spear into the shield of the best of the Akhaians. Pandaros throws his spear at Diomedes' shield, piercing the shield and going into his corselet. Diomedes then hurls his spear into Pandaros' skull, killing him, with Aineias' taking up a defensive position over the body. In book 20 Aineias drives his spear against Akhilleus' shield, piercing only the first two layers. Akhilleus then throws his spear through Aineias' shield, but without striking him. Then a more specific motif occurs in each duel, used only here in the poem. Diomedes in book 5 and Aineias in book 20 each hefts a huge stone, a χερμάδιον, to hurl at his opponent (5.302–4 = 20.285–87 with substitution of Αἰνείας for Τυδεΐδης). Diomedes strikes Aineias in the hip, inflicting a serious wound, but in book 20 it is Aineias who is about to hurl the stone, threatening to wound Akhilleus.

f. The duel is deprived of a climax when a deity intervenes through a pivotal contrafactual, carrying off Aineias

> And now Aineias, lord of men, would have perished,
> had not Aphrodite, daughter of Zeus, thought quickly,
> who bore him to Ankhises when he was a shepherd,
> she poured her white arms around her son,
> and covered him, her bright robe a fold before him.
>
> (5.311–5)

> And then Aineias would have hurled the boulder as he rushed on,
> hitting his helmet or shield, which would ward off mournful destruction
> and the son of Peleus at close hand would have deprived him of life,
> had not Poseidon, the earthshaker, thought quickly.
>
> (20.288–91)

Homeric epic is fond of this form of syntax, pivotal contrafactuals ("and now X would have happened had not Y intervened"), occurring some sixty times, especially designed to prevent a climax harmful to an important character, or favorite hero. Although the syntax is well studied in terms of generic occurrences (Lang; de Jong; Morrison 1992a and b), its tendency to serve larger structural functions remains underappreciated (Louden 1993: 185–86, 196–97; 1999a: 123–27). Here, the parallel passages, occurring at the same point in their respective sequences, mark the end of Aineias' active involvement. Though his encounters leave little lasting effect on the respective *aristeiai,* they look ahead to his future importance as the key Trojan survivor of the war. In a further indication of the episode's importance, Akhilleus' encounter with Aineias is mentioned in the games in book 23 (292).

Although Aphrodite's rescue of her son is to be expected, the rescue of the Trojan Aineias in book 20 by Poseidon, a staunchly Greek partisan, is not. Part of the effect gained, however, is further elevation of Aineias' status: more important deities than his mother are concerned with his destiny, a further reminder of Laomedon's troubled background (20.297–308; discussed in chapter 6). Diomedes' *aristeia* begins with the same specific motif, a Greek-partisan god saving the first Trojan victim of the best of the Akhaians through a pivotal contrafactual. The motif appears only in these two passages in all of the *Iliad*. Diomedes' first opponents are the two sons of Phegeus (5.9–21), a priest of Hephaistos. Diomedes slays the first and is on the point of dispatching Idaios, the second, when Hephaistos intervenes through the same syntax:

> Even so he [Idiaos] would not have escaped the black death-spirit
> had not Hephaistos caught him away and rescued him, covered in night.
>
> (5.23–24)

Because of its several parallel motifs, Hephaistos' rescue of Idaios is an anticipatory echo of Poseidon's saving Aineias.

⮌

6. The best of the Akhaians' exploits are accompanied by a Greek-partisan god's defeat of a Trojan-partisan god

Fighting between the gods, or theomachy, is more pronounced and climactic in Akhilleus' sequence, but there are prominent instances in Diomedes' *aristeia*. The basic dynamic underlying most of the *Iliad*'s theomachies is the relatively easy defeat of the Trojan-partisan deities by those aiding the Akhaians, a divine parallel for the overwhelming victory the best of the Akhaians achieves over the Trojans. The key event in both sequences is Athena's defeat of Ares (5.793–867; 21.391–414). Also present is a motif common to ancient Near Eastern myth: the gods of a doomed city abandon it as its destruction approaches (see especially 22.213, and the discussion of Aphrodite below). These episodes are discussed at length in chapter 6.

⮌

7. The best of the Akhaians three times attacks Apollo, while he protects a Trojan hero, but gives way on his fourth attempt

With the blessing of deities loyal to the Akhaians, Diomedes and Akhilleus both attack Apollo, the most important pro-Trojan god, while he keeps Aineias safe from Diomedes in book 5 (436–44) and Hektor safe from Akhilleus in book 20 (445–48). Diomedes' sequence goes to this episode immediately after motif 5, the encounter with Aineias, while in Akhilleus' sequence a brief episode with Polydoros intervenes (20.407–18), after which Hektor, outraged at his death, wants to confront Akhilleus (20.419 ff). Earlier, Apollo commanded Hektor not to face Akhilleus alone (20.376–79). The two sequences employ several specific verbal parallels, as underlined:

Three times he rushed forth, striving to kill him,
but three times Apollo smote his shining shield;
but when he sped on a fourth time, like a god.
Apollo the far shooter addressed him, a fierce order.

(5.436–39)

Three times he rushed forth, swift-footed bright Akhilleus,
with his bronze-tipped spear, but three times he struck the deep mist.
But when he sped on a fourth time, like a god.
he [Apollo] spoke winged words to him, a fierce order.

(20.445–9)[16]

The motif keeps Aineias safe due to the larger issue of his destiny as a sur-
vivor of the war, but keeps Hektor safe to postpone his meeting with Akhil-
leus for its climax in book 22.

The underlying numerical pattern of the motif is common to Near East-
ern traditions. Gordon (1967: 70) notes Homeric epic's and the Old Testa-
ment's frequent use of "the climaxing of '3' by '4,'" citing several passages
in Amos and Proverbs. West (1997: 363) notes a further, specific Old Testa-
ment parallel in the story of Balaam (Num 22:21 ff), having in common not
only the three, then four, but the divine boundary in the climactic fourth:

He has consented to go to Moab to advise the king, and he is on his way there,
riding on a donkey. A Messenger of Yahweh stands to block his way, visible at
first only to the donkey. Three times Balaam tries to press forward, and three
times the donkey shies back at the sight of the divinity. Finally Yahweh opens
Balaam's eyes . . . then he is frightened and says he will go back.

Very like the *Iliad*'s repeated pattern, three unsuccessful (and "incorrect")
attempts to proceed against a deity (the Messenger, or angel, a close equiva-
lent to Apollo) are followed by a fourth movement away from the divine
character, which is seen as correct behavior.

a. He is called δαίμονι ἴσος *("like a god") only during his* aristeia *and, with
one exception, only when he attacks a Trojan-partisan deity*

Commentators have noted possible patterns behind deployment of the
phrase, δαίμονι ἴσος, "like a god," Pucci (132) asserting that "the formula
seems to indicate a hero in the moment of his *aristeia*." Closer examina-
tion suggests more-specific restraints on its use. All nine occurrences of
the phrase occur in the *aristeiai* of Diomedes (5.438, 459, 884), Patroklos

(16.705, 786), and Akhilleus (20.447, 493; 21.18, 227). Eight of these nine occur when the respective best of the Akhaians attempts to attack Trojan-partisan deities (Apollo, Ares, and Xanthos, in all occurrences except 20.493). The phrase is a unique index of the best of the Akhaians, and of the specific subgenres of myth the narrative employs. If Diomedes and Akhilleus (and Patroklos; discussed in chapter 3) are "like a god" when they attack another god, the narrative is briefly turning to a theomachian modality to underscore the might of the best of the Akhaians as he powers his way against the Trojans.[17]

b. The best of the Akhaians fights and wounds another Trojan-partisan god, causing the wounded deity to ask another god for help

In Diomedes' sequence this group of motifs (6–7b) is doubled, as he first attacks Aphrodite, and later Ares, under Athena's direction. The doubling underscores the shaky nature of the divine support on the Trojan side, that two of the three Trojan-partisan gods are victimized by a Greek hero. Diomedes triumphs not only over a goddess dubiously qualified in warfare but also over a more potent deity in Ares. When Aphrodite rescues Aineias, Diomedes' charioteer, Sthenelos, goes straight for the famous horses, while Diomedes boldly pursues Aphrodite, wounding her in the hand, as she bears Aineias. He rebukes her, telling her face-to-face that her gender makes her unfit for warcraft (5.348–51),[18] a view validated by Zeus afterward when he tells Aphrodite to leave the war to Athena and Ares. While Apollo carefully retrieves Aineias, Aphrodite seeks out Ares, asking him to lend her his horses to return to Olympos.

In Akhilleus' sequence, a few brief episodes come after the conclusion of the encounter with Aineias, before his fight with Xanthos. In Diomedes' sequence, a similar series of brief encounters immediately *precedes* his lengthy encounter with Aineias. Shortly into book 21, however, Akhilleus encounters Xanthos, a pro-Trojan deity, the thematic parallel to Diomedes' tangle with Aphrodite. The narrative carefully prepares for the encounter with the river by mentioning Xanthos throughout the first half of book 21 (21.2, 18 ff, 122 ff, 136–38, 145–47, 184–93). At the end of his encounter with Lykaon, Akhilleus insults Xanthos (21.130). His subsequent encounter with Asteropaios (discussed below as motif 8), himself descended from the river Axios (21.141–43), serves as transition to the fight with Xanthos.

While we can recognize the same basic motif in Akhilleus' encounter with Xanthos, the heroic tenor of the episode is quite distinct from the clashes in book 5, which have a comic modality (discussed in chapter 6). The river is angered because Akhilleus has dammed his waters with Trojan corpses. Initially, Akhilleus agrees to cease harming Xanthos' waters, but vows to continue slaying Trojans. The Trojan-partisan Xanthos then attacks him, rolling his currents against him in the riverbed, sending a wave after him on the plain. For Xanthos' attack on Akhilleus, the *Iliad* uses the verb πλάζω (*plazo*, 21.269), "strike, drive," the same verb the *Odyssey* uses to articulate Poseidon's hostility to Odysseus.[19] Akhilleus is so distressed by Xanthos' repeated attacks that he cries out to Ζεῦ πάτερ (273).[20] Poseidon and Athena respond, reassuring him. Almost immediately the tables are turned, as Xanthos/Skamander calls on Simoeis for aid because of the savage man he now faces (21.314). In their pleas for help, both Aphrodite and Xanthos compare the best of the Akhaians with a divine opponent, Aphrodite asserting Diomedes would fight even with Zeus (5.362), Xanthos stating that Akhilleus rages equal to the gods (21.315).

Diomedes' second encounter, when he attacks Ares, is more openly theomachian, as Athena not only prompts the whole episode but serves as his charioteer (5.837 ff) and guides his spear (5.836 ff). Diomedes is never in any real danger, with Athena at his side, and the partially comic modality of the event is underscored when Zeus mocks Ares' humiliation (5.889–91, discussed at greater length in chapter 6, subgenre 11c).

∽

8. The best of the Akhaians duels with and defeats a great Lykian warrior

The narrative pattern, as noted above, positions the best of the Akhaians in duels with leaders of each of the three Trojan contingents: the Trojans, the Dardanians, and the allies. Between the encounter with Aineias, leader of the Dardanoi, which comes first, and the climactic encounter with Hektor, which comes last, the best of the Akhaians defeats a leader of the third contingent, the most important of the Trojans' allies, the Lykians.[21] These leaders are the three quality opponents who face the best of the Akhaians, most of the other warriors being lesser known (and comparatively expendable). After Diomedes defeats Ares to conclude book 5, book 6 continues with several quick slayings by different characters and Helenos' sending Hektor into Troy (discussed in chapter 6, subgenre 9), as prelude to the extended scene between Diomedes and Glaukos. As in the encounters with Aineias, lengthy verbal preliminaries signal the scene's importance. Diomedes speaks first, a challenging query about Glaukos' identity and lineage (6.119 ff). During Glaukos' lengthy reply, Diomedes realizes that their ancestors were bound by the sacred ties of hospitality (6.215–31), and declares that they should thus refrain from fighting each other and exchange gifts instead. Combat preempted, Diomedes nonetheless defeats Glaukos in the controversial exchange of armor in which he gains arms worth eleven times more than those he gives, Zeus having deluded Glaukos.

The conclusion of the encounter has probably provoked more discussion than any other episode in the *Iliad*, except the duals in book 9.[22] The dialogue itself serves many purposes, a key one being a transition out of the violent acts central to Diomedes' *aristeia*. As Edwards (1987: 202) notes, "it bridges the difference in tone between the killings on the battlefield and the emotional meetings within Troy." But why is Glaukos so easily victimized, and why does Zeus appear to endorse his victimization by "stealing his wits?" Edwards (1987: 206) suggests that the one-sidedness of the exchange, Diomedes getting gold for bronze from Glaukos, resembles the more violent outcome of many duels and "echoes the usual ending of exploits such as those of Diomedes, stripping the armor from a corpse." The narrative pattern emphasizes that Diomedes besting Glaukos is the first of a series of three, parallel encounters, the others being Patroklos and Sarpedon (16.419–683, discussed in chapter 3) and Akhilleus and Asteropaios (21.139–204). The outcomes of these parallel encounters help explain otherwise unusual tendencies present in this scene and confirm Edwards' suggestion. In both of the other two episodes, the best of the Akhaians not only defeats the Lykian champion, but slays him and strips his armor. After slaying Sarpedon, Patroklos and his companions strip his armor and take it back to the ships (16.663–65). After slaying Asteropaios, Akhilleus also strips his armor (21.183). Before Patroklos slays Sarpedon, Zeus, after painful deliberation, explicitly endorses this outcome of their duel. Throughout Akhilleus' *aristeia*, Zeus implicitly supports the Greek hero's acts, as Akhilleus himself argues in his triumphant vaunt over the slain Asteropaios about how the descendants of Zeus are greater than the offspring of rivers (21.184–99). It is thematic for the Trojans to lose in exchanges of arms in the *Iliad* (discussed again in a later motif, *17. Hektor exchanges armor with the best of the Akhaians*). This unique exchange both affords victory to the best of the Akhaians and forms the end of Diomedes' *aristeia*, concluding his role in the initial sequence.

While the Lykians nominally drop out of the poem after Sarpedon's death and are not mentioned after book 17, nonetheless Akhilleus' combat with Asteropaios (21.139–204) is an instance of the same motif, if slightly adapted, offering numerous links with Diomedes' encounter with Glaukos. Although Asteropaios is said to be leader of the Paionians, when first mentioned in the *Iliad* he has been chosen by Sarpedon to accompany him and Glaukos as the bravest of the allied fighters (12.101–4). Citing this, and other passages, Bryce (244) regards Asteropaios as a Lykian. Asteropaios is again associated with Glaukos at 17.216–17, and in the games for Patroklos he is again associated with Sarpedon (23.799–808), when Akhilleus offers their armor as prizes in the single combat (Shannon 76). When the Paionians are mentioned in the Catalogue, they have the same epithet as do the Lykians, τηλόθεν, "from afar" (2.849, 877).

Beyond these thematic associations between Asteropaios and the Lykians, his encounter with Akhilleus shares a number of close structural and rhetorical parallels with the Glaukos/Diomedes episode, most of which elements occur only in these two contexts. In each scene the two warriors approach each other, described in an identical formula (6.121–22 = 21.148–49, differing only in the names). Both times the Greek warrior speaks first, asking his opponent's identity (6.123, 21.150), commenting on how daring his opponent is to face him (6.126, 21.150), and noting, in an identical formula (6.127 = 21.151, found only in these two contexts), "it is the children of the doomed who oppose my force." Both Glaukos and Asteropaios reply with the same otherwise unique formula (6.145 = 21.153, other than the names), wondering why their lineage is questioned. Richardson (67) underscores the many similarities the two contexts share when he asserts that Asteropaios' "opening question was more effective as an introduction to Glaukos' famous comparison of men to leaves (6.145). Like Glaukos, Asteropaios too gives his parentage but not his name, which would be unnecessary."

Undaunted, Asteropaios stands up to Akhilleus. Unique in his ambidexterity, hurling spears with each hand, he is the only opponent to wound Akhilleus. But Akhilleus slays him as he attempts to retrieve one of his spears, leaving his corpse on the riverbank. In Akhilleus' sequence, this encounter also serves as transition into motif 7b, his fight with the river Xanthos, whereas in Diomedes' sequence, the peaceful, if exploitive, exchange of arms by Diomedes concludes his participation in the narrative pattern, as Aias becomes the "best of the Akhaians" for the motifs involving Hektor.

9. The greatest Trojan warrior, Hektor, meets his mother, sister-in-law, and his wife, Andromakhe, near the Skaian Gates, and the women, especially Andromakhe, who predicts his death and worries about their son, Astyanax, ask him not to return to battle

a. Andromakhe and Helen refer to Hektor as their brother

At this point each sequence shifts its focus to Hektor. He is the best of the Akhaians' final, most important opponent. But before Hektor faces him, he hears pleas from close female relatives not to return to battle. In book 6 the

The *Iliad:* Structure, Myth, and Meaning

episodes are full of foreboding, pointing, implicitly, to Hektor's death. In the final sequence, Hektor's scenes with his female relatives are doubled. Two episodes—book 22, before his final duel with Akhilleus, and book 24, when his corpse is brought into Troy for the funeral—depict Hektor with the women in his life. Book 23 intervenes between these two episodes, as (in our analysis) an expanded version of another motif (*20. Both sides mourn their dead and construct a tomb*). In one of several contrasts, the scenes in book 6 take place within the city, whereas in book 22 Hektor is outside. In book 6 Helenos' directive that he enter the city and ask their mother to sacrifice to Athena turns the focus to Hektor. Helenos asks for a prayer to Athena to restrain Diomedes, "most powerful of the Akhaians" (κάρτιστον Ἀχαιῶν, 6.98), periphrasis for "the best of the Akhaians." On entering the city (while Diomedes' encounter with Glaukos unfolds), Hektor is met by the Trojan wives and daughters, a segue to his intimate meetings with the women of his own family. Their concern over possible deaths of their loved ones (6.239–41) looks ahead to Hekabe's concern for him here, and everyone's concern for him in book 22.

Then Hekabe and Laodike meet him. His sister Laodike is "most beautiful of the daughters" (θυγατρῶν εἶδος ἀρίστην, 6.252, 3.124). In book 24 Hektor's sister Kassandra, first to see him when his corpse is brought into the city (24.699), is also singled out for her beauty, "like golden Aphrodite" (ἰκέλη χρυσῇ Ἀφροδίτῃ, 24.699), and elsewhere described with the same formula as Laodike (13.365). Hektor's two sisters are the only named characters described by this formula.[23] Hekabe introduces a darker, more serious mood,[24] assuming Hektor is in trouble and that he has come to pray. She describes the Greeks as δυσώνυμοι, "accursed" (6.255). She asks him to stay with her (6.258; cf. 22.38), drink wine to restore his strength, and offer libation to Zeus. Hektor rejects her request to drink wine (below as motif 9b), but relays Helenos' directive to propitiate Athena with prayer and sacrifice.[25]

Trying to locate Andromakhe, he finds Paris, chiding him for being at home, but has a lengthier conversation with Helen, suggesting she is the real focus of the scene.[26] Like Hekabe, Helen also asks him to stay with her and rest a while (6.354). Helen's speech to Hektor is quite close to her lament in book 24. In each case Helen's first words to Hektor, "My brother by marriage" (δᾶερ ἐμεῖο, 6.344, 354; ἐμῷ θυμῷ δαέρων πολὺ φίλατε πάντων, 24.762), call attention to her family ties to him. She wishes she had perished before ever coming to Troy (6.345–48, 24.764) and draws sharp contrasts between Hektor and Paris (6.350 ff, 24.762 ff).

Hektor has unexpected difficulty finding Andromakhe, who is simultaneously searching for him. He learns she has gone to the tower, in fear.

Her panic parallels her distraught state in book 22, when she learns of his death (μαινομένη ἐικυῖα, "seeming like a crazed woman," 6.389; μαινάδι ἴοη, "like a Maenad," 22.460). She has gone to the tower to attempt to see Hektor (πύργῳ ἐφεστήκει, 6.373, πύργον . . . ἔστη, 22.462–63).They finally meet each other before the Skaian Gates (6.392–92), while an attendant holds Astyanax, whose name is explained, "for Hektor alone saved Ilion" (6.403).[27] The explicit equation of Hektor's life with the preservation of the city emphasizes Troy's impending doom, since a string of motifs here points to his looming death. Andromakhe's first words, "your own force [μένος] will destroy [φθίσει] you" (6.407), are an accurate prediction of Hektor's death (cf. her comment at 22.457–58) and of her impending status as a widow (χήρη, 6.408), much as in 22 she acknowledges his death and her status as widow (χήρην, 22.484). She notes that Akhilleus slew her father and her seven brothers, making Hektor a substitute for all her male relatives, implicitly pointing ahead to Akhilleus' slaying of Hektor as well, her last remaining adult male relative. She then declares "Hektor you are my brother" (6.430). Asking Hektor to pity her (6.431, 407; cf. 24.82), and to stay at the tower (6.431), she furthers her focus on his impending death, and its consequence for her. But as Hekabe could not, Andromakhe is unable to persuade him to change his battle strategy[28] (and his relatives will be unable to persuade him to return to the city in book 22). As Hektor takes his leave of Andromakhe, she and the women servants stir up lamentation in the house, convinced they will never see Hektor alive again (6.499–502), a further link between this scene and those in books 22 and 24.

The narrative pattern suggests parallels between Andromakhe and Helen in their interactions here with Hektor. In book 6 Hektor only encounters Helen because he is looking for Andromakhe. Both designate him as their "brother" (δᾶερ, 6.344, 354; 24.762; κασίγνητος, 6.430), in some extended or symbolic sense. Each argues for a unique relationship with him. Helen acknowledges that it is her fault that Hektor has to fight (6.355–56). Andromakhe argues persuasively that Hektor is for her not only husband but brother and father. We return to these parallels in chapter 2, arguing that when Helen looks out from the tower in book 3, the scene is modeled on Andromakhe's doing so in books 6 and 22.

In Akhilleus' sequence, Hektor's meetings with his female family members appear in more complex, highly developed form. Hektor's relatives appear in three separate scenes, attempting to persuade him not to fight Akhilleus (22.38–89), distraught after Akhilleus has slain him (22.415–514), and mourning him in ritual (24.716–75); in book 6 most characters combine these functions in a single speech. Furthermore, Priam, not onstage in book 6, is the first to speak to Hektor in book 22. Nonetheless, his speech conforms to the same dynamic visible in the other speeches in books 6 and 22. Priam's appearance in book 22 (25–78) is an anticipatory doublet of his later role in book 24 (analyzed in the subsequent motif, *19. Priam, disturbed over his son's mortal combat, drives out to the middle of the battlefield to propose a truce to care for the dead*). As the family member most closely involved with the retrieval of Hektor's corpse (also evident in books 3 and 7, as discussed in chapter 2), his speech here (22.38–76), especially his dwelling on the after-effects of Hektor's death, marks the narrative turning a corner to focus on Hektor's death. Priam and Hekabe each have a speech before Hektor faces Akhilleus and after he has been slain, whereas Andromakhe is restricted to speaking only after Hektor is slain, for greater dramatic effect, and because it parallels their almost having missed each other in book 6. In the fully tragic sequence of book 22, they *do* miss each other until it is too late: Hektor is already dead when she looks for him (22.450–64), much as Andromakhe earlier predicted (6.407). In twice comparing Andromakhe with a madwoman (6.389, 22.460) and in her accurate prediction of Hektor's death (6.407), the *Iliad* figures Andromakhe as the same mythic type that the post-Homeric tradition uses for Kassandra.

In book 22, as in book 6, Hektor is before the Skaian Gates (6.393, 22.6), though now on the outside, the wall *separating* him from his family. Priam is first to speak, attempting to persuade his son not to face Akhilleus. His speech closely parallels Andromakhe's in book 6, as he asks Hektor not to face the best of the Akhaians, lists male relatives whom Akhilleus has already slain (22.44–52; 6.413–30), asks Hektor to come and stay within the city (22.56; 6.431) and to pity him (22.59; 6.431), and sketches out the grim circumstances of his life after Hektor's death, the central topics of Andromakhe's earlier speech.[29] Hekabe follows, also asking Hektor to pity her (22.82) and her breasts that suckled him, to come within the walls (22.85), again concluding by sketching out the grim consequences of his death (22.86–89). To endow her scene at the end of book 22 with greater suspense, and as a thematic parallel to Hektor and Andromakhe having difficulty meeting each other (6.365–95), Andromakhe is kept out of this scene, her speech postponed until after Hektor's death. Priam and Hekabe each have a second speech, Priam's (22.416–28) closely anticipating his actions in book 24, focusing on his need to leave the city and meet with Akhilleus, whereas Hekabe's in effect begins the lament. Andromakhe's speech (22.477–514), after the narrator's lengthy description of how she has not yet heard of Hektor's death, picks right up from her book 6 speech, focusing on her and Astyanax's wretched circumstances in the wake of Hektor's death and the abuse of his corpse. We analyze the speeches in book 24 below in connection with motifs 19 and 20.

b. His fear of shame counters their attempts at persuasion

Hektor's reaction to his closest female relatives' (and Priam's in book 22) pleas that he stay within the city is virtually the same in both sequences: he is unpersuaded (though ironically he will be persuaded by his brother, who is, in both sequences, a figure he should not trust):

> οὐδέ με πείσεις.
> you will not persuade me.
> (6.360)

> οὐδ᾽ Ἕκτορι θυμὸν ἔπειθον.
> and they did not persuade Hektor's heart.
> (22.91)

Hektor's reason is the shame he feels especially before the Trojan women, and the same formula is repeated in both sequences (αἰδέομαι Τρῶας καὶ Τρῳάδας ἑλκεσιπέπλους, 6.442 = 22.105; cf. 22.155). Hektor is consistently motivated by his sense of shame (αἰδώς) and fear of what others will say about him. In book 6 he further specifies his fear of being branded a coward (6.443), while in book 22 he specifies the assumed source of reproach, Poulydamas, if he were now to enter the city (22.100; since Poulydamas is not distinguished as a character until book 11, he is not be mentioned in book 6).[30]

✍

10. As a result of the plotting of Apollo and Athena, the best of the Akhaians now encounters Hektor in a duel to decide the whole war

For the remainder of the initial sequence, Aias replaces Diomedes as the "best of the Akhaians." The *Iliad* confirms him as best of the Akhaians several times (7.50; cf. 7.182–83, 73; 2.768–69), but glosses over his replacing Diomedes by having lots drawn to determine his selection, and by having Diomedes' *aristeia* conclude in a nonheroic manner through the encounter with Glaukos and Hektor's scenes in Troy. When his lot is chosen, this would probably be understood as representing the gods' choice. This section of each sequence (and book 16 in the middle sequence, discussed in chapter 3) now turns to the duel with Hektor, the climax to the *aristeia*. In the initial sequence, Diomedes plays Akhilleus' role as it pertains to the general deeds of an *aristeia*, encounters with enemy warriors other than the greatest Trojan. Aias, however, has a thematic function throughout the *Iliad* as the Akhaian who is capable of defeating Hektor (as he himself thinks, 7.192), and thus replaces Diomedes as the narrative pattern arrives at the climactic encounter between the best of the Akhaians and the greatest Trojan warrior.

In both sequences Athena and Apollo, the gods most active in aiding the respective sides, set up the climactic duel. As discussed in chapter 7, Athena and Apollo each have the traditional role of the deity who has a special mentor relationship with the hero. In book 7, Athena, alarmed at Hektor's reemergence from Troy, heads toward Troy and is met by Apollo (7.20), who suggests a cessation to the general fighting for the day, proposing a duel between Hektor and whomever the Greeks choose, to which Athena agrees. The gods' actions here (in book 7) have been criticized as poorly motivated,[31] but the narrative pattern reveals that the scene is an element in a recurring complex, with parallel actions in books 21–22. The events in the first half of book 7 should thus be seen as a first statement, a less heated rehearsal of the same themes that will come with greater intensity and a more climactic function at the end of book 21 and through most of book 22.

In books 20–22 Athena and Apollo repeatedly act to arrange the climactic confrontation, first by postponing any premature encounters between the two figures, then by ensuring they *do* meet. Early in Akhilleus' *aristeia*, Apollo commands Hektor not to fight with Akhilleus (20.376–78) for the time. Violating this divine interdiction (which in most myths would bring disaster on the violator) out of anger when he sees his brother Polydoros slain, Hektor hurls his spear at Akhilleus. But when Athena prevents it from striking the protagonist, Apollo whisks Hektor away (20.437–44), not to reappear until book 22. The incident looks ahead to the final encounter in book 22 and is a miniature of much of the *Iliad:* Hektor is unable to wound the best of the Akhaians and, in confrontations with him, is only kept alive by divine intervention. At the end of book 21 (538 ff), Apollo's rescue of all the other Trojan warriors, so Akhilleus' only target will be Hektor, produces much the same result as his suggestion of a general cessation of fighting, except for the lone duel in book 7. As a final distraction, he spurs Agenor on to face Akhilleus, but when the Greek hero closes in on him, Apollo whisks him away to safety, and, assuming Agenor's form, deceives (δόλῳ, 21.599) Akhilleus on a wild chase, during which all the other Trojans take refuge within the city walls. However, having prevented hostilities against the remaining Trojans, Apollo abandons Hektor, just when Athena approaches Akhilleus to give him decisive aid, λίπεν δέ ἑ [Hektor] Φοῖβος Ἀπόλλων / Πηλεΐωνα δ' ἵκανε θεὰ γλαυκῶπις Ἀθήνη (22.213–14), the poem's most emphatic juxtaposition of the two deities' opposing roles.

Athena, who largely agreed with Apollo's suggestions in book 7 and followed his lead, now assumes the more active role in insuring that Hektor will face Akhilleus. Her help and intervention are greater and more decisive than either deity's in book 7. Appearing to Akhilleus in a theophany as herself,[32] she offers her aid, using dual forms to express her working together with the hero (νῶϊ, 22.216; δηώσαντε, 22.218).[33] But she then appears to Hektor in human form, as Deïphobos, offering to help take a stand against Akhilleus. While persuading Hektor, she suggests theomachian tones in her highly negative characterization of Apollo (22.220–21)[34] and closely mirrors Apollo's use of deception against Akhilleus (21.599). The specific nature of her intervention against Hektor, however, comes under our next motif.

a. Hektor is persuaded by his brother to battle the best of the Akhaians

Before facing the best of the Akhaians, in each sequence Hektor first has a conference with his brother, which gives him confidence to face the Greek hero. At the end of book 6, after the ominous description of Hektor's servants mourning him while alive (which prefigures his actual death in Akhilleus' sequence), assuming he will not return from battle (6.500–502), he meets Paris, now "brimming with courage and strength"[35] and compared to a horse galloping in his pride. After their brief meeting, Hektor has a renewed optimism for his success in the war (6.526–9).[36]

In the middle of book 22 Athena serves the same function by taking the form of Hektor's brother Deïphobos. As noted earlier, Akhilleus' sequence has greater interaction by the gods, evident in Hera and Poseidon performing a role played by a mortal in the earlier motif, *5c. A corresponding consultation takes place on the Greek side.* Approaching Hektor, Athena as Deïphobos addresses him with the same opening half line with which Paris addresses Hektor at the end of book 6 (ἠθεῖ᾽, ἦ μάλα δή σε, 6.518 = 22.239), the sole occurrences of this formula. The intimate brotherly address is the first indication that the two scenes share the same underlying emotional dynamic. In each scene the pattern uses the same formula to depict Hektor's "brother" reversing his downcast mood and making him eager to face battle (μέμασαν πολεμίζειν ἠδὲ μάχεσθαι, 7.2–3; μεμαῶτε μαχώμεθα, 22.243), with Hektor and "brother" the subject in each phrase.

In both instances Hektor's "brother" is an unreliable figure, whose agenda is quite different from his own. In the previous scene in book 6, Paris displays his fundamental irresponsibility in the war, his bizarre absence from the duel with Menelaos strongly undercutting any claims he might have to heroism. Even Helen complains of his recklessness (ἄτη, 6.356). Consequently, we should feel some unease when, fraternal camaraderie notwithstanding, Hektor so easily joins the confident mood exhibited by

Paris (7.2–3), who moments before was enjoying himself in the bedroom instead of fighting in the war that he himself has caused. In book 22 the brother's unreliability is even greater in Athena's deception, in which she pumps Hektor full of false confidence in order to lead him to his death. In chapter 7 I argue that her deception is a traditional Near Eastern subgenre of myth present in Ugaritic and Old Testament myth. Athena's deception is paralleled by Apollo's deception of Akhilleus (21.599–22.9), and in the middle sequence, his striking Patroklos (16.791, discussed in chapter 3). In both sequences, then, but more obviously in the final sequence, Hektor's highly unreliable brother gives him a false confidence to help him face the best of the Akhaians.

↜

11. Panic seizes Hektor on first seeing the best of the Akhaians, prompting his retreat, which normally would be back into the army

Although in both sequences Hektor feels confident just before facing the best of the Akhaians (7.3, 22.243), in each case as soon as he sees Aias/Akhilleus, uncontrollable panic seizes him. In book 7 Hektor is unable to bear the sight of Aias striding toward him, and wishes to escape into the ranks, momentarily forgetting that the special terms of the duel (which he himself has called) prevent him from blending back into the army. Here, if only briefly, the encounter with Aias veers into the psychological modality that will become more prominent in Akhilleus' sequence in the dream simile (22.199–204):

> A fierce trembling [τρόμος] crept into the limbs of each of the Trojans,
> and the heart in Hektor himself was beating hard;
> but it was no longer possible to flee or to withdraw
> back into the host of soldiers, since he had challenged in his will to fight.
>
> (7.215–18)

In Akhilleus' sequence the same motif occurs, with the same subject, τρόμος, "trembling," but the motif is considerably expanded, as now Hektor, unable to bear the sight of Akhilleus in his divine armor, is seized by panic and flees,

> and trembling [τρόμος] took hold of Hektor, as he saw him, and he could not dare
> to remain there, but left the gates behind, and he went in flight.
>
> (22.136–37)

Unlike in book 7, where the terms of the duel serve to inhibit his flight, there is now no army standing around to impede his impulse, and Hektor flees. His flight is a lengthy expansion of the motif, as Hektor not only panics but dashes three times around the city walls in his fear, the expansion being marked in ring compositional fashion (οὐδ' ἄρ' ἔτ' ἔτλη, 22.136; οὐδέ ποτ' ἔτλην, 22.251). In place of the assembled troops witnessing the duel in book 7, the gods are now the audience (22.166–85). Then follows the dream simile (22.199–204), an extraordinary technique to mark Hektor's extraordinary panic and isolation. Then Akhilleus signals to the other Greeks not to harm Hektor (22.205–7), one of the few instances in his *aristeia* where the presence of other Greeks is acknowledged, but here used to further isolate Hektor.

⤳

12. Hektor asks the best of the Akhaians to swear an oath to return the corpse of the defeated to his companions, undefiled, but deprived of its armor

In both scenes Hektor displays special concern with the treatment of the slain warrior's corpse. Before the duel with Aias, Hektor specifies that should the Akhaian hero slay him, his body is then to be freely given back to the Trojans (7.77–80), and should the Akhaian warrior be slain, his people could heap up a burial mound for him (7.84–86). Because he announces these terms before the Greeks have determined who will face him, there is no rebuttal or rejection of his request. The Greeks tacitly agree to the terms. Because the duel is halted before either contestant is slain (discussed below), the concerns are less prominent in the encounter with Aias. However, when seen as a constituent element in the narrative pattern, the first instance acquires added foreboding, since the audience hears this as a repeated concern by Hektor. Akhilleus will utterly reject such agreements.

In Akhilleus' sequence, where the duel results in Hektor's death, the same concerns form one of the poem's climaxes and prompt some of its central moral dilemmas. Here the stark difference in the divine economy points to Akhilleus' rejection of Hektor's request. In book 7 Athena largely goes along with Apollo's suggestions about the duel (7.24–43), but in book 22 it is Athena who dominates the outcome. Because Hektor makes his request immediately after his consultation with Athena disguised as Deïphobos, his concerns are already subordinated to Athena's deception, Zeus having already hefted his scale, Apollo having already abandoned him (22.213). Hektor asks Akhilleus to swear oaths by the gods (22.254–55), invoking Zeus as witness to his terms, as in book 7 (7.76). He announces that if he should slay Akhilleus he would not defile his corpse but, having taken his arms, would return the corpse to the Akhaians, and he bids Akhilleus do the same (22.254–58). Both scenes employ similar formulae for Hektor giving the corpse back to the Akhaians, νέκυν . . . ἀποδώσω, / ὄφρα . . . Ἀχαιοί (7.84–85), νεκρὸν Ἀχαιοῖσιν δώσω πάλιν (22.259). Both scenes employ the same formula for obtaining the slain foe's armor, τεύχεα συλήσας (7.78, 82), συλήσω κλυτὰ τεύχε᾿ (22.258), although κλυτὰ in book 22 continues the implicit emphasis on how those same arms, divinely made, help signify Hektor's death. However, where the book 7 scene includes tacit Greek acceptance of such terms, in book 22 Akhilleus rejects all such agreements (22.261–67), pointing to the atrocities he will soon commit on Hektor's corpse. The motif is doubled, occurring a second time in Akhilleus' sequence. Immediately after Hektor receives his fatal wound, but while he still has the strength to speak, he again requests honorable burial, repeating lines used in the book 7 challenge:

> but give my body back to be taken home, so the Trojans
> and the Trojans' wives can give me my share of fire when I have died.
> (22.342–43 = 7.79–80)

Kirk notes some of the larger parallels between the two episodes: "Both direct repetition and loose similarity are probably deliberate underlining Hektor's obsession with this matter and giving ironical point to his emphasis on the present [the duel in book 7 with Aias] occasion" (Kirk 1990: 244).

⟆

13. The best of the Akhaians has a unique shield

Elsewhere in the epic considerable attention is given to the exceptional shield that the best of the Akhaians wields. Now as the confrontation nears, the shield looms large endowing the best of the Akhaians with virtual invulnerability. Akhilleus himself notes the parallel between Aias' shield and his own armor (18.193–94), "nor do I know of any other whose renowned [κλυτὰ] armor I could wear, / except for the shield of Aias son of Telamon." Parallels between Aias' and Akhilleus' shields are frequent and thematic throughout the *Iliad*. Diomedes, best of the Akhaians for books 5–6, also serves as an instantiation of the motif, though in less significant contexts.[37]

As Aias arms to meet Hektor, he is not given a full arming scene, though he does don all his armor. This is because the narrative pattern places the arming scene at the beginning of the *aristeia*. Instead, the narrator emphasizes his shield (7.219–24), described as "like a tower [πύργον]." Whether this refers to size, shape, or function, Aias' shield is the only one in the *Iliad* so described. It is further distinguished in receiving a brief account of its maker, Tukhios, and his making of the shield. The same formula is used of Hephaistos fashioning Akhilleus' shield, κάμε τεύχων (7.220, 19.368). Aias' shield figures thematically throughout the poem as a concretization of his might (and looks ahead to his defensive prowess around Patroklos' corpse in book 17). In Akhilleus' sequence the shield takes on even greater importance, with the greater divine involvement typical of the final sequence. Because Hektor stripped Akhilleus' armor from Patroklos' corpse, Akhilleus needs new arms, and, accordingly, Thetis arranges for Hephaistos to fashion him a new set. The finished work, a divine product, strikes awe in humans. None but Akhilleus can even look directly at it (19.14–16). I place this motif at this point in the narrative pattern (though it can be regarded as a subset of the arming scene) because the best of the Akhaians' special shield conveys his relative invulnerability in the encounter. Whereas Hektor's own vulnerability is emphasized when he goes up against the same figure. The shield's importance thus increases as the climactic encounter nears.

❧

14. When Hektor strikes the best of the Akhaians, his spear is driven back by the special shield

The duels with Aias and Akhilleus are quite brief, once preliminary verbal exchanges are finished. In book 7 Hektor initiates the action immediately after his speech to Aias, by hurling his spear at him, which fails to pierce his massive shield:

> So he spoke, and having brandished it, hurled the long-shadowing spear,
> and hit the terrible seven-ox-hide shield of Aias
> at the outermost bronze, which was its eighth layer,
> and the tireless bronze spear went cleaving six folds
> but it was held fast in the seventh skin.
>
> (7.244–48)

A few lines later, the motif is repeated a second time, with greater emphasis on the failure of Hektor's spear, as the spearhead is now bent back:

> The son of Priam then struck the middle of the shield with his spear,
> but the bronze did not break through, and the spearhead bent back.
>
> (7.258–59)

Although an unsuccessful spear throw is not infrequent in the *Iliad*, the narrative pattern lends additional significance to it here because of the shield's special nature and the aura of invulnerability it confers upon the best of the Akhaians. Hektor's inability to pierce the shield is symptomatic of his overall failure in the encounter. We could say that in other contexts the motif is generic, but when it happens to Hektor against the best of the Akhaians, the motif is marked.[38]

In the final sequence Akhilleus throws first with the spear, missing Hektor, but the spear is then retrieved by an invisible Athena. Just before Hektor realizes Athena has deceived him by pretending to be his brother Deïphobos (22.297–99), he throws his spear at Akhilleus, striking his shield (22.290), but failing to inflict any damage, just as in his duel with Aias (7.244–46):

> So he spoke, and having brandished it hurled the long-shadowing spear,
> and he struck the middle of the shield of the son of Peleus and did not miss,
> but the spear was driven back [ἀπεπλάγχθη] from the shield, and Hektor was enraged.
>
> (22.289–91)

The same formula (22.289 = 7.244, and 22.273)[39] initiates the motif in each sequence, and the upshot of each scene is the same: the best of the Akhaians' unique shield prevents Hektor's best throw from wounding or even grazing his opponent.

Furthermore, the verb, ἀποπλάζω, depicting Hektor's failure against Akhilleus' divine shield, is significant. In the *Odyssey* πλάζω (*plazo*), and its compounded forms, almost always express divine agency.[40] The central use depicts Poseidon's divine wrath against Odysseus, (πλάζει δ' ἀπὸ πατρίδος, *Od.* 1.75). When a mortal is the subject, the verb is in the passive voice; when an immortal, such as Poseidon, is subject the verb is active (Louden 1999a: 73). Here, since a mortal spear is driven away by the immortal shield, the passive is used. The shield, then, expresses divine agency's helping Akhilleus against his mortal opponent. When Hektor's cast of the spear is in vain at the end of each sequence, it is terminal; he will have no second chance.

15. Hektor's imminent defeat is emphasized by a pivotal contrafactual, which demonstrates his dependence on Apollo

As in Aineias' encounter with the best of the Akhaians (motif 5f), a pivotal contrafactual signals the impending conclusion of the combat. I repeat my assertion that pivotal contrafactuals often mark larger structural components (Louden 1993: 190–98; 1999a: 77) hence their inclusion here as a second, separate motif. But whereas the narrative pattern's earlier contra-factuals were used to rescue Aineias,[41] this pair marks Hektor's danger and imminent defeat—how dependent he is on Apollo, how helpless he is without him against the best of the Akhaians. In book 7 the "and now . . . had not" structure is further used to mark the end of the encounter and to help gloss over Hektor's apparent loss. In that duel's final action, Aias hurls a great stone at Hektor, which knocks him sprawling to the ground, prompting Apollo's intervention:

> And he [Hektor] was stretched out, sprawling,
> driven next to his shield; but at once Apollo raised him up straight.
> And now they would have struck each other at close range with swords,
> had not heralds, messengers for Zeus and men,
> come, one for the Trojans, and one for the bronze-tunicked Akhaians.
>
> (7.271–75)

Because of Aias' blow, Apollo's brief but crucial intervention is necessary even to keep the duel going, if only to its immediate end, the abruptness of which has seemed puzzling to many. "It is a startling anti-climax" (Kirk 1990: 271). But despite the sense of anticlimax, it is clear that Aias would have been victorious if the combat had gone on any longer.[42] The only wounds suffered in the fight are those Aias inflicts on Hektor, discussed below as motif 16. The stone Aias throws is not only bigger than that hurled by Hektor, but he appears to throw it harder (7.268–69). The episode serves some larger purposes in suggesting the greater trajectory of the plot. If Hektor would have been defeated by *this* best of the Akhaians, he will surely be no match for Akhilleus in the final sequence.

In Akhilleus' sequence, as in Aias' duel, Apollo's intervention is necessary even to enable Hektor to continue the duel. Akhilleus now chases a panicked Hektor (with all the repetitions of "swift-footed Akhilleus" here expressing their accumulated force), who would be unable to flee, would be slain in flight, and die a cowardly death, if not for Apollo's help:

> But how could Hektor have fled out from the mark of death,
> had not Apollo come near him for the last, and final
> time, who stirred force [μένος] into his vigorous knees?
>
> (22.202–4)

The passage has been criticized for a variety of reasons (e.g., Richardson 128–29, who also cites Leaf), for commentators have failed to see the parallels with the incident in book 7. Together the two passages depict Apollo's aid as essential to enable Hektor to face the best of the Akhaians.[43] Though pivotal contrafactuals are common in Homeric epic, out of the forty in the *Iliad*, the two identified as motif 15 (7.271–75, 22.202–4) are the only instances in which Hektor is saved through this construction.[44] Implicitly, when Apollo's support is withdrawn, he is easily defeated by the best of the Akhaians. As motif 13 suggests an invulnerability associated with the best of the Akhaians, so motif 15 implies considerable vulnerability in Hektor, should Apollo not offer his full support. When Apollo does abandon him (22.213), Hektor's defeat is certain. Apollo's doing so is a subset of a typical motif, or subgenre of myth, the deities of a city abandoning it shortly before its impending destruction, common in Near Eastern myth (West 1997: 74, 76), as discussed in chapter 6.

⌒

16. In the duel's climax, the best of the Akhaians wounds Hektor in the neck with his spear

In both contexts after Hektor's ineffective spear throw, the best of the Akhaians responds with a most effective thrust, wounding Hektor in the same, highly vulnerable location, his neck. Aias' spear thrust is effective, if unremarkable, receiving scant attention in the poem, or from commentators:

> the spearhead went through, and struck him [Hektor] as he was
>   rushing on,
> and cutting through, it reached his neck, and black blood spurted up.
>   (7.261–26)

In Akhilleus' case, this particular spear thrust has been carefully prepared for, the spear itself singled out in unique fashion throughout the poem. No other warrior can manage Akhilleus' Pelian ash spear (μελίη, μείλινος), which Cheiron gave his father (16.141–44). As Shannon (83–84) points out, its use is further restricted in the opponents Akhilleus wields it against. Though using it against both Aineias and Asteropaios, he fails to strike either with it. Of all the Trojan warriors he goes up against, the ash spear, wielded only by Akhilleus, slays only Hektor:

> right there bright Akhilleus drove with his spear, as he [Hektor] was
>   rushing on,
> the spearpoint went straight through his vulnerable neck,
> but the ash spear, heavy with bronze, did not cut through his windpipe.
>   (22.326–28)

The two passages share five common elements, as underlined and numbered in brackets,

ἤλυθεν ἐγχείη, στυφέλιξε δέ μιν μεμαῶτα,   [1, 2]
τμήδην δ᾽ αὐχέν᾽ ἐπῆλθε, μέλαν δ᾽ ἀνεκήκιεν αἷμα   [3, 4, 5]
                                    (7.261–62)

τῇ ῥ᾽ ἐπὶ οἷ μεμαῶτ᾽ ἔλασ᾽ ἔγχεϊ δῖος Ἀχιλλεύς,   [2, 1]
ἀντικρὺ δ᾽ ἁπαλοῖο δι᾽ αὐχένος ἤλυθ᾽ ἀκωκή·   [4, 5]
οὐδ᾽ ἄρ᾽ ἀπ᾽ ἀσφάραγον μελίη τάμε χαλκοβάρεια.   [3]
                                    (22.326–28)

The *Iliad* has a specific verb, δειροτομέω, to refer to a warrior slitting an enemy warrior's throat. At the end of book 21, Agenor uses it in his soliloquy, in a scene generally agreed to parallel and foreshadow the circumstances of Hektor's duel with Akhilleus.[45] Agenor fears that Akhilleus will slit his throat, δειροτομήσει (21.555). All instances of δειροτομέω and ἀποδειροτομέω in the *Iliad* have Akhilleus as their subject (18.336; 21.89, 555; 23.22, 174; cf. Richardson 61). Though not figuring in his duel with Hektor, the verb articulates Akhilleus' special role in the *Iliad* as the throat slitter,[46] the climactic instance of which is his mortally wounding Hektor in the neck.

We should also note the motif's occurrence in the games in book 23, when Diomedes duels Aias. Though both heroes are, at different times in the narrative pattern, the best of the Akhaians, here it is Diomedes, not Aias, who is about to win the duel by wounding his opponent in the neck:

> The son of Tydeus then, over the top of the great shield
> kept grazing his [Aias'] neck with his spearpoint.
>   (23.820–21)

That Aias is now in the defeated position perhaps points to his death at Troy, while Diomedes will return home victorious and alive. In chapter 2, in a discussion of Priam's role, and in chapter 6, in a discussion of sacrifice, we consider why Hektor dies of a neck wound (rather than some other kind of wound). In chapter 6 we observe a further instance of the same motif on the divine plane, when Athena defeats Ares (21.406).

17. Hektor exchanges armor with the best of the Akhaians

After the best of the Akhaians has defeated Hektor, an exchange of arms follows. The motif is dependent upon Hektor's earlier concern, expressed in the previous motif, *12. Hektor asks the best of the Akhaians . . . to return the corpse . . . undefiled, but deprived of his armor.* In his own verbal preliminaries, then, Hektor himself suggests this is the likely outcome of the duel. The tone varies considerably between the two contexts since in book 7 Hektor is alive, defeated, but without serious injury, whereas in book 22 he is dead, a passive participant in the exchange. Hektor's proximity to death in the book 7 duel has been suggested in the earlier scenes with his female relatives and at the end of the encounter ("who were not expecting to see him alive," 7.310). Even the weapons exchange is emblematic of Hektor's vulnerability and of the best of the Akhaians' superior force. Hektor gives Aias a weapon that could be used against him, whereas Aias gives him something that can receive a weapon, rather than inflict a wound:

> having spoken thus he [Hektor] gave him a silver-studded sword,
> together with a scabbard and a well-cut baldrick:
> while Aias gave a sword belt, bright with purple.
>
> (7.303–5)

In book 22 Akhilleus now retrieves from Hektor Akhilleus' own armor, which he (Hektor) had earlier taken from Patroklos:

> And he pulled the bronze spear out from the body,
> and he set it apart, but from the shoulders he stripped
> the bloodied armor.
>
> (22.367–69)

We return to this motif in chapter 3, as it figures in Hektor's duel with Patroklos, and in chapter 5, in discussing exchanges of armor in Old Testament myth.

18. The best of the Akhaians is honored for his victory (by his commander in chief) at a feast

After the best of the Akhaians defeats Hektor, a celebratory mood prevails, resulting in a victory procession back to the ships. In book 7 the Greek warriors lead Aias to Agamemnon ("The well-greaved Akhaians led Aias, rejoicing in his victory, back to bright Agamemnon" 7.311–12), who then hosts a banquet in honor of the best of the Akhaians (7.314–22). At the feast, Agamemnon bestows especial honor upon Aias:

> and he showed honor to Aias with long cuts from the tenderloins,
> did the hero, the son of Atreus, wide-ruling Agamemnon.
>
> (7.321–22)

Akhilleus' sequence contains the same motif, though with two key differences. First, too much friction remains for Agamemnon to host such a feast honoring Akhilleus. With Agamemnon playing a less prominent role, then, Akhilleus himself acts as the leader of the camp for much of books 23 and 24. Second, the feasting motif is complicated by Akhilleus' mourning for Patroklos. Akhilleus announces and leads the procession to the ships and camp in much the same spirit as the men in book 7 convey Aias:

> And now let us go, Akhaians, singing the victory song,
> and let us return to the hollow ships, and let us lead him (Hektor).
>
> (22.391–92)

The formula, ἀείδοντες παιήονα κοῦροι Ἀχαιῶν (22.391), also occurs at 1.473, after Odysseus has accomplished the sacrifice to Apollo.[47] Subsequently, much of book 23 functions as an extended victory feast. Before heading back to his tent, however, Akhilleus first abuses Hektor's corpse (discussed in chapter 5). But after reaching camp, he serves a feast for all the Myrmidons (23.29–34). *Then* his men escort him to Agamemnon, parallel to the Akhaians escorting Aias to Agamemnon (εἰς Ἀγαμέμνονα δῖον ἄγον, 7.312 = 23.36). Now a second feast is immediately prepared, repeating a formula used in the book 7 feast (δαίνυντ', οὐδέ τι θυμὸς ἐδεύετο δαιτὸς ἐΐσης, 7.320 = 23.56).[48] Richardson (166) remarks on the sequence: "The funeral feast of the Myrmidons here precedes the burial, an order which seems unusual." But as we will observe in motif 19, book 7 offers the same sequence of events, which also leads immediately to a funeral. The funeral games contain another instance of the motif, as Akhilleus offers to host a feast for the participants in the armed combat, Diomedes and Aias (23.810).

19. Priam, disturbed over his son's mortal combat, drives out to the middle of the battlefield to propose a truce to care for the dead

The final two motifs are highly involved and are explored again in chapter 2 in connection with Priam's trip outside the city in book 3. Motif 19 is doubled both in book 7 and again in books 22–24. In book 7 the Greeks *and* the Trojans hold parallel council scenes, at which Nestor first suggests a truce, and then Priam, in a separate scene, follows with his own suggestion. In spite of Nestor's having preceded him, the motif is more closely associated with Priam because he plays the same role, developed to a much greater extent, in books 3 and 24, whereas Nestor has no role in the other episodes. There is doubling in the final sequence because book 22 contains a short episode in which Priam states his intended course of action (22.415 ff.), but does not follow through with it until book 24, separated by the lengthy doings concerning Patroklos' funeral. Patroklos' funeral itself serves as a doublet for the preparations and execution of Hektor's funeral, which concludes the poem. Awareness of the narrative pattern, in the parallels books 22–24 provide to book 7, helps address and clarify certain supposed problems often thought to exist in Nestor's proposal.[49]

At the victory feast for Aias, Nestor proposes (7.327–37) a respite from battle to gather and burn (νεκροὺς . . . κατακήομεν, 7.332–33) the many recently slain Akhaians, because Diomedes' *aristeia* prompted a level of carnage parallel to that in Akhilleus' *aristeia*. Nestor additionally suggests that the resultant funeral mound could serve defensive purposes if they add towers to it (πύργους ὑψηλούς, 7.338). The proposal has often been criticized as out of place, as a later addition. Why build a defensive wall now, in the tenth year of the war? Nestor's suggestion of the defensive wall is predicated upon his proposal for the funeral pyre for the dead. The collective funeral mound will itself form the wall he proposes (7.336–39). His central proposal, then, is tending to the dead and performing funeral rituals for them. To better understand the larger function of Nestor's proposal, we need to consider its place in the narrative pattern. The final scene of the *Iliad* will be the funeral of Hektor. It is toward this scene that the whole poem, as well as the narrative pattern that informs it, is aiming to conclude its plot. Shortly before Hektor's funeral, and deeply intertwined with it, is the funeral for Patroklos (23.109–91). Just as Patroklos' death leads to Hektor's death, so are their funerals closely paralleled. Nestor's, and Priam's, proposals to halt the war (Nestor: πόλεμον . . . παῦσαι, 7.331; Priam: παύσασθαι πολέμοιο, 7.376) briefly, to allow for burial, look ahead to the much larger pauses and more detailed descriptions of the funerals for Patroklos and Hektor. The narrative pattern thus uses a motif that functions in a climactic way in books 23–24, but it is somewhat less smoothly adapted to a different, less dramatic context in book 7.

When Nestor specifies relatives gathering bones (ὀστέα . . . ἄγη, 7.334–35) after the bodies have been burned away,[50] he invokes one of the *Iliad*'s most powerful images. It will occur again in Hektor's funeral, eleven lines before the end of the poem (ὀστέα λευκὰ λέγοντο, 24.793). The image is central to Patroklos' funeral, which parallels Hektor's (ὀστέα . . . λέγωμεν, 23.91, 224, 239; ὀστέα λευκὰ / ἄλλεγον, 23.252–53). The *Iliad*'s thematic use of similar phrases (ὀστέα + a form of λέγω) suggests that the notion of loved ones gathering bones from a funeral pyre is central to the end of the narrative pattern. Perhaps most potent of all occurrences of the formula is the simile ("as a father mourns burning the bones of his child," 23.222), which must be taken as evoking Priam.[51] When Akhilleus is compared to a father grieving for his son, unexpectedly, this simile suggests the common ground that will be found between Akhilleus and Priam late in book 24. Nestor's image at 7.334–35 thus looks ahead thematically to the outcomes of the funerals of both Patroklos and Hektor and should not be regarded as an addition.

In the parallel Trojan assembly Priam makes the same suggestion, proposing to send heralds to the Greek camp, asking for a truce to allow them to burn their dead (νεκροὺς / κήομεν, 7.376–77). Priam sends his herald, Idaios, and does not himself meet with the Greeks, as he does in books 3 and 24. As a result of the *aristeia* of the best of the Akhaians in books 5–6 (and 20–22), numerous Trojans have perished and require burial. A much smaller number of Greeks was slain.[52] Hence Nestor's rationale ironically underscores that Priam's role is the more principal for this particular motif (evident in his appearing in the motif three times, as opposed to only once for Nestor). With some irony, Hektor is the first character to introduce burial mounds as a theme (7.84–86).

Before suggesting the truce, Priam instructs the Trojans, "and remember the watch, and let each man be wakeful" (7.371), which Kirk criticizes, arguing that it is borrowed from 18.298.[53] However, the tone of 7.371 corresponds precisely to this moment in Akhilleus' sequence, evoking the mood and atmosphere, the menace and vulnerability the Trojans feel after Hektor has died (22.415 ff), and especially Priam's dangerous journey out into the enemy camp to meet with Akhilleus. In book 7 these possibilities are only suggested, through the extended parallel structure that is the narrative pattern. Hence Priam's detail is a part of a chain that has greater importance in the later sequence but fits less smoothly in the book 7 context. In 7.371 the story line has the greater sequence of the narrative pattern in mind and states only briefly a specific point that will be developed at much greater length in book 24. Books 6–7 offer further indication that the Trojans were greatly alarmed over Hektor's possible, even likely death in the duel with Aias (7.310; cf. 6.500–502). In book 7 the scene is bifurcated into a preliminary trip by Idaios, Priam's herald (7.381), who meets with Diomedes (who even here serves to parallel Akhilleus) and Agamemnon. In book 24 (24.178, 281, 304) Priam and Idaios make the journey together. In book 7 Priam is clearly outside the city (7.427),[54] participating in rituals at the pyre (7.427–29), but his actual departure from Troy is not depicted, unlike in books 3 and 24.

Books 22 and 24 (and book 3, discussed in chapter 2) have a much fuller version of the motif, centered upon Priam and his attempt to retrieve Hektor's corpse from Akhilleus. As the scene shifts from Akhilleus defiling Hektor's corpse (22.395–404), it pauses briefly on Hekabe (405–7) before resting on Priam, in an extreme state of mourning (22.408 ff.). He asks his family members to let him go outside of the city to supplicate Akhilleus, implicitly to retrieve Hektor's corpse. Richardson (149), who regards Priam's speech as anticipating the actual supplication in book 24, notes some parallels: "[T]here too he reminds him of his father Peleus (22.420–1 ~ 24.486–92), and again speaks of his lost sons (22.423–8 ~ 24.493–502)." There follow a speech by Hekabe and an extended focus on Andromakhe, discussed below under the final motif. All of book 23 focuses on the funeral and subsequent games for Patroklos, which should be regarded as an expanded doublet of Hektor's funeral (though also as the conclusion to the middle sequence, books 8–17), and it is analyzed under the following motif. In some senses it intrudes into its present location, much as having Nestor in book 7 make the suggestion to care for the dead before Priam does.[55] That is, in some thematic respects book 24 begins as if following directly after the end of book 22.

Much of book 24, however, focuses closely and at length on Priam's dilemma: how can he retrieve Hektor's corpse and secure the peace and safety necessary for the very funeral rituals Hektor himself was so anxious about? Typical of Akhilleus' sequence, but absent from book 7, Priam receives significant divine aid. In a divine council (24.23–76, 98–120, 143–59), marking a significant pivot in the plot, Apollo, much as Athena in the *Odyssey*'s first divine council (1.45–62), redirects the gods' attention to a larger moral issue, the gap between Hektor's numerous sacrifices to the gods and their present disregard of his corpse. Though Hera objects to some of Apollo's suggestions, Zeus validates his comments about Hektor's sacrifices (24.66–70), an index of a character's piety in myth,[56] and sets in motion a means to retrieve his corpse.[57] While dispatching Thetis to inform her son, he sends Iris to prepare Priam for his momentous, nighttime journey, to ransom Hektor. As Zeus' instructions to Iris dictate, Priam must do much of the work himself, accompanied by only one old man (the herald, Idaios), though receiving divine assistance from Hermes. It is Akhilleus, however, not Priam, who first raises the possibility of a truce to allow for Hektor's funeral, volunteering to restrain his forces (24.656–58). In reserving for Akhilleus this crucial point, the narrative allows him credit for the moral climax of the poem, as the hero undergoes a reversal from his recent abuse of Hektor's corpse to respectfully restoring it to Priam. We focus on Akhilleus' morality in chapter 5.

⌒

20. Both sides mourn their dead and construct a tomb

The doubling continues, growing out of the greater parallels between the deaths and funerals of Hektor and Patroklos, which parallels are intertwined in Akhilleus' macabre abuse of Hektor's corpse on Patroklos' tomb (24.15–17). Greater drama and suspense result in having Hektor's burial, rather than Patroklos', conclude the poem, as the fast-approaching doom awaiting Troy does not even need to be stated at poem's end, so closely is the city's survival linked to the life of its greatest warrior. Nestor's suggestion in the opening sequence for a mass tomb (τύμβον δ' ἀμφὶ πυρὴν ἕνα χεύομεν, 7.336) and the subsequent construction of a defensive wall on the tomb become the funeral and mound (τύμβον . . . εὐρύν θ' ὑψηλόν τε τιθήμεναι, 23.245–47) for Patroklos in Akhilleus' sequence. Priam's suggestion in book 7 for a truce to burn the fallen Trojans in 7 becomes his quest to obtain the corpse of the fallen Hektor in book 24. References to Patroklos' burial rituals occur through book 23.

In book 7 the Trojans eagerly await the return of Idaios (7.414–17), Priam's herald, to learn whether a truce has been arranged, as in book 24 they eagerly await the return of Priam himself (24.697–712). Priam's leading role is evident, not only in prompting the motif but in the larger management of the mourning. In both sequences the mourning threatens to get out of control, unless Priam intervenes. In book 7 Priam himself supervises the collection of the bodies but limits the public mourning:

> But great Priam would not allow them to weep; but in silence
> though grieving in their hearts, they piled up the bodies on the funeral
> pyres,
> and having burnt them in the fire they made their way back to sacred Ilion.

(7.427–29)

In book 24, after Kassandra observes him entering the city, having retrieved Hektor's corpse, a huge crowd gathers to mourn, such that Priam intervenes through a pivotal contrafactual to limit the public mourning:

> and now all the day until the sun went down
> they would have mourned Hektor, shedding tears in front of the gates,
> had not the old man [Priam] addressed the people from his seat,
> "Let my mules come through; but after that
> have your fill of mourning, when I bring him home.
>
> (24.713–17)

The same dynamic recurs an additional time toward the end of book 24, when, after the three lamentations, the city's inhabitants break into mourning, such that Priam redirects their attention toward the necessary gathering of wood (24.776–81).

When Akhilleus asks Priam how much time he would need to carry out Hektor's funeral, Priam mentions the difficulty in obtaining wood because of the Trojan' current circumstances (οἶσθα γὰρ ὡς κατὰ ἄστυ ἐέλμεθα, τηλόθι δ' ὕλη / ἀξέμεν ἐξ ὄρεος, 24.662–63). Both sequences employ parallel expressions for the gathering of the wood and other tasks connected with the funeral pyres of Hektor and Patroklos. Priam's comment contains the basic formula used throughout, a form of ἄγω + ὕλη (7.418, 420; 23.50, 111, etc.). At 24.784 the basic formula occurs with a thematic qualification, a comment on the immense supply of wood gathered for Hektor's pyre, "for nine days they were bringing a prodigious amount of wood," ἐννῆμαρ μὲν τοί γε ἀγίνεον ἄσπετον ὕλην. A variation is also used to describe the similar amount of wood piled upon Patroklos' pyre (23.127: παρακάββαλον ἄσπετον ὕλην).

Awareness of these formulas helps resolve an obscurity in Nestor's original proposition (τύμβον δ' ἀμφὶ πυρὴν ἕνα χεύομεν ἐξαγαγόντες / ἄκριτον ἐκ πεδίου, 7.336–37). Since antiquity commentators have been puzzled by ἄκριτον, uncertain as to what it modified or described.[58] I suggest on the basis of the parallels cited above that Nestor is using the same formula found in both the gathering and piling of timber for the funerals of Hektor and Patroklos. Though ὕλην or ξύλα are absent, ἄκριτον implies one or the other, as object of ἄγω as in the other passages with ἄσπετον ὕλην to designate the amount of timber to be gathered and burned (23.127, 24.784). The poem offers one earlier conjunction of ἄσπετον and ὕλην which also suggests thematic associations with the passages under discussion. At 2.455 as the Greeks march against the Trojans, the gleam from their armor is compared to a conflagration that destroys a forest, Ἠΰτε πῦρ ἀΐδηλον ἐπιφλέγει ἄσπετον ὕλην. In this simile early in the poem, the only other collocation of ἄσπετον and ὕλην, the gleam of the Greeks' armor and the destructive flames to which it is compared may carry with it the suggestion of the flames that will ignite the pyres of Hektor and Patroklos.

In book 7 Nestor proposes building a wall on the mass funeral mound to keep the Greeks safe. In books 23–24 the mound that the Greeks construct for Patroklos also implicitly marks their safety because, with Hektor now slain (whose death is the requisite consequence of Patroklos' own death), the possible threat the Trojans might present to the Greeks is drastically lessened.

The mourning element, almost nonexistent in book 7, is most elaborate in the final books. In the initial sequence on the Greek side, it is suggested only in Nestor's note that the bones of the deceased are to be gathered and stored so that they can be returned to loved ones back in Greece (7.334–35). In books 23–24, however, Akhilleus and Priam lead their peoples in elaborate rituals. Akhilleus will not wash before the heroic feast of motif 18 until Patroklos has been cremated. In book 24 we should recognize the closing speeches as an adapted form of the earlier motif, *9. The greatest Trojan warrior, Hektor, meets his mother, sister-in-law, and his wife, Andromakhe,* and *9a. Andromakhe and Helen refer to Hektor as their brother.* Helen is here the last of the speakers. Again, we can detect a surprising parallel with book 7. At the same assembly at which Priam proposes the truce to bury the dead, Antenor proposes returning Helen (7.348–64), shortly after Hektor's apparent loss to Aias. At the poem's end, Helen serves as a segue to the Greek triumph, pointing ahead to her going home with the Greeks.[59] Helen is final in the speeches in 24 because that is as close as Akhilleus' sequence gets to the restoration of Helen to Menelaos, the actual consequence that will follow soon upon Hektor's death.

༄ ༄ ༄

CHAPTER TWO

The Overture

Book 3 is usually thought to serve a retrospective function, recounting episodes through which the *Iliad* replays and evokes issues associated with the beginning of the war. Though it undoubtedly does serve such a function, this is not its only purpose. While evoking earlier events, book 3 simultaneously introduces many of the poem's central structures, the motifs and type-scenes that recur in later episodes, even in the conclusion of the epic. In this sense, as Edwards (1987: 188) notes, book 3 introduces "the future as well as the past," or, as Owen (28) puts it, it is "retrogressive and progressive at the same time" and contains "the shadows of coming events." Book 3 is almost entirely composed of motifs from the narrative pattern as analyzed in chapter 1, the string of motifs and type-scenes that underlies books 4–7 and 20–24. But since book 3 precedes these two sections of the poem, it *introduces* these motifs and, hence, serves as an overture by acquainting the audience with central components of the *Iliad*'s plot.

Each of the five sections of book 3, Paris' duel with Menelaos (3.1–120, 314–82), Helen and the *teikhoskopia* (3.121–244), Priam's participation in the sacrifice and oaths (3.245–313), and the aftermath of the duel (3.383–461), presents, in miniature, relevant selections of the principal narrative pattern. Paris' duel with Menelaos, though looking back to the root cause of the war, also provides an initial statement of those portions of the narrative pattern depicting Hektor's duel with the best of the Akhaians, but with Paris in Hektor's role. The *teikhoskopia* (a frequently criticized section of book 3) contains motifs from the narrative pattern involving reactions to Hektor's death, with Helen in Andromakhe's role, anxious at the Trojan wall in book 22. Priam's trip outside the city in book 3 to witness the oath-taking ceremony on the battlefield employs the same motifs that will be developed on much larger scale in books 22 and 24 (and the brief instance in book 7), when he sets the terms of mourning and retrieves Hektor's corpse. Book 3 provides a sketch of the narrative pattern, with special emphasis on it's conclusion: Priam, concerned over the mortal combat of his son, meeting with the leader of the Greek camp. By noting how much of the narrative pattern underlies Paris' duel with Menelaos, and the other episodes that make up book 3, we can better understand book 3's relation to book 7 and to the concluding books of the poem.

If book 3 is an overture, why doesn't it occur at the very beginning of the *Iliad?* As Stawell argues (50), the narrator is eager "'to secure a hearing' by a vivid scene at the outset": to ensure that it has our attention, the *Iliad* first gives us "a sudden fierce and hasty action, which we feel is bound to have momentous consequences," the quarrel between Akhilleus and Agamemnon. Having accomplished this task in book 1, the poem addresses other necessities in book 2 (discussed in chapter 3). Then, by replaying the roots of the war and sketching out the larger design of the rest of the epic, book 3 skillfully interweaves elements that serve opposite functions, retrospective and premonitory.

While the encounter between Paris and Menelaos is paradigmatic for the war, at the same time it serves as foil for most of the poem's fighting. Though neither man is in the first rank of fighters, in having the two warriors with competing claims to Helen fight each other, the narrative offers simultaneously a version of the war's cause and its possible conclusion. Yet in having Paris defeated so easily in the first duel, the narrative points ahead to eventual Trojan defeat, to Akhilleus' easy defeat of Hektor in the concluding duel, itself the embodiment of Troy's fall. Though not a first-rate warrior, Menelaos nonetheless embodies the Greeks, and the greater justice of their cause, as Paris embodies the Trojans' greater culpability and recklessness in provoking the war. The poem underscores this by selecting their duel for the most prominent articulation of Zeus as guarantor of the sanctity of hospitality (3.354). At one level Paris' easy defeat exemplifies the moral that hospitality myths illustrate, punishment for those who transgress the sanctity of hospitality (discussed in chapter 6).

In using Paris to introduce motifs in which Hektor will later figure, book 3 is employing antitypes. Although Hektor and Paris are logically parallel as brothers, as the two most prominent sons of Priam, they are opposites in most other respects, such as heroism and sense of honor. Frye (49–52, 366) and others use the terms "high mimetic" as opposed to "low mimetic" to indicate such disparities in characterization. Typically, characters in an epic or tragedy are high mimetic, better than the audience, as Aristotle suggests in the *Poetics*. However, the *Iliad*'s scenes involving Paris tend to be low mimetic, presenting a character less moral than the audience. Throughout this study I use the term *parody* to indicate such differences between what the audience expects to see in a character in epic and how Paris instead behaves. In book 3 (and elsewhere, as discussed in chapter 3), Paris functions as a parody of Hektor, and a parody of heroic values in general.

Paris and Helen are the central married couple in terms of why the war started and is still being waged, but Hektor and Andromakhe are the central married couple in terms of the *Iliad*'s plot, the war's impact on the losing side, and the audience's sympathy. As the only two married couples the poem depicts (except much older couples, such as Priam and Hekabe, and Antenor and Theano), they offer both a natural symmetry and polarity with each other.[1] Paris is the Trojan who begins the war, while Hektor is the Trojan whose death signals its imminent conclusion, for without him the fall of Troy is imminent, as the poem's conclusion implies. The two men are further linked as brothers, and by the reciprocal roles they play in *10a. Hektor is persuaded by his brother to battle the best of the Akhaians*. As Paris and Hektor frame most of the poem in their losing duels (as the first and last Trojans depicted fighting), and all of its fighting, so their wives' appearances in adjacent contexts are similarly linked. Helen seems to share in Paris' culpability for causing the war: by presenting something of a replay of their initial encounter, a passage at the end of book 3 implies that she went with him willingly (3.441–48). Andromakhe, on the other hand, is one of the poem's most tragic and most sympathetic characters. Helen's plight in book 3, though evoking neither descriptor, nonetheless prefigures much of Andromakhe's predicament in book 22. She is the wife of the Trojan who is now in a duel to resolve the entire war. Helen's prominence at the end of book 3 also looks ahead to her prominence at the end of both sequences of the narrative pattern, visible in Antenor's remarks at 7.348–53, and in Helen's own speech for Hektor at 24.762–75. Book 3 uses the "marriage" of Paris and Helen as a parody of the marriage of Hektor and Andromakhe.

While book 3 quickly suggests much of the pattern, it sometimes subordinates its elements to the present needs and concerns of the narrative in book 3. As a result, book 3 does not present all the motifs from the narrative pattern together in one unbroken sequence but mainly employs motifs from the second half of the narrative pattern (motifs 9–19).[2] It first offers a brief startup of the duel with elements corresponding to Hektor's duels with Aias and Akhilleus (motifs 10–18), then focuses on Helen, foreshadowing Andromakhe's circumstances in books 6 and 22. The *teikhoskopia* segues from Helen to a focus on Priam, who leaves the city to participate in a ritual with his enemy and returns with a sacrificial victim, circumstances that look directly to Priam's role in book 24 (motif 19). Only then does the narrative return to Paris' duel with Menelaos (again corresponding to Hektor's duels with Aias and Akhilleus), employing motifs from earlier in the pattern. This somewhat zigzagged presentation of the pattern's sequence of motifs has no doubt hindered recognition of the relation of book 3 to the rest of the poem.

Book 3 also employs motifs that, though not part of the principal narrative pattern, occur in *one* of the separate sequences, in Hektor's duel with Aias in book 7, or in his duel with Akhilleus and its aftermath in books 22 and 24, suggesting additional ties between book 3 and the concluding section of the narrative pattern. While commentators have noted considerable common ground between the book 3 duel and that in book 7 between Hektor and Aias, they usually omit the parallels with Hektor's duel with Akhilleus. Book 3 concludes with Agamemnon's insistence that Helen be restored to Menelaus (3.458–60). Helen gives the final speech in book 24 because that is as close as Akhilleus' sequence gets to the restoration of Helen to Menelaos, the actual consequence that will follow soon upon Hektor's death.[3]

In terms of the motifs of the narrative pattern, book 3 falls into five sections:

I.   Paris agrees to face Menelaos in a duel to determine the war (3.1–120: motifs 11, 10a, 12)
II. Helen, his wife, learning of the fearful duel, goes to the tower to view the battlefield (3.121–244: motifs 9, 9a)
III. Priam leaves the city to take part in a ceremony with the leader of the Greeks (3.245–313: motif 19)
IV. Paris duels with Menelaos (3.314–82: motifs 2, 14, 16, 5f, 15)
V.   In the duel's aftermath, Paris lives and Helen comes to him (parody) (3.383–461: motif 9)

I. Paris agrees to face Menelaos in a duel to determine the war

This first section (3.1–120) employs motifs from the narrative pattern depicting Hektor as he faces the best of the Akhaians in a duel to determine the war, with Paris for Hektor, and Menelaos for the best of the Akhaians.[4] This section also features motifs found in *one* of the two sequences, in Hektor's duel with Aias or in his duel with Akhilleus. After book 2's lengthy catalogs, book 3 opens with the promise of immediate combat, the two armies facing each other for the first time in the poem. However, the narrative quickly shifts its focus away from the amassed armies to motifs from Hektor's duels. One formula first suggests that the action will shift to a duel: Οἱ δ᾽ ὅτε δὴ σχεδὸν ἦσαν ἐπ᾽ ἀλλήλοισιν ἰόντες ("and when they were near, going toward each other," 3.15), a line occurring especially in the *aristeiai* of

Diomedes and Akhilleus to introduce *individual* encounters (5.14, 850; 6.121; 20.176; 21.148; 22.248).[5] Its next-to-last occurrence (22.248) marks Hektor's decision to stand and face Akhilleus. The formula is the first of many details linking Paris' duel with Hektor's duels with the best of the Akhaians. In book 22 the formula occurs between motifs 11 and 12 of the narrative pattern.

Leaping out in front of the ranks, Paris challenges the best of the Akhaians to face him in combat. The formula that articulates his challenge (προ-καλίζετο πάντας ἀρίστους, 3.19) is used three times of Hektor's challenging the best of the Akhaians, a prelude to his duel with Aias (7.150, 285; cf. 7.39, 50). The formula does not, however, occur in book 22. The rest of the Trojans are safely within Troy, removing the need for any such challenge.

In this duel Menelaos functions as the best of the Akhaians, a role he serves throughout book 3 (and in book 17, as discussed in chapter 3). Though not a warrior on a par with Akhilleus, Diomedes, or Aias, Menelaus is a natural embodiment of the Greek side as the man on whose behalf the war is fought and the one with the strongest personal motive against Paris. In addition to serving in those motifs that feature Hektor, Paris also parallels Aineias in his close relationship with Aphrodite, evident in another motif from the pattern that book 3 introduces, as discussed below. As he strides out to meet Paris, Menelaos is like a lion (3.23–27). Just before he faces Aineias in his *aristeia*, Diomedes too is compared to a lion as he slays and despoils two victims (5.161–65). The same dynamic begins Akhilleus' sequence. An imminent clash between the two armies (20.156–58) turns instead into a duel between Aineias and Akhilleus (20.158–60), the latter being compared to a lion (20.164–75). Both similes depict the Greek hero as a lion so intent on his prey that he can endure attacks from others, including humans (20.166–73, 3.23–28), and in both, the humans are characterized by the same epithet ("vigorous," 20.167, 3.26).[6]

A prominent motif from the pattern immediately follows the lion simile: *11. Panic seizes Hektor on first seeing the best of the Akhaians, prompting his retreat . . . back into the army.* Although Paris initiates the duel (as does Hektor in book 7), he panics as soon as he sees Menelaos, dashing back into the Trojan ranks (3.30–38). Paris' reaction thus confers a certain parodic air on the episode.[7] Here, as in Hektor's sequences, the same word is used for "panic," τρόμος (3.34, 7.215, 22.136).

Book 3 (3.38–76) proceeds with another motif from the narrative pattern, though slightly modified, *10a. Hektor is persuaded by his brother to battle the best of the Akhaians.* After Paris' shameful retreat, Hektor criticizes his brother in a scene categorized by Fenik (1968: 26, 49–51, 155) as a rebuke pattern. As a result of Hektor's rebuke Paris is now willing, even eager, to fight Menelaos. Consequently, we have an ironic variation on motif 10a, with Paris as the parallel for Hektor, as we should expect, but Hektor himself as the brother who persuades "Hektor" to face the best of the Akhaians in the duel to decide the war.

Book 3 continues with a motif found in Akhilleus' sequence, but only hinted at in the book 7 duel, *The leader of the Greek forces prevents his men from harming Hektor so that the duel may proceed unimpeded.* In book 22, shortly before the duel, Akhilleus signals to his men not to throw projectiles at Hektor (22.205–6), lest they deprive him of his own claim to victory over Hektor. In book 3 the Greeks are also attempting to hurl projectiles and shoot arrows at Hektor when he proposes the duel between Paris and Menelaos, until Agamemnon commands them not to (3.79–80). The motif, Greeks attempting to hurl projectiles at Hektor and needing to be restrained by their leader, does not occur in book 7, which duel has a stronger sense of decorum, from the civility between Athena and Apollo to the heralds intervening to conclude the contest. Book 7's closest parallel is Agamemnon seating his troops so that they will listen to Hektor's proposal (7.57).

Though not present in book 7, book 3's instance of the motif is framed by other structures that are present in the book 7 sequence. The lines immediately preceding those quoted above recur in both contexts, depicting in book 3 how glad Hektor is that Paris will fight Menelaus and in book 7, that he himself will duel with Aias:

> So he spoke, and Hektor was greatly cheered having heard his speech,
> and going into the middle he was restraining the ranks of the Trojans,
> having taken his spear by the middle, and they all were seated.
> $(3.76–78 = 7.54–56)$

The lines immediately following the motif depict Hektor as he sets forth the terms of the duel:

> And Hektor spoke to both sides,
> "Listen to me, Trojans and well-greaved Akhaians."
> $(3.85–86 = 7.66–67)$

This last parallel cannot be present in book 22 since, again, all the Trojans are within the walls.

Book 3 continues with several elements from another motif occurring in the same section of the pattern as above, *12. Hektor asks the best of the Akhaians to swear an oath to return the corpse of the defeated to his companions, undefiled, but deprived of its armor.* This section of book 3 also utilizes elements that occur in close proximity to motif 12 in one, but not both, of the two sequences.

Though Hektor does not here specify the treatment of the slain warrior (3.86–94) he announces the terms of the duel's outcome, a rough equivalent to his concern within the pattern for burial rites for the duel's loser. The line introducing his speech and the first line of Hektor's speech in which he specifies burial agreements both recur in book 7 (3.85–86 = 7.66–67).

The next line in book 3 contains a motif that recurs just before Hektor is about to face Akhilleus in book 22. In each context Hektor asserts Paris' responsibility for starting the war:

Ἀλεξάνδροιο, τοῦ εἵνεκα νεῖκος ὄρωρεν
(3.87)

Ἀλέξανδρος . . . ἥ τ᾿ ἔπλετο νείκεος ἀρχή
(22.115–16)[8]

These are the only two passages in the *Iliad* stating that Paris begat the strife, though his earlier deeds are elsewhere referred to (and 3.100 is close to being a restatement).[9] In each case Hektor makes his remark while the best of the Akhaians is nearby, Menelaos (3.87) and Akhilleus (22.115–16).

Because Hektor does not articulate the possibility that the duel may result in the death of either combatant, but merely refers to a victor (3.92), a full instantiation of motif 12 cannot occur here. However, Menelaos, in his response to Hektor's speech, puts the result in starker terms, emphasizing the likelihood of death, returning the narrative's focus to the (likely) death of the Trojan in the duel (3.100–101). This brusque, even defiant response, rebuffing Hektor's emphasis on a peaceful resolution to the conflict (3.93–94), parallels Akhilleus' attitude in book 22 (22.261–72, 345–54), when he will not agree to Hektor's requests on the treatment of the fallen warrior. In books 3 and 7 the immediate response to Hektor's speech is the same, a somewhat strained silence (Ὣς ἔφαθ᾿, οἱ δ᾿ ἄρα πάντες ἀκὴν ἐγένοντο σιωπῇ, 3.95 = 7.92).

Menelaos agrees to the duel, but adds his own stipulations: a sacrifice is to be performed before the duel, with Priam present to oversee the oaths (3.103–10). These points serve as a transition into Priam's segment, book 3's third section, in our analysis. When Menelaos finishes enumerating the sacrifice (Trojans are to bring two lambs for sacrifice, Greeks one), both sides, hoping for an end to the war, remove their armor, and clear a space for the duel. The resultant space created around the duel (3.113–15) parallels those in books 7 and 22, duels that unfold with no interference from any other warriors. Hektor then sends a herald to retrieve Priam and the lambs for sacrifice.

~

II. Helen, his wife, learning of the fearful duel, goes to the tower to view the battlefield

But instead of moving on to Priam, the narrative unexpectedly focuses on Helen, the principal subject of book 3's second section (3.121–244). Helen's making her way to the tower to see the duel makes central use of the narrative pattern's motifs 9 and 9a, Hektor depicted with his closest female relatives, including his wife. In terms of the narrative pattern, Helen functions here as a parody (which becomes more pronounced in the fifth section of book 3) of Andromakhe. To reach Helen, however, the second section follows two parallel messengers. Hektor sends a herald to Troy to fetch Priam (3.116–17), while Iris is sent to Helen to tell her of the duel about to be fought on her behalf. Why Iris is sent is unspecified, but the closest parallel is Zeus' dispatching her to summon Priam in book 24 (24.143–59). The parallels have not been noted by commentators, perhaps because of the indirection in book 3: after Iris appears to Helen, we follow Helen, who then goes to Priam to tell him that he is to leave the city to oversee rites for his son's duel. In book 24 Iris appears directly to Priam, telling him to leave the city to ransom his son's corpse, his son having died in a duel with the best of the Akhaians.[10] Again book 3 employs a motif found in one, but not both, of the sequences.

Some motifs are used only here to depict Helen and in books 6 and 22 to depict Andromakhe. When Iris comes to Helen, she takes the form of her sister-in-law, Laodike (3.122). The kinship term, γάλοως, "sister-in-law," is closely associated with both Andromakhe and Helen.[11] It is twice used of Andromakhe, when Hektor is looking for her (6.383) and when she has fainted after seeing his corpse dragged about the city (22.473). The only other occurrence in the *Iliad* is in Helen's eulogy for Hektor (24.769), when she notes that if any of her sisters-in-law spoke harshly to her, Hektor would always restrain them. The word γάλοως is always used in connection with either Helen or Andromakhe and always of their association with Hektor or, as at 3.122, of Helen's association with Hektor's stand-in, Paris. Helen herself is Hektor's sister-in-law.

When Iris/Laodike reaches Helen, she, as Andromakhe after Hektor's duel with Akhilleus, is weaving at the loom: ἥ δὲ μέγαν ἱστὸν ὕφαινε (3.125); ἀλλ' ἥ γ' ἱστὸν ὕφαινε μυχῷ (22.440). The *Iliad*'s only other collocation of ἱστὸν, "loom," and ὕφαινε, "weave," is also used of Andromakhe, at roughly the same point of the initial sequence (6.456), when Andromakhe and Hektor converse. The parallels extend to the item each is presently weaving, δίπλακα πορφυρέην ("a bright, folded robe," 3.126, 22.441, the *Iliad*'s only two instances of the collocation). The same compound verb, occurring only in these two passages in the *Iliad,* depicts them at their work, ἐνέπασσεν (3.126), ἐν δὲ θρόνα ποικίλ᾿ ἔπασσε (22.441, tmesis).

Each wife then engages in conversation about her need to see her husband's duel. Although in book 3 it is Iris/Laodike who raises the point and in book 22 it is Andromakhe, the first line of each respective speech contains several common elements:

δεῦρ᾿ ἴθι, νύμφα φίλη, ἵνα θέσκελα ἔργα ἴδηαι

(3.130)

δεῦτε, δύω μοι ἔπεσθον, ἴδωμ᾿ ὅτιν᾿ ἔργα τέτυκται

(22.450)

Iris/Laodike goes on to tell Helen of the combatants in the duel and the reason for fighting:

But Alexander and Menelaus, dear to Ares,
will fight for your sake with their great spears;
you will be called wife of he that has won.

(3.136–38)

In book 22 Andromakhe expresses her fear about the assumed combatants:

But I'm dreadfully
afraid that bright Akhilleus will chase daring Hektor,
having cut him off, alone, away from the city onto the plain,
and put on end to his painful bravery.

(22.454–57)

As a result of the conversation about her husband's duel, each wife then rushes from her chamber in a highly emotional state, seeking a spot from which she might observe the duel. Helen rushes out into the street, crying (3.142). Andromakhe hurries forth like a woman possessed (22.460). Each woman is accompanied by attendants, described with similar formulas, ἅμα τῇ γε καὶ ἀμφίπολοι δύ᾿ ἕποντο (3.143); ἅμα δ᾿ ἀμφίπολοι κίον αὐτῇ (22.461).[12] In this tense state, both wives reach the tower (3.145, 154; 22.462), where each encounters a throng of people.

In Helen's case, the throng is Priam and the elders, who are briefly described in lines that form a transition to the *teikhoskopia* (3.146–52). Helen's urgent desire to see her husband fighting retreats into the background as she approaches them, and their talk instead focuses on Helen's beauty (3.156–60). In her subsequent conversation with Priam, neither character makes any mention of the duel, nor does the rest of this section treat the subject at all (since Iris mentioned it) until the herald Idaios summons Priam (3.249 ff). Although the *teikhoskopia* has often been criticized as out of place, an improper use of a type-scene better employed in the first rather than in the tenth year of the war (e.g., Kirk 1985: 286–87), its beginning and ending parallel Andromakhe's circumstances in books 6 and 22.

On the other hand, the leisurely pace of the *teikhoskopia* fits the occasion: the armies have ceased their fighting and await Priam, who is unaware, as yet, that he is to take part in the oath-swearing ceremony. There is no denying the anachronistic tenor of Priam's asking the identities of the leading Greeks in the tenth year of the war; nonetheless, as the scholia note (Erbse 389), the special circumstances of the occasion—the warriors having removed their armor, and waiting, motionless, for the preliminaries to the duel—allow better opportunity than would have been usual for the Trojans to view the individual Greek warriors. Helen patiently fields his questions about Agamemnon, Odysseus, and Telamonian Aias, and volunteers the identification of Idomeneus (3.230–33).

At this point (3.234), however, the tenor of the scene shifts, as Helen, no longer merely answering Priam but volunteering her own thoughts, announces that she can see all of the best of the Akhaians, except her brothers. The narrator then informs us that both brothers have already died, though Helen, scanning the battlefield, is unaware of this. As this section concludes the *teikhoskopia*, the entire digressive panorama has been leading up to just this scene—an anxious Helen,[13] unable to spot her male relatives, and feeling partly to blame for their possible danger. This is precisely Andromakhe's predicament at the end of book 22, when, as did Helen, she frantically rushes to the tower to see the outcome of the duel between Hektor and the best of the Akhaians: "She stood on the wall, looking about, and she saw him" (ἔστη παπτήνασ' ἐπὶ τείχεϊ, τὸν δ' ἐνόησεν 22.463). In book 3 Helen comments:

> and now I see all the quick-glancing Akhaians
>
> . . . .
>
> but I cannot see the two marshalers of the hosts,
> horse-taming Kastor and Polydeukes, good with his fists.
>
> (3.234–37)

Helen and Andromakhe are further linked in these episodes in the emphasis placed on their connections to brothers and brothers-in-law. Helen refers to Hektor as her brother-in-law (δᾶερ, 6.344), while Andromakhe refers to Hektor as her brother (κασίγνητος, 6.430). Helen and Andromakhe are both trying to see their "brothers," who, unknown to them, are already dead.

⟿

III. Priam leaves the city to take part in a ceremony with the leader of the Greeks

When the heralds Hektor sent reach Priam, book 3 resumes the thread involving his participation in the sacrifice and oath-taking ceremony, employing elements from motif 19 of the narrative pattern: *19. Priam, disturbed over his son's mortal combat, drives out to the middle of the battlefield to propose a truce to care for the dead.* As earlier noted, book 3's first section concludes suggesting the focus on Priam will follow immediately, but instead Helen's section intervenes. Because of this, the first two elements of Priam's pattern (motifs a and b below) occur earlier, at the beginning of Helen's sequence, or what we have labeled section II (3.121–244), while the rest of his pattern resumes as soon as the *teikhoskopia* ends. Book 7 contains a very brief instance of the same group of motifs shortly *after* the conclusion of the duel between Hektor and Aias, just as books 22–24 place the corresponding elements *after* the conclusion of Hektor's duel. Book 3, then, by placing Priam's business and the focus on Helen *before* the duel, alters the usual sequence, which has hindered recognition of its relation to events in books 7, 22, and 24. Because section III (3.245–313) offers the most complex correspondences with the narrative pattern (especially with motifs in books 22 and 24) of any of the five sections, we analyze it in greater detail.

a. Iris comes with word of what is happening outside the city involving Priam's son

Iris' unmotivated appearance to Helen in book 3 has prompted criticism.[14] Parallels with Iris' approach to Priam in book 24 suggest that her chief function in book 3 is prompting Helen to go to Priam. As soon as the *teikhoskopia* concludes, with Helen failing to spot her brothers, Hektor's messengers arrive, enclosing the entire Helen section in a larger ring compositional structure:

Hektor sends heralds to get lambs and Priam: 3.116–17
      Helen goes to Priam: 3.121–244 (= section II)
Heralds, having obtained lambs, approach Priam: 3.245–46[15]

In book 24 Iris comes directly to Priam, announcing herself as Zeus' messenger (24.173). This motif does not occur in book 7, though Antenor's comments at the impromptu assembly (7.345–79) are the closest parallel. However, most of what transpires at that assembly is an instance of the following motif.

b. Priam is seated, surrounded by a group of men cast as opposites to his son, in a scene infused with a strange atmosphere

When Iris, or Helen prompted by Iris, reaches Priam, he is seated, surrounded by a large group of men, in a scene infused with a strange atmosphere. In book 3 (3.146) the scene owes its peculiarity to Helen's transcendent beauty, to unusual qualities assigned the elders gathered about Priam (whose voices are compared to cicadas' chirping), and the weird juxtaposition of Priam's seeming cheerfulness with the seriousness of the upcoming duel. The elders as a group are opposites to Paris, too old to fight and taking no active part in the war. But they are ineffectual when they try to suggest a course of action opposed to his.

In book 24 Priam is surrounded by all nine of his surviving sons (24.161), including Paris (though they are not named until 24.249–51). Priam marks them as opposites to Hektor by wishing they had all died in his place (24.253–54), and referring to them as "wicked children, disgraces" (24.253), whereas Hektor, along with the also-slain Mestor and Troilos, he describes as his "best [ἀρίστους] sons" (24.255). Much about Priam's trip to meet with Akhilleus will have a surreal quality,[16] but such a modality begins with Iris' message that Priam himself will go through the Greek lines to see Akhilleus.

In book 7 the impromptu assembly gathers outside Priam's doors. All are seated, in accordance with usual assembly decorum, except the speaker. The tone is again unusual, evident in the unique description given the council, "the assembly . . . in terrible disorder" (ἀγορὴ . . . δεινὴ τετρηχυῖα, 7.345–46), in Antenor's proposal to give Helen back (7.350–53), in Paris' rejection of the proposal (ironic when Paris insists of Antenor, "Surely the gods themselves have ruined your brain," 7.360), and in Priam's too-easy acquiescence to Paris' position.

c. "Iris" tells him to go out of the city to the battlefield because of a duel involving his son

As noted above, book 3 reverses the order governing the other two sequences by having Priam's scenes precede his son's duel. In book 3 the messenger is the herald Idaios, who tells Priam of the duel, that Paris and Menelaos are to fight to determine the war, and that Priam is to go outside the city to oversee the ceremonies involving the duel. The verb Idaios uses of Priam going down to the plain is καταβῆναι (*katabenai*, 3.253), the verb that gives the name, *catabasis*, to the subgenre of myth that depicts a descent to the underworld.

In book 7 there is, initially, no messenger reporting to Priam. Rather, at first Priam tells Idaios to report to Menelaos and Agamemnon (7.372). However, Idaios later reports back from the Greek camp (7.416), having received replies from Diomedes and Agamemnon about the terms of the truce. Here the duel is less directly involved because the truce is called as a consequence of Diomedes' *aristeia*, but in the narrative pattern Aias has the duel with Hektor. In Akhilleus' sequence, his duel with Hektor concludes his *aristeia*, but in the initial sequence these functions are split among Aias and Diomedes.

In book 24, with the climactic duel between Priam's son Hektor and Akhilleus long ended, the messenger Iris tells Priam that Zeus bids him to ransom Hektor's corpse from Akhilleus as the unresolved final terms of their duel. Thus, as a result of the duel, he must leave the city, as in books 3 and 7, a trip suggesting passage to the underworld.

d. Priam shudders on hearing the message

In books 3 and 24 (but not 7) Priam shudders on first hearing the messenger's report about the disposition of the terms of his son's duel and his own role in it (ῥίγησεν δ᾽ ὁ γέρων, 3.259; τὸν δὲ τρόμος ἔλλαβε γυῖα, 24.170).[17] The motif is not present in 7, which entire episode moves at a brisker pace than those in 3 and 24. In fact, no description of any kind is given of the Trojans' reaction to Idaios' report of his meeting in the Greek camp (7.414–17). Instead, both sides immediately prepare to gather their dead and collect wood for a pyre. Sheppard (38) is the only previous commentator to note the parallel in books 3 and 24: "Meanwhile the sacrificial beasts are ready, and the heralds fetch King Priam. He shivers as he rises, then drives out through the Scaean gates, down to the plain. This picture is the poet's subtle preparation for Priam's visit to Achilleus."

e. He orders others to prepare his vehicle

In book 3 this motif follows immediately after the prior one (3.259–60). In book 7 the motif does not occur, for, as with motif IIIc, Idaios is the only character whose coming and going are depicted. Priam is depicted giving other orders (as discussed below), but his preparations for departure from and return to the city are omitted. In book 24, the lengthiest and most elaborate of the episodes, Priam gives two sets of directions to have his vehicle made ready (24.189–90, 263–64), the second necessary because his sons fail to carry out the first set of orders (Richardson 293).

f. He mounts his vehicle, which he himself drives

Though we might expect an aged figure such as Priam to have a chariot driver, in the two fullest depictions, in 3 and 24, Priam drives, holding the reins. In book 3 he is shown mounting his chariot and grasping the reins (3.261 = 3.311). In book 7, as with motifs IIIc and e, the rapid pace omits any description of his departure from Troy (if there had been such a description, it would probably have come after 7.417). In book 24 there are in fact two vehicles, but Priam is depicted mounting and driving his chariot (24.322, 326).

g. An aged attendant or herald accompanies him

In all three episodes an aged helper accompanies Priam. While there are some variations in his role, Idaios appears only in these three scenes and is the main version of the figure who accompanies Priam (though in book 3 Antenor acts as the aged attendant). Idaios' sole reason for being in the *Iliad* seems to be to aid Priam (and Hektor) at this stage of his narrative pattern. His name may derive from "timber" (ἴδη), as noted by Herodotus and Theocritos, suggesting a possible connection with the wood-gathering scenes at this same juncture of the narrative pattern (see chapter 1, motif 20). In book 3, Antenor rides in the chariot with Priam, but Idaios also accompanies him out to the battlefield, as he and another herald bring the sacrificial victims and mixing bowl out from the city (though their actions are not fully described). Idaios' first mention by name in the poem is only a few lines earlier (3.248), and previously he is referred to as κῆρυξ (3.116, both Idaios and a second herald, unless it is the Greek Talthybios, as at 7.277, are signified here, and at 3.245). Of the two Trojan heralds in book 3 only Idaios is named, and only Idaios speaks (3.250–58), relaying the terms of the duel directly to Priam. Antenor then gets into the chariot with Priam. Though not depicted, Idaios and the unnamed Trojan herald must accompany them in a second vehicle, since they are present at the ceremony at 3.268 and 3.274, having brought the lambs and mixing bowl. Why is Antenor in this episode as Priam's attendant but not in the parallel scenes in books 7 and 24? His taking part in the ceremony is a natural outgrowth of his prominence in the *teikhoskopia*. His role here parallels his speaking up at the assembly in book 7 (347–54), when he serves as an attendant to Priam but in an entirely different capacity.[18]

Idaios' prominence at the end of the book 7 duel is a natural result of his role in the overall pattern, anticipating his task in book 24. Idaios and Talthybios, the Greek herald, break up the duel between Hektor and Aias (7.274–76), with Idaios taking the more prominent role. Idaios speaks to the warriors, telling them to cease fighting, to give way to the night (7.279–82), while Talthybios is silent. Given Hektor's own parallel with the sacrificial victims, a tie or link between Idaios and Hektor is perhaps briefly suggested when Hektor sends Idaios into the city to obtain the sacrificial victims (3.116).

In book 24 Zeus himself orders Idaios' participation (24.148–51), which Iris then relays (24.177–80), typical of the greater divine involvement characterizing Akhilleus' sequence. Zeus directs that Priam be accompanied only by an old herald, one who will drive the mules and wagon that will retrieve Hektor. Zeus also specifies that Hermes take part (24.153 ff). Hermes' scene with Priam in book 24 is not part of the *Iliad*'s narrative pattern but resembles a motif in the *Odyssey*'s extended narrative pattern: "*A divine helper appears, advising him how to approach a powerful female figure*" (Louden 1999a: 4–6). Since the motif occurs three times in the *Odyssey* (Hermes to Odysseus, *Od.* 10.277, and Athena to Odysseus, 7.19 and 13.221), and only once in the *Iliad*, there is greater likelihood that the *Iliad* borrows the motif from the *Odyssey*, from its narrative pattern, rather than vice versa, as is usually argued.[19] Hermes can also be seen as a divine parallel to Idaios. Hesiod calls Hermes "herald of the gods" (*Works* 80). It is Idaios who first spots Hermes (24.351–52). The two characters are mentioned consecutively (24.689–90), in a natural association (cf. 24.468–71).

h. He drives away from the city, out into the battlefield

Thus accompanied, Priam leaves the city, driving out across the battlefield, himself driving the horse-drawn chariot, in all three sequences. These three instances are the only times in the *Iliad* that Priam leaves the city, though the circumstances vary considerably. In book 24 this is a dangerous enterprise, crossing enemy lines alone, whereas in books 3 and 7 truces are in effect as a result of the respective duels, allowing Priam to proceed without fear. In book 3 Priam drives his chariot (3.263), accompanied by Antenor, to oversee the sacrifices and oaths before the duel has taken place. In book 7, though Priam is not shown driving out of the city, he is depicted on the battlefield the day after the duel to gather corpses (7.418–29). In book 24, after the duel in which Hektor dies, Priam drives out with Idaios driving the mule-drawn wagon, crosses the battlefield, and goes through the enemy camp to Akhilleus' tent. In book 24 this motif is greatly expanded by the meeting with Hermes, who becomes Priam's driver for the rest of the trip. In both books 3 and 24 the arrival is signaled by a variation on a formula:

'ἀλλ' ὅτε δή ῥ' ἵκοντο μετὰ Τρῶας καὶ Ἀχαιούς.
(3.264)

'ἀλλ' ὅτε δή πύργους τε νεῶν καὶ τάφρον ἵκοντο.
(24.443)

'ἀλλ' ὅτε δὴ κλισίην Πηληϊάδεω ἀφίκοντο.
(24.448)[20]

i. He is disturbed about the mortal combat of his son

In each sequence, Priam is disturbed about the deadly consequences of his son's duel, beforehand, in book 3, and afterward, in book 24. In both contexts Priam makes a speech about how much he has to endure with regard to his son's (probable) death. In book 3 Priam declares that he cannot bear to watch Paris fight Menelaus (οὔ πω τλήσου', 3.306). Priam uses a similar phrase when he meets Akhilleus: "I have endured such things as no other man" (ἔτλην δ' οἷ' οὔ πώ τις ἐπιχθόνιος βροτὸς ἄλλος, 24.505).[21] Priam's remarks in book 3 (3.304–9) serve as a short version of his speeches to Akhilleus in book 24. Kirk (1985: 309) notes the parallel with book 24: "Thus the present passage *Il.* 3.306 foreshadows the passionate sensitivity Priam will reveal both before and after Hektor's death, in books 22 and 24." Priam's concern, overt in books 3 (22) and 24, is expressed by other characters in book 7, as Priam himself does not appear until the assembly, after the duel has already taken place (7.345 ff). Book 7 does not give a perspective on the duel from inside Troy, as do books 3 and 24. Instead Hektor himself emphasizes concern with burial before the duel (7.77–86), his concern looking ahead to the same predicament in Akhilleus' sequence. All the Trojans are anxious when he emerges (unexpectedly) alive from the duel with Aias, (7.307–10).

j. In connection with his son's duel, Priam participates in a ceremony with the leader of the Greek camp

Prominent in books 3 and 24, this motif is somewhat altered in book 7, with Idaios, Priam's herald, present at the meeting, in place of Priam. In book 3 the ceremony serves as the specific impetus for Priam's trip outside the city, whereas in book 24 other more-pressing factors explain why Priam goes forth. Both instances of the ceremony (books 3 and 24) involve sacrifices, oaths, and exchange of the sacrificial victims (analyzed below as the next motif). Priam's herald, Idaios, is present in all three contexts.

In book 3 Menelaos requests Priam's presence at the oath taking and sacrifice, to hold the Trojans to the terms of the duel, a mechanism for ending the war. Although Menelaos, as we have seen, sometimes serves as the best of the Akhaians in book 3, Agamemnon presides over the ceremony. Its purpose is to establish a temporary cessation of fighting; however, the threat of resumed battle hangs over the proceedings in Agamemnon's vow to fight for the ransom (3.290; cf. 3.286) and finish the war, should the Trojans fail to uphold the terms of the agreement. Alluding to the negative outcome of the duel, the narrator notes that Zeus will not bring about the wishes of those present (3.297–302). Heralds, Idaios among them, take part in the ritual (3.268, 274).

Also central to the ceremony is Agamemnon's oath (3.276–91) to Zeus, in which he invokes Helios, the rivers, earth, and chthonic deities who take vengeance on those who break oaths, as witnesses to the ceremony between Greeks and Trojans. Both Greeks and Trojans hope that whoever first violates the oaths will spill his brains, a graphic parallel to Agamemnon's pouring a libation of wine (3.297–301). Both passages not only look ahead to Pandaros' breaking of the oath in book 4 but to earlier thematic Trojan wrongdoing, by Paris and Laomedon (21.443–60, discussed at length in chapter 6).

In book 7, at the ceremony that corresponds to those in books 3 and 24, Idaios meets and speaks with Agamemnon and Diomedes (7.381–413), both of whom can be seen as the best of the Akhaians. Pledges are also emphasized, as Agamemnon, as in book 3, again invokes Zeus to witness the pledges secured in the meeting (7.411; cf. 3.298–301).

Implicitly the ceremony in this motif is between the leaders of the two peoples (or his proxy, Idaios, in book 7). Akhilleus has this role in book 24 (and throughout book 23), becoming the Akhaians' leader when he goes to battle in book 20, and remaining leader through the end of the poem. Typical of the greater divine involvement in Akhilleus' sequence, Zeus himself, through Iris, requests Priam's presence (24.117–19, 145–58).

In book 24 several actions—ceremony, meeting, and an agreement—parallel the earlier meetings between Priam (and/or Idaios) and the Greek leader. Most ceremonial is Akhilleus' presiding over the cleaning and preparation of Hektor's corpse (24.582–90) and his subsequent sharing of a meal with Priam. The actual ransoming of Hektor happens fairly quickly. Prompted by Priam's mention of what Peleus would suffer, Akhilleus, thinking of his own father, agrees to return Hektor's corpse to Priam. The climax of the visit is thus their shared meal and Akhilleus' hospitable reception. Given hospitality's status as a sacred institution in ancient myth, Greek and biblical, the sensitivity Akhilleus displays serves as a key index of his humanity, even more than his high-minded arbitration of the contests and prizes in the funeral games for Patroklos.[22] Akhilleus displays a wide range of consideration for the aged leader, from his initial attempt to console him, to his gentle insistence that they share a meal together, to his reassurance that he intends him no harm. The episode's pacing thus suggests that, as the job is already accomplished, the more important event is really the contact between the two men.

Akhilleus' parable of Niobe is, in some respects, a formal equivalent of Agamemnon's prayer in book 3. We could classify both discourses as "the leader of the Akhaians invokes the gods to correct Priam's behavior." Although Agamemnon's prayer is aimed at the Trojan warriors rather than Priam, nonetheless, he specifies both Priam and Priam's children in his description of those who might break the agreement (3.288). Agamemnon invokes a number of gods to prevent the potential misbehavior of a parent and his children. Ultimately Priam will pay for earlier transgressions by Laomedon and Paris, and for Pandaros' breaking of the treaty Agamemnon now engineers through this prayer (see chapter 6). Niobe is punished explicitly for previous transgression against the gods (24.607–8, 611, 614–17), provoking a divine wrath (24.605–6). The main common theme, however, is the children Niobe has lost, as Priam has lost Hektor, and the previous sons both he and Akhilleus mention (24.479, 495–98, 520–21). While their parallel loss of a number of children closely links Niobe and Priam, so does the implicit destruction coming Priam's way, partly engineered by the gods, as it was for Niobe. Niobe is not obliterated, but she survives, transformed into stone. Priam, though doomed to die, survives as a monument of sorts, as the *Iliad* confers upon him the eternal presence a statue has.

The ceremony culminates in the shared meal, which Akhilleus earlier urged (24.601) and again presses, after narrating the story of Niobe (24.618). Akhilleus himself prepares the meal, a feature more usual in theoxenies (cf. Lot and Sara in Gen 18; Baucis and Philemon in Ovid, *Metamorphoses* 8.611–724); Akhilleus himself sacrifices/slays the sheep (σφάξ', 24.621). Akhilleus, not Priam first raises the issue of a truce (also Agamemnon's concern in book 3), again revealing leadership and sensitivity to Priam's needs. Akhilleus prefaces his generous offer with a sarcastic comment (24.649–50) so as not to seem as if he is being too kind and intimate, as a way to maintain his heroic identity. He confirms his intentions by gently touching Priam on the wrist (24.671–72), a gesture of reassurance (as noted by Richardson 346 but almost as often misunderstood as his sarcasm) that he will hold the Greeks to the terms Priam has specified. The penultimate scene in the poem, the episode reaffirms Akhilleus as the moral man who is capable of restoring order, as he does in book 1 (see chapter 5).

k. The slain victim(s), wounded in the throat by the leader of the Greek camp, is (are) placed in his vehicle

Each meeting concludes with Priam returning to Troy, conveying corpses given him during the ceremony by the leader of the Greeks. In book 3 the slain victims are the lambs sacrificed by Agamemnon to safeguard the oaths between the Trojans and the Greeks. Commentators have wondered why Priam takes these sacrificial victims back into the city, when, in a seemingly parallel incident, a sacrificed boar is hurled into the sea (19.266–68). When Priam conveys the sacrificed lambs back to Troy in book 3, his unusual action foreshadows his retrieval of the slain Hektor in book 24. The parallels extend to the cause of death: Hektor dies of a wound to the neck, as do the slain lambs in book 3. In both instances the leader of the Greek camp wields the instrument that slits the necks of the victims. In book 3 Agamemnon with his knife (μάχαιρα) first cuts the hairs off the lambs' heads (3.271–73),[23] then slays them by slitting their throats. The narrative continues with an unusual focus on the suffering of the sacrificed lambs:

> and then he set them on the ground, gasping for breath,
> losing their life, for the force of the bronze had taken it away.
>
> (3.293–94)

Kirk (1985: 307) notes the peculiarity: "The actual death of sacrificial victims is nowhere else in Homer so graphically described." The narrative pattern reveals that the unusual pathos of the scene prefigures the climactic scenes of Priam's retrieval of Hektor's corpse. Here book 3 continues its function as an overture by briefly striking the notes and phrases that will return with greater seriousness and development at the poem's end. Like the sacrificed lambs in book 3, Hektor also dies of a wound to the throat, a motif in the narrative pattern (*16. In the duel's climax, the best of the Akhaians wounds Hektor in the neck with his spear*):

> and where the collarbones keep the neck from shoulders, his throat
> was exposed, where the soul's destruction is swiftest.
>
> (22.325–26)

There is some overlap of common formulas describing Hektor's death and the sacrificed lambs: τάμε χαλκοβάρεια ("the heavy with bronze [spear] cut," 22.328)[24] and τάμε νηλέϊ χαλκῷ ("[Agamemnon] cut with pitiless bronze," 3.292). Hektor is able to speak to Akhilleus, though fatally wounded (ἀσπαίροντας, 22.337), a graphic parallel to the dying lambs' painful gasps (λαυκανίη, 3.293). In a further link, the word ὀλιγοδρανέων only occurs twice in the *Iliad*, and in all of archaic epic (Richardson 138), of Hektor's throat (22.325), just before Akhilleus slits it, and of Priam (24.641) as he drinks Akhilleus' wine, having successfully ransomed his son (24.641–42). In book 3 the victim's throats are slit in Priam's presence; in Akhilleus' sequence, the victim's throat is slit, but Priam reclaims the victim much later, due to the development of the funeral motifs, which in this sequence first center around Patroklos.

Why would Hektor's corpse be paralleled to sacrificial victims? In some broad respects Hektor can be seen as a sacrificial victim, probably to Athena, the deity, after Hera, most eager for the destruction of Troy, most actively engaged in ensuring its fall. She intervenes personally to engineer Hektor's death (22.214–99—a motif of the narrative pattern, *10. As a result of the plotting of Apollo and Athena, the best of the Akhaians now encounters Hektor in a duel*). In book 6 when Hektor brings word from Helenos that the Trojans are to sacrifice and pray to Athena (6.237–85), he declines to participate in the sacrifice, saying it would not be right because he is "splattered with blood" (αἵματι . . . πεπαλαγμένον, 6.267–68). The conjunction of his blood-splattered state with Athena's refusal to listen to the Trojans' prayer in book 6 seems to prefigure his death, and Athena's own role in bringing it about. The *Odyssey* confirms this view in Athena's injunction to Odysseus that she expects to see the "threshold of his palace splattered with the suitors' blood." Her declaration repeats the same basic formula as at *Il.* 6.268:

αἵματι τ᾽ ἐγκεφάλῳ τε παλαξέμεν ἄσπετον.
(*Od.* 13.395)

αἵματι καὶ λύθρῳ πεπαλαγμένον εὐχετάασθαι.
(*Il.* 6.268)

Both passages feature, in similar word order and formulas, a blood-spattered violence associated with Athena. The conjunction of Hektor's blood-splattered state with Athena's refusal to grant the Trojans' prayer in book 6 evokes his death and her role in bringing it about. The narrative pattern thus associates Hektor's blood-splattered state before Athena in book 6 with his destruction at her hands in book 22.[25] Immediately before causing his death, Athena discusses Hektor with Zeus, who himself associates Hektor with sacrifice, noting how many he performed on Mount Ida, and on the Trojan acropolis (22.170–72).

If Hektor suggests a sacrificial victim for Athena, from the city's perspective he is the sacrifice that doesn't work, opposite to scapegoat figures such as Oedipus or Christ, whose sacrifices make their communities safe. As such, Hektor is part of a larger pattern of the Trojans' failed relations with the gods, a key instance of their inability to curry divine favor, their failure to make themselves abide by sacred agreements. As Laomedon cheated and betrayed Poseidon and Apollo (21.443–60), as Paris ruptured the sanctity of hospitality, so the Trojans, in the present time of the poem, violate the sacred agreement for which the lambs were sacrificed. Hektor is part of this thematic chain of events, and pays the price for Pandaros' breaking of the sacred oath. In a sense, Hektor *is* the blood-splattered sacrifice that Athena accepts in book 22, having earlier rejected the robe offered to her in book 6. As Priam oversees the sacrifice of the lambs in book 3, in some respects he also oversees the conclusion of Hektor's sacrifice.[26]

l. He returns home safely

In book 3 Priam returns home immediately after placing the sacrificial victims in his chariot, accompanied, as before, by Antenor:

> and so he himself [Priam] got in, and was holding the reins from behind;
> and Antenor mounted the well-wrought chariot alongside him,
> the two then went back returning to Ilion.

> (3.311–13)

Verse 3.313 is used again, with slight modification, of the throng that accompanies Priam and Idaios as they head out to meet Akhilleus in book 24 but then turn back to the city as the other two go on (3.313 = 24.330). In book 24 Hermes' presence significantly complicates the departure, since he serves as Priam's driver until they reach the river Xanthos (24.691–94). Priam and Idaios then drive themselves back, depicted in a couplet (24.696–97) that serves as ring composition with 24.323–24.

m. And, carefully limiting the mourning, oversees the terms of the truce

While this last motif is absent in book 3, in books 7 and 24 Priam limits potentially excessive mourning by others. In book 7 Priam is on the battlefield, overseeing the Trojans as they gather the corpses, reining in the passions of some who would have engaged in lengthier displays of grief (7.427).

Akhilleus' sequence has these elements in the most fully developed form. Priam expresses his concern about the duel and Hektor's likely death even before the duel begins (22.37–76). Immediately after the duel (22.412–28) a grieving Priam wishes to go claim the body, but book 23 intervenes before the rest of the expected sequence is carried out. In book 24 Priam vents such concerns at length before setting out, and again, face to face before Akhilleus. On returning to the city, Priam limits the displays of grief by those seeing the corpse (24.713–18), just as at 7.427 (see chapter 1). His careful supervision of the events connected with the funeral reaches to the final lines of the epic.

⤿

IV. Paris duels with Menelaos

After introducing thematic material that looks ahead to the very end of the poem, book 3 resumes the thread with which it began, Paris' duel with Menelaos. Although the fourth section (3.314–89) employs key motifs from the narrative pattern, its focus on Paris, an antitype to Hektor, features a parodic modality that undercuts and alters the force of some motifs. Chapter 3 argues that the middle sequence of the narrative pattern, books 8–17, parodies the narrative pattern in the initial and final sequences. In this respect book 3 introduces narrative strategies that will become prominent in the middle books. In book 3 a parodic sensibility is evident near the beginning of section IV in the anonymous prayer both sides utter hoping that Paris will die in the duel:

> whichever man has wrought these acts for both sides,
> grant that he having perished enter the house of Hades.
>
> (3.321–22)

This inverts, or parodies the tremendous concern the Trojans voice for Hektor before he duels Aias in 7 and Akhilleus in 22. Though his death could end the war, and though both sides wish for it, Paris does not die within the *Iliad*. Hektor, in some ways, dies in his place, paying the price for Paris' and Pandaros' wrongdoing.

Hektor and Odysseus first clear a space for the duel (3.314–15). As the duel would finally begin, the narrative employs motifs from near the very beginning of the narrative pattern, though slightly adapted. Book 3 next employs 2. *The best of the Akhaians arms himself as prelude to his* aristeia, but reverses its application, using it not of a "best of the Akhaians" but of the Trojan who started the war, Paris. Paris' arming scene is built out of the same basic components as the other three scenes, including Akhilleus', the shin guards (3.330–31 = 19.369–70, 11.17–18, 16.131–32), the breastplate (3.332 = 19.371), the bronze, silver-studded sword (3.334–35 = 19.372–73), the shield (3.335), the crested helmet (3.336–37), and the spear (3.338).[27] Despite the generic resemblances between this arming scene and the others, the valence is entirely different, since Paris is the character most antithetical to the best of the Akhaians.[28]

Having won the lot, Paris first hurls his spear. Though he strikes Menelaos' shield, his spear bends back,[29] an instantiation of *14. When Hektor strikes the best of the Akhaians, his spear is driven back by the special shield.* The same formula describes Paris' and Hektor's two throws at the best of the Akhaians, προΐει δολιχόσκιον ἔγχος/καὶ βάλεν (3.346–47 = 7.244–45, 22.290–91). Menelaos prays to Zeus before retaliating (3.351–54), his prayer articulating a key moral issue, that Paris ruptured the sacred institution of hospitality. Menelaos now throws and hits his target, a six-line sequence that occurs verbatim when Aias hurls his spear at Hektor (3.355–60 = 7.249–54), reinforcing Menelaos as a "best of the Akhaians." Though his spear pierces Paris' shield, the Trojan is able to dodge the shaft and escape harm. Frustrated, Menelaos then strikes Paris' helmet with his sword, only to have his blade shatter (3.363). Now enraged, Menelaos grabs Paris by his helmet, almost strangling him by his chin strap, a unique dilemma in the poem. Though Kirk (1985: 319) regards the chin strap as "a slightly ponderous explanation," the details, emphasizing how tender Paris' neck is under his chin, are an adapted form of *16. In the duel's climax, the best of the Akhaians wounds Hektor in the neck with his spear.* The three neck wounds suggest an ascending progression in the gravity of the injuries from book 3 to 7 to 22: Paris almost strangled by his chin strap in book 3; Hektor grazed in the neck by Aias' spear (τμήδην δ' αὐχέν' ἐπῆλθε, 7.262); and Hektor mortally wounded in the throat by Akhilleus' spear, which passage repeats the same epithet used of Paris' chin (ἁπαλοῖο δι' αὐχένος, 22.327; ἁπαλὴν ὑπὸ δειρήν, 3.371).[30]

Although Menelaos has the upper hand, as will Aias and Akhilleus over Hektor, the duel breaks off with Paris' helmet spinning over to the Greeks' side,[31] and Aphrodite intervening to save him. Her saving Paris combines two motifs from the narrative pattern, *5f. The duel is deprived of a climax when a deity intervenes through a pivotal contrafactual, carrying off Aineias, and 15. Hektor's imminent defeat is emphasized by a pivotal contrafactual.* In spite of their similar underlying syntax, the two different sets of pivotal contrafactuals have quite different forces and functions.[32] Those involving Aineias (5.311–15, 20.288–91) serve to emphasize that he will survive the war and that he is the offspring of Aphrodite. For Hektor, on the other hand, the contrafactuals (7.271–75, 22.202–4) emphasize his defeat and the consequent fall of Troy, embodied in his death.

The incident thus anticipates both motifs in the narrative pattern. In Aphrodite we have the same deity who intervenes for Aineias, saving him for the future. But this passage also serves as a divine intervention that marks the defeat of the Trojan involved in the duel, Hektor in books 7 and 22. A formula common to Aphrodite's book 3 intervention for Aineias and Poseidon's book 20 intervention serves as a further link between this section of book 3 and the larger narrative pattern, "easily, since (s)he is a god, and (s)he covered him in a great mist" (3.381 = 20.444).

～

V. In the duel's aftermath, Paris lives and Helen comes to him (parody)

When Aphrodite sets Paris down in his fragrant bedroom,[33] book 3 extends Paris' unheroic qualities and develops them into full-blown parody, or mock epic. Most of the fifth section (3.382–461) serves as a parody of the narrative pattern's 9. *The greatest Trojan warrior, Hektor, meets his mother, sister-in-law, and his wife, Andromakhe, near the Skaian Gates, and the women, especially Andromakhe, who predicts his death and worries about their son, ask him not to return to battle.* Paris functions as a parody of Hektor, Helen as a parody of Andromakhe, and Aphrodite, having assumed mortal guise, as a parody of the other females that speak with Hektor in book 6 (Hekabe, Theano, and Andromakhe's housekeeper). The conclusion of section V introduces elements that will be used in Hera's deception of Zeus, allowing book 3, in its function as an overture, to introduce again the parodic quality of the middle books (8–17), in which book 14 extends parody to the divine economy.

Section V opens with Helen on the tower (3.384), where Andromakhe will be for Hektor's duels (6.373; cf. 22.447). Andromakhe's two appearances in the *Iliad* are tragic, in book 6 full of foreboding for his possible death in the duel, in book 22 serving as the *Iliad*'s means for conveying the consequences of Hektor's death. Helen by comparison suffers no long-term ill consequences from Paris' defeat. Indeed, the whole reason for the war is to "defeat" Paris, to restore Helen to Menelaos, as the duel in book 3 acts out for the audience. In this sense, Paris' defeat serves to figure the restoration of Helen to Menelaos, a development more typical of a comic narrative, a "happy" ending. Hektor at this point in the narrative pattern, before both duels, is strongly motivated by a sense of shame (αἰδέομαι Τρῶας καὶ Τρῳάδας, 6.442 = 22.105), whereas Paris' desire for Helen is more important to him than either the terms or outcome of the duel. He does not care if people find his behavior shameless, as Helen herself comments (6.351).

Assuming the form of an old maidservant, Aphrodite urges Helen to come to Paris in their bedroom. In bringing the couple together, she parallels Hektor's housekeeper in book 6 (6.382–89), who tells Hektor where Andromakhe has gone, allowing them to meet. The parallel is again parodic, since Aphrodite brings the couple together to have sex, whereas the housekeeper helps Hektor find Andromakhe to allow Andromakhe to voice her concern for him. Aphrodite functions here as a go-between, or pander.[34] As the housekeeper, she tells Helen "you would not think that he had come from having fought with a man, but that he was going to a dance" (392–93). While meant to arouse Helen, Aphrodite's words are ironic for the audience, since in the *Iliad* comparing a warrior to a dancer is normally an insult (15.508, 24.261). The word Aphrodite selects to emphasize Paris' sexual allure, στίλβων, "gleaming" (3.392), links this scene with Hera's seduction of Zeus in book 14.[35] When Hera seduces Zeus, he draws a golden cloud about them, glistening (στιλπναί, 14.351) with dew. Both episodes focus on negative consequences of sexual desire.[36] Hera arouses Zeus' desire only in order to deceive him, to disobey his proclamation forbidding divine intervention against his plan. Aphrodite, by provoking Helen's desire for Paris, similarly furthers a course destructive to Troy, a reenactment of the crime that brought the Greeks to Troy.

Surprisingly, Helen recognizes the goddess and rebels against her (3.399–412). Key events in Greek myth often come to pass in accord with Dodd's formulation of overdetermination: a mortal and a god are both responsible for making something happen. The climax of each Homeric epic is a key example: Akhilleus slaying of Hektor with Athena's aid; Odysseus slaying the suitors with Athena's help. However, by having Helen resist and initially refuse Aphrodite,[37] this episode problematizes the norms of overdetermination, and possibly even parodies it. It resembles the strangely comic situations Euripides develops by subjecting a traditional myth to a contemporary realism, as in the *Ion*. Aphrodite's response to Helen's surprising behavior is to threaten a divine wrath, which quickly snaps Helen partly back into line. Aphrodite's threatened divine wrath, however, seems more a divine parallel for marital squabbles than the divine wraths of Athena and Hera, which will lead to the destruction of Troy (see chapters 6 and 7).

Helen's brief revolt stems from her awareness that to go to Paris under such circumstances (his failing to honor the terms of the duel) would be shameful, drawing reproaches from the Trojan women (3.410–12). This is a parody of 9b. *His fear of shame counters their attempts at persuasion* (6.442,

22.105), though it applies to Hektor in the narrative pattern. Helen thus comes close to stating Hektor's usual position on feeling shame before the Trojan women as his motivation for dueling the best of the Akhaians. Unlike Hektor, however, Helen will nonetheless do what her sense of shame tells her not to do. Aware, then, of the shamefulness of seeing Paris now, but bullied by Aphrodite to do so, she addresses him with abuse, wishing he had died in the duel (3.428). Her wish parodies the concern Andromakhe feels for Hektor in books 6 and 22, closer to a soap opera depiction of marital squabbles. She clearly regards Paris as having lost the duel (3.429), as Hektor loses in books 7 and 22, and her description of his defeat (ἀνδρὶ δαμεὶς κρατερῷ) parallels depictions of warriors, including Hektor, defeated by Akhilleus.[38] Helen regards Paris' earlier boasts that he would defeat Menelaos as absurd (3.430–31). But after her biting criticism, Helen relents, telling Paris not to face Menelaos again, lest he be slain, a closer parallel to Andromakhe's concern for Hektor.

In his response, Paris concedes his defeat, but ascribes it to Athena's aid to Menelaos (3.439). Though the episode does not depict Athena aiding Menelaos, Paris' assumption that she did parallels the explicit help Athena will give to Akhilleus when he fights Hektor, and of which Hektor will be fully aware (15.614; 20.94; 22.270, 446). It is thus a partial instance of *10. As a result of the plotting of Apollo and Athena, the best of the Akhaians now encounters Hektor in a duel to decide the whole war,* offering further support for seeing Menelaus in book 3 as the best of the Akhaians (as he is again in book 17). In admitting defeat, Paris omits dealing with the terms of the duel: if he has lost, he must give Helen back, as the terms clearly dictate. In failing to acknowledge this, he continues his thematic irresponsibility. Paris' assertion that the Trojans, too, have the gods on their side (3.440) is ironic. Book 3 presents Aphrodite as the god most closely concerned with the Trojans, a god who will be defeated by the best of the Akhaians in book 5 (5.334–430). In preferring erotic dalliance with Helen to salvaging his reputation on the battlefield, Paris puts his own desire ahead of the needs of his people, as when he first brought Helen to Troy. As Aphrodite's use of στίλβω helps link this scene with Hera's deception of Zeus, so Paris uses the same rhetorical technique that Zeus will (οὐ γάρ πώ ποτέ μ' ὧδε . . . ὡς σέο νῦν ἔραμαι καί με γλυκὺς ἵμερος αἱρεῖ, 3.442–46; cf. 14.315–28) to express his lust for Helen.[39]

Milton uses Paris' desire for Helen as a model for Adam's postlapsarian lust for Eve. Book 3 depicts Paris and Helen's relationship as based almost entirely upon sex and little else. For Milton, an astute Homeric commentator,[40] Paris' lust is Satanic. In *Paradise Lost*'s exploration of the Fall, Milton models Adam's desire to have sex with Eve (after having eaten the fruit) on Paris' own articulation of his lust:

For never did thy Beauty since the day
I saw thee first and wedded thee, adorn'd
With all perfections, so inflame my sense
With ardor to enjoy thee, fairer now
Than ever, bounty of this virtuous Tree.

(9.1029–33)

Miltonists usually connect the passage with Zeus' similar declaration to Hera in book 14,[41] but the ties are much closer with Paris, since both Adam and Paris refer to their first encounters, and Zeus does not, nor do Paris and Adam include a catalog of like exploits, which is Zeus' chief concern.

Paris is shameless, literally described so, indifferent to what other people think about him. In this respect he fully instantiates the parodic tone of the fifth section of book 3, functioning as a parody of Hektor, who *is* motivated by his sense of shame and concern for what others will say (6.442 = 22.105). Hektor is ultimately the only force keeping Helen with Paris, the force allowing them to make love as they do here. The book ends as everyone on the battlefield searches for the mysteriously vanished Paris, hateful to Trojan and Greek alike, and Agamemnon declaring Menelaos the winner. In accord with the agreed-upon terms, the Trojans should return Helen and her possessions (3.456–61).

As a suggestive miniature of much of the poem, book 3 parallels the initial and final sequences in ending with the idea of giving Helen back (7.348–53; in book 24 this is figured in having Helen deliver the last funeral oration: she speaks last because she will soon return to the Greeks). Menelaos has won a symbolic victory, one that predicts the triumph of the best of the Akhaians. But the divine council that opens book 4 diverts our attention away from the issue of whether the Trojans should now return Helen, as Agamemnon demands. The simmering, theomachian tensions, culminating in Hera articulating her furious wrath against Troy, result in Zeus acceding to her request to have the Trojans violate the sacred oaths over which Priam presided. Pandaros will serve as another Paris, embodying the worst failings of the Trojans, their irresponsibility, their culpability, their violation of sacred agreements.

CHAPTER THREE

The Middle Sequence

Parody of the Narrative Pattern

Every time they went out to do battle the Lord brought disaster on them,
as he had said when he gave them his solemn warning;
and they were in dire straits.
—JUDGES 2:15

Much as parts of book 3, the middle sequence employs the motifs of the narrative pattern in inverted form, and a type of parody, though not necessarily comic, prevails in books 8, 11–17.[1] The Greeks suffer repeated defeats, and Hektor is victorious. Zeus' intervention in book 8 establishes the new tone. Whereas Diomedes and Akhilleus are unequivocally victorious in their *aristeiai,* in the middle sequence Agamemnon is wounded and driven from battle in his. Whereas Aias and Akhilleus triumph over Hektor with ease, without injury, Patroklos is slain by the Trojan. The audience knows, however, that this is a temporary inversion of the normal state of affairs. Early in book 11 Zeus sets the limits of the middle sequence, declaring to Hektor that, once Agamemnon is wounded, Hektor shall be victorious until the sun goes down (11.192–94). But Hera will speed up the sun's setting, prematurely ending Hektor's one day of support (18.239–41). Zeus' temporary favoring of Hektor, beginning in book 8, and ending in book 17, defines the middle sequence.

The sequence is primarily structured around two *aristeia,* Agamemnon's, which occurs early in the middle books, and Patroklos', the aftermath of which concludes the middle sequence. As in books 4–7, in which Diomedes serves in the motifs associated with Akhilleus' general *aristeia,* but Aias serves as the best of the Akhaians who defeats Hektor, the middle sequence also bifurcates the best of the Akhaians into two warriors, Agamemnon and Patroklos. Agamemnon's *aristeia* concentrates on motifs from the beginning of the narrative pattern, while Patroklos' *aristeia* replays a beginning of the narrative pattern but then employs motifs from the end of the pattern, including the duel with Hektor. Although both Agamemnon and Patroklos meet with some success in their *aristeiai*, they fall short of the achievements of Diomedes/Aias and Akhilleus. Agamemnon and Patroklos are characters with more failings, or lapses in judgment, than Diomedes and Akhilleus. Diomedes in his *aristeia* observes limits on fighting with the gods and is not prone to displays of excessive cruelty. Agamemnon, on the other hand, does lapse into occasional cruelty,[2] and Patroklos' inability to observe limits on opposing the gods is a key failing. Other differences in the general tone of books 11–17 result from the far different purposes that the middle part of the poem serves: to depict the Greeks in a state of desperation from which only Akhilleus will be able to save them.

The wounding of key *Greek* heroes is thematic through the middle sequence, climaxing in the death of Patroklos. By contrast, no Greek warrior suffers a significant wound in the final sequence; in the initial sequence, Greek wounds are simply not a prominent element. Paris' ability to wound several Greeks also serves as a key barometer of the middle books' inversion of the values that dominate the rest of the poem. Unable to harm Menelaos, and clearly defeated by him in book 3, in the middle sequence Paris meets with substantial success, driving several key Greeks from battle. His wounding of Makhaon (11.506–7) is a central pivot toward Patroklos' death. Paris' success in this sequence thematically parallels and predicts Hektor's victory over Patroklos as the climax of the middle sequence. In short, in the middle sequence *the Trojans are victorious,* an inversion, or parody, of the narrative pattern in the initial and final sequences, and of the war's outcome.

The parodic modality reaches its highest pitch in the depiction of the divine economy. In book 14, midway between the *aristeiai* of Agamemnon and Patroklos, Hera briefly assumes control of the executive function, through methods that constitute the major scandal of Homeric depictions of deity.[3] Whereas the initial and final sequences depict divine tensions through straightforward theomachy, book 14 uses more indirect means, a parody of theomachy. Hera is able to achieve temporary mastery over Zeus by diverting and deceiving him with her lovemaking. Her deception is successful because Zeus succumbs to his own sexual desire. To depict this surprising episode, the *Iliad* employs parodies of Near Eastern cosmogonic myth (see chapter 7).

The parodic qualities of the middle sequence begin in book 8, as discussed below, but are also present in book 10, the *Doloneia*. In chapter 4 we analyze books 9–10 for their parallels with books 1–2 and 18–19, forming the introductory pattern. As Petegorsky (178) has shown, the middle books focus on strategies involving deception or disguise, beginning with the embassy to Akhilleus, where Akhilleus himself, refusing Agamemnon's overtures, suggests that the Greeks turn to μῆτις, *metis* ("cunning, strategy," 9.423), since he will no longer help them. Hera's deception of Zeus continues the use of cunning and deception as a strategy in the middle sequence. The climax of the middle books, however, the death of Patroklos (who enters battle *disguised* as Akhilleus), reveals the ultimate failure of deception as an alternative to Akhilleus' might.[4] Parody is further present in the continual undercutting of Hektor's accomplishments, a feature seen throughout the middle sequence. While Hektor achieves various triumphs in books 8 and 11–17, the *Iliad* thematically undercuts his acts and implies criticism of his choices.

Although parody serves as a dominant organizing device in the middle sequence, a few specific thrusts of the narrative pattern remain unchanged. Aias, for instance, continues his thematic role as the best of the Akhaians who defeats Hektor, best of the Trojans. This role comes to the fore during the deception of Zeus (14.409 ff), when he comes close to slaying Hektor. Such episodes tend to be curtailed, however, compared with a major set piece such as the *Patrokleia*.

Book 8: A Miniature of the Middle Sequence

At the end of the first sequence, Aias' defeat of Hektor looks ahead to Hektor's death by Akhilleus' spear. The truce to reclaim bodies and the building of the wall look ahead to the extended truce in 24 and the funerals of Patroklos and Hektor. Given the pattern of motifs in the initial and final sequences, the middle sequence begins with two surprising variations. First, it skips over the entire introductory pattern (which will occur in full in books 9–10) focusing instead on the first motif of the *principal* pattern (*1. When theomachian frictions surface at a divine council, Zeus dictates the permissible level of divine intervention*), which, in the other two sequences, comes *after* the introductory pattern. Book 8 develops theomachy to a considerable degree, employing it three times (8.1–46, 198–211, 350–488). Only then do books 9–10 present the introductory pattern. After this detour, book 11 resumes with the second motif of the principal narrative pattern (*2. The best of the Akhaians arms himself as prelude to his* aristeia) to launch Agamemnon's *aristeia*. In book 8's second unusual tendency, it functions as an overture for the middle sequence, much as book 3 does for the principal narrative pattern. In other words, all of the key developments to follow in books 11–17 are first briefly sketched out or suggested in book 8. In particular, it is in book 8 that the Greeks are first threatened with defeat (Morrison 1994: 211).

Book 8 begins with an initial instance of theomachy (8.1–46), much as at the beginning of book 4. Though no actual fighting occurs (nor in book 4), the episode is clearly theomachian in the threats and blunt abuse the gods hurl at each other. As in books 4 and 20–21, Zeus imposes clear limits on subsequent divine involvement. Indeed, his speech putting limits on the extent to which other deities may intervene (4.7–17) contains the strongest theomachian elements. Zeus threatens one of two options for gods intervening to help either side. Either the god will be struck (πληγεὶς, 8.12),[5] by Zeus himself, and return to Olympos disgraced, or Zeus will hurl the offender down to Tartaros to be confined there. Being confined to Tartaros is the end result of large-scale theomachy elsewhere in Greek (Hesiod, *Theogony*, 868) and other myth (*Paradise Lost*, 2.69, 6.55, etc.). Zeus goes on to suggest a third theomachian alternative, pitting himself against all the other Olympians combined, the account of the golden chain (8.18–27).

After this initial, carefully limited, instance of theomachy, however, book 8 segues into a different subgenre of myth altogether, one frequent in OT myth (e.g., Deut 28:25, 28; Judg 4:15; 1 Sam 7:10; Isa 13:4–8; cf. Gen 11:7; Exod 23:27 ff), but occurring only here and in book 17 in all of the *Iliad*: the chief god intervenes to inspire panic or rout, reversing the tide of battle.[6] Zeus' direct intervention in mortals' affairs, when he leaves Olympos to act, is rare in Homeric epic, occurring only once in the *Odyssey* (12.405–19), and only twice in the *Iliad*, in book 8 to initiate the middle sequence, and again in book 17 to conclude it.[7] Descending to Ida to observe the fighting (8.66–67), at noon,[8] Zeus takes out his scales (as he will again in book 22 to mark Hektor's end), to weigh the fates of the two armies. He then hurls blazing lightning in the midst of the Greek army, inspiring fear (8.75–77). Panic and a general flight ensues among the Greeks, setting the tone for the woundings and retreats that typify the middle sequence. Though infrequent in the *Iliad*, the motif is frequent in OT myth and is exemplified in the following passage: "As Samuel was offering the sacrifice and the Philistines were advancing to the attack, the Lord with mighty thunder threw the Philistines into confusion. They fled in panic before the Israelites" (1 Sam 7:10). This first move by Zeus, *against* the Greeks, sets in motion the entire middle sequence, culminating in the death of Patroklos eight books later. For the rest of the middle sequence, until the end of book 17, the Greeks rather than the Trojans will be under attack (see Morrison 1994). In essence, Zeus' panicking the Greeks with thunder is the opposite of motif 3 from the narrative pattern (*3. A god places* μένος, *"battle might," in him as he goes to face the Trojans*). Zeus' thunder takes *menos* away from the Greeks.

These quick opening scenes (8.1–98) establish the reversal of fortunes, Greek losses, that characterize the middle sequence, while the rest of book 8 serves as an overture for the sequence, introducing the major motifs to come in the next several books. Kirk (1990: 293) has commented on a further tendency of book 8: "It is characteristic of the Book as a whole that most of its actions and initiatives, whether divine or human, are soon abandoned or reversed."[9] This stop-and-start tendency is not only typical of book 8, but characterizes the middle sequence as a whole. After Zeus' intervention causes the Greek retreat, Diomedes single-handedly initiates a counter-movement that successfully restores momentum to the Greek side. So successful is Diomedes that he is in danger of routing the Trojans (8.118–31), forcing Zeus to intervene a second time, now hurling a bolt of lightning in front of Diomedes' chariot (8.133–36). Zeus' second intervention, a doublet of the first, makes his aid to the Trojans, and to Hektor in particular, patently obvious to the Greeks.[10] Nestor counsels immediate retreat to Diomedes, reasoning that since Zeus openly favors Hektor, they do not have a chance to oppose him. Book 8 here first instantiates a central thrust of the middle sequence: Zeus' favoring of Hektor, which will be articulated more explicitly in book 11 (11.181–209), and marks, roughly, the beginning and ending of the middle sequence.

In another indication of parody, when Nestor urges Diomedes to flee, he is reluctant to do so, fearing Hektor's ridicule (8.139–50). This is an inversion of two motifs from the principal pattern, *9b. His (Hektor's) fear of shame counters their attempts at persuasion*, and *11. Panic seizes Hektor on first seeing the best of the Akhaians*. In the initial and final sequences, Hektor is the anxious, terrified warrior, but in the inverted middle sequence, Diomedes, a Greek who serves as a best of the Akhaians, is depicted in a manner fitting the Trojans in the other sequences. The outcome of the motifs differs as well. Nestor reassures Diomedes that no Greek will think him a coward for fleeing now (8.151–56). Whereas in the first and third sequences, a terrified Hektor receives no counsel to deal with his shame and panic.

When Hektor then reviles Diomedes (8.160–66), as the Greek had feared, Diomedes again considers ignoring Zeus' favor to Hektor, which Nestor has clearly perceived. Hence, Zeus thunders three more times, the third instance of this same motif (8.170–71). Hektor now comments to his troops on the obvious favor Zeus bestows upon him (8.175–76). Confident because of Zeus' aid, Hektor asks for fire to burn the Greek ships (8.181–83), the first instance of a motif that governs much of the middle sequence and which becomes entangled in Patroklos' life.

After Hektor's curious address to his horses (8.185–90),[11] perhaps parody of a different sort, the narrative shifts to a divine council between Hera and Poseidon (8.198–211), which serves a number of functions. In an angry Hera (as the result of Zeus' intervention), the narrative again signals a theomachian modality. The subsequent description of Olympos shaking as she leaves her throne (8.199) points ahead to her success later in the sequence when she deceives Zeus. Frustrated with Zeus' plan to help Hektor, Hera approaches Poseidon to elicit his aid for the Greeks, violating Zeus' earlier order. As Fenik (1968: 223) notes, Hera's consultation anticipates her consultation with Athena later in this book (8.350 ff). Poseidon's brief appearance looks ahead to his larger role later in the middle sequence (13.10–38, 83–125, 206–45). The Greek wall is also mentioned here (8.213), an entity that will gain in importance throughout the sequence.

As Hektor is about to set fire to the ships, a pivotal contrafactual heightens the moment:

> And now he might have kindled their balanced ships with the hot flame,
> had not the goddess Hera set it in Agamemnon's heart
> to rush in with speed himself and stir the Akhaians.
>
> (8.217–19)

In an inversion typical of the middle sequence, the pivotal contrafactual presents Hektor as the significant threat that needs to be contained. The middle sequence will thwart Hektor's desire to set fire to a ship until near the end of book 15, but it uses the motif as a central organizing device repeatedly until then. Hera intervenes (reminiscent of her prompting Odysseus to contain Agamemnon's blunder in book 2), inciting Agamemnon to marshal the host. So effective is his speech that even Zeus is persuaded (8.245–46) not to carry the destruction to the level he had intended. Agamemnon's role here prefigures his prominence and *aristeia* in book 11. The description of the layout of the Greek ships, as Agamemnon mounts Odysseus' centermost ship to speak, will be repeated right before his *aristeia* (8.222–26 = 11.5–9).

With Diomedes leading, the Greeks launch a successful counterattack, including a brief *aristeia* by Teukros (8.266–310). Though enjoying momentary success, Teukros is repeatedly unable to hit Hektor, once because Apollo fouls his arrow (8.311). Implicitly Hektor now has the favor of both Zeus and Apollo, a functional parallel to Akhilleus' having the implicit favor of Athena and Zeus (and Hera) in book 22. Accordingly, he seizes a huge stone (χερμάδιον: 8.321) and strikes Teukros on the neck (8.326), wounding him and driving him from battle. Teukros' brief *aristeia* introduces the dominant inversion of Greek *aristeiai* in the middle sequence. After an initial period of success, the Greek hero is driven from battle, wounded, as will happen to both Agamemnon and Patroklos. Second, Teukros' neck wound is an inversion of a key motif from the narrative pattern, *16. In the duel's climax, the best of the Akhaians wounds Hektor in the neck with his spear.* A further formula links Hektor's wounding of Teukros with his own neck wound at the hands of Akhilleus, τῇ ῥ᾽ ἐπὶ οἶ μεμαῶτ᾽ (first half of 8.327 = first half of 22.326), used of Teukros and Hektor respectively, as each is wounded (Kirk 1990: 324–25). Hektor thus ends both Teukros' brief *aristeia* and the whole Akhaian counteroffensive.

There follows yet another instance of theomachy, the most fully developed of book 8. Hera consults with Athena (8.350–488), Athena suggesting that they arm and enter battle, against Zeus' edict (8.7 ff). But when they do so (8.381–96), an angry Zeus sends Iris to threaten them with severe punishments, including being struck by his lightning. In her report, Iris goes beyond Zeus' actual remarks to insult Hera (κύον ἀδεές, "fearless bitch"), which underscores the theomachian modality. Chagrined, they return to Olympos where Zeus, in book 8's most explicit statement of theomachy, repeats his threat to strike (πληγέντε, 8.455) them with lightning should they violate his edict. Having reiterated his threat Zeus goes on to declare that tomorrow an unstoppable Hektor will slay Patroklos (8.470–76). Zeus' prophecy, reaching up to the climax of book 16, underscores that book 8 is a miniature of the whole middle sequence. The theomachy concludes with Zeus's mentioning Tartaros (8.481), a veiled threat aimed at Hera, as Zeus' earlier reference (8.13), where he would hurl any Olympian who broke his edict against interfering in battle.

In book 8's final scene, set off by the onset of night (8.485–88), Hektor holds a Trojan assembly (8.489–542), not far from the Greeks' ships. Even the assembly's location typifies the inverted values that characterize the middle sequence: the Trojans are confident enough to spend the night close by the Greek camp. The assembly looks ahead to books 9–10 and 18. Hektor's reference to the many Trojan fires (8.508) anticipates the Greeks' anxiety when they see the same fires during the night (9.77, 232–34; 10.12). Hektor's extravagant desires (discussed below) prefigure his wishes in the Trojan assembly in book 10 (and in book 18) and his tendency to make foolish boasts.

Commentators rarely discuss whether it is *wise* for Hektor to try to burn the Greeks' ships in the first place. The audience knows that most of the Greeks were recently eager to sail home at a moment's notice (2.154). If Hektor destroys a significant portion of their fleet, he destroys the option of having them leave. He helps ensure that they remain, with no alternative other than to keep trying to sack Troy. Hektor, caught up in a quest for his own glory and reputation, seems unable to envision what might actually be the best course for his troops and city. Hektor begins and ends his speech on fantastic notes, which are a mixture of whimsy and arrogant presumption. He opens saying that he thought he would have destroyed (8.498) the

Greeks' ships and all of the Greeks, if night had not come so quickly. This extraordinary claim is indicative of Hektor's bizarre, fantastic perspective in the middle sequence. He closes his speech wishing he was immortal and ageless, honored as are Athena and Apollo (8.538–40). He will later make similar remarks to Aias, wishing even that he was the son of Zeus (13.825–27), as book 8 again looks ahead to later developments in the middle sequence. Coming from Hektor (as opposed to coming from, say, Akhilleus), these are hubristic remarks.[12] Hektor's wish to be immortal is ironic, since his death will come soon, a climax of the poem. The audience knows that Hektor's present success is due to Zeus' aid, lasting only a day.

In a divine reaction to his speech and subsequent Trojan offerings, the gods reject the Trojans' sacrifices, as Athena earlier rejects Theano's offering (6.311):

> But the blessed gods took no part of it,
> They did not wish to; for sacred Ilion was very hateful to them,
> as was Priam, and the people of Priam of the strong ash spear.
>
> (8.550–52)

Though the lines have long been regarded as suspect, having been borrowed from the pseudo-Platonic *Alcibiades II* (Kirk 1990: 340), they belong to the subgenre of apocalyptic myth, as do many passages in the *Iliad* (explored at length in chapter 6). The book closes with another depiction of the Trojans' myriad fires (8.554–63), which will provide the air of menace the Greeks feel in books 9–10.

Book 8 thus takes up one day, which goes by quickly, a short version of the extremely long day that will occupy books 11–17 (and part way into book 18). In this last regard, the structure of the middle sequence closely parallels the overall structure of the initial sequence. Both feature a day that passes quickly at the beginning of the sequence (most of book 1) and a very lengthy day (books 2–7, 11–17) that constitutes the bulk of the sequence. The final sequence is the opposite: one day occupies most of the initial books (19–22), with more days passing during the closing two books.

Book 11

Having noted book 8's function as a miniature of the middle sequence, we now note inversions of the narrative pattern in books 11–17 (with books 9–10 discussed in chapter 4). After opening with a unique (for the *Iliad*) dawn formula, Eos leaving Tithonos' bed (11.1–2), which evokes a tragic sense of mortality that typifies the middle sequence, book 11 proceeds with a string of motifs from the principal pattern. The first is a variation on *3. A god places* μένος, *"battle might," in the best of the Ackaians as he goes to face the Trojans.* While Athena and Thetis spark the *aristeiai* of Diomedes and Akhilleus (5.1–2, 19.37; cf. 19.353–54), Eris performs the same divine function at the beginning of Agamemnon's *aristeia*. Eris hurls "great strength" (σθένος, 11.11) into each of the Akhaians. In a further parallel with Athena, Eris here holds the τέρας πολέμοιο in her hands (11.4), much as Athena holds the aegis (5.738) during Diomedes' *aristeia* (2.446).[13] But Eris is a very different goddess than Athena. Whereas Athena embodies victory in war, Eris embodies strife—in the *Iliad*, strife between Agamemnon and Akhilleus. Her presiding over Agamemnon's *aristeia*, as Athena does for Diomedes and Akhilleus, is an editorial comment on the Greek king, a reminder that he bears responsibility for the quarrel with Akhilleus. Zeus hurls her among the Greek ships, as Zeus will also do with Ate (19.130).[14] As the only deity present when Agamemnon's *aristeia* is about to begin, Eris embodies how the Greeks are temporarily without Zeus' support, and her epithet, πολύστονος, "full of sorrows," suggests the losses the Greeks will suffer in the middle sequence.

Eris' two appearances frame an arming scene for Agamemnon (11.16–44): *2. The best of the Akhaians arms himself as prelude to his* aristeia. His arming proceeds in the usual order (greaves, corselet, sword, shield, helmet, spear),[15] with corselet and shield receiving the greatest elaboration (19–28, 32–40). However, in a departure from the *aristeiai* of Diomedes and Akhilleus, and a sign of the inverted thrust of the middle sequence, the narrator now devotes significant space to depicting the Trojans as they prepare to do battle. The first such passage (11.56–66), in contrast to descriptions in earlier books (e.g., 3.2–7), depicts Hektor leading the Trojans.

Shortly after Eris' second appearance (11.73–77), Agamemnon begins his *aristeia* (*4. Thus inspired, he begins an* aristeia, *through which he will earn fame*). His *aristeia* proceeds, initially, with many elements in common with Akhilleus' *aristeia*.[16] As in the earlier motifs, however, Agamemnon's *aristeia* is inverted or parodic. His heroic deeds seem appropriately those inspired by Eris rather than Athena. His main advances against the Trojans are close to atrocities (11.95 ff, 146 ff).[17] B. Hainsworth (235) notes his characteristic tendencies: "Agamemnon is especially savage with the sword (a slashing weapon), see his treatment of Peisandros (11.146), but only here is the dramatic effect of his spear-thrust described." Fenik (1968: 84) adds further comment (on 11.146–47): "[G]risly slayings are typical for Agamemnon. . . . Heads are cut off again at 261, 202, and 14.496."

Zeus sends Iris to command Hektor to stay out of the fighting until Agamemnon is wounded (11.181–82).[18] Hektor receives attention unusual for a

Trojan during an *aristeia* by the best of the Akhaians. Zeus promises his support until the sun sets, support that will result in the death of a best of the Akhaians, Patroklos. This constitutes the strongest inversion of the middle sequence: a Trojan will perform the most significant slaying of the sequence. Hektor suggests this function in Agamemnon's *aristeia* as well. Though he does not wound Agamemnon, it is in Zeus' command to him that we first learn Agamemnon's *aristeia* will end in his getting wounded (11.191–92, 206–7), opposite the virtually unscathed *aristeiai* of Diomedes/Aias and Akhilleus in the principal pattern.[19] Almost immediately after Iris relays Zeus' directions to Hektor, Agamemnon is wounded. Two brothers, sons of Antenor, are Agamemnon's only opponents after Hektor's scene with Iris. Agamemnon slays both. Before he dies, however, the second brother, Koon, is able to inflict the wound (11.252) that drives Agamemnon from battle, ending his *aristeia*.[20] Because Antenor and Priam closely parallel each other, perhaps even being doublets,[21] Agamemnon's wounding Antenor's son in the neck (11.240) in the climax of his *aristeia* is a version of *16. In the duel's climax, the best of the Akhaians wounds Hektor in the neck with his spear.* Koon, son of Antenor, wounding Agamemnon, best of the Akhaians, anticipates Hektor, son of Priam, and his wounding of the next "best of the Akhaians," Patroklos.

Agamemnon's *aristeia* ends quickly, without impact comparable with those of Diomedes or Akhilleus, and Hektor now launches an *aristeia*. A Trojan *aristeia* is very unlikely in the initial sequence and is absent entirely from the final sequence. Furthermore, Hektor enters battle (11.284–85) with the support of Zeus. He rallies the Trojans by noting that Zeus has promised him glory (11.288–90), an inversion of a motif normally applied to the best of the Akhaians: *4. Thus inspired, he begins an* aristeia, *through which he will earn fame.* Although Hektor's closest divine relationship is with Apollo (discussed below, and in chapter 7), as he enters battle he is equated with Ares, βροτολοιγῷ ἶσος Ἄρηϊ (11.295). This is an instantiation of another motif normally associated with the best of the Akhaians in *his aristeia: 7a. He is called* δαίμονι ἶσος, *only during his* aristeia *and, with one exception, only when he attacks a Trojan-partisan deity.* In the *Iliad*, Ares is thematically associated with defeat when he fights with other gods (5.793–867, 21.391–414; cf. 5.385–91; and see chapter 6). Hektor's depiction as being like Ares thus suggests his eventual defeat at the hands of someone who is aligned with Athena, Akhilleus. The Iliadic Ares resembles the iconography of the Ugaritic Baal, a storm god (discussed in chapter 7). Twice, in the initial stages of his *aristeia*, Hektor is compared to a blustering storm, (11.297–98, 305–9). Ares is described as a storm in the first theomachy (5.864–67), just after his defeat by Athena and Diomedes. Although the storms to which both Hektor and Ares are compared are powerful forces, the comparisons nonetheless suggest a strong, but chaotic, power unable to achieve strategic result. In a further link, the epithet, κορυθαίολος, "with glancing helm," is restricted only to Hektor and Ares.[22]

Hektor now slays ten men, but without elaboration by the narrator (11.301–3), which reticence may be intended to undercut his accomplishment (B. Hainsworth 257). With the Greeks now in retreat, a pivotal contrafactual (11.310–12), which signals limits to Hektor's accomplishment, restates the same dynamics found in the pivotal contrafactual in book 2 (Odysseus preventing the Greeks from fleeing homeward, 2.155 ff). In each context, the passage follows an episode in which Agamemnon is prominent but fails to achieve his objective, leaving the Greeks retreating to their ships. Odysseus then limits the damage, containing a crisis (discussed in chapter 4 as *12. Odysseus succeeds in restoring order in a second or later Greek assembly*, and *13. The introductory pattern concludes with a summons to battle, for which Odysseus is largely responsible*). The final line of the contrafactual closely recalls the circumstances of the episode in book 2, "and now the Akhaians in their flight would have fallen on their ships" (11.312). Odysseus now summons Diomedes, continuing their pairing in books 8, 10, and 19. The passage is crucial, immediately halting the progress of Hektor's *aristeia*, as Odysseus, in a sense, agent of Athena, here contains Hektor, agent of Ares. Although in book 8 the same pair is unsuccessful in halting a Greek flight, a comparison of the contexts suggests that Odysseus is the one who can halt a flight, and Diomedes cannot.[23]

Both *aristeiai*, Agamemnon's and Hektor's, are short, quickly curtailed, and probably intended to counterbalance each other (B. Hainsworth 260). The careful symmetry suggests a stalemate between the two sides for the middle sequence, a stalemate tipped only temporarily in the Trojans' favor by Zeus' promise of success to Hektor. Diomedes and Odysseus are themselves aware (11.318–19) that Zeus now favors the Trojans. After Diomedes and Odysseus bring his brief *aristeia* to an end, Hektor attempts a counterattack, but Diomedes drives him out of battle with a successful spear cast (11.342–67).

Diomedes' driving Hektor out of battle and boasting that he might slay him (11.365–66) suggest parallels with Akhilleus' defeat of Hektor. Nonetheless, the momentum shifts back to the Trojans, typical of the stop-and-start nature noted above in book 8. Paris now hits Diomedes with an arrow, wounding him in the foot (11.377), a unique injury that suggests a thematic parallel to Paris' (non-Iliadic) wounding of Akhilleus (B. Hainsworth 267). The wounded Diomedes, protected by Odysseus, removes his arrow, and his charioteer drives him to safety. Odysseus, left alone, is, in a sense, abandoned by Diomedes (11.399–400), an inversion of their respective roles in the book 8 retreat. Cut off and alone against the Trojans, Odysseus slays five, before being wounded by a sixth opponent, Sokos. Book 11 thus quickly presents the wounding of Agamemnon and Diomedes, who both serve as versions of the best of the Akhaians, and of Odysseus, who, though not serving as the best of the Akhaians, figures prominently in the introductory pattern (discussed in chapter 4). When Athena prevents his wound from being lethal, Odysseus then slays Sokos, his sixth Trojan in this episode (11.446–58).

Victorious but wounded, Odysseus, again surrounded by Trojans and cut off from the Greeks, calls for help. Menelaos summons Telamonian Aias, who is compared to a flooding river, fed by Zeus (11.492–96). Hektor and Aias in this scene effectively neutralize each other, but the Greeks again suffer a setback as Paris inflicts a second significant injury, wounding Makhaon, the healer. Only in the inverted modality of the middle sequence does Paris, a character so lacking in traditional heroism, inflict significant casualties. A pivotal contrafactual highlights the moment, a crucial scene in the overall architectonics of the poem:

> But the Akhaians would never have yielded the way,
> had not Alexander, husband of fair-tressed Helen,
> stopped Makhaon, shepherd of the host, in his bravery,
> hitting him on the right shoulder with a three-pronged arrow.
>
> (11.504–7)

When Idomeneus sees that Makhaon is wounded, he urges Nestor to drive him to safety (11.510–20). As Nestor does so, Akhilleus sends Patroklos to inquire about the wounded man (11.597–643). While Nestor then detains Patroklos, he suggests that Akhilleus send Patroklos into battle in his stead (11.795–803). Although Patroklos will not be able to act on the suggestion until book 16, the narrative initiates that course of events through the contrafactual in which Paris wounds Makhaon.

As Hektor, at Kebriones' urging, now targets Aias, the middle sequence continues to invert prominent motifs from the narrative pattern. Zeus makes Aias panic (11.543–46), an inversion of *11. Panic seizes Hektor on first seeing the best of the Akhaians, prompting his retreat.* Aias' retreat proves more dignified and orderly than those of Hektor (7.216–18, 22.136 ff) and Paris (3.31–32), because it enables him to rescue other Greeks in the vicinity. When Eurypylos steps in to aid Aias, Paris wounds him as well, again leaving Aias surrounded and vulnerable. The fifth Greek to be wounded and driven from battle, and Paris' third victim, Eurypylos also figures in initiating the *Patrokleia*. As Paris' wounding of Makhaon prompts Patroklos' visit with Nestor, so Eurypylos' arrival will delay his return to Akhilleus (11.804–15.390). In tending to Eurypylos, Patroklos acts as a substitute for Akhilleus (hinting at his own role as a best of the Akhaians), because Eurypylos assumes that he must know some of the same remedies that Akhilleus has learned (11.830–31). Shortly before this, Hektor is described plying his chariot over fallen corpses, a motif that will later apply to Akhilleus (11.534–37 = 20.499–502). The graphic image is yet another instance of the inversions that govern the middle sequence. Book 11 concludes with the Trojans, particularly Paris, having inflicted upon the Greeks their most severe casualties so far in the poem.

Book 12

Most of book 11's tendencies continue in book 12, with an additional emphasis on Hektor's shortcomings in strategy concerning the wall, evident in Poulydamas' difference of opinion. Glaukos and Sarpedon become prominent, looking ahead to Patroklos' slaying of the latter in book 16 (motif 8). The climax of book 12, Hektor's ill-advised, but successful, assault on the Greek wall looks ahead to Patroklos' ill-advised assault on the walls of Troy in book 16. The attempt on the wall is presented as a series of three efforts, by Asios, Sarpedon, and Hektor, an instance of "the scale of ascending importance" (Kakridis 1949: 28). The three attempts, presented as rather short for Asios (12.110–72), very lengthy for Sarpedon (12.290–412), and rather short again for Hektor's final though successful effort (12.413–72), parallel the deployment of the three sequences, in which the second middle sequence (books 8–17) is significantly longer than the initial (1–7) and final (18–24) sequences. The destruction of the wall is first briefly set in a future, apocalyptic context. After the war is over, and the Greeks have returned home, Poseidon and Apollo, angry that they built the wall without sacrificing to the gods, turn all the local rivers against the wall for nine days, destroying it, and washing it into the sea (12.6–35) (see Scodel 1982 and chapter 6).

The dynamic that first emerges here between Poulydamas and Hektor will govern the middle sequence (and into Akhilleus' sequence). Poulydamas gives reasonable advice. When Hektor follows his suggestions, all is well. When he does not, he meets with disaster. That Hektor is in need of advice is implicit throughout these scenes. In a simile comparing Hektor to a powerful lion or boar, the animal is slain because of its own courage (ἀγηνορίη δέ μιν ἔκτα, 11.46), recalling Andromakhe's earlier charge (φθίσει τὸ σὸν μένος, 6.407). On this first occasion in which Poulydamas offers advice, Hektor uncharacteristically accepts it (see B. Hainsworth 325), leading to success in negotiating the ditch, crucial to the attempt on the wall. After the curious catalog of Trojans and allies who will take part in the attempt (11.88–107), all agree to follow Poulydamas' advice except Asios, who, in what follows, serves as an example of what happens when Poulydamas' advice is ignored. The narrator asserts that Asios is a νήπιος, "a fool," and predicts that Idomeneus will slay him soon afterward (12.110–17). Asios' unsuccessful attempt (12.110–72), which ignores Poulydamas' plan to attack in formation, now follows (12.118–73). Asios thus personifies the dangers of excessively individual bravery, and of rejecting Poulydamas' advice.

The first attempt having failed, an augury (12.200–209) prompts a second, more typical exchange between Poulydamas and Hektor. The Trojans shiver as they behold an eagle bit by the blood-red serpent it holds in its claws. Poulydamas argues that the omen foretells disaster for their attempt on the wall, should they pursue it. In his reply (12.231–50), Hektor charges Poulydamas with cowardice, bluntly advancing his own erroneous interpretation. But the Trojans were "correct" when they shivered, and Poulydamas' analysis was clearly accurate. Hektor has become Asios, from the previous episode, and Paris, who similarly rejects Antenor's advice (12.231 = 7.357). As commander of the Trojan forces, Hektor's relationship with Poulydamas is reminiscent of Agamemnon's turbulent relationship with Kalkhas (discussed in chapter 5).

After Hektor prevails in his argument, the Lykians initiate a second, lengthier attempt on the wall. After a tour de force description of the fierce battle that ensues following Asios' failed attempt, a pivotal contrafactual opens Sarpedon's attempt:

> But never would the Trojans and glorious Hektor then
> have breached the gates of the wall and the great bolt,
> had not Zeus the deviser prompted his own son, Sarpedon,
> against the Argives, like a lion among curved-horn cattle.
>
> (12.290–93)

As we have seen throughout books 8, 11–12, Hektor's temporary victories are ascribed entirely to Zeus' intervention, a condition that holds throughout the middle sequence. Sarpedon's Hephaistos-fashioned shield is described (12.294–97), serving as a brief arming scene, as before an *aristeia*, and an inversion of *13. The best of the Akhaians has a unique shield*. Sustained emphasis now falls on the Lykians in general, leading to some of the best-known lines in the poem, Sarpedon's address to Glaukos on heroic duty (12.310–28). Both heroes then lead the Lykians (12.330) in an assault on the wall. This second attempt shifts from likely success to failure, however, when Glaukos is wounded. Sarpedon is nonetheless able to pull down some of the wall's structure (12.397–99) before Aias and Teukros drive him back. But Sarpedon is able to accomplish what he does only because Zeus protects him (12.402–3).

When Hektor leads the third attempt, he is successful, smashing the wall by hurling a great stone. His hefting of the stone (χερμάδιον) is depicted through a formula (οἶοι νῦν βροτοί εἰσ'· ὁ δέ μιν ῥέα πάλλε καὶ οἶος, 12.449 = 5.304 = 20.287) found in the *khermadion* sequence, motif 5e. Though this is Hektor's great triumph, the narrative firmly undercuts his accomplishment, a regular tendency of the middle sequence. Not only is Zeus said to tilt the previously even battle in Hektor's favor (12.437), he intervenes again to lighten the stone that Hektor hurls to smash the gates (12.450). But most telling is that Hektor inflicts his most serious damage not on enemy warriors but on inanimate gates and wall.

The attack results in no loss of Greek life. Yet, in some integral way, Hektor's and the others' attempts on the wall, and their dismantling of it, are closely bound up with their own deaths. The Greek wall seems to serve as a larger boundary, almost as a line of demarcation between life and death for the Trojans. It can be no accident that the three leaders of the three assaults on the Greek wall all die in the same order as that in which they made their attempts: Asios (13.389), Sarpedon (16.502), Hektor (22.361).[24] As Scodel (1982) has argued, the destruction of the wall (as described at 12.3–35) draws on a tradition of Near Eastern apocalyptic myth, but the wall has a more immediate link to destruction within the present time of the poem. Morrison (1994: 210 ff) notes a further inversion of the middle books: the Trojans' attack on the Greek wall is depicted as the siege of a city.[25] Thus in a certain sense, Hektor's and the others' assaults on the walls and setting fire to the ships prefigures the fall of Troy, the dismantling of *its* walls, and the attendant conflagration. It is perhaps for this reason, the link between the Greek wall and the death of the Trojans, that book 12 first describes the wall in such apocalyptic terms (12.3–35). In book 7 the Greeks built the wall and ramparts as a parallel and counterpart to the Trojans' funeral activities: *20. Both sides mourn their dead and construct a tomb.* The wall thus has intrinsic connections with mortality.

Book 13

Book 13 opens by again underscoring Hektor's dependence on Zeus for his success: "And Zeus brought Hektor and the Trojans near the ships." The immediate corollary to this is that if Zeus wavers in his support, or even in his attention (as he will in book 14), Hektor will be unable to sustain his success. Zeus now does look away, trusting that his proclamations at the last divine council (8.10 ff) will keep any Olympian from intervening. As he gazes on foreign peoples, Poseidon intervenes to help the Greeks.

Poseidon's role in book 13 parallels and predicts Hera's in book 14 (Edwards 1987: 241, 247). Each Greek-partisan god rebels against Zeus' earlier decree, a miniature *theomachy*, while Zeus is distracted or otherwise occupied. Essentially Poseidon here serves as Hera's agent, working against Zeus in her place. The rich description of his arrival (13.17–38) conveys the importance of his intervention (Janko 1992: 45–46). Assuming the form of Kalkhas (who has not been mentioned since 2.322), Poseidon thereby revives as a theme the friction between the prophet and Agamemnon, which helps motivate the beginning of the *Iliad*.[26] After urging the Aiante to set an example and fight off Hektor, he strikes them with his staff, filling them with *menos* (13.59–61), making them nimble of foot, a slightly altered instance of *3. A god places* μένος *(5.125, 5.136) in the best of the Akhaians*.

Telamonian Aias in particular (13.78–79) seems filled with *menos*, as at the beginning of an *aristeia*, signaling that some of what transpires here replays the dynamics of his defeat of Hektor in book 7. Poseidon as Kalkhas gives a second exhortation to the Greek army, asserting that Agamemnon is responsible for their present difficulties because he dishonored Akhilleus (13.111–13). The friction between the "seer" and his king parallels Poseidon's rebellion against Zeus on the divine plane. Hektor, compared to a boulder loosened by a storm-fed river (13.136–42), now leads a Trojan attack, continuing the Hektor-as-storm comparison that runs throughout the middle sequence. Hektor's initial assault, however, is unsuccessful, as the boulder, coming to a halt in the middle of the plain, implies. There follows a number of give-and-take encounters in which neither side can develop sustained momentum. Tellingly, however, Aias prevents Hektor from making off with the armor of Amphimakhos, a slain Greek (13.190–94), maintaining his thematic role as the best of the Akhaians who defeats Hektor. The Aiante retrieve Amphimakhos' corpse, predicting Aias' later retrieval of the slain Patroklos.

Poseidon makes a third exhortation, now assuming the form of Thoas, targeting Idomeneus with his speech (13.219–20, 232–38), and prompting the last Greek *aristeia* until Patroklos. The disguised Poseidon replays Agamemnon's role from books 2 and 4, marshaling and rousing the troops. The lengthy prelude to the *aristeia* includes a brief arming scene (13.241–45), an instantiation of *2. The best of the Akhaians arms himself as prelude to his* aristeia. Other elements follow from the narrative pattern, used in the encounters with Aineias. Poseidon's speech includes the rhetorical figure, *"where now are*" (ποῦ τοι, 13.219; cf. 5.171). A lengthy consultation scene follows (13.246–329), also employing elements from consultation scenes in the narrative pattern (motifs 5a, c). As Idomeneus goes on to exhort his own troops, he suggests thematic parallels with Aias and Akhilleus (13.321–25), as noted in chapter 1.

As a final transition into the *aristeia* proper, the narrator summarizes the conflict between Poseidon and Zeus as ἔριδος κρατερῆς, "a powerful strife" (13.358), which implies a theomachy, if lacking actual violence between the two gods. As such the reference is an adapted version of the first motif, which begins *1. When theomachian frictions surface at a divine council.* Much as the larger narrative is an ἔρις (*eris*) myth, strife between Akhilleus and Agamemnon (see chapter 5), so the divine conflict is between Zeus and Poseidon in this book. Prompted by Poseidon, Idomeneus begins his *aristeia*, by slaying two Trojans, including Asios, the leader of the first attempt on the wall. Poseidon further intervenes to strike terror into Alkathoos (13.434–45), Idomeneus' final victim. When Idomeneus eventually retreats, after Aineias enters, the episode develops into a complex of duels in which the Greeks gradually gain the upper hand, as Poseidon intended.

When the Greeks do regain the upper hand, the *Iliad* offers its central articulation of the war as an ethical cause. Menelaos enters battle, upset at Deipuros' death, wounding Helenos, and slaying Peisandros (13.581–619). Vaunting over these deeds, Menelaos frames the whole war in an ethical perspective, depicting the Trojans as having committed various offenses against him. Chief among these is violating the sanctity of hospitality and acting out of hubris (13.633) to such an extent that Zeus, in a divine wrath, will destroy the city (13.624–25), an apocalypse of similar scope to Sodom and Gomorrah (Gen 19):

> Arrogant Trojans, insatiate of the fierce war cry,
> nor are you lacking in other outrage and disgrace,
> such as the sort you committed against me, you wicked dogs,
> nor were you at all afraid of the terrible wrath of high-thundering Zeus,
> god of hospitality, who will some day utterly destroy your steep city.
>
> (13.621–25)[27]

The narrative now shifts to Paris, with deft irony at his expense. Like Menelaos, Paris enters battle upset over the death of an acquaintance (13.660–62). Like Menelaos, he is provoked by his feelings about hospitality, the slain acquaintance having been his guest friend, ξεῖνος (13.661). But Paris and Menelaos occupy opposite positions with regard to hospitality. Paris' transgression of hospitality, making off with his host's wife and stealing a number of his possessions, not only provoked the war but, within the mythological world view of the *Iliad*, insures that Paris and his people will suffer consequences.[28] Menelaos, as no other character in the poem, has been wronged in this regard. Paris, as no other character in the poem, has not only ruptured a sacred institution and thus committed an offense before Zeus himself, but he continues to act in ways that serve to link his present, often irresponsible, actions to his original sin, as it were (e.g., 3.382–461). By having Paris express outrage that his acquaintance by hospitality dies, book 13 thus imbues his words with considerable irony and sly humor at his expense.[29]

Book 13, continuing its concern with some of the moral issues relevant to the war, closes with a focus on Hektor (13.673–837). The third installment of the dynamic between Hektor and Poulydamas uses a pivotal contrafactual to underscore Hektor's need to heed Poulydamas' advice:

> And then the Trojans would have gone away from the ships
> and huts, painfully, back to windy Troy,
> had not Poulydamas standing alongside spoken to daring Hektor.
>
> (13.723–25)

The passage underscores Poulydamas' importance to Trojan success in the middle sequence. In this third of his four speeches, noting Hektor's frequent failure to listen to reason (13.726), Poulydamas advises him to consult with the other Trojan officers. The episode looks ahead to Poulydamas' final, but unsuccessful, attempt to persuade Hektor, in book 18. Poulydamas presciently refers to Akhilleus' likely return to battle (13.746–47), which will again be the central topic of their discussion in book 18.

Hektor's response is complex. While he agrees with Poulydamas' recommendation that he consult with the Trojan officers, he seems overconfident, overly reliant on his own heroism, which was Andromakhe's earlier concern (6.407). When the other Trojans assemble around Poulydamas, Hektor goes off alone to ascertain the status of the other Trojan groups, finding only wounded or slain Trojans (13.761–64). The passage suggests his later isolation (22.98–104), when he is cut off from everyone else, realizing Poulydamas' advice to return to Troy was correct. Of the officers, only Paris is unwounded, actively leading his men. Instead of approving, however, Hektor lashes out at Paris (13.765–87), abusively dressing him down in terms that, while appropriate to Paris in books 3 and 6, are inappropriate here since Paris is displaying leadership. Of Hektor's misplaced reaction, Janko (1992:

141) notes, "We may read into it his alarm, vexation and guilt that he caused these losses by plunging on regardless of whether others were keeping their formation." Hektor is taking out on Paris his own conflict with Poulydamas. When he and Paris make a further attempt on the wall, they are repulsed by Aias, who asserts that the Greeks will sack Troy before the Trojans take the Greeks' ships (13.815–16). When Aias' declaration is confirmed by an augury (13.821–23), Hektor goes on to wish again that he could be called Zeus' son and honored as are Apollo and Athena (13.825–27). Hektor's hubris and presumption, like that of a Pentheus or Hippolytos in a classical tragedy, instantiate Menelaos' depiction of the Trojans' collective hubris (13.621 ff).

Book 14

Book 14 extends the middle sequence's inversions to parody of the divine economy. Whereas Poseidon led the divine rebellion in book 13, Hera, who is *the* divine rebel in the *Iliad* (see chapter 6), assumes the leading role in book 14. Hera's acts embody and typify the inverted values of the middle sequence. Her temporary ability to advance her agenda in book 14, contrary to Zeus' will, is a divine parallel to Hektor's temporary victories in the middle books, a short-term phenomenon, contrary to the eventuality of Troy's defeat. Book 14 has a ring compositional design that emphasizes Hera's rebellion by placing it in the center of an A B C B A structure (Janko 1992: 149). Book 14 begins by first continuing some narrative threads left suspended in book 11. Nestor, still tending Makhaon, seeks Agamemnon and finds him wounded with Diomedes and Odysseus (14.1–40). A brief council scene follows (14.41–152), like that in book 9. Agamemnon, continuing the defeatist line he has often sounded since book 2, fears his men will no longer fight for him. Regarding the wall built at Nestor's suggestion as ineffective, he suggests returning to Greece. But Odysseus rebuffs him (reprising his role in the introductory pattern, *12. Odysseus succeeds in restoring order in a second or later Greek assembly,* discussed in chapter 4), even insulting him (14.84–85, 95). Odysseus does so without reprisal, where Akhilleus cannot in book 1. He has greater authority by virtue of his age, speaking ability, and role as strategist. Agamemnon accepts Odysseus' "harsh rebuke" (14.104–5), agrees not to recommend flight, and asks for another plan. Diomedes asserts that they must return to battle, though wounded. Poseidon, assuming the form of an old man, then comes to Agamemnon reassuring him.

Hera now reestablishes herself as the chief divine rebel, as before in books 1, 4, and 8. In her rebellion, Hera crosses a line not crossed by the other

Greek-partisan gods, Poseidon and Athena. She openly lies to Zeus and Aphrodite, thereby providing a model for Milton's depiction of Satan in *Paradise Lost*, rebellious and openly dishonest with the supreme god.[30] Her epithet here, χρυσόθρονος, "golden-throned" (14.153), though also used of Eos and Artemis (Dee 2001: 140), may, in this context, allude to her contesting the divine seat of power.[31] Her view of Zeus here, "and he was quite hateful to her" (14.158), suggests a divine hatred that approaches the Satanic.[32] Unconstrained by the presence of other gods, as at earlier divine councils, Hera exudes hatred of Zeus and of his steerage of the poem's plot thus far (see chapters 6 and 7).

As she initiates her deception of Zeus, the *Iliad* shifts into an ironic modality more characteristic of the *Odyssey*. In planning to *deceive* Zeus (ἐξαπάφοιτο, 14.160), Hera's technique resembles Odysseus' in the second half of the *Odyssey*, to appear less than she is, and so more easily lull her opponent into a posture in which he may be caught off guard. But Odysseus uses this method against the suitors, impious men who have demonstrated that they are outside the norms of civilized culture, whereas Hera is lying to the god of the cosmos himself. The closest parallel is the *Ate* narrative (19.91–136), in which she seeks similar results (to deceive Zeus) and is described by many of the same terms. Because Hera's deception is directed against Zeus, the episode is rife with allusions to divine rebellion and theomachy. Retreating to her private chamber, Hera dresses and does her toilette (14.178–87), a parody of a warrior's arming scene (Morris 1992: 20; Janko 1992: 173–74).

To ensure success Hera enlists the aid of two other deities, Aphrodite and Hypnos. Hera acknowledges that Aphrodite is angry (κοτεσσαμένη, 14.191, also a theomachian reference) with her because they support different sides in the war. When Aphrodite answers, eager to grant Hera's request, she calls her the daughter of great Kronos (14.194), a further implicit reference to theomachy, because Kronos was defeated by Zeus in the first theomachy. Hera is described as δολοφρονέουσα, "lying," to Aphrodite, also used of her in the *Ate* narrative (14.197 = 19.106). Hera asks Aphrodite to give her desire and yearning, which she notes can even *subdue* the gods (δαμνᾷ ἀθανάτους, 14.199), yet another suggestion of theomachy. But she claims that she needs these powers to reconcile Ocean and Tethys, a patent fiction. She embeds in this request a reference to Zeus' defeat of Kronos (14.203–4), a theomachian reference, as is the fictitious quarrel between Okeanos and Tethys. Unaware of her own irony, and herself deceived and exploited by Hera, Aphrodite says she grants the aid because Hera sleeps in the arms of Zeus (14.213).

"Desire," concretized as a garment worn about her breasts,[33] Aphrodite now removes and lends to Hera. Pictured on it are many powers including persuasion, said to steal the wits even of the thoughtful (14.217), again an implicit theomachian reference. Hera, having placed it in her bosom, now approaches Hypnos. Unlike with Aphrodite, Hera bluntly tells Hypnos her agenda. But he proves a harder sell, having suffered repercussions from an earlier, parallel incident. Hera had him put Zeus to sleep when Heracles sacked Troy (again suggesting the *Ate* narrative), which enabled Hera to harass Heracles at sea on his return voyage. Knowing he escaped Zeus' subsequent divine wrath only when Night intervened (in a pivotal contrafactual, 14.258–59), Hypnos demurs. When Hera offers marriage to one of the Graces, Hypnos agrees. Hera's support from other deities parodies a full theomachy directed against Zeus.

When they return to Mount Ida, Hypnos conceals himself in a lofty pine, while Hera makes for the peak of Gargaros, instantly rousing Zeus' desire. When he asks her where she is headed, she repeats the lie (δολοφρονέουσα, 14.300 = 14.197 = 19.106) about reconciling Okeanos and Tethys, adding a further lie that she has come to ask his permission before doing so (14.301–11). Ironically, Zeus refers to his arousal in a term that suggests defeat in a theomachy (ἐδάμασσεν, 14.316), repeated by the narrator when he is asleep on the peak of Gargaros, after making love (δαμείς, 14.354). This same verb often denotes the defeat of a warrior on the battlefield (e.g., 3.437, 22.40). Zeus' succumbing to his own desire points to Paris' irresponsible return to bed at the end of book 3 (14.314 = 3.341; 14.315a = 3.442a, etc.).

With Zeus now asleep after making love, Hypnos speeds to Poseidon, urging him to seize the moment and defend the Greeks. Poseidon, just as at 13.44 ff and 14.147–52, rouses the Greeks against Hektor and the Trojans. In doing so, Poseidon occupies the position Athena will in Akhilleus' sequence, the pro-Akhaian deity who stirs the best of the Akhaians against Hektor. The expected confrontation between the two armies turns into a duel between Hektor and Telamonian Aias, the best of the Akhaians in book 7, the figure capable of defeating Hektor. Hektor hurls his spear, striking Aias' shield but failing to wound him (Fenik 1968: 124–25), a passage that offers brief instances of two motifs: *13. The best of the Akhaians has a unique shield*, and *14. When Hektor strikes the best of the Akhaians, his spear is driven back by the special shield*. In a brief instance of a *khermadion* sequence (5e in the narrative pattern), Aias hurls a great stone at Hektor, wounding and disorienting him. With both sides then trying to seize his body, the Trojans, Dardanians, and Lykians are able to retrieve it. But with Hektor out of the fighting, the Greeks are emboldened, and Aias Oileus takes the initiative. There follows a series of tit-for-tat slayings by both sides, until the book concludes with the Trojans in panicked retreat and the Greeks executing a mass slaying. Hera has successfully reversed the direction of the middle sequence.

Book 15

As book 15 begins, the Trojans halt their flight, and Zeus awakes, seeing Poseidon among the Greeks, and Hektor vomiting blood. Realizing Hera's deception, he sends Iris to command Poseidon to withdraw from the battlefield and Apollo to instill *menos* in Hektor. Zeus now proclaims the climax of the middle sequence, that Hektor shall slay Patroklos (15.65), and of the final sequence, Akhilleus' slaying Hektor (15.68), and even events falling beyond the end of the *Iliad*, the sack of Troy (15.71).[34] Zeus reiterates his promise to Akhilleus.

When Hera returns to Olympos, as Janko (1992: 240) notes, she "overtly advises submission, but covertly stirs up revolt. . . . Rather than acknowledge Zeus's superiority, she says that he *asserts* it." Hera now serves as divine *provocateur*. She does not act directly contrary to Zeus but goads Ares into breaking his command by informing him of the death of his son, Askalaphos. Hera's ability to continue subverting Zeus' will continues the central inverted tendencies of the middle sequence. Athena restrains Ares, warning that Zeus would strike him with lightning (15.117). The verb she uses, πλήσσω, denotes defeat in a theomachy (see chapter 7). Iris now relays Zeus' command to Poseidon, suggesting the threat of theomachy (15.179, πολεμίξων). Though Poseidon takes offense at Zeus' threat, he acquiesces in a manner that allows him to save face.

Zeus next orders Apollo, essentially, to redirect the middle sequence back to where it had been before Hera and Poseidon's interventions helped the Greeks and hurt the Trojans. Their intervention, spanning much of books 13–14, gives the middle sequence its greater length, ten books, compared with the seven books composing the first and third sequences. Apollo is to wield the aegis to rout the Greeks and then instill *menos* in Hektor, an inversion of *3. A god places* μένος, *"battle might," in him (the best of the Akhaians)*. Having done so, Apollo then promises Hektor the kind of divine aid (15.254–61) normally reserved for the (Greek) protagonist in Homeric epic (e.g., *Od.* 13.393–96).

As he returns to battle Hektor is compared in similes to a horse and a lion, the second of which is typical of the best of the Akhaians as he initiates an *aristeia* (5.161, 11.113, 16.487, 20.164). But when Thoas, the Greek counselor sees him, he is surprised that Aias had not killed him (15.289; cf. Hektor slain by Akhilleus, 22.446), an instantiation of Aias' central role as thematically capable of defeating Hektor. After Thoas recommends a Greek retreat, Hektor leads the Trojans on, while Apollo wields the aegis, routing the Akhaians (15.320–27, 365–66). Apollo now, in effect, repeats Zeus' hurling thunder among the Greeks at 8.75–77, which initiated the middle sequence, to panic them into retreat and temporary defeat.[35] A compound of πλήσσω (ἐνι πλήξαντες, 15.344) depicts the Greeks in their god-sent confusion. Hektor and the Trojans, with Apollo's aid, now storm the wall. Apollo takes *menos* away from the Greeks (15.493; cf. 15.594–95).

After a brief scene in which the proximity of battle finally prompts Patroklos to leave Eurypylos (15.390–405) and return to Akhilleus, Hektor and the Trojans fight Aias and the Greeks to a stalemate. Hektor, addressing his men by the three divisions (15.425–28, 486), exhorts them to retrieve the armor of his slain cousin, Kaletor. The middle sequence thus initiates a key concern, retrieving the armor of a fallen comrade, which will climax in Hektor's recovery of armor from Patroklos. As Apollo wielding the aegis restores the equilibrium of the middle sequence to where it had been in book 8, Teukros enters (15.436), reprising his role at 8.309–29 (Fenik 1968: 227; Janko 1992: 277). Zeus, in a pivotal contrafactual, prevents him from slaying Hektor (458 ff). Teukros then has an arming scene (15.479–83), again presenting the second motif, *2. The best of the Akhaians arms himself as prelude to his* aristeia.

The fighting having reached an equilibrium, in which neither side gains noticeable advantage, the narrator notes that Zeus will regard his promise to Thetis fulfilled when Hektor sets fire to a ship (15.596–600). This will constitute Hektor's greatest success in the middle sequence, and the end of Zeus' explicit support (15.601–2). The narrator goes on to note, in a classic statement of overdetermination, that Hektor himself will shortly be slain (Παλλὰς Ἀθηναίη ὑπὸ Πηλεΐδαο βίηφιν, 15.614). Hektor is unaware that this short-term success, the burning of a ship, will lead to long-term defeat.[36] When Hektor grabs hold of one of the ships, in a speech meant to rouse the Trojans (15.718–25), he asserts that the Greek ships had come contrary to divine will, that the Trojan counselors' cowardice had prevented him from destroying them earlier. After Hektor's misguided focus on burning the ships (Agamemnon proposed earlier the same day to return home, 14.74–81), book 15 ends with Aias exhorting the Greeks to resist the attack.

Book 16

As book 16 begins, Patroklos finally returns to Akhilleus (having intended to do so since 11.651), restoring the poem's focus on the protagonist for the first time since 11.614. Seeing Patroklos crying, Akhilleus surmises something is amiss with Patroklos' or his own father (16.13–16):

He was shedding [χέων] warm tears [δάκρυα] like a fountain with black
   water,
which pours dark water down a sheer rock face.

(16.3–4)

The episode, through some intriguing parallels, points ahead to Priam's re-
trieving Hektor's corpse by making Akhilleus think of his own father (see
motif 19 in chapter 1). The description of Patroklos resembles Akhilleus' ac-
count of the weeping Niobe:

>   shedding tears [δάκρυ χέουσα],
> now somewhere in the rocks, in remote mountains,
> in Sipylos, where they say are the beds of goddesses,
> the nymphs, who make their way about Akheloos,
> there, though now a stone, she broods on her griefs from the gods.

(24.613–17)4

Patroklos' weeping before Akhilleus like water down the face of a rock is
quite close to Niobe's weeping over her stone face in Akhilleus' descrip-
tion. Akhilleus' response to Patroklos is pity (ᾤκτιρε, 16.5), his same response
to the mourning Priam (οἰκτίρων, 24.516). The weeping and links with the
aftermath of Hektor's death introduce the tragic qualities that will domi-
nate Patroklos' *aristeia*, the point at which Akhilleus' rash wish, that Zeus
make the Greeks suffer, ironically causes his best friend to die.[37]

Patroklos will serve as the final best of the Akhaians before Akhilleus
(Menelaos identifies him as "the best of the Akhaians" shortly after his
death, 17.689). As the initial sequence bifurcates the best of the Akhaians
into Diomedes, who has a great *aristeia*, and Aias, who defeats Hektor in
a duel, the middle sequence bifurcates the best of the Akhaians into Aga-
memnon and Patroklos, each of whom has complementary personal rela-
tionships with Akhilleus. Agamemnon interacts with Akhilleus in his public
life, especially his public conflicts, whereas Patroklos interacts in his private
life. By contrast, Diomedes and Aias (except for participation in the em-
bassy in book 9) lack close personal interaction with Akhilleus in the *Iliad*.
When Akhilleus accedes to Patroklos' request to send him into battle wear-
ing his arms, he stipulates that Patroklos not accomplish too much, lest he
deprive Akhilleus of glory, and not to attack Troy by himself, lest Apollo
come against him (16.89 ff). The negative commands function in book 16
like divine interdictions (Louden 1999a: 14, 18–19, 92–95, etc.). Patroklos,
unable to observe the commands, will thus bring on his own death.

Patroklos' *aristeia* contains the middle sequence's fullest deployment of motifs from the narrative pattern, but also maximizes the inversions that characterize this sequence. A fully developed instance of *2. The best of the Akhaians arms himself as prelude to his* aristeia launches his *aristeia*. But Patroklos' arming scene (16.130–54) maintains the middle sequence's inversions in his inability to wield Akhilleus' spear (16.140–44). Although both Aias and Akhilleus wound Hektor in the neck with their spears, Patroklos is unable to take the relevant weapon and will himself be slain by Hektor. The narrative pattern's first motif (*1. When theomachian frictions surface at a divine council, Zeus dictates the permissible level of divine intervention*) is also evident in the encounter between Hera and Zeus in book 15 (and her subsequent interference with Ares). Immediately following Patroklos' arming scene, Akhilleus marshals the Myrmidons (16.155–209), an instance of the final motif from the introductory pattern, *13. The introductory pattern concludes with a summons to battle* (discussed in chapter 4). What is normally the final motif of the introductory pattern here overlaps with motifs from the beginning of the principal narrative pattern. More intriguing is the variation on the next motif from the pattern, *3. A god places* μένος *(5.125, 136) in the best of the Akhaians as he goes to face the Trojans.* Here Akhilleus himself plays the role played elsewhere by a deity (Athena in books 5 and 19, and Eris in 11), and instills *menos* in the best of the Akhaians (16.210).[38]

After this cluster of four motifs from the narrative pattern, book 16 delays the start of Patroklos' *aristeia*, pointing ahead to its failure through departures from the usual motifs. Akhilleus makes a compound prayer to Zeus (16.233–48), who grants the first part, but rejects the second, which asks for Patroklos' safe return. When Patroklos then addresses and exhorts the Myrmidons, as Janko (1992: 353) shows, he gives strong indications that he will be unable to uphold Akhilleus' interdictions. To emphasize that Patroklos' death is interwoven with Hektor's, the narrative interweaves references to Hektor. While Patroklos prepares, the Trojans are able to drive Aias back and set fire to a ship (16.101–22), but Hektor's actual accomplishments are minimized, as Janko (1994: 330) notes: "Hektor's failure to harm Aias is telling; like his defeat by him while Zeus sleeps at 14.402ff.—he is not even given the honour of being first to set a ship ablaze."

Initially, Patroklos' *aristeia* resembles the beginning of Diomedes'.[39] Both *aristeiai* open with a detailed description of one killing (16.287–96, 5.9–29). After slaying the significantly named Pyraichmes, "Fire-spear" (Janko 1992: 354), as his first victim (16.287–93), marking an end to the Trojans' threat to burn the ships, Patroklos single-handedly triggers a Trojan retreat, resembling the rout Akhilleus will cause after slaying Asteropaios (Janko 1992: 355). Patroklos then slays Areilykos, initiating a series of individual

Greeks who slay individual Trojans (16.306 ff), a technique also found at the start of Diomedes' *aristeia*. As Fenik (1968: 192) and Janko (1992: 356) note, there is considerable overlap between the other Greeks involved in these two series. In book 5 Diomedes is first, as Patroklos is here. Menelaos, Meges, Meriones, and Idomeneus, among others, then follow suit in each case (though not in exactly the same order). Such series do not occur in books 20–22 because in Akhilleus' *aristeia* the focus remains entirely on his own exploits.

Whereas Patroklos' *aristeia* begins successfully for him, Hektor faces an immediate reversal of his recent fortunes. In a simile he is paralleled with a shepherd who endangers his flock because of his foolishness (ἀφραδίηισι, 16.354).[40] Immediately thereafter, Aias drives against the Trojans. A series of three cloud/storm similes (16.297–300, 363–66, 384–92) now builds forcefully from a cloud clearing to allow a burst of light, to Zeus bringing on a hurricane, to Zeus, angry at disrespectful mortals, bringing about apocalyptic destruction.[41] The progression of the similes suggests the larger tempo of the war, leading up to Akhilleus' *aristeia,* and ultimate Greek victory (beyond the plot of the *Iliad*). The progression of the similes also implies that Zeus' support of Hektor, the defining factor of the middle sequence, is coming to an end.[42]

At this point in the initial and final sequences, the best of the Akhaians duels Aineias in a lengthy episode (*5. He encounters the second greatest warrior on the Trojan side, Aineias, leader of the Dardanians, a–f*). Perhaps so as not to lessen the focus on Hektor, the middle sequence omits the encounter with Aineias, who appears only a few times in books 11–15 (13.459–541; 14.425; 15.332), never playing a very prominent role, until briefly in book 17.[43] Accordingly, those portions of the narrative pattern do not figure in Patroklos' *aristeia*. But rather than dispense entirely with motifs associated with him, Patroklos' *aristeia* incorporates several into motif 8 from the narrative pattern, the best of the Akhaians' encounter with a Lykian hero.

After Patroklos single-handedly slays a series of twelve Trojans (16.399–418), his *aristeia* turns to its lengthiest episode (16.419–683), the encounter with Sarpedon, *8. The best of the Akhaians duels with and defeats a great Lykian warrior*. Patroklos' slaying of Sarpedon forms the climax of the three encounters, succeeding Diomedes and Glaukos, Akhilleus and Asteropaios. Akhilleus has the climactic series involving Hektor, the best of the Trojans, but Patroklos is given the next most significant victory. A divine consultation between Zeus and Hera signals the encounter's importance. Sarpedon first declares that he will find out who it is that causes so much evil for the Trojans, as Aineias had said about Diomedes (16.424 ff = 5.175 ff). Concerned for his son, Zeus proposes a divine rescue, a slightly adapted form of

5f. The duel is deprived of a climax when a deity intervenes through a pivotal contrafactual, carrying off Aineias. Zeus' verb for the rescue is essentially the same as in the first statement of this motif, when Aphrodite rescues Paris (ἀναρπάξας, 16.437; ἐξήρπαξ', 3.380). But Hera suggests that Sarpedon be taken to Lykia as Zeus wishes, but only after dying at Patroklos' hands. In Hera's firm disagreement, and suggestion of friction among the gods if Zeus were to rescue Sarpedon (16.443, 445–49), the episode instantiates *1. When theomachian frictions surface at a divine council, Zeus dictates the permissible level of divine intervention.* It is Hera, not Zeus who dictates the terms of Sarpedon's disposition, appropriating the executive function, as in book 14, continuing the inversions that define the middle sequence.

Zeus responds by pouring down a bloody rain as a tribute for Sarpedon (16.459; cf. the beginning of Agamemnon's *aristeia*, 11.53), a sign of his mourning and an indication of the greater bloodshed that is to come.[44] The link with Agamemnon's *aristeia* also points to Patroklos' pending failure, because Agamemnon was the only previous best of the Akhaians driven from his *aristeia* seriously wounded. Sarpedon's death, though quite heroic, is anticlimactic. The preliminaries (chiefly the divine council), and the immediate consequences (the *ate* of Patroklos) are developed in greater depth and are of greater consequence than the combat (16.462–81) and death (16.482–502), again true of the motifs associated with Aineias in the narrative pattern. The mention of tree cutters (16.485, 663), after the slain Sarpedon falls like a tree (16.482–84), may look ahead to preparations for the two funerals that close the poem, Patroklos' (23.119, 315) and Hektor's (24.784), in their emphasis on collecting wood.[45] Before dying, Sarpedon's speech (16.492–501) reiterates and elevates the issue of reclaiming the arms and corpse of the fallen warrior (a combination of two motifs: *12. Hektor asks the best of the Akhaians to swear an oath to return the corpse of the defeated to his companions, undefiled, but deprived of its armor,* and *17. Hektor exchanges armor with the best of the Akhaians*). These two motifs are central to the deaths of both Patroklos and Hektor and reverberate through the remainder of the poem.

The narrative now focuses on Glaukos (16.508–63), an odd development within an *aristeia* by a best of the Akhaians. Apollo heals Glaukos (16.528) of his earlier wound and then instills him with *menos* (16.529), an inversion of *3. A god places* μένος, *"battle might," in the best of the Akhaians as he goes to face the Trojans.* Rousing other warriors, Glaukos rebukes Hektor, much as Hektor had Paris, demanding that they prevent Sarpedon's arms from being taken, an adaptation of *10a. Hektor is persuaded by his brother to battle the best of the Akhaians.* Zeus, marking his son in special ways, now intensifies the fighting around Sarpedon by bringing on night (16.568–69).

After fierce back-and-forth fighting (16.570–607), exchanges between

Aineias and Meriones, Zeus considers how to bring about Patroklos' death (16.644–52) when he problematizes his slaying of Sarpedon by taking his armor.[46] The episode, an inversion of *17. Hektor exchanges armor with the best of the Akhaians,* prefigures Hektor's donning of Akhilleus' arms, which Zeus himself will condemn (17.200–205). After Patroklos gives Sarpedon's arms to his companions, he is deluded, under the influence of *ate* (μέγ' ἀάσθη / νήπιος, 16.685–86; ἄτη, 16.805), and in violation of Akhilleus' interdiction (16.686–87). In his connection with *ate* Patroklos is again linked with Agamemnon (who is thematically subject to *ate*). The *Iliad* shows other options for a warrior in such circumstances when Akhilleus slays Andromakhe's father but does not despoil him (σεβάσσατο γὰρ τό γε θυμῷ, 6.417), burying him with his armor (see chapter 5). Patroklos is now targeted by Zeus (16.688–91).

In a final triumph, Patroklos slays a handful of Trojans, until Apollo draws near. At this decisive juncture, book 16 employs several motifs from the narrative pattern, most of them inverted in accord with the middle sequence. In his delusion Patroklos violates Akhilleus' edict against attacking Troy and goes against Apollo in so doing, exemplifying *7. The best of the Akhaians three times attacks Apollo, while he protects a Trojan hero, but gives way on his fourth attempt.* The same context continues with *7a. He is called* δαίμονι ἶσος *only during his aristeia and . . . only when he attacks a Trojan-partisan deity* (16.705). Apollo intervenes by way of a pivotal contrafactual unique in the *Iliad:*

> And then the sons of the Akhaians would have taken Troy
> by Patroklos' hands, for he was rushing with his spear,
> had not Phoibos Apollo stood upon the high-built
> tower, intending destruction for him, and helping the Trojans.
>
> (16.698–701)

Homeric epic usually employs pivotal contrafactuals to save or rescue a key character. But here Apollo (16.701, 711) intervenes to destroy a hero, not aid him. Apollo's response, his intervention *against* Patroklos, is an inversion of *15. Hektor's imminent defeat is emphasized by a pivotal contrafactual, which demonstrates his dependence on Apollo* (16.703–6; cf. 5.436–39, 20.445–48). In keeping with the inverted modality of the middle sequence, only here does the encounter with Apollo lead to the death of the best of the Akhaians. Apollo's role here is an exact counterpart of Athena's role in book 22, when she helps cause Hektor's death.

The nexus of motifs involving Andromakhe (motifs 9, 9a) cannot occur in full, since Hektor and Andromakhe are not onstage together between books 6 and 22. But Patroklos' *aristeia* nonetheless appears to allude to these motifs. Hektor is curiously depicted as almost inside the city, inside the

Skaian gates (16.712), wondering whether to bring the army within the walls (16.714), close to Andromakhe's suggestion that he defend the city from within the walls (6.433–34). Apollo then takes the form of Asios, Hekabe's (16.718) brother. This only mention of Hekabe between books 6 and 22 briefly suggests Hektor's meetings with his female family members. In his address to Hektor, Apollo shames him into going back out (16.722), close to two motifs: *9b. His fear of shame counters their attempts at persuasion*, and *10a. Hektor is persuaded by his brother to battle the best of the Akhaians*. Apollo's comments also resemble the disguised Athena's remarks before Hektor faces Akhilleus (22.229–46).

Encouraged by the disguised Apollo, Hektor makes for Patroklos with a determination (16.731–32) that would normally characterize the best of the Akhaians, in *his aristeia* (particularly Akhilleus' pursuit of Hektor). Patroklos' last victim is Kebriones, Hektor's chariot driver, whose death is closely bound up with Patroklos' own death, as Patroklos' death will be tied to Hektor's. The bitter fighting over his corpse employs formulas used of Akhilleus lying dead.[47] As with Sarpedon, the Greeks strip the armor from Kebriones, and the narrative repeats Apollo's intervention, combining two motifs: *7. The best of the Akhaians three times attacks Apollo, while he protects a Trojan hero, but gives way on his fourth attempt* (16.784–86), and *7a. He is called δαίμονι ἶσος only during his* aristeia *and, with one exception, only when he attacks a Trojanpartisan deity* (16.786). Now Apollo moves against Patroklos, striking him with his hand (πλῆξεν, 16.791), then striking him a second time, sending his helmet flying. When Hektor recovers it and dons it, the *Iliad* again links improper seizing of arms with resultant death (16.799–800). When Apollo fouls the rest of Patroklos' arms, *ate* seizes him (16.805), allowing him to be wounded in the back by Euphorbos and finished off by Hektor, who approaches only after seeing Patroklos already wounded. Many of the remaining motifs are now irrelevant, given the profound turnabout: the best of the Akhaians has died. Patroklos has unexpectedly fulfilled Akhilleus' wish to harm the Akhaians.

Book 17

In book 17, perhaps the *Iliad*'s darkest book,[48] the middle sequence presents its grimmest inversions, the immediate consequences of the death of the best of the Akhaians. The prolonged fighting over Patroklos' body and armor (which is shaped by awareness of an account of Akhilleus' death, the struggle for *his* arms and corpse—see Edwards 1991: 62, 90) reworks and inverts several key motifs from the narrative pattern. Hektor's anxiety about possible mistreatment of his corpse should he be slain (*12. Hektor asks the best of the Akhaians to swear an oath to return the corpse of the defeated to his companions, undefiled, but deprived of his armor*) is a vital motif in the initial and final sequences. The initial and final sequences both conclude with motifs concerning mourning and the treatment of the slain: *19. . . . to propose a truce to care for the dead,* and *20. Both sides mourn their dead and construct a tomb.* Much of book 17 inverts these three motifs from the narrative pattern.

In having the most-recent best of the Akhaians die in book 16, the poem has created a void. Akhilleus cannot serve this function until the final sequence begins, in book 18. Into this vacuum, perhaps surprisingly, steps Menelaos. But the *Iliad* has twice earlier hinted at just such a move. In book 3, the overture for the narrative pattern, Menelaos serves as best of the Akhaians in his duel against Paris (see sections I and IV in chapter 2). Menelaos was also the first to volunteer to duel Hektor in book 7, a similar point in that sequence (7.94–103), as here. Confirming his status as stand-in for "the best of the Akhaians," Athena appears to him (17.553–73), suggesting parallels with Akhilleus and employing another motif from the narrative pattern. Athena assumes the form of Phoinix, Akhilleus' close associate (whom we argue in chapter 4, motifs 5 and 6 of the introductory pattern, parallels Patroklos as *a companion dear to Akhilleus*). Her descent recalls her appearance to Akhilleus in book 1 (ἦλθε δ᾽ Ἀθήνη/οὐρανόθεν, 1.194–95; Ἀθήνη/οὐρανόθεν καταβᾶσα, 17.544–45). After conferring with Menelaos, she puts βίη (*bie*, "might"), in his shoulders and knees, a variation of *3. A god places* μένος *in him as he goes to face the Trojans.* The book opens, however, with Menelaos' encounter with Euphorbos, which curiously anticipates Hektor's duel with Akhilleus. When Euphorbos attempts to strike Menelaos, his spear is bent back by the latter's shield (17.44–45): *14. When Hektor strikes the best of the Akhaians, his spear is driven back by the special shield.* He counters by fatally stabbing Euphorbos in the neck (17.47–49): *16. In the duel's climax, the best of the Akhaians wounds Hektor in the neck with his spear.* The formula describing Menelaus wounding Euphorbos is the same as when Akhilleus wounds Hektor (17.49 = 22.327). A disguised Apollo now refers to Menelaos' slaying Euphorbos, as "he slew the best of the Trojans" (Τρώων τὸν ἄριστον ἔπεφνε, 17.80), confirming the combat as a brief instantiation of *the best of the Akhaians slays Hektor, best of the Trojans.*

Book 17 also revisits Hektor's lapses of judgment, and their negative consequences. Menelaos repeats his thematic position of asserting higher moral ground, as at 13.621–25 (cf. 3.351–54), by rebuking Euphorbos: "[I]t is not a good thing for an arrogant man [ὑπέρβιον] to boast" (17.19). Hektor squanders Zeus' favor by acting as Dolon does in book 10 (discussed in chapter 4), pursuing Akhilleus' horses, and wishing to be like the gods, as before in the middle sequence (8.538–40, 13.825–27). Apollo, now in the form of Mentes, urges Hektor to confront Menelaos, instead of vainly pursuing Akhilleus' horses (17.75–81). When Hektor does pursue Menelaos and Patroklos, the former enlists the aid of Aias. Hektor attempts to decapitate Patroklos' corpse (17.126), ironically suggesting a thematic parallel for Akhilleus' abuse of his own corpse. His attempt is an inversion of *12. Hektor asks the best of the Akhaians to swear an oath to return the corpse of the defeated to his companions, undefiled, but deprived of his armor.* But when he sees Aias approach, Hektor quickly withdraws, an adaptation of *11. Panic seizes Hektor on first seeing the best of the Akhaians, prompting his retreat* (ἐς ὅμιλον ἰὼν ἀνεχάξεθ' ἑταίρων, 17.129; ἑτάρων εἰς ἔθνος ἐχάξετο, > 3.32).

Hektor's retreat draws a biting rebuke from Glaukos, who threatens to send the Lykians home unless they try to win Patroklos' corpse so as to be able to ransom Sarpedon. Glaukos thus raises (17.159–63) the issue that will be central to book 24, the ransoming of the corpse of a great warrior, ironically doing so with Hektor, whose corpse will become the principal instantiation of the theme. As he does with Poulydamas, Hektor does not take Glaukos' criticism to heart, but instead uses it to justify more outrageous behavior on his own part. He puts on Patroklos/Akhilleus' divine armor, a surprising parody of *17. Hektor exchanges armor with the best of the Akhaians,* prompting Zeus to condemn his poor judgment (οὐ κατὰ κόσμον, 17.205).

Hektor dons the arms of Akhilleus, which fit him well (17.210) and possibly give him divine powers (17.211; cf. 19.386). He then offers to divide half the spoils (including Akhilleus' arms, implicitly) with whoever takes possession of Patroklos' body, after overwhelming Aias (17.230). The unrealistic offer again suggests parallels with the *Doloneia* (discussed in chapter 4). In his offer to reward handsomely whoever defeats Aias, Hektor seems almost aware of Aias' thematic ability to defeat him throughout the poem. Aias has Menelaos summon Aias Oileus, Idomeneus, and Meriones. As a fierce battle for Patroklos' corpse unfolds, Zeus is angry (μίσησεν) at the Trojans' attempt (17.272). This is as close as Zeus gets to displaying a divine wrath against an individual in the *Iliad*[49] and serves as prelude to his actual intervention below (17.593–96).

The Trojans score an initial success, routing the Greeks but not slaying any, and seize the corpse, until Aias, implicitly designated as a "best of the Akhaians" (17.279–80), counters, panicking the Trojans. After Aias then slays two and Hektor one, a further rout of the Trojans is only prevented by Apollo, again acting through a pivotal contrafactual (17.319–22), an instantiation of *15. Hektor's imminent defeat is emphasized by a pivotal contrafactual, which demonstrates his dependence on Apollo.* The passage suggests Aias is capable of sacking Troy single-handedly, as are Patroklos and Akhilleus.

Although Apollo disguises himself as Ankhises' herald, Periphas, Aineias recognizes that a god has spoken and rouses the Trojans to a counterattack. Aineias slays Leokritos, but the counterattack against Aias is short-lived, with more Trojans than Greeks dying in the fierce fighting.

While an intense battle rages, Akhilleus as yet knows nothing of Patroklos' death. The occasion, with the Greeks inglorious if they return without Patroklos, and apparently about to die, is given greater pathos by the unique scene with Akhilleus' immortal horses, refusing to return, weeping (17.426–40). Zeus, moved by the horses' plight, that they, immortal, were given to a mortal and witness such suffering, utters the *Iliad*'s most trenchant observation on human existence: "[F]or there is nothing more wretched than a man" (17.446–47). I take Zeus to refer to Hektor, the impending tragic results stemming from his vain pursuits and reckless choices.[50] Affirming that he shall not mount them, but that they instead will bear Automedon back to camp, Zeus reiterates that his support for the Trojans ends at sunset.

In spite of Apollo's warning, Hektor enlists Aineias' aid in a final vain effort to win Akhilleus' horses (17.483–91). In his foolish pursuit, Hektor now resembles Dolon.[51] Athena, in the form of Phoinix,[52] comes to inspire Menelaos. Apollo, in turn, spurs on Hektor, briefly giving the Trojans the upper hand. After Aias sends Antilokhos to tell Akhilleus that Patroklos has died and that Hektor has the armor, Menelaos hefts Patroklos' corpse, with Meriones' help, while Aias guards their retreat. Their success is underscored by one of the series of burning-city similes (17.736–41; cf. 18.207–13, 21.522–24, 22.410–11).[53] In this first of the series, houses in a city burn, with no explanation given for the fire's cause. But the next two similes develop the image of a city burning due to its having provoked a divine wrath (21.523), sacked by a surrounding army. Menelaos and Aias successfully recover Patroklos' body, and bring the middle sequence, with its focus on improper treatment of the dead, to a close. The simile briefly points beyond any motifs in the narrative pattern, arcing toward the sack of Troy.

Book 17 closes the middle sequence not only by utilizing and emphasizing motifs from the end of the narrative pattern but by linking itself to book 8, the sequence's first book, through ring compositional arrangement of an unusual motif. We noted how rare is Zeus' intervention in book 8 when he twice hurls lightning on the Trojan plain, to rout the Greek forces and initiate the inverted modality of the middle sequence. In ring composition, signaling the conclusion of the middle sequence, he makes his only other intervention in the *Iliad*. Now shaking his aegis (17.593–96), he hurls thunder and lightning to rout the Greeks again.[54] The middle sequence thus ends much as it began. Zeus terminates the temporary aid given the Trojans, which inverted the *Iliad*'s usual priorities.

⥲⥲⥲

CHAPTER FOUR

The Introductory Pattern
The Best of the Akhaians Calls an Assembly

Chapters 1–3 established and analyzed the *Iliad*'s principal narrative pattern as it underlies books 4–7 and 20–24, how book 3 provides a miniature preview of it, and how books 8, 11–17 offer it in an inverted form. We now consider those books that begin the three sequences. Books 1–2, 9–10, and 18–19, share a number of parallels. Thetis appears only in books 1 and 18, and her crucial prophecy is articulated in 9; Hephaistos also appears only in 1 and 18. Parallels have long been noted between books 2 and 10: their night-time settings, the unheroic characters Thersites and Dolon, the prominence of Odysseus, and his triumph over both figures. The assembly in book 19 appears to answer that in book 1, while the council in 9 attempts to do so but fails. Odysseus performs diplomatic missions, leads delegations, and restores order at assemblies in these same books. Nestor is also prominent in these same contexts (though both characters appear in other books as well). Two of the *Iliad*'s three most important marshaling scenes occur in 2 and 19.[1] Books 1, 9, and 18 serve both as Akhilleus' main entrances and exits, and the occasions for his most important decisions. He meets with Athena and Iris in books 1 and 18.

An introductory pattern underlies each pair of books, as the principal narrative pattern underlies the remainder of the poem. We analyze the introductory pattern separately because it functions separately. Only in these books is Akhilleus onstage in all three sequences. After these books (1–2, 9–10), he remains offstage in most of the first two sequences. The opening sequence further marks off the introductory pattern by interposing book 3, separating books 1–2 from books 4–7 of the principal narrative pattern. In the middle sequence books 9–10 come after book 8, which instead first offers an overture for that sequence.

The *telos* or goal of the introductory pattern is to assemble the army and, following a marshaling scene, send it off to do battle, led by the best of the Akhaians. Each of the three sequences, however, has a different way of arriving at this objective, offering considerable variety, just as each sequence of the principal narrative pattern is distinct with a unique modality. In keeping with its governing tendencies, the middle sequence gives books 9–10 an inverted or parodic relation to the introductory pattern as it appears in 1–2 and 18–19. Books 18–19 employ the various motifs in very different order than do 1–2 and 9–10 because Akhilleus' return to battle is unique, marked by unusual variations or expansions on elements common to the other sequences, but now stated in their climactic form, with greater divine involvement.[2] Hephaistos' fashioning Akhilleus' shield is a key instance of this tendency. One section of book 18, lines 148–242, concludes the preceding episode from book 17 but "spills over" into the middle of book 18, further complicating this book's intricate structure. Books 1 and 19 offer valuable parallels for addressing the notorious problem of the duals in book 9 (discussed below as motifs 5 and 6). The variations the three sequences play on the same set of underlying motifs are best seen in the different outcomes for Akhilleus. The assembly in book 1 results in Akhilleus' withdrawal, whereas the failed embassy in 9 indirectly prompts the insertion of Patroklos.[3] The assembly in 19 results in Akhilleus' return to battle and the marshaling of the host for war, the "normal" result of the introductory pattern, if the quarrel with Agamemnon had not intervened.

Although the order of the motifs may vary in a given sequence, due to differing needs of each sequence, the introductory pattern consists of the following motifs:

1. *The best of the Akhaians calls an assembly to address a crisis that interferes with the war against the Trojans.*
2. *In the course of the assembly, Agamemnon's leadership is challenged, if not preempted.*
3. *Agamemnon exercises reckless judgment (*ate*) against the best of the Akhaians.*
4. *Nestor attempts to restore order between the best of the Akhaians and Agamemnon.*
5. *Agamemnon dispatches Odysseus to lead a delegation that includes* two *heralds to return a companion dear to Akhilleus.*
6. *Akhilleus (and Patroklos) receives the delegation hospitably.*
7. *Akhilleus articulates his conflict about fighting, unfair distribution of winnings, and a slight to his honor and changes his resolve about fighting in the war.*
8. *Akhilleus thinks of Thetis and considers her prophecies about his destiny.*
   a. *Hephaistos serves a mediating function that helps further Thetis' agenda.*

9. *Night falls as a juncture between the two books.*

10. *The Trojans, led by Hektor, hold an assembly to plan their strategy (2, 10, and 18).*

11. *At the assembly, Hektor makes a foolish boast.*

12. *Odysseus succeeds in restoring order in a second or later Greek assembly against an Akhilleus figure.*

13. *The introductory pattern concludes with a summons to battle, for which Odysseus is largely responsible.*

∽

1. The best of the Akhaians calls an assembly to address a crisis that interferes with the war against the Trojans

In the initial sequence the crisis takes the form of Apollo's wrath against the Greeks, which results in the god slaying first livestock (1.43–50) and then the Greeks themselves (1.51–53). The divine wrath and subsequent plague have arisen because Agamemnon mistreated Khryses, Apollo's priest. Agamemnon had won Khryseis, Khryses' daughter, and refused to give her back when the priest came to ransom her. The incident reveals not only Agamemnon's responsibility for provoking the crisis but his poor leadership in dealing with subsequent complications. Instead of agreeing with Khryses' plea, Agamemnon rejects him, angrily and abusively (1.11, 25–33). The real crisis, then, at the start of the poem, is *Agamemnon's* anger at Apollo's priest, not Akhilleus' wrath (see subgenre 3 in chapter 5). But it is Akhilleus, the best of the Akhaians, not Agamemnon, who calls the assembly (ἀγορήνδε καλέσσατο λαὸν Ἀχιλλεύς, 1.54) to address the crisis. Agamemnon should be calling the assembly because the crisis afflicts his army. Akhilleus does so because of divine impetus: Hera is troubled over the Akhaians' suffering (1.55–56). Akhilleus thus has the support of a powerful god, whereas in the opening scenes Agamemnon goes against, and provokes, a powerful god, Apollo.

In book 9, on the other hand, a chastened Agamemnon calls the assembly. This time the crisis is Akhilleus' withdrawal, arising from the aftermath of the book 1 assembly and Zeus' subsequent intervention in book 8, which has demoralized the Greeks. As we noted in chapter 3, in the middle sequence Agamemnon himself functions as the best of the Akhaians in his *aristeia* in book 11. So in book 9, in his belated recognition of his responsibility for his army's problems, he himself calls the assembly.

In the final sequence the order of the motifs differs, with the assembly coming later, whereas in books 1–2 and 9–10, the assembly activities open the sequences. In the final sequence the assembly comes after the scenes involving Hephaistos and the shield, among others. As in the initial sequence,

Akhilleus calls the assembly. The sense of crisis, caused by Greek losses during Akhilleus' absence, is lessened, as Akhilleus is returning to battle, but he seeks first to declare an end to his wrath against Agamemnon. As in the initial sequence, the assembly has a divine impetus: Thetis tells Akhilleus to hold it (19.34).

Two sets of recurring formulas reinforce the parallels between the three assembly scenes. The first depicts the convening of the assembly:[4]

ἀγορήνδε καλέσσατο λαὸν Ἀχιλλεύς
(1.54)

κλήδην εἰς ἀγορὴν κικλήσκειν
(9.11)

εἰς ἀγορὴν καλέσας ἥρωας Ἀχαιούς
(19.34)

After the best of the Akhaians summons the host to an assembly, he then rises, making the first speech, also described in a recurring formula:

ἀνιστάμενος μετέφη πόδας ὠκὺς Ἀχιλλεὺς
(1.58)

ἂν δ᾽ Ἀγαμέμνων / ἵστατο
(9.13–14)

ἀνιστάμενος μετέφη πόδας ὠκὺς Ἀχιλλεὺς
(19.55 = 1.58)

⌒

2. In the course of the assembly, Agamemnon's leadership is challenged, if not preempted

In book 1 Akhilleus implicitly challenges and appropriates Agamemnon's leadership by having called the assembly. He suggests that the Greeks are unable to wage war and deal with the plague at the same time (1.59–61) and will be driven home unvictorious unless they deal with the plague. His term for being driven back, παλιμπλαγχθέντας (1.59), implies that the gods have turned against them, since a divine wrath is usually implicit in this verb's deployment.[5] Though Akhilleus may intend his statements as a rhetorical ploy, he shocks the assembly, and Agamemnon in particular, by implying that the Greeks might return home without achieving their objective. In so doing, he opens the door to his later vow to leave, by figuratively depicting the Greeks as fleeing (θάνατόν γε φύγοιμεν, 1.60). Akhilleus is unnecessarily confrontational in singling out Agamemnon as his sole addressee, Ἀτρεΐδη (1.59), pronouncing his name as the first word he utters in the poem. By opening the assembly in a confrontational manner Akhilleus immediately puts Agamemnon on the defensive. Commentators typically downplay Akhilleus' role in provoking Agamemnon and, ironically, problematizing the assembly that he himself has called.[6]

When Agamemnon asks for another gift to replace Khryseis, whom he only now agrees to return to her father (1.116–20), Akhilleus blocks his course. Having singled Agamemnon out in his opening address (1.59), he now escalates the tension by insulting him, "greediest of men" (1.122), ruling out any possibility that the army will repay Agamemnon for his loss of Khryseis. As before, Akhilleus makes the occasion a personal confrontation with Agamemnon, whereas Agamemnon has not yet addressed Akhilleus or mentioned him by name. Akhilleus, as in the parallel scene in book 19, is impatient, knows that Agamemnon is responsible for provoking Apollo's wrath, and therefore believes his own forthright approach will expedite a solution.

Akhilleus' confrontational approach and insult, however, invite retaliation from Agamemnon, now provoked into answering Akhilleus and his invective. Having put forth a straightforward proposal for compensation, Agamemnon sees Akhilleus block this course and foment a personal confrontation. Provoked, Agamemnon makes a veiled insult, accusing Akhilleus of trying to cheat him (1.132), of keeping his own winnings, while, he, Agamemnon, goes without. However, by agreeing to return Khryseis to her father, Agamemnon acts to put the issue behind him to address the troops' concern, but threatens to replace his loss by taking another warrior's prize, Akhilleus', or Aias', or Odysseus' (1.135–39). Again, Akhilleus raises the stakes, increasing his confrontation with Agamemnon and, in so doing, loses focus of the greater threat to the army. He shifts the issue into dangerous new territory by questioning the purpose of the entire expedition. In so doing, he points ahead to a later motif: 7. *Akhilleus articulates his conflict about fighting, unfair distribution of winnings, and a slight to his honor and changes his resolve about fighting in the war.* He reasons that, since he has no personal quarrel with the Trojans, he and the others are here to honor the Atreidai (1.158–59), but if Agamemnon now disrupts the system of exchange on which that honor rests, he will go home (1.169–70).

In book 9 the two positions are reversed. It is now Agamemnon who raises the issue of the Greeks leaving, and Diomedes (a best of the Akhaians) who challenges Agamemnon and even belittles his lack of leadership. Reflecting his loss of power and authority, Agamemnon begins the assembly with a more inclusive and tactful address to his audience than in book 1: "Friends, leaders and counselors of the Argives" (9.17). His proposal, which repeats his test from the book 2 assembly (9.18–28 = 2.111–18 = 139–41),[7] though now meant in earnest, puts him in the position Akhilleus occupies in the book 1 assembly, of threatening to go home at once. Each speaker, Akhilleus in book 1 and Agamemnon in book 9, uses a modal first-person plural of φεὺγω (Akhilleus: φύγοιμεν, 1.60; Agamemnon: φεύγωμεν, 9.27) to raise the possibility of returning home with the war unfinished. As Akhilleus erupted in book 1 (though over other issues), Diomedes now lashes out at Agamemnon, casting his words back at him, φευγόντων σὺν νηυσὶ φίλην ἐς πατρίδα γαῖαν (9.47 = 9.27, except the form of φεύγω). As in books 5–6, Diomedes is here a thematic parallel of Akhilleus, a stand-in for the best of the Akhaians, until the embassy visits with Akhilleus himself.

In book 19 Akhilleus again convenes the assembly by addressing Agamemnon first, Ἀτρεΐδη (19.56), but here the specific address is less provocative and more forthrightly urgent, reflecting Akhilleus' impatience throughout the scene. His wrath against Agamemnon has been over since he learned of Patroklos' death, and he now officially proclaims its passing. But throughout the scene he is largely indifferent to Agamemnon, opposite his bearing in books 1 and 9, and could care less about the transfer of gifts, with which this assembly is so concerned.

～

3. Agamemnon exercises reckless judgment (ate) against the best of the Akhaians

In book 1, perceiving that Akhilleus has challenged his leadership, Agamemnon angrily explodes at him, having earlier lost his temper at his priest, Kalkhas (see chapter 5), and treated Apollo's priest, Khryses, abusively. Kalkhas emphasizes Agamemnon's potential to lose his temper, when he hesitates to explain the reason for Apollo's wrath:

> For when a king is angry at a lesser man, he is mightier;
> for even if he should swallow his wrath down for that day,
> to be sure he keeps his resentment, until it reaches a climax,
> within his chest.
>
> (1.80–83)

Though Kalkhas speaks to his immediate predicament, that he will anger Agamemnon by pointing out that *he* caused Apollo's wrath by abusing

Khryses, the passage is thematic, also suggesting Agamemnon's relationship with Akhilleus. Akhilleus may not fit the "lesser man" description as well as Khryses, but Nestor (1.277–81) does assert that he is less kingly (βασιλεύτερος or φέρτερος) than Agamemnon.

His anger roused, turned away from Kalkhas and against Akhilleus, Agamemnon responds to Akhilleus' objections by implying that he is a coward (φεῦγε, 1.173; cf. 1.179–80), a reckless charge against a hero such as Akhilleus. Continuing an insult-laced tirade, Agamemnon declares he will seize Briseis from Akhilleus to replace Khryseis (1.181–87). In subsequent dialogue with Athena, Akhilleus characterizes Agamemnon's actions as *hubris* (1.208), which Athena seconds (1.214). Later, to his mother, Thetis, Akhilleus refers to Agamemnon's actions as *ate*, the first time the word is used in the *Iliad*:

> that the son of Atreus, wide-ruling Agamemnon, may recognize
> his recklessness [ἄτην], that he dishonored the best of the Akhaians.
>
> (1.411–12)

Henceforth, throughout the poem, *ate* and related derivatives will be closely associated with Agamemnon, embodying his reckless judgment, particularly with regard to Akhilleus.

In the council in book 9, a somewhat repentant Agamemnon, partially aware of the damage he caused in the book 1 assembly, makes explicit his association with *ate*, "Zeus, the son of Kronos, has bound me with a grave recklessness [ἄτη] . . . and now he has devised a wicked deception [ἀπάτην]" (9.18–21). In his second speech in the book 9 council, he articulates a cluster of references to *ate* that look ahead to his extended digression on the same in book 19:

> Old man, not at all falsely did you describe my recklessness [ἄτας],
> I was deluded [ἀασάμην], and I do not deny it
>
> . . . .
>
> but since I was deluded [ἀασάμην], trusting in my wretched wits.
>
> (9.115–19)[8]

In the assembly in book 19, after Akhilleus renounces his wrath, Agamemnon responds with his lengthy etiological account about Ate (19.87–137), employing twelve *ate*-derived forms: ἄγριον ἄτην, 88; πρέσβα Διὸς θυγάτηρ Ἄτη, ἣ πάντας ἄαται, / οὐλομένη, 90–91; Ζεὺς ἄσατο, 95; Ἥρη θῆλυς ἐοῦσα δολοφροσύνης ἀπάτησεν, 97; ἀάσθη, 113; εἷλε Ἄτην κεφαλῆς λιπαροπλοκάμοιο, 126; Ἄτην, ἣ πάντας ἄαται, 129; Ἄτης ᾗ πρῶτον ἀάσθην, 136;

ἀασάμην, 137. We have noted throughout this book that Akhilleus' sequence has greater divine involvement, including gods even in contexts in which the other sequences do not. So here, unique in the *Iliad*, Ate is personified, a goddess, powerful enough to delude Zeus (see subgenre 5 in chapter 5). Implicitly, then, is it any wonder that a king of men, Agamemnon, succumbed to a mere human manifestation of it?

∽

4. Nestor attempts *to restore order between the best of the Akhaians and Agamemnon*

In book 1, in the poem's first divine intervention, Athena (sent by Hera) prevents Akhilleus from acting on his impulse to slay Agamemnon (1.173–87). Although she asks him to refrain from this strife (ἔριδος, 1.210), she validates his position in the quarrel (see subgenre 4 in chapter 5). Athena here fulfills her typical role in heroic myth as mentor to the hero, giving him advice in person (see chapter 7). But after she departs, Akhilleus insults Agamemnon again (1.225),[9] escalating the confrontation by declaring that Agamemnon will regret what he has done to the best of the Akhaians. Into this dire impasse, Nestor intervenes. His initial strategy, hoping to unite both Greeks against their common enemy, is to point out that this quarrel would delight the Trojans. Proclaiming his credits as a speaker who has advised legendary heroes of the past, he asks Agamemnon not to take Briseis and asks each man to let go of his anger (1.282–83). His credentials as speaker and counselor notwithstanding, Nestor fails to get either man to heed him, and the assembly indecorously dissolves.[10] There is considerable irony at Nestor's expense in the emphasis given his preeminence as a honey-tongued orator (1.248–49), only to have him fail to persuade either Agamemnon or Akhilleus.

In the middle sequence, Nestor proves more effective, but with qualifications. In a replay of the dynamics from the assembly in book 1,[11] Agamemnon makes a proposal; Diomedes, as Akhilleus in book 1, strongly objects to it, and Nestor mediates between the two figures. Agamemnon proposes that the army go home, owing to the despair that grips the Greek camp after book 8. Diomedes, taking the remark personally (as Akhilleus makes the book 1 assembly a personal confrontation with Agamemnon), compares it with Agamemnon's provoking him in the marshaling scene in book 4, replaying the dynamics of the book 1 assembly in the friction between the best of the Akhaians and his commander. Here the roles are reversed from book 1. It is Diomedes who tells Agamemnon, "Go ahead and go home. I and Sthenelos will stay and fight." Unlike in book 1, Nestor is able to manage this confrontation successfully. As B. Hainsworth (66–67) notes, "Nestor showers the speech with praise, excuses it, and then ignores it." Diomedes, younger and less stubborn than Akhilleus, is easily overruled by Nestor. But, as in book 1, Nestor's strategy for reconciliation between Agamemnon and Akhilleus fails (discussed under the following motif).

In the final sequence, as in both earlier sequences, tempers flare as Akhilleus is again involved in a dispute (19.146–237). But Nestor has no role in the assembly, and remains offstage, so to speak. Why? In book 19 the assembly must lead to success. Akhilleus will return to battle, if only from personal motives. Because Nestor has been unable to achieve reconciliation between Agamemnon and Akhilleus in either of the first two sequences, in the final sequence a successful restoration of order between Akhilleus and Agamemnon is left to another character. Odysseus, who is associated with success throughout the *Iliad*, will impose a reconciliation (discussed below as *12. Odysseus succeeds in restoring order in a second or later Greek assembly, against an Akhilleus figure*).

↬

5. Agamemnon dispatches Odysseus to lead a delegation that includes two heralds to return a companion dear to Akhilleus

↬

6. Akhilleus (and Patroklos) receives the embassy hospitably

In the initial and middle sequences, these motifs compose the most involved part of the introductory pattern. Due to the complexity of these portions of books 1 and 9, we will treat these two motifs at length and together. In each case Odysseus leads a delegation shortly after an assembly or council has met that focuses on Akhilleus (1.57–305, 9.11–176, 19.45–276). In each case Odysseus' delegation attempts to solve a problem or reach a solution. Odysseus' essential function in the *Iliad* and in the larger Trojan War saga is that of the successful problem solver, whether devising the Trojan horse to end the war or using his diplomatic skills, as in his handling of the assembly in book 2 and in the instances of the motifs under discussion (except in book 9). The delegations also accomplish an additional purpose beyond their interaction with Akhilleus: the members perform a sacred function or purifying ritual. The parallels between the three sequences are startling, and provide valuable tools for addressing two well-known problems in the book 9 embassy to Akhilleus: the notorious duals, and Akhilleus' remark on the "hateful man" (9.312).

In book 1 the delegation is bifurcated into two separate scenes (1.308–17,

318–48), two separate delegations.[12] First, Agamemnon dispatches Odysseus to lead (ἐν δ' ἀρχὸς ἔβη πολύμητις Ὀδυσσεύς, 1.311) a large delegation (including twenty rowers) entrusted with returning Khryseis to her father. Immediately after this, Agamemnon sends the two heralds, Talthybios and Eurybates, to Akhilleus' tent to take away Briseis (1.320–26) (*a delegation that includes two heralds*). Both of these separate, but parallel, scenes share specific features in common with the later delegations in books 9 and 19. No duals are used to describe Odysseus' delegation. He not only returns Khryseis to her father, but accomplishes the more important objective of appeasing Apollo's wrath. In this instance, Odysseus performs the sacred or purifying function in the various rituals undertaken in connection with the hecatomb. Though this is the first delegation, it is a variation on the others in that Odysseus restores the woman not to Akhilleus but to her father, a priest of Apollo (on whose behalf Akhilleus had intervened). In spite of these differences, this first delegation predicts and parallels the others, being particularly close to the delegation in book 19. In both scenes Agamemnon's possession of a woman, who rightfully belongs somewhere else, causes drastic problems. When he releases the woman, Odysseus restores her to the man with whom she belongs. Odysseus' offering the hecatomb to Apollo, appeasing his wrath against the Greeks, suggests parallels with Akhilleus ending his wrath with Agamemnon. Apollo and Akhilleus occupy similar positions in the two episodes, as the figure whose wrath causes great harm to the Akhaians until he is assuaged or moves beyond his anger.[13]

In the second delegation in book 1, when Agamemnon sends the heralds, Eurybates and Talthybios, to Akhilleus, he uses the same word he will to the delegation Odysseus leads in book 19 (κρατερὸν δ' ἐπὶ μῦθον ἔτελλε, 1.326; cf. ἐπιτέλλομαι, 19.192). Only here is Odysseus *not* the leader of the delegation that proceeds to Akhilleus' tent. He cannot be, since he simultaneously leads the larger, more elaborate, and time-consuming delegation to restore Khryseis to her father and to appease Apollo's wrath. Instead, this delegation consists of two heralds, Talthybios, who performs the sacred function of the delegation in book 19, and Eurybates, a member of the delegation of five in book 9. Akhilleus, when he later recounts these events to Thetis, neatly juxtaposes the two delegations (1.389–92), revealing how easily they serve as complementary, bifurcated instances of the same motif. Here the usual function of restoring a companion to Akhilleus is reversed: Agamemnon has dispatched the heralds *to take away* "a companion dear to Akhilleus."

The two heralds are consistently referred to by duals as they take Briseis away from Akhilleus (τώ οἱ ἔσαν κήρυκε καὶ ὀτρηρὼ θεράποντε, ἔρχεσθον, 1.321; τὼ δ' ἀέκοντε βάτην παρὰ θῖν' ἁλὸς ἀτρυγέτοιο, 1.327; ἱκέσθην, 1.328;

τώ, 1.330; τὼ μὲν ταρβήσαντε καὶ αἰδομένω, 1.331; στήτην, 1.332; σφῶϊν δὸς, 1.338; τὼ δ᾽ αὖτις ἴτην, 1.347). Not only are Eurybates and Talthybios frequently described by duals, but some of the formulas expressing the duals reappear, problematically, in the book 9 delegation (discussed below). If we were to combine both delegations in book 1, Odysseus returning Khryseis to her father and propitiating Apollo's wrath, and Eurybates and Talthybios going to Akhilleus' tent to take away Briseis, the resulting composite would be very close to the book 9 delegation.

In book 9 the delegation, which hopes to assuage Akhilleus with Agamemnon's gifts, consists of Odysseus, Aias, Phoinix, and two heralds, Eurybates and Odios. Two of these five, Odysseus and Eurybates, each take part in one of the two complementary delegations Agamemnon sends in book 1. Thereafter, in a notorious discrepancy, what Schadewalt called "Surely the greatest problem in the whole of the *Iliad*,"[14] the narrator repeatedly refers to this group of five using the dual number (9.182 ff). While many explanations have been proposed, none has proved persuasive, though significant contributions have been made, especially by Boll, Segal, B. Hainsworth, and Edwards. Boll (1917–18, 1919–20) first suggested the relevance of the passage in book 1 (1.327–47) in which duals depict the heralds, Talthybios and Eurybates, as they approach Akhilleus to claim Briseis. Segal (101–14), building on Boll, argues that the book 9 duals, like those in book 1, refer to the two heralds, Eurybates and Odios. B. Hainsworth (86) suggests that the duals in book 9 "survive from an archetype in which they were grammatically appropriate." Edwards (1991: 263) notes similarities between scenes in books 1 and 19: "In structure the transfer of gifts [to Akhilleus in book 19] is much like the restoration of Khruseis to her father." Building on these observations, I note additional significant parallels between the four episodes (1a and b, 9, 19). I note the tendency for Odysseus to be depicted with duals throughout the *Iliad* and call attention to his herald, Eurybates, who is key to at least a partial solution of the problem.[15]

The book 9 delegation is unique, not only in the controversial duals. This delegation, as part of the middle sequence, is governed by the inverted, or parodic, qualities that shape books 8–17. Consequently, this delegation *has* to fail and is doomed from the start. Such is the result of Zeus' honoring Akhilleus' request from book 1 and resolve to aid Hektor in books 8–17. Akhilleus will not end his strife with Agamemnon until he learns of Patroklos' death, no matter what members of the delegation—Odysseus, Phoinix, or Aias—might say. The book 9 delegation signals its failure early. Only here does Nestor, not Agamemnon, take charge of the process of forming the delegation, select its members, and utter ἐπέτελλε (*epetelle*, 9.179), dispatching the delegation. When Nestor, thematically ineffectual at mediating between Akhilleus and Agamemnon, formulates and directs the delegation, its chances for success are further diminished. Nestor's ineffective speech in the assembly in book 1 parallels his ineffective instructions to the delegation in book 9. Odysseus will attempt to clean up the subsequent mess, as he does in book 2 and again in book 19. Nestor selects Phoinix, Aias, and Odysseus, and the two heralds, Eurybates and Odios (9.168–70). Talthybios, Agamemnon's herald, appearing in delegation scenes in both books 1 and 19, does not take part in the embassy in book 9. B. Hainsworth (83) suggests, "The presence of Talthubios, Agamemnon's usual herald, might in this delicate situation have appeared provocative." Though Nestor designates Phoinix as leader of the delegation (9.168), two other formulas in the episode indicate Odysseus is the leader to and from Akhilleus' tent (ἡγεῖτο δὲ δῖος Ὀδυσσεύς, 9.192; ἦρχε δ᾽ Ὀδυσσεύς, 9.657). Variations of this last formula designate Odysseus as leader in all three delegations in which he appears (Ὀδυσεὺς . . . ἦρχε, 19.248; cf. ἐν δ᾽ ἀρχὸς ἔβη πολύμητις Ὀδυσσεύς, 1.311). Inside Akhilleus' tent, though Aias nods to Phoinix (9.223), it is Odysseus who speaks first, confirming his role as the delegation's leader.

Nestor chooses Phoinix for the delegation because of his close relationship with Akhilleus. After the delegation finishes its speeches, Odysseus and the others depart, leaving Phoinix with Akhilleus. Khryseis, Briseis, and Phoinix, despite their different genders, occupy similar roles, all being versions of a figure who shares an intimate emotional bond with Akhilleus and sleeps in his tent. The delegations in books 9 and 19 *return a companion dear to Akhilleus,* Phoinix in 9, and Briseis in 19, the climax of the series, whose return officially marks the end of the quarrel between Akhilleus and Agamemnon. In book 1 Odysseus returns Khryseis, but to her father, Khryses, while Eurybates and Talthybios take Briseis *away* from Akhilleus. Odysseus leading Phoinix to Akhilleus, with the result that he will stay with him, thus anticipates Odysseus restoring Briseis to the hero in book 19 and replays Odysseus leading Khryseis to Khryses in book 1.[16] In book 9 all delegation members perform the sacred function (9.171–76), washing their hands, pouring libations, and making prayer to Zeus. This scene is the counterpart to the sacrifice of the boar, and prayer, in 19 (19.250–75) and, on a larger scale, the hecatomb and prayer to Apollo in 1 (1.309–17).

Let us now note the formulas, including the duals, found in the second delegation in book 1 (with the two heralds) and in book 9:

a. *1.322:* ἔρχεσθον <u>κλισίην Πηληϊάδεω Ἀχιλῆος</u>.
   9.166: ἔλθωσ᾽ ἐς <u>κλισίην Πηληϊάδεω Ἀχιλῆος</u>.
b. * *1.327:* τὼ δ᾽ ἀέκοντε <u>βάτην παρὰ θῖν᾽</u> ἁλὸς ἀτρυγέτοιο.
   9.182: <u>Τὼ δὲ βάτην παρὰ θῖνα</u> πολυφλοίσβοιο θαλάσσης.

c. * *1.328* = *9.185:* Μυρμιδόνων δ’ ἐπί τε κλισίας καὶ νῆας ἱκέσθην.

d. *1.329:* τὸν δ’ εὗρον. *9.186:* τὸν δ’ εὗρον.

e. *1.334:* χαίρετε. *9.197:* χαίρετον.

Not only is there a considerable number of parallel items,[17] but all of the common elements occur in the same order, suggesting a similar underlying conception, or rubric, shapes each passage. The verbs in the asterisked items b and c include two of the problematic duals in the book 9 episode.[18] In each instance the duals designate a group that includes the herald Eurybates. In the two bifurcated instances of the delegation motif in book 1, then, we have Odysseus leading the delegation most parallel to the version of the motif in book 19, and the herald Eurybates taking part in the delegation closest in diction to the episode in book 9. An additional thematic parallel links the visit of Talthybios and Eurybates with the delegation in book 9. In both instances Akhilleus greets the delegation hospitably when it first arrives (1.334–35, 9.196–98), whereas in book 19 he is impatient or indifferent.

The final instance of the motif, the book 19 delegation, since it is largely successful, best demonstrates what is supposed to happen in the other three instances. At an assembly, Agamemnon dispatches Odysseus to convey Briseis to Akhilleus and the many gifts earlier promised (in the parallel scene at 9.120–57). Agamemnon’s verb for his order is ἐπιτέλλομαι (*epitellomai,* 19.192), used in each case to set the delegation in motion (1.326, 9.179, 19.192). Agamemnon then gives a second command to his herald, Talthybios, to prepare a boar for sacrifice to Zeus and Helios (19.196–97), constituting the sacred function, or purifying ritual, also performed by each delegation. In an additional link with the sacred function performed by Odysseus (when restoring Khryseis to her father), the sacrificed boar is here thrown into the ocean (19.267–68); as in book 1, his men wash themselves and throw their washings into the ocean (1.313–14; cf. Kirk 1985: 85). Odysseus restores Briseis to Akhilleus (19.246, 279–82) as part of a public reconciliation, and Akhilleus will return to battle. After Odysseus carries out the exchange of gifts, including Briseis, *a companion dear to Akhilleus,* Agamemnon and Talthybios perform the sacrifice before the assembled troops (19.249–68), and the wrath of Akhilleus against Agamemnon is officially over, the delegation scene a success.[19]

No duals are used of the book 19 delegation, although relevant duals occur earlier in the book 19 assembly, involving Odysseus (τὼ δὲ δύω σκάζοντε βάτην, 19.47), as discussed below. Of the three parallel episodes in books 1, 9, and 19, diplomacy is least necessary in book 19. Briseis is being returned to Akhilleus, who is now more concerned with Patroklos and Hektor. Neither persuasion, as in book 9, nor a show of force, as in book 1, is necessary in this last instance of the motif, which segues quickly into the poem's most potent *aristeia*. This delegation is quite large. Seven helpers are specified (19.238–40), apparently selected by Odysseus.

Let us summarize the analysis thus far. The episode in book 9 is one of four instances of a motif we have characterized as, *5. Agamemnon dispatches Odysseus to lead a delegation that includes two heralds to return a companion dear to Akhilleus*. These four instances are, 1a: Odysseus returns Khryseis, 1b: Talthybios and Eurybates remove Briseis, 9: Odysseus returns Phoinix, and 19: Odysseus returns Briseis.[20] The first scene, 1a, most resembles the last, 19. In each scene Odysseus restores a young woman, whom Agamemnon has been keeping, to her father, or Akhilleus, both times ending a wrath (Apollo's, Akhilleus') that has been ruinous to the Greeks. In both 1a and 19 no dual forms are used to refer to the delegations. The second scene, 1b, is closest to the second to last, 9. Akhilleus greets both delegations with similar courtesy (1.334, 9.197), a factor not present in 1a and 19. Dual forms are used to depict both of these delegations. A herald named Eurybates takes part in each scene. The four scenes occur in ring compositional order, typical of Homeric epic:

1a (1.307–18), 1b (1.320–48)   9 (9.178–669)   19 (19.238–49)
                  1a > 19   1b > 9

Ring composition should not be thought of only from the perspective of the audience, as something for listeners to perceive, but also from the composer's perspective. Such larger structures impose order and meaning onto an epic and are facets of the poem's larger architecture.[21]

It is time now for a closer look at the herald Eurybates, who occupies a significant position not only in the delegation motif, but in the controversial duals. He is one of the five composing the delegation in book 9, and he takes part in 1b, both of which delegations are referred to by duals. But who is he? A herald named Eurybates is three times mentioned in the *Iliad*, in two of the scenes under discussion, and in the assembly in book 2, as well as once in the *Odyssey* (19.244–48). In all of these contexts except *Il*. 1.320, Eurybates is clearly identified as Odysseus' own herald. Just before Odysseus restores order in the assembly in book 2, Eurybates accompanies Odysseus, retrieving his cloak, which the hero threw off in haste, as he dashed to prevent the Greeks from running to their ships. Eurybates is here designated Ἰθακήσιος (2.184), suggesting that he has worked with Odysseus even before the war, perhaps functioning as his herald in Ithaka. This is confirmed in Eurybates' one mention in the *Odyssey*, when Odysseus gives a detailed description of him,

rounded in his shoulders, dark skinned [μελανόχροος], wooly headed,
Eurybates was his name; and Odysseus honored him beyond
his other companions, because he knew fitting things in his mind.

(19.246–48)

Because a disguised Odysseus here describes Eurybates to prove to Penelope his close acquaintance with Odysseus, his focus on Eurybates' appearance, and Odysseus' relationship with him, suggests Penelope is also well acquainted with the herald, or why go into such detail? Thus in the *Odyssey*, Odysseus' relation with Eurybates predates the war. Eurybates, though mentioned only a few times, may have deeper roots in Homeric epic than is generally realized.

A few particulars of this unique description suggest parallels with Odysseus. Describing Eurybates as "dark-skinned," Odysseus himself is elsewhere referred to as μελαγχροιής (*Od.* 16.175), a synonym. These are the sole occurrences of each word in the *Odyssey* (μελανόχροος occurs once in the *Iliad*, 13.589, of beans). Like Eurybates, Odysseus is also described as short (*Il.* 3.193, 210). Priam likens Odysseus to a ram (3.196), and, though the comparison seems based on Odysseus' movement, it may also reflect on his hair, suggestive of οὐλοκάρηνος in the description of Eurybates. Antenor adds that Odysseus' impressive speaking ability made the Trojans overlook his less impressive physical appearance (3.221–24). The same is implicitly true of Eurybates, a figure of diplomacy entrusted with important missions, though he does not conform to aristocratic ideals of physical beauty. In addition to these corporeal similarities, as Russo (90) notes, the phrase ὅτι οἱ φρεσὶν ἄρτια ᾔδη (19.248) suggests deeper parallels between Odysseus and Eurybates, an emotional or intellectual affinity. In short, Odysseus has a fitting herald, who resembles himself. We can now better understand why Eurybates takes part in the second delegation in book 1, which takes Briseis away from Akhilleus, when Odysseus is elsewhere occupied leading the first delegation. The only time Odysseus does not take part in and serve as leader of a delegation, a herald closely associated with him, who resembles him in several ways, does take part, occupying Odysseus' usual slot.

However, commentators have traditionally assumed that the Eurybates at *Il.* 1.320 must be a different character than Odysseus' herald, some other herald with the same name, belonging to Agamemnon, though this is his only mention in either epic.[22] In support of this traditional interpretation is 1.321: τώ οἱ ἔσαν κήρυκε καὶ ὀτρηρὼ θεράποντε. The οἱ implies that, in this description at least, both heralds, Talthybios and Eurybates, take orders from Agamemnon. The scholia on 1.320 also assert that this Eurybates is not

Odysseus' own herald. As far as I know, however, there is no evidence, other than the oi at 1.321, though the scholia's assertion has been accepted without question by most Homerists for over two millennia. In spite of the oi, and against the scholiasts, I argue that the Eurybates at 1.320 is Odysseus' herald, not a separate figure mentioned only here, but part of the larger nexus of thematic parallels we have noted. The assumption that the Eurybates of book 1 must be a separate figure has prevented commentators from noting the broader thematic parallels. The narrator may refer to Eurybates here as Agamemnon's herald simply to emphasize his authority as he sends this delegation to impose his will on Akhilleus. The heralds themselves perform this task against their will, compelled by Agamemnon (τὼ δ᾿ ἀέκοντε, 1.327). Among its many kings and several scenes of diplomacy, the *Iliad* has the herald Talthybios, named nine times, closely associated with Agamemnon, and another herald, Eurybates, associated with Odysseus, who frequently carries out diplomatic functions himself.

Excursus: The Hateful Man (ekhthros)
Before proceeding with our argument on the duals in book 9, we first apply some of the parallels observed to address another well-known ambiguity in the book 9 delegation scene. After Akhilleus hospitably receives the delegation (9.196–222), Odysseus is first to speak, appealing to Akhilleus on many different grounds, but with greatest emphasis on Agamemnon's offer of gifts. In closing, however, Odysseus suggests that if Agamemnon remains too hated (ἀπήχθετο, 9.300) by Akhilleus, he might return, nonetheless, to win glory (μέγα κῦδος ἄροιο)[23] by defeating Hektor. In reply, Akhilleus articulates his disgust with a man who says one thing, but means another:

> For as hateful [ἐχθρός] to me as the gates of Death is he
> who hides one thing in his heart, but speaks another.
>
> (9.312–13)

Commentators are divided on whether Akhilleus here refers to Agamemnon or Odysseus.[24] Thematic parallels we have already noted from book 1 help clarify relevant issues. On the basis of the parallels in book 1, and the *Iliad*'s very specific pattern of employment of the word *ekhthros*, Akhilleus clearly aims his remark at Agamemnon.

In book 1, when the heralds Eurybates and Talthybios approach his tent in order to seize Briseis, Akhilleus is well aware that they have come ordered by Agamemnon. Accordingly, he feels no hostility against them, as he explicitly states:

Welcome, heralds, messengers of Zeus and of men,
come nearer; you are not at all to blame in my eyes, but Agamemnon.

(1.334-35)

Akhilleus is no fool. He is fully aware that Agamemnon is behind their action, has ordered the heralds to do what they are now doing. He does not rejoice when he sees them arrive (1.330), but he fully understands why they have come, does not lose his temper with them, and, before either party utters a word, is shown to comprehend the situation (αὐτὰρ ὁ ἔγνω ᾗσιν ἐνὶ φρεσὶ φώνησέν τε, 1.333).

When the delegation arrives in book 9, Akhilleus greets them with full courtesy, in lines that partly parallel his greeting to the delegation in book 1:

Welcome, very dear men arrive; it must be urgent;
these are my dearest Akhaian friends, even in my anger.

(9.197-98)

Ushering them in and offering hospitality,[25] Akhilleus repeats how close to him are the men who have come, "for these who have come into my chamber are my closest friends" (9.204), all serving as very close parallels to his greeting to the delegation in book 1 (1.334-35). Following the greeting, Akhilleus continues with exemplary hospitality, himself performing some of the tasks, loosely aligning the episode with such hospitality myths as Baucis and Philemon, and the Eumaios episodes in the *Odyssey*, in which a genial host reveals his morality by waiting on his guests, who may be on some divine mission.[26] After they have feasted, Odysseus speaks first, a lengthy speech (9.225-306), which Akhilleus will easily recognize, as he does of the delegation in book 1, as representing Agamemnon's point of view. Just as in 1.333-36, when Akhilleus does not blame the heralds, knowing Agamemnon is to blame, so at 9.312-17 he does not blame the delegation with Odysseus, Phoinix, and Aias, fully cognizant that they have been sent by Agamemnon. In his reply, in which he rejects Agamemnon's offer, Akhilleus begins with his ambiguous remark (9.312-13). In much of the rest of his own speech, Akhilleus repeatedly criticizes Agamemnon in very strong terms (e.g., μ' ἀπάτησε, 9.344; ἐφυβρίζων, 9.368). His subsequent characterization of Agamemnon as an arrogant deceiver thus supports the view that 9.312-13 also targets Atreides.

To assume, then, that Akhilleus criticizes Odysseus in his remark presupposes a rather imperceptive Akhilleus, unable to understand that Odysseus, just as the heralds in book 1, is carrying out what Agamemnon has ordered. Since Akhilleus knows that Odysseus is often entrusted with diplomatic missions of this sort (3.205–24, 11.766–89: Akhilleus himself is in the audience for this earlier visit; cf. 2.272–73), it is highly unlikely that he would be unaware that Odysseus here serves a diplomatic function,[27] a mouthpiece for Agamemnon.[28]

To have Akhilleus criticize Odysseus also assumes that the composer, at this crucial juncture, introduces a *new* strife, between Akhilleus and Odysseus, at the risk of diminishing, even obfuscating, the primary theme of the poem, and of book 9 in particular—the bitter *eris* between Akhilleus and Agamemnon. In fact, the *Iliad* repeatedly pairs Odysseus and Akhilleus as figures opposed to Agamemnon, not to each other. While losing his temper at Akhilleus in the assembly in book 1, Agamemnon also briefly threatens to seize the concubine of Odysseus or Aias (1.138), before deciding to take Briseis from Akhilleus himself. The passage briefly conjures up an Odysseus potentially as wronged by Agamemnon as Akhilleus is. A more specific pairing of Akhilleus and Odysseus follows in book 2. The narrator notes that Thersites "was especially hateful [ἔχθιστος] to Akhilleus and Odysseus" (2.220). Much as Akhilleus, Odysseus is highly critical of Agamemnon's leadership (4.329–63 and especially 14.82–108, discussed below with motif 12). In this respect, Akhilleus and Odysseus have considerable common ground as critics of Agamemnon. Perhaps most revealing of all, however, is the bifurcation of the delegation scene in book 1. The only delegation that Odysseus does not lead is the one that goes to Akhilleus' tent to take Briseis away. It follows that if the *Iliad* intended strife between Akhilleus and Odysseus as a theme, it would have had Odysseus lead the delegation that seizes Briseis, giving Akhilleus reason to harbor resentment against him in book 9. Instead, the poem appears to have gone out of its way to minimize possible conflict between the two epic protagonists by having Odysseus not take part in the one delegation that proves offensive to Akhilleus. It is clear, then, that except for their exchange of words in book 19 (199–237; see motif 12 below), the *Iliad* has *minimized* conflict between Akhilleus and Odysseus, even where it could have developed such conflict, if desired.[29]

We conclude this section by noting that the *Iliad* employs Akhilleus' adjective, *ekhthros,* only under very specific circumstances, as part of a specific pattern. Akhilleus is the only character in the *Iliad* who uses the word, and it is line initial each time he pronounces it, clearly for emphasis. One of these instances is only sixty-six lines later in Akhilleus' same speech, "hateful [ἐχθρὰ] to me are his gifts; I honor them at the value of a splinter" (9.378). There is no question that here Akhilleus uses the same adjective, in the same speech, to refer to Agamemnon. In book 16, instructing Patroklos before sending him into battle, Akhilleus again uses *ekhthros,* again line initial, "nor have I heard the voice of the son of Atreus, speaking from / his hateful [ἐχθρῆς] head" (16.76–77). Again there is no question that Akhilleus uses the same word, in the same position, to refer to his hatred of Agamemnon. The only other occurrence of the adjective in the entire *Iliad* is the passage under question (9.312), which, like the other two (both of which unambiguously refer to Agamemnon), is line initial and spoken by Akhilleus.

Ekhthros is a word of strong emotion, expressing bitter personal animus. Both Agamemnon and Akhilleus lose their tempers and insult each other in front of the assembled troops. Both engage in acts that put themselves above what is best for the army (Agamemnon by refusing to return Khryseis, causing the deaths of hundreds, perhaps thousands of his troops: 1.10, 51–53;[30] Akhilleus by asking Zeus to cause deaths in the army [1.409–10], which will culminate in the death of Patroklos). Odysseus, on the other hand, is not depicted as losing his temper in the *Iliad* in a large public assembly, or acting to advance his own agenda. Here in book 9, as before at the assembly in book 2 (discussed below as motif 12) Odysseus works to restore order and unite the army. If Odysseus is attempting to "deceive" anyone here, it is Agamemnon, not Akhilleus, since he appears to censor some of Agamemnon's speech (9.158–61) out of tact, knowing that certain remarks would offend Akhilleus.[31] It seems clear, then, that the *Iliad* reserves *ekhthros* to designate Agamemnon as the target of Akhilleus' wrath, and only during their quarrel (*eris*).

HAVING ESTABLISHED THE PARALLELS between the four episodes, and the central involvement of Odysseus and Eurybates, let us review the variations found between the four different instances. In three of the four scenes Odysseus is the leader of the delegation, and so designated (1.311, 9.657, 19.248). The only delegation he does not lead is that in the second scene in book 1 in which Eurybates and Talthybios take Briseis away from Akhilleus. Odysseus cannot take part in this scene because he simultaneously leads the delegation that restores Khryseis to her father. This seems deliberate, a tactful move on the part of the *Iliad*, not to associate Odysseus with the act which will so infuriate Akhilleus. In three of the four scenes *a companion dear to Akhilleus* is returned, and in the fourth, taken away. Khryseis is restored to Khryses, not Akhilleus, but her return occurs because of Akhilleus' intervention. Odysseus in book 9 leaves Phoinix with Akhilleus and, as the climax of the series, restores Briseis to him in book 19. In three of four instances heralds are involved (Eurybates and Talthybios in 1, Eurybates and Odios in 9, Talthybios in 19).

We now summarize the unusual aspects of the book 9 delegation (other than the duals), when compared with the other three instances of the motif. The herald Odios appears only here (9.170) in all of Homeric epic. Aias has no counterpart in the other delegations. Nestor dispatches this delegation, whereas Agamemnon does so in all other instances. In the other three instances, a woman is conveyed by the delegation (Khryseis, Briseis, Briseis), but here it is Phoinix. In book 9 there is no distinction between the delegation conveying the companion dear to Akhilleus and those taking part in the sacred ritual. All five men perform both functions, whereas in book 1 the two functions are bifurcated into entirely separate scenes (1.308–17, 318–48), and in book 19 Odysseus leads the delegation, while Talthybios prepares the boar for sacrifice. This last difference partly accounts for the larger number of participants in the book 9 delegation: one delegation serves tasks performed by two separate delegations in 1, while in 19 Odysseus and Talthybios separately handle the different tasks. In book 19 neither herald who took Briseis away, Eurybates and Talthybios, has a part in returning her, which, like having Odysseus not take away Briseis, seems intentionally tactful.

The parallels in the other delegations suggest that the likeliest participants in the book 9 delegation would be Odysseus, the usual leader, Eurybates, the herald closely associated with him, and Phoinix, *the companion dear to Akhilleus*.[32] If this analysis is correct, we might expect the dual forms to refer, in some way, to these three characters. We have indirect confirmation that the duals include Odysseus because he is designated by duals thematically throughout the *Iliad*, regularly paired with a few different characters on different occasions. Two such episodes are additional, retrospective, instances of the delegation motif. An embassy to Troy to attempt a diplomatic means for Helen's release consisted of Odysseus and Menelaos, which pair is described by a dual (ἄμφω δ᾽ ἑζομένω, 3.211; cf. 11.139–40). This delegation, no doubt sent by Agamemnon, led by Odysseus (3.216–24), conforms to the general shape of the four delegations in the *Iliad*, except that its audience was Trojans, not Akhilleus. Both Menelaus and Odysseus make speeches (unsuccessful, as in book 9). If the delegation had been successful, they would have taken Helen back to Greece, providing the other usual slot of a female being conveyed, as with Khryseis and Briseis.

In a further retrospective account of a delegation, Nestor and Odysseus visited Patroklos (and Akhilleus) before the war. In this episode Odysseus and Nestor are twice designated by duals (11.767, 776). The scene exhibits additional parallels with the book 9 delegation. Patroklos and Akhilleus receive both delegations. Akhilleus has the same reaction to the delegation's arrival in each case: "And Akhilleus stood up, surprised" (11.777 = 9.193). There is a further parallel in that, because the delegation is successful, Patroklos, *a companion dear to Akhilleus*, will now go off with them.

For the apparent oddity of Phoinix, a male, playing in the book 9 delegation the role elsewhere assigned a female, we have only to consider another aspect of Patroklos, part of the audience for several delegation scenes. In Phoinix's lengthy, paradigmatic tale of Meleager's wrath within the book 9 delegation (9.529–99), as Kakridis noted,[33] Kleopatra plays the same role as will Patroklos in the "ascending scale of affection," the two characters' names being reversed forms of the same compound. We have, then, Phoinix, himself in a role usually filled by a woman, telling the tale of a woman's action, which a member of his audience, Patroklos, will himself shortly parallel.

In other episodes, Odysseus is consistently paired with Diomedes, and each time, the pair is referred to by duals. Examples include the *Doloneia,* in which Odysseus and Diomedes are designated by duals at least six times (φωνήσαντε, 10.349; κλινθήτην, 10.350; τὼ μὲν ἐπιδραμέτην, 10.354; τὼ δ᾽ ἀσθμαίνοντε κιχήτην, 10.376; ἀψάσθην, 377; τὼ δὲ βάτην προτέρω, 10.469), and a brief episode in the Wounding of the Chiefs in book 11 (τί παθόντε, 11.313). Book 19 also uses sets of duals involving Odysseus and Diomedes (τὼ δὲ δύω σκάζοντε βάτην Ἄρεος θεράποντε, 19.47; ἔγχει ἐρειδομένω, 19.49). This second-to-last formula, τὼ δὲ . . . βάτην (19.47) is one of the problematic dual formulas in book 9 (9.182, 192) and is also used of the second delegation scene in book 1 (1.327). Because these dual forms in book 19 occur at the start of the assembly at which Odysseus will be ordered to lead the delegation, they are relevant to those in books 9 and 1. Because Odysseus leads three of the four instances of the type-scene, and even the earlier embassy to Troy before the war, it seems probable that the duals must include him as one of their referents.

I argue that Eurybates, Odysseus' herald, or Phoenix is the other character most likely to be the subject of the duals in book 9. In all of the thematically parallel scenes using duals, either Odysseus or Eurybates is involved. In book 9, both take part. Outside of book 9 the two characters are closely associated: in book 2, when Odysseus halts the Greeks' flight toward their ships after Agamemnon's disastrous performance, and in the *Odyssey* (19.244–48). In book 1 of the *Iliad,* the two characters perform closely parallel roles. Consequently, because of the underlying structures and parallels that constitute the delegation motif, some of the book 9 duals are based on formulas that, in another conception of the scene, referred to Odysseus and Eurybates, the characters who occupy these thematic slots in all instances of the type-scene.

Wordplay on the name Eurybates strengthens his association with the duals used in these scenes. When Agamemnon dispatches the two heralds to take Briseis away from Akhilleus, his command is shortly followed by a dual form of βαίνω that echoes the name Eurybates, ἀλλ᾽ ὅ γε Ταλθύβιόν τε καὶ Εὐρυβάτην προσέειπε . . . / τὼ δ᾽ ἀέκοντε βάτην παρὰ θῖν᾽ ἁλὸς ἀτρυγέτοιο (1.320–27). A similar collocation occurs in book 9, κηρύκων δ᾽ Ὀδίος τε καὶ Εὐρυβάτης ἅμ᾽ ἑπέσθων . . . / τὼ δὲ βάτην (9.170–82).[34] If it seems unlikely that Homeric epic would refer to a king and his herald with a dual, we have only to note the episode that concludes the poem, in which Priam and Idaios, are referred to with duals (τὼ μὲν ζευγνύσθην . . . κῆρυξ καὶ Πρίαμος, 24.281–82), revealing the appropriateness of such a formation. We also adduce another formation in the *Odyssey*, when τὼ βήτην (17.200) is used of Odysseus and his swineherd Eumaios, another figure with more than a little in common with Eurybates. Since the alternate form βήτην (instead of βάτην) is also used in the *Iliad* (8.115; 12.330; 14.281, 285; 16.327; 17.492; 23.685), even an alternate form of the entire formula, τὼ δὲ βήτην (8.115, 17.492, 23.685), in place of τὼ δὲ βάτην, it appears that, when Eurybates is involved in the scene, the *Iliad* may have intentionally selected the more effective form (βάτην) for the wordplay generated.

One passage containing a dual can be seen as referring to all three characters we argue are the most expected participants in the book 9 delegation: Odysseus, Eurybates, and Phoinix. In the verse, τὼ δὲ βάτην προτέρω, ἡγεῖτο δὲ δῖος Ὀδυσσεύς (9.192), the dual could refer specifically to Eurybates and Phoinix, with Odysseus being specified as the third character. Could this line have generated some of the other duals? The same line, because it does not specify any of the individuals involved except Odysseus (though wordplay on the name Eurybates is possible), could have been used in other epics for other delegations. The same formula could have been used in a possible earlier version of the episode in book 9, in which neither Aias nor Odios took part. I suggest that many of the other duals derive from formulas originally designating Odysseus and Eurybates when they were not conveying someone or were on their return from a successful conveyance, having left a third party, such as Phoinix or Briseis.

Our analysis thus suggests that the *Iliad* has a consistent form for the delegation motif in which the expected participants are Odysseus, his herald, Eurybates, and a person dear to Akhilleus whom the other two are conveying. Traditionally, commentators have made Phoinix out to be problematic, the least qualified to take part in the delegation.[35] Our analysis, on the contrary, argues that he serves a typical function, parallel to Briseis, as *a companion dear to Akhilleus*. Phoinix will now stay the night in Akhilleus' tent (9.617–21), as Briseis used to, and will again. There are further parallels between the two characters as speakers. While Briseis has no speaking part in the book 1 scene, in book 19 she makes an eloquent lament for Patroklos (19.287–300), comparable, in some ways, with Phoinix's moving speech in book 9. Each speaker, Phoinix and Briseis, demonstrates a marked emotional intimacy to Akhilleus. Almost as if to underscore the parallels between the two characters, as Briseis finishes her lament for Patroklos (19.300), Phoinix is in close proximity (19.311), one of the few times he is mentioned outside of the book 9 delegation.[36]

If Aias and Odios may not have been part of the original conception of the delegation in book 9, why are they there? The one herald, Eurybates, has been doubled, as in book 1 (Eurybates *and* Talthybios), perhaps to suggest the additional importance of this, the poem's most fully developed delegation. It is possible that paired heralds, both in 1b and 9, reflect Near Eastern influence. Gordon (1965a: 110), commenting on the two heralds in 1b, notes that sending messengers in pairs is common in Ugaritic epic (e.g., *Baal Cycle*), and suggests a parallel in the Old Testament 2 Kings 5:23). As for Aias, another reason for seeing him as an addition is the *Iliad*'s usual tendency to keep the first two "best of the Akhaians," Diomedes and Aias, apart from Akhilleus. Aside from the unique funeral games for Patroklos, Akhilleus is rarely onstage together with either Diomedes or Aias. If Aias is an addition, his presence undeniably deepens and strengthens the scene. Not known either for his speaking or diplomacy in Homeric epic, he suggests parallels with Menelaos in the earlier delegation to Troy. Antenor succinctly notes Menelaos' speaking style:

> Indeed, Menelaos spoke forth rapidly,
> with few words, but very clearly, since he was not
> a man of many words, nor did he stumble in his speech.
>
> (3.213–15)

In Menelaos, the earlier delegation led by Odysseus featured a speaker with a style like that of Aias, suggesting that such a speaker is a traditional element of a delegation scene. Where both Menelaos and Odysseus proved ineffectual, however, Aias, of the three speakers in the book 9 delegation, ironically is the most effective in persuading Akhilleus. After Phoinix's speech, Akhilleus softens his resolution from leaving immediately, to "tomorrow, when the dawn appears, / we shall *discuss* whether we are to return or stay" (9.618–19). But after Aias' shorter, more direct appeal, Akhilleus talks of returning to battle, if Hektor sets fire to the ships (9.650–53), a considerable concession. If Aias is the odd man out, the composer's decision to develop the book 9 scene far beyond the others necessitated including an additional speaker, whose direct style of speaking prevents the delegation from being an entire disaster, but leaves Akhilleus just enough room to deepen his own tragic circumstances.

7. Akhilleus articulates his conflict about fighting, unfair distribution of winnings, and a slight to his honor and changes his resolve about fighting in the war

In book 1 Akhilleus makes his complaint not to the embassy but, immediately after its departure (1.348), to his mother, Thetis. He complains to her that Agamemnon has dishonored him, by taking Briseis. He speaks at length (1.365–412, the longest speech of book 1), an initial sounding of his themes in book 9. He gives fuller background than does the principal narrator of the events leading up to Agamemnon's taking Briseis away (see Rabel 50–55). Akhilleus then requests Thetis to ask Zeus to cause the Akhaians to die, to make Agamemnon recognize his mistake (*ate*). His perspective parallels his rejection of Agamemnon's embassy in book 9. Akhilleus implicitly reaffirms to Thetis his earlier threat to sit out the war.

In book 9 Akhilleus' lengthy rejection of Agamemnon's offer, the heart of the tragedy that is the *Iliad*, has been interpreted in a number of ways.[37] It is an angry complex of conflicting perspectives. My own view is that both antagonists are wrong or mistaken, but in different ways. Akhilleus is wrong to reject the offer and does so out of anger, smoldering resentment at Agamemnon. Akhilleus recognizes that Odysseus is here not to speak for himself but to convey Agamemnon's perspective. His recognizing that Odysseus functions as a proxy infuriates him.[38] Akhilleus is a prisoner of his anger, unable to reason adequately, lacking the self-control that an Odysseus typically has. At this point his anger becomes οὐλομένη (1.2). So powerful is Homer's artistry that many readers are reluctant to find fault with his protagonist. Agamemnon is wrong to offer compensation that is flawed.[39] In spite of Akhilleus' repeated emphasis on just distribution and compensation, what he really wants from Agamemnon is an admission of wrongdoing (ἣν ἄτην, 1.412), more than material goods, and he will reject any offer lacking such an admission.[40] Agamemnon *has* made such an admission to others (e.g., 9.115 ff) but not to Akhilleus' face. In book 9 Agamemnon does not even make his offer to Akhilleus' face but through a proxy, Odysseus.

In books 18–19 Akhilleus changes his position on fighting in the war when he learns of Patroklos' death. Hearing Patroklos has died, Akhilleus wishes for his own death, but only after he has slain Hektor (18.88–93). He reaffirms this change of heart several times (18.114–15, 334–35; 19.68–70), and symbolically reenters the fighting, when, at Iris' behest, and aided by Athena, he appears by the ditch and shouts (18.217–37), enabling the Greeks to recover Patroklos' corpse. Akhilleus makes public his change of mind at the assembly (19.56–68), which he has convened for just this purpose.

8. Akhilleus thinks of Thetis and considers her prophecies about his destiny

In book 1 Akhilleus calls on his mother as soon as the embassy leaves (1.351). After he summarizes the reasons for his strife with Agamemnon, he asks her for help, reminding her how she has claimed that Zeus is in her debt. In reply, Thetis is quite explicit about Akhilleus' swift-approaching destiny. Describing him as swift fated beyond all men (ὠκύμορος . . . περὶ πάντων, 1.417),[41] she emphasizes how tragic his destiny is, that he is to be exceedingly short-lived (1.416). Although she makes no explicit link with his dying at Troy, her comments in book 1 are a thematic parallel to her later, more-explicit remarks that he will perish if he remains in the war.

In book 9 the highly expanded delegation scene incorporates motifs that in books 1 and 18–19 occur outside of the delegation, most notably, the scene involving Thetis. Though not onstage, the poem's climactic articulation of her prophecy is given at this point in the narrative. Akhilleus relates his present choice, between accepting or rejecting Agamemnon's offer, to his mother's prophecy,

> For my mother, the goddess, silver-footed Thetis, tells me
> twofold are the destinies I carry toward the day of my death. Either,
> if I stay here and fight about the city of the Trojans,
> my homecoming is destroyed, but I will have eternal fame;
> if I return home to my own fatherland,
> my noble fame perishes, but I will have a long life
> and the end in death will not come for me quickly.
>
> (9.410–16)

Thetis' prophecy is presented in more-explicit terms than when she is onstage in book 1. Although the prophecy assumes a choice, it is ironic that Akhilleus, so motivated by anger, does not really make a choice as much he is driven by his own emotions (as he comes close to admitting in the next scene with Thetis, 18.107–11). Similarly, when he decides to return to battle in book 18, it is out of revenge and anger. His mother's prophecy is a factor more for the audience, than for Akhilleus himself.

In books 18 and 19, as in book 1, the scenes with Thetis occur outside of the delegation scene but in close proximity to it. When Antilokhos informs him of the death of Patroklos, Akhilleus cries out, and his mother hears him (18.36 = 1.358). As Edwards (1991: 147) notes, "Perhaps this is more than simple formular repetition, as the earlier meeting of Thetis and her son is recalled by her words a little later (74–7)." Before leaving the Nereids, Thetis prophesies that she will never receive her son again in Phthia (18.59–60). Some of Thetis' first remarks to Akhilleus here also occur in the book 1 scene (18.73–74 [first half of 74] = 1.362–63 [first half of 363]). Shortly thereafter Thetis explicitly links Akhilleus' death with Hektor's (18.96). The *Iliad* thus juxtaposes Akhilleus' decisions whether to leave (books 1 and 9) or return to battle (book 18) with his mother's prophecies.

a. Hephaistos serves a mediating function that helps further Thetis' agenda

Hephaistos serves a few distinct mediating functions in the *Iliad*. At the end of book 1, Thetis' visit to Zeus, to get him to agree to Akhilleus' request, results in Hera's resentment and anger, and much subsequent divine conflict (discussed in chapter 6). But Thetis' visit also prompts Hephaistos' first appearance in the poem. As Hera's resentment of Zeus' meeting with Thetis threatens festivities on Olympos, Hephaistos intervenes (1.571) to divert her. His opening remarks are reminiscent of Akhilleus' in the book 19 assembly:

> if then you two *quarrel* with each other *on account of* mortals
> εἰ δὴ σφὼ ἕνεκα θνητῶν ἐριδαίνετον ὧδε.
>
> (1.574)

> we were enraged in spirit-eating *strife on account of* a maiden.
> θυμοβόρῳ ἔριδι μενεήναμεν εἵνεκα κούρης.
>
> (19.58)

Hephaistos cautions Hera against fighting with Zeus by recalling how, when he attempted to aid her in an earlier quarrel, Zeus hurled him from Olympos (1.586–94). We might characterize these events as follows: in book 1 after meeting with her son Thetis gets pivotal aid for him from Zeus, who is in her debt, and Hephaistos appears shortly afterward, discussing how he was once thrown from heaven by Zeus. In book 1 the link between Thetis and Hephaistos is indirect. It will be explicit and developed in greater depth in book 18.[42] In book 18, after meeting with Akhilleus, Thetis goes to Hephaistos (who is in her debt, because of her aid when he had been thrown from heaven) to get armor that will enable Akhilleus to return to battle. This motif, so clearly present in books 1 and 18, is absent in book 9. Why? Perhaps to increase Akhilleus' sense of isolation and alienation in book 9, no gods are present, not even Thetis, nor the highly sympathetic Hephaistos. In spite of the motif's absence from book 9, we treat it as part of the introductory pattern because of its importance in book 18, which scene is paralleled and foreshadowed by the scene at the end of book 1.

⤚

9. Night falls as a juncture between the two books[43]

Books 1 and 9 end with a string of similar motifs, culminating in the fall of night, whereas book 18 shares some of these features but lacks others. In book 1 we follow Thetis to Olympus, staying there while Zeus, Hera, and the others retire for the night. The close of book 1 keeps Hephaistos before us in his mediating between Hera and Zeus and, as the gods retire, in the reminder that he fashioned their homes. Book 2 opens with a wakeful Zeus, deliberating on how to realize his promise to Thetis.

Book 9 ends with two sets of characters retiring for the night. First Phoinix and Akhilleus are shown bedding down. Then the embassy, minus Phoinix, reaches Agamemnon, reports its failure, and each man then retires to his tent for the night.

Book 18 complicates the onset of night, the next night after that in books 9–10. After commanding Akhilleus not to enter battle until she returns with Hephaistos' arms, Thetis announces (18.136) she will return at dawn. Before night falls, however, the fierce struggle for Patroklos' corpse resumes (18.148 ff), essentially a postponed section of the middle sequence. After Iris comes to Akhilleus, advising him to stand at the ditch and yell, and Athena aids him as he does so, Akhilleus routs the Trojans with his shout.[44] As soon as the Greeks retrieve Patroklos, Hera brings on a premature night, spurring on a less-than-willing Helios (18.239–41). Hera's unique (within the poem) action is typical of the heightened level of divine interaction in Akhilleus' sequence, and of the greater intensity of expression on the composer's part.[45] The deity in the poem who most hates the Trojans (e.g., 18.367), Hera prematurely ends the day of glory Zeus promised to Hektor (18.239–42; discussed at Edwards 1991: 174). These acts begin to suggest how ruthlessly the deck will be stacked against Hektor when he encounters Akhilleus. All night the Greeks mourn Patroklos (18.315, 354); dawn opens book 19.

In books 2 and 10, thematically parallel events follow the onset of night. Both books begin in much the same way, with Zeus in the former and Agamemnon in the latter, unable to sleep.[46] While book 10 has long been criticized for its anomalies, I take the position that though it clearly differs from the rest of the poem at the lexical level, at the level of theme book 10 contains typical, traditional material that would have been part of the earlier tradition out of which the *Iliad* evolved.[47]

The *Iliad:* Structure, Myth, and Meaning

～

10. The Trojans, led by Hektor, hold an assembly to plan their strategy

In response to recent changes of fortune or position by the Greeks, the Trojans hold an assembly. The Trojans' assemblies in books 2 (2.788), 10 (10.299), and 18 (18.243–313) should be seen as counterparts to the Greek gatherings in books 1, 9, and 19, though in book 2 the motif is present in only minimal form. After the catalog of Greek forces, Iris comes to Troy, in the form of the Trojan lookout, Polites (2.786–91). The Trojans are already holding an assembly (ἀγορὰς ἀγόρευον: 2.788) outside Priam's doors. Although no motivation is given for the occasion of this particular assembly, it serves as a pretext for quickly marshaling the Trojan warriors. Iris, as Polites, announcing that the Greeks are assembled in a great force, directs Hektor to have the leaders of the various allies give orders to their men. Perhaps in a sign of things to come, not Priam but Hektor dissolves the assembly (2.807–8).

In book 10 the Trojan warriors remain outside the city for the night, confident from their success in book 8. When Hektor calls an assembly (10.299–332), only the warriors, as opposed to any of the Trojan elders—Priam, Antenor, or the six others earlier named as men of counsel (3.146–49)—are there to take part. The same is true of the book 18 assembly (18.242–314). By now, however, Poulydamas has emerged as a figure capable of giving sound advice.

Compared with the Greeks, the Trojans are at a considerable disadvantage in their assemblies. Typically for the Greeks, if an assembly or council falters or becomes confused, either of two, senior, experienced counselors, Nestor or Odysseus, can intervene to steer it toward a reasonable objective, soothing egos along the way, if necessary. Hektor, however, typically holds sway over the Trojans' assemblies, and, as noted above, in the assemblies in books 8 and 18, none of the older Trojan counselors is present, since the assemblies are held on the battlefield, near the Greek camp. Rarely persuaded by the more sensible Poulydamas, Hektor, focused on his own reputation, is unable to keep the big picture in mind with regard to the possible outcome of specific military strategies or the larger war (see chapters 3 and 6). This is established as a typical Trojan dynamic early in the poem when Antenor, perhaps the most sensible of all the Trojans (see chapter 6), is dismissed and overruled by Paris (7.347–65), the most irresponsible character in the poem. By having Paris prevail in one assembly, and Hektor repeatedly overrule Poulydamas in others, the *Iliad* implicitly criticizes the Trojans' ability to reason and rein in irresponsible impulses.

11. At the assembly, Hektor makes a foolish boast

Hektor does not make a boast in the Trojan assembly in book 2, nor is any actual report given of the discussion. However, he is the focal point of the assembly, as noted above, in that Iris/Polites addresses her/his remarks mainly to Hektor (2.802–6). The brief scene ends with the impression that Hektor is firmly in charge. We are not told if Antenor or Poulydamas is present. We include the motif, though absent in the opening books, in the narrative pattern because of its prominence in the assemblies in books 10 and 18.

In book 10 Hektor calls the assembly (10.299–300) to get a volunteer for an intelligence mission, a close counterpart to the Greek decision,[48] in the absence of participation or aid from Akhillean *bie,* to employ Odyssean *metis.*[49] In eliciting a volunteer, Hektor is more emphatic about the prize he would award than he is about the mission itself. He promises, for the man who would spy out whether the Greeks are still guarding their ships, the horses "which are the finest of those by the swift ships of the Akhaians" (10.306). Implicitly, these would be Akhilleus' horses. Zenodotus' text was even more explicit on this point, having Hektor promise "those which carry the blameless son of Peleus" (see B. Hainsworth 185). Dolon, the son of a herald (10.314), volunteers.[50] To verify the reward, he asks Hektor to swear an oath that he will give him Akhilleus' horses and chariot (10.321–23), and Hektor so swears. Hainsworth observes, "Hektor's ready acquiescence in Dolon's ridiculous demands underlines Trojan arrogance in anticipated victory" (see B. Hainsworth 188).

In book 18 (242–314) the Trojans again hold a nighttime council (ἐς δ' ἀγορὴν ἀγέροντο). In this last Trojan assembly, Hektor's foolishness is even more strongly depicted, the disastrous consequences all the greater. Near panic now reigns among the Trojans (πάντας γὰρ ἔχε τρόμος, 18.247), because of Akhilleus' recent appearance. Poulydamas is first to speak (18.249–53). Though well aware that they would have to swallow some of their pride to do so, he prudently recommends that they retreat back into the city. The audience knows Poulydamas' suggestion is reasonable, even correct. But, in a tragic narrative, a character's mistakes are seen as avoidable only in retrospect, and the heroic code by which he lives will make it difficult for Hektor to do as Poulydamas suggests. Hektor rejects Poulydamas' argument with the same formula Paris used in his rejection of Antenor's suggestion to give Helen back to the Greeks: "Poulydamas, no longer do I like what you say to me" (18.285 = 7.357). Hektor therefore aligns himself, to some extent, with the most irresponsible character in the poem. We know that Hektor is here mistaken, if not deluded, because the temporary favor Zeus promised him (11.186–94) is now over, with the setting of the sun, hastened by Hera (18.239–42), right before the Trojans hold this assembly. Hektor goes on to make the foolish boast that he will face Akhilleus and not run from him. The Trojans' reaction, that they applaud Hektor and ignore Poulydamas, partly reflects Athena's influence: "Fools, for Pallas Athena had taken their wits" (18.311).[51]

⌒

12. Odysseus succeeds in restoring order in a second or later Greek assembly against an Akhilleus figure

In each sequence, if not in quite the same order in all three, Odysseus restores order among the Greeks by confronting a figure who in some respects resembles Akhilleus or, as in book 19, is Akhilleus himself. In books 2 and 19 he does so at the Greek assembly, whereas in book 10 he does so on an escapade plotted at and immediately following a council. There is a comic or parodic modality in all three scenes. Book 2 is perhaps the most significant of these scenes. This is Odysseus' first speaking role in the poem, a key instance of his success in the face of Agamemnon's repeated failures of leadership and Nestor's failed attempt at mediation in the assembly in book 1. Odysseus' success in these three scenes can be seen to prefigure his role as the sacker of Troy.[52]

Book 2 begins with Zeus pondering how to fulfill Akhilleus' request and destroy many of the Greeks. His first solution is to send a dream to Agamemnon, a dream described as οὖλον, "destructive" (2.6, 8), a thematic link to οὐλομένην, of Akhilleus' wrath (1.2). When the dream reaches the sleeping Agamemnon, it takes Nestor's form. While the dream is thereby more credible to Agamemnon, as commentators have suggested (Kirk 1985: 116), there may be irony at Nestor's expense. Agamemnon proceeds to call a council, reporting the dream to Nestor, among others, adding his own idea to use this occasion to test the army's resolve. Nestor, by seconding this dubious plan, repeats his ineffectual role from book 1, unable to prevent Agamemnon from acting in a way that will hurt, not help, his troops and their cause. Agamemnon dissolves the council and has the heralds summon a full assembly.

When Agamemnon holds forth at the assembly, he declares that Zeus has deceived him (ἄτη, 2.111; ἀπάτην, 2.114), but is unaware of the extent of the deception. This serves as a doublet of the earlier motif: *3. Agamemnon exercises reckless judgment* (ate). Books 2 and 10 (but not 19) tend to repeat material from earlier in the introductory pattern, having second councils or assemblies, though using them for different effect than before. As he deceives his troops Agamemnon claims that the Trojans' allies drive him, πλάζουσι (2.132), from his goal of sacking the city. Having earlier provoked Apollo's wrath, Agamemnon is now being blocked by Zeus himself. Hence πλάζουσι in his test/deception of his troops ironically refers to the actual opposition of divine forces against Agamemnon.

When Agamemnon suggests to the troops that they should now return to Greece, his plan backfires, everyone not at the council jumping at the chance to go home. Odysseus, prompted by Athena, contains Agamemnon's disastrous motion. Hera dispatches Athena to halt the Greeks' flight to their ships in the *Iliad*'s first pivotal contrafactual, which not only halts Agamemnon's disastrous gambit but highlights Odysseus' subsequent role. As commentators note, Athena does not, as Hera directed, go to each man and persuade him not to flee. She goes only to Odysseus. Much as in the second half of the *Odyssey*, Odysseus now carries out an agenda directed by the goddess. Hurrying to carry out her command, to restrain the Greeks from fleeing, Odysseus sheds his cloak, which is caught by Eurybates, his herald, repeating their association in the delegations in books 1 and 9. But when all have returned to the assembly and take their seats, apparently ready to hear Odysseus out, Thersites speaks.

Commentators have argued that Thersites functions as a parody of Akhilleus.[53] He is described as "in strife with kings" (ἐριζέμεναι βασιλεῦσιν, 2.214), much as Akhilleus with Agamemnon. Thersites makes arguments more than a little like Akhilleus' in books 1 and 9, using a similar speaking style. His first word is a vocative to Agamemnon, as Akhilleus began the first speech of the assembly in book 1. He goes on to articulate issues Akhilleus raised: inequitable distribution of war winnings and Agamemnon's attachment to slave women. In closing, he repeats a line Akhilleus hurled at Agamemnon in his most insult-laden speech (2.242 = 1.232). Thersites, however, is a resolutely unheroic figure. Within the heroic ethos of the *Iliad*, such statements coming from a man with no standing as a warrior do not have the same force as when Akhilleus utters them. Thersites is fiercesome in words but not deeds. Odysseus answers Thersites first in words, then in deed. He repeats the narrator's description of Thersites as striving with kings (2.214, 247), asserting that Thersites should not do so. Denouncing Thersites, Odysseus dashes him with the scepter.

Having quelled strife from an Akhilleus-like figure, and winning full support in so doing (2.270–77), Odysseus addresses the assembly. Significantly, the narrator now introduces him as Odysseus, "the city sacker" (ὁ πτολίπορθος, 2.278). Athena, again by his side, now takes the form of a herald who silences the host. Though the herald is unnamed, the form Athena has taken must be that of Eurybates, mentioned a short time earlier (2.184).[54] Odysseus' speech is a masterpiece of rhetoric.[55] Though the army has reason to chafe, it had omens confirming that Troy was to fall in the present year, and no reason to doubt the omens. Odysseus concedes the lure of going home but contains it in his highly effective antistrophe or *conversio* on νέεσθαι, "to return" (2.288, 290, 291, 298).[56]

As was his thrashing of Thersites, Odysseus' speech is wildly popular among the assembled troops (2.333–35). But, since Akhilleus will not return to battle until book 20, and Zeus has yet to cause the Greeks to suffer as promised, the *Iliad* moves quickly to contain the momentum of Odysseus' success. Though Odysseus has just saved him from a disaster, Agamemnon has no reaction. Instead, Nestor makes a derivative speech, reworking Odysseus' emphasis on the earlier omens (2.349–53), and closing with the suggestion that the troops be placed in order by clan. Having given no reaction to Odysseus, Agamemnon praises Nestor, saying he surpasses the other Akhaians in speaking (2.370). The episode thus replays Agamemnon's poor decision making and Nestor's curious lack of efficacy. As such the scene also instantiates, if under the surface, friction between Odysseus and Agamemnon, which resurfaces at 4.329–63 and especially 14.82–108. Taplin (90) well contrasts the relative merits of Odysseus and Nestor in this scene:

> Odysseus . . . takes over Agamemnon's sceptre and uses it assertively; he rallies everyone with socially appropriate sentiments; he silences Thersites to the approval of all. . . . His speech . . . meets with great approval. Nestor is perhaps not such an unqualified success . . . he utterly fails to heal the dispute because he defers too much to Agamemnon. . . . After Odysseus' calm, cogent speech, Nestor supplies emotive bluster at 2.336–68, and Agamemnon lavishes praise on it.

Odysseus not only prevents the army from running to the ships but also thwarts Zeus' first attempt at fulfilling his promise to Akhilleus.

Book 10 replays similar dynamics, Odysseus defeating an Akhilleus figure, in the *Doloneia*. Commentators have noted larger structural similarities between books 2 and 10. Haft (38) observes:

> The *Doloneia* also bears the same relationship to Book 9 as *Iliad* 2 does to its preceding book: the Embassy and *Iliad* 1 focus upon Achilles; in his absence, the *Doloneia* and *Iliad* 2 thrust his "rival" Odysseus into prominence. In Book 10, Odysseus uses his *metis* to win for himself and Diomedes a triumphant return from behind enemy lines. In Book 2, Odysseus single-handedly prevents the demoralized Greeks from leaving Troy in disgrace.

Rabel (66, n. 13) makes a similar argument, "Odysseus will perform a similar role in book 10, the *Doloneia*, the contents of which . . . recall the crisis of book 2." Dolon, though not a Greek, is, nonetheless, a parodic version of Akhilleus in the emphasis placed on his swiftfootedness (ποδώκης, 10.316), and in his obsession to possess Akhilleus' horses and chariot (10.321–23, 392–93).[57] Their considerable differences notwithstanding, Dolon's parallels with Akhilleus are quite specific. B. Hainsworth (186) notes of Dolon's epithet ποδώκης, "it is remarkable that this epithet is otherwise strictly confined in the singular to Akhilleus." Physical shortcomings suggest other parallels between Dolon and Thersites (εἶδος μὲν ἔην κακός, 10.316; cf. 2.216–19). Both are unheroic characters whose attempts to compete in the heroic arena—whether verbally, as in Thersites' case, or physically, as with Dolon—are ludicrous. There is a tremendous gap for each character between what he would accomplish and what he can actually accomplish. Since Dolon is the son of a herald (10.315), the episode continues Odysseus' thematic association with heralds, also evident in his encounter with Thersites.

As Odysseus and Diomedes are about to capture Dolon, Odysseus is again described as "the city sacker" (ὁ πτολίπορθος, 10.363), the only other time in the *Iliad* he receives this epithet, other than in the book 2 assembly, immediately after his trouncing of Thersites (see Haft 45–50). As Odysseus and Diomedes pursue Dolon, they are repeatedly referred to with dual forms (10.349, 350, 354, 360, 361, 364, 376), a thematic link with Odysseus' mission in book 9.[58] Dolon's first words (10.378–81), begging to be taken alive, reveal his cowardice, the gap, as with Thersites, between his words and his actual abilities. Though Thersites is a Greek, he functions almost as an enemy in the assembly by threatening the precarious unity Odysseus has just instilled. Because Dolon is a Trojan, his parallels with Akhilleus notwithstanding, and therefore an actual enemy, Odysseus' and Diomedes' trouncing of him goes to a level beyond Thersites'. Dolon is slain, beheaded, his head still talking as it lurches off his neck.

In book 19 Odysseus again contains a figure who strikes a heroic pose in the assembly. This time, however, the figure is no parody of Akhilleus, but Akhilleus himself. After Agamemnon's lengthy *Ate* narrative (19.91–133), Akhilleus replies with a distinct lack of decorum, insulting Agamemnon and his gifts in his disdainful references (19.147–48; see Edwards 1991: 253). Impatient, and uninterested in Agamemnon's desire to display the astonishing quantity and value of his gifts, Akhilleus urges an immediate return to battle. Odysseus strongly disagrees with Akhilleus.

While commentators, ancient and modern, generally misunderstood this confrontation between Odysseus and Akhilleus, recent scholarship has demonstrated that "the meal is a regular part of the sequence of joining battle."[59] Hence, Odysseus is correct in insisting that the army follow its usual procedures, observed elsewhere in the *Iliad*. But his insistence on procedure is much more than this. The meal has great symbolic value, an army reunited in chain of command and purpose.[60] Though intended to serve this purpose, the assembly in book 19 fails to do so, due to residual ill will between Agamemnon and Akhilleus, *until* Odysseus insists upon this greater display of unity. The directness of the confrontation is signaled by Odysseus' highly assertive opening line to Akhilleus, the same formula Agamemnon casts at Akhilleus in the assembly in book 1 (19.155 = 1.131) after Akhilleus has challenged and insulted him. Unlike either Agamemnon or Akhilleus in book 1, however, Odysseus neither loses his temper nor employs insults, but firmly objects to Akhilleus' preferred course of action. Odysseus' actions here parallel his accomplishments in the assembly in book 2. In each scene Odysseus contains an Akhilleus, but his concern is to restore order to the army, not to pursue a personal grievance. In books 2, 10 (and 9), and 19, Odysseus acts not to win glory for himself but to advance the army's collective objective.

When Odysseus finishes stating his reasons why the army should first join in a common meal, after a public declaration of the end of the feud, Agamemnon praises him (19.185–97). But Akhilleus, unpersuaded, continues to object. Resolute, the embodiment of the grizzled veteran, Odysseus speaks again,[61] noting that, though Akhilleus is better with the spear, he himself is wiser and knows more things. His second speech is difficult and dense, insisting on the need for a prepared, well-fed army, because the realities of war may not allow another meal soon. Akhilleus now has no response; Odysseus has prevailed.[62] Though the defeat is a small one for Akhilleus, Odysseus' victory is no mere formality, but a restoration of order, much as in book 2, something Agamemnon is unable to accomplish, and in which Akhilleus is simply not interested. Odysseus' performance here is a miniature of the dynamics of the Greek victory over Troy. Akhilleus will bring Hektor down with his spear, but Odysseus will devise the ultimate victory over the city. Odysseus' actions associated with this motif prefigure his role as the sacker of Troy.

Although the meal is an important part of the sequence of motifs, Akhilleus, through his insistence on being Akhilleus, so to speak, has it both ways. He does not take part in the meal but receives divine sustenance anyway (19.347, 353). Because he does not take part in the meal, and the narrative closely focuses on him for most of the final sequence, we do not get a depiction of the meal. Akhilleus' concession that the others at least can have their meal is somewhat akin to the conclusion of a comedy such as the *Dyskolos* in which the *senex iratus* who has been standing in the way of the plot's resolution by refusing to agree to the marriage, now partakes, if reluctantly, in the wedding feast. In this sense, then, there is a hint of the parodic modality that typifies the parallel encounters between Odysseus and Thersites and Dolon.

Nestor's lack of participation in the assembly in book 19 is noteworthy. In some respects Odysseus and Nestor are complementary figures in the *Iliad.* Both excel at speaking in the assembly; both are respected for their wisdom and strategy. Each attempts to mediate between Agamemnon and Akhilleus. In the *Odyssey,* Nestor comments on their shared qualities:

> While I and shining Odysseus were there not ever
> did we speak at cross-purposes, in the assembly, nor in the council,
> but having [ἔχοντε][63] one mind and with prudent planning
> we would devise the things that were best for the Argives.
>
> (3.126–29)

In the assembly in book 1, Nestor is ineffectual. In the council in book 2, he supports Agamemnon's ill-advised plan to test his troops deceptively. Odysseus has to clean up the resultant mess. In book 19 Nestor's ineffectual tendencies are kept offstage. Conversely we are now able to see why Odysseus does not speak up and cannot take part in the book 1 assembly: *because it has to be a failure.* When Odysseus takes part in the main assemblies of the narrative pattern, he prevails.[64] Perhaps Nestor's main weakness is that he is too closely tied to Agamemnon's self-interest. Odysseus' greatest strength is that he has the army's interest, success in the war, as his motivation, and reserves personal confrontation with Agamemnon for episodes outside of the assemblies (as at 4.349–55 and 14.82–108).

13. The introductory pattern concludes with a summons to battle, for which Odysseus is largely responsible

In all three sequences, Odysseus' ability to contain the dissenting Akhilleus figure and restore order over the Greek army lead more or less directly to the marshaling of the Greek army for battle. In book 2 this process continues in Nestor's peculiar speech (2.337–68; see Kirk 1985: 150–51), which, though oddly ignoring everything Odysseus said, nonetheless builds on the order he has instilled. Indeed, this marshaling scene is only possible because of Odysseus' recent actions. Nestor suggests that the troops be arranged by tribe and clan (363–68), and Agamemnon agrees. As the troops leave the assembly, they take their meal by their shelters (2.399 ff), the meal serving in the initial sequence as it does in book 19 (see J. B. Hainsworth 161–63). Having eaten, and sacrificed, the Greeks assemble, depicted in that highly expanded, almost 300-hundred-line-form we know as the Catalog of Ships. Whatever its genesis, or earlier history, whenever its composition, the passage serves as the poem's most highly developed depiction of the regular motif of the Greek forces being marshaled for battle (J. B. Hainsworth 161, 175).

As is clear from the parallels in books 19–20, Diomedes' *aristeia* could come immediately after the marshaling scene at the end of book 2. Instead, the *Iliad* interposes book 3 as an overture, as discussed in chapter 2, presenting digressive materials that simultaneously look back to the beginning of the war and introduce key scenes from the end of the narrative pattern.[65] Book 4 starts anew on the divine plane, the tensions depicted there paralleling, on smaller scale, the full theomachy that will erupt in books 20–21 (counterpart to books 8 and 14 in the middle sequence). The episode concludes with Zeus' directing Athena to cause the Trojans to break the truce established for Paris' duel in book 3. Pandaros' subsequent wrongdoing re-establishes that the Greeks have the moral high ground. The wounding of Menelaos ends the section of the poem in which he has been prominent and foreshadows the wounding of Agamemnon and Patroklos. Agamemnon now has renewed purpose to attack the Trojans, as will Akhilleus in the final sequence.

Book 4.221 ff, in serving up a second marshaling scene, essentially brings the narrative pattern back to where the introductory pattern leaves off in book 2.[66] Provoked by the outrage Menelaos has suffered, Agamemnon, in one of his finer displays of leadership, himself now marshals the troops. His insulting of Diomedes (4.365–421) briefly serves to recapitulate some of the key motifs in books 1–2, the tensions between the best of the Akhaians (a role now played by Diomedes) and Agamemnon (*2. In the course of the assembly, Agamemnon's leadership is challenged;* and *3. Agamemnon exercises reckless judgment against the best of the Akhaians*). Agamemnon is more successful at motivating his troops using anger and provocation, rather than deception, as he attempted in book 2. Book 4 also reworks key narrative techniques by employing similes similar to those which ushered in the book 2 catalog (4.275–82, 422–39, and 452–56).

In the middle sequence, the *Doloneia* concludes with Odysseus and Diomedes returning to the Greek camp, victorious and laden with spoils. The two heroes then take a meal (10.578). Book 11 begins with dawn, and—after Zeus sends down the goddess, Eris (11.3)—the narrative hastens to an arming scene for Agamemnon (11.16 ff). Though lacking a marshaling scene, the underlying sequence nonetheless is clearly intact. Odysseus' triumph over Dolon in short order leads to the army's setting off for battle, prepared for an *aristeia* by the best of the Akhaians.[67]

The transition at the end of book 19 is the smoothest. After the assembly breaks up (19.309), there is a brief scene in which Akhilleus, accompanied by friends, mourns Patroklos. In a briefer scene, Zeus has Athena instill nectar and ambrosia in Akhilleus, an altered instantiation of the meal that Akhilleus has been refusing. A general arming scene immediately follows, the focus soon shifting to Akhilleus' arming, the climactic version of all such scenes in the poem. As J. B. Hainsworth (160–61) points out, the only interruption in the usual sequence of the themes depicting armies joining battle, is the unexpected dialogue Akhilleus holds with his horses. As book 20 begins, the arming scene immediately resumes. Akhilleus' anger will now provoke him to do what he could have done back in the initial sequence. His chances for success are aided by Hektor, who in his recklessness has kept his men on the plain.

CHAPTER FIVE

༶ঌঌঌঌ

Subgenres of Myth in the *Iliad* I

Greek literature is a Near Eastern literature.
—M. L. WEST

ঌ

1. Siege myths

The *Iliad* is set against a background of siege myth,[1] a myth depicting a hostile force encamped before a city intending to sack it. Frequent elsewhere in Greek myth—for example, Heracles' earlier sack of Troy and traditions of the Seven against Thebes—siege myth probably existed in Greek culture at least as early as the Mycenaean era, as depictions of sieges on the silver rhyton from Mycenae and a Theran fresco suggest.[2] Homeric epic bears unmistakable signs of Near Eastern influence, as we will see throughout chapters 5–7. Siege myths are quite common in older Near Eastern traditions, including *Lugulbanda and the Thunderbird, Gilgamesh and Aka, Enmerkar and the Lord of Aratta* (all Sumerian), and *Kirta* (Ugaritic). But in no extant Near Eastern tradition is siege myth more common than in Old Testament (OT) myth. Throughout the books of conquest (Deut–2 Kings) and the prophetic books (Isaiah-Malachi) dozens of sieges are depicted.

In myth a city is besieged because its people have offended the gods. If the attacking force is successful, it is because the gods support them. In this respect *all* siege myths are holy wars, divinely provoked, divinely decided, "If disaster strikes a city, is it not the work of the Lord?" (Amos 3:6; cf. Ezek throughout). Yahweh's frequent epithet, "the God of Hosts," embodies this principle and cuts both ways, supportive of the Israelites' armies when they are the attackers, supportive of enemy armies when the Israelites, because of their wrongdoing, are besieged. Compare Knox and Russo (352–53): "Classicists will doubtless be reluctant to apply the notion of 'Holy War' to the well-greaved Achaeans. . . . The definition of Holy War . . . required simply that the summons to war—and thus the assurance of victory—come from God Himself. This is precisely what has occurred in Agamemnon's dream." Although modern Homeric criticism, in my view, tends to downplay the larger sacred dimensions of the *Iliad*, comparison with OT myth helps bring out moral thrusts of the poem's plot, which are at times latent, at other times explicit. There is considerable common ground in the forms of wrongdoing the *Iliad* attributes to the Trojans and which OT myth depicts in the inhabitants of the besieged city (see *8. Trojan misconduct* in chapter 6).

Siege myths tend to come in two different types: some identify with the attacking force, which tend to be heroic, and the others identify with the besieged, which tend to be laments. The *Iliad* has both types, but the majority of the poem is given to the heroic deeds of the attacking Greeks. Lament is closely identified with the Trojans, and surfaces primarily in the speeches of Andromakhe, Priam, and Hekabe, as they envision their fates after the sack of Troy. OT siege myths feature the same dichotomy, using the heroic mode to portray the Israelites in the conquest of Canaan (Joshua) and in their battles with the Philistines and other nearby peoples (e.g., 1 and 2 Sam), but switching to lament when they are besieged (Lam and the prophetic books). In the prophetic books, the OT thus turns to those subgenres of myth which the *Iliad* uses to depict the Trojans' plight, whereas in the books of conquest the OT employs the subgenres of myth the *Iliad* employs to depict the Greeks. The high style of heroic siege myths focuses on an individual, Heracles, Patroklos, or Akhilleus, as capable of sacking Troy single-handedly.[3] In OT myth the high style is only used of the Israelites (Josh–2 Chron), never of their attackers.

In the OT, lament siege myths are marked by a greater realism than the heroic style, which, for *its* effects, depends on the miraculous, the deeds of heroes and gods. When the Israelites are besieged, the myths delineate the specific weaponry, strategy, and situations of the attackers, a less heroic and more mundane view of the victors. For the besieged, the horrors of deprivation of food and water, rationing of supplies, and even cannibalism replace the heady, positive view conveyed by narratives identifying with the attackers. The *Iliad* approaches these topics only to depict Troy *after* it has been sacked (in forward-looking speeches by Andromakhe, Priam, and Hekabe). Since the *Iliad* downplays the perspective of the besieged, except in a few key scenes, it never mentions siege weapons or strategies, except briefly and, most surprisingly, does so of the Trojans when *they* assault the Greek wall (B. Hainsworth 344–46). This constitutes one of the weirder ironies of the poem and must be deliberate.[4] Occasional acknowledgment of siege conditions does surface, as at 22.154–56, when the narrator notes how the Trojan women, before the Greeks came, used to wash clothes in the springs along which Akhilleus now chases Hektor. Andromakhe's concern about where the wall might be breached (6.434) is another such passage.[5] The greater realism in the OT's depictions of the besieged Israelites perhaps reflects the different eras in which the two different genres are set. Like the *Iliad*, OT myths of conquest are set in a past several centuries before the narratives took their final shape, allowing for a more idealized, marvelous, heroic mode, whereas the laments in the prophetic books are written with the events they depict in a more recent past.

A passage from Ezekiel demonstrates the greater realism OT myth uses to depict sieges from the perspective of the besieged: "Draw a city on it, the city of Jerusalem: portray it under siege, erect towers against it, raise a siege-ramp, put mantelets in position, and bring up battering-rams on every side" (Ezek 4:1–2). The passage, in its pronounced self-awareness, shows how familiar the genre of siege myths was to the ancient OT audience. If the *Iliad* were not so dominated by the heroic, miracle-filled mode used of the attacking Greeks, it might have such a description, written from Andromakhe's or Priam's perspective. Of the many siege myths in the OT, most relevant to the *Iliad* are Genesis 14, 34; Habakkuk 1–3; Judges 19–20; Ezekiel 25–28; and Nahum 2–3, each of which can be seen, in some ways, as a miniature *Iliad*.

Two traditional features of siege myths are the excesses or atrocities of the attackers and the horrible sufferings of the conquered. Because the *Iliad* concludes before the actual sack of Troy, depictions of the attackers' excesses are limited to brief conjectures made by various Greeks about their expected assault on Troy. When Menelaos briefly considers honoring Adrestos' plea to be taken alive, Agamemnon dissuades him:

> Did the Trojans really do best by you in your house?
> Let none of them escape sheer destruction at our hands,
> not even the babe whom a mother carries in her womb;
> let them all perish from Troy, unwept, without a trace!
> (6.56–60)

Although the passage has been regarded as extreme in its cruelty,[6] OT myth offers close parallels for treatment of the besieged. Several passages resemble Agamemnon's exhortation: "Then Menahem . . . destroyed Tappuah and everything in it and ravaged its territory . . . because it had not opened its gates to him, and he ripped open every pregnant woman there" (2 Kings 15:16; cf. Hosea 13:16; 2 Kings 8:12; Amos 1:13).

Nestor exhorts the Greek troops in book 2 by having them imagine what sounds like a mass rape of the Trojan women (see Kirk 1985: 153), after they have sacked the city:

Therefore let no one be eager to return home
until he lies next to a wife of the Trojans
and avenges the mournful struggles of Helen.

(2.354–56)

Again OT myth offers a parallel in the apocalyptic description of the sack of Babylon: "All who are found will fall by the sword, all who are taken will be thrust through; their babes will be battered to death before their eyes, their houses looted and their wives raped" (Isa 13:15–16). The circumstances depicted in Genesis 34 (in which Dinah can be seen to parallel Helen, Shechem Paris, Hamor Priam, and Jacob's sons the Greeks) also suggest parallels to Nestor's and Agamemnon's remarks, though rape is not specified on the part of the attackers:

> Then two days later, while they were still in pain, two of Jacob's sons, Simeon and Levi, full brothers to Dinah, later arming themselves with swords, boldly entered the town and killed every male. They cut down Hamor and his son Shechem and took Dinah from Shechem's house and went off. Jacob's other sons came in over the dead bodies and plundered the town which had brought dishonour on their sister . . . they carried off all the wealth, the women and the children and looted everything in the houses. (Gen 34:25–29)

In OT myth, such practice is often (though not in Gen 34) the command of god, as set forth in Yahweh's specific directives in Deuteronomy:

> When you advance on a town to attack it, make an offer of peace. If the offer is accepted and the town opens its gates to you, then all the people who live there are to be put to forced labour and work for you. If the town does not make peace with you but gives battle, you are to lay siege to it and, when the Lord your god delivers it into your hands, put every male in it to the sword; but you may take the women, the dependents, and the livestock for yourselves, and plunder everything else in the town. You may enjoy the use of the spoil from your enemies which the Lord your god gives you. (Deut 20:10–14)

This is a form of the ban (*herem*), the presumption that everything in the conquered city becomes sacred to Yahweh. The full-scale slaughter, which includes civilians, apparently functions as a sacrifice to Yahweh.[7] In the ban's fullest form, all men, women, and children, all living creatures in the besieged city, are to be slain by Yahweh's command: "Go now, fall upon the Amalekites, destroy them, and put their property under ban. Spare no one; put them all to death, men and women, children and babes in arms, herds and flocks, camels and donkeys" (1 Sam 15:3). Indeed, according to these rules for war, some trees are accorded higher status than the enemy population:

> When in the course of war you lay siege to a town for a long time in order to take it, do not destroy its trees by taking an axe to them, for they provide you with food; you must not cut them down. The trees of the field are not people, that you should besiege them. But you may destroy or cut down any trees that you know do not yield food, and use them in siege-works against the town that is at war with you, until it falls. (Deut 20:19–20)

The Iliadic passages (6.55–57, 2.354–56) are far from extreme when considered within an ancient Near Eastern context, less extreme than the OT passages quoted above, and others like them (cf. Josh 7:21, 10:28–32; Ps 137:7–9; Ezek 9:5–6; Isa 13:15–16).[8]

When similar incidents are reported from a vantage point sympathetic to the conquered, the OT turns to the lament, well represented throughout Jeremiah, Lamentations, and Ezekiel. We quote at length from Lamentations' depiction of the fall of Jerusalem:

> . . . once queen among provinces,
> now put to forced labour!   1:1
> Her adversaries have become her masters,
> her enemies take their ease.
> Her young children are gone,
> taken captive by an adversary.   1:5
> Is there any agony like mine,
> like these torments which the Lord made me suffer.   1:12
> The Lord treated with scorn
> all the mighty men within my walls;
> he marshalled rank on rank against me
> to crush my young warriors.   1:15
> The elders of Zion sit on the ground in silence;
> they have cast dust on their heads
> and put on sackcloth.[9]   2:10
> You summoned my enemies from every side,
> like men assembled for a festival;
> on the day of the Lord's anger
> no one escaped, not one survived.
> All whom I have held in my arms and reared
> my enemies have destroyed.   2:22

My eyes ache
because of the fate of all the women of my city.   2:51
We are like orphans, without a father;
our mothers are like widows.   5:3

Here are many of the same images and motifs which the *Iliad* associates with
Priam (22.38–76, 416–28; 24.239–47, 253–64, 486–506), Hekabe (22.82–
28, 431–36; 24.748–59), and especially Andromakhe (6.407–39, 22.477–514,
24.725–45).[10]

⤚⤳

2. The exterminating angel slays many on the battlefield[11]

Although siege myths provide the context in which the *Iliad* is set, they func-
tion more as a *generic* backdrop for the plot rather than provide the specific
issues the *Iliad* explores. The traditional subgenre of myth that actually sets
the *Iliad* into motion is a type in which a god, angry because of perceived dis-
respect, sends a pestilence or plague against a people, often against an army.
In OT myth, Yahweh may himself send the plague, but often an *exterminat-
ing angel* is dispatched to do this. Yahweh or the angel then sends a disease
in some unspecified manner or is depicted shooting arrows into the host.
To initiate its plot, the *Iliad* combines both types in its depiction of Apollo.
    Apollo, angry at Agamemnon (discussed below as *3. The king who quar-
rels with his prophet*), is first described broadly as stirring up an evil sickness
against the Greek army (1.10, 61). Later, when bringing about the plague, he
shoots his arrows (1.42, 46), first at Greek livestock, but then at the Greek
army:

> then sending firm-pointed arrows at the men themselves
> he kept striking them; the teeming fires for the corpses were always
>   burning.
> For nine days the god's arrows went back and forth through the army.
>   (1.51–53)

Although the *Iliad* does not specify the number, Greek casualties are exten-
sive. In OT myths, Yahweh sends a plague after perceiving a lack of respect:
"How much longer will this people set me at naught? . . . I shall strike them
with pestilence" (Num 14:11–12). Like Apollo, Yahweh, or an angel doing
his bidding, shoots his arrows to bring on the plague: "He loosed arrows,
he sped them far and wide,/his lightning shafts, and sent them echoing"
(2. Sam 22:15; cf. Ps 18:14, 38:2, 64:7–9, 106:29, 144:6). A passage in Isaiah

is very close to the *Iliad*'s description of Apollo: "The angel of the Lord went out and struck down a hundred and eighty-five thousand men in the Assyrian camp; when morning dawned, there they all lay dead" (Isa 37:36).[12] OT myths often specify the large number of casualties the exterminating angel inflicts, "seventy thousand people died" (2 Sam 24:15); "That night the angel of the Lord went out and struck down 185,000 in the Assyrian camp" (2 Kings 19:35); "The Lord sent a pestilence throughout Israel, and seventy thousand Israelites died" (1 Chron 21:14).[13]

Several OT instances involve the Assyrian king, Sennacherib. Most relevant is 2 Chron 32:21: "So the Lord sent an angel who cut down every fighting man, leader, and commander in the camp of the king of Assyria, so that he withdrew disgraced to his own land." This is the state of affairs Agamemnon fears for the first several books of the *Iliad*, and to which Akhilleus alludes in his very first words in the poem:

> Son of Atreus, now I think, having *been driven back* [παλιμπλαγχθέντας],
> we must return home, if we are to escape death.
>
> (1.60–61)

In Homeric epic, the verb πλάζω (*plazo*) and its compounds, in the passive voice, designate mortals who have provoked a divine wrath (see Louden 1999a: 69–103 and chapter 1). Although Sennacherib is a historical figure, the OT writers depict him using traditional motifs and subgenres of myth, which depictions are neither realistic nor historical, but effective vehicles to illustrate moral cause and effect central to the goals of ancient myth. Agamemnon thus parallels not only a specific subgenre of myth in the OT but a specific figure within that subgenre, Sennacherib, the commander in chief who, because he has offended god, sees his army afflicted by the exterminating angel.[14]

a. God pities the dying mortals and arranges to have the plague checked

Both the *Iliad* and OT myth use the same mechanism for halting the destruction visited by the exterminating angel. A god takes pity on the deaths among the host and calls off the plague. In the *Iliad*, it is Hera who so intervenes: "Hera . . . for she was concerned for the Greeks, because she saw that they were dying" (1.55–56). The OT has several instances in which Yahweh, concerned about the welfare of the Israelites, halts or calls off the god-sent plague. Perhaps closest to the *Iliad* is a passage from Samuel: "The Lord sent a pestilence throughout Israel from the morning till the end of the appointed time; from Dan to Beersheba seventy thousand of the people died.

The angel stretched out his arm toward Jerusalem to destroy it; but the Lord repented of the evil and said to the angel who was destroying the people, 'Enough! Stay your hand'" (2 Sam 24:15–16)[15] In OT myth only Yahweh can start or stop such destruction whereas in Homeric polytheism Apollo and Hera can do so independently. As argued, in chapter 7, Hera has a unique role among the *Iliad*'s deities: to attempt to usurp Zeus' position. In having Hera end the plague, which we might expect Zeus to do, the *Iliad* offers its first hint that Hera will contest Zeus' executive function.

b. The hero intervenes to check the god-sent plague

Both OT myth and the *Iliad* feature an additional means of checking the god-sent plague: a mortal intervenes to appease the offended god, whose wrath caused the plague. Such a man is highly ethical by the standards of his community. He has a special relationship with god and moves to restore his community to correct behavior in the eyes of the gods. In the *Iliad*, this is none other than Akhilleus himself, who, prompted by Hera, calls an assembly to deal with the plague's destructive consequences (1.54–61). Homeric scholarship has not, in my view, sufficiently appreciated the moral dimension of Akhilleus' actions here. The OT parallels and the *Iliad* itself suggest that the consequences of Apollo's plague have been severe. Akhilleus thus saves people from harm, not as a warrior, as expected in a heroic poem such as the *Iliad*, but through his observance of correct behavior with the gods. This moral dimension in Akhilleus is again emphasized in the account he gives his mother, Thetis: "At once I bid them to propitiate the god" (1.386).

Two OT instances involve the character Phineas, in circumstances surprisingly parallel to those in the *Iliad*. In Numbers 25, Yahweh sends a plague against the Israelites for their worship of Baal and other gods, and because an Israelite man then has sex with a Midianite woman. Agamemnon prompts the plague in *Iliad* 1 by his relationship with Khryseis. Then Phineas enters the narrative:

> When Phineas son of Elazar, son of Aaron the priest, saw him, he got up from the assembly and took a spear, and went into the alcove[16] after the Israelite and the woman, where he transfixed the two of them, the Israelite and the woman, pinning them together. Then the plague which had attacked the Israelites was brought to a stop; but twenty-four thousand people had already died. (Num 25:7–9)

As in the *Iliad*, Numbers here has the same two subgenres of myth (*2. The exterminating angel slays many on the battlefield; 2b. The hero intervenes to check the god-*

sent plague) occurring in sequence and in close succession. Yahweh himself comments on Phineas' behavior: "Phineas . . . has turned my wrath away from the Israelites; he displayed among them the same jealous anger that moved me, and therefore I did not exterminate the Israelites in my jealous anger" (Num 25:11). The events are recounted again in Psalms:

> Their deeds provoked the Lord to anger,
> and plague broke out amongst them;
> but Phineas stood up and intervened,
> and the plague was checked.
> This was counted to him as righteousness
> throughout the generations ever afterwards.
>
> (Ps 106:29–31)

Akhilleus' and Phineas' narratives have the following four motifs in common: their communities have offended god, and now suffer from a god-sent plague; the god is offended because a man has a woman from outside of the community, to have sexual relations with her (*Il.* 1.31); the righteous man intervenes by standing up at an assembly; and his action brings about an end of the divine wrath, propitiating the god. Different as Phineas and Akhilleus may be in other respects, they serve in the same role in the same subgenre of myth, the ethical man who rights his community's relations with the offended god. Phineas' weapon is the spear, Akhilleus' special weapon in the *Iliad*. Phineas is also mentioned in warring contexts (Judg 20:28), and his close relationship with Yahweh is proverbial (1 Chron 9:20). Akhilleus does not slay Agamemnon, as Phineas does the unnamed Israelite, but considers doing so (*Il.* 1.191).

David, in an additional OT instance of this subgenre (2 Sam 24), combines the roles of Agamemnon and Akhilleus; he is not only the king who provokes the god-sent plague but also the righteous man who acts to avert it: "When David saw the angel who was striking down the people, he said to the Lord, 'It is I who have sinned, I who committed the wrong; but these poor sheep what have they done?'" (2 Sam 24:17). Aware of his own culpability (seventy thousand people die, 2 Sam 24:15), he acts to end the crisis that he has caused: "He [David] built an altar to the Lord there and offered whole-offerings and shared-offerings. Then the Lord yielded to his prayer for the land, and the plague in Israel stopped" (2 Sam 24:25). The parallels extend to the end of the crisis. David's propitiation of Yahweh, parallel to Akhilleus' role in dealing with the plague, is essentially the same type-scene as Odysseus' propitiation of Apollo's wrath and plague (*Il.* 1.440–74).

Andromakhe recounts how when Akhilleus killed her father, he did not despoil him, "for he showed respect in his heart" (σεβάσσατο γὰρ τό γε θυμῷ, 6.417). This is a rare instance in Homeric epic of a word, σέβας, central to the later Greek ethical vocabulary. Although the *Iliad*'s central focus is on Akhilleus' quarrel with Agamemnon, his moves to avert the plague afflicting the Greeks, and his respectful treatment of Eetion, occur before the quarrel with Agamemnon, and may thus be more indicative of Akhilleus when not engaged in a bitter quarrel. Such a view of Akhilleus, as concerned with the good of his community, with what is fair and proper, is confirmed by his behavior in books 23 and 24: his adjudication of the games and his reception of Priam. Much of the present time of the *Iliad*, except books 1, 23, and 24, may thus depict an atypical Akhilleus.[17]

∽

3. The king who quarrels with his prophet

The main provocation for Akhilleus' quarrel with Agamemnon is Agamemnon's earlier quarrels with Khryses, Apollo's priest, and with his own prophet, Kalkhas (see Hernandez 323–30). Both episodes, crucial for the trajectory of the *Iliad*'s plot, are instances of a common subgenre of myth, *The king who quarrels with his prophet*. Evident in Homeric epic also in Iphikles' imprisonment of the prophet Melampous (*Od.* 11.291–97, 15.225–40) and elsewhere in Greek myth in the friction between Oedipus and Teiresias, this mythic subgenre is even more common in the OT. Especially close to the *Iliad*'s depiction of Agamemnon with Kalkhas (and Khryses) are the myths of Ahab's relationships with the prophets Elijah (1 Kings 17–19, 21) and Micaiah (1 Kings 22).[18]

When Akhilleus summons the assembly to address the problem of Apollo's plague (*2b. The hero intervenes to check god-sent plague*), he encourages the army to consult a prophet, conjecturing that Apollo is angry over a neglected sacrifice (1.64–66). Kalkhas says he can explain why Apollo is angry enough to send a plague but fears a king will be angry at him if he does so (1.76–83). In his subsequent offer of protection to Kalkhas, Akhilleus asserts that he will protect Kalkhas from any powerful Greek, even Agamemnon. His safety assured, Kalkhas declares that Apollo is angry because of Agamemnon's disrespectful treatment of Khryses, Apollo's priest. In front of the assembly, Agamemnon lashes out at Kalkhas, losing his temper at his prophet. Agamemnon earlier exhibited similar behavior in his dealings with Apollo's priest. When the latter attempted to ransom his daughter from the Greek king, Agamemnon treated him abusively (1.11, 24–33). Because the rest of the army respects Khryseis' cause (1.22–23), Agamemnon is established as exercising poor judgment by his disrespect of religious authority. Replying to Khryses, Agamemnon contemptuously calls him "old man," ignoring his position as Apollo's priest. By so doing, Agamemnon himself provokes the divine wrath (1.9), indirectly insulting Apollo. Angry at Agamemnon's disrespectful treatment of his priest, Apollo visits the plague on the Greek army (1.9–10).

Agamemnon's abusive treatment of a priest, Khryses, and a prophet, Kalkhas, shows a side of him that becomes clearer through comparison with OT myth. In the OT, Ahab acts toward his prophets in much the same way that Agamemnon does toward Kalkhas and Khryses. After an encounter with an unnamed prophet who antagonizes him, "The king of Israel [Ahab] went off home and entered Samaria sullen and angry" (1 Kings 20:43). Ahab provokes divine wraths by worshiping Canaanite gods (1 Kings 16:33), putting him on a collision course with Yahweh's prophets, Elijah and Micaiah. The conflict intensifies when Jezebel, Ahab's wife (who has more than a little in common with Klytaimnestra), has some of Yahweh's prophets slain, and Yahweh causes a drought, resulting in the following exchange: "As soon as Ahab saw Elijah, he said to him, 'Is it you, you troubler of Israel?' 'It is not I who have brought trouble on Israel,' Elijah replied, 'but you and your father's family, by forsaking the commandments of the Lord and following Baal'" (1 Kings 18:17–18). Ahab's subsequent problems result from his allowing the worship of the gods, Baal and Asherah, against Elijah's wishes.

Like Ahab, Agamemnon has thematic problems with the gods. The *Iliad* repeatedly associates him with Ate, a negative, contentious figure (discussed below). Eris (Strife), who resembles Ate in many respects, functions as the tutelary deity over his *aristeia* (11.3 ff, 73 ff, discussed in chapter 4). Zeus himself, because of his relationship with Thetis and Akhilleus, forms an agenda counter to Agamemnon for most of the initial and middle sequences, even intentionally deceiving him (below, *5. God sends the king a deceiving spirit*). Agamemnon's actions at the beginning of the poem not only offend Apollo, but put him on the wrong side of Zeus, much as Yahweh turns against Ahab.[19]

a. The king accuses his prophet of prophesying only evil

So close are the two traditions, Greek and OT myth, in their use of this mythic subgenre that they share specific verbal parallels. Both kings, Agamemnon and Ahab, in their anger at their prophets, accuse them of prophesying only evil for their kings. In his furious response to Kalkhas' proclamation that he, Agamemnon, has provoked Apollo's wrath and plague, the Greek king responds:

Seer of evils, not ever have you uttered a good thing for me;
always it is dear to you to prophesy evils.

(1.106–7)

Agamemnon's anger at Kalkhas may allude to Kalkhas' earlier prophecy
at Aulis, that the king had to sacrifice his daughter (not mentioned in the
Iliad). Twice in the OT Ahab makes virtually the same, verbatim remark to
his prophet Micaiah. When deliberating whether or not to attack the city
Ramoth-gilead, Ahab seeks the advice of many prophets: "'There is one
more,' the king of Israel answered, 'through whom we may seek guidance
of the Lord, but I hate the man, because he never prophesies good for me,
never anything but evil. His name is Micaiah'" (1 Kings 22:8). Shortly there-
after, when Micaiah has uttered a prophecy that confirms Ahab's view of
him, Ahab repeats: "Did I not tell you that he never prophesies good for
me, never anything but evil?" (1 Kings 22:18).[20]

In the most extreme instances of this subgenre, the king attempts to have
the prophet slain or thrown into prison. Agamemnon does not go this far,
but Kalkhas fears something of this sort (1.76–83), without protection from
Akhilleus. Ahab has Micaiah thrown into prison (cf. the prophet Melam-
pous in *Od.* 11.291–97, 15.225–40). King Zedekiah has the prophet Jere-
miah imprisoned repeatedly (Jer 32:2, 37:15–16), threatened with death
(Jer 26:8), flogged, and put in stocks (Jer 20:2). King Jehoiakim attempts
to slay the prophet Uriah (Jer 26:21).

4. The king, who has offended god, quarrels with his greatest warrior (or eris*)*

Akhilleus' role as the righteous man who averts the divine wrath causes his
quarrel with Agamemnon, who himself had caused the wrath through his
offensive behavior. By agreeing to protect Kalkhas, which the prophet re-
quests in a way that suggests it would require heroic behavior (εἴ με σαώσεις,
1.83), Akhilleus deflects Agamemnon's anger away from the prophet and
onto himself. His quarrel with Agamemnon is thus predicated upon his
agreement to protect the prophet. The *Iliad*'s own term for their quarrel is
eris, "strife" (ἐρίσαντε, 1.6; ἔριδι, 1.8; 1.277; cf. 2.214, 5.740, etc.).[21] Hesiod,
in the *Works and Days*, offers evidence for viewing the term as a specific sub-
genre of myth. According to Hesiod, there are two kinds of *eris* (*Works and
Days* 11–46). One is essentially a positive kind of competition and is good for
a society. The other is negative and can cause strife within a group. Hesiod's
second, negative *eris*, fits the quarrel between Akhilleus and Agamemnon.

While *eris* is expected to exist between Greeks and Trojans, it is inappropriate between a commander and his greatest warrior. The rest of books 1–17 of the *Iliad*, all of the first two sequences, are thus framed by an *eris* myth. Books 18–24 (the final sequence), on the other hand, restore *eris* to its correct application, outside the community, Greeks against Trojans. As noted, Eris is also personified as a deity, closely associated with Agamemnon (discussed below). The *Iliad* employs a unique epithet, θυμοβόρος, "eating at the heart," to underscore the deadly effect of strife (Hogan 25–26).

Beyond the initial friction of their being on opposite sides in the case of Apollo's divine wrath, Agamemnon and Akhilleus share the additional tension, common to heroic myth, between a hero who is greater than his king, but remains his subject and wields less political power as a result. In Greek myth, the most noted instance of this relationship is Herakles and Eurystheus (cf. Perseus and Polydektes, Jason and Pelias, et al.). Akhilleus' circumstances approach those of Herakles in that he is the son of a deity and, in this respect, of higher status than Agamemnon, and he enjoys the special regard of Zeus. He also has Athena's full support, key to a hero's success in Greek heroic myth, and Hera's. There is pathos in Zeus' regard for Akhilleus because he knows that in a sense Akhilleus is the son that was to have been his child. Since Thetis was destined to bear a son more powerful than his father, if Zeus' son, Akhilleus would have become the new ruler of the cosmos (see Slatkin 70 ff, 101–7). Akhilleus is thus *like* the special son of Zeus that Herakles is. Agamemnon, on the other hand, is thematically on the wrong side of god, offending Artemis before the war, provoking Apollo's wrath and plague, on the wrong side of Zeus because of his quarrel with Akhilleus, and associated with such strife-provoking deities as Ate, the Baleful Dream (2.6), and Eris, who initiates his *aristeia*.

OT myth offers a key instance of this subgenre of myth in the troubled relations between Saul and David. Saul may thus be grouped with Ahab and Sennacherib as figures whom the OT depicts using largely the same subgenres of myth that the *Iliad* uses for Agamemnon. A troubled figure, Saul suggests all of Agamemnon's negative tendencies, though, like the Greek king, he is also capable of considerable heroism. The kings' parallels fall into two categories: how they provoke the gods, and how they quarrel with the hero. Ultimately the two categories overlap since the hero is the chosen one of god. In his strained relations with the prophet Samuel, Saul is also another instance of *3. The king who quarrels with his prophet.*

Before David is a factor, Saul earlier offends Yahweh (as Agamemnon Artemis), which provokes his fractious relationship with his prophet, Samuel. Through Samuel, Yahweh commands Saul to sack the city of Amalek, putting everything under the ban, allowing no survivors (1 Sam 15:1–3). But after sacking the city, Saul spares both the king, Agag, and the best livestock. Yahweh regrets having made Saul king: "He has not obeyed my instructions" (1 Sam 15:11). Samuel regrets having anointed Saul as king (1 Sam 15:10–11). Saul then erects a memorial for his victory (1 Sam 15:12), desiring fame, much as a Homeric warrior. But Samuel confronts Saul over his partial violation of the ban: "Because you have rejected the word of the Lord, he has rejected you as king" (1 Sam 1:23). Within the *Iliad*, Agamemnon's alienation of Zeus, because of his quarrel with Akhilleus, places him in a similar predicament for books 2–18.

Like Agamemnon, who has an *aristeia* in book 11 (discussed in chapter 3), Saul essentially has an *aristeia* in 1 Sam 11:6–15 and demonstrates his heroic capabilities. When the Ammonites besiege Jabesh-gilead, Saul acts: "When Saul heard this, the spirit of God suddenly seized him" (1 Sam 11:6). This is a close equivalent to the *menos* expressions that initiate *aristeiai* in the *Iliad* (chapter 1, *3. A god places* μένος *in him as he goes to face the Trojans*). Such expressions, and subsequent *aristeia*, are especially common in Judges (discussed below as subgenre 6). The heroic tales in Judges suggest the same raw stuff from which the *Iliad* must have derived (cf. Niditch 16, 90 ff), but in Judges the myths are stated quickly and simply without the elaboration with which the *Iliad* develops its themes and type-scenes. The pace of Saul's *aristeia* is somewhat different; he first rouses the other Israelites to follow him by slicing an ox into pieces, distributing them through Israel, and threatening to do the same to the oxen of anyone who does not follow him. Alter (62) argues the motif is borrowed from Judges 19, which episode, discussed below, is one of the closest OT analogues to the larger story of the Trojan War. Similarly, Saul's defeat of Amelek suggests a miniature *Iliad* with his *aristeia* and successful outcome (though missing the key element of the foreign woman).

After this initial success, however, Saul's career becomes problematic, because of his failure to carry out the ban in full and his resultant rejection by Yahweh and by his prophet Samuel. 1 Samuel now focuses on the friction between the rising hero, David, who has Yahweh's blessing, and Saul, who has lost such divine support, much as the *Iliad*'s depiction of strife between Akhilleus and Agamemnon. In further specific motifs Saul has in common with Agamemnon, he treats priests disrespectfully (1 Sam 21.9–13, 13:11–14), has difficulties with sacrifices (1 Sam 13:9 ff, 14:31 ff), is compelled to sacrifice his own child (1 Sam 14:36–45; cf. Iphigeneia at Aulis), must himself perform a human sacrifice (1 Sam 15:33), causes friction in how he distributes war winnings (15:8–97), generates severe frictions under his rule

(1 Sam 11:10–15), is at times very dispirited (1 Sam 28:1–7), and is jealous of the hero (1 Sam 16:14–23, 18:5–9).[22]

In the fullest degree of such strife the king would attempt to have the hero slain (as with motif 3 in chapter 1), which Saul does (1 Sam 19:1 ff).[23] Agamemnon thus falls short of the degree to which Saul goes, but there are parallels in the delegation he sends to Akhilleus (1.320 ff; see esp. 1.330) and the men Saul sends to David who attempt to seize him (1 Sam 19.20). As Gunn (680) notes, "whatever Saul attempts to turn against David rebounds against Saul." The sentiment well describes how things go for Agamemnon as a result of the quarrel. In response to Saul's animosity toward him, David ends up working for the enemy, the Philistines, somewhat as Akhilleus' specific request that Zeus aid the enemy Trojans inflicts suffering among his own people. The strife between Saul and David is set against a broad backdrop of war against the Philistines, that most Greek of OT peoples.[24] As part of an attempted reconciliation, both Saul and Agamemnon offer a daughter's hand in marriage to the hero whom they have estranged (*Il.* 9.144–48; 1 Sam 17 ff; 2 Sam 3:13). As Gunn (680) notes of Saul and David, "King and competitor each forswear all hostile intent toward the other, but they keep their distance and go their own way," a fitting description of Agamemnon and Akhilleus in the final books of the *Iliad*. The strife between Agamemnon and Akhilleus has tremendous impact on the narrative pattern. The quarrel provides motifs 1–7 of the introductory pattern (see chapter 4) and causes the first two sequences of the principal narrative pattern (books 4–8, 10–17) to have substitutes for Akhilleus.

↪

5. God sends the king a deceiving spirit

Another subgenre, frequent in OT myth, again involves the two characters closest to the *Iliad*'s depiction of Agamemnon, Ahab and Saul. As earlier noted, all three figures participate in subgenre 3. *The king who quarrels with his prophet.* A king who does not heed his prophet tends to estrange himself from (the) god(s). The Saul narrative succinctly formulates this turn of affairs, "The spirit of the Lord had forsaken Saul, and at times an evil spirit from the Lord would seize him suddenly" (1 Sam 16:14). Agamemnon's close association with *ate*, "recklessness" (both as a description for his poor judgment and as divine personification of same at 19.91–136), with the goddess Eris, *and* with the deceptive dream in book 2 are all instantiations of this same subgenre, a king deceived by a god-sent spirit.

After agreeing to Thetis' request that he honor Akhilleus and destroy many Akhaians, Zeus sends a destructive (οὖλος) dream to Agamemnon. When the dream appears to Agamemnon, it deludes him into thinking that if he attacks now, he can sack Troy, contrary to Zeus' actual intent, "Fool, he did not know what things Zeus was devising" (2.38). At a subsequent council (2.50–84), Agamemnon relates his dream, but adds his own idea of testing the troops by suggesting that they give up and go home.

The story of Ahab in 1 Kings closely parallels the *Iliad*'s depiction of Agamemnon in book 2, even to specific details of the two kings' situations. Each king contemplates the sack of a city, Agamemnon camped before Troy, Ahab before Ramoth-gilead. As noted above, Ahab is not fond of a prophet, Micaiah, their relations serving as an instance of subgenre *3a. The king accuses his prophet of prophesying only evil.* At an assembly at which different prophets give their views, all recommending that Ahab attack Ramoth-gilead now, Micaiah relates his different vision:

> I saw the Lord seated on his throne, with all the host of heaven in attendance on his right and on his left. The Lord said, "Who will entice Ahab to go up and attack Ramoth-gilead?" One said one thing and one said another, until a spirit came forward and, standing before the Lord, said, "I shall entice him." "How?" said the Lord. "I shall go out and be a lying spirit in the mouths of all his prophets." "Entice him; you will succeed," said the Lord. "Go and do it." (1 Kings 22:19–22; also 2 Chron 18:18–24; cf. Judg 9:23).

The divine council evidences the polytheistic background of OT myth. In spite of Micaiah's depiction of Yahweh's actual design,[25] Ahab agrees with the other prophets; is *deluded* by the "lying spirit"; attacks the city, which just like Agamemnon, he presumes is his for the taking; and is slain in his attempt.[26] The verb here rendered "entice" (the Hebrew root *pth*) can also be rendered "deceive" (see esp. 2 Sam 3:25, Jer 20:7). The Septuagint uses ἀπατάω of Yahweh (ἀπατήσεις, III Kings 22:22 = 1 Kings 22:22) as he dispatches the spirit to deceive Ahab, the same verb the *Iliad* uses three times, associated with Agamemnon (9.344, 375; 19.97) and with Zeus (in the related noun, ἀπάτη, 2.114).

Agamemnon and Ahab thus pursue parallel trajectories through several consecutive subgenres of myth: *3. The King who quarrels with his prophet; 3a. The king accuses his prophet of prophesying only evil; 5. God sends the king a deceiving spirit.* Saul also participates in subgenre 5 as well, in a number of brief instances. When Saul is rejected by Samuel and God, the narrator notes, "The spirit of the Lord had forsaken Saul, and at times an evil spirit from the Lord would seize him" (1 Sam 16:14). After strife between Saul and David escalates, the king is again visited: "The next day an evil spirit from God seized on Saul" (1 Sam 18:10). Saul is, in fact, routinely harassed by such spirits, always said to be sent by God (1 Sam 16:16, 23; 19:9; cf. *Il.* 19.130–31 where Zeus is said to hurl *ate* down among mortals).

Agamemnon frequently participates in this mythic subgenre, for his associations with Ate and Eris, two negative, contentious deities, thematically parallel the deceiving Dream of book 2. Ate, or Delusion, embodies his flawed decision making, as is evident in his narrative about her in book 19. Eris, or Strife, embodies his quarrel with Akhilleus. Most parallel to the OT instances is Agamemnon's lengthy mythical narrative about Ate (19.88–137). Here a fully personified Ate, an immortal daughter of Zeus, is a close equivalent of the OT's evil spirit. In his myth, Ate embodies and causes reckless judgment, even in Zeus, prompting an oath that allows Eurystheus to have power over Herakles, his special son. After realizing that he has been deceived by Hera, Zeus hurls (19.130) Ate out of Olympos, so that she enters mortals' affairs (19.131). Agamemnon thus provides an etiology for deluded behavior (such as his own and Saul's). On one occasion Agamemnon connects *ate* with Zeus, as if Zeus sent it upon him, much as the OT passages about Saul ("Zeus, the great son of Kronos, bound me with a heavy recklessness [*ate*]," 9.18). This instance hints at personification, as in OT "evil spirit" passages.

The personified Eris, or Strife, also closely associated with Agamemnon, is a further instance of this same subgenre. In her only appearance, Zeus hurls (11.3) Eris into the Greeks' midst, much as he hurls Ate, and personally sends Dream to Agamemnon. Eris has a slightly more "heroic" aspect than Ate or Dream.[27] As noted in chapter 4, she serves a tutelary function over Agamemnon's *aristeia* at *Il.* 11.3 ff (cf. 11.73–74). Elsewhere described as Ares' sister (4.441), Eris can embody certain aspects of war and shares one epithet with Athena (λαοσσόος) (Dee 2001). But instead of presiding over the successful *aristeiai* of Akhilleus and Diomedes, as does Athena, Eris instead presides over the first Greek *aristeia*, which results in the hero being seriously wounded.[28]

In an additional parallel, occurring in the same context in the sagas of Saul and Agamemnon, both David and Akhilleus are depicted as accomplished musicians. After saying he is plagued by *ate* (9.18, 115, 116, 119), Agamemnon sends the delegation to meet with Akhilleus in book 9. When Odysseus, Aias, and Phoinix approach the hero,

> Him they found delighting his heart with a high-pitched lyre,
> beautifully fashioned, with a silver bridge,

which he had taken from the spoils when he sacked the city of Eetion,
he delighted his heart with this lyre, singing epics of heroes.

(9.186–89)

This is as close as the *Iliad* gets to a self-referential portrayal of an epic tradition in process. David hears himself depicted as the subject of an incipient oral epic tradition, in a popular refrain:

> At the homecoming of the army and the return of David from slaying the Philistine, the women from all the cities and towns of Israel came out singing and dancing to meet King Saul, rejoicing with tambourines and three-stringed instruments. The women, as they made merry sang to one another:
> 'Saul struck down thousands,
> but David tens of thousands.'
> Saul was furious, and the words rankled. (1 Sam 18:6–8; cf. 1 Sam 29:5)

The passage is a microcosm of the conflict between Saul and David, with Saul's anger, jealousy, and David's greater success and popularity, all further fueled by the song. The occasion is the moment after the hero's *aristeia*, as at *Il.* 7.314 ff, and 22.391 ff. Again the enemy is the Philistines, most Greek of OT peoples. Elsewhere, David himself also performs music and song, much as Akhilleus:

> And whenever an evil spirit from God came upon Saul, David would take his lyre and play it, so that relief would come to Saul. (1 Sam 16:23)

> He [Saul] fell into a frenzy in the house, and David played the lyre to him as he had done before. (1 Sam 18:10)

These passages link David's singing with our previous mythic subgenre. Both Akhilleus and David are depicted as performers of what is no doubt heroic saga, while they themselves serve as the central hero of an epic tradition. Akhilleus is not depicted as playing before Agamemnon, but the delegation he sends briefly hears Akhilleus play a song, right after Agamemnon complains about being deluded by Ate (9.18, 115, 116, 119).

The OT parallels reveal Dream, Eris, and Ate are all instances of the same subgenre, an "evil spirit" sent by god to delude the king who has lost divine favor — Agamemnon, Ahab, and Saul. The *Iliad*'s association of Agamemnon's anger with his poor judgment (see the motif in chapter 4, *3. Agamemnon exercises reckless judgment* (ate) *against the best of the Akhaians*) again parallels OT myth's depiction of Saul, having fits when the Evil Spirit comes and raging at David.

⌒

6. The great hero and his exceptional qualities

The first five subgenres of myth we have considered are those which set the plot of the *Iliad* in motion over books 1–2. These have more to do with decision making than fighting and are less involved with the typical subject matter of a myth depicting warriors at war. We now turn to those mythic subgenres associated with heroic actions, the accomplishments, motivations, and predicaments of the central hero. As before, OT myth, especially Joshua– 2 Chronicles, is rich in parallels for most of the specific subgenres of myth that compose the heroic substance of the *Iliad*'s plot.

a. The hero's personal relationship with the deity

Central to heroic Greek myth is the hero's personal relationship with the gods. In Homeric epic a hero's personal relationship with Athena in particular is key to his greatness.[29] Akhilleus enjoys special relationships with several gods—Athena, Thetis, and Zeus—and has the unwavering support of Hera and Poseidon. His face-to-face meetings with Athena (1.197 ff, 19.352 ff, 21.284 ff; cf. 18.203 ff) and Thetis (1.360–428, 18.70–148, 19.4– 39, when she places *menos* in him, a role normally taken by Athena) are relatively unique in the *Iliad*. The only other Greek hero who meets face-to-face with an undisguised Athena is Diomedes (5.793 ff), one of the two (with Aias) successful stand-ins for Akhilleus as "best of the Akhaians." The first words spoken to Akhilleus in the *Iliad* are "Akhilleus, dear to Zeus" (1.74). This is no mere honorific. Though Zeus never meets with Akhilleus in person, he honors his request, going to great lengths to cause harm to the Greeks by so doing. The principal narrative pattern outlined in chapter 1 points to his special relation to deity: *3. A god places* μένος *in him as he goes to face the Trojans.*

It is much the same in OT myth. Yahweh marks his special relationship with a chosen hero through his singular favor, as he addresses Joshua before the conquest of Canaan: "As long as you live no one will be able to stand against you: as I was with Moses, so shall I be with you; I shall not fail you or forsake you" (Josh 1:5). As Boling (1982:123) notes, the formulaic phrase "Yahweh is with you" derives from the older epic sources on which the Deuteronomic authors draw. We might compare Poseidon's speech (in the presence of Athena) to Akhilleus during his fight with the river:

Do not be afraid, son of Peleus, nor be so anxious,
such are we two of the gods who stand beside you to help you

. . . .

We grant you the winning of glory.

(*Il.* 21.288–89, 297)

Zeus does not make such direct personal appearances to the hero, in neither
the *Iliad* nor the *Odyssey*, much as Yahweh usually has an angel meet with
the hero. Joshua not only enjoys the support of Yahweh, as Akhilleus does
Zeus, but a rough equivalent of Athena also appears to him as he is about
to besiege Jericho: "When Joshua was near Jericho he looked up and saw
a man standing in front of him with a drawn sword in his hand. Joshua
approached him and asked, 'Are you for us or for our enemies?' The man
replied, 'Neither! I am here as captain of the army of the Lord'" (Josh 5:13–
14). Perhaps the climactic OT example is the favor Yahweh shows Joshua
after he defeats the Amorite kings at Gibeon (Josh 10:12–14).

As in the *aristeiai* of Diomedes and Akhilleus, the OT depicts fighting by
the gods to parallel the hero's great deeds, a further sign of his special rela-
tion with the gods. Of Joshua's meeting, Miller (131) notes, "the very pres-
ence of this figure declared that the ensuing conquest was sacral and that
Israel's army would be led by Yahweh's divine army." Athena suggests this
function when serving as Diomedes' chariot driver (5.837–57), and when
she appears to Akhilleus at *Il.* 19.341–56 (cf. the angel's appearances to
Elijah in 1 Kings 19). Chapter 1 noted how fighting between gods paral-
lels the hero's *aristeia: 6. The best of the Akhaians' exploits are accompanied by a
Greek-partisan god's defeat of a Trojan-partisan god.* The closest OT parallel is
the account in Judges 4–5 of the fight between the Israelites and Sisera, a
Canaanite general, by the waters of Megiddo:

The stars fought from heaven,
the stars in their courses fought against Sisera.
The torrent of Kishon swept him away,
the torrent barred his flight, the torrent of Kishon.

(Judg 5:20–21)

Perhaps the most intriguing of heroic OT passages is the obscure and el-
liptic mention of Shamgar: "After Ehud there was Shamgar, *son of Anath*. He
killed 600 Philistines with an ox-goad, and he too delivered Israel." (Judg
3:31; cf. Judg 5:6). Although this is one of the OT's few mentions of Anat,
a Canaanite war goddess, there is no consensus as to what "son of Anath"
means. Archaeological evidence suggests the phrase implies membership

in a special warrior group (Shupak 517–25). My own view is that it was originally meant literally, a remnant from a time when Israelites still worshiped the goddess (as they continued to worship Anat's brother Baal, her father, El, and his wife, Asherah), whose cult center, Anathoth (Josh 21:18, 1 Kings 2:26, etc.), was only a few miles from later Jerusalem. Shamgar as son of the war goddess Anat would thus parallel how some heroes fighting at Troy are the sons of gods (Akhilleus, Sarpedon, Aineias). In Joshua's encounter with the angel, OT myth suggests parallels for Athena's relation with the Homeric hero, while Shamgar has as a mother the deity who serves as counterpart to Athena herself.

Other key OT examples of the hero's special relation with deity include the myths of Gideon, Othniel, and Samson. Gideon's myth includes the same type-scene of an angel reassuring the hero: "The angel of the Lord appeared to him and said, 'You are a brave man, the Lord is with you . . . Go and use this strength of yours to free Israel from the Midianites'" (Judg 6:12–14). This again calls to mind Athena's and Poseidon's reassuring Akhilleus during his fight with the river Xanthos (*Il.* 21.284–98). Gideon's real, or earlier, name is Jerubaal, which literally means, "May Baal take action." As the *Oxford Study Bible* (Suggs et al. 254) notes, the name would originally have belonged to "a worshipper of Baal not a foe" (see M. Smith 1990: 11–13). As with "Shamgar, son of Anath," the Gideon/Jerubaal myth seems to derive from when the Israelites were polytheistic and worshiped the Canaanite pantheon (discussed in chapter 7) or was borrowed from a non-Israelite tradition that later made him into a worshiper of Yahweh. Judges 7 has further episodes of Yahweh's special relation with Gideon/ Jerubaal (cf. 1 Sam 23:1–5).

A god speaking on the hero's behalf at a divine council is perhaps the most important sign of the hero's special relationship with god. The *Iliad* uses this motif most importantly when Thetis speaks with Zeus in book 1, though their conversation suggests a more intimate exchange than is typical for a divine council. Thetis gets Zeus to validate Akhilleus' wish, prompting books 2–17 of the *Iliad*. The *Iliad* has this defining scene near the end of book 1 (1.495–531), whereas the *Odyssey*, in Athena's complaint to Zeus about how Odysseus' suffers, has it at the beginning of the epic (1.45–95). In *Gilgamesh*, Shamash maintains a similar relationship with the hero and speaks on his behalf at divine councils. Similarly, in the *Aqhat*, Baal speaks with El on behalf of the protagonist.

In a further sign of his special relationship, an immortal feeds the hero in a crucial encounter. In the *Iliad*, when Akhilleus refuses to eat until he has avenged Patroklos, Athena comes to him and instills him with nectar and ambrosia for his coming *aristeia* (*Il.* 19.347–56). Elijah, an OT prophet depicted in ways typical of heroic myth, is fed and kept alive by an angel during his strife with Ahab:

> While he slept, an angel touched him and said, "Rise and eat." He looked, and there at his head was a cake baked on hot stones, and a pitcher of water. He ate and drank and lay down again. The angel of the Lord came again and touched him a second time, saying "Rise and eat; the journey is too much for you." He rose and ate and drank and, sustained by this food, he went on for 40 days and 40 nights to Horeb, the mount of God. (1 Kings 19:5–8)

As before, the Homeric Athena serves functions for which OT myths employ an angel.

b. The hero's great fame

When Akhilleus tells the delegation Thetis' prophecy, he uses the phrase, "imperishable fame," κλέος ἄφθιτον (9.413). A motif in chapter 1 discussed how the best of the Akhaians pursues fame: *4. Thus inspired, he begins an aristeia, through which he will earn fame.* Hektor voices similar concerns in his remarks about fame when he sets the terms for the duel at *Il.* 7.80–91. Although Homerists have made much of the notion that epic's concern with "heroic fame" may be inherited from Indo-European culture,[30] it is clear that non-Indo-European peoples had very similar notions. Gilgamesh tells Enkidu, before facing Humbaba, "If I should fall, I shall have won fame. People will say, Gilgamesh grappled in combat with ferocious Humbaba."[31] This is essentially Hektor's position in the *Iliad*—that his heroic fame, even if he is slain by Akhilleus, is more important to him than his family. Some aspects of the economy of heroic fame in the *Iliad* may derive from Near Eastern traditions and not necessarily reflect Indo-European derivation.

OT myth also depicts concern for the hero's great fame, although in many contexts the preferred position is that heroic fame is more proper for Yahweh, because of *his* great deeds, and less a proper concern for a mortal hero. Genesis briefly suggests a whole heroic age, much as Hesiod's two bronze Ages (*Works and Days* 143–73): "When the sons of the gods had intercourse with the daughters of mortals and children were born to them, the Nephilim were on the earth; they were heroes of old, people of renown" (Gen 6:4). Much as in Hesiod, a divine wrath and apocalypse ends this race. In the heroic myths about the conquest of Canaan and battles with the Philistines, however, the heroic ethos and its concern for fame reemerges. We have seen David depicted as the subject of heroic lays while alive and himself singing epic material. OT myth continues a concern for heroic fame in

Joshua, Gideon, and Samson, who sings of his *own* heroic exploits against the Philistines: "With the jaw-bone of a donkey I have flayed them like donkeys; with the jaw-bone of a donkey I have slain a thousand men" (Judg 15:16). Joshua also earns heroic fame: "The Lord was with Joshua, and his fame spread throughout the country" (Josh 6:27). After David is installed as king, Yahweh tells his prophet Nathan to tell him, "I shall bring you fame like the fame of the great ones of the earth" (2 Sam 7:9). David himself composes a heroic lay for Saul and Jonathan ("How are the warriors fallen on the field of battle!" 2 Sam 1:17–27), conferring eternal fame upon them (cf. 2 Sam 3:33–34). OT myth's concern with heroic fame is most frequent in contexts in which the Israelites battle the Philistines. We earlier noted Saul's memorial for himself (1 Sam 15:12), which finds parallels in Hektor's comments on setting up a funeral mound for a slain Akhaian to promote his own fame (*Il.* 7.86–91); the pine memorial Gilgamesh takes from Humbaba's trees (end of tablet 5); and Akhilleus' funeral mound, ostensibly for Patroklos. In one OT passage (Isa 56:5), Yahweh confers eternal fame upon mortals, but for reasons of faith rather than heroic deeds: "I shall give them everlasting renown; an imperishable name."

c. The great hero's aristeia

The greatest single accomplishment of the hero, in the *Iliad*, is his *aristeia*, during which he, inspired by god, slays a great number of the enemy. Much of Joshua and Judges is organized around the notion of an *aristeia* (though the Bible does not use the Greek term), as well as parts of 1 and 2 Samuel and 1 and 2 Chronicles. Typically, the great hero "delivers" his people from danger, in both traditions, through an *aristeia*. The biggest difference in OT instances of this subgenre is the scarcity of duels, which are confined to clashes between the Israelites and the Philistines. Thus while many sections of Joshua and Judges could be called *aristeiai*, they lack this feature, which typifies a Homeric *aristeia*. That difference aside, Joshua's exploits in Joshua 10 and those of Othniel in Judg 3:10, Jephthah in Judg 11:29–33, and Samson in Judg 14:19, can all be seen as *aristeiai*.

As in the *Iliad*, an *aristeia* in the OT typically begins with God inspiring the hero to perform exceptionally. To depict this, the *Iliad* has the *menos* passages (as at *Il.* 5.2), in which a deity, usually Athena, instills *menos* ("spirit," "courage") in a hero, resulting in his *aristeia*. The OT equivalent includes multiple examples: "The spirit of the Lord came upon him [Othniel] . . . He took the field, and the Lord delivered King Cushan-rishathaim of Aram into his hands" (Judg 3:10); "Then the spirit of the Lord came upon Jephthah . . . Jephthah made this vow to the Lord: 'If you will deliver the Ammonites into my hands, then the first creature that comes out of the door of my house to meet me when I return safely shall be the Lord's; I shall offer that as a whole offering'" (Judg 11:29–31; cf. Judg 14:6, when Samson slays a lion bare-handed, and Judg 15:14–15, when he slays a thousand Philistines). Brief passages in 2 Samuel and 1 Chronicles summarize other such incidents (2 Sam 23:8, 18, where Abishai slays 300; 1 Chron 11:11, where Jashobeam also slays 300), which contain enumerated slayings of enemy warriors in even greater numbers (e.g., 10,000 at Judg 3:29, led by Ehud) than the *Iliad* assigns Akhilleus or Diomedes in their *aristeiai*.[32]

Often the great hero has a special weapon with an unusual history of ownership. In OT myth this is particularly true of David, who appropriates the great sword of Goliath, the Philistine, after slaying him (1 Sam 21:8–9). Other OT heroes, both Israelite and enemy, occasionally are so depicted, in formulaic terms ("whose spear had a shaft like a weaver's beam," 2 Sam 21:19; 1 Chron 11:23) that are close equivalents of the epithets and formulas that compose Homeric epic and are the hallmark of an inherited oral epic tradition.[33] In the *Iliad* and *Odyssey* this is especially true of Akhilleus and Odysseus, who use special weapons about which the poems provide extensive accounts (*Il.* 19.387–91; cf. 16.139–44; *Od.* 21.11–41).

The great hero signals his prowess as a warrior in pivotal duels with enemy champions. Such duels form the high style of heroic myth, the climax of a Homeric *aristeia*. The most important duels decide an entire conflict, as that of Paris and Menelaus in *Iliad* 3 is explicitly supposed to do (but does not), and as that of Hektor and Akhilleus implicitly does. All but one of the OT's duels involve the Philistines, the best known of which is David and Goliath (1 Sam 17).[34] Their encounter is built entirely out of traditional elements that occur in the *Iliad*'s three most important duels, as commentators have noted (de Vaux 24–28; Niditch 91, 96, 105). We can deduce a common sequence of motifs underlying the three Iliadic duels and the duel of David and Goliath (see also West 1997: 214, 370, 376). The David and Goliath narrative particularly resembles Hektor's duel with Aias in book 7, but also shares features with the duels of Paris and Menelaus (book 3), and Hektor and Akhilleus (book 22).[35]

A. The enemy champion initiates the duel, boasting that he will fight any opponent and thereby decide a larger conflict between two warring peoples

The Philistine Goliath parallels Hektor in recklessly initiating a contest that he will lose, while the Israelites parallel the Greeks, as having the more rightful cause.

I am the Philistine champion and you are Saul's men. Choose your man to meet me. . . . Here and now, I challenge the ranks of Israel. Get me a man, and we will fight it out. (1 Sam 17:8–10)

> For the best of the Panakhaians are here among you,
> whomever of these whose heart bids him to come forth to fight me,
> let him come forth to be the champion against bright Hektor.
> $(Il.\ 7.73–75)^{36}$

The terms used to designate the hero who participates in the duel are quite parallel. De Vaux (124) defines the Hebrew phrase, *ish habbenayim*, usually translated as "champion," as "a man who steps out to fight between the two battle lines . . . one who enters into single combat between two armies drawn up in line of battle . . . one who takes part in a fight between two . . . the champion in a single combat." "Champion" (*ish habbenayim*), then, functions as a close equivalent of Homeric *promakhos*, and its short form *promos*, the generic term for a champion in Homeric epic,[37] used of Hektor in book 7 and Paris in book 3 (προμάχιζεν Ἀλέξανδρος: *Il.* 3.16).

A1. The enemy's challenge contains an "if clause" which posits the terms should the opponent win

> If he should take my life with the thin-edged bronze,
> having stripped my armor let him carry it to the hollow ships,
> but give back my body to be taken home again.
> $(Il.\ 7.77–79)$

If he defeats and kills me in fair fight, we shall become your slaves. (1 Sam 17:9)

B. There is a description of both combatants' armor

Samson's helmet, breastplate, greaves, dagger, shield, and spear are described (1 Sam 17:5–7), to which a sword is added (but not mentioned until 17:51). Other than the dagger, these are the same items found in a Homeric arming scene (greaves, corselet, sword, shield, helmet, spear; see chapters 1, 2, and 3). The final item, receiving the greatest elaboration in both traditions, is the spear. The Homeric order possibly ends with spear because of the climactic role Akhilleus' spear plays in wounding Hektor: *16. In the duel's climax, the best of the Akhaians wounds Hektor in the neck with his spear* (see chapter 1). The word the OT uses of Goliath's helmet, *koba*, "is a non-Semitic word, and thought by some to be of Indo-European origin" (McCarter 1985: 292).

Because the *Iliad* has already given us a full arming scene for Paris (3.330–38) and lengthy depictions of the Greeks arming themselves en masse on the same day as Hektor's duel with Aias, Hektor does not have an arming scene here. Aias receives a slightly adumbrated arming scene,[38] focusing mainly on his shield and menacing gait. Hindson (154) compares the description of the armed Aias (*Il.* 7.206–24) with the account of Goliath (1 Sam 17:5–7, 38–40, 45). Stager (169) compares Goliath's armor with that depicted on the Mycenaean Warrior Vase.

C. The duel will decide the larger conflict between the two peoples

This is quite explicit in the case of Goliath, Paris' duel with Menelaos, implicit in Hektor's with Akhilleus (*Il.* 3.70–75, 90–94; cf. 22.410–11). Goliath's explicit enunciation of the motif suggests a context like the end of the Trojan War: "If he defeats and kills me in fair fight, we shall become your slaves; but if I vanquish and kill him, you will be our slaves and serve us" (1 Sam 17:9).

D. All of the hero's own people (Israelites, Greeks) are afraid to respond

When Saul and the Israelites heard what the Philistine said, they were all shaken and deeply afraid. (1 Sam 17:11)

When the Israelites saw the man they fell back before him in fear. (1 Sam 17:24)

So he [Hektor] spoke, and all of them stayed stricken to silence
in shame of refusing him, and in fear to take up his challenge.
(*Il.* 7.92–93)

E. The hero (David/Aias) answers the challenge

The hero distinguishes himself in his eagerness to respond to the enemy's challenge. David boldly volunteers, "Let no one lose heart! I shall go and fight this Philistine" (1 Sam 17:32), whereas Aias is chosen out of nine volunteers (*Il.* 7.161–69), which would be understood as an expression of the gods' will:

Friends, look, the lot is mine, and I myself rejoice
in my heart, since I think I will prevail over brilliant Hektor.
(*Il.* 7.191–92)

F. The hero makes his own vaunt, claiming god(s) on his side

This motif is more polemical in the OT narrative but is nonetheless present in the *Iliad*. In an oft-repeated motif, OT narratives seek to demonstrate Yahweh's supremacy over other gods. Hence David's victory here over Goliath implies the same, as Hindson (23–24) notes: "The idea of battle by 'championship' suggested to Israel by Goliath was of Aegean origin and implied that whichever had the strongest god would win the contest and any further battle would be unnecessary for the winner would be obvious. This explains why the Philistines fled when Goliath fell." David declares in advance that his victory will signify exactly this: "You have come against me with sword and spear and dagger, but I come against you in the name of the Lord of Hosts, the God of the ranks of Israel which you have defied." (1 Sam 17:45). Although in the *Iliad* both sides worship the same group of gods, individual gods fight against one another (as discussed in chapter 6), and Greek-partisan gods defeat Trojan-partisan deities, particularly in Athena's defeats of Ares (5.799–863, 21.391–415; cf. Apollo's desertion of Hektor, 22.213). Aias' vaunt, however, cannot mention the gods' partisanship because Athena and Apollo have just agreed not to interfere in the duel (7.17–43), opposite their involvement in book 22.

> But come, while I don my armor of war,
> you all pray to Lord Zeus, the son of Kronos,
> each of you in silence, that the Trojans not hear;
> or openly out loud, since we fear no one,
> for no eager man will force me in pursuit unwilling.
>
> (*Il.* 7.193–97)

> Hektor, now you will clearly see, one on one,
> of what sort are the best/bravest [ἀριστῆες] among the Danaans
> · ·
> for such are we who will stand up against you;
> and we are many; but start the fight and the battle.
>
> (*Il.* 7.226–32)

F1. The hero vows to leave his slain opponent's corpse for the birds and dogs

David's adherence to this traditional motif is startling:

> The Lord will put you into my power this day; I shall strike you down and cut your head off and leave your carcass and the carcasses of the Philistines to the birds and the wild beasts. (1 Sam 17:46)

Come, I shall give your flesh to the birds and beasts. (1 Sam 17:44)

The *Iliad* sounds this motif as a general theme ("the anger of Peleus' son, Akhilleus . . . which . . . gave their bodies to the delicate feasting of dogs, of all birds," *Il*. 1.1–5), but the climactic statement is reserved for the duel between Hektor and Akhilleus:

> I have unstrung your knees; therefore the hounds and birds
> shall rip you disgracefully.
>
> (*Il*. 22.335–36; cf. 22.354)

G. The hero easily defeats the enemy champion, knocking him to the ground with a stone

In both traditions the disparity between the lengthy preliminaries and the surprisingly brief encounter is anticlimactic. Goliath never gets off a blow, never sees his defeat coming, as David slings a stone into his forehead, mortally wounding him (1 Sam 17:49–50). The episode minimizes the size of the stone, thereby maximizing Yahweh's agency. The duel between Hektor and Aias is also short. The participants quickly exchange spear throws, spear thrusts, and hurl stones. In each case Aias' response is more powerful and more threatening. Aias' toss of a huge stone (7.268), the more traditional form of the motif, knocks Hektor to the ground, so that Apollo has to help him to his feet (7.270–72).

H. The enemy champion is defeated by a neck wound

After knocking Goliath down, David cuts his head off with the Philistine's own sword (1 Sam 17:51). In the *Iliad*, Aias wounds Hektor in the neck with his spear (7.262). Though not a mortal wound, as noted in chapter 1, the incident anticipates Akhilleus' later lethal wounding of Hektor in the neck by spear (22.327). Menelaos defeats Paris by clenching his chinstrap around his throat (3.371–72; see chapter 2). Goliath's name may reflect the centrality of the throat wound in these traditions. McCarter (1985: 285) notes a variant from the Septuagint, which he thinks preserves the more likely original reading: "Then if he attacked me, I would grab him by his *throat*, knock him down, and kill him," where most OT texts have "beard" in place of "throat."[39] Here David is comparing slaying Goliath to slaying a lion or bear, in which "throat" would make a better parallel than beard, applicable to both animals, and to Goliath. While there is no consensus on a derivation for Goliath's name, if the Philistines are an Indo-European people, possibly even Mycenaean Greeks, his name may reflect this. A posited Indo-European root could work and, if correct, suggests wordplay in the OT account: *gwel-*(3), with the basic meaning of "swallow," for verbal, "throat," for nominal derivatives, the same root from which "gullet" derives (Watkins 234). "Goliath," if accurately rendering a Philistine name, may derive from this root.[40]

H1. *The victorious hero commits an atrocity*

As noted, David proceeds to decapitate Goliath. Diomedes does this to Dolon (*Il.* 10.455–57). In Hektor's duel with Aias the combatants are prevented from going further, but Hektor himself attempts to decapitate Patroklos (17.126). After Akhilleus slays Hektor, he commits numerous atrocities on the corpse (22.395–405, 463–65) but stops short of decapitation.

I. *The enemy troops are disheartened at their champion's defeat*

In the OT account, "When the Philistines saw the fate of their champion, they turned and fled" (1 Sam 17:51). The circumstances of Hektor's duels with Aias and Akhilleus do not allow for this (in the former a truce is in effect, in the latter all other Trojans are safely in the city). But shortly before Hektor faces Akhilleus, the motif occurs when Akhilleus defeats the Lykian champion, Asteropaios,

> But he [Akhilleus] went after the horse-driving Paionians,
> who had fled in panic by the eddying river
> when they had seen their greatest man [ἄριστον] in the fierce battle
> subdued by force by the sword and the hands of Akhilleus.
>
> (*Il.* 21.205–8)

In a final parallel, while both duels are composed of traditional motifs, the motifs are employed in ways that prompt similar criticisms. Chapter 1 noted criticisms directed at book 7 — that the duel is redundant coming so soon after book 3's duel between Paris and Menelaus.[41] Similar questions haunt David's duel with Goliath (Yadin 373–95). 2 Sam 21:19 asserts that another hero, Elhanan, slew Goliath. This has led some scholars to assume, as McCarter (1985: 291), that "certain details of the Elhanan tradition have attached themselves artificially to an unrelated story of a duel of David's own."[42] Another possibility, according to McCarter (ibid.) is that an earlier version of the duel had no Goliath but an anonymous Philistine opponent: "[M]ost scholars . . . now assume that he was anonymous in the original version of the story. The name [Goliath] was imported from 2 Sam 21:19" (cf. de Vaux 122 n. 1). The duel is interrupted by a lengthy digression (1 Sam 17:12–30) about David that contradicts episodes before and after in its depiction of David's relation with Saul. McCarter (1985: 303) concludes that the digression "originally existed as an independent narrative."[43]

OT myth contains other heroic duels, though not depicted at length or in as much detail as David's with Goliath. Most involve David's associates (2 Sam 21:15–22, 23:8–39; cf. 1 Chron 11:10–41), several of whom are depicted as full-scale heroes, winning heroic fame, taking part in duels with opposing champions, and having *aristeiai*.[44] The key difference with the *Iliad*'s heroic narratives is length and development. In the *Iliad* each standard motif may be expanded and developed into a lengthy episode, whereas OT myths tend to state motifs without development or elaboration. The opponents of David's heroes are almost always Philistines (de Vaux 126–27), said to be descended from the Rephaim (see esp. 2 Sam 21:16–22), a race of legendary giants.

A "heroic three" (2 Sam 23:8, 16, 17) are mentioned, Jeshbaal/Ishbosheth, Eleazar, and Shammah, heroes in David's service. The first, Jeshbaal/Ishbosheth, "brandished his spear over eight hundred, all slain at one time" (2 Sam 23:8), an *aristeia* without elaboration. As with Gideon/Jerubaal, Jeshbaal is named for the Canaanite god, Baal. Later writers changed his name to Ishbosheth, to obscure the connection with an earlier polytheistic tradition.[45] Eleazar also fought against the Philistines and "rained blows on the Philistines until, from sheer weariness, his hand stuck to his sword" (2 Sam 23:10), again suggesting an *aristeia*, in capsule form. Shammah (2 Sam 23:11–12) also fought against the Philistines and again can be credited with an *aristeia*. A group of thirty heroes associated with David are also mentioned (2 Sam 23:13, 18, 19, 22, 23), approaching the *Iliad*'s notion of a gathering of heroes. Benaiah is described at greatest length, "a hero of many exploits. It was he who slew the two champions of Moab, and who once went down into a pit and killed a lion on a snowy day" (2 Sam 23:20). In facing "champions" Benaiah is victorious in the kind of duel as between Hektor and Aias, and David and Goliath, and has a similar epic fame ("He was more famous than the rest of the thirty," 2 Sam 23:23).[46]

As in the *Iliad*, OT heroic duels are articulated by means of formulas, stock repeated elements, suggesting origins in an oral tradition. Conflict with the Philistines brings out those heroic motifs most relevant to the *Iliad*. The Israelite hero is undaunted when facing the enemy: "He stood his ground" (2 Sam 23:10, 12; 1 Chron 11:14—all fights against Philistines). David fights not only against the Philistines but, for a time, *with* them as well (1 Sam 21:10 ff), perhaps learning their heroic culture. Several other formulas involve spears. The spear of the great enemy hero is exceptional: "spear as big as the beam of a loom" (1 Chron 11:23); "whose spear had a shaft like a weaver's beam" (1 Sam 17:7, 21:19; 1 Chron 20:5, describing Lahmi, Goliath's brother). Three of the four enemy heroes are Philistines, the fourth, Egyptian. The weight of the spear may be specified: "and its head which was of iron, weighted 600 shekels" (1 Sam 17:7); "whose bronze spear weighted 300 shekels" (2 Sam 21:16). The great Israelite hero typically wields his spear in an extraordinary manner, reminiscent of an Iliadic *aristeia*—for example, "[Abishai] it was who brandished his spear over three hundred dead" (2 Sam 23:18; 1 Chron 11:20), and Jashobeam "who brandished his spear over 300 men" (1 Chron 11:11).

7. The hero as the ethical man who has unjustly suffered wrongs

A key issue that myths address is the existence of undeserved suffering on the part of *moral* men. How can it be, if the gods are just, that a man who acts as he should, suffers catastrophic reversals of fortune? OT myth addresses this dilemma in the book of Job. As Moscati (44–45, 84–85, 132–33, 258) convincingly demonstrates, the "unjust sufferings of the righteous man" is a well-attested Near Eastern subgenre of myth, extant in several different cultures (Sumerian, Akkadian, Babylonian, and Egyptian, in addition to OT myth).[47] The authors of the book of Job have been influenced by these or other earlier instances of this subgenre (see Pope lvi–lxxi; Gable et al. 57–59). When Agamemnon sends a delegation to attempt to reason with the estranged hero in book 9, the *Iliad* turns to this traditional subgenre of myth to portray Akhilleus, slightly modifying the subgenre to accommodate it within the larger framework of the Trojan War. The protagonist of the *Sumerian Wisdom Text: Man and His God* suggests Akhilleus' view of Agamemnon in book 9: "The man of deceit has conspired against me" (Pritchard, 590.37).

There are other generic links between the book of Job and the *Iliad*. Job suggests epic affinities by opening with a divine council, that most epic of type-scenes.[48] The two councils in Job are quite like that which opens the *Odyssey*. The principal deity opens the council, which then becomes a two-character discussion about the protagonist (*Od.* 1.26–95; Job 1:6–12, 2:1–6): "The day came when the members of the court of heaven took their places in the presence of the Lord, and the Adversary, Satan, was there among them" (Job 1:6). As in *Gilgamesh*, the *Aqhat*, the *Iliad*, and the *Odyssey*, the divine council features the principal god discussing the fate and fortunes of the protagonist with another deity. Yahweh himself makes Job the topic of conversation, and, much as Zeus cedes to Athena's wishes in the *Odyssey* (*Od.* 1.84–95), he gives Satan power to do as he pleases to affect the protagonist. Their discussion, as well as Satan's intent, also suggests the frictions between Zeus and Hera in the *Iliad*.[49] Satan hopes to undermine Yahweh and show that he is wrong or capable of error, as Hera is diametrically opposed to Zeus throughout the *Iliad*.

The bulk of *Iliad* 9 and Job present us with a heretofore prosperous, ethical man who, having met with adversity, is now brooding and isolated. As earlier noted, as the hero with a special relation with god, Akhilleus is a moral man by the standards of his culture (evident in his propitiation of Apollo). Pope (xvi), referring to the descriptions of Job as "blameless and upright" (1.1) and "the greatest man in all the East" (1.2), notes "the Prologue introduces the hero as a man of exemplary rectitude and piety." Both Job and Akhilleus are pious, ethical men, leaders in their communities, who have suffered what appear to be capricious reversals beyond their comprehension. There is a difference in degree: Job has been shaken more by his misfortune. But the biggest difference between Job and *Iliad* 9 is the identity of the character who has wronged the ethical man. For Akhilleus, this is Agamemnon. For Job, unaware of the role of Satan, who suggests parallels with Ate in deluding Agamemnon, it is Yahweh himself against whom he rails. This key difference is a large one and confers upon the book of Job much of its theological depth and complexity. Job's predicament is therefore more difficult, his tests more severe, than Akhilleus'. Book 9 of the *Iliad*, by contrast, contents itself with exploring ethical behavior largely between mortals, set within a larger context of a heroic siege myth. But Job, though a self-contained myth, alludes to siege myth in Job's figurative comparison of his critics to invading warriors, "they raise their siege-ramps against me; to destroy me they tear down my crumbling defences, and scramble up against me unhindered; they burst in as through a gaping breach" (Job 30:12–14).[50]

In each myth a delegation of three associates comes to the estranged protagonist,[51] to try to talk him out of his present isolation, to return to the community to which he belongs. The delegations that visit them commiserate, up to a point, but are critical of the protagonists' perceived aloofness. The speeches and advice which Odysseus, Phoinix, and Aias make to Akhilleus suggest parallels with those of Eliphaz, Bildad, and Zophar to Job. In each myth, Akhilleus and Job make speeches in response to each of the three speakers of the delegation. The first speaker of each delegation warns the ethical man of the dangers of giving too free a rein to his angry mood. Eliphaz thus advises Job, "Fools are destroyed by their own angry passion, /

and the end of childish resentment is death" (Job 5:2). Odysseus, first to speak in his delegation, similarly warns that Peleus himself must have told Akhilleus, "Keep your great-hearted spirit within your chest, for regard for others is better; and leave off ruinous strife!" (9.255–57).

Both delegations react similarly, frustrated when the protagonists reject their arguments and advice. In the *Iliad* such sentiments are confined to Aias, who, to increase the force of his criticism, directs his comments to Odysseus, snubbing Akhilleus:

> For Akhilleus
> has made his great-hearted spirit savage [ἄγριον] in his chest,
> hard-hearted [σχέτλιος], nor does he care for his comrades' friendship.
> (9.628–30)

We can compare the exasperated complaints of Eliphaz: "Would a sensible person give vent to such hot-air arguments / or puff himself up with an east wind?" (15:2), and "and pour out such mouthfuls of words?" (15:13).[52] Bildal is even more direct, like Aias, in his frustration at Job's rejection of their arguments: "What do you mean by treating us as no more than cattle?" (18:3).

For his part, Job, much like Akhilleus, keeps returning to a perceived lack of respect. He complains to Bildad of mistreatment by his friends, "How long will you grieve me and crush me with words? You have insulted me now a dozen times and shamelessly wronged me" (19:2–3). He complains further of mistreatment by Yahweh:

> he has stripped me of all honor
> and taken the crown from my head.
> (Job 19:9)

Akhilleus' central complaint, directed at Agamemnon, expresses a rough parallel, that the latter has dishonored him:

> the coward and the brave man are held in the same honor;
> the shiftless man and he who toiled hard die in the same way.
> (*Il.* 9.319–20)

Earlier, both Akhilleus and Nestor are even more explicit: "He [Agamemnon] dishonored me (Akhilleus: 1.355–56), "You [Agamemnon] have dishonored . . . him (Akhilleus: 9.109–11).

Both protagonists express similar positions on the finality of death:

As a cloud breaks up and disperses,
so no one who goes down to Sheol ever comes back.

(Job 7:9–10)

But when a human being dies all his power vanishes;
he expires, and where is he then?
As the waters of a lake dwindle,
or as a river shrinks and runs dry,
so mortal man lies down, never to rise
until the very sky splits open.
If a man dies, can he live again?
He can never be roused from this sleep.

(Job 14:10–12)

but the soul of a man cannot return, neither seized as plunder,
nor taken by force, once it has gone past the fence of his teeth.

(*Il.* 9.408–9)

Job and Akhilleus are both confident that they are correct in their re-
lations with god. Akhilleus reiterates his rejection of Agamemnon's offer
and the honors that it suggests by asserting his conviction that Zeus already
honors him: "I think I am already honored in Zeus' ordinance" (9.608). Job
imagines a possible face-to-face meeting with Yahweh, "No; God himself
would never set his face against me. There in his court the upright are vin-
dicated, and I should win from my judge an outright acquittal" (23:6–7; cf.
"even now my witness is in heaven," 16:18; "What is the lot prescribed by
God above, the portion from the Almighty on high?" 31:2). Both the book of
Job, and Akhilleus in book 9, may be characterized more specifically as fol-
lows: *The hero, driven outside the norms of his society by his sufferings, is approached
by friends who try to counsel him, but he refuses to listen, and finds their offers insulting.*
Homeric epic has thus selected a common subgenre of myth, extant in many
Near Eastern traditions, to depict Akhilleus' alienation.[53] Ironically, Akhil-
leus' strife with Agamemnon, resulting in being deprived of Briseis, springs
from his own ethical behavior: *2b. The hero intervenes to check the god-sent plague.*

〜〜〜

CHAPTER SIX

Subgenres of Myth in the *Iliad* II

ἅζομαι· οὐδέ πη ἔστι κελαινεφέϊ Κρονίωνι
αἵματι καὶ λύθρῳ πεπαλαγμένον εὐχετάασθαι.

I am reverent; it is not right to pray to the black-clouded
son of Kronos when I am spattered with blood and gore.
—IL. 6.267–68

〜

8. Trojan misconduct

Far from framing its plot as a simplistic tale of good (Greeks) versus evil
(Trojans), the *Iliad* provokes considerable sympathy for such Trojan char-
acters as Andromakhe, Priam, and Hektor. So skillful at engaging our sym-
pathies is the poem that occasional readers fail to see the less sympathetic
traits with which the poem also colors the Trojans.[1] While the *Iliad* suggests
kindly qualities in many Trojans, it uses not only Paris but even Hektor as
examples of recklessness and arrogance, showing why the whole city, from
the perspective of a myth, has offended the gods and will be destroyed. To
depict Trojan misconduct, the *Iliad* employs the same subgenres of myth
as OT depictions of mortals' failings. The *Iliad* presents, as Schein (1997:
353) observes, "a consistent pattern in which the Trojans initiate not only
the battle but the war, as aggressors and transgressors who are morally re-
sponsible for their own ruin."

a. Previous Trojan wrongdoing: Laomedon and inherited guilt

As often in OT myth, the Trojans' difficulties begin at least a generation
earlier, in wrongdoing by Priam's father, Laomedon. Though figuring only
in the *Iliad*'s background, Laomedon nonetheless embodies a nexus of Tro-
jan treachery, thematic throughout the poem. Most important is the occa-
sion when he cheated and threatened violence against the gods themselves,

Poseidon and Apollo. In the *Iliad*'s brief, elliptic account, Poseidon notes (21.441–57; cf. 7.452–53) how he and Apollo worked for Laomedon for a year, Poseidon building the city walls, Apollo tending the flocks. When they finished, however, Laomedon refused to pay them, threatening to punish, torture, and sell them into slavery. The account omits details such as why the two gods were working for Laomedon and whether they had assumed human form. This same subgenre of myth, in which a god works for a mortal, also occurs in the story of Apollo sentenced to work for Admetos as punishment by Zeus (Euripides' *Alcestis*, 1–2, 6–8, which lies behind Iliadic accounts of Eumelos' excellent horses: *Il.* 2.763–67, 23.288–89). Admetos thus represents a positive form of the same subgenre of myth, a mortal who properly treats the god who is working for him and is then rewarded.[2] In its bare outlines, the myth resembles a theoxeny, in which the gods come to test mortals by appearing in disguise, as in Genesis 18–19; in *Odyssey* 1, with Athena's disguised appearance among the suitors; and in much of the second half of the *Odyssey*.[3] In Apollodorus' account, Apollo and Poseidon are in human guise, out to test Laomedon's arrogance (Ἀπόλλων γὰρ καὶ Ποσειδῶν τὴν Λαομέδοντος ὕβριν πειράσαι θέλοντες, εἰκασθέντες ἀνθρώποις II v 9). Laomedon's apparent threat to disfigure them (21.455) may imply that he thinks they are mortals. Although we cannot be certain of all the details that lie behind our account, the *Iliad*'s brief sketch resembles a negative theoxeny, in which mortals who offend the disguised god(s) will be punished.

Regardless of the form Poseidon and Apollo assumed, Laomedon is revealed as a liar and a cheat who breaks contracts, which, since contracts involve oaths sworn by the gods, reiterates his contempt for the gods. If he was aware that his workers were gods, his actions equate him with those eternally punished in Tartaros. Although this specific subgenre of myth is not attested in the OT, consider Yahweh's complaint about the king Jehoiakim, and his subsequent punishment:

> Woe betide him who builds his palace on unfairness
> and completes its roof-chambers with injustice,
> compelling his countrymen to work without payment,
> giving them no wage for their labour!
>
> . . . .
>
> He will be buried like a dead donkey,
> dragged along and flung out
> beyond the gates of Jerusalem.
>
> (Jer 22:13, 19)

Laomedon establishes the Trojans as breakers of sacred oaths, and prefigures their present-time breaking of sworn oaths in book 4 (discussed below). Such cheating is thematic on Laomedon's part. Tlepolemos and Sarpedon relate how Herakles came to Troy, and sacked it, to obtain Laomedon's prized horses, which the Trojan king had promised but then refused to give him (5.640–51; cf. 14.250–51, 15.26–29). There is again, no doubt, the breaking of an oath, sworn by the gods. Even worse, Laomedon was in Herakles' debt, since he had earlier defeated a sea monster that had threatened Troy (20.145–48). In cheating Herakles, he cheats the hero who had saved his daughter, Hesione, and his city.

Laomedon is also paradigmatic for the Trojans' imminent victimization and defeat. In a third incident to which the *Iliad* alludes, Ankhises steals some of Laomedon's famous horses (5.268–72). Thus, in two of the three episodes, Laomedon's horses, which are in some way central to, or even the secret of his reign (much as Aietes' possession of the Golden Fleece), are taken from him. When Herakles sacks Troy, he goes on to slay Laomedon and all of his sons, except Priam. The Trojans themselves, and their allies, are fully cognizant of Laomedon's wrongdoing, as Sarpedon concedes to Tlepolemos:

> Tlepolemos, truly, he [Herakles] destroyed sacred Ilion
> because of the foolishness of Laomedon, a haughty man,
> who rebuked with a nasty word one who had treated him well.
> (5.648–50)

In the loss of his horses, Laomedon thus prefigures both how Priam's fabulous possessions will be plundered by Agamemnon's Greeks, and how Priam himself, and his sons, will be slain at the hands of Greek heroes.

In Laomedon the *Iliad* personifies the ancestral wrongdoing of the Trojans. By the standards of ancient myth, his offenses against the gods may already be enough to doom the city. In his treachery and defeat, Laomedon implies a trajectory and a thematic cause and effect operative for the Trojans: break oaths, as they do in the present time of the poem (4.70 ff), and Troy will be sacked. As in OT myth, divine retribution for such offenses does not necessarily come quickly. As Lefkowitz (151) notes, "Because the gods can take a longer view than short-lived mortals, they are content to wait to administer their justice and to postpone revenge even for several generations." OT myth illustrates the same principle in Solomon. Because he participates in the worship of other gods, including "Ashtoreth, goddess of the Sidonians," Yahweh decides to take the kingdom away from him. But

Yahweh waits until after Solomon dies, and takes ten tribes of the kingdom away from his son, Rehoboam (1 Kings 11:34).

The example of Laomedon suggests that inherited guilt is operative in the *Iliad*. It is central to OT myth, as Yahweh explicitly articulates in Exodus:

> [I, God] one who punishes children and grandchildren to the third and fourth generation for the iniquity of their fathers. (Exod 34:7)

> For I, the Lord your God, am a jealous God, punishing the children for the sins of the parents to the third and fourth generation of those who reject me. (Exod 20:5)

Belief in inherited guilt is common in ancient cultures, offering a solution to the apparent injustice of why a good man might suffer, if he himself has committed no wrong: one of his ancestors did, and he is paying the penalty. Hesiod's *Works and Days* implies a belief in inherited guilt and ties it to the descendants of a man who has falsely sworn an oath (282–84; see West 1978: 140, 216–17). It is clear that Homeric epic presupposes the counterpart of inherited guilt, that a deity who aided a great hero is predisposed to aid the son of that hero, as Athena aids Diomedes in the *Iliad* (e.g., 5.800–813) and Telemakhos throughout the *Odyssey*. The *Iliad*'s use of Laomedon to figure collective Trojan wrongdoing thus implies the workings of inherited guilt, that his descendants will pay for his repeated offenses against the gods.

OT myths frequently depict Yahweh causing cities to be sacked if its citizens worship other gods. To do so involves breaking an oath. OT myth thus offers a figure parallel to Laomedon, Zedekiah, a king of Judah, whom Yahweh punishes for his oath breaking: "The Lord God says: As I live, he has made light of the oath sworn in my name and has violated the covenant he made with me. For this I shall bring retribution upon him. Because he has broken faith with me I shall throw my net over him, and he will be caught in the meshes; I shall carry him to Babylon and bring him to judgment there" (Ezek 17:19–20). Yahweh proceeds to pronounce judgment on Zedekiah for his oath breaking: "And you, impious and wicked ruler of Israel, your fate has come upon you in the hour of final punishment. . . . Ruin! Ruin! I shall bring about such ruin as never was" (Ezek 21:25–26). The Israelites are thematically depicted as subject to such punishments if they violate oaths. When Yahweh finds them worshiping Canaanite deities, he abandons them, handing them over to their enemies, for violating a covenant and sworn agreement: "In his anger the Lord made them the prey of bands of raiders and plunderers; he sold them into the power of their enemies around them, so that they could no longer stand against them" (Judg 2:14; cf. 2 Kings 17:20). In one passage, breaking oaths is prelude to apocalyptic desolation:

> People swear oaths and break them;
> they kill and rob and commit adultery;
> there is violence, one deed of blood after another;
> Therefore the land will be desolate
> and all who live in it will languish
> with the wild beasts and the birds of the air.
>
> (Hosea 4:2–3)

b. Paris: A man's desire for a foreign woman brings destruction on his people

In the *Iliad*'s more immediate past, Paris embodies recklessness and violation of sacred trusts, again offenses against the gods. In the myth of Paris' Judgment, briefly mentioned at 24.25–30, the *Iliad* offers an etiology for the divine wraths of Hera and Athena. Poseidon's opposition is explained by Laomedon's outrageous dealings with him, but Paris is directly responsible for offending the two powerful goddesses, to whom Troy and its people are now hateful (ἀπήχθετο). The *Iliad* refers to his choice among the three goddesses as his *ate* (24.28), his "delusion," and notes that he "insulted the goddesses" (νείκεσσε θεάς, 24.29) when they came to him.[4] The notion of Paris' "judgment" is itself ironic, since he is thematically depicted as incapable of prudent judgment (e.g., 3.440, 7.360).

Paris is the most ironic character in the *Iliad*. An ironic and parodic tone attends him in book 3, and his greatest feats occur in the parodic middle sequence (e.g., 11.506–7). His divine champion is Aphrodite, not Athena, as for Akhilleus, Odysseus, and Diomedes, or Apollo, as for Hektor. As such, his principal motivation is desire, or lust, graphically portrayed at the end of book 3, opposite the heroic fame sought by most of the poem's warriors. He is portrayed as seeing nothing wrong in this. Like the suitors in the *Odyssey* (see esp. *Od.* 21.288–310 and Louden 1999a: 39–40), Paris often makes statements intended as criticisms of others but which ironically describe himself. In one of the *Iliad*'s most subtle notes, he is said to be moved when a man who was his guest friend dies (13.660–61, discussed below), ironically suggesting he values hospitality. Typically a warrior makes ironic statements at the expense of another character, such as a warrior's boast over a fallen foe. Patroklos, for example, asserts that he did not know the Trojans were such expert acrobats as he watches a slain warrior fall to the ground (16.745–50). Paris, however, makes comments that redound upon himself. Earlier,

Paris wonders if the gods have not ruined the brains of the eminently sensible Antenor (7.360), when the same seems truer of Paris himself.

OT myth offers rich parallels for Paris' key action, obtaining Helen, and thereby bringing ruin on his own people. Perhaps closest is the account of Shechem's rape of Dinah in Genesis 34 (see Pitt-Rivers 146–61). Shechem, a Hivite prince, sees Dinah, Jacob's daughter, desires her, and rapes her. But feeling affection for her, he asks his father, Hamor, to arrange a marriage. When Hamor meets with Jacob, Jacob's sons learn what has happened and are angry. Hamor appeals to them, citing Shechem's love, offering not only to form an alliance between the two peoples, but to cede them land and pay any bride-price they wish.[5] Jacob's sons lie to Hamor and Shechem, saying they will allow the marriage, only if Hamor has all the males of his people circumcised. Agreeing, Hamor informs his people of the alliance, and his men agree to be circumcised. However, while the Hivites recover from circumcision, Dinah's brothers, Simeon and Levi enter the town, killing every male, including Hamor and Shechem, and reclaim Dinah. The revenge concludes with general plundering: "Jacob's other sons came in over the dead bodies and plundered the town which had brought dishonour on their sister. They seized flocks, cattle, donkeys, whatever was inside the town and outside in the open country; they carried off all the wealth, the women, and the children, and looted everything in the houses" (Gen 34:27–29). The narrative serves as a miniature *Iliad*, using a number of the same motifs found in the larger Trojan War saga (see Niditch 107).

Not only does the common motif underlie both, that stealing a woman from another people leads to war, but the roles of several main characters are quite similar. Shechem is the sensualist that Paris is, overwhelmed by desire, thinking little of the consequences of his act. He does attempt to make some amends, beyond what Paris offers in the *Iliad*. The fathers of the reckless men, Hamor and Priam, are quite similar. Hamor's generosity, magnanimity, and gracious conduct, all parallel Priam's chief positive qualities. These parallels suggest a certain naiveté in the Trojan patriarch, to which his other positive qualities may blind us. Hamor is perhaps too easily gulled into thinking all is well, as is the case of the Trojans when they accept the Horse, though outside of the *Iliad*. Dinah's brothers act much as the Greek brothers, Agamemnon and Menelaos, and those who had sworn oaths to aid Helen. The successful attack by Shechem's people also parallels the Greek victory in its use of deception and trickery, the ruse of circumcising the males, and Odysseus' wily strategy, the Trojan Horse.

The parallels between the story of Paris and Helen and OT myths thus suggest a specific subgenre of myth, *A man's desire for a woman outside his culture brings destruction on his own people*. Agamemnon, in his desire and improper retention of Khryseis, is also an instance of this type (under *2b. The hero intervenes to check the god-sent plague*). We earlier noted a further OT example of this subgenre, the account in Numbers 25 of the Israelite who marries a Midianite woman, bringing a divine wrath and plague on his people, and causing the death of 24,000, until Phineas rights things by slaying the offender. Pitt-Rivers (137–38) formulates a general description of the mythic type, operative throughout the OT: "[T]he violation of Yahweh's proscription of marriage alliance with foreign women does not pay; it is always followed sooner or later by disaster." Thus, to marry a foreign woman leads to a divine wrath: "Yahweh's injunctions to avoid entanglements with foreign women are plain: explicit in prescription and demonstrated by outcomes which are the result of divine anger." Paris provokes the divine wraths of Hera and Athena when he obtains Helen, since his doing so is a consequence of having chosen Aphrodite over them at the "Judgment." Solomon and Ahab (in his marriage to Jezebel) serve as additional instances in OT myth of the man who improperly marries outside of his people.

A further relevant OT myth is the Gibeah outrage, the shocking narrative in Judges 19–20 of a rape, followed by vengeful destruction of the guilty city. The myth offers a considerable number of significant parallels with the *Iliad* and the greater Trojan War saga (Niditch 16). A concubine, after an argument with her Levite husband, returns to her father's house in Bethlehem. After four months, her husband goes to retrieve her and is hospitably entertained for several days by her father. Leaving with her on the fifth day, the husband decides to pull into an Israelite town, Gibeah, within Benjamin, when night falls. No one offers them hospitality, until an old field worker takes them in. A mob gathers, beating on the door and demanding to have sex with the guest. The old man instead offers his virgin daughter and the guest's concubine. Up to this point, the narrative appears modeled on Genesis 19.[6] When the mob does not heed him, the Levite thrusts his concubine outside, to be raped by the mob all night. When she dies the next morning, her husband, unaware that she is dead, tells her to get up. Then, taking her corpse home, he cuts her body into twelve pieces, distributing the pieces through Israel. After the assembled Israelites learn about the crime, they send an embassy to Benjamin, demanding that the perpetrators be handed over. When the Benjamites will not, 400,000 Israelites besiege Gibeah. The Benjamites slay 22,000 Israelites on the first day, and 18,000 on the second. Phineas, whom we earlier paralleled with Akhilleus (*2b. The hero intervenes to check the god-sent plague*) is now present among the Israelites. On the third day the Israelites plot an ambush. Pretending to retreat, they draw the Benjamites out, surround them, and slay 25,100. The narrative sums up the resultant destruction: "The Israelites then turned back to deal with the other Benjamites, and put to the sword the people in the towns and cattle, every creature they found; they also set fire to every town within their reach" (Judg 20:48).

Here no single Paris, but a mob, modeled on those inhabitants of Sodom and Gomorrah who threaten Lot's angelic visitors in Genesis 19, outrages the woman. A hospitality myth, as in Genesis 19, the Gibeah account features Israelites who react much as do the Greeks in the Trojan War saga. Both assemble as a nation to deal with the violation of one of their wives by outsiders. Both first send embassies to obtain restitution before resorting to war but are refused. Both peoples then besiege the perpetrator's cities, but meet with setbacks and defeats instead of victory. The first two days of defeats for the Israelites form a neat parallel to the middle sequence (books 8–17), its many Greek woundings and casualties. Most intriguingly, at this point, after sustained losses and defeats, the parallel character Phineas/Akhilleus (*2b. The hero intervenes to check the god-sent plague*) appears as the narratives now pivot to the successful attack. Both peoples sack the respective cities through deception and trickery, both pretending to retreat in order to catch the wrongdoers' cities off guard, as they panic, fleeing before the onslaught of the attackers. As Niditch (108–9) notes, the same term, *nebalah* ("folly"; cf. *ate*), is used to denote the outrageous conduct here and in the myth of Shechem (Gen 34:7 and Judg 19:23, 20:6, 10). The rape of Shechem and the outrage at Gibeah thus employ key motifs common to the Trojan War saga, but without the larger framework of heroic myth in which the *Iliad* sets them.

Paris commits further offenses beyond obtaining Helen, a married woman and one from outside his community. He also stole a number of possessions from Menelaos. Frequent reference to the incident (7.350, 363–64, 389–90, 400; 11.125–25; 13.627; 22.114–16; and probably 3.97, 354), another way by which Paris wronged his host, and callously endangers his people by having these ill-gotten gains in their midst, underscores its function as a further cause for war. In all these ways, Paris is a fuller embodiment of *ate* than is Agamemnon. The *Iliad* minimizes Paris' time onstage, however, because too great a focus on him would turn the epic into a different kind of work, with a more satiric tone. He is simply too antiheroic—responsible for bringing disaster upon his people and irresponsible in failing to help resolve the problems he has caused.

Paris' stolen goods involve other Trojans in his wrongdoing, particularly Antimakhos. When Agamemnon slays two of Antimakhos' sons, Peisandros and Hippolokhos, in his *aristeia*, the narrator notes that Antimakhos had received more gold than anyone else from Paris. Once his support is bought by the gold, Antimakhos then backs Paris when he refuses to return Helen to the Greeks. His sons, both unheroic characters, are driving a chariot, not fighting, when, losing control of the reins, they are caught by Agamemnon. They plead with him to take them alive, noting how much wealth lies in Antimakhos' house (11.131–35). The gold they refer to is implicitly that which Paris gave their father, stolen from Menelaos. Rejecting their plea, Agamemnon further charges that Antimakhos had recommended murdering Menelaos (11.138–41), when he and Odysseus came on the earlier embassy (discussed in chapter 4). Though the murder was not carried out, it reveals considerable treachery in Antimakhos since embassies were under divine protection. Antimakhos' name, perhaps "opposed to fighting" (von Kamptz 56), suggests his unheroic qualities, similar to the lack of heroism seen in his sons.

Achan's violation of the ban parallels Paris' recklessly bringing home illicit items that jeopardize his city. When Joshua attacks Jericho he places the city under the ban (Josh 6:17), but Achan subsequently takes some of the plunder for himself. Yahweh, in a consequent divine wrath (Josh 7:1), causes Joshua's men to suffer defeat and threatens to abandon the Israelites if they do not deal with the violation (Josh 7:12): "The man who is taken as the harbourer of forbidden things must be burnt, he and all that is his, because he has violated the covenant of the Lord and committed an outrage in Israel" (Josh 7:15). Confronted, Achan details the goods he has taken in violation of the ban: "Among the booty I saw a fine mantle from Shinar, two hundred shekels of silver, and a bar of gold weighing fifty shekels; I coveted them and I took them" (Josh 7:21). In violating the ban, bringing improper, alien goods into his home, and provoking a divine wrath, Achan endangers his whole community. The term here translated as "outrage" is *nebalah*, used in two other passages suggesting parallels with Paris (the rape of Shechem and the outrage at Gibeah, Gen 34:7 and Judg 19:23; 20:6, 10), and suggesting a similar range of behavior as Homeric *ate*, which is closely associated with Paris. To end the crisis, Joshua and the Israelites stone Achan and his children (Josh 7:24–25). This action saves the community, solving the crisis. By contrast, the Trojans do not address the consequences of Paris' actions, except one halfhearted attempt discussed below. Paris thus performs the typical functions of a few OT malefactors rolled into one: Achan, in bringing in improper goods that endanger his community; the unnamed Israelite who marries a Midianite woman (Num 25); Shechem, carried away by lust for Dinah; and even the mob in Judges 19.

Does the *Iliad*'s frequent mention of Paris' theft imply, if only at a thematic level, that other Trojan wealth consists of ill-gotten gains? Were some of Laomedon's riches acquired illicitly? At the very least, the wages he should have paid to Poseidon and Apollo but kept resembles Achan's violation in Joshua. We adduce two OT passages about Tyre, a city with a status like Troy's:

> By great skill in commerce
> you have heaped up riches,
> and with your riches your arrogance had grown . . .
> I am about to bring foreigners against you,
> the most ruthless of nations,
> they will draw their swords against your fine wisdom
> and defile your splendour.
>
> (Ezek 28:5–7)

> Tyre, who built herself a rampart,
> has amassed silver like dust
> and gold like the dirt on the streets.
> But the Lord will take from her all she possesses . . .
> and the city itself will be destroyed by fire.
>
> (Zech 9:3–4)

The great wealth and prosperity of Troy seem arrogant, prompting divine resentment.

c. Paris' violations of hospitality

Within the broader context of Greek myth, as evident in the *Odyssey*, Paris' gravest wrongdoing is his violation of hospitality. We noted the two most relevant OT hospitality myths, Genesis 18–19 and Judges 19–20. In Greek myth the safety and rights of guests and hosts are sacred, protected by Zeus Xeinios, as he is referred to at *Il.* 13.624–25. The *Iliad* invokes the sacred dimension of hospitality more often than is generally realized. Perhaps the three most important passages are 13.621–27, 3.351–54, and 6.55–60. When Menelaos slays Peisandros, he gives the moral justification for the war in his vaunt over the slain foe:

> Reckless [ὑπερφίαλοι] Trojans, greedy for the terrible war cry,
> nor are you lacking in other outrage [λώβης] and disgrace [αἴσχεο],
> such as how you outraged me, cowardly dogs, nor did
> you fear the horrible wrath [μῆνιν] of Zeus the hospitality god
> who will some day destroy your steep city.
>
> (13.621–25)

Menelaos refers to the Trojans (ὑπερφίαλοι, "reckless") and their wrong-doing (λώβη, "outrage," λωβέομαι) in terms quite like those in OT myth and adds further moral condemnation, typical of the OT, in "you did not fear the stern wrath of thundering Zeus/[guardian] of Hospitality." OT myth commonly links, as does Menelaos, lack of fear of god with the wicked: "A wicked person . . . sees no need to fear God" (Ps 36:1). Lack of the fear of god is tied to the possibility of taking another man's wife, as Abraham notes while wandering in Egypt: "There is no fear of God in this place, and I shall be killed for the sake of my wife" (Gen 20:11). As Menelaos states, Zeus will destroy Troy, but only in accord with Lefkowitz's (151) formulation of the Olympian's sense of time in "a longer view."

Menelaos' prayer to Zeus, before his duel with Paris, is another key in-dicator of the *Iliad*'s use of hospitality myth:

> Lord Zeus, grant that I punish him who first wronged me,
> shining Alexander, and subdue him beneath my hands,
> so that anyone of future generations may shrink
> from wronging a host [ξεινοδόκον] who had received him hospitably.
>
> (3.351–54)

As the wronged host, Menelaos sounds this central moral justification for the war. His terms for Paris' violation of hospitality resemble those in the account of Laomedon's treatment of Herakles (5.650).

In a third key passage, Agamemnon exhorts Menelaos not to show mercy to a Trojan in his power, because of Paris' violations of his hospitality:

> O Menelaos, my brother, are you so concerned on behalf of
> these men? Did your house receive such good treatment from
> the Trojans? Let none of them flee complete destruction
> at our hands, not even the young warrior that a mother might carry
> in her womb, let him not escape, but let them all
> utterly perish from Ilion, vanished and unwept.
>
> (6.55–60)

The *Iliad* never depicts Zeus commenting on Paris' violation of hospitality, or most of the Trojans' other transgressions (a notable exception is when Hektor dons Akhilleus' armor: 17.205), but neither in the *Odyssey* does he comment on the suitors' many infractions. Zeus Xeinios will act to uphold the sacred reciprocity of hospitality, but, as in the *Odyssey*, he does not *person-ally* intervene, nor does he have a rapid schedule for punishment (discussed below on 4.160–61). His doing so falls outside of the *Iliad*'s plot, though the event is alluded to (below as *13. Apocalypse: A wrathful god destroys an arrogant city*).

There are Trojans who recognize and address Paris' wrongdoing and recklessness. The *Iliad* figures the ethical Trojan in Antenor. In some respects he is a doublet of Priam. Like the patriarch, Antenor is father to twelve sons taking part in the war, many slain in the course of the poem. One son, Agenor, is also a doublet for Hektor,[7] strengthening the parallels between the two fathers. But more important is Antenor's function as the moral Trojan, whose ethics are evident in everything he does. In book 3 he informs Helen how he hosted Menelaos and Odysseus when they came to Troy in the earlier embassy.[8] Already known to the Greeks as an honorable man, Antenor takes part in the oath-taking ceremony in book 3. Theano, Antenor's wife, leads the prayer and sacrifice to Athena in book 6. Though Theano's sacrifice is unsuccessful, as is Antenor's attempt to deal with Paris in book 7, the examples of correct behavior lie in Antenor's household.

His most significant scene is the Trojan assembly held after Aias defeats Hektor in the duel in book 7. Antenor opens the meeting with a forceful suggestion:

> Come then, let us give Argive Helen and all of her possessions
> back to the sons of Atreus. Now, as it is, we are fighting, having
> violated our sworn oaths; therefore I do not expect anything better
> to happen to us, unless we act in this way.
>
> (7.350–53)

Antenor proves unsuccessful, but in making the attempt he aligns himself with a figure noted above, the man who removes an improper alien woman, whose presence has put his community at risk. Phineas fills this role in the OT, Akhilleus himself in *Iliad* 1, in restoring Khryseis to her father. Though voted down, Antenor establishes, if only briefly, a moral course that could save the Trojans. He is also the only Trojan to comment on how they have violated the oaths sworn in book 4 (discussed below), and how this violation reflects upon them. Antenor here acts as Priam *should* have acted, as the moral man who sets his community right, confronting his people's wrongdoing and resultant problems. Priam, sympathetic as he is, generous, gracious, even heroic in book 24, does not. When it comes to addressing the grave problems facing his people, Priam is passive, inactive, and nowhere criticizes Paris for taking Helen (unless indirectly at 24.248–54). Antenor's name, "the man who is opposed," is opposed to (the impropriety of) his own people.[9]

d. Present-time wrongdoing by the Trojans: Pandaros

Wrongdoing by the Trojans is not confined to the past, or to Laomedon and Paris. Other Trojans, including Pandaros, Dolon, and Hektor himself, display similarly reckless behavior, needlessly putting their community at risk. These instances of present-time wrongdoing add to the city's already substantial legacy of wrongdoing and the number of sacred institutions they have violated. In these respects, the Trojans, collectively, occupy a moral position similar to the suitors in the *Odyssey*, though the *Odyssey*, typical of romance, makes the suitors more uniformly negative and villainous than the Trojans as a body. But the common root of the suitors' and Trojans' wrongdoing is the violation of hospitality.

Book 4 is the *Iliad*'s most forceful depiction of present-time wrongdoing by the Trojans. It is a natural continuation of Paris' shocking scene at the end of book 3: the man who endangered his city by bringing Helen to Troy is now making love to her, ignoring his duel with Menelaos and its sworn terms. The fractious divine council concludes with Zeus directing Athena to have the Trojans break the truce (4.70–72), violating the sacred oaths sworn with such ceremony (3.276–301). Finding Pandaros, Athena suggests he might win glory and gifts from Paris,[10] should he now shoot Menelaos. Pandaros is thus not only a doublet for Paris, as an archer and breaker of sacred conventions, but a thematic parallel to Antimakhos, who recommended slaying Menelaos on a diplomatic mission and received gifts from Paris as compensation for his support (11.138–41). Easily persuaded, Pandaros ignores the consequences of this action.

After a lengthy description of his bow, underscoring the importance of his action, Pandaros shoots, wounding Menelaos. But Athena, who helped provoke the incident, prevents the arrow from causing a fatal wound. Agamemnon reassures Menelaos in one of the poem's central articulations of a moral framework for the war:

> Still, the oath is not in vain, and the blood of the lambs,
> the pure libations, and the pledged right hands, in which we placed our
> trust.
> For if the Olympian has not immediately brought this to completion,
> eventually [ὀψὲ] he will, and they will pay a great price,
> with their own heads, their wives, and their children.
> For I know this well in my heart and soul,
> the day will come when sacred Ilion will be destroyed
> and Priam, and the host of Priam of the great ash-spear;
> and Zeus, the high-seated son of Kronos, dwelling in the sky,

himself will shake his dark aegis over them all, in anger [κοτέων]
at this deception. These things shall not go unaccomplished.

(4.158–68)

Agamemnon understands Zeus' timetable, as many modern commentators
do not, that if not now, then in the future, Zeus will punish the Trojans for
transgressing the sworn oaths.

Pandaros' individual treachery now expands to include the Trojans as a
whole, for they attack unexpectedly en masse (4.221), while the Greeks are
still unarmed. Marshaling the troops to avenge the Trojans' treachery, a
miniature of the beginning of the war, in effect, Agamemnon makes a sec-
ond speech sounding moral tones central to the poem:

For Zeus the Father will not be a helper to those that are false [ψευδέσσι];
but those very ones who first violate sacred oaths,
truly, vultures shall feed on their tender flesh,
and we, then, will lead off their wives and infant
children on our ships, when we sack the citadel.

(4.235–39)

As Agamemnon rouses his troops to attack the Trojans for Pandaros' trans-
gression, Idomeneus reiterates the Trojans' offense and its consequences:

Stir up the other flowing-haired Akhaians
so we can fight immediately, since the Trojans
violated the oaths; in turn there will be sorrows and death
for them, because they first trampled on the oaths.

(4.268–71)

In OT myth if peoples and cities, even Israel, violate sacred contracts,
Yahweh hands them over to plunderers: "He will abandon Israel because of
the sins that Jeroboam has committed and has led Israel to commit" (1 Kings
14:16). The specific act of breaking oaths, which in the *Iliad* is associated
with Laomedon and Pandaros, is repeatedly singled out as leading to the
destruction of a city in OT myth:

People swear oaths and break them;
they kill and rob and commit adultery . . .
Therefore the land will be desolate
and all who live in it will languish.

(Hosea 4:2–3)

OT myth consistently depicts the operation of collective guilt, also at work in the *Iliad*. In myth, a city must be punished, even destroyed, because of the wrongdoing of a group or even an individual (cf. Hesiod, *Works and Days*, 240–41, discussed below).

e. *General arrogance and* hubris *by the Trojans: Dolon*

Two types of recklessness on the battlefield are figured in Dolon and Hektor. When Hektor calls a nighttime council, he offers as reward for carrying out a spy mission the finest horses and chariot the Akhaians have (10.305–6). Although he does not specify which horses are the best, it is well known that these are Akhilleus' horses, said to be immortal (10.402–4; 17.76–77, 441–55). In promising something he cannot possess, Hektor is reckless, if not dishonest. Agreeing to the risky mission, Dolon has Hektor swear that he will give him Akhilleus' horses and chariot (10.321–23). Dolon is presumptuous in his desire for Akhilleus' divine horses and in his boasts of what he will be able to accomplish when he reaches Agamemnon's ship, where the best (of the Akhaians) are assembled (10.326–27). However, Dolon's arrogance only endangers himself, not those around him. But Hektor knowingly swears a false oath to Dolon (10.329–31) so that he will risk his life. Although commentators have largely ignored Hektor's false oath,[11] it establishes him as a thematic parallel to Pandaros, and Laomedon, as a violator of sacred oaths. The narrator emphasizes Hektor's act, "he swore a false oath" (ἐπίορκον ἐπώμοσε, 10.332). The specific wording of his oath has an ironic secondary meaning for the audience, that *none* of the Trojans will ever possess Akhilleus' horses (10.330–31), including Hektor, when he later pursues them in vain.

Dolon is a type of character also present in the *Odyssey* in Leodes, the suitor, and Elpenor, member of Odysseus' crew. All three are self-deluding characters, who pursue vain desires and are utterly lacking in heroic potential.[12] When Dolon perceives Odysseus and Diomedes coming toward him, he hopes (ἔλπετο, 10.355) that they are Trojans. Both Elpenor, whose name is cognate with the verb, and Leodes, are closely associated with related words. When Odysseus learns that Dolon desired Akhilleus' horses (10.401), he notes how improper such a desire is. Dolon's self-delusion and vain desires are exactly what the *Odyssey* represents in Leodes and Elpenor (Louden 1999a: 40–41). Asking to be ransomed, both Dolon and Leodes are beheaded, with the same formula (*Il.* 10.457 = *Od.* 22.329). Before dying, however, Dolon turns coward, betraying the positions of the other Trojans. The episode is thus a disaster for the Trojans and looks ahead to the unsuccessful plans Hektor will formulate in books 12 and 18.

f. General arrogance and hubris by the Trojans: Hektor

Hektor, more than any other single character, embodies the Trojans' positive *and* negative characteristics. In one of the *Iliad*'s more subtle accomplishments, readers are so taken by Hektor's sympathetic qualities that they are reluctant to acknowledge his less favorable tendencies. Closer inspection reveals that Hektor shares a number of parallels with Dolon, that he misleads his followers, not on some grand cause, but for his own selfish objectives. Like Dolon, Hektor deludes himself, desires things he has no business desiring, and does both thematically throughout the poem. Books 8 and 17, the beginning and concluding books of the middle sequence, are designed to emphasize Hektor's shortcomings.

Throughout the middle sequence, Hektor repeatedly loses sight of more important objectives, such as saving his family and city, focusing instead on issues less connected with defeating the Greeks and more involved with his own glory. Shortly after Zeus intervenes to establish the inverted course of the middle sequence, Hektor addresses his horses, declaring his desire to capture Nestor's shield, and Diomedes' Hephaistos-fashioned corselet (8.191–97). Hektor's stated reason for pursuing these two items is that, if he does so, he hopes (ἐελποίμην, 8.196) the Greeks would then return home. But how would this follow? Because Hektor will have captured two pieces of armor, the Greeks will be so demoralized as to give up the war and return home? This absurd assumption is typical of how Hektor misreads the temporary favor Zeus grants him. Hektor's use of ἔλπω (and at 8.526, 17.488, discussed below) aligns him with Dolon (10.355), as pursuing vain desires.

Hektor then pursues an even more misguided course: to burn the Greeks' ships. Curiously absent from Homeric criticism is any assessment of whether Hektor *should* try to burn the Greeks' ships? Hektor's attempt to do so characterizes and shapes much of the middle sequence. But if he wants to prevent the sack of Troy, surely cutting off a possible Greek retreat is not the wisest course. His first attempt is unsuccessful, prevented by Hera, through a pivotal contrafactual (8.217–18). At the assembly, Hektor asserts that he would not only have destroyed the Greeks' ships today but slain all of the Greeks, if night had not come so quickly (8.498–500), a repetition of his earlier unrealistic assessment but even more exaggerated. In this speech, Hektor again uses ἔλπω (8.526) of his wish to drive the Greeks away and concludes wishing that he "were immortal and ageless . . . honored as Athena and Apollo" (8.638–40). Hektor not only repeats Dolon's tendency toward unrealistic desires, but in his wish to be honored as a god, *to be a god,* Hektor swells to an arrogance, a *hubris*, that, in a traditional ancient culture will not go unpunished.[13] Book 8 thus highlights, three times, Hektor's tendency to make faulty assessments of the Greeks' fortunes, and to respond with a dubious course of action. Hektor later repeats the wish to be immortal, honored as Athena and Apollo (13.827 ff = 8.540 ff; 13.825–26 is close to 8.538–39).

The middle sequence further figures Hektor's hubris in his relation with Poulydamas. As noted in chapter 4, when Hektor listens to Poulydamas, for example, at 12.60–80, all goes well. But Hektor rarely heeds Poulydamas' advice (B. Hainsworth 325). Hektor refuses to heed Poulydamas' sensible interpretation that an augury they see portends serious casualties for the Trojans (12.200–209). The rest of the Trojans react with horror when they see it (12.208), but Hektor ignores the warning and instead belittles all use of augury. As B. Hainsworth (343) notes, "to any pious mind his words would represent a fatal delusion."

Zeus himself, his mentor god Apollo, and Hera all criticize Hektor's arrogance and misguided desires. During the struggle for Patroklos' corpse Hektor repeatedly pursues Akhilleus' horses rather than the armor, or the corpse itself, repeating Dolon's vain desire. According to Janko (1992: 421), "Hektor longs to win Akhilleus' divine pair . . . his greed gives Menelaos the chance to defend Patroklos' body and armour." The scene embodies Hektor's shortcomings, losing sight of larger objectives to pursue something for himself. When he persists, Apollo reprimands him:

> Hektor, so now you hurry chasing unattainable things,
> the horses of talented Akhilleus, which are very difficult
> for mortal men to control and drive,
> for anyone other than Akhilleus, whom an immortal mother bore.
>
> (17.75–78)

Apollo notes that Hektor's pursuit of Akhilleus' horses, by allowing Menelaos to slay Euphorbos, has cost the life of one of his men.

Apollo's reprimand is prelude to stark editorial comment by Zeus. When he does win Akhilleus' armor from Patroklos' corpse, Hektor attempts to decapitate Patroklos (17.126), an act that aligns him with Aias Oileus (*Il.* 13.202–5), destined to be slain by Poseidon for his blasphemy (*Od.* 4.499–511). When Telamonian Aias approaches, however, Hektor retreats, an instantiation of Aias' thematic tendency to defeat him. After Glaukos upbraids him for abandoning Sarpedon's corpse, Hektor dons Akhilleus' arms, as Zeus watches, decrying his act as improper (οὐ κατὰ κόσμον, 17.205). Hektor now marshals the Trojans in an attempt to seize Patroklos' body, each man vainly hoping (ἔλπετο: 17.234) to be the one to do it. But Zeus, hating (μίσησεν, 17.273) the prospect of the Trojans defiling the corpse, addresses Akhilleus' horses, object of Hektor's vain desires, and declares that he will not allow Hektor to mount them (17.448–49):

> for there is nothing more wretched than man,
> of all the things that breathe and move upon the earth.
>
> (17.446–47)

I take the couplet, as did the ancient commentator (Edwards 1991: 107: bT), to refer to vain hopes, and that Zeus particularly intends Hektor's vain hopes and how those lead to his death. The *Odyssey* employs a parallel remark, in a context with a similar dynamic. The disguised Odysseus warns Amphimakhos of the destruction that awaits mortals who misbehave as the suitors do:

> The earth rears nothing less worth regard than man,
> of all the things that breathe and move upon the earth.
> for never does he think he will suffer evil later
> while the gods provide him talent, and make his knees spring.
>
> (*Od.* 18.130–33)

In the extended *theoxeny* that shapes the beginning and ending of the *Odyssey* (Louden 1999a: 22–23, 25–27, 95–97), Odysseus here plays the role normally played by a god, carrying out divine punishment against those who have violated hospitality. It thus parallels Zeus' pithy remark, a warning on the consequences of inappropriate actions.[14]

Hektor offers surprisingly close parallels to Dolon. Both Dolon and Hektor die soon after they express the same vain desire, to possess Akhilleus' divine horses. Against the combined divine perspectives of Hera, Apollo, and Zeus himself, Hektor continues to pursue Akhilleus' horses, under Dolon-like self-delusion, again expressed by the same verb, ἐελποίμην (17.488).

In OT myth Yahweh frequently punishes such presumption and arrogance as Hektor embodies. In Ezekiel Yahweh criticizes the ruler of Tyre for assuming he is like a god, and implies that such behavior provides cause for his city to be sacked:

> In your arrogance you say,
> "I am a god;

I sit enthroned like a god on the high seas."
Though you are a man and no god,
you give yourself godlike airs. . . .
Because you give yourself godlike airs,
I am about to bring foreigners against you,
the most ruthless of nations;
they will draw swords against your fine wisdom
and defile your splendour. . . .
When you face your attackers,
will you still say, "I am a god?"
You are a man and no god
in the hands of those who lay you low.
                                        (Ezek 28:1–9)

Such passages are common in the prophetic books, as in Yahweh's reason for allowing Israel to be sacked by Assyria:

I abhor the arrogance of Jacob . . .
I shall abandon the city and its people to their fate.
                                        (Amos 6:8)

Yahweh's declaration of Jerusalem's destruction offers a parallel to the eventual sack of Troy as resulting from the arrogance of Laomedon, Paris, Dolon, and Hektor:

I have wiped out this arrogant people;
their bastions are demolished,
I have destroyed their streets;
no one walks along them.
Their cities are laid waste,
abandoned and unpeopled.
                                        (Zeph 3:6)

More explicitly apocalyptic is Yahweh's threat of destruction for Babylon:

I shall bring disaster on the world
and due punishment on the wicked.
I shall cut down insolent pride
and bring down ruthless arrogance.
                                        (Isa 13:11)

⌒

9. Hektor's death as drawing on myths of human sacrifice

Because of their many transgressions—these of Laomedon, Paris, Antima-
khos, Pandaros, Dolon, and Hektor—the Trojans are thematically unsuc-
cessful in their attempts to curry divine favor (except Aphrodite's), with-
out which they must lose the war. Their loss of divine favor is emphasized
in book 6, in the sacrifice to Athena, which the goddess rejects (6.311; cf.
8.548–52). Yahweh frequently refuses to accept sacrifices in OT myth:

> When you bring me your
> whole-offerings and your
> grain-offerings
> I shall not accept them.
>   (Amos 5:22)

The extra-Homeric tradition offers additional depictions of Athena aban-
doning the Trojans. Burkert (1983a: 158) notes that Athena abandoned Troy
"when Odysseus and Diomedes carried off the Palladion."[15] Apollo deserts
Hektor (22.213) as he is about to face Akhilleus. In Near Eastern myth, the
last resort for a city under siege, or other dire calamity such as famine, is
human sacrifice, particularly sacrifice of the king's son. By such means the
beleaguered city wins back divine favor. Hektor's death may be influenced
by such myths. Our analysis in chapter 2 demonstrated that Priam's re-
trieval of Hektor's corpse in book 24 parallels his retrieval of the sacrificed
lambs in book 3 (see section III: *k. The slain victim[s], wounded in the throat by
the leader of the Greek camp, is [are] placed in his vehicle*), suggesting some equa-
tion of Hektor and sacrificial victims.

   Why might the *Iliad* parallel Hektor's death with a human sacrifice?
Hektor serves as the agent for the unsuccessful offering to Athena in book 6,
which episode not only has links with Hektor's own death (noted in chap-
ter 1), but his behavior seems problematic in other ways, as do details of
ritual procedure. Helenos tells him to go to the city to arrange a sacrifice
to Athena to save the Trojans from Diomedes (6.86–96), whose successful
aristeia parallels Akhilleus' later deeds (including slaying Hektor). As Kirk
(1990: 163) observes, "For the commanding officer to withdraw from the
field to organize prayers for his army's safety is unusual by Homeric stan-
dards." Although Helenos dictates that the sacrifice to Athena consist of
twelve heifers (6.93), Hektor announces that he will have the Trojan women
perform a hecatomb (6.115).[16] When he reaches Hekabe, Hektor refers to

the sacrifice as "things to be sacrificed" (θυέεσιν: 6.270). It is unusual within the formulaic nature of Homeric epic for Hektor to use such varied terms. Does his variety of terms indicate discomfort with the sacrifice or suggest that he is proceeding incorrectly?

Meeting Hekabe, Hektor declines her offer to pour a libation saying it would be wrong for him to do so, since he is "splattered with blood and gore." Is his declining to take part offensive to Athena? The special robe Hekabe selects for the sacrifice was obtained by Paris in Sidon when he returned with Helen (6.290–91). The robe, a result of Paris' favoring Aphrodite over Athena in the Judgment of Paris (cf. *Il.* 24.28–30), might also be offensive to Athena. The formula used of Hekabe's retrieving the robe is repeated of Priam when he fetches goods to ransom Hektor's corpse from Akhilleus (6.288 = 24.191; cf. Kirk 1990: 198). In another departure from Helenos' instructions, Hekabe meets with Theano, priestess of Athena and wife of Antenor. Kirk (1990: 165) notes her unique status: "No other priestess is mentioned in Homer." Like her husband, Theano serves as an example of a moral Trojan by virtue of her unique office as priestess of Athena.[17] Theano places the offering on the knees of Athena's statue and prays to the goddess as ῥυσίπτολι, "city saver," an epithet used only of Athena (Dee 2001: 135), to break Diomedes' spear (6.306). But Athena rejects the offering and prayer. Her not breaking the spear of Diomedes suggests Athena's aid to Akhilleus when he will kill Hektor with his spear. As Antenor is unable to persuade the Trojan council to have Paris return Helen, Theano, by offering Athena an item tainted by its connection with Paris, is doomed to failure.

As we briefly argued in section III (k) of chapter 2, Hektor broadly suggests a sacrificial victim to Athena (Hektor himself is part of the θυέεσιν), the deity, after Hera, most eager for the destruction of Troy, and most actively engaged in ensuring its fall. We can recover a fuller sense of the formula used when he, splattered with blood, declines to participate in the libation to Athena by noting similar phrases from the *Odyssey*. The formula also occurs in the *Odyssey* when Odysseus, under Athena's supervision, slays the suitors (22.402, 23.48):

αἵματι καὶ λύθρῳ πεπαλαγμένον ὥς τε λέοντα.
spattered with blood and gore like a lion.
(*Od.* 22.402 = 23.408)

αἵματι καὶ λύθρῳ πεπαλαγμένον εὐχετάασθαι.
to pray spattered with blood and gore.
(*Il.* 6.268)

In the most important passage from the *Odyssey*, Athena declares what she expects:

αἵματι τ᾽ ἐγκεφάλῳ τε παλαξέμεν ἄσπετον
your immense floor [to be] spattered with [the suitors'] blood and brains.

(Od. 13.395)

Virtually a command from Athena, this first instance of the formula in the *Odyssey* calls the other two into being.

Homeric epic thus offers four passages (*Il.* 6.268; *Od.* 13.395, 22.402, 23.48; cf. *Od.* 20.354) featuring the same basic word order and formulas, depicting Athena's involvement with a blood-splattered hero. All three Odyssean passages refer to Odysseus slaying the suitors, an act he carries out as directed by Athena. In the *Iliad*, Hektor utters the formula to initiate an unsuccessful sacrifice to the same goddess, who will shortly bring about his own death. The formula is exclusively associated with Athena in both epics.[18] Athena directs Hektor's death at Akhilleus' hands, much as she directs Odysseus' victory over the suitors. Hektor's blood-splattered state in book 6 prefigures his death and Athena's role in bringing it about in book 22. Put another way, Athena not only causes Hektor's death; this is another way of saying she demands it, a death resembling human sacrifice.

Morris (1995: 231) notes an Ugaritic prayer, understood to depict a form of human sacrifice, asking the gods to save a besieged city:

> O Baal, drive away the strong one from our gate,
> The warrior from our walls!
> The bull, O Baal, We shall sacrifice [to thee],
> the vow, O Baal, we shall fulfill,
> A [(?*kr*) male or firstborn?] we shall fulfill [as vow].

As Morris (1995: 238–39) notes of the prayer, "its language and occasion are most closely matched . . . in the special rites ordered by Hektor from the women of Troy." Morris observes that because the robe Theano selects is Sidonian, it comes from the same people as does the Ugaritic prayer.[19] The Ugaritic prayer suggests Helenos' instructions, "So she [Athena] might hold back from sacred Ilion the son of Tydeus" (6.96), and Theano's prayer, "Athena, our city's defender . . . break the spear of Diomedes" (6.305–6).

Hektor is part of a larger pattern of divine failures on the Trojans' part, their inability to curry divine favor, their inability to make themselves abide by sacred agreements. As Laomedon cheated Poseidon and Apollo, as Paris ruptured the sanctity of hospitality, so Pandaros and the Trojans, in the present time of the poem, violate that sacred agreement for which the lambs are sacrificed (3.275–301). Hektor is part of this thematic chain of events, himself paying the price for Pandaros' violation of the sacred oath. In a sense, Hektor *is*, in book 22, the blood-spattered sacrifice that Athena now accepts, having earlier rejected the offering in book 6. Hektor's "sacrifice" for Athena marks the accomplishment of her desire, the fall of Troy. As Priam oversees the sacrifice of the lambs in book 3, he oversees the conclusion of Hektor's "sacrifice" when he brings his corpse back to Troy, as earlier he retrieved the sacrificed lambs (3.310–13), their throats slit. Priam, who has to sacrifice his son at the end of the war, thus suggests a complement to Agamemnon, the king who sacrificed his child to begin it.

Though we are primarily concerned with placing the *Iliad* in a Near Eastern context, comparative Indo-European evidence also suggests Hektor's possible connection with human sacrifice. When Hektor declines his mother's request to participate in the ritual, he emphasizes, as we have noted, that his blood-spattered state makes it unseemly to do so. The verb that articulates his refusal is ἅζομαι (*hazomai*), often translated "I am reverent/in awe." The verbal root is productive in Greek, leading to related words having to do with religious practice and, sometimes, sacrifice. The cognate in Sanskrit, *yajati*, has, as one of its primary meanings, "sacrifice." When Hektor utters this verb, then, is it a possible double entendre of some kind, affirming his connection with a sacrifice he does not intend, almost as if he is declaring that he is *herem*, "sacred to god?"

Human sacrifice is more common in Near Eastern myth (see Morris 1995: 231–36). Indeed, some scholars argue that instances of human sacrifice in Greek myth are borrowed from or influenced by the Near Eastern myths (e.g., Morris 1995: 231–237). OT myth is rich in references to human sacrifice. The myth of Abram's near sacrifice of Isaac only works if the audience assumes Isaac is actually in danger of being sacrificed.[20] Yahweh's command that all firstborn sons are to be sacrificed to him (Exod 22:29–30, 13:2, 13) also suggests OT narratives are reacting to inherited traditions that express familiarity, even some acceptance of, human sacrifice. Very like Agamemnon's sacrifice of Iphigeneia is Jephthah's sacrifice of his daughter in Judges 11. First described as "an intrepid warrior" (Judg 11:1),[21] Jephthah is one of the principal heroes depicted in Judges. His myth is composed entirely of traditional motifs, recognizable in the Greek myths of Meleager and Agamemnon.[22] After earlier having slighted him, a council of elders asks him to lead its army (cf. Meleager, *Il.* 9.543 ff). Agreeing, he vows, if successful in battle, to sacrifice the first creature coming out his door when he returns (11:30–31). He is successful and has an *aristeia:* "Then the spirit of the Lord came upon Jephthah" (Judg 11:29), "He routed them with very great slaughter" (Judg 11:33). When he returns home, however, his daughter comes out to meet him. Though he despairs, when she hears of the vow she willingly accepts her fate, if she can first roam the hills with her companions (Judg 11:34–37).[23]

The OT myth of human sacrifice most relevant to Hektor is the siege of King Mesha of Moab. When King Mesha rebels from Israel, the kings of Israel, Judah, and Edom, combine to wage war against him. Mesha, now besieged, is soon reduced to desperate measures, much as Priam in the *Iliad:* "Meanwhile all Moab had heard that the kings had come to wage war against them, and every man, young and old, who could bear arms was called out and stationed on the frontier" (2 Kings 3:21). The Israelites and their allies advance, after razing all nearby towns. Mesha, assuming all is lost, takes a final, drastic step: "When the Moabite king saw that the war had gone against him . . . he took his eldest son, who would have succeeded him, and offered him as a whole-offering on the city wall" (2 Kings 3:26–27). Mesha's eldest son parallels Hektor's status as Priam's most important son. The sacrifice is effective, "There was such consternation among the Israelites that they struck camp and returned to their own land" (2 Kings 3:29). As Robinson (37) explains,

> The sacrifice was offered to Chemosh the god of Moab. Their defeat would have been looked upon by the Moabites as a punishment from their god for some national sin. So this most costly offering was made to appease the anger of the god. It was made on the city wall in full view of the Israelites in order that the anger of Chemosh might be turned away from the Moabites and towards their enemies.

As Robinson (38) further notes, this "implies that the Israelites were so convinced of the efficacy of the sacrifice that they lost all confidence in their own cause." Human sacrifice recurs twice more in 2 Kings (16:3, 21:6; cf. 1 Kings 16:34).[24] In the former passage, Ahaz, a king of Jerusalem, sacrifices his own son: "He even passed his son through the fire according to the abominable practice of the nations whom the Lord had dispossessed in favour of the Israelites." Robinson (203) suggests that human sacrifices "were condemned . . . as implying powers which were believed to lie outside the control of Yahweh."[25]

Niditch (42), speaking of the ban (*herem*) in OT myth, when the Israelites slay all the inhabitants of a city, soldiers and civilians, men, women, and children, brings together several relevant issues, arguing that human sacrifice is implicit in the ban and provides

> a culturally pervasive notion of what soldiers are doing in vowing to eliminate all of the enemy. . . . They are offering human sacrifices to the deity. The enemy

is usually imagined to be slaughtered by sword in the denouement of battle and not prepared Aztec-style for a separate sacrificial ritual. . . . Nevertheless, the deaths are perceived as sacrifices to God in exchange for help in war.

Although the *Iliad* does not state that the mass slayings Akhilleus, Patroklos, and Diomedes commit in their *aristeiai* are offerings to the gods, much of Iliadic warfare is in accord with the ban (see discussion of 6.56–60 in chapter 5). The *Iliad* clearly reveals the gods, particularly Athena, as aiding and desiring the slaughter, particularly Hektor's.[26]

Closely connected with his slaying of Hektor, Akhilleus slays twelve Trojans, dedicating them to Patroklos.[27] This is human sacrifice. Homeric criticism is rather silent on the act. Each time Akhilleus or the narrator refers to his sacrifice of the twelve, the same verb is used, ἀποδειροτομέω, literally, "to slit the throat" (18.336; 23.22, 174).[28] The terminology implies thematic parallels both with Akhilleus' slaying of Hektor, stabbed in the neck with his spear, and the sacrifice of the lambs in book 3, whose throats were slit. Each time the sacrifice of the twelve occurs it is paired with a reference to Akhilleus' slaying of Hektor (18.334–37; 23.21–23, 174–83), again implying parallels between the two acts. The *Iliad*, in imposing a predominantly heroic, warrior framework and modality upon its many different subgenres of myth, may have reworked a motif that in earlier epic tradition applied to a god but now adheres to a mortal, Patroklos.

~

10. Divine councils

We now turn to subgenres of myth in which gods are the principal agents. Generally, these subgenres offer parallels on the divine plane for events on the mortal plane. As the *Iliad*'s mortals hold assemblies, quarrel, and fight wars, so do its deities. Perhaps the most definitive such subgenre for epic is the divine council (though they also appear in myths other than epics), in which the gods meet to discuss or debate the fate of the protagonist and his people. Divine councils construct the parameters of an epic's plot by defining the boundaries of mortality in a given myth. At some point in an early divine council, the chief god utters his decree or prophecy concerning what the protagonist will suffer or accomplish.

The *Iliad*'s divine councils are in many respects highly innovative when placed alongside those in *Gilgamesh* and the *Odyssey*. Frequent in the *Iliad* are divine consultations at which Zeus is *not* present (2.155–66; 5.29–36, 355–431, 711–67; 7.17–43; 8.198–211, 350–484; 14.188–281, 354–60; 15.90–217; 18.35–65, 369–467; 20.67–78, 112–54, 293–317; 21.214–501). Frequent in the

Iliad, but absent from the *Odyssey* and *Gilgamesh*, are divine councils in which the will of the chief god is resented and openly challenged. In the *Odyssey*, Zeus successfully accommodates the differing divine perspectives of Helios, Athena, and Poseidon, talking all three down from an intended destruction of apocalyptic proportions to a more reasonable, more contained level of punishment (12.376–89, 13.125–58, 24.472–86; see Louden 1999a: 23–25, 70–71, 98–102). These divine councils depict the same dynamic as one in *Gilgamesh*, between Anu and Ishtar (VI iii–iv).[29] Kalypso, somewhat grudgingly, accepts Zeus' command, as delivered by Hermes (5.138–44), to let Odysseus return. The *Iliad*'s very first divine meeting has Hera resenting Zeus' authority (1.539 ff).

Divine councils are surprisingly well represented in OT myth.[30] Israelite monotheism evolved out of an earlier polytheism, and a significant portion of OT myth reflects and retains the earlier polytheistic beliefs (see, e.g., M. Smith 2001: 17). Many earlier OT myths present a fully polytheistic conception, revolving around the central members of the Ugaritic/Canaanite pantheon: El, Asherah, Baal, Anat, all named in the OT (discussed at length in chapter 7), as well as other deities worshiped in the vicinity (Chemosh and Molech). Occasionally, figures such as Sun, Moon, and Death, are mentioned in ways that demonstrate that they were not just personified but thought of as deities.[31] Later compilers have retrojected monotheism onto the myths from the earlier periods, but have not completely effaced the polytheistic foundation from which many OT myths derive. Frequent in this earlier polytheistic framework are divine councils.

Psalms retains instances of a traditional type, the principal god presiding and passing judgment over immortals:

> God takes his place in the court of heaven
> to pronounce judgment among the gods.
> (Ps 82:1)

Such passages (cf. Ps 89:5–7, 1 Kings 22:19) are influenced by earlier Canaanite/Ugaritic depictions of El, presiding over the Ugaritic pantheon (discussed in chapter 7). Also present in OT myth are those more typical of Iliadic divine councils, in which the will of the chief god is being challenged. That in Job, discussed in chapter 5 (subgenre 7) is a chief instance of this type: "Once again the day came when the members of the court of heaven took their places in the presence of the Lord, and the Adversary was there among them" (Job 2:1). The Adversary (Satan) goes on to challenge Yahweh's position about Job, hoping to undermine it, if not prove him wrong. This is close to the posture Hera adopts throughout divine councils in the *Iliad*, best seen in the retrospective divine council at *Il.* 19.100–113.

These two divine councils (Job 2:1–7; *Il.* 19.100–13) offer a number of close parallels. In each case the principal deity (Yahweh, Zeus) convenes the divine assembly to make an announcement about a special mortal (Job, Heracles). In each case an immortal is opposed (the Adversary, Hera) to the principal deity's plans for the mortal and sets out to thwart them. The opposed immortal first bandies words with the principal god, attempting to trip him up verbally (Job 1:9–11, 2:4–5; *Il.* 19.106–12). The antagonistic immortal then leaves the divine council to cause problems for the mortal, Hera causing Herakles to grow up in servitude to Eurystheus, the Adversary afflicting Job with boils to make him doubt Yahweh.

Perhaps the other OT divine council most relevant to those in the *Iliad* in which Zeus' will is contested is in Isaiah:

> Bright morning star . . .
> You thought to yourself:
> I shall scale the heavens
> to set my throne high above the mighty stars;
> I shall take my seat on the mountain where the gods assemble
> in the far recesses of the north.
> I shall ascend beyond the towering clouds
> and make myself like the Most High.
>
> (Isa 14:12–14)[32]

Although a mortal is probably intended, one who has demonstrated Hektor-like arrogance and presumption, the author of Isaiah appropriates an older subgenre of myth to frame his statement, that of the divine challenger who will be cast out of heaven and thrown into the underworld: "Instead you are brought down to Sheol, into the depths of the abyss" (Isa 14:15); "Sheol below was all astir to greet you at your coming" (Isa 14:9). Zeus' threats to cast down to Tartaros Hera, or any other deity who rebels, belong to this same specific subgenre, as discussed below.[33]

⌒

11. Divine conflicts

a. Divine disagreement: Resentment of the chief god

Why are there divine conflicts in the *Iliad?* All the gods know that in the larger siege of Troy, the Greeks will be victorious, and the city will be sacked. However, there are reversals along the way, postponing the inevitable Greek triumph. Only Zeus is portrayed as always fully cognizant of this larger picture, that *temporary* aid to Hektor does not alter or jeopardize eventual Greek victory. Hera, and next in degree, Athena and Poseidon, typically lose sight of the bigger picture, violently overreacting to any aid Zeus gives Hektor, even when the aid is strictly limited, as in the one day of support to Hektor (8.470, 11.185–94).[34] In this sense, Hera and Athena reveal themselves as unfit for rule, unable to balance the back-and-forth rhythms of the war, unable to keep the bigger picture and ultimate outcome in mind. Their respective positions, Zeus' larger perspective versus Hera's and Athena's excessive bias and shortsightedness, present motives for divine conflict in the *Iliad*. Additionally Apollo, Ares, and Aphrodite favor the Trojans, putting them in opposition to Hera, Athena, and Poseidon.

The lowest level of divine conflict in the *Iliad* is provocation, a god deliberately setting out to rile another, typically concerning perceived interference with eventual Greek victory. Most scenes of divine provocation occur in the initial sequence. The *Iliad* has a formula for divine provocation, "to rile with abusive words" (ἐρέθῃσιν ὀνειδείοις ἐπέεσσιν, 1.519, of Hera; cf. 4.5–6, of Zeus; 5.419, of Athena and Hera; cf. νείκησεν . . . ὀνειδείοις ἐπέεσσιν, 21.480; and Hera's nasty speech to Apollo at 24.55–63, which Zeus characterizes as ἀποσκυδμαίνω). Although the *Iliad* features several deities at times antagonistic toward Zeus, Hera is his most frequent antagonist, provoking, verbally abusing, and raging against him.

Hera's quarrel with Zeus serves as a divine parallel for the *eris,* or strife, between Akhilleus and Agamemnon (on *eris* see chapter 5, subgenre 4). In having a formidable wrath, and bitter resentment against her king, Hera parallels Akhilleus. In having his leadership frustrated by his own sexual desire, or following sexual desire at an inopportune time, Zeus parallels Agamemnon. Zeus' foolish deception in book 14 forms a surprising parallel to Agamemnon's poor judgment in his inappropriate desire for Khryseis (and Briseis; see esp. 1.113–14). Through his own lapse, Zeus allows Hektor to suffer, paralleling the harm Agamemnon causes his own troops through his desire (1.50–52).

In other significant ways, however, Zeus is far more like Akhilleus, and Hera more like Agamemnon. As the most powerful god, and greatest divine warrior, Zeus parallels Akhilleus, the most heroic warrior. He is also linked to Akhilleus in being indebted to Thetis, and because he came close to being the father of Akhilleus, out of his own earlier desire for the Nereid.[35] As is evident in her solicitous regard for him throughout the poem, Hera has close links with Agamemnon. The strife between Akhilleus and Agamemnon, though bitter, never escalates into physical violence (though without

The *Iliad:* Structure, Myth, and Meaning

Athena's intervention at 1.194–98, Akhilleus might have slain Agamemnon), which finds a parallel in Zeus and Hera not facing each other in the general theomachy in book 21.

b. Rebellion against the chief god

Divine rebellion is a direct challenge to the rule or authority of the principal god. It differs from theomachy in that it usually has as its specific goal an attempt to seize the position of the chief god, which may not necessarily involve full battle, or even physical force. Theomachy, on the other hand, is actual combat between gods. Hera, for a time, is successful in seizing and usurping Zeus' power during the deception in book 14 and its immediate aftermath, though she does not participate in any theomachy against him. In Near Eastern myth, divine rebellions often figure in creation myth, when one generation of gods supplants or supersedes another, and the same is true of OT myth, in passages mainly found in Psalms (e.g., 18:7–15, 74:13–15, 77:16–19, 89:10, 104:4–7). Out of many Near Eastern instances of divine rebellion, the *Enuma Elish* offers the most relevant parallels to the *Iliad*, Tiamat serving as a close parallel to Hera. Both female deities lead rebellions; much as Hera in the *Iliad*, Tiamat is thematically depicted as having a fierce wrath:

> When Tiamat heard this,
> She was furious and shouted at her lover;
> She shouted dreadfully and was beside herself with rage.
>
> (I 234)[36]

The *Enuma Elish* has many similar passages ("Tiamat . . . is raging out of control," 247; "Tiamat who raged out of control," 252; "She went wild, she lost her temper," 253; "They are working up to war, growling and raging," 237, 245), which, together, depict Tiamat as like the Iliadic Hera in her anger, and in how she vents it.

Hera rebels specifically over Zeus' short-term policy, as promised to Thetis, of helping Hektor and the Trojans in the middle sequence. Rebellion against Zeus' decrees, but not actual violence between gods, characterizes the divine economy in the middle sequence. Poseidon and Athena join her rebellion, following her lead (14.356 ff), but playing roles that involve less direct confrontation with Zeus. Hera also elicits the aid of Hypnos, who is fully aware of his participation, and Aphrodite, who (like Zeus himself) is unaware that Hera is deceiving her. Hera's rebellion thus involves a considerable cast of other divine characters but is parodic, consistent with the dominant tone of the middle sequence. In having Hera win Hypnos over to her side by offering him a reward, the *Iliad* parodies the tradition, as in Hesiod's *Theogony*, in which the successful god in a theomachy achieves victory by persuading figures such as Briareos to come over to his side for a reward (*Theogony* 617 ff). In the *Theogony*, Zeus is such a figure, and his successful leadership in the Olympians' own rebellion against the Titans is emblematic of his executive skills throughout his reign. Hera's own leadership, however, revolves largely around the use of deception. After her successful rebellion, Hera temporarily usurps Zeus' position. The *Iliad* uses the verb δολοφρονέω ("to devise deceits") to refer to a god who carries out divine rebellion and particularly associates the verb with Hera (14.197, 300, 329; 19.106; cf. related nouns at 19.97, 112; cf. 15.14).

OT myth generally prefers theomachy to the lower-intensity divine conflicts. But the immortal who instigates and leads a divine rebellion is essentially what has become Satan in later parts of OT myth or the Devil in New Testament myth. The OT uses the tradition of myths of divine rebellion in the account in Isaiah 14, quoted above, in which a foreign leader presumes to set his throne among the gods. Revelation contains the fullest account of divine rebellion in the New Testament (Rev 12.7–9), an account that features several motifs in common with divine rebellions in the *Theogony*.[37]

c. Theomachy, or violence among the gods

I define theomachy as a wrathful god fighting with another god or gods. The *Iliad*'s word for this, as for the quarrel between Agamemnon and Akhilleus, is *eris* (ἔρις), "strife" (20.47, 55, 66; 21.360, 385, 390, 394; cf. 18.107).[38] The parallel reveals theomachy's tendency to parallel principal aspects of the plot. The *Iliad*'s expression for theomachy is "the gods come together in strife," θεοὺς ἔριδι ξυνεῖναι (θεῶν ἔριδι ξυνιόντων, 20.66; θεοὺς ἔριδι ξυνιόντας, 21.390; cf. θεοὺς ἔριδι ξυνελαύνεις, 21.394). The *Theogony* uses the same formula to describe the war between the Olympians and the Titans (θεῶν ἔριδι ξυνόντων, 705). Two other formulas describe single combat of one god with another, ἰσοφαρίζειν μένος ("to match power against," 21.194, 411), and ἀντιφέρεσθαι (μένος) (1.589: 21.482, 357, 488). Of the gods, Ares is particularly associated with *eris*. Treated with contempt by Zeus (his comment about how dear *eris* is to him, 5.891) and defeated, laughably, by Athena, Ares' association with *eris* suggests a negative commentary on *eris* itself. Hera functions thematically as the deity with a divine wrath against another god. Angry with Zeus through much of the poem, Hera is also angry at Apollo (24.55), Hephaistos (18.395–97), Ares (21.413), Artemis (21.479), and perhaps Xanthos (21.331). Hera's junior partner, Athena, also displays anger at Zeus (4.23), at Ares (21.393), and Aphrodite (5.419).[39] At the core of the *Iliad*'s theomachies, the conflict between Athena and Ares parallels Akhilleus' violent duel with Hektor.

Theomachies display a variety of moods. Often comic, at times allegorical, such scenes appear at odds with the *Iliad*'s tragic presentation of Akhilleus, Hektor, and Andromakhe. Other episodes are serious, seething with threats and potent wraths. Why such stark differences? There are distinct categories of theomachy. Three basic oppositions suggest a simple but useful typology. Most important is time: first, theomachies are either set before mortals yet exist, or concurrent with them; second, Zeus takes part in the theomachy, or does not; third, the theomachy is either god against god, god against goddess, or goddess against goddess. These three distinctions establish and define the specific type of theomachy involved, whether serious or comic, present or retrospective.

The *Iliad*'s different categories of theomachy serve different narrative purposes, depending on the respective category. Present and retrospective are strongly opposite types of theomachy, differing in tone, and whether or not they represent serious threats to Zeus' reign. In retrospective theomachies, the tone is serious, the threat to Zeus' reign real. In retrospective incidents, Zeus *is* presented as in danger of being defeated (*Il.* 1.393–412, and 15.18–24; see also 15.78–149). In retrospective theomachy, Zeus uses violence against other gods, as he punishes, strikes, hurls lightning at, or imprisons in Tartaros defeated deities. As in Hesiod's *Theogony*, the *Enuma Elish*, and Yahweh's combat with Rahab/Leviathon, serious theomachies are normally part of creation myths, set near the beginning of time, before mortals yet exist. These early, premortal theomachies help shape the universe, and tend to be very etiological. Such, for example, are the two theomachies in Hesiod's *Theogony*, the generational conflict between the Titans and the Olympians (*Theo.* 617–819) and the final battle between Zeus and Typhoeus (*Theo.* 821–80), serious conflicts in which Zeus has to earn victory. Some of the retrospective theomachies briefly alluded to in the *Iliad* belong to this type, occurring long ago, perhaps before the creation of mortals. This is especially true of that theomachy upon which so much of the *Iliad*'s plot depends, when Thetis rescued Zeus under siege from the other Olympians (1.397–406). Retrospective theomachies do not parallel aspects of the *Iliad*'s plot.

Present-time theomachy is opposite, tending toward the comic because in a world with mortals the general notion of *any* god being defeated has comic potential, so contrary to the standard conceptions of deity, from a mortal's perspective. In present-time theomachy, the defeat of Zeus in particular is presented as an absurdity (though this may not *seem* so since in the retrospective accounts he is in serious danger). Poseidon declares how manifest Zeus' actual power is: "I would not be willing that the rest of us fight with Zeus, the son of Kronos, since he is much stronger" (8.210–11). Zeus affirms as much, in more emphatic terms (8.17–27). Zeus does not take part in the full theomachy of books 20–21. He would easily defeat any opponent, and has no interest in defeating Hera, or the others, in actual combat. His not taking part in the general theomachy in books 20–21 is a thematic parallel both to Akhilleus' one-sided victories in his *aristeia* and duel with Hektor and to Akhilleus *not* competing in the games in book 23, because he would easily win all or most of the events. In present-time conflicts, Zeus is capable of defeating all of the other Olympians together.

Many of the *Iliad*'s present-time theomachies are indirectly linked with the retrospective theomachy when Thetis came to Zeus' aid. Zeus honors Akhilleus' request to help the Trojans and harm the Greeks (and thereby provokes Hera's wrath) because he owes Thetis a favor for her aid when the other gods were against him (1.397–406). Zeus thus prompts the *Iliad*'s present-time theomachies by paying off his debt from the retrospective theomachy and is fully aware of the link between the earlier and present conflicts (1.518–21). In present-time theomachies Zeus never strikes, hurls out of Olympus, throws lightning at, or confines to the underworld any other deity, though these are the typical outcomes of retrospective divine conflicts (as at 1.591, 15.18–24). In the *Iliad*'s present time, no deity temporarily defeats Zeus through violent means or by binding him, as is the case in retrospective theomachies. Hera temporarily subdues Zeus (δαμείς, 14.353), but not by violence or binding, usual theomachian means, but by lying and manipulating him through sex. Zeus limits himself to verbal threats about possible physical punishment (15.17).[40] Present-time theomachies do parallel central aspects of the *Iliad*'s plot.

While friction between Zeus and Hera is thematic and runs through most of books 1–17 of the *Iliad*, episodes of theomachy are largely confined to books 5, 20, and 21, the same respective point in the initial and final sequences. Divine conflicts that parallel the heroic duels of mortal warriors are, in the *Iliad*, the climactic type of theomachy, reserved for the *aristeiai* of Diomedes and Akhilleus. They cannot occur in the middle sequence, because of its inverted tendencies, and since Agamemnon's and Patroklos' *aristeiai* are less successful.[41] Athena's defeat of Ares is the central such encounter. Their two duels (5.793–867.21.391–414) serve as the divine parallel for Akhilleus' defeat of Hektor. In the two very different war gods, the impulsive Ares associated with the Trojans and the strategic Athena associated with victory and with the Homeric hero in particular, the *Iliad* figures the mortals' conflict on the divine plane. The combat between the two war gods is a typical instance of present-time theomachy, with its comic modality.

Each deity embodies the temperament and likelihood of success for the mortal warriors on the respective sides. Because of his close association with strife (*eris*), Ares is the *Iliad*'s theomatic figure of theomachy second only to Hera. He embodies the chaos and fury of war, but not strategy, or victory, with which Athena is associated. Athena occupies a unique position in Homeric epic as the warrior god who mentors the hero, both Akhilleus and Odysseus. When she easily defeats Ares at 21.400–414, her victory incorporates potent thematic parallels associated with Akhilleus: she wounds Ares in the neck (21.406), the only neck wound in all the theomachian episodes. Athena's wounding Ares in the neck parallels and anticipates Akhilleus' slaying Hektor, by a fatal neck wound (22.321–27). Athena's encounter with Ares employs stock ingredients found in mortal combat: the challenging vaunt (21.393–99), a reference to previous combat between the two foes (21.396–99), an ineffective thrust with the spear (21.400–401), the hurling of a great stone (21.403–6), and the victor's vaunt (21.410–14).[42] A description of Ares' hair fouled in the dust (21.407) parallels key images and vocabulary used shortly afterward of Akhilleus' treatment of Hektor's corpse (22.401).

Ares' laughably easy defeat by Athena encapsulates the coming fall of Troy itself, inevitable after Akhilleus slays Hektor. Ares' divine defeats are absurdly easy, incapable of generating pity (e.g., 5.888 ff). He initiates the combat with Athena (ἦρχε γὰρ Ἄρης, 21.391), parallel to Hektor's initiating his duel with Aias, and even to Paris as having begun the war (νείκεος ἀρχή, 22.116; cf. Menelaos' complaint at 13.621–25). Ares' slim-to-nothing chance of defeating Athena parallels Hektor's self-delusion and helplessness before Akhilleus. Ares occupies a position common in Near Eastern myth, the defeated god of the enemy people.[43] Athena's victory predicts the ease with which Akhilleus proceeds in his *aristeia*, and the slaying of Hektor, as well as serving as an accurate assessment of the real disparity between the Greek and Trojan forces when Akhilleus is fighting. Ares, on the other hand, is the poem's thematic divine loser, defeated not only by Athena, but by a mortal, Diomedes (5.792–867) and, in a retrospective account, by the giants Ephialtes and Otos (5.385–91).

Hephaistos' and Xanthos' duel is the one present-time theomachy that is not comic. To depict this archetypal, elemental struggle between fire and water, the *Iliad* reverts to the retrospective serious type, associated with creation myth. Hephaistos' victory again embodies the coming Greek victory, his fires prefiguring the apocalyptic conflagration that awaits Troy. The description at 21.333–38 of how Hera and Hephaistos will now cause a tremendous fire to burn not only Xanthos but the Trojans may allude to an episode in the sack of Troy outside of Homer, in which Hera, the deity with a relentless divine wrath against Troy, and Hephaistos, the god of fire, jointly cause Troy's fiery inferno. When Xanthos admits defeat, he uses the *Iliad*'s standard formula for a divine duel, "not any one of the gods could match you," οὔ τις σοί γε θεῶν δύνατ' ἀντιφερίζειν (21.357; cf. 1.589; 21.482, 488). Xanthos himself links his defeat by Hephaistos to Troy's coming conflagration, "when all of Troy burns by the ravenous fire" (21.375; see Richardson 84).

After Athena defeats Ares, Aphrodite intervenes to help him (21.415–34), much as their respective encounters with Diomedes are intertwined (5.355–63). As with Ares, the *Iliad* thematically depicts Aphrodite in an unflattering light, an embodiment of key Trojan failings, those of Paris, in particular, as Ares embodies Hektor's shortcomings. She shares with Ares the dubious distinction of being driven from battle by a mortal. Further, she is singularly criticized as unfit for taking part in war (5.348–49, 428–29).[44] Athena strikes her in the breasts (21.424), signaling that their encounter, along with the next between Hera and Artemis, is the oldest catfight in Western literature. Though the encounter is not heroic, Athena vaunts over her victim, now lying side by side with Ares: "May all the Trojans' helpers be such as these are" (21.428–29). The theomachies in books 20–21 thus parallel the war: deities partisan to the Trojan side who participate in divine conflicts are all defeated.

Unlike the previous face-offs, the encounter between Apollo and Poseidon (21.435–69) remains solely a verbal exchange. Why? Unique among its treatment of Trojan-partisan deities, the *Iliad* depicts Apollo respectfully. He has wraths against mortals in the *Iliad* (Agamemnon, Patroklos, and Akhilleus) but not against gods.[45] Unlike Ares, Aphrodite, and Artemis, he is never depicted being struck or defeated. Consequently, the scene bestows a certain dignity upon both gods, especially after the comic modality, and defeats, of the previous scenes. Poseidon wins implicit victory (as Artemis notes with chagrin at 21.472), if only at the verbal level, since the *Iliad* chooses this occasion to reiterate some of the greatest Trojan wrongdoing: Laomedon's treachery, his refusal to pay the two gods their promised wage for building the walls of Troy, and his threat to disfigure them.[46] By reminding Apollo of Laomedon's iniquity, and calling the Trojans ὑπερφίαλοι "arrogant, overbearing" (21.459), Poseidon evidences the greater right on the Greek side and undermines Apollo's support for the Trojans.

When Artemis intervenes to criticize Apollo for not fighting Poseidon, Hera accosts her in a second catfight (21.470–96). Yet another Trojan-partisan deity is defeated and treated with disrespect in the comic modality of present-time theomachy. Artemis reviles her brother (νείκεσε: 21.470), a potent root (νεῖκος: "strife") resonating with central themes in the poem. Since they are both Trojan-partisan deities, she suggests a divine parallel with Hektor's disagreements with Poulydamas. Like the Trojans, in their larger strife with the Greeks, Artemis initiates this conflict through her own reckless behavior. When Apollo refuses to reply to her taunt, Hera intervenes, challenging Artemis with the theomachian formula, μένος ἀντιφέρ-σθαι (21.482, 488), her final lines (487–88) parodying heroic vaunts (εὖ εἰδῇς; cf. 20.213, 6.150). Quickly disarming Artemis, Hera strikes her with her own bow, underscoring her easy superiority, while the Mistress of Beasts flees, weeping. A defeated Artemis, reduced to behaving like a girl, now runs, crying, to Zeus, a doublet of the similarly defeated Aphrodite crying to Dione (5.370–74).

A further noncombative exchange, between Hermes and Leto (21.497–504), concludes the theomachies. Hermes graciously concedes victory to Leto, declaring his refusal to fight with her, as a wife of Zeus. The encounter parallels Apollo's refusal to fight Poseidon, though now the roles are reversed (the Greek-partisan god is respectful): a response to Artemis' role in the previous encounter, his graciousness countering her rudeness. His comments about victory are ironic ("boast to the gods that you bested me with superior force," 21.500–501; cf. his ironic remarks to Priam, 24.362–71, 379–85, 390–404, 433–39) and parody the notion of theomachy. Resident in his graciousness is the implicit, unquestioned Greek victory, sounded again at the divine level.

Hera's deception of Zeus in the middle sequence is the only present-time conflict involving Zeus, and unique in several respects. No actual violence is involved, but her preliminaries, at her toilette, parody a divine arming scene (cf. Athena at 5.734 = 8.384; see Janko 1992: 174). Zeus is unaware, as she seduces him, that she is engaging him in conflict. Zeus does not appear to have a wrath against Hera in these scenes, making the conflict one-sided. While Hera is victorious (ὕπνῳ καὶ φιλότητι δαμείς, 14.353), theirs is a conflict between two beings who are basically on the same side, in most respects, in terms of the larger Trojan War. They put aside their friction and do not oppose each other when general theomachy erupts in books 20–21, just as Akhilleus and Agamemnon, who are otherwise united in war against the Trojans, move past their strife in book 19 for Akhilleus' return to battle in book 20.

The *Iliad* uses gender to reinforce the comic modality in present-time theomachy. The most comic divine encounters all involve at least one female; a few involve two or more. Athena, Hera, Aphrodite, Artemis, and Leto all figure in at least one comic theomachy. Of male deities, only Ares (twice) and Zeus figure in comic theomachies (cf. Hermes' encounter with

Leto). While Ares serves as the most ludicrous divine figure in the poem, and Zeus is briefly lampooned in Hera's comic victory, neither of the other two most important male gods, Poseidon or Apollo, takes part in a violent theomachy. The *Iliad* thus does not contain a present-time theomachy between two male gods except for Hephaistos versus Xanthos, which, as noted, reverts to the retrospective type of theomachy. The patriarchy behind these myths apparently finds greater comedy in divine combat that involves goddesses.

To sum up, retrospective theomachies are serious, involve Zeus in violence, and do not mirror central aspects of the *Iliad*'s plot. In retrospective theomachy, defeated rebellious deities are associated with the underworld, a tradition also found in the OT (e.g., Isa 14:15), and the *Theogony* (729). This tradition is alive in the *Iliad*'s present-time conflicts in Zeus' threat, clearly aimed at Hera (8.13–16). Present-time theomachies, on the other hand, are comic, do not involve Zeus in violence, and are used to parallel and amplify central issues in the poem. The three sequences of the narrative pattern differ in the type of divine conflicts they employ. The initial sequence features provocation, as at 1.519, 4.5–6, and 5.419. The closest to actual theomachy is the assistance Athena gives to Diomedes as he attacks Aphrodite and Ares (5.330, 855). Rebellion, but not physical conflict, characterizes theomachy in the middle sequence. Hera moves beyond provocation to rebellion by way of deception (δολοφρονέουσα, 14.197, 300, 329; κακὰ μήσαο, 14.253, 15.27). In the parodic middle sequence is Zeus engaged and "defeated." Only the final sequence has actual present-time theomachy. In this climactic sequence, which has greater divine involvement, violence breaks out with the comic modality typical of present-time theomachy. But the conflicts pose no threat to Zeus, who does not even take part. Strife between Zeus and Hera ends with the end of the middle sequence (other than the retrospective account in Agamemnon's *Ate* narrative, 19.91–136, in which Hera uses deception, as in the middle sequence). Akhilleus' return to battle, marking the end of his strife with Agamemnon, coincides with the end of strife between Zeus and Hera.

HOMERIC EPIC CLEARLY INHERITS many features of theomachy from earlier Near Eastern myth, where it is a frequent mythic subgenre (*Enuma Elish*, the *Baal Cycle*, *Anzu Epic*, and so on). Theomachies associated with theogonic and creation myths are probably the most widely known, such as Marduk's defeat of Tiamat in the *Enuma Elish*, the combat in the *Anzu* epic, and others (probably *Ninurta*, although the species of his opponent, Azag, is unclear; see Jacobsen 237). Less well known, but relevant, are theomachies in Ugaritic myth, which we will discuss in chapter 7 but may sketch out here. The

Baal Cycle depicts Baal in combat with both Yam, god of the sea, and Lot, the sea dragon (an earlier form of OT Leviathon), as well as Mot, god of death. The encounters, in their broad outlines, are generically similar to Marduk's combat with Timat in the *Enuma Elish*.

Among other Near Eastern traditions, OT myth also has many instances, if brief, of divine conflict and theomachy.[47] As in the *Iliad*, OT theomachies serve several different functions. General theomachian passages, tantalizing in their brevity, such as the following description of Yahweh, suggest the *Iliad*'s serious, retrospective accounts of Zeus' battles:

> who humbled the gods of old
> and subdued the ancient powers.
> (Deut 33:27)

Instances of this serious type, set near the creation of the cosmos before humans exist (as in Hesiod's *Theogony*), are rather frequent (Ps 74:13–15, 77:16–19, 89:10; Isa 27:1, 51:9–10; Job 26:12–13; 2 Sam 22). Scattered passages depict Yahweh's primordial defeat of a giant serpent known as Leviathan, or Rahab.[48] The incident is simultaneously cosmogonic and theomachian, depending on one's interpretation of the dragon's species. The serpent may be seen as primordial, perhaps a Near Eastern dying god, out of whose corpse some of the earth is fashioned, as in Cross' (111) description, "when the dark powers of chaos and evil are subdued and the new heavens and earth created." References in Job appear to confirm such a reading, depicting a Yahweh "who by himself spread out the heavens and trod on the back of the sea monster" (Job 9:8).[49] These parallel Marduk's defeat of Tiamat in the *Enuma Elish*, and Zeus' victory over Typhoeus.

OT myth is fond of putting this primordial theomachy to different uses. Prophetic literature may even project the same encounter into a future time:

> On that day the Lord with his cruel sword,
> his mighty and powerful sword, will punish
> Leviathan that twisting sea serpent;
> he will slay the monster of the deep.
> (Isa 27:1)

Elsewhere, as Cross (108) notes, this same myth is superimposed on the era of mortals, to add further meaning to the exodus from Egypt:

> Was it not you who hacked Rahab in pieces
> and ran the dragon through?

Was it not you who dried up the sea,
the waters of the great abyss
and made the ocean depths a path for the redeemed?

(Isa 5:9–10)

Another instance suggests a scene in the *Iliad*'s general theomachy in books 20–21, as well as suggesting a general affinity with the Homeric Hymns:

I call to mind the deeds of the Lord;
I recall your wonderful acts of old . . .
The waters saw you, God,
they saw you and writhed in anguish;
the ocean was troubled to its depths.

(Ps 77:11–16)

As Dahood (231) notes, the watery personification (*tehomot*) here rendered as "depths" is etymologically related to the name Tiamat, the Babylonian water serpent Marduk defeats in the *Enuma Elish*. The waters' terrified reaction suggests Hades' response to the general theomachy in the *Iliad:*

And from beneath, Aidoneus, Lord of those below, was terrified,
afraid he leapt from his throne and cried out, lest Poseidon,
the Earthshaker, break open the earth.

(*Il.* 20.61–63)

Edwards (1991: 293–95) notes many elements in this passage that also occur in theomachies in Hesiod's *Theogony*.

Though best known from Hesiod's *Theogony* (820–68), the *Iliad* draws on Zeus' defeat of Typhoeus at 2.780–83 in a simile that serves as climax for the catalog of the Greek contingents:

and so then they went as if the all the lands were consumed by fire,
and the earth moaned, underneath, as if struck by Zeus who delights in
    thunder,
angered, as when he lashed the earth about Typhoeus
in Arimoi, where they say are now Typhoeus' haunts.

(*Il.* 2.780–83)

A defeated Typhoeus remains alive imprisoned beneath the earth, as with Zeus' threats to cast rebellious deities down to Tartaros (*Il.* 8.13–16). The *Iliad* here links Zeus' theomachian defeat of Typhoeus to the coming Greek victory over the Trojans, to energize a later, warrior context,[50] much as OT myth (Isa 5:9–10) parallels Yahweh's defeat over Leviathan/Rahab with the Israelites' success over Egypt.

Similar to the *Iliad*'s use of theomachy to parallel the triumph of Greek heroes in their *aristeiai*, OT myth includes gods taking part in war to accompany Israelite victory in mortal warfare. In the "Song of Deborah," a form of theomachy accompanies the defeat of the Canaanite king Sisera:

> Kings came, they fought;
> then fought the kings of Canaan
> at Taanach by the waters of Megiddo;
> no plunder of silver did they take.
> The stars fought from heaven,
> the stars in their courses fought against Sisera.
>   (Judg 5:19–21)

In a similar vein, shortly before Joshua is to sack Jericho, a siege myth, as is the *Iliad*, a "man" appears to him: "When Joshua was near Jericho he looked up and saw a man standing in front of him with a drawn sword in his hand. Joshua approached him and asked, 'Are you for us or for our enemies?' The man replied, 'Neither! I am here as captain of the army of the Lord'" (Josh 5:13–14). As Cross (70) notes, Joshua here encounters his heavenly counterpart, much as Akhilleus and Diomedes meet with Athena while they prepare to attack the Trojans.

Like the *Iliad*, OT myth largely maintains the same distinction between serious, retrospective theomachy and comic, present-time theomachy (though, as noted, retrospective theomachies can also be given present-time application). Comic, present-time theomachy is well represented in the OT, with one key difference: the non-Yahwist gods are kept offstage. The actual theomachy, Yahweh's defeat of another god, also takes place offstage, while onstage a *proxy* theomachy is enacted between *agents* of the two deities, the prophets or divine icons of the respective gods. Such proxy theomachies include the prophet Elijah's defeat of 850 prophets of the gods Baal and Asherah and the Ark's destruction of Dagon's sacred icon.

OT myth's most fully developed, comic, present-time theomachy is Yahweh's defeat of Baal, enacted through Elijah's defeat of the prophets of Baal and Asherah in 1 Kings 18. The Israelite King, Ahab, precipitates the conflict by erecting a temple to Baal and a sacred pole for Asherah (1 Kings 16:29–33), though continuing to worship Yahweh. Ahab's actions provoke the prophet Elijah, an instantiation, as noted, of *3. The king who quarrels with his prophet* (in chapter 5). Jezebel, Ahab's Phoenician wife, has some of

Yahweh's prophets slain (1 Kings 18:4), further exacerbating the conflict between Ahab and Elijah. By marrying a Phoenician woman Ahab violates Yahweh's general proscription against marrying foreigners, and parallels Paris in endangering his community by bringing a foreign woman into its midst (*8b. A man's desire for a foreign woman brings destruction on his people*).

Elijah prompts a confrontation between Yahweh and Baal by declaring that there will be no rain or dew for years, unless he commands it (1 Kings 17:1). "The issue was which of the two gods controls the rain" (Suggs et al. 365). In the third year of the subsequent drought, Yahweh instructs Elijah to confront Ahab, after which he will bring rain (1 Kings 18:1). Elijah challenges Ahab to summon the 450 prophets of Baal and 400 of Asherah to meet him on Mount Carmel (1 Kings 18:19), the contest serving as a proxy theomachy between Yahweh and Baal.[51] When all gather on Mount Carmel, Elijah challenges the prophets of Baal and Asherah to prepare a bull for sacrifice and to ask their gods to light the fire for the sacrifice, while he will do the same with another bull (1 Kings 18:21–24). When Baal's prophets try, but receive no answer, Elijah ridicules their god: "At midday Elijah mocked them: 'Call louder, for he is a god. It may be he is deep in thought, or engaged, or on a journey; or he may have gone to sleep and must be woken up'" (1 Kings 18:27). Elijah prepares his altar, and the sacrifice, praying to Yahweh. Immediately, Yahweh sends fire, consuming the sacrificed bull. Elijah then has the 850 prophets seized and slaughtered (1 Kings 18:40). Now, Elijah tells Ahab, Yahweh will send rain, and a great storm follows.

Comic in Elijah's mocking tone and the failure of the Canaanite prophets, this present-time theomachy resembles those in the *Iliad* in how it parallels frictions on the mortal plane. Here the more usual parallels with human war are adapted for religious conflict. Elijah's comic theomachy parallels not war between peoples but conflict and friction *within* the Israelite community, the choice between worship of Yahweh, as embodied in Elijah, and worship of the Canaanite deities, led by Jezebel. Instead of the defeated god's warriors dying, his *prophets* do. The deaths of the Canaanite prophets at Elijah's hands thus parallel the Trojans' death toll at Akhilleus' hands. Yahweh's defeat of Baal also has an elemental dimension, the prominence and power of fire and water, and the control of both. In this respect, the encounter suggests elements of retrospective theomachy as well. Yahweh's ability to create fire on the water,[52] and then make rain, replays his ancient defeat of the waters, which in the *Iliad* is also present in slightly altered form in Hephaistos' defeat of Xanthos (21.328–84).

In the ark's defeat of the sacred icon of the Philistines' god, Dagon, 1 Samuel offers a further instance of comic, present-time theomachy by proxy. Here the Philistines, that Aegean people whom biblical archaeologists argue are Mycenaean Greeks,[53] twice defeat and rout the Israelites (1 Sam 4:1–3), the second time slaying 30,000 and seizing the ark (1 Sam 4:10–11). The ark serves various functions in OT myth: repository for the tablets Moses received (Deut 10:5), footstool or podium for Yahweh (McCarter 1980: 108), and a visible sign of his presence, but also a force in war, protecting the Israelites, scattering their enemies before them. In this latter sense, as McCarter and others note, the ark functions in OT myth much as the Palladium of Athena does in Trojan War myth.[54] Although the *Iliad* does not mention the Palladium, the Cyclic epic, the *Little Iliad* (see West 2003: 122–23, 130–33), and Apollodorus (*Epit.* 5.13) include its capture by the Greeks as necessary for the Greeks to sack Troy. As McCarter (1985: 24) explains, a theomachian conception lies at the heart of such myths: "[A] victorious army regarded the capture of its enemy's gods as a demonstration of the superior power of its own gods. Accordingly the captured images would be placed in the temples of the victor's gods as spoils of war, a gesture that evinced the inferiority of the enemy's gods." The Philistines, having captured the Ark, set it inside Dagon's temple in Ashdod, beside his image. The theomachy is thus by proxy, between the two icons, and takes place offstage.

The next morning, the Philistines find Dagon's icon lying face downward before the ark. They right the image, but the following morning again find it face down, now with its head and hands broken off. Dagon's twice-repeated posture in defeat loosely parallels Ares, defeated by Athena, "and having fallen he [Ares] covered seven measures, and his hair was in the dust,/ and his armor rattled around him" (*Il.* 21.407–8). The theomachy also includes a fanciful, clearly parodic, etiology (see McCarter 1985: 122) which, for the OT authors, further cements Yahweh's victory over the Philistine god: "That is why to this day the priests of Dagon and all who enter the temple of Dagon at Ashdod do not set foot on Dagon's platform" (1 Sam 5). Subsequent events display Yahweh's power as he sends plagues upon the Philistines (a variant of chapter 5's 2. *The exterminating angel slays many on the battlefield*), until they voluntarily surrender the ark.[55]

In a further specific subset of present-time theomachy common to OT myth and the *Iliad, The great hero defeats the enemy's god(s)*. The *Iliad* employs this subgenre when Diomedes defeats both Aphrodite and Ares, and Akhilleus fights the river Xanthos (5.330, 855; 21.211 ff). OT myth offers the same subgenre, though again by proxy, in Samson's defeat of the same Philistine god, Dagon, in Judges 16. The Philistines display Samson, captured and blinded, at a public sacrifice to Dagon: "The lords of the Philistines assembled to offer a great sacrifice to their god Dagon. . . . The people when they saw him, praised their god, chanting: 'Our god has delivered our enemy into our hands, the scourge of our land who piled it with our dead'"

(Judg 16:23–24). But Samson prays to Yahweh, who grants him strength (in chapter 1, see *3. A god places* μένος *in the hero*), enabling him to pull down the pillars of Dagon's temple, slaying all the Philistines.[56] Aided by Yahweh, Samson slays the Philistines and defeats their god.

Formulaic passages in the prophetic books evidence an additional aspect of OT theomachy: gods defeated and driven into exile by Yahweh, paralleling Athena's defeat of Ares, and Apollo's abandonment of Troy (22.213). Jeremiah's prophecies against foreign nations, which connect the Philistines with Crete (Jer 47:4), specify the defeats of several other gods. After Yahweh defeats them and their peoples, "Milcom will go into exile" (Jer 48:7), "Kemosh will go into exile" (Jer 51:44), and "I shall punish Bel in Babylon" (Jer 51:44), says Jeremiah. Similarly Isaiah prophesies Yahweh's victories over other gods when he declares, "Bel has crouched down, Nebo stooped low" (Isa 46:1), the former being another name of Marduk, the latter being his son, a god of wisdom (Suggs et al. 755).

d. Gods punishing gods (as a result of theomachy)

Gods who are defeated in theomachies are subject to punishment and loss of status. The most extreme option occurs only in retrospective theomachies, such as Hesiod's account in the *Theogony*, and the book of Revelation's war in heaven (Rev 12:7–9): defeated gods are imprisoned in the underworld. The *Iliad*'s present-time theomachies allude to confinement in the underworld, but only as a threat. In the fractious divine council at *Iliad* 8.2 ff Zeus threatens two punishments for any Olympian who breaks his command against intervening in the war:

> Struck [πληγείς] he will make his way to Olympos with difficulty,
> or, having seized him, I will hurl him into gloomy Tartaros.
>
> (8.12–13)

The first option, to be struck (πληγείς: 8.12) by Zeus, is the *Iliad*'s most typical way of depicting Zeus' defeating another god after a conflict. The *Iliad* uses the verb πλήσσω (*plesso*), "smite, strike," to depict Zeus punishing a god who has committed offense. Other typical examples in the *Iliad* include Zeus restating this threat to Athena and Hera (οὐκ ἂν ἐφ' ὑμετέρων ὀχέων πληγέντε κεραυνῷ / ' ἂψ ἐς Ὄλυμπον ἵκεσθον, 8.455–56), and his similar threat to Hera after she deceived him (πρώτη ἐπαύρηαι καί σε πληγῇσιν ἱμάσσω, 15.17).[57] The *Theogony* also employs *plesso* in Zeus' defeat of Typhoeus, πλῆξεν ἀπ' Οὐλύμποιο (855). Derivatives of the verb remain associated with divine punishments in later formations including *plague*, a god-sent disease. The second option (8.13), Zeus hurling the offender into Tartaros (8.13), restates the ancient motif of confining the defeated deity in the underworld. Homeric epic particularly associates *plesso* with Zeus' lightning, his most frequent means for inflicting punishment (as at 8.455: πληγέντε κεραυνῷ).

↜

12. God panics the army by hurling lightning, reversing the tide of battle

In OT myth Yahweh frequently intervenes to affect the outcome of war by hurling thunder against an enemy army and routing it. Though frequent in the OT, the *Iliad* employs this subgenre of myth sparingly. The main instance is Zeus' sole intervention on the battlefield, when he hurls lightning before the Greeks (8.75–77, 133–36; cf. 17.595), routing them, and initiating the middle sequence during which the Trojans are victorious. Of the *Iliad*'s gods, only Zeus has the ability to hurl lightning. Nonetheless, other Olympian gods participate in this same basic motif, instilling panic or terror in an army through some other means. For instance, Apollo routs the Greeks by hurling Phobos (panic/rout) among them (17.118). Phobos itself is often personified as an attendant or son of Ares, along with Deimos (4.440, 11.37, 15.119). Poseidon also instills terror once in an individual warrior (13.434–35). In addition to frequent instances of Yahweh's routing armies with his thunder (discussed below), OT myth also has personifications as attendants for him in war, much like Ares, as at Habukkuk 3.5: "Pestilence stalks before him, and plague follows close behind."

The *Iliad*'s main use of this subgenre is quite pivotal: it initiates the middle sequence with its inverted values of temporary Trojan victory. After forbidding other Olympians to interfere, and casting his divine scales to affirm his decision to help the Trojans and harm the Greeks, Zeus hurls lightning against the Greeks (8.76). Greek heroes including the Aiante, Idomeneus, Agamemnon, and Odysseus, instantly turn and flee, the generic result, as comparison with OT myth reveals (e.g., Amos 2:16). When Nestor is left vulnerable to Trojan attack, Diomedes stays his ground to help him, causing Zeus to thunder a second time, before his chariot (8.133–35). In the resulting panic, both Nestor and his horses are afraid (8.136, 138).

Such scenes are common in OT myth. Very indicative, though not specifying thunder as the specific agent for the rout, is Yahweh's declaration in Exodus: "I shall send terror of me ahead of you and throw into panic every people you find in your path. I shall make all your enemies turn their backs towards you. I shall spread panic before you to drive out the Hivites, the Canaanites, and the Hittites in front of you" (Exod 23:27–28). Judges, in one of the oldest sections of the OT, offers a typical instance, suggestive of *Iliad* 8 in many respects: "And the Lord threw Sisera and all his chariots and army into panic-stricken rout before Barak's onslaught; Sisera himself dismounted from his chariot and fled on foot" (Judg 4:15). As a result of Yahweh's sending panic into the army, Sisera's immediate predicament suggests Nestor's circumstances and those of the other heroes who flee in *Iliad* 8. For the specific parallel of a god hurling thunder to cause such panic, 1 Samuel has the following instance: "As Samuel was offering the sacrifice and the Philistines were advancing to the attack, the Lord with mighty thunder threw the Philistines into confusion. They fled in panic before the Israelites" (1 Sam 7:10). Given the likely association of the Philistines with Mycenaean Greeks, here the motif may be applied against the same people as it is at *Iliad* 8.76 ff.[58] Miller (116) offers a general explanation for the use of divine routs in OT myth: "the tradition of holy war in which victory was believed to be accomplished, not by might of numbers and weapons but by terror (cf. Ex. 23:27 ff, Josh. 2:9) and dread (cf. Deut. 2:25, 11:25) which Yahweh wrought upon the enemy, that caused them to melt . . . before the Israelites."[59]

Such passages are also common in the prophetic books. In Jeremiah, Yahweh threatens revenge against the Ammonites, "I am bringing terror on you from every side, / says the Lord God of Hosts; every one of you will be driven headlong / with no one to rally the fugitives" (Jer 49:5). Zechariah prophesies a day when Yahweh will destroy all the nations that fought against Israel: "On that day a great panic sent by the Lord will fall on them" (Zech 14.13). OT myth also depicts Yahweh throwing panic against the Israelites, as Zeus does against the Greeks in *Iliad* 8. Amos speaks of Yahweh's coming punishment against Israel: "On that day the bravest of warriors will throw away his weapons and flee" (Amos 2:16). Elsewhere Yahweh himself warns the Israelites that their enemies will rout them if they fail to keep his commandments, "I shall set my face against you, and you will be routed by your enemies" (Lev 26:17; cf. Deut 28:25).

⌐⌐

13. Apocalypse: A wrathful god destroys an arrogant city

I define apocalypse as a wrathful god's mass destruction of mortals who have committed offense against him (though the destruction may include mortals who have committed no offense). The larger Trojan War saga culminates in the destruction of Troy, and the *Iliad* clearly designates this event as an apocalypse. Apocalyptic myths exist in three different degrees of destruction. A full apocalypse depicts the destruction of the entire human race, as in the passing of some of Hesiod's ages (*Works and Days* 138) and the OT myth of the flood (Gen 7–10). But the middle degree, the destruction of an entire city, is the most common, as in the myth of Sodom and Gomorrah (Gen 19), Ovid's Baucis and Philemon (*Metamorphoses* 8.618–724), and the destruction of Troy. Zeus and Hera define the middle degree of apocalypse in their cavalier discussion on the topic of destroying separate cities (4.40). In Greek myth it is especially Zeus' wrath that triggers either a full-scale or a middle-degree apocalypse. Also found is a smaller, contained apocalypse, when Zeus talks another wrathful deity down to a less violent degree of punishment, punishing only those humans who have actually committed offense, as each of the *Odyssey*'s three sequences (Helios at *Od.* 12.43, 77–88, Poseidon *Od.* 13.158–64, and Athena *Od.* 24.472–86) concludes.[60] In all three degrees of apocalypse, a typical figure, the "one just man," and his immediate family, survive (discussed below as subgenre 14). To provide a context for better understanding apocalyptic myth, we turn first to Hesiod's *Works and Days*, then the *Iliad*'s examples and Near Eastern parallels, especially OT myth, which is particularly fond of apocalypse.

The *Works and Days* offers brief instances of full apocalypses and a more detailed account of the middle degree of apocalypse, a wrathful god's destruction of a city. In his myth of the Ages, Hesiod's second generation, the silver race, after provoking the gods' wrath by failing to honor them, is destroyed through a full apocalypse: "Zeus, the son of Kronos, thus angered, hid them away" (137–38). Though vague and elliptic, the account makes clear that the entire race was destroyed (the earth covered it over, 140), with no mention of a "one just man" figure surviving. Hesiod predicts that his own iron age, the fifth such generation, will also meet its end in an apocalypse. In a lengthier account (174–201) of his age's wrongdoing, which has violated hospitality, he specifies that "Zeus will destroy this race" (180). Sinclair (22–23) compares details here (181 ff) to an apocalyptic passage at Mark 13:12.

But it is in a subsequent passage on *hubris* that Hesiod's use of apocalypse is most relevant to the *Iliad*. While the just flourish, says Hesiod, and so do their cities, Zeus punishes the arrogant (οἷς δ᾽ ὕβρις τε μέμηλε: 238), and their cities:

> For often an entire city is taken away[61] because of one bad man,
> the one who transgresses [ἀλιτραίνει] and devises reckless things.
>
> (240–41)

Hesiod here invokes the type of apocalypse upon which the *Iliad* is predicated: Troy is destroyed for offenses committed by key individuals, especially Laomedon and Paris. "Reckless things" (ἀτάσθαλα) is a moral term in Homeric epic, denoting behavior that needlessly brings danger on a community, that goes against the gods' designs, much like "sin." Related, cognate words are used of Paris (ἄτης, 24.28) and Hektor (ἀτασθαλίῃσιν, 22.104), while a similar, but noncognate term is used of Laomedon (ἀφραδίῃσιν, 5.649). Hesiod goes on to depict the destruction Zeus will visit on the city of the arrogant man:

> For the son of Kronos brings great suffering upon them from heaven,
> hunger and plague, and the people perish,
> and the women do not bear children, and the houses dwindle,
> through the designs of Olympian Zeus; at another time
> he destroys their numerous army, or their city walls,
> or the son of Kronos takes away their ships on the sea.
>
> (242–47)

Here are the typological kernels of the myths of Thebes (243–44) and Troy (246: *Iliad*, 247: *Odyssey*).

Although the devastation falls outside the plot's present time, the *Iliad* alludes to the apocalyptic destruction on many occasions. The key transgressions of Laomedon (breaking a sworn oath and cheating the gods), Paris (bringing a foreign, married woman among his people, plundering Menelaos' goods, and violating hospitality), Pandaros (breaking a sworn oath), and Hektor (self-delusion, presumption, and *hubris*), conspire to turn the gods against the city and people. Although many gods in the *Iliad* express anger at a given mortal, in apocalyptic passages Zeus himself is the wrathful god, angry not at a Trojan hero but at Troy, or the Trojans collectively. One of the most traditional of such passages is the following simile of Zeus as storm god:

> As when all the black earth is weighted down by a tempest
> on a late summer day, when Zeus pours down overwhelming waters
> raging against men who have stirred him to anger [κοτεσσάμενος χαλεπήνῃ]
> because they pass crooked decrees in violent assembly,
> and drive righteousness away, and care nothing for the gods' regard,
> and all their rivers swell their current to full spate,
> and the mountain streams rip channels in the hillsides
> and dash groaning headlong down from the mountains,
> down to the raging sea, so that the works of men are destroyed.
>
> (16.384–92)

Zeus's cause for anger, and hence his reason for apocalyptic destruction, is close, as many have noted (e.g., West 1978: 217) to the passage from the *Works and Days* (240–47). Essentially this is Hesiod's city of the arrogant man. Though Troy is not here named, the enumerated wrongs are reminiscent of those committed by Laomedon and Paris: Zeus' anger at these wrongs prompts and channels the fury of natural forces, storm, rivers, and streams, to destroy man-made works, a city and its walls.[62]

When Pandaros wounds Menelaos in book 4, thus breaking the truce and sworn oaths, he extends earlier Trojan transgressions by Laomedon and Paris. Agamemnon prophesies that Zeus will be so angered as to doom Troy to destruction:

> For if the Olympian does not bring it to pass at once,
> then he will later, and they will pay with a great penalty,
> with their own heads, with their wives, and with their children,
> For I know this well, in my mind and heart,
> there will be a day sacred Ilion will be destroyed,
> and Priam and the people of Priam of the ash spear,
> for Zeus, the son of Kronos, seated aloft, who dwells in the heaven
> himself will shake his dread aegis, enraged [κοτέων]
> at this deception [ἀπάτης]. These things will not be unaccomplished.
>
> (4.160–68)

Agamemnon's powerful image of an angry Zeus will not occur in the present time of the *Iliad*, where Hera and Athena occupy such divine positions. But as we have noted, and as Agamemnon seems well aware, in the apocalypse, it is Zeus who is moved to anger, not Hera or Athena. In both passages, Zeus' anger is rendered by the verb κοτέω (*koteo*), which, as Walsh (23–29, 50, 52–53, 79, 97, 101) shows, the *Iliad* uses of long-term anger, often of the angers immortals have against mortals. The apocalyptic destruction of Troy is thus presented as the end of a long process, not Zeus' momentary response to a specific occurrence.[63]

Menelaos' tirade against the Trojans, as he stands over the slain Peisander, complements the previous passage in several respects:

> You are not lacking in insult, nor in other outrage,
> such as you committed against me, you dogs, nor in any way did
> you fear the violent wrath [χαλεπὴν . . . μῆνιν] of Zeus the thunderer,
> the god of hospitality, who someday will sack your sheer citadel.
>
> (13.622–25)

The two brothers are of one mind. Both assign apocalyptic destruction of Troy to an angry Zeus, outraged by Trojan misconduct. Both are aware, as many modern commentators are not, that Zeus' timetable is not immediate. I repeat Lefkowitz's (151) formulation, "Because the gods can take a longer view than short-lived mortals, they are content to wait to administer their justice and to postpone revenge even for several generations." Menelaos here reacts out of frustration, much as he does in the abortive duel with Paris, where he also invokes Zeus' connection with hospitality (3.351–54). Personally violated by Paris to prompt the war, Menelaos is more focused than many on its end, as Janko (1992: 122) notes, "full of . . . grief and indignation based on his sense of injustice. . . . His faith in Zeus will eventually be vindicated."

Hektor, when he foolishly rejects Poulydamas' suggestion to return to the city, speaks of Zeus' wrath, and how it has already harmed Troy:

> For before, mortal men always used to speak of the city
> of Priam as rich in gold, rich in bronze,
> but now our houses' beautiful heirlooms are destroyed,
> and many possessions make their way, sold, to Phrygia
> and fair Maionia, since great Zeus grew hateful [ὠδύσατο].
>
> (18.288–92)

Similar to the irony in Paris' awareness that Athena helps the Greeks 3.439–40, Hektor is aware that Zeus' anger is directed against Troy but deludes himself as to what this implies, just as the final sequence, which will result in his own death, begins. Hektor does not specify how Zeus' anger is manifest, but parallels in OT myth help us fill in the ellipsis (Ezek 28:5–7; Zech 9:3–4, discussed below). Hektor means that Zeus has sent the Greek army against Troy. Zeus' anger here thus initiates the process that will culminate in the apocalypse. According to Poseidon, Zeus "hates Priam's race" (ἤχθηρε, 20.306), which, considering how many relatives this involves, is close to saying he hates the Trojans, and again implies a pending apocalypse.

Although Zeus' wrath marks the apocalyptic destruction of Troy, other gods' wraths play a supporting role when not directed at an individual but at the Trojans, collectively. Chief among these is Hera, whose wrath is twice linked with a Troy consumed by flames. As she reminds Poseidon, she and Athena have sworn oaths not to prevent the apocalyptic conflagration that awaits the city:

> For truly we two have sworn many oaths, I and
> Pallas Athena, before all the immortals,

never to ward off the evil day from the Trojans
when all of Troy should be consumed by devouring fire,
burning, and the Ares-like sons of the Akhaians light the fires.

$$(20.313–17)$$

In a second passage (21.374–6 = 20.315–17), the river Xanthos swears an oath to Hera (to get her to call off Hephaistos and his fires) that he will not prevent Troy's apocalyptic destruction, repeating her connection with the coming conflagration.

A further passage links the apocalyptic destruction of a city with a collective divine wrath:

As when the smoke going up rises to the wide heaven,
the smoke of a city on fire, and the gods' wrath [μῆνις] sends it up,
which sets toils upon everyone, and hurls griefs upon many,
so Akhilleus sets toils and griefs upon the Trojans.

$$(21.522–24)$$

Although the city is again unnamed, because the gods' wraths and subsequent fire are paralleled with Akhilleus, the apocalypse is implicitly the destruction of Troy.

Two additional passages (12.10–34, 7.446–63) use apocalyptic terms to refer to the coming destruction not of Troy but of the Greek wall. The former passage suggests links with Zeus' storm simile, while the latter marks the end of the initial sequence. Both passages assign the gods' destruction of the wall to the Greeks' failure to have offered hecatombs when they built it. The book 7 passage is a small divine council between Zeus and Poseidon very like three parallel scenes in the *Odyssey* (12.376–88, 13.125–60, 24.472–87), in which Zeus talks an offended god out of carrying out apocalyptic destruction. All three *Odyssey* passages, and *Iliad* 7.446–63, end sequences of their respective narrative patterns.[64] Thus, *Iliad* 7.446–63 belongs to a family of type-scenes with apocalyptic connotations, the earliest of which is Anu talking Ishtar out of destroying Uruk (*Gilgamesh* VI iii–iv; cf. *Homeric Hymn to Demeter* 310–13). On this occasion Poseidon complains about a loss of respect, as in the three Odyssean passages, but he does not threaten angry destruction. Here, as is typical of the type-scene, Zeus is careful to restore Poseidon's sense of respect and also specifies the destruction—that Poseidon destroy the Greeks' wall after they leave Troy. Zeus' initiating the wall's destruction thus parallels his responsibility for Troy's destruction.

The passage in book 12 has fully developed apocalyptic references, not just generic affiliations. The *Iliad* chooses this moment to evoke not only the destruction of Troy but the end of an era. Poseidon and Apollo will destroy the Greeks' wall after the war, after the Greeks have left, and after many heroes, demigods, have died. Only here (12.23) in all of Homeric epic is the term *hemitheoi* (demigods) used for heroes (Scodel 1982: 34–40, 48). The method of destruction, as at *Iliad* 16.384–92, is the combined forces of several storm-fed rivers, after Zeus has rained for nine days. In both passages, the rivers flow down from the mountains (ἀπ᾽ Ἰδαίων ὀρέων, 12.19; ἐξ ὀρέων, 16.392) to the sea (ἅλαδε, 12.19; ἐς δ᾽ ἅλα, 16.391), to destroy the works of mortals (12.26, 16.392). The passage thus depicts Zeus supervising Poseidon and Apollo in the destruction of the wall. The episode is the *Iliad*'s only mention of Poseidon's trident (12.27; B. Hainsworth 320), the instrument Vergil depicts him using in the destruction of Troy (*Aeneid* 2.610). Commentators (e.g., Scodel 1982: 40, 45, and Nagler 149–55) have tended to lump all apocalypses together and perhaps misunderstood the level of destruction implied here. The *Iliad* points to the destruction of a city, not an angry destruction of an entire race. The *Iliad* thus does not here draw on *the* flood myth, as has been claimed, but on the middle degree of apocalypse, destruction of a city (discussed below).

An additional passage depicts Troy, Priam, and his people as hated by the gods. The lines are not found in ancient manuscripts of the *Iliad*, but preserved in the pseudo-Platonic *Alcibiades* II (Kirk 1990: 340):

> But the gods took no part in it [the sacrifice],
> and they did not want it; for sacred Ilion was hateful [ἀπήχθετο] to them
> and so was Priam and the people of Priam of the stout ash spear.
>
> (8.550–52)

Though the lines may be suspect, their theme is entirely traditional. The gods' rejection of a sacrifice is a frequent subgenre of myth, occurring elsewhere in the *Iliad* when Athena rejects a Trojan sacrifice (6.311), and more frequently in OT myth, where it is often associated with a coming apocalypse. Jeremiah has several relevant examples, including the following passage, relevant to *Iliad* 8.550–52 and 6.311: "Though they sacrifice whole-offering and grain-offering, I shall not accept them. I shall make an end of them with sword, famine, and pestilence" (Jer 14:14). Here, as in *Iliad* 8.550–52 and 6.311, a god's rejection of a sacrifice is prelude to his bringing destruction upon a people through war. Similarly, Hosea links Yahweh's rejection of sacrifices with his helping an invading army destroy a people:

> They go with sacrifices of sheep and cattle
> to seek the Lord, but do not find him,

for he has withdrawn from them . . .
Now an invader is set to devour their fields.

(Hosea 5:6–7)

OT myth is rich in similar passages of Yahweh rejecting a sacrifice or prayer, linked with apocalypse (Jer 11:14, 44:16–19; Hosea 4:19, 8.13; Amos 5:22; Micah 3:4).

Perhaps in no mythic tradition is apocalypse more common than in OT myth. Though most frequent in the prophetic books, OT myth incorporates apocalypses from Genesis on. There are instances quite close to the passages at *Iliad* 12.10–34 and 16.384–92, in which Yahweh uses water, rivers, or ocean to set in motion the middle degree of apocalypse, the destruction of a city. Ezekiel provides relevant examples:

> For the Lord God says: "When I make you a desolate city, like cities where no one lives, when I bring the primeval ocean up over you and the great waters cover you, I shall thrust you down with those who go down to the abyss, to the dead of all the ages; I shall make you dwell in the underworld . . . I shall bring destruction on you, and you will be no more. (Ezek 26:19–21)

> In my rage I shall unleash a storm-wind; rain will come in torrents in my anger, hailstones in my fury, until all is destroyed. I shall overthrow the wall which you have daubed with whitewash and level it to the ground, laying bare its foundations. . . . I shall vent my rage on the wall and on those who daubed it with whitewash. (Ezek 13:13–15)

As at *Iliad* 12.10–34, these passages depict the common form of apocalypse in which a wrathful god destroys a city, as Zeus in the *Iliad*. The passage from Ezekiel 13 has a similar focus on a wrathful god destroying a specific wall as *Iliad* 12.10–34 (cf. Lam 2:8–9; Isa 25:12). Isaiah offers another passage, relevant to *Iliad* 12.10–34 and 16.384–92:

> The Lord has one at his bidding, mighty and strong,
> like a sweeping storm of hail, like a destroying tempest,
> like a torrent of water in overwhelming flood
> he will beat down on the land with violence.
>
> (Isa 28:2)

The "one" is usually thought to be an Assyrian king (Suggs et al. 731–32), whom Yahweh leads against the Israelites in apocalyptic imagery, much as Athena accompanies the best of the Akhaians against the Trojans in the *Iliad* (cf. Ezek 43:2–3).

OT myth particularly figures the destruction of Tyre, similar to the *Iliad*'s depiction of Troy, as having wealth that has bred arrogance:

> Your [Tyre's] commerce grew so great
> that lawlessness filled your heart
> and led to wrongdoing . . .
> I kindled a fire within you,
> and it devoured you.
> I reduced you to ashes on the ground.
> (Ezek 28:16–18)

> Tyre, who built herself a rampart,
> has amassed silver like dust
> and gold like the dirt on the streets.
> But the Lord will take from her all she possesses;
> he will break her power at sea,
> and the city itself will be destroyed by fire.
> (Zech 9:3–4)

As Zeus for Troy, Yahweh is here depicted causing apocalyptic conflagration to punish the city's arrogance.

Much as the *Iliad*, OT myth often employs apocalyptic machinery to depict an angry god leading an army to lay waste to a city. Typical is the account of Babylon falling to Cyrus:

> The Lord of Hosts is mustering a host for war.
> They come from a distant land, from beyond the horizon,
> the Lord with the weapons of his wrath,
> to lay the whole earth waste . . .
> The day of the Lord is coming,
> that cruel day of wrath and fierce anger,
> to reduce the earth to desolation
> and destroy all the wicked there . . .
> All who are found will fall by the sword,
> all who are taken will be thrust through;
> their babes will be battered to death before their eyes,
> their houses looted and their wives raped.
> (Isa 13:4–16)

The concluding lines are quite close to Priam's grim prophecy in his plea to Hektor to come within the walls rather than face Akhilleus alone:

[Me] accursed, whom the father, son of Kronos, will waste
on the threshold of old age, in a miserable way, having beheld many
evils: my sons slain, my daughters dragged off,
their bedchambers ravaged, my own children
dashed to the ground in terrible slaughter.

(22.60–64)

Though Isa 13:4–16 refers to Babylon, the same generic elements well fit Troy in the *Iliad*.[65]

The *Iliad* points to, but does not depict, Troy's apocalyptic destruction. The initial sequence concludes with Poseidon and Zeus discussing the destruction of the Greek wall, an indirect reference to the apocalypse awaiting Troy. The middle sequence concludes with the fierce fighting compared to apocalyptic conflagration rushing on an unnamed city:

like a savage fire, rushing on a city of men,
blazes, stirred up suddenly, and the houses are destroyed
in the great blaze, for the force of the wind roars upon it.

(17.737–39)

The end of the final sequence lacks a deliberate figuring of the apocalypse. Instead, in a potent instance of Homeric epic's selectivity, the poem concludes with the funeral of Hektor, leaving unspoken the transition to Troy's destruction, a foregone conclusion with Hektor, *Upholder* of the city, dead.[66] In this respect the *Iliad*'s conclusion is an instance of aposiopesis, or paralipsis, an event deliberately not described, more emphatic in its omission. Hektor's corpse burning on its pyre (24.787) thus thematically parallels, and is a miniature of, the coming apocalyptic conflagration that awaits Troy.[67]

↝

14. The one just man

Although the *Iliad* concludes with Hektor's funeral, it has earlier alluded to a positive outcome arising from Troy's apocalyptic destruction. The most frequent result of apocalyptic myth is the survival of a traditional figure, the "one just man."[68] Rewarded by the gods for his piety, he survives the apocalypse, which was directed at mortals who had committed offense. Known from the very ancient Near Eastern myth of the Deluge, the designated survivor, Ziusudra/Atrahasis, was early incorporated into the *Gilgamesh* epic as Utnapishtim. Best known in OT myth from Noah (who is clearly based on the earlier myth of Ziusudra/Atrahasis), this figure is common in both

Greek and OT myth. Other versions of the figure in Greek myth include Deukalion, Dardanos, Baucis and Philemon, even Telemakhos,[69] while OT myth, in addition to Noah, has Lot, Enoch (Gen 5),[70] and probably Daniel (Ezek 14:14).[71] We will establish the conventional aspects of the figure before noting how Aineias serves this same function in the *Iliad* and greater Trojan War myth. Neglecting the mythic type, commentators have otherwise been at a loss to account for, convincingly, the several unusual traits the *Iliad* gives Aineias.[72]

The one just man typically has a personal relationship with god (*Atrahasis* I vii [Dalley 18–19]; Noah, Gen 6:9, 13, etc.; Enoch, Gen 5:22–24, Lot, with angels, Gen 14). He is often descended from a relative especially favored by god (Lot is Abraham's nephew, Gen 11:27; Enoch is seventh in descent from Adam). In some cases the close relationship with god develops because the one just man has displayed exemplary morality (Lot gives the disguised angels hospitality, as do Baucis and Philemon for Jupiter and Mercury). Genesis foregrounds these qualities in Noah ("a righteous man, the one blameless man of his time," Gen 6:9) before relating his myth. An immortal advises him how to avoid the coming catastrophe. He may attempt to warn others of the destruction, but if he does, they do not heed him. He and his immediate family not only escape the subsequent apocalypse, but he is given some special status, resembling the gods in some way.

In his account of Enoch in *Paradise Lost*, Milton draws on the various biblical references as well as apocryphal texts. Although his version is a few millennia later than the texts we are considering, he skillfully brings together the key motifs associated with such figures in a way that helps us understand how the *Iliad* draws on this traditional type in its depiction of Aineias (11.665–710):

> . . . one rising, eminent
> In wise deport, spake much of Right and Wrong,
> of Justice and Religion, Truth and Peace,
> And Judgment from above; him old and young
> Exploded, and had seiz'd with violent hands,
> Had not a Cloud descending snatch'd him thence
> Unseen amid the throng . . .
> The only righteous in a World perverse . . .
> Him the most High
> Rapt in a balmy Cloud with winged Steeds
> Did, as thou saw'st, receive, to walk with God
> High in Salvation and the Climes of bliss

Exempt from Death; to show thee reward
Awaits the good, the rest what punishment.

Two passages in the *Iliad* cement Aineias' status as this traditional figure, if only in a germinal form, which Vergil was to exploit more fully as his *"pius Aeneas."*

Aineias' duel with Akhilleus is deprived of a climax, as discussed in chapter 1 (motif 5f), when Poseidon intervenes through a pivotal contrafactual. But why does Poseidon, a Greek-partisan god, rescue Aineias (20.291–340), just as the theomachian tensions that accompany Akhilleus' *aristeia* are building? Even more unusual, though not usually discussed by commentators, why is Hera, given her relentless hatred of all things Trojan, not opposed to Poseidon saving Aineias (20.310–12)? In chapter 1 we noted a thematic parallel in Hephaistos, a Greek-partisan god, saving the Trojan Idaios in Diomedes' *aristeia* (5.23–24). Poseidon gives specific reasons for saving Aineias, which corroborate the subgenre of myth we have mentioned. Poseidon declares that Aineias is ἀναίτιος (*anaitios*, 20.297), "guiltless." I follow Edwards (1991: 325) in taking this as a reference to Laomedon's having cheated Poseidon and Apollo. Shortly before, Aineias gives his lineage (20.215–40), showing his descent from Assarakos, whereas Laomedon, and therefore Priam and his children, are descended from Ilos.[73] As Poseidon implies, Aineias is thus not tainted by the inherited guilt which affects most Trojans (above, subgenre 8a). Poseidon further declares that Aineias is fated to survive (20.302). These two details, as well as other traits noted below, identify Aineias as a "one just man."

The whole episode of Aineias' encounter with Akhilleus has general apocalyptic overtones. Aineias declares to Akhilleus, of lineages and family lines in general, "Zeus makes great or diminishes the prowess in men" (20.242). The sentiment is close to Hesiod's *Works and Days* 5–7, a generalization about Zeus' helping and harming mortals, a specific subset of which is his role in causing apocalyptic destruction. When Hera does not object to Poseidon's proposal to save Aineias, she reiterates that she and Athena have sworn to not prevent the Greeks from burning and destroying Troy (20.310–17). In confirming her support of the apocalyptic conflagration of Troy, she implicitly confirms that Aineias is not part of the coming destruction. There is a further hint of Aineias' association with the apocalypse where the narrative pattern would lead us to expect, the parallel for Aineias' encounter with Akhilleus, his earlier duel with Diomedes. As Aineias converses with Pandaros about the destruction Diomedes wreaks in his *aristeia*, he wonders if the best of the Akhaians is not some god:

Unless it is some god, enraged [κοτεσσάμενος] at the Trojans
angry [μηνίσας] because of sacrifices. The wrath [μῆνις] of a god is a
difficult thing.

(5.177–78)

As Walsh (23–29, 50, 52–53, 79, 97, 101) argues, *koteo* denotes a long-term
anger, just the kind motivating a god for an apocalypse, and used of Zeus in
an apocalyptic passage discussed above (4.168). Poseidon gives as an addi-
tional reason for saving Aineias Zeus' wish for a continuation of Darda-
nos' line (20.303–5). Dardanos is Zeus' own son. In some accounts Darda-
nos himself is a survivor of a great flood (Gantz 560), suggesting he too
may be an instance of the one just man, and giving him specific parallels
with Noah. The episode thus refers four times to Aineias' unique status
as a major Trojan hero who survives the apocalypse. Outside of Homer,
Apollodorus relates that when the Greeks were sacking Troy, they spared
Aineias on account of his piety (οἱ δὲ Ἕλληνες αὐτὸν διὰ τὴν εὐσέβειαν εἴασαν,
Epitome V.21).

Of the several instances of the one just man in OT myth, Lot, survivor
of the apocalypse at Sodom and Gomorrah, most closely parallels Aineias.
Lot and Aineias both survive in part because they are related to another
mortal favored by god (Abraham, Gen 19:29; Dardanos).[74] Both survive
the middle-degree apocalypse, the destruction of a city; both doomed cities
having particularly violated hospitality, though neither Aineias nor Lot
takes part in the violation. Genesis 19 is a theoxeny, in which Lot demon-
strates his morality by offering hospitality to the disguised angels.[75] Each
has face-to-face discussions with the immortals, receiving advice on how to
survive. At the conclusion of Aineias' aborted duel with Akhilleus (20.322–
29) Poseidon hurls him to safety, landing at the far edge of battle, among
Trojan allies. Poseidon then addresses him (20.332–39), advising him not
to face Akhilleus and to avoid him until he dies. But then, directs Poseidon,
Aineias is to reenter battle with confidence, because no one will be able
to slay him. Poseidon thus resembles the angels in Genesis 19, coming to
warn and advise Lot. His hurling Aineias also suggests Yahweh's taking up
to heaven, or rescue, of Enoch (Gen 5:24).[76] As Edwards (1991: 328) notes,
"Poseidon's words twice repeat the prediction that Aineias is fated to sur-
vive the war." Poseidon's dialogue with Aineias thus has apocalyptic asso-
ciations, the advice of the immortals to the one just man, which has been
adapted to fit the present context of the *Iliad*, but more typically would deal
with his survival of the apocalypse itself.

If we adduce the *Aeneid*, the parallels are even closer. Both Lot and
Aineias lose their wives, while the men escape apocalyptic destruction with

their offspring. The *Cypria* and the *Little Iliad* (West 2003: 104, 136) name Aineias' wife Eurydike, while Lot's wife, typical of OT myth,[77] is never named. Orpheus' Eurydike suffers a fate similar to Lot's wife: each dies unable to resist a divine interdiction against looking back. Does the same association go back to Aineias' Eurydike? Some of the details in Vergil's depiction of Creusa may thus be quite ancient. The name of Aineias' son, Askanios, occurs in the *Iliad* (2.862, 13.792), but of a Phrygian, a Trojan ally.[78] West (2003: 16) argues that the *Odyssey*'s account of the Sack of Troy (8.500–520) is so close to the epitome of the *Sack of Ilion* that the Homeric tradition knew some similar version of the basic episodes. All this suggests that the *Iliad* is aware of a larger tradition about Aineias, not necessarily heroic epic, but myths that would align Aineias closer to the patriarchal narratives of Genesis.

As the *Iliad* figures Akhilleus not only as a hero but also as other mythic types (*7. The hero as the ethical man who has unjustly suffered wrongs*), so it figures Aineias not only as a warrior but as the one just man, descended from a line Zeus favors more than Hektor's. In so doing the *Iliad* left the door open for Vergil to develop and exploit more fully Aineias' relation to this traditional figure. In addition to depicting Aineias as the one just man, Vergil will also figure him in other subgenres of myth common to OT myth but absent from the *Iliad*, those used for Moses (*Aeneid* 1, 3, 5–6), and Joshua (*Aeneid* 7–12).

❦❦❦

CHAPTER SEVEN

The *Iliad*'s Divine Economy, the Goddess Anat, and the Homeric Athena

The whole picture of the gods in the Iliad is oriental.
—M. L. WEST

This final chapter explores the *Iliad*'s divine economy from three perspectives. First, I argue that three central deities in epic divine economies (Zeus, Athena, Apollo for the *Iliad*) function as an "epic triangle" around the hero.[1] Second, I note the chief functions Iliadic gods serve, how they relate to each other and to the chief mortal characters. Third, I place the *Iliad*'s divine economy alongside the Ugaritic/Canaanite[2] pantheon, drawing on the texts recovered from Ras Shamra and evidence from OT myth, Cyprus, and Egypt. Why compare the *Iliad*'s divine economy to that in the Ugaritic myths? Commentators have often noted similarities between the Homeric divine economy and various Near Eastern divine pantheons. In chapters 5 and 6 we noted parallels especially with OT myths, arguing that they form the closest overall comparanda for the *Iliad*'s chief subgenres of myth. OT myths themselves, and depictions of their deity, draw heavily on earlier Canaanite/Ugaritic myth (e.g., see M. Smith 1990, 2001). Closer consideration of Ugaritic myth has much to offer Homeric studies.[3] The Ugaritic pantheon is the Near Eastern divine economy most similar to the *Iliad*'s.[4] I then turn to a specific focus on Athena. The Ugaritic goddess Anat can serve as a hermeneutic for understanding the Homeric Athena, especially certain episodes that have been thought controversial.

We can better define the *Iliad*'s divine economy, and Athena's position therein, by briefly noting how it resembles and differs from the divine economies of two other epics, *Gilgamesh* and the *Odyssey*.[5] In these epics three particular deities, who serve in a triangular relationship, have the most significant impact on the structure of the poem due to their specific relationships with the hero. The three gods embody three type-scenes concerned with the epic hero: divine council, theophany, and divine wrath. The divine council, presided over by a "sky father" figure, typically meets to discuss the hero's fate. The sky father supports the hero but does not personally intervene on his behalf. The hero receives personal visitation, theophany, from a second deity who serves as his mentor. A third deity has the opposite relation with the hero, a divine wrath against him, but does not usually appear to him face-to-face. In *Gilgamesh* Anu, the sky father, convenes and presides over divine councils which concern the fate of the hero (I ii, VII i). Shamash is the hero's mentor, or advocate, who appears in theophany to Gilgamesh (V i, VII i), while Ishtar develops a divine wrath against him (VI iii).[6] The triangle of deities also functions as a metaphor for a legal configuration. The two opposing lesser deities are defense (Shamash) and prosecuting (Ishtar) attorneys before the supreme judge (Anu). The *Odyssey* has Zeus, Athena, and Poseidon in the same respective functions. Zeus, the sky father, presides over divine councils (1.26–95, 5.3–42, etc.); Athena mentors the hero, serves as his advocate, and appears in theophany to him (1.48–62, 3.231, 7.18–78, 13.221–439, 16.157–76, 22.205–40); and Poseidon has a divine wrath against him (1.20–21, 68–79; 5.282–96, 339–41; 8.565; 13.126–60). Although there are many other deities in the poem, these three define the most important functions of the divine economy.[7]

But the *Iliad*'s divine economy is more complex than the *Odyssey*'s because of three complicating factors: Hektor's function as a second hero, episodes of theomachy, and Thetis' prominence. In spite of these factors, at its core the *Iliad*'s divine economy has the same triangular relationship. Zeus is again the sky father who convenes divine councils and supports the hero; Athena, the mentor who advises the hero on heroic action; and Apollo, the deity with a divine wrath against the hero:

Zeus
(sky father and judge who
presides over divine councils)

Apollo   Athena
(wrathful, prosecuting attorney)   (mentor, theophany, advocate)

Akhilleus

However, Apollo's wrath against Akhilleus is not as decisive a factor in the present time of the *Iliad* as Ishtar's in *Gilgamesh,* or Poseidon's in the *Odyssey.* In the *Iliad,* Apollo normally remains quite composed in comparison with Ishtar and Poseidon. His wrath against Akhilleus surfaces only briefly (22.7 ff, 24.32 ff). It's full force is postponed until after the end of the poem, as in Hektor's dying remarks ("on that day when Paris and Apollo will slay you, noble though you are, at the Skaian gates," 22.359–60). Apollo will help slay Akhilleus, the complement to Athena's helping Akhilleus slay Hektor (the two climactic instances of overdetermination in Trojan War myth), but not within the *Iliad*.

The *Iliad* affirms Akhilleus' triangular relationship by replicating it around two of his surrogates. Thus Diomedes in book 5 receives a theophany and full support from Athena (5.792 ff) and is hindered by Apollo (5.437–44). In the games in book 23 Athena again helps Diomedes and Apollo hinders (23.382–400, a miniature of the poem's divine economy: Diomedes wins the chariot race with Athena's aid, despite Apollo's interference). At 23.357 Diomedes is again the "best of the Akhaians." Patroklos, on the other hand, is a greater target for the divine wrath of Apollo. As Athena with Hektor, here the angry deity helps cause the death of the hero (16.788–93), even the death of a best of the Akhaians.

But, in the first complication imposed on this governing triangle, the middle sequence treats Hektor as a principal hero who enjoys the favor of Zeus. Consequently the *Iliad* also has an epic triangle around Hektor—the same three deities, in fact, but with the positions of Apollo and Athena reversed:

Zeus
(supporter of the hero who presides over divine councils)

Athena   Apollo
(wrathful, prosecuting attorney)   (mentor, theophany, advocate)

Hektor

A frequent formula, αἴ γὰρ, Ζεῦ τε πάτερ, καὶ Ἀθηναίη, καὶ Ἄπολλον (*Il.* 2.371, 4.288, 7.132, 16.97; *Od.* 4.341; 7.311; 17.132, 235; 24.376) articulates the twice-recurring epic triangle.[8]

A significant difference, however, is Zeus's more active role. He does not merely preside over divine councils but personally intervenes on Hektor's behalf, in books 8 and 15, at the beginning and near the ending of the middle sequence. Zeus does not directly intervene in the initial or final sequences to help Akhilleus, nor does he for Odysseus in the *Odyssey* (though his direct intervention for Hektor amounts to *indirect* intervention on Akhilleus' behalf). Second, unlike Apollo with Akhilleus, Athena's wrath has real consequences in the present time of the *Iliad* and leads directly to Hektor's death in book 22. While Apollo offers Hektor significant aid from time to time (especially at 15.59–63, 220–62; he places *menos* in Hektor: 15.60), he deserts him (22.213) when Hektor needs him most, an instantiation of a regular motif in Near Eastern myth: *The gods of the doomed city abandon its inhabitants* (see West 1997: 72–76). Because of their opposing roles in both triangles we might expect Athena and Apollo to confront each other in a theomachy in the *Iliad*. But the opposed deities, mentor and wrathful, do not confront each other in any of the epics under discussion, *Gilgamesh*, the *Odyssey*, or the *Iliad*. Instead the sky father mediates between them, as judge and arbiter, ensuring that each of their perspectives is respected. In a final difference, Hera, as a result of her rebellion against Zeus, especially during the middle sequence, serves as a second wrathful deity opposed to Hektor.

Athena is the only deity other than Zeus to appear in all three Homeric "triangles," for Odysseus, for Akhilleus, and for Hektor (cf. her close relationship with Herakles and Tydeus, until he offends her). Zeus rarely acts or intervenes himself, allowing the younger generation of gods to carry out the busier aspects of the plot. Athena mediates between Zeus and the epic hero, embodying divine will toward him. She serves as a divine version of the epic protagonist in each poem, having Akhillean characteristics in the *Iliad* but Odyssean qualities in the *Odyssey* (see Louden 1990: 180–219).

The second distinguishing factor noted above, episodes of theomachy, adds great complexity to the *Iliad*'s divine economy. Thematic theomachy, in which Hera contests Zeus' executive function (paralleling the strife between Agamemnon and Akhilleus) and Athena defeats Ares (paralleling the Greeks' war against the Trojans), leads to greater intervention by other gods than in *Gilgamesh* or the *Odyssey*, neither of which has any real parallels for Iliadic theomachy.[9] Not only Hera's contesting Zeus' executive function, but vocal and active participation from Athena, Poseidon, and Ares, and the general theomachy that erupts after Hephaistos' combat with Xanthos, crowd the *Iliad*'s divine economy beyond the central structures governing *Gilgamesh* and the *Odyssey*. The *Iliad* imposes theomachian relationships on many of the gods that do not normally exist outside of the poem.

Hera's contesting of Zeus' executive function is particularly evident in how frequently she commands or dispatches other deities to perform her behests. The *Iliad* reveals this as a dominant theme early (1.195), when Hera, not Zeus, sends Athena to contain Akhilleus' anger at Agamemnon in the first assembly. It is Hera who dispatches Athena to prevent the Greek flight (2.155–56) after Agamemnon's disastrous testing of the troops.[10] Zeus' first words in the poem point to her potential to resent his decrees (1.518–19). In book 14 she briefly usurps the executive function. As prelude to seizing power, she again serves an executive function by sending Hypnos to incapacitate Zeus. Hera's seizing power thus results in temporarily turning the battle in the Greeks' favor and temporary incapacitation of Hektor (thematically parallel to her harming Herakles, 15.26–28). She also takes the leading role in the divine council at 16.431–61, and Zeus follows her suggestion, a reversal of most divine councils in Homeric epic (cf. 4.62–66). However, her own approach to the executive function is too partisan and extreme to have any real stability. The executive function usually seeks a balance between opposed divine forces (as Zeus achieves at 24.65–76) and does not itself occupy an extreme position, as does Hera.

Thetis' key role as Akhilleus' divine parent, confidante, and source of prophecy is a further complication beyond the traditional triangle,[11] partly obscuring Athena's role as his mentor. There is some overlap in their dual roles as Akhilleus' confidante (even Hera and Poseidon briefly have this function, but never face-to-face with Akhilleus), although the poem carefully signals Athena's prime role as mentor by having her make the first theophany (1.194 ff) and the climactic one when she guides Akhilleus' slaying of Hektor (22.214). Thetis' influence leads her to have several scenes in which she meets with gods, including Zeus, Hephaistos, and the Nereids.

Aphrodite, in her relations with Aineias, replicates Thetis' role as the goddess mother of the special hero.[12] Though never depicted as intimately as Thetis with Akhilleus, her rescue of Aineias (5.312) establishes her as the same basic type. But, in her relations with Paris, which the *Iliad* develops at greater length, Aphrodite parodies the same divine function. All her appearances in the *Iliad* have a parodic modality. When she saves Paris in book 3 and deposits him in his fragrant bedroom (3.382), instead of on the battlefield (as Poseidon does Aineias at 20.328), the point is clear: Paris is a champion in the bedroom, not on the battlefield. When Aphrodite disguises herself as a maid to bring Helen to Paris, they have sex, while everyone else wonders where Paris is and what has become of his duel with Menelaos.[13] In books 5 and 21 Aphrodite is twice defeated, by Diomedes and by Athena. While her defeats embody the overall Trojan defeat, they also underscore her irrelevance to those heroic acts with which the *Iliad* is primarily concerned.

As a transition to discussion of the Ugaritic gods, we turn to Hephaistos. We noted in chapter 4 some specific facets of his role in the *Iliad* (*8a. Hephaistos serves a mediating function that helps further Thetis' agenda*), and in chapter 6 his role in the general theomachy in book 21. But Hephaistos serves two highly traditional functions, broader than the plot of the *Iliad,* typical of a craftsman god in Near Eastern myth. He crafts divine weapons for the hero or the gods and builds the divine dwellings of the gods (cf. Tvashter in Vedic myth). The *Iliad* makes several references to his having built the gods' residences on Olympos (1.606–8; 14.166–68, 338–39; 18.369–71; cf. 11.76–77).[14] He also fashioned the scepter of Zeus (2.101–2), a symbol of the supreme god's power and authority.[15] As for divine weapons, the *Iliad* famously depicts Hephaistos' fashioning Akhilleus' new armor (18.469–612), endowed with divine powers.

Hephaistos has a close analogue in the Ugaritic god Kothar. Like Hephaistos, Kothar fashions divine residences for the gods and forges special weapons for gods and heroes. In the *Baal Cycle*, Kothar builds a palace for Yamm, the sea god. Though the *Iliad* does not specify that Hephaistos constructed Poseidon's palace, the description of the sea god's palace (13.21–22) involves terms that are elsewhere closely associated with the craftsman god, κλυτὰ . . . χρύσεα . . . τετεύχαται, ἄφθιτα, "renowned . . . fashioned of gold, imperishable" (κλυτά, 18.144, 147; 19.10; χρύσεα, 14.239, 18.418; τεύχω, 2.101, 14.166; ἄφθιτον, 2.46, 14.238; see Nagy 1979: 179). Toward the end of the *Baal Cycle*, Kothar fashions a divine palace for Baal, after his triumph over other gods. Also in the *Baal Cycle*, Kothar (KTU 1.2 IV 11–21, in M. Smith) fashions weapons for Baal for his combat with Yamm. In the *Aqhat*, Kothar fashions the special bow wielded by the titular hero and coveted by the goddess Anat.

A place name, Kaphtor suggests the possibility that Kothar and Hephaistos are themselves linked. The Ugaritic myths say Kothar has thrones in Memphis and Kaphtor. As Morris (1992: 94) notes, "The identity of Kaphtor has been accepted as Crete." OT myth asserts that the Philistines came from Kaphtor/Crete (e.g., Gen 10:14). Morris (1992: 79–84) argues that the two craftsman gods are linked: "On a literary level, Kothar's connection with Kaphtor intensifies his close relationship with Hephaistos. Their epithets, creations, and specialties overlap too closely for coincidence" (94–95). In a further parallel, Morris (1992: 82–83) compares the suffering caused by the bow Kothar makes for Aqhat and the armor Hephaistos makes for Akhilleus. One might also parallel the relationships between Athena and Hephaistos, on the one hand, and Anat and Kothar, on the other.[16] Kothar and Hephaistos are not the only Ugaritic and Greek gods who may be linked.

The Ugaritic / West Semitic Goddess, Anat

The *Baal Cycle* and the *Aqhat*, along with references in OT myth and other sources, consider interactions of the goddess Anat with the other Ugaritic gods and with mortals. Awareness of Anat and her relationships helps illuminate several episodes in the *Iliad* and provides contexts for analyzing some of Athena's more controversial characteristics. Consideration of the Ugaritic divine pantheon also brings out further parallels between Homeric and OT myth because four of the principal Ugaritic deities are named in OT myth: El, a sky father figure who presides over divine councils; his wife Asherah, mother to many of the other gods; Baal, a war and storm god; and Anat, war goddess.[17] Modern readers of the Bible tend to be unaware that the Israelites' monotheism evolved out of an earlier polytheism; as M. Smith (2001: 17) notes, "this monotheism emerged only midway through Israel's history. It was heir and reaction to a long tradition of Israelite polytheism." When the Israelites are depicted worshiping Baal, or Asherah, they are probably worshiping a contingent of the Canaanite pantheon because these were not monotheistic gods who existed in isolation. Other Ugaritic gods also figure in the OT, including Yamm, or Sea (*yam*, Exod 14:21; personified at Prov 8:29; Ps 74); Mot, or Death (*maweth*, personified at Isa 28:15 as King of Sheol); and Lot, the dragon (= Leviathan, Job 41:1; Ps 74:14; Isa 27:1). Many scholars think that the OT Yahweh is heavily influenced by older depictions of both El and Baal. OT myth also implies that Yahweh himself was formerly a son of El (Ps 82; cf. Deut 32:8–9; see M. Smith 2001: 48–49).

A war goddess, a young maiden who acts out of wrath against both gods and mortals, Anat is a prominent member of the Ugaritic pantheon. Anat was "originally a north-west Semitic goddess" (P. L. Day 63), worshiped by the Canaanites, but also worshiped in Egypt (the favored deity of Ramses II, worshiped through Greek and Roman periods) and Cyprus. P. L. Day (75) characterizes Anat as "a warrior and a patron or guardian of warriors and royalty." Miller (45) asserts that "Anat was the warrior goddess *par excellence*." Parallels with Athena quickly become apparent. Like Athena, Anat is said to be a maiden/virgin, *btlt* (though the precise meaning of the term is problematic).[18] But perhaps Anat's most distinguishing hallmark, and the one that has elicited the most discussion, is her "bloodthirsty" nature.[19] I argue that Athena, in Homeric epic, also shares this defining characteristic, as does Yahweh. Taken together, the three deities suggest that divine bloodthirstiness is a traditional feature of ancient myth.

Parallels between Athena and Anat have occasionally been noted by others but not pursued at great length. But Homerists tend to be unaware, with rare exceptions,[20] of Ugaritic myth. Ugariticists have neglected Athena because the post-Homeric Athena is often seen as a goddess of wisdom. Thus Walls (29), in one of the few comparative studies of Anat, argues: "Athena is always described in Greek myth as calm and thoughtful, never overcome by blind fury or battle frenzy." But several Homeric episodes we have already discussed counter his assertion. A few scholars have argued for common ground between Anat and Athena (Gordon 1967: 38; Lipinski 309–13; Du Buisson 48–55; Jones 10, 67; Eaton 16, 76, 127), though not in detail, or with sustained arguments. Considine (107, 138)[21] briefly compares Anat's anger at El with Athena's at Zeus. But it is ancient evidence that most strongly confirms the goddesses' basic equivalence. In a bilingual, Phoenician and Greek, inscription from Larnaka, Cyprus, as P. L. Day (68) notes, "Anat is named in the Phoenician portion of a bilingual text . . . that names Athena in the corresponding place in the Greek portion of the inscription."[22] Also on Cyprus, at Idalion, there was a joint sanctuary for both goddesses, Anat and Athena.[23] Du Buisson (54) notes a less certain, but tantalizing, link. Lycophron refers to Odysseus' theft of Athena's Palladium as κλῶπα Φοινίκης θεᾶς, "the thief of the Phoenician goddess" (*Alexandra* 658). The scholiast on the passage clarifies, "in Corinth Athena the Phoenician (φοινίκη ἡ Ἀθηνᾶ) is worshipped." A "Phoenician Athena" seems to be Anat.[24]

Not every aspect of the two goddesses is completely parallel, nor is my analysis intended as a comprehensive overview of Anat. Certain aspects of Anat and her myths remain uncertain due to lacunae in the texts, the relatively limited number of surviving narratives, and their, at times, uncertain references and meanings. I limit myself to those facets of Anat relevant to the Homeric Athena.[25] After reviewing the Ugaritic and Homeric parallels, we consider attestations of Anat in OT myth.

Anat and Athena share many generic features, in addition to the more specific details and interactions in which we are interested. Both goddesses have certain masculine tendencies, are closely involved with their fathers, and have no relation with their mothers. In Anat's case, her mother's identity is not known, but it appears certain that Asherah, El's wife, mother of many other Ugaritic gods, and parallel to Hera, is not her mother. M. Smith (2001: 56–57, 226, n. 17) reports a conjecture that Anat's mother was a concubine of El. If true, this suggests parallels with Metis, Athena's mother, who can be seen as Zeus' concubine, and with whom Athena has no relationship.

Anat and Athena have a similar iconography as the spear-wielding goddess.[26] Keel and Uehlinger (88) describe a thirteenth-century (B.C.E.) cylinder seal from Bethel in which Anat is depicted holding a lance. In a scarab found in Jerusalem, Anat "sits side-saddle on a horse that is striding over a fallen enemy" (Keel and Uehlinger 88; cf. *Il.* 5.840–41, 855–57). Wyatt (1984) includes a rendering of a stela from Ugarit in which Anat sits on a throne, holding a spear or javelin in each hand. The *Iliad* and *Odyssey* offer a potent repeated description of Athena wielding her spear:

she ascended the blazing chariot and seized her *spear,*
heavy, great, and stout, with which she subdues the ranks
of heroes, those at whom she of the mighty father is angered [κοτέσσεται].

$$(Il. 5.745-47 = 8.389-91; cf. Od. 1:99-101)$$

Discussing the formula "she of the mighty father," Walsh (45) argues, "This epithet suggests Athena's role as an angry god." The verb expressing her anger here (κοτέω), signifies, in Walsh's (29) view, "a long-term anger outside of the immediate battle's context." As she first appears to Telemakhos in the *Odyssey,* she has her spear (*Od.* 1.104), after a repetition of the formulaic lines above (*Od.* 1.99–101 = *Il.* 5.745–47). In black-figure vase paintings, Athena is depicted at the moment of her birth as springing from Zeus' head, fully armed, already wielding her spear. Descriptions from the *Homeric Hymns* (28.9: σείσασ᾽ ὀξὺν ἄκοντα, 28.9) strengthen the connection.

Both goddesses have temples. Although this is a generic parallel, a curious detail suggests a more specific correspondence. The *Baal Cycle* mentions Anat's temple only briefly: "The gates of Anat's house are closed" (Parker 107). As M. Smith elaborates, "Anat's 'house' here presupposes a fortified temple located on her sanctuary-mountain (or more specifically, an acropolis?). Cf. Yahweh's sanctuary or 'holy mountain' in Exod. 15:13, 17–18; Ps. 48:2–3" (in Parker 167, n. 43). The *Iliad* briefly depicts Theano, Athena's priestess, opening the doors of Athena's temple on the Trojan acropolis (*Il.* 6.297–98). Theano goes on to sacrifice—in this, the only sacrifice to Athena depicted in the *Iliad,* and only mention of her temple—special robes:

intricately fashioned robes, the work
of Sidonian women, which godlike Alexander himself
brought back from Sidonia, when he had sailed across the broad sea.

$$(Il. 6.289-91)^{27}$$

The women who made the robes offered in sacrifice to Athena are from the culture that worshiped Anat.

Anat and Athena's Relations with Other Gods

Parallel passages in the myths offer the most striking correspondences between Anat and Athena and define the goddesses' unique identity. The *Baal Cycle* depicts Anat interacting with other gods, especially Baal and El, while the myth of *Aqhat* depicts Anat also interacting with mortals. A few episodes involving Athena include her interactions with Zeus and Ares, a

bloodied Hektor initiating an unsuccessful sacrifice to her, and her decep-
tions of Pandaros and Hektor.

El, the sky father figure, heads the Ugaritic pantheon, known from many
OT theophoric names, even the name Israel. El combines functions that in
Greek myth are split between Zeus and Kronos (cf. Mondi 159). El is the
creator, the Father, presiding over divine councils, giving edicts, but not
actively performing feats.[28] Like Kronos, El has three sons who separately
have power over the sky (Baal), the sea (Yamm), and the dead (Mot), much
as the three brothers, Zeus, Poseidon, and Hades.[29] The *Baal Cycle* depicts
these younger gods as often in conflict with each other, with El remain-
ing largely above the fray; as Mullen (4) notes, "El remained the head of
the Canaanite pantheon, ruling as king over the younger cosmogonic gods.
The battles of these younger deities for kingship concerned the rule of the
cosmos, not supremacy over the gods. El alone sat as king and judge over
the younger gods, his children." El is a more aged and less vigorous figure
than Zeus. When not arbitrating divine disputes, or leading divine coun-
cils, he presides over banquets, or drinking parties. Though a more vigor-
ous figure, the Iliadic Zeus largely replicates El's three functions of presid-
ing over divine councils, arbitrating divine disputes, and leading drinking
parties (*Il.* 1.584–602; cf. 4.2–4), which suggest the Near Eastern *marzeah*
(see Cross 39; M. Smith 1994: 140–44).

Anat and Athena are both addressed as "daughter" at divine councils by
their respective fathers. In each case the goddess is causing friction, and the
sky father would defuse the tension. In Anat's case, she puts pressure on El,
even threatening violence against him, to have a home built for Baal. El re-
sponds:

> I know you, O daughter, that you are furious.
> Among goddesses no scorn is like yours.
>
> (CTA 3 v 27–29, in Parker 117)

In Athena's case, Zeus forbids intervention by the other Olympians, so he
can honor Akhilleus' request to make the Greeks suffer,

> Take heart, Tritogeneia, my child; I do not speak from anger
> in any way, but I wish to be kind to you.
>
> (*Il.* 8:39–40)

Both respective sky fathers send divine messengers to their daughters, to
summon them (Anat: Parker 92–94; Athena: *Il.* 8.398–425).

In the *Baal Cycle* Anat's interaction with El can be confrontational and fractious. In this myth, Baal fights both Yamm (sea) and Mot (death), theomachies resembling episodes in Hesiod's *Theogony*, and in the *Iliad*. When Anat has an audience with El to demand that he have a palace built for Baal, she threatens him:

> I will smash your crown
> I will make your beard run with blood,
> The gray hair of your beard with gore.
>
> (CTA 3 v 23–25, in Parker 117)

Anat repeats the same formulaic threat to El in the *Aqhat* (Parker 63) when she denounces Aqhat for not giving her his bow (discussed below). El responds calmly, as we have earlier noted:

> I know you, O daughter, that you are furious,
> Among goddesses no scorn is like yours.
>
> (CTA 3 v 27–29, in Parker 117)

Mullen (68) ascribes Anat's demeanor to her identity as a war goddess, noting that El is not disturbed by her verbal onslaught: "[H]e seems to accept the threat as the normal manner in which 'Anat makes a request" (65). I suggest Anat's confrontational manner with El in these myths can be explained as thematically paralleling the central conflicts that structure the two myths (*Baal Cycle, Aqhat*), Baal's battles with Yamm and Mot, and Anat's strife with Aqhat.

While Athena does not directly threaten Zeus (4.20–21), several encounters suggest Anat's interactions with El.[30] When Zeus deliberately provokes Athena and Hera in the divine council opening book 4 (4.5–19), the goddesses are angry, seething:

> So he spoke, but Athena and Hera muttered at him,
> as they sat nearby, plotting evils for the Trojans.
> At this point Athena was silent, and did not say anything,
> resenting Zeus the Father, and a savage anger took hold of her.
>
> (4.20–23)

Athena's anger (χόλος . . . ἄγριος) and animosity suggest Anat's furious manner with El.

In book 8, when Zeus aids the Trojans against Athena's wishes, her resentment resurfaces. Zeus threatens to strike and imprison in Tartaros any deity who would go against his plan to aid the Trojans (8.5–27). When the Trojans inflict casualties on the Greeks because of Zeus' aid, Athena speaks to Hera, reminiscent of Anat with El:

> . . . but my Father rages, with evil thoughts,
> the wicked rogue, always thwarting my desires,
> nor does he recall in the least how often I saved
> his son, beaten down by Eurystheus' labors . . .
> But now he hates me. . . . There will be a time
> when he will again call [me] his dear bright-eyed girl.
> But now harness for us the single-hooved horses
> while I enter the house of aegis-bearing Zeus
> to arm myself for war.
>
> (*Il.* 8.360–76)

Athena neatly skirts the central issue: she intends to violate Zeus' decree and enter the war, though he threatened to punish any god who would oppose his edict. Her emotional, confrontational assessment of Zeus, and her own headstrong tendencies, suggest Anat's antagonism toward El. Elsewhere she persists in characterizing Zeus in an intractable, confrontational manner, as when she predicts to Ares how an enraged Zeus will seize them all, guilty or not of violating his edict (15.135–37). Though more disciplined in the *Odyssey*, there too she briefly resembles Anat's confrontational style with El when she accuses Zeus of hating Odysseus (ὠδύσαο, 1.62).[31]

As her attitude to Zeus resembles Anat's behavior with El, Athena's interactions with Ares suggest Anat's relations with her brother, Baal. Prototypically Near Eastern, Baal, a storm and war god, is the most dynamic member of the Ugaritic pantheon. From a Greek perspective, Baal combines aspects of Zeus and Ares. He is at once a powerful force in the sky, hurling thunderbolts, and an impetuous, youthful figure, a god of war, who is more than once defeated by other gods. Some of his epithets are reminiscent of Zeus': "the rider of the clouds" (also used of Yahweh, Ps 68:4, 33), "the cloud gatherer." Though the focal point of Ugaritic myth, he is a figure of some tension since he is not a son of El but of Dagon (the principal Philistine god, according to OT myth). On Zeus suggesting a composite of Baal and El, Ugaritic scholars argue that OT depictions of Yahweh draw on combined traditions of El, the ruling father, source of wisdom, presiding over divine councils, and dispensing justice, and Baal the vigorous storm god, who leads his people to victory in war (e.g., Mondi 172; M. Smith 1990: xxiii, 21–22, 64).

Anat and Baal, Athena and Ares

Anat, Baal's (half?) sister, has a close relationship with him.[32] They are both gods of war, and Anat is his close ally, typically coming to his aid when Baal struggles against a powerful opponent. In the *Baal Cycle*, Anat lists a catalog of fierce opponents she fought and defeated on Baal's behalf:

> Surely I fought Yamm, the Beloved of El,
> Surely I finished off River, the Great God,
> Surely I bound Tunnan and destroyed him.
> I fought the Twisty Serpent,
> The Potentate with Seven Heads,
> I fought Desire, the Beloved of El,
> I destroyed Rebel, the Calf of El,
> I fought Fire, the Dog of El,
> I annihilated Flame, the Daughter of El
> That I might fight for silver and inherit gold.
> (CTA 3 iii 37–47, in Parker 111)

The *Iliad* suggests a parallel in Athena's complaint about her support for Herakles, the labors she helped him overcome on Zeus' behalf:

> Nor does he [Zeus] recall in the least how often I saved
> his son, beaten down by Eurystheus' labors.
> He would always cry out to heaven, and Zeus
> sent me forth from heaven to offer him aid.
> For if I had thought these things in my shrewd wits
> when he sent him into the close-gated house of Hades
> to bring out of Erebos Hades' loathsome hound,
> he never would have escaped the steep currents of Styx.
> (*Il.* 8.362–69)

Anat intercedes on Baal's behalf in other ways as well. When Yamm's messengers declare that Baal is to pay tribute to Yamm, he is disturbed ("Then Prince Baal is shaken"), lashes out, and strikes the messengers. But as he does so, Anat and the god Athtart restrain him, after he has seized two weapons:

> His right hand Anat seizes,
> His left hand Athtart seizes.
> (CTA 2 i 39, in Parker 101)

Though there is no consensus as to why they do so, it seems likely that Anat and Athtart are trying to prevent him from getting himself into further trouble, making a bad situation worse.³³ The *Iliad* has two episodes in which Athena takes Ares by the hand to prevent him from fighting. When Ares sees Diomedes slay two men, sons of Dares, a priest of Hephaistos, he is angered. But Athena takes him by the hand (χειρὸς ἑλοῦσ᾿, 5.30), getting him to agree to leave the fighting to mortals. Athena suggests, as an additional means of persuading Ares to comply, that they should avoid Zeus' anger (μῆνις, 5.34). Her management of Ares looks ahead to a second, complementary episode.

In a second, more developed episode, Ares is unaware that his son, Askalaphos, has been slain (13.521–25). When Zeus forbids further divine intervention (15.110–12), Hera provokes Ares by informing him of his son's death. An emotional Ares seeks revenge, even if it means being struck (πληγέντι) by Zeus' lightning. But Athena intervenes to restrain him, preventing Zeus' wrath, which she and the narrator describe as severe (15.121–22). She takes his spear from his hand (χειρὸς ἑλοῦσα, 15.126), affirming her own position as the spear-wielding god (*Il.* 5.745–47 = 8.389–91; *Od.* 1.99–101), as well as his helmet and armor. Compare M. Smith's (1994: 311) interpretation of events in the passage from the *Baal Cycle*, "Just as Baal seizes . . . the weapons in his hand . . . Anat seizes his right hand." In each myth, Anat and Athena intervene in the same setting, a gathering of the gods, to disarm and restrain Baal/Ares. Athena takes no other god by the hand in Homeric epic. According to her own interpretation, Athena here saves Ares from the wrath of Zeus, which suggests parallels with Anat helping Baal in contexts in which he is defeated. Although this scene seems an inversion of their normal relations in the *Iliad*, it may depict their usual relations outside of it, in which Athena does show sisterly consideration for him, like Anat to Baal. The *Iliad*'s depictions of the gods are subordinated to the larger theme of strife between the Greeks and Trojans.

Elsewhere in the *Iliad* Athena and Ares work as a complement, as evident in the book 15 episode, and suggest teamwork reminiscent of Anat and Baal's joint efforts. The two are frequently paired as complementary figures embodying war, from the marshaling of the troops on the first day of fighting (4.439), to Zeus' telling Aphrodite to leave the works of warfare to Athena and Ares (5.430; cf. 5.332–33), from the description of the fierce fighting around Patroklos' corpse (17.398), to Akhilleus' pairing of the two when he seeks to rally the Greeks during his *aristeia* (20.358). But perhaps most important is their pairing in the two cities at war (18.516–19) on the shield Hephaistos makes for Akhilleus. This remarkable episode displays a number of sustained parallels with Ugaritic myth and culture. On parallels to Akhilleus' shield, Edwards (1991: 203) notes: "The nearest monumental parallels are bronze shields found in Crete, which may have come from Asia Minor or from Cyprus, and Phoenician silver and bronze bowls." Edwards (1991: 204–5) further notes a Phoenician silver dish that has a depiction of a city under siege. In the *Aqhat*, discussed below, Kothar makes the weapon, a bow, for the hero Aqhat, as Hephaistos here fashions arms for Akhilleus. These sustained parallels and connections raise the possibility that the depiction of the sibling war gods Athena and Ares on Akhilleus' shield is influenced by a Phoenician iconographic tradition of the sibling war gods Anat and Baal.

Not only is Ares' interaction with Athena reminiscent of Baal's with Anat, but a few of the *Iliad*'s depictions of Ares invoke parallels with a Baal tradition, including two passages suggestive of Ares as a *storm* god. When Diomedes, with Athena guiding, stabs Ares with his spear, he howls in pain and rises to heaven like a storm cloud:

> Just as a black mist appears out of the clouds,
> an ill wind that stirs up after a hot spell,
> so bronze Ares seemed to Diomedes, son of Tydeus,
> as he rose up into the heavens with the clouds.
>
> (*Il.* 5.864–67)

A second passage affirms the Iliadic Ares' affinity with storms. As a send-off for Akhilleus' *aristeia*, Athena gives a shout to rouse the Greeks:

> And Ares was shouting from the other side, like a black storm,
> urging the Trojans.
>
> (*Il.* 20.51–52)

Both storm passages occur in theomachian contexts, in which Ares is defeated by Athena, loosely paralleling Baal's defeats by the gods Yamm and Mot in the *Baal Cycle*.

Ares' and Baal's thematic tendency to be defeated points to a most curious parallel. Baal not only is defeated twice, but even temporarily dies, a characteristic of older Near Eastern gods normally thought alien to the Homeric conception of deity. But more than once in the *Iliad*, Ares is depicted as near death. When the *Iliad* notes his defeat by the giants, Otos and Ephialtes, it dramatizes the event through an unusual pivotal contrafactual:

> And now Ares, insatiate of war, would have *perished* [ἀπόλοιτο],
> had not [their] stepmother, beautiful Eëriboia,
> sent word to Hermes.
>
> (5.388–90)

Homerists usually argue that the startling "would have perished" is an error of some sort,[34] perhaps a misapplied formula. I suggest possible influence of a Baal tradition on the Homeric Ares. The Giants had held him in painful bonds (3.387, 391).[35] Homeric epic clearly implies parallels between being held in bonds and being in the underworld.[36]

A further passage suggests the Iliadic Ares has more in common than is generally realized with older Near Eastern gods such as Baal. Immediately after the storm simile given above, when Ares, wounded by Athena and Diomedes, rises to Olympos, he complains of his sufferings to Zeus:

> Then he [Diomedes] rushed like a god upon *me*,
> but my swift feet bore me away, otherwise there I had
> long suffered pains *among the dread corpses*,
> or remained alive, but weak from the blows of the bronze.
> (5.884–87)

In the second passage in which Athena takes him by the hand, Ares adds the detail, that he would risk Zeus' anger:

> struck by Zeus' lightning
> and *lie there with the corpses* in the blood and dust.
> (15.117–18)

Taken together the three passages corroborate an Iliadic tradition that associates a defeated Ares with death and/or with being in the underworld, much as Baal, in the *Baal Cycle*. Mot and El command Baal to descend to the underworld, and thus die:

> Be counted among the inmates of hell;
> And you will know, O God, that you are dead.
> (Parker 148)

> For dead is Mightiest Baal,
> Perished the Prince, Lord of the Earth
> (Parker 153)

Ares and Baal share additional tendencies. Both come across as foolhardy, prone to make boasts that they cannot uphold, which involve them with Athena and Anat. Handy (102) asserts of Baal:

> While it is true that he is presented in the myths as a mighty, virile deity, he also is shown to possess a vast amount of what may only be called stupidity. . . . First,

when . . . he issued a challenge to Mot. For a deity who could prevail in a contest with Mot this would be reasonable, though boastful, action to take, but Baal was incapable of withstanding the attack by Mot and the challenge was merely foolhardy. Baal ended up in the realm of the dead from which his sister Anat had to extract him.

Ares cuts much the same figure in his brash challenge to Athena (21.393–99), threatening to pay her back for what she and Diomedes have done to him. Instead, Athena easily defeats him, as in book 5. In both traditions, there is tension and strife between Ares and Zeus, and Baal and El. After Ares complains to Zeus about Athena's treatment of him, Zeus responds strongly:

> Don't whimper sitting next to me, you hypocrite;
> you are most hateful of the gods to me, of all the Olympians,
> for always strife is dear to you, and wars and fighting.
>
> (*Il.* 5.889–91)

Near the beginning of the *Baal Cycle*, El appears to command Yamm to drive Baal from his throne, and denounces him, "Thus he reviles me" (KTU 1.1 IV 23).[37]

To see Ares as a more serious figure one needs to step outside of the *Iliad*. Mondi (186) notes resemblance to a Baal tradition in the *Homeric Hymn to Apollo*'s depiction of Apollo entering Olympos:

> at whom the gods tremble as he enters the house of Zeus,
> and they all spring up from their sets when he comes
> near . . . and she [Leto] leading him, shows him a seat.
>
> (2–9)

Mondi (186) shows that Apollo here resembles Baal in his relations with El: "There is a redistribution of the familiar mythic functions here: Zeus is represented as the patriarchal El type, with Leto playing the role of his consort; it is Apollo who is the young and dynamic regent." There are traces of this kind of depiction of Ares at the end of the scene we just considered, Ares' complaint to Zeus. After having been attended to, now Ares "was sitting beside Zeus, son of Kronos, exulting in his glory" (*Il.* 5.906). The formula "exulting in his glory" (κύδεϊ γαίων) is used twice elsewhere of Zeus himself, once of Briareus, the hundred-handed monster (1.405). Only in this phrase is Ares the triumphant briefly suggested (cf. Miller [34–35] discussing Baal's triumphant return to his palace after defeating Mot).

Much about Ares seems more at home in a Near Eastern context. In a further parallel, Ares and Baal both have a similar band of divine attendants involved in their warrior pursuits. Ares is unique among the Olympian gods in the *Iliad* in this respect.[38] His two sons, Deimos and Phobos, accompany him into battle, along with Eris (4.440; at 11.37 they are on Agamemnon's shield; at 5.739 Phobos is on Athena's shield, with Eris, Alke, and Ioke). Ares orders his sons to harness his horses and chariot when he briefly plans to avenge the death of Askalaphos (15.119); at 13.299 Phobos, alone, accompanies Ares. Baal has a divine squad of "his seven lads," or "his seven attendants" (CTA 6.VI.8 and CTA 5.V.8–9; see Miller 18). Elsewhere "the helper-gods of Baal" are mentioned. Miller suggests that "they may have assisted Baal in various ways."[39] OT depictions of war settings use similar conceptions. Habakkuk depicts invading Babylonians much as the Homeric Ares accompanied by Deimos and Phobos: "Fear and terror go with them" (Hab 1:7). Perhaps more surprising, however, is a brief depiction of Yahweh in a similar fashion: "Pestilence stalks before him, and plague follows close behind" (Hab 3:6).[40]

Anat and Athena as Bloodthirsty in War

In their most salient, and definitive, parallel, Anat and Athena both demonstrate a bloodthirsty appetite for war. Scholarship on Anat has focused on this as a controversial divine attribute. The same tendency in Athena has provoked less comment. Burkert's (1985: 140) remark on her "primitive ferocity" is an exception. I argue that divine bloodthirstiness is a typical aspect of deity for the period, even present in depictions of Yahweh.

The cardinal passage for Anat occupies a curious, not fully understood position in the *Baal Cycle*. The passage (KTU 1.3 II 3–30) does not further the narrative about Baal, or recount an episode that is part of the overall sequence, but rather is a set piece, almost outside of the rest of the narrative, a formulaic depiction of the goddess, similar in function to the passage from Athena's arming scene given above (5.745–47 = 8.389–91). Mortals are more prominent here than anywhere else in the *Baal Cycle*,[41] bringing the passage closer to Homeric epic. Other aspects of the passage are reminiscent of Athena in *Iliad* 6 and *Odyssey* 13:

> And look! Anat fights in the valley.
> Battles between the two cities.
> She smites peoples of the seashore
> Strikes the populace of the sunrise.

Under her, like balls, heads,
Above her, like locusts, hands,
Like locusts, heaps of warrior-hands.
She fixes heads to her back,
She fastens hands to her belt.
Knee-deep she gleans in warrior-blood,
Neck-deep in the gore of soldiers.
With a shaft she drives away captives,
With her bow-string, the foe.

And look! Anat goes to her house,
The goddess takes herself to her palace,
For she is not sated with her fighting in the valley,
With battling between the two cities.
She arranges chairs for the soldiery,
Arranges tables for the hosts,
Footstools for the heroes.
Hard she fights and looks about,
Battling Anat surveys.
Her innards swell with laughter,
Her heart fills with joy,
The innards of Anat with victory.
Knee-deep she gleans in warrior-blood,
Neck-deep in the gore of soldiers,
Until she is sated with fighting in the house,
With battling between the tables.

(KTU 1.3 II 3–30)[42]

The passage presents a number of problems. As M. Smith (1995: 369) notes, "one major exegetical question . . . involves the nature of the fighting in the second half of the text." Smith (1995: 373) continues more specifically: "As the second half of the passage describes her, Anat is not satisfied with fighting and she destroys her captives. The question is whether or not her destruction involves consumption of her enemies, although there is no explicit indication that Anat eats her enemies." If she does, *why* would Anat devour the warriors? What would her action mean? Wyatt (1998: 248), who assumes she does, suggests that the cannibalism is a depiction of war: "Anat's particular form of flesh-devouring savagery is a graphic image of war personified."

The *Iliad* provides some relevant contexts for exploring Anat's possible cannibalism, hinting at similar behavior in Athena, and in Hera. The Iliadic

Hera has several tendencies in common with Anat, a propensity for anger, the motif of a goddess having suckled a hero (apparently alluded to at 5.393; cf. 24.58),[43] and an association with cannibalism. Often in the *Iliad*, Hera is linked with Athena, as the Olympians most eager for Troy's destruction. They often operate in tandem, from Hera's dispatching Athena to restrain Akhilleus (1.194–95), to their angry muttering at Zeus (4.20–24 = 8.457–60), to their joint arming scenes (5.720–51, 8.381–93).[44] In book 4 Zeus associates Hera with potential cannibalism, "even if you would devour Priam and his children raw . . . then would you sate your wrath" (4.34–6).[45] Zeus' address reflects an El-like perspective on Anat. From an Ugaritic viewpoint, Anat's definitive qualities, while primarily located in Athena, are occasionally bifurcated into Hera, Athena's comrade in the war.[46]

The Homeric Athena is also depicted in contexts suggestive of cannibalism. Her arming scene, noted above (5.736–47, 8.384–91), suggests parallels with the depiction of Anat's feast. Athena's interactions with the suitors and their feasts in the *Odyssey*, and with Hektor's bloody sacrifice in *Iliad* 6, offer additional contexts. Athena's arming scene has an undercurrent of violence. Her reason for arming is to go against Zeus' orders and intervene in the war. In the first scene, she dons Zeus' aegis, adorned with the Gorgon's head, and a helmet, adorned with "the foot soldiers of a hundred cities" (5.744). As in Anat's feast, a fierce goddess goes to war as if, by virtue of her helmet, she is leading hundreds of warriors into battle with her. Athena now takes hold of a spear, "the spear with which she *subdues* the ranks of heroes, those at whom she is angry [κοτέσσεται]" (5.745–47 = 8.389–91). In the *Iliad*, the Greek verb rendered here as "subdues," δάμνησι, often denotes not only defeat but a warrior's death (as at 5.653; 11.444, 820; 16.816, 848; 22.55, 271, et al.). The formulaic description therefore suggests Athena not only threatens the warriors with her deadly spear but is capable of slaying them, just as Anat is with her lance. The set piece is a token of Athena's power and habits as generally understood. In the present time of the *Iliad*, Hektor and Pandaros are warriors whose death Athena causes, both slain by spear (22.325–61, 5.290–96). There is a brief hint of cannibalism at Hektor's death. Before dying, he is concerned that dogs will devour his corpse (22.339). But when he pleads with Akhilleus to prevent this, Akhilleus wishes he himself were able to eat Hektor's corpse raw (22.346–47). Since Akhilleus here carries out an agenda directed by Athena, does his wish reflect a similar if unspoken desire in Athena?

In the *Odyssey*, Athena is depicted even closer to Anat as she personally directs the slaughter of the suitors. When she descends from Olympos to set the *Odyssey*'s plot in motion, she seizes her spear, described in lines echoing her arming scenes in the *Iliad*:

she seized her mighty spear, tipped with a sharp bronze point,
heavy, great, and stout, with which she *subdues* the ranks
of heroes, those at whom she of the mighty father is angered.

(*Od.* 1.99–101)

The *Odyssey* continues with a depiction of Athena developing a divine wrath against a large body of warriors, the suitors.[47] Arriving in Ithaka to meet with Telemakhos and discuss his long-absent father, a disguised Athena complains strongly about the behavior of the 108 suitors in the hall:

What feast is this, why this throng? What does it have to do with you?
Is it a banquet or a wedding, since it is no communal meal.
How <u>arrogantly</u> [ὑβρίζοντες] they seem to strut about in their feasting
all through the palace. Were a pious man to encounter them,
he'd be deeply offended, seeing such disgraceful conduct.

(1.225–29)

Athena here serves as the disguised god who witnesses mortals' transgression of the sacred tenets of hospitality, the mythic subgenre theoxeny. The *Odyssey* later gives explicit definition of the mythic type:

For the gods, likening themselves to guests from abroad,
becoming all different sorts, go among the cities,
observing men's arrogance and good conduct.

(17.485–87)

Such is Athena's position when she complains to Telemakhos, just as the disguised angels in Genesis 19 and the disguised Jupiter and Mercury in Ovid's *Metamorphoses* (8.619–724). Her divine wrath is now directed against the suitors for the remainder of the poem. The *Odyssey* depicts the suitors as warriors, trained in the use of the spear (*Od.* 4.626 = 17.168).

Two passages depict Athena moving against the suitors while they are feasting, suggestive of Anat's bloody feast. To help Telemakhos slip away to visit Nestor, Athena incapacitates the suitors:

She went to the palace of godlike Odysseus,
and there she poured sweet sleep on the suitors, and struck [πλάζε][48]
them as they were drinking, dashing the cups from their hands.

(2.394–96)

The brief episode neatly foreshadows the poem's climax, the death of the suitors, jointly executed by Odysseus and Athena. In a second passage shortly before they will die, Athena disorients them, again while they feast:

> In the suitors Pallas Athena
> stirred up wild laughter, and dashed [παρέπλαγξεν] their minds.
> Now they were laughing with jaws that were not their own.
> The meat they were eating was splattered with blood, their eyes were
> full of tears, their cheer now seemed like lamentation.
>
> (20.345–49)

Both passages bring together elements prominent in Anat's bloody feast. The war goddess acts violently against a warrior band while it attends a feast.

While the *Odyssey* does not have contexts suggesting cannibalism in Athena, other than the juxtaposition of her bloodshed with feasting, it does depict her as having a bloodlust like Anat. As noted in chapter 6, when Athena instructs Odysseus to proceed against the suitors, she declares that she expects "his immense floor to be splattered with [the suitors'] blood and brains" (*Od.* 13.395). When Odysseus slays the suitors, under Athena's supervision, the same bloody description, "splattered with blood and gore," recurs twice (*Od.* 22.402 = 23.48), of Odysseus. These passages taken together are quite suggestive of Anat's bloody feast, but with the violent bloodshed transferred to Odysseus.[49] The *Iliad* itself utters the formula as Hektor initiates a sacrifice to Athena (*Il.* 6.268).

Anat and Aqhat: Athena and Hektor (and Paris and Pandaros)

Anat is often criticized for the perceived cruelty with which she treats the hero Aqhat, for deceiving him and leading him to his death. Again Athena offers a close parallel in her deception of Hektor in *Iliad* 22 and in her exploitation of Pandaros (*Il.* 4.88–5.296), who, like Aqhat, is an archer.[50] Such cruelty is a traditional characteristic of ancient deities and is also present in OT depictions of Yahweh who deceives Ahab and leads him on to his death (1 Kings 22).

I offer a summary of the *Aqhat*. The childless Danel performs a ritual, which moves Baal to intervene with El, to ask him to bless Danel with a son. After later entertaining the Katharat, goddesses of birth, Danel makes love to his wife, who becomes pregnant with Aqhat. During her pregnancy, the god Kothar visits, bringing a bow he made. After a break in the text, Aqhat, now a young man, is at a feast with the gods, including Anat. Desiring his bow, she offers him wealth and immortality in exchange. He arrogantly rejects her offer, telling her to go to Kothar and have him fashion one for her, asserting that women have no part in bows. Threatening him, Anat meets with El to secure his permission for Aqhat's death. Anat next arranges with a mercenary soldier, Yatipan, to take Aqhat's bow and slay him. In the form of a bird of prey, he kills Aqhat but loses or destroys the bow in the process. As a blight strikes the region, Danel and his daughter Pughat are performing rituals when two messengers approach who tell them how Anat caused Aqhat's death. Danel then asks Baal to dispatch birds of prey so he can search their bellies for Aqhat's remains. When Danel buries the remains, he returns home, to mourn Aqhat for seven years. The mourning completed, Pughat asks his blessing to avenge Aqhat. When Danel agrees, she dons warrior garb beneath her clothes, and heads for Yatipan's camp. Yatipan receives her, and they are drinking in his tent when the narrative breaks off. Most scholars assume she slays Yatipan, avenging Aqhat, and ending the blight on the region. Some assume that Aqhat is subsequently brought back to life (cf. Hippolytus).

The *Aqhat* has left oblique traces in OT myth. Gordon (1965b: 156) argues that Kohath (Gen 46:11) is the same name as Aqhat. Though little is said of Kohath (also at Exod 6:16, 18; 1 Chron 15:5), he is the uncle of Moses and Aaron. Kohath's sister as mother of Moses may suggest a greater importance in earlier traditions for Kohath, and that Israelite tradition here draws on Ugaritic, for both Aqhat and his sister. The Daniel mentioned at Ezek 14:14 is thought to be the same character as Aqhat's father, Danel.

The myth in its full arc employs the epic[51] triangle identified above, with El as sky father, Baal as mentor deity, and Anat as the god with a divine wrath against the hero:

El
(sky father, judge)

Anat   Baal
(wrathful)   (mentor)

Aqhat

As always, the two opposed gods, Anat and El, do not confront each other. In the *Aqhat*, they are separated by time, since Baal intervenes to help bring about the birth of Aqhat, and Anat intervenes only after he has become a man. Ugaritic myth handles time much as does OT myth. The narrative goes linearly through its episodes, quite different from the selectivity of Homeric epic, which tends to focus on short units of time, some of which are treated in a nonlinear manner, rather than depict a twenty-year span in sequence.

The *Aqhat* exhibits an extensive homology with parts of the *Iliad*, several characters exhibiting specific parallels. Not only do Anat and Athena act out similar roles, and Aqhat and Hektor (with Paris and Pandaros as additional thematic parallels to Hektor), but in each case the father of the doomed hero is a well-known patriarch, Danel and Priam, who has the sky father's sympathy. Each goddess works closely in tandem with a warrior, Yatipan and Akhilleus (and Diomedes), to cause the death of the hero at whom she is angry. In spite of the goddesses' animosity, each hero, Aqhat and Hektor, enjoys the favor of the sky father. The *Iliad* especially parallels Anat's relations with Aqhat in Athena's treatment of Hektor and the archer Pandaros. While the *Aqhat* has been subjected to a variety of interpretations, a consensus is emerging that sees the title character as an example of human presumption or arrogance, who is punished by the wrathful god, Anat.[52]

Aqhat and Paris: A God Offers a Mortal
A Choice between Kingship, Immortality, Riches

Although the *Aqhat* has, as prelude, his father's pious request for his birth, Kothar's visit, and other brief episodes, Aqhat's tragedy begins with Anat's desire for his bow. Aqhat holds a feast or banquet, attended by mortals and gods.[53] The text offers few details about the feast, nor do we possess enough other myths with similar contexts to know the conventions for such a gathering. Since it appears that Anat is a guest, the context suggests vague parallels with theoxenic myth, except that the goddess is not in disguise. In any case, hospitality, and the behavior of host and guest, all seem to be issues. Greek myth is rich in disputes breaking out at feasts (Akhilleus and Odysseus at *Od.* 8.76; Prometheus and Zeus in the *Works and Days;* the Centaurs and Lapiths at *Od.* 21.295–303), but none that is particularly close to the *Aqhat*.

Anat pursues her desire of his bow through an instance of a well-attested subgenre of myth: *A god offers a mortal a choice between kingship, immortality, riches, or other options.* Anat's offer of fabulous wealth, or immortality, to Aqhat, finds parallels in other Ugaritic myth, in the myth of Solomon, and even the temptation of Christ. Ugaritic myth has the same mythic type in *Kirta,* when El appears to the title character in a dream (1. CAT 1.14 35–

43, in Parker) and offers him a choice between kingship, such as El's, or wealth.[54] Like Aqhat, Kirta desires sons and rejects the other offers (1. CAT 1.14 ii 4–5). I summarize the rest of *Kirta* for its additional parallels with Paris' role in Trojan War myth.[55] El directs Kirta to raise an army and besiege the city, Udum, to demand the king's daughter, Huraya, "Who's as fair as the goddess Anat." But, on his way to lay siege to Udum, Kirta stops in Tyre, vowing to dedicate a statue to Asherah, if he is successful. Reaching Udum, he attacks the surrounding towns, until Pabuli, king of Udum, offers him ransom. Kirta rejects Pabuli's offer of riches, demanding his daughter, Huraya. Obtaining his bride, Kirta spares the city and returns home. But seven years later, after Huraya has borne several sons, Asherah remembers Kirta's unfulfilled vow and makes him gravely ill. When he is finally healed, his eldest son attempts to seize the throne. The text concludes with Kirta cursing his son (which may or may not be the actual ending of the myth; see Greenstein, in Parker 10).

In Solomon's dream (1 Kings 3:5–15), Yahweh appears to him and asks what he should give him. In this instance, the god does not list the options ahead of time. Solomon answers "a heart with skill to listen, so that he may govern your people justly and distinguish good from evil." Yahweh then replies with the full set of options he apparently intended, noting that Solomon did not ask for long life, wealth, or for the death of his enemies. The first two of these options are those Anat offers Aqhat. When Solomon chooses wisdom, Yahweh grants him the other three options as well.

In Matthew and Luke, the devil tempts Christ by offering him three options (Matt 4; Luke 4:1–13). In Matthew the devil first suggests that Jesus, who has fasted for forty days, turn stones into bread. Then, setting him on the top of the temple at Jerusalem, he bids him to throw himself down, to be saved from harm by the angels. Finally, from a mountaintop he shows him all the kingdoms of the world and offers him kingship over all, if Christ will bow down to him. The first two options are unique, but the third, the offer to the hero of kingship over all, occurs in other instances of the mythic subgenre. Like Kirta, and Solomon, Christ rejects the options. Though the Gospels, and probably the author of Q before them,[56] put the traditional mythic type to a slightly different purpose, the underlying similarities remain clear, especially in the last option, kingship over all.

Though different contexts and details serve different functions in myths of the hero's choice, the main purpose of the episodes is to suggest the hero's moral qualities through his choice, much as Aristotle argues of a protagonist in a tragedy (*Poet.* 1450b). The hero defines himself, and reveals his governing qualities, through his selection. Danel, Kirta, Solomon, and Christ each select the correct option, which in all their cases (but not in all instances of the subgenre) is "none of the above." The earlier instances may also be understood as temptations, as in the myth of Christ.

A particularly well-known instance of this subgenre of myth initiates the Trojan War. Though Troy has inherited guilt from Laomedon's crimes against the gods, the tragedy of Troy's present generation, and the death of Hektor, begin with the Judgment of Paris, to which the *Iliad* briefly alludes (24.28–30).[57] The Judgment of Paris has strong parallels with the other examples, the *Aqhat, Kirta,* Solomon's Dream, and the Temptation of Christ, both in the basic type-scene and in the divine wraths that result from it. The *Iliad*'s brief reference to the Judgment seems intended to account for Hera's and Athena's divine wraths against Troy. Aphrodite is specified as offering a gift, which implies that the other goddesses do as well. Short though it is, the allusion suggests the closest parallels with Aqhat's interaction with Anat. The *Iliad* implies that Paris misbehaves in the Judgment when it states, "he insulted/reproached/quarreled with the goddesses," νείκεσσε Θεᾶς (24.29). The root νεικ-, "strife," resonates throughout the *Iliad* to denote characters exercising poor judgment, bringing conflict among their own people. The term would have been apropos in the *Aqhat* to describe Aqhat's treatment of Anat. The passage also refers to the Judgment as Paris' *ate* (24.28), the delusion or recklessness that the *Iliad* associates particularly with Agamemnon and Paris.

The *Cypria* and Apollodorus offer more details' specifying the other goddesses' gifts. Hera offers kingship over all (βασιλείαν πάντων); Athena, victory in war (πολέμου νίκην). Hera's offer (βασιλείαν πάντων) is quite close to the devil's final option for Christ (πάσας τας βασιλείας τοῦ κόσμου, Matt 4:8; cf. Luke 4:5). Paris is a negative example of the subgenre, as is Aqhat, making the incorrect choice, whereas Kirta, Solomon, and Christ are positive, making the correct choices. In saying yes to Aphrodite Paris spurns two more-powerful goddesses, Athena and Hera. Choosing *either* of their offers would have been a correct choice, beneficial to his city or people. In choosing the gift of Aphrodite, and an illicit choice (a *married* Helen), Paris reveals himself as immoral, a selfish sensualist, unconcerned with future repercussions of his act, bringing disaster on his city.[58] We noted in chapter 6 (*8b. Paris: A man's desire for a foreign woman brings destruction on his people*) the mythic type in the OT, which provokes a divine wrath against the people who take her in (cf. Gen 34).

Paris and Aqhat both bring troubles upon themselves through their roles in this subgenre of myth. Each Paris/Aqhat offends the parallel goddess, Athena/Anat, in this face-to-face encounter and later suffers the consequences of her divine wrath. The *Iliad*'s implication that Paris provokes or strives with the goddesses (νείκεσσε Φεᾶς, 24.29) resembles Aqhat's arrogance with Anat. Although the *Iliad* does not depict Paris' death, other sources (Apollodorus, *Epitome* 5:8; *Little Iliad,* argument 2) tell us that Philoktetes slays Paris in a duel. In the *Iliad,* such duels typically involve divine aid. As noted in chapter 1 Athena has the thematic role of aiding the best of the Akhaians in his duel with the central Trojan hero. This suggests that Athena should be understood as having a hand in Paris' death, as Anat does for Aqhat. Paris, like Aqhat, is an archer (discussed below).

The *Kirta* suggests additional parallels of Kirta with Paris in the divine wraths both provoke as they obtain their foreign brides. Paris provokes not only Athena's anger but the wrath of Hera as well. Kirta provokes the wrath of the equivalent Ugaritic goddess, Asherah. Each does so not only in conjunction with obtaining his foreign bride but in connection with a stop at a Phoenician city—Sidon, in Paris' case, and Tyre, for Kirta. After Paris leaves Sparta with Helen, a wrathful Hera sends a storm, driving him to Sidon (*Cypria,* argument 2; Apollodorus, *Epit* 3.4). He then sacks the Phoenician city, Sidon. Kirta, on his way to besiege Udum, to win Huraya as his bride, stops in Tyre to vow to dedicate a statue to Asherah, if he is successful in winning his bride. But Kirta later forgets his vow, and Asherah is apparently the cause of his subsequent illness.

Athena's and Anat's Intervention to cause Hektor's and Aqhat's deaths

As Anat does for Aqhat, Athena herself arranges for Hektor's death. Though set in motion long before,[59] Hektor's death is triggered by a unique divine council resembling Anat's meeting with El to plan Aqhat's death. While Akhilleus chases Hektor around Troy, the gods are likened to spectators watching a footrace (22.157–66), from which the divine council develops, with Zeus, as usual, presiding. Although Zeus opens the council noting his own feelings for Hektor, wondering if the gods should not allow him to live (22.168–72), Athena redirects the discussion, shifting the topic away from the specific case of Hektor, who has Zeus' sympathy, to the general issue of whether a *mortal* should be allowed to escape death (22.178–81).[60] Having obscured Hektor through her general reference, Athena then issues something of a threat: if Zeus lets a mortal escape death, "Do it; but all we other gods will not approve." Quickly backpedalling ("I do not speak at all with fervor, but I wish to be kindly to you"), Zeus gives Athena permission to handle the situation as she sees fit, "Act in accord with the mind within you, and do not hold back" (22.185).

The discussion, both Athena's aggressive approach and Zeus' deferential tone, are much like those of Anat to El (CTA 18 i 15–19; Parker 63–64), noted above. Having left the feast at which Aqhat insulted her, Anat goes to El, and threatens to use violence against him, if he will not allow her to punish Aqhat (1.18.11–12). The only other deity in Homeric epic to address Zeus so boldly is Hera (16.440–49), who, as we have seen, not only shares functions with Athena but resembles Anat in a few particulars, most notably her association with cannibalism. In his reply, El is introduced as "The Gracious One, the kindly god" (Hallo's translation, 348), close to Zeus' assertion that he wishes to be kindly (ἤπιος) to Athena. El continues:

[(so then) go ahead and] lay hold of what you desire,
carry out what you wish.

                    (CTA 18 i 18–19, in Hall, 348)

The lines could hardly be closer to Zeus' deference to an Athena eager to cause Hektor's death, "Act in accord with the mind within you, and do not hold back" (*Il.* 22.185).

Athena then descends from Olympos while Akhilleus continues to chase Hektor. When Zeus weighs the two heroes' fates, and Hektor's sinks, Apollo deserts him. Athena now appears to Akhilleus, openly, in a full theophany, the central type-scene in which the mentor deity participates, delineating her relationship with him. She speaks words of encouragement to Akhilleus, much as Shamash to Gilgamesh (*Gilg.* V i, SBV), and Athena to Odysseus (*Od.* 22.232–35). She speaks of their proposed teamwork, using dual forms to link herself and the hero as subjects (*Il.* 22.216, 218; cf. *Od.* 13.372–72, 439). But in her subsequent appearance to Hektor, she does not appear as Athena but assumes the form of Deiphobos, his brother.

Athena's appearance to Hektor is a parody of theophany. She *pretends* to aid and reassure the hero, in order to lead him to his death. He is unaware of her dialogue with Akhilleus. As "Deiphobos" Athena offers false encouragement, addresses him as "dear brother" (ἠθεῖ', 22.229),[61] and makes a false offer of aid, selling her deception through her guise as his brother. As with Akhilleus, she uses dual forms (22.231, 243–45) to describe her proposed teamwork with Hektor. But these falsely intimate their cooperation, as does her account of how relatives attempted to restrain her from coming out. Her deception validates, falsely, Hektor's own uncertain circumstances as book 22 begins. Finding (false) assurance from Athena, Hektor agrees with her plan to face Akhilleus, together, as he thinks. Hektor only realizes her deception when, after hurling his only spear without harming Akhilleus, he calls "Deiphobos" to retrieve it for him (22.294–96). Hektor immediately recognizes Athena's hand in his deception, "but Athena has utterly deceived me" (ἐμὲ δ' ἐξαπάτησεν Ἀθήνη, 22.299). Akhilleus goes on to slay Hektor, almost as an anticlimax, a key instance of overdetermination.

There are intriguing parallels in Anat's deception of Aqhat. After meeting with El to obtain permission for Aqhat's death, as Athena does with Zeus, Anat meets with Aqhat. Then, the text is severely damaged. All we know for certain is that Anat addresses Aqhat as "brother,"[62] Athena's first word to Hektor when she appears to him to lead him to his death. Anat then apparently invites or challenges him to go hunting. But when the text resumes, Anat is meeting with the mercenary warrior, Yatipan. The two discuss how to kill Aqhat, concluding with Anat's description of his death:

> I myself will soar amongst the hawks,[63]
> above Aqhat [I'll] position you.
> Strike him twice on the head,
> three times above the ear,
> Pour out [his] blood like one emptying [a bucket],
> [pour it out] on his knees like one slaughtering [an animal],
> so that his life force rushes out like wind,
> like spittle his vitality,
> like smoke from his nostrils.
>
> (CTA 18, in Hallo 349–50)

The actual slaying of Aqhat (which repeats the lines above) has little in common with Hektor's death and is closer to Apollo's helping to slay Patroklos (Apollo strikes Patroklos in the back and shoulders, 16.791–92).

Aqhat's and Hektor's Disrespect to Anat and Athena

Aqhat treats Anat with contempt in their face-to-face encounter when she offers him wealth or immortality. To Anat's offer of riches for the bow, Aqhat tells her to obtain the goat horn and buffalo sinews from which a bow might be made and take them to Kothar, who could then make her a bow. His disdain is evident in his use of imperatives to her and in cataloging the components of a bow, which smacks of presumption and sarcasm. His arrogance escalates. When Anat responds by offering eternal life, he accuses her of attempting to deceive him:

> Maid, don't beguile me:
> To a hero your guile is slime.
> (CAT 1.17 vi 34–35, in Parker 61)

Suggesting her offer of immortality is false, even dishonest, Aqhat adds the further insult that bows are for warriors, not women (vi 39–41). Diomedes makes a similar remark, but to Aphrodite (*Il.* 5.348–51), not to Athena. It is clear that the *Iliad* validates Diomedes' criticism of Aphrodite (Zeus affirms it, *Il.* 5.428–30, a comment also reminiscent of Aqhat's words). By contrast, Aqhat is in error, and arrogant, to make the charge against Anat (as Diomedes would be, had he made the charge against *Athena*). Aqhat's insolence suggests Gilgamesh's disrespectful response to Ishtar (*Gilgamesh* VI i–iii). But Gilgamesh is clearly correct to say no to a relationship with Ishtar (as his knowledge of her earlier lovers reveals), though wrong to say no so arrogantly.[64]

Chapter 6 noted instances of Hektor's arrogance which suggest disrespect to Athena. Twice Hektor wishes he were "honored as Athena and Apollo are honored" (8.538 = 13.827). The wish is not only presumptuous,[65] but reveals Hektor's ignorance of his actual relations with Athena. The audience knows Athena and Hera are committed to bringing about Troy's destruction, that Zeus' aid to Hektor (in books 8–15) is for only a day. Does his declining to take part in the sacrifice to Athena (*Il.* 6.266–68) constitute disdain for her? Hektor's excuse, that he is too bloodied, is not persuasive.[66] He substitutes Zeus, in place of Athena (whom Helenos designated as the deity to be propitiated, 6.88–96), as the object of the sacrifice (6.266), which again could be taken as disrespectful to Athena. Hektor repeatedly violates the armor of the best of the Akhaians, Athena's *protégé*. In his challenge to duel with the best of the Akhaians, Hektor boasts he will hang his slain opponent's captured armor in the temple of Apollo (7.82–83) after declining to take part in the rituals to Athena. When Hektor achieves his goal, after Patroklos is slain, he dons Akhilleus' armor (17.194–205), which Patroklos had worn during his own *aristeia*. Though we are not shown Athena's reaction, Zeus is highly critical (17.201–6). Like Pandaros, whom Athena helps Diomedes slay after he breaks the sacred oath, Hektor swears a false oath (10.329–31).

Athena's Intervention to cause Pandaros' Death

Athena's intervention to cause the death of the archer, Pandaros, parallels her deception of Hektor, and is even closer to the Anat/Aqhat episode. Richardson briefly notes parallels between her deceptions of Pandaros and Hektor and manipulation of the suitors in the *Odyssey*, most of the contexts we argue suggest Athena's parallels with Anat.[67] When Athena encourages Pandaros to break the truce, she mentions gifts he would receive from Paris.

The gifts are tainted goods, likely the possessions Paris stole from Mene-
laus' house, linking Pandaros with Paris' irresponsible behavior. Athena has
a wrath against both archers, as Anat does against Aqhat. Athena encour-
ages Pandaros to make a prayer to Apollo, κλυτότοξος, "famed for the bow"
(4.101). Pandaros' bow is then described, made of goat horns, from a goat
he shot himself.[68] Kirk (1985: 341–42) and others argue that it would have
been a composite, of horn and sinew bound together: "These composite
bows are Asiatic in type and origin." Aqhat contemptuously suggests that
Anat take ibex horns, buffalo sinews, and bull's tendons to Kothar if she
wishes to have a bow made. Gordon (1965b: 264) argues for specific paral-
lels between the bows of Pandaros and Aqhat:

> Illustrious bowmen are often described in Homer. Some of them, like Pandarus,
> received their divinely fashioned bows as gifts from some god; quite like Aqhat,
> whose bow was made and given by Kothar-and-Hasis. The composite bow made
> with the bull's sinew (*Il.* 4.122, 151) and horn of the wild ibex (*Il.* 4.105) is essen-
> tially the same as the composite bow described in the Ugaritic legend of Aqhat.

Having provoked the incident, Athena then prevents the arrow from caus-
ing serious harm to Menelaus, reiterating that her primary concern was to
have Pandaros break the oath. Having violated the sacred oath, Pandaros
is doomed to die.

In a sequel to the episode, Athena brings about his death. Since the *Iliad*
can use present-time episodes to allude to future events,[69] Pandaros' death,
and Athena's role in it, may allude to the death of Paris. Pandaros reappears
in Diomedes' *aristeia*, wounding the erstwhile "best of the Akhaians" (5.103)
with an arrow. We argued in chapter 2 that Menelaus serves as the "best of
the Akhaians" in his duel with Paris in book 3. In injuring Diomedes and
Menelaus with his arrows, Pandaros thus wounds *two* best of the Akhaians.
Pandaros' wounding Diomedes is often compared with Paris' wounding
Diomedes in the heel (11.369–400; see, e.g., Kirk 1985: 64), reinforcing the
parallels between Pandaros and Paris, and prefiguring Paris' eventual
wounding of Akhilleus. When Diomedes then prays to Athena for help,
and the goddess reassures him, he resumes his winning ways, slaying sev-
eral Trojans, and prompting Aineias to seek out Pandaros, and his bow.
Pandaros, who thought he had slain Diomedes, criticizes himself for re-
lying too much on his bow (5.205), now thinking it was bad luck to have
brought it to Troy (5.209), vowing to destroy it (5.212–16). When Aineias
and Pandaros now encounter Diomedes, the archer throws his spear, which
merely glances off the Greek hero's shield. When Diomedes throws, how-
ever, Athena herself guides his spear (5.290), sending it into Pandaros'

mouth, slicing off his tongue (5.291–93). Pandaros' earlier breaking the truce and sacred oaths provides a pretext for his gruesome death. When the oaths were sworn, both Greeks and Trojans hoped that whoever should break the truce would have his brain poured on the ground as the wine poured in libation (3.298–301).

The *Doloneia* offers additional parallels in Athena's role, and in its use of bows and archery. While chapter 6 considered Dolon as an example of Trojan arrogance, a self-deluding, nonheroic, character, we now note thematic parallels between the *Doloneia* and Athena's interaction with Pandaros and Hektor. Dolon is an archer (10.459). Only here in all the *Iliad* does Odysseus carry a bow (Petegorsky 195), lent by another archer, Meriones (10.260). Dolon's name ("cunning contrivance") ironically embodies the sort of deception associated with Athena and Odysseus,[70] not with the Trojans. Athena does not personally intervene with or appear to Dolon, but she is mentioned throughout the episode (10.245, 274–96, 460–64, 482, 497, 507–12, 516, 553, 571, 578–79), puts *menos* in each Diomedes (10.366) and Odysseus (10.482), sends an omen, and appears in theophany to them. Odysseus and Diomedes both pray and promise sacrifices to Athena, while Dolon neither prays nor vows offerings but vainly hopes for Akhilleus' divine horses as reward for his mission. When they intercept him, he foolishly mistakes them for comrades. His mistake suggests Hektor, deceived by Athena's pose as his brother, and Anat's brotherly invitation to Aqhat to hunt, all prelude to the hero's death.

To sum up, Anat and Athena both participate in the same subgenre of myth, arranging for the death of a young hero who has offended them. Anat's supervising the death of Aqhat parallels Athena's association with Hektor and Pandaros (and Paris, by extension; cf. Dolon). The hero has previously acted arrogantly, shown disrespect to the goddess. Aqhat does so at the choice scene, Hektor as outlined above, and Pandaros in his easy transgression of the truce and the oaths sworn to uphold it (though his arrogance is not directed against Athena personally). The goddess works with another warrior — Yatipan, Akhilleus, or Diomedes — to bring about the death of the offending hero.

In Athena's case, such behavior is part of her thematics not only in the *Iliad* but in extra-Homeric myth. She deceives other heroes and leads them to their deaths, even Greek heroes. Her treatment of Telamonian Aias offers the closest parallels to the episodes we have noted. Aias serves as an instance of the "best of the Akhaians" and thus might be expected to have Athena's full support. However, in contrast to her close teamwork with Diomedes and Akhilleus, she agrees not to intervene in Aias' duel with Hektor in book 7 (7.29–35). In the *Odyssey*, she works against Aias by helping Odysseus win the contest for Akhilleus' arms (*Od.* 11.547). In Sophocles' *Ajax*, Athena treats Aias much as Anat does Aqhat. Aias arrogantly (774–77) rejects her offer of help, implying he needs no assistance from the gods.[71] Under a now wrathful (656, 757, 776–77) Athena's direction, Aias takes part in the kind of blood-spattered carnage (χειροδαίκτα σφάγι᾽ αἱμοβαφῆ, 219) so typical of Anat and the Homeric Athena. Athena's deception parallels Anat's leading Aqhat to his death by inviting him, as a "brother," to go hunting. Aias' delusion is called *ate* (307, 976), as Hektor calls Athena's having posed as his brother (*Il.* 22.299). In his delusion he believes that he has slain Odysseus, Agamemnon, and Menelaus, and that Athena is his ally in all this (92–93, 117), when her real design is to destroy him, as Athena did with Hektor, and Anat with Aqhat. In disorienting and deluding Aias (51–52) Athena parallels how she works against the suitors (*Od.* 2.395–96, 20.345–49; cf. *Il.* 18.311). Athena has similar interactions against other heroes, from Aias Oileus (*Od.* 3.109; 4.499–511, 502: ἐχθόμενός περ Ἀθήνῃ; cf. *Il.* 23.774–75) to Tydeus.[72]

The Magic Bow: Aqhat, Philoktetes (Paris, Pandaros), Eurytos, and Odysseus

Without Aqhat's divine bow, fashioned by Kothar, Anat would have no interest in him, nor develop a divine wrath against him. Homeric epic has a few instances of a hero with a special bow, and Athena, not Apollo, is involved with most such heroes. Philoktetes and his special bow loom large in the overall Trojan War saga. The *Iliad* does not mention his bow but notes that he led a company of archers and that the Akhaians would soon need him (2.718–25), implying awareness of the tradition that his bow is required to sack Troy. Sophocles' *Philoktetes* repeatedly asserts that Troy cannot be taken unless he returns to Troy and slays Paris with his special bow (1426–27). Sophocles assigns Odysseus, Athena's protégé, the task of obtaining the bow.

As in the *Aqhat*, possession of the god-fashioned bow proves unlucky for its owner, as Philoktetes laments (776–78), and as Pandaros complains (*Il.* 5.209). Odysseus serves as the agent of Athena, both in her larger agenda of destroying Troy, and in using deceit to try to obtain the bow. In all these ways Odysseus moves against Philoktetes to obtain his divine bow much as Anat goes against Aqhat to obtain his.[73] Athena parts Hektor from his spear by playing on his erroneous assumption that she will retrieve it after he has thrown in vain (*Il.* 22.293–99). Philoktetes received his divine bow from Herakles, but Apollo gave the bow and arrows to Herakles (Apollodorus 2.4.11). J. B. Hainsworth (359, in Heubeck) notes, "The bow, naturally a gift of Apollo . . . is the characteristic weapon of Herakles in Homer." In the *Nekuia*, Herakles is shown using not his club, prominent in later myth, but his bow (*Od.* 11.607). Herakles thus parallels Pandaros, receiving a special bow from Apollo which causes problems for its owner (J. B. Hainsworth 359–60, in Heubeck)

In the *Odyssey*, Odysseus asserts that of the archers who fought at Troy only Philoktetes was better than he (*Od.* 8.219–20). He mentions Herakles and Eurytos as archers of note in another respect, as competing with the gods in their archery (ἀθανάτοισιν ἐρίζεσκον περὶ τόξων, 8.224). Odysseus notes that Eurytos challenged Apollo to compete in archery, and the angry god then killed him. Eurytos' encounter with Apollo is thus yet another Greek myth suggesting parallels with the *Aqhat*, though featuring Apollo, not Athena, as the god who develops a wrath against a presumptuous archer. The *Iliad* mentions Eurytos once more (2.596), associating him with Thamyris, who boasted that he could surpass the Muses in song, cementing Eurytos as arrogantly competing with the gods. The *Odyssey* intertwines all these figures by noting that the bow and arrows Odysseus uses to slay the suitors (a scene reminiscent of Anat's feast) are the gift of Iphitos, Eurytos' son (*Od.* 21.11–41). In doing so, the *Odyssey* implies parallels between Philoktetes' bow, which helps effect the Greeks' conquest of Troy, and Odysseus' bow, used for slaying the suitors, which marks the end of the greater Trojan War saga, and of the heroic era. Both bows are associated with Eurytos and Herakles before they make their way to Philoktetes and Odysseus. Odysseus successfully wields the bow on a day sacred to Apollo (*Od.* 21.258–59), and with the explicit help of Athena, suggesting he can *balance* the two opposing gods of the Homeric epic triangle.

Myths about archers thus exist in two types, positive or negative, depending on the archers' relations with the gods.[74] Aqhat, Pandaros, Eurytos, and Paris are negative, having contentious relations with the gods, as does the Iliadic Teukros. Teukros, Telamonian Aias' brother, competes against Meriones in archery at the funeral games for Patroklos (23.859–83). But when he fails to vow a sacrifice to Apollo before he shoots, Apollo makes his shot miss (23.865). Zeus also fouls his shot when he attempts to wound Hektor (15.458–73; see Richardson 268). Teukros is thus another instance of the negative type, thematically depicted as having a god make him miss his shots. Odysseus, Meriones, and Philoktetes, on the other hand, are positive instances, all linked with each other, exemplifying correct relationships with the gods. Of all the heroes in Greek myth Odysseus enjoys the closest relations with Athena (e.g., *Od.* 13.296–306; *Il.* 10.245), and does not incur divine wrath when he uses the bow. Meriones lends Odysseus a bow in the *Doloneia* (10.260), successfully shoots and slays Harpalion, Paris' guest-friend (13.650), and defeats Teukros in the archery contest (23.850–83). He is thus not only associated with Odysseus, but his slaying of Harpalion parallels and foreshadows Philoktetes' slaying of Paris. Although Philoktetes resembles Aqhat in suffering for having a divine bow, in slaying Paris, and returning home from Troy without complications (*Od.* 3.190, the *Odyssey*'s way of saying no god had a divine wrath against him), he is a positive example. All three positive archers defeat negative archers: Philoktetes defeats Paris; Meriones, Teukros; and Odysseus, Dolon.

Hektor and Aias, though not archers, both have brothers of the negative archer type, Paris and Teukros. Perhaps because of their archer brothers, Greek myth has drawn Hektor and Aias into the rubric of arrogant archer myths. Scholars have conjectured that Hektor was not originally part of the Trojan War saga, but that Paris was the central Trojan warrior. If so, some of the tradition's oldest or deepest motifs would still be constructed around Paris, though Hektor has since evolved into the *Iliad*'s central Trojan character. At the core of the *Iliad*, then, remains an archer, Paris, who has offended Athena (νείκεσσε, 24.29). But in the present-time of the poem it is Athena's wrath against Paris' brother, Hektor, that serves as a climax of the poem, while Paris' own death falls outside of the poem, to be brought about by another archer Athena supports, Philoktetes. Paris' own death, however, and Athena's likely role in helping to bring it about, seem prefigured in her helping Diomedes slay the archer Pandaros, a doublet of Paris. Anat's interactions with Aqhat, her wrath provoked by his disrespect, and her interest in his divine bow thus offer contexts for each of the Iliadic figures: Paris, Pandaros, Hektor, and the barely mentioned Philoktetes. Athena's surprising prominence in archer myths, instead of Apollo, may be a natural subset of her tendency to mentor the Greek hero, whose success often depends on his relationship with Athena. But it also suggests the influence of an Anat tradition on the Homeric Athena.

Anat in Old Testament Myth

Though OT myths feature the Canaanites and Israelites worshiping much of the West Semitic pantheon, particularly Baal, El, and Asherah, they do not depict the worship of Anat. But Anat and her traditions are nonetheless evident in the OT, in proper names, in specific subgenres of myth, and in violent behavior assigned to Yahweh. There are also instances where commentators suspect allusions to Anat though she is unnamed. Mention of Anat in the OT generally seems associated with the Philistines. OT redactors have a tendency to portray the Philistines as worshiping Dagon to the exclusion of the other deities in their pantheon, unrealisti-

and enjoy personal relationships with a mentor god. Elsewhere in Judges, a hero such as Samson is inspired by god ("The spirit of the Lord suddenly seized him," Judg 14:6; cf. 3:10, 6:34, 11:29, 13:25, 14:19, 15:14) and performs acts, such as slaying hundreds of warriors, which in the *Iliad* would be an *aristeia*. From an Iliadic perspective, Shamgar is a hero, who performs an *aristeia* because of his connection with Anat. Shamgar and Samson both perform their *aristeiai* against the Philistines, that OT people connected by many with Mycenaean culture. In the *Iliad* the consummate deity for inspiring an *aristeia* is Athena, who places *menos* in Diomedes (5.2, 125, which equals the third motif in the principal narrative pattern, *3. A god places* μένος *in him as he goes to face the Trojans*). The mention of Anat in conjunction with Shamgar's fighting the Philistines may thus suggest an actual intersection of Israelite and Greek mythic traditions.

According to Suggs, Sakenfeld, and Mueller (248), the term rendered as "Judge" denotes a man who can "bring the people back from idolatry," who delivers Israel back to the true faith. Why, then, would OT myth assign such a role to a heroic character explicitly connected with Anat, a non-Yahwist deity, part of a polytheistic pantheon? The discord between Shamgar's connection with Anat and the role he has been given as a "judge" suggests that the redactors of the text at this stage are using traditional elements of heroic myth but putting them together in profoundly contradictory ways. This is not the only such instance. Another Judge who is cast in a very traditional heroic mold is Gideon (Judg 6–8), whose real name is Jerubaal (Judg 6:32), a clearly theophoric name, which the text claims means "let Baal plead." However, "a person with this name, which really means 'May Baal take action,' would be a worshipper of Baal not a foe. Other difficulties in the Gideon stories indicate that several different sources have not been perfectly fused" (Suggs et al. 254). Both Shamgar and Gideon/Jerubaal thus appear to be traditional heroes who originally had little or no connection with Yahwist religion, but which OT myth incorporates nonetheless as examples of heroic valor.

Anat, Rameses II–IV, and the Philistines

Anat was the favored deity of the pharaohs, Rameses II–IV. Her status in Egypt thus deserves consideration since Egypt influenced Israelite culture and Greeks had contact with Egypt during this period as well. In a review of the royal inscriptions Shupak (519) notes that "Anath is revealed to have been primarily a goddess of war and to have been associated in particular with Pharaoh, in her capacity as the sovereign's personal protectress." Anat's personal relationships with Egyptian pharaohs parallel the personal relationship Athena has with Homeric kings such as Odysseus and Akhilleus. Rameses II (1304–1237) had a sword inscribed "Anat is Victory" and named his hunting hound "Anat is Protection."[81] Both aspects of the war goddess, victory and protection, are also specific attributes of war with which Athena is associated in Homeric epic.[82]

Ramesside Egypt also had contact with the Philistines. Rameses II fought against a coalition of Sea Peoples which may have included the Philistines and apparently what the *Iliad* knows as Lykians (Hindson 18) and other peoples allied with the Trojans—Dardanians, Mysians, and Pedasians (Hindson 38). We know for certain that Rameses III (1198–1166) fought and defeated a group of Sea Peoples which did include the Philistines (Shupak 520). After their defeat by Egypt, the Philistines settled on the Palestinian coast (Hindson 109) and commenced extensive interaction with the Israelites. Stager (157) refers to "the same confederacy of Sea Peoples, or Mycenaean Greeks, who invaded the coastlands and the island of Alashiya (Cyprus) around 1185–1175." Though rarely noted by Homerists, the *Odyssey*'s allusions to Greek raids on Egypt (*Od.* 14.257–86, 17.426–43) accord well with Egyptian records of the Philistines and other Sea Peoples during the reign of Rameses III.

Additional evidence suggests an Anat tradition has influenced OT myth, even where she is not named. Why would Israelite myths draw on and preserve aspects of an Anat mythic tradition? M. Smith (2001: 23), quoting Stith Thompson, posits a reason for general influences of this kind: "While old myths were commonly readapted in ancient Israel, new myths are rarely attested. Stith Thompson remarked of new myths: 'It is always easier to borrow a myth or tale than it is to construct a new one.' Israel generated relatively few new myths, and the majority of them drew on older mythic material." Other OT myths feature characters and incidents reminiscent of Anat's myths, suggesting that an Anat mythic tradition remained productive in Israelite tradition as a source or model.

The Philistines Dedicate Saul's Armor in the Temple of Ashtoreth

When the Philistines rout the Israelites and kill Saul's three sons, including Jonathan, Saul then falls on his own sword. The next day, the Philistines come upon his body: "They cut off his head and stripped him of his armour. . . . They deposited his armour in the temple of Ashtoreth and nailed his body on the wall of Beth-shan" (1 Sam 31:9–10). The behavior here ascribed to the Philistines resembles an incident in the *Iliad*, Hektor's comments before his duel with Aias, which, as noted in chapter 5, is the closest analogue to David's duel with Goliath (1 Sam 17). When he establishes terms for the duel, Hektor specifies how he will treat the enemy's corpse and armor, should he win:

> But if I should kill him, and Apollo should grant me glory,
> having stripped off his armor, I'll bear it back to sacred Ilion,
> to hang it up in the temple of Apollo the farshooter,
> but I'll give his corpse back to the strong-benched ships.
>
> (*Il.* 7.81–84)

In vowing to hang Aias' arms up in Apollo's temple, Hektor is once more on the wrong side of Athena. But Hektor's obsession with proper care for the slain warrior, ironically pointing to the abuse that awaits his own corpse, encapsulates a custom that parallels the Philistine practice. When the tale is retold in 1 Chronicles, the Philistines are said to hang his armor up in the temple of Dagon, not Ashtoreth (1 Chron 10:10). The discrepancy can be attributed to the tendency of OT redactors to focus exclusively on Dagon, as if the Philistines were monotheists.

Commentators have suggested that the temple in which the Philistines hang Saul's armor would, in fact, have been a temple of Anat. As P. L. Day (75) explains, "Given Anat's clear portrayal as a warrior and a patron or guardian of warriors and royalty in extrabiblical sources, and given that we know she had a temple in Beth Shan, it makes good sense to suggest that the armour of a vanquished warrior-king would be brought to her temple by the grateful victors."[83] Day (66–67) further notes that the Egyptians left records of their worship of Anat in both Gaza and Beth Shan, which were important Egyptian military outposts at the time (cf. Eaton 30). Hektor himself will be slain, his corpse defiled almost as is Saul's, his armor seized by a hero close to Athena, much as the Philistines may here consecrate Saul's arms to Anat.

Jael, Deborah, Pughat (Aqhat's Sister), and Anat

The two references to "Shamgar, son of Anat," frame another myth that has been linked with Anat, Jael's murder of Sisera. We mentioned Jael as the wife of Heber, a Kenite (a people associated with the Canaanites). Shamgar and Jael are mentioned in a parallel construction (Judg 5:6), implying links between the two figures. Within OT myth Jael belongs to a subset of foreign women who turn against their own people to help the Israelites; Rahab is another prominent example (Josh 2). Yahweh puts the Israelites under the power of Jabin, a Canaanite king (Judg 4:1–2), whose general is Sisera. A battle develops between the Israelites, led by Barak, and Sisera's ten thousand men. When Yahweh hurls panic against the Canaanites (see subgenre 12 in chapter 6), they are routed, and Sisera flees, much as the Greeks in *Iliad* 8. As Barak chases him, Sisera seeks refuge in Jael's tent. Jael comes out to greet him, invites him in, and tells him not to worry (Judg 4:17–18). She then covers him (which may imply hiding him) and gives him some milk, which, because of its soporific qualities, probably implies cunning on her part (Boling 1975: 114). After he falls asleep, she takes a tent-peg and pounds it into his temple with a mallet (Judg 4:21, 5:26), crushing his skull.

Jael's actions are reminiscent both of Anat's deception of Aqhat and of Pughat's (Aqhat's sister) preparing to slay Yatipan, her brother's slayer. When Anat arranges to have Aqhat slain, she first invites him, deceptively, to go hunting. Jael's use of deception, in violation of hospitality (which is clearly sacred in Gen 18–19, as in Greek myth), suggests the cruelty commentators perceive in Anat's deception of Aqhat, leading him to his death (see Johnson). The scene of her murder of Sisera, a tent, is the same as Pughat's murder of Yatipan, except there the tent is Yatipan's own. Jael's act, as Pughat's, involves deception and violation of the usual rules of hospitality. But it is their female gender that most bonds Jael and Pughat and makes them distinct in extant Near Eastern myth. Homeric epic lacks a prominent female heroine who can be seen as a hypostasis of the goddess, as is Odysseus, but the *Aqhat* may imply that Pughat is such a figure for Anat, and Jael may be in OT myth.

The same episode suggests further links with an Anat mythic tradition in Deborah, the prophetess who advises the Israelites how to defeat Sisera. Her status as prophetess deserves comment. Female prophets are quite rare in OT myth. Huldah (2 Kings 22:14–20) is apparently the only other prophetess in the OT (unless we count Jezebel, discussed below). She figures in a context where most of the Israelites are depicted as worshiping Baal, Asherah, and the rest of the Canaanite polytheistic pantheon (which would include Anat).[84] A world of difference separates Deborah from Huldah, however. Deborah formulates plans and not only advises but orders (Judg 4:14) the Israelite commander. As the sole female in OT myth who leads a people in war, Deborah thus serves functions similar to those Anat embodies in her mythic tradition.[85] The existence of a female prophet, within such a strongly patriarchal tradition, probably implies polytheism (as with both Jezebel and Huldah) and connection with a goddess. It is thus reasonable to suggest that Deborah was originally a priestess of Anat,[86] as the Iliad depicts Theano as Athena's prophetess (6.298–311). Perhaps Deborah's closest OT counterpart is Jezebel, priestess of the goddess Asherah. But Jezebel serves, more typical of patriarchal OT myth, as a negative example of female authority and power, of what can go wrong when a woman rules, like Klytaimnestra in Greek myth.

Violent Depictions of Yahweh, Suggesting an Anat Tradition

Depictions of Yahweh's violence are another means by which an Anat tradition may have influenced, and left traces on, OT myth. Yahweh is occasionally depicted acting in ways characteristic of Anat: eager for violence on a large scale, with imagery suggestive of divine cannibalism, and deceiving a character to lead him to his death. M. Smith (1990: 64), who notes many such connections, sums up the basic situation, and a possible explanation for it: "By the biblical period, the savage, grisly descriptions of battle accorded Anat in the Late Bronze Age became one way to describe Yahweh, the divine warrior."[87] I adduce Eaton's (73) earlier assessment:

> The tone and imagery of these [Anat] passages are echoed in some descriptions of the fury and wrath of Yahweh in the Old Testament. . . . A section of the book of Isaiah (63:1–6) represents Yahweh wearing garments which are red with the gore of the sinful whom he has destroyed. There can be little doubt that the use of such imagery was something which Israel shared with its pagan neighbors.

It is a reflex of the traditional nature of ancient myth to *borrow* formulas, type-scenes, and subgenres of myth from earlier traditions, putting the elements together in a new way, but without fully effacing connections with the earlier tradition.

In the passage Eaton notes, which several commentators have associated with depictions of Anat, Yahweh is portrayed as a divine warrior, much like Anat or Athena, answering a prophet's question about his grisly appearance:

> Why are your clothes all red,
> like the garments of one treading grapes in the winepress?
> I have trodden the press alone,
> for none of my people was with me.
> I trod the nations in my anger,
> I trampled them in my fury,
> and their blood bespattered my garments

and all my clothing was stained . . .
I stamped on peoples in my anger,
I shattered them in my fury
and spilled their blood over the ground.

(Isa 63:2–3, 6)

Not only are Yahweh's blood-spattered garments, soiled with the blood of humans he has slain, reminiscent of Anat in the tableau of her feast, but the phrase "their blood bespattered my garments" is quite close to the recurring Homeric formula associated with Athena (*Il.* 6.268; *Od.* 22.402 = 23.408; cf. *Od.* 20.354) and her thematic depiction, "she subdues the ranks / of heroes, those at whom she of the mighty father is angered" (*Il.* 5.745–47 = 8.389–91; *Od.* 1.99–101). As MacKenzie (187) notes, "This is the theophany of Yahweh the warrior judge . . . the imagery of Yahweh marching in blood-stained garments is somewhat appalling."[88]

Psalms offers a similar depiction, suggesting parallels with the tableau of Anat after she has slain warriors at the feast (CTA 3.2.3–30):

God himself smites the heads of his enemies,
those proud sinners with their flowing locks.
The Lord says, "I shall fetch them back from Bashan,
I shall fetch them from the depths of the sea.
that you may bathe your feet in blood,
while the tongues of your dogs are eager for it."

(Ps 68:21–23)[89]

Specific images found in this passage occur in other depictions of Yahweh's violent acts in OT myth.[90]

Elsewhere OT myths' violent depictions of Yahweh mix imagery of the feast and the preparation of the vintage with the aftermath of decisive victories in battle. The resultant combination suggests divine cannibalism, at least at a figurative level:

I shall make my arrows drunk with blood,
my sword will devour flesh,
blood of slain and captives,
the heads of the enemy princes.

(Deut 32:42)

Yahweh's weapons, which will eat human flesh and drink human blood, are given cannibalistic associations.

In Second Isaiah, an apocalyptic description of Yahweh's divine wrath against the entire world culminates in a depiction that mixes sacrificial and cannibalistic imagery:

> for the Lord's anger is against all the nations
> and his wrath against all their hordes;
> he gives them over to slaughter and destruction.
> Their slain will be flung out,
> stench will rise from their corpses,
> and the mountains will run with their blood. . . .
> The Lord has a sword sated with blood,
> gorged with fat, the fat of rams' kidneys,
> and with the blood of lambs and goats;
> for the Lord has a sacrifice in Bozrah,
> a great slaughter in Edom.
>
> (Isa 34:2–4, 6)

The passage suggests not only the practice of the ban (*herem*) but the juxtaposition of slaughter with feasting in Anat's tableau and Athena's arranging to slay the suitors in connection with their feasting.

In some depictions of Yahweh's violence suggestions of cannibalism are transferred to the Israelites:

> Behold a people rearing up like a lioness,
> rampant like a lion;
> he will not couch till he has devoured the prey
> and drunk the blood of the slain.
>
> (Deut 23:24)

Ezekiel contains a unique example of transferred cannibalism and thirst for blood, combined with sacrificial imagery. Though here Yahweh is depicted as addressing birds and beasts, the direct address, in human speech, aligns the animals with the Israelites: "You will sate yourselves with fat and drink yourselves drunk on blood at the sacrifice which I am preparing for you. At my table you will eat your fill of horses and riders, of warriors and fighting men of every kind" (Ezek 39:19–20). As Zimmerli (309) notes, this amounts to a reversal of the usual positions in a sacrifice: "[I]n the normal sacrificial meal the fat and the blood are reserved for Yahweh." Thus the slaughtered are clearly sacred, a sacrifice to Yahweh. Again a similar combination of motifs is present as in Anat's tableau and Athena's managing the suitors' destruction.

In at least one instance, the suggestion of cannibalism attendant upon Yahweh's victories is transferred to the defeated enemy people themselves (see M. Smith 1990: 63):

> I shall make your oppressors eat their own flesh,
> and they will be drunk with their own blood
> as if with wine.
>
> (Isa 49:26)

The previous passages, and more like them,[91] depict Yahweh in ways close to Anat's portrayal in Ugaritic myth. Because many scholars have shown how Israelite myths are at least in part derived from an earlier West Semitic tradition, it stands to reason that the resemblances between Anat and violent depictions of Yahweh are not coincidence but reflect some indebtedness, partial derivation from an Anat tradition.

Commentators have also argued for connections between the Anat mythic tradition and another type of violence associated with Yahweh in OT myth, the ban. As discussed in chapter 5, the ban (*herem*) is the extreme form of warfare in which Yahweh demands the slaughter of all the inhabitants of a city, including civilians. The Mesha stele gives independent testimony to the same practice among a neighboring people, the Moabites (Smelik 35). Here the god demanding the deaths of all the inhabitants of a city is Kemosh (attested in OT myth; e.g., Num 21:29). In the surviving inscription, King Mesha relates Kemosh's command that he attack the cities of Atarot and Nebo:

> and I killed all the people [from] the city as a sacrifice for Kemosh. . . . And Kemosh said to me: Go, take Nebo from Israel. And I went in the night and I fought against it from the break of dawn until noon, and I took it and I killed [its] whole population, seven thousand male citizens and aliens, and female citizens and aliens, and servant girls; for I had put it to the ban for Ashtar Kemosh.[92]

Smelik (38) notes how close the conception is to accounts of the ban in OT myth and specifically compares the passage with 1 Sam 15:3, Yahweh's command to defeat Amalek and put everything under the ban. The Mesha stele thus demonstrates that such practice was not confined to Israel and that the ban was carried out in very similar ways by other peoples. We suggested in chapter 5 that occasional passages in the *Iliad* might also be seen as suggesting related practices (6.55–57, 2.354–56).

M. Smith (2001: 162) posits a relationship between the ban and an Anat tradition, noting that the specific term, *hrm*, used for the ban, is also used of

Anat: "The bloody battle, represented in Ugaritic tradition by the goddess Anat, may provide an insight into the mythos behind the biblical ban (BH *herem*; Ugaritic *hrm) utilized by Iron Age Levantine monarchies (Israel, Judah, and Moab). The same root applies to Anat's warfare in CAT I.13." Smith (ibid.) argues that the Anat texts "suggest how the deity was seen to conduct *hrm* warfare":

> To judge from Anat's "*herem*," it is possible that behind Yahweh's warfare lies the mythos that when the king defeats and slaughters his enemies, Yahweh is understood as fighting for the king and destroying his enemies in battle, and then slaughtering the enemy captives following battle.

Such a conception is implicitly at work in the *Iliad* when Athena assists Diomedes and Akhilleus in the violent acts that constitute their *aristeiai*.

Anat's interactions with mortals and gods in the *Aqhat* and the *Baal Cycle* thus provide a context through which to view the Homeric Athena. Many of what are regarded as Athena's more striking features in Homeric epic —her use of deception against mortals, resentment of Zeus, bloodthirstiness or "primitive ferocity" (Burkert 1985: 140)—all have close equivalents in earlier depictions of Anat. The Anat myths offer close parallels to Athena's divine interactions: her relation with her father El suggests Athena's with Zeus; her relationship with Baal is particularly suggestive of Athena's with Ares and offers contexts for understanding Ares' unusual association with defeat and death in the *Iliad*. Her deception of Aqhat belongs to the same subgenre of myth as Athena's treatment not only of Hektor but of parallel figures, Pandaros, Paris, and Aias. The myths of Anat thus not only supply us with contexts in which to place Athena, but they help us understand the specific subgenres of myth that the *Iliad* has selected to articulate Athena's role in the Trojan War. Anat's particular association with bloodthirsty violence offers contexts for Athena's connections with similar acts and helps us understand why a bloodied Hektor parallels the sacrificial lambs in books 3 and 24. Though not as prominent in OT myth as Baal, El, or Asherah, the Anat myths provide a context for considering specific forms of divine violence ascribed to Yahweh in OT myth. Anat's similarities with Athena also function as a further link between Homeric Akhaians and the Philistines of OT myth. The two goddesses were linked in antiquity.[93] There is no agreed upon etymology of Athena's name. The Mycenaean form was *atana*, as in the compound *atanapotinija*, "Mistress Atana." Atana is only a simple metathesis away from Anat.

Conclusion

This study has sought to provide two sets of tools, two different contexts, for understanding the *Iliad*. The first context, and tool, is the narrative pattern, introductory and principal, in its three sequences. The thrice-recurring string of interconnected type-scenes and motifs provides a context for interpreting a given episode by offering three parallel scenes for most of the motifs in the pattern. As we have seen, particularly in our analysis of the duals in book 9, the parallels can be quite valuable in helping to establish the conventions and norms of a given context, such as which characters are most likely to participate in a specific type of episode. The narrative pattern demonstrates that an *aristeia* by the best of the Akhaians is structured around having him face three champions—Dardanian, Lykian, and Trojan. The narrative pattern reveals how significant neck wounds are woven into the tapestry of the *Iliad*, from Hektor's duel with Aias, ending when a spear grazes his neck, to Athena, a goddess who wields the spear, inflicting a neck wound on Ares, to the climax of Akhilleus' *aristeia*, the lethal wound his special spear inflicts on Hektor. Nestor's suggestions for building the wall and declaring a truce to gather the dead, so often criticized as a later addition, can now be seen to point to the truce that allows the recovery of Hektor's corpse, each scene recurring as the final motif in its respective sequences of the pattern. The narrative pattern thus serves as a hermeneutic for these and many other episodes.

Recognition of the narrative pattern reveals the unique function of book 3. The duel between Paris and Menelaus and other episodes not only invoke the roots of the war, as is commonly held, but rehearse the three major duels to come, familiarizing the audience with key motifs from the narrative pattern. Paris, as Hektor's brother, and Menelaus, as a best of the Akhaians, are depicted in motifs that occur again when Hektor duels Aias, when Hektor slays Patroklos, and when Hektor is slain by Akhilleus. The *Iliad* initiates the series of neck wounds associated with Hektor when Menelaus almost strangles Paris by his chin strap. When Helen looks out from the wall and cannot see her brothers, she prefigures Andromakhe looking in vain for the slain Hektor. Book 3 thus incorporates key motifs from the narrative pattern and first sounds some of the *Iliad*'s most stirring themes as an overture for the epic.

Variations between the narrative pattern's sequences reveal significant use of parody in the *Iliad*. Motifs that occur in the initial and final sequences in their usual function are inverted in the middle sequence, sometimes with humorous results, as in Hera's seduction of Zeus. Other inversions reverse fundamental dynamics in the poem: Hektor and the Trojans now defeat the Greeks, if only temporarily. Paris, who himself parodies the typical relationships and choices of a warrior, and clearly loses the duel in book 3, here meets with his greatest success, wounding Diomedes and Makhaon. In the initial sequence Hektor's concern with proper treatment of the slain warrior's corpse is vivid. But he himself violates such observances when he attempts to decapitate Patroklos. Aphrodite's relations with Aineias and Paris parody Thetis' and Athena's with Akhilleus.

The repetitions of the three sequences reveal the thematic functions of specific characters, such as Odysseus and Telamonian Aias. Odysseus repeatedly restores order, often after a blunder by Agamemnon. Thus in book 1 Odysseus conducts the hecatomb to appease Apollo's wrath (after Agamemnon provoked it), and Odysseus restores order at the assemblies in books 2 and 19. Although Akhilleus slays Hektor, Aias has the thematic role as *the best of the Akhaians defeats Hektor*, because he plays this role several times from book 7 on. Nestor, though a respected figure, is revealed to be thematically ineffective at mediating between Agamemnon and Akhilleus. The *Iliad* thus implies an opposition between Odysseus and Nestor, as the successful and ineffectual counselors on the Greek side.

The existence of the narrative pattern has significant ramifications for the study of the transmission of the *Iliad*. The three sequences, and the parody of the pattern in book 3, together underlie virtually the entire epic. Since such close correspondences could hardly be the result of later additions or rhapsodic contributions, the pattern reveals a persistent stability at the core of the *Iliad*. Its central themes appear to have remained intact, apparently in the sequence in which we have them. Even the *Doloneia*, though likely subjected to some later handling to account for its differences at the lexical level, employs the same motifs (e.g., *Odysseus succeeds in restoring order ... against an Akhilleus figure*) and at the same place in the middle sequence as we would expect on the basis of the parallels in books 2 and 19. This study thus confirms West's (2004) recent assessment of the textual transmission of the *Iliad*:

[I]n my view (and that of most Homerists) what the tradition gives us is not a "mass of multiple versions" but a single version that has suffered trivially from interpolation and corruption. That single version may indeed bear the imprint of differing versions that its author, an oral poet by profession, had recited on different occasions. But he laboured to produce a single, coherent written version, and, the more deeply one studies the *Iliad*, the more one is impressed by the measure of his success in doing so . . . there is no evidence for any materially "different versions" of these epics, only for trivial variation and amplification at the verbal level.

Although West here ventures conclusions about the process that I do not fully share, my analysis of the narrative pattern in chapters 1–4 supports his assertions about the stability of the *Iliad*.

CHAPTERS 5–7, in which we broke the *Iliad* down into specific subgenres of myth, established another context for understanding the epic. Near Eastern traditions, especially OT and Ugaritic myth, feature the same specific subgenres of myth and thus offer the most useful contexts for interpreting the *Iliad*. Several of the first subgenres we analyzed establish the prominent tendencies of the characters of Akhilleus and Agamemnon. The selectivity the *Iliad* exercises in emphasizing one type of mythic vehicle over another is one of the best hermeneutic tools for eliciting meaning from it. *The king who quarrels with his prophet* establishes Agamemnon as having problematic relations with the gods (except for Hera, who remains devoted to him). Akhilleus, on the other hand, is first established as a highly moral figure, *The hero intervenes to check the god-sent plague,* who acts not out of self-interest but on behalf of the army. But the *Iliad* selects *eris*, the bitter quarrel, as the mythic type that frames much of the subsequent action. In doing so, the *Iliad* gives note that it is a tragedy (as opposed to the *Odyssey*'s romance) and that, in this respect, Akhilleus serves as a negative example (we are not to emulate his behavior) because of the horrible consequences of his wrath. Agamemnon's surprisingly close parallels with Ahab and Saul particularly demonstrate the value of turning to OT myth to provide a context for the *Iliad*. In David and Phineas, OT myth features characters who act in some of the same subgenres of myth as does Akhilleus in the *Iliad*.

Viewing the *Iliad*'s divine economy through the context of the Ugaritic divine economy reveals not only Athena's close parallels with Anat but parallel dynamics between gods: Anat and El and Athena and Zeus, Anat and Baal and Athena and Ares. Athena's unique association with the "blood-spattered" formula, her apparent bloodthirsty nature, her interactions with Pandaros and Hektor all find close parallels in the myths of Anat. The *Iliad*'s puzzling thematic association of Ares with death and dying, especially in the pivotal contrafactual (5.388–89; cf. 5.884–87; 15.118), again suggests motifs prominent in depictions of the Ugaritic Baal.

ALTHOUGH BEYOND THE SCOPE of this study, the myths of Anat may also give us clues about *why* Greek and OT myth are so similar. The introduction noted three different theories to account for the parallels between Greek and Near Eastern myth. I would posit some kind of direct contact between Greek culture and a West Semitic people or peoples, diachronic contact extending over large periods of time. Some version of the people we think of, from the Greek point of view, as Phoenicians, seems the likeliest candidate. The similarities between Anat and Athena, as agents in specific subgenres of myth and as goddesses worshiped in a joint temple on Cyprus, suggest not casual points of contact between the Greeks and Phoenicians but a long-range symbiosis, an extensive cultural interchange (cf. West 1997: 4, 588). If we accept some overlap between the Philistines and Mycenaean Greek culture, David, many of whose acts are traditional motifs in myth, can be seen as a symbol of the cultural contact between the Greeks and West Semitic cultures.

Because there were earlier means of recording West Semitic myths as texts, it seems likely that the Greeks were more in debt to the Phoenicians than vice versa in terms of learning or acquiring the specific subgenres of myth used in the *Iliad*. But it is possible that the Phoenicians or Israelites also borrowed or learned subgenres of myth from the Greeks. In ways that have not yet been sufficiently appreciated (but see de Vet, and West 1997: 590–606), Near Eastern parallels with Homeric epic clearly problematize some aspects of how oral Homeric epic may be. Although I remain committed to the position that seeing the *Iliad* and the *Odyssey* as oral-derived texts is the best way to account for their defining features, we cannot rule out the possibility that Homeric epic was exposed to Near Eastern myths as *written* texts.

I offer a few additional observations which may serve as clues to the means of cultural interaction behind these parallels. Of all the books of the Old Testament, my analysis suggests that 1 Kings and Ezekiel are closest to the *Iliad,* either in having the most mythic subgenres in common or closest in how they employ the same subgenres. Agamemnon and 1 Kings' Ahab share numerous parallels; both participate in several of the same subgenres of myth, as do, conversely, the prophets with whom they interact, Elijah, Micaiah, Kalkhas, and Khryseis. 1 Kings is one of the most polytheistic books of the OT, depicting the Israelites worshiping the gods of the Ugaritic/Canaanite pantheon—Baal, Asherah, and others. There is even a divine council (1 Kings 22:19), a quintessentially epic and polytheistic episode.

Ezekiel probably contains more descriptions and details of sieges and city sackings than any other book of the Bible, which gives it a natural affinity with the *Iliad,* whose generic framing mythic subgenre is siege myth. Ezekiel not only mentions the Philistines and links them to Crete (Ezek 25:16) but refers to Cyprus (= Kittim, Ezek 27:6), and even the Greeks, in the OT's usual word for Greek culture, Javan (= Ionian; Ezek 27:13), thus bringing together in brief compass many of the elements of our study. The particular resemblances between 1 Kings and Ezekiel and the *Iliad* may imply something about a mechanism of contact between Greek and Israelite culture, or something about the time or place in which these texts reached not necessarily the same form in which we have them but an earlier state of relative completion. But until more studies sift through such possibilities, it is advisable to remain open to a variety of theories about the nature of the contact between ancient Greece and the Near East. Undoubtedly, demonstrated common ground between the *Iliad* and OT myth also has significant ramifications for the study of the Bible, but that will have to wait for a future project.

○⌒⌒⌒

Notes

Introduction

1. Lowenstam 1993: 11: "[E]ach Homeric poem is organized on the principle of repetition."

2. See the passages quoted at Louden 1999a: xv–xvii.

3. Heiden (1996: 7–16) offers a convenient summary of Wade-Gery, Davison, Schadewalt, Taplin, and Stanley, before adding his own argument. Heiden (1996: 8, n. 10) also notes additional proponents of a three-part structure in the *Iliad*.

4. Again see Heiden 1996: 8 for a chart of the divisions argued for by Wade-Gery, Davison, Schadewalt, Taplin, and Stanley, and (21) for his own delineation of three parts.

5. On bifurcation as a Homeric technique, see Louden 1999a: 7, 138, n. 7; further discussion in chapter 1.

6. Motifs are numbered as listed near the beginning of chapter 1.

7. Due (5), for instance, asserts "Briseis, Helen, Andromache, and Hecuba . . . these four women are the only women who speak in the *Iliad*," leaving out Theano (and Hektor's housekeeper).

8. Cf. Kirk 1985: 253: "Thus the poetical tradition remained conscious that the whole Trojan force consisted of three elements: (i) the Troes proper, from the city of Ilios and perhaps a few other places in the vicinity; (ii) the Dardanoi or Dardanioi, from the foothills of Ida, (iii) the allies, ἐπίκουροι, from farther afield."

9. Austin 1975: 273. Though his comment was on the *Odyssey*, the same is true of the *Iliad*.

10. Lowenstam 1993: 11: "[T]he method is to develop and elaborate upon ideas and motifs by putting them through a series of permutations in order to perceive at the end their true value and meaning. In music, the fugue develops themes in the same way, and one can draw parallels between the literary and musical methods."

11. However, we can sometimes turn to myths that survive in texts later than Homer and establish contexts thereby. For examples, see especially, Slatkin.

12. I follow Janko's (1982) relative chronology of Homer and Hesiod.

13. See, e.g., Louden 1996a and 1999b, which explore Indo-European relexes, themes, and myths in Homeric epic.

14. See especially Considine, Burkert, Mondi, West, and Morris among others, and Gordon before all of them.

15. Although some OT scholars occasionally refer to OT "epic," e.g., Cross 123, 143, 182, 293; Niditch 90, 92, 105.

16. See Louden 1999a: 95–99 on the *Odyssey*'s basic affinity to Genesis 18–19.

17. Among many others, see Stager 152–69; Brug 9; and Hindson. OT scholars commonly associate the Philistines with Mycenaean and/or Homeric Greeks. A whole book needs to be written on the OT Philistines and the *Iliad;* here I make only intermittent passing connections.

18. Quoted by Morris 1995: 244.

19. Griffin 1980 also makes useful observations on parallels between the *Iliad* and OT myth.

20. My definition partly builds on the discussion of Kirk 1974: 27.

21. Cf. Yamagata, and Feeney 6: "As a first point, these gods are quite immoral"; Feeney 3: "The problem of how to read the gods in epic is a problem of fiction before anything else."

22. Cf. *Od.* 18.132. It is interesting that Van Erp Taalman Kip omits these two lines but gives the rest of Agamemnon's remarks here (387–88).

23. Burkert 1983b: 53: "[I]n fact I do not know of another passage in Homer which comes so close to being a translation of an Oriental text"; and 54: "It looks as if Homer were alluding to *Enuma elis* directly."

24. Burkert 1992: 91: "There is hardly another passage in Homer which comes so close to being a translation of an Akkadian epic."

CHAPTER 1. *The Principal Narrative Pattern*

1. In the final sequence a few of the motifs occur earlier, in books 18 and 19.

2. On the general tendency, see Louden 1999a: xvii.

3. I thank W. G. Thalmann for reminding me about this point.

4. On Diomedes, during books 5–6, as a stand-in or surrogate for Akhilleus, see Edwards 1987: 8, 198.

5. See Armstrong for general discussion of the *Iliad*'s arming scenes.

6. Edwards 1991: 200: "The making of the armour by Hephaistos can formally be considered a relocated expansion of Akhilleus' arming scene, which will be resumed at 19.369."

7. See the recurring formula in Judges used of most of the heroes, including Samson, e.g., 3.10, of Othniel: "The spirit of the Lord came upon him"; cf. 15:14, etc., and descriptions of Shamash's aid to Gilgamesh.

8. See Louden 1999a: xvi–xvii and Lord 69. For discussion of a similar instance of motifs occurring in slightly different order in two thematically parallel episodes in Homeric epic, see Louden 1999a: 32–35.

9. Edwards 1991: 330: "[E]xcept for passing refs. such as those in 20.374, 21.32, and 22.3–4, nothing more is heard of the Greek army until after the death of Hektor, an almost surrealistic concentration of the audience's attention upon Akhilleus."

10. Edwards (1991: 303) briefly notes the parallel.

11. Again, Edwards (1991: 303) notes the parallel.

12. See Parks for a comparison of flyting in Homeric and Old English traditions.

13. The formula, however, also occurs in seven other passages (6.122, 517; 10.36; 11.604; 21.149; 22.249; 24.634).

14. For a complete schematic of the royal Trojan Houses going back to Dardanos, see Edwards 1991: 316.

15. On the "one just man" as a mythic type, see Louden 1999a: 69–70, 96, 98, 132. We give fuller coverage of the topic in chapter 6, subgenre 14.

16. In chapter 3 we discuss the motif in Patroklos' *aristeia*, 16.702 ff.

17. I disagree with Lowenstam (1981: 76) who, following Muellner, argues that the *daimon* of the epithet is specifically Ares. I think the narrative pattern thematically identifies the best of the Akhaians with victorious pro-Akhaian deities, of whom Athena is the most important.

18. The "woman's work" motif is also found in the *Aqhat* epic, Parker 62.

19. For discussion of πλάζω, see Louden 1999a: 69–103.

20. Akhilleus' cries form a thematic parallel to the description of Herakles doing so (8.364–65, also followed by a reference to Herakles having to escape a lethal body of water, οὐκ ἂν ὑπεξέφυγε Στυγὸς ὕδατος αἰπὰ ῥέεθρα, 8.369).

21. See Kirk 1990: 163 on the Lykians as standing for all of the allies.

22. See Scodel 1992 and Fineberg for a sampling of the extensive bibliography.

23. The only other instance of the formula describes an unnamed daughter of Agamemnon (13.378).

24. Schadewalt (129, in Wright and Jones) notes that "A new mood, heavy with anxiety, is heard in the concern of a mother."

25. We consider the sacrifice to Athena as a specific subgenre of myth in chapter 6.

26. Cf. Odysseus's (in *Od.* 11) having a lengthier conversation with his mother Antikleia than with Teiresias, and the brief discussion in Louden 1999a: 12.

27. For further discussion of this and other etymological wordplays in Homer, see Louden 1995.

28. We discuss Andromakhe's recommendations for battle strategy in chapter 6.

29. See Kakridis 73–74 for a brief comparison of the two scenes.

30. Milton seems to draw on Hektor in these scenes for his characterization of Satan at *Paradise Lost* 4.81–87.

31. Kirk, in Fenik 1978: 22: "The divine intervention is not well motivated"; cf. Kirk 1990: 230–31.

32. In chapter 7 we discuss theophany as characteristic of a mentor deity in heroic myth.

33. Cf. the duals used to express the close teamwork between Athena and the other Homeric protagonists at *Od.* 13.372–73, 439.

34. Athena's tone is reminiscent of divine frictions in the *Baal* epic, discussed in chapter 7.

35. Schadewalt 129, in Wright and Jones.

36. Ibid.

37. The motif may also be present in the special corselet Diomedes has, though mentioned only in a frequently criticized passage (8.195: δαιδάλεον θώρηκα, τὸν Ἥφαιστος κάμε τεύχων), on which see Kirk's note, 1990: 8.191–97.

38. An additional occurrence of the motif at 14.402 is discussed in chapter 3.

39. The same formula occurs another four times (3.355, 5.280, 11.359, 17.516).

40. Most commonly, the verb πλάζω expresses divine hostility against a mortal. For discussion, see Louden 1999a: chap. 4.

41. The rescue of a hero is one of the dominant reasons for their employment throughout the Homeric corpus, on which see Louden 1993.

42. Cf. Kirk 1990: 271: "The surprise is the greater since Aias is apparently winning, having suffered no real damage from his opponent."

43. The same motif occurs in the middle sequence in books 14–15, as discussed in chapter 3.

44. An exception is a highly altered instance at 15.458; for complete figures, see Louden 1993. The *Odyssey* offers the only other instance in Homer of a pivotal contrafactual involving a rhetorical question (4.441–44).

45. See, among others, Fenik 1968: 213–14 and Edwards 1987: 50–52.

46. Cf. 20.455 where Akhilleus also slays Dryops by stabbing him in the neck.

47. Kirk 1985: 103: "Here [1.473] and at 22.391–92 it is a song of rejoicing; in the latter Apollo is not mentioned, but here the rejoicing is coupled with praise of the god . . . compare the processional hymn led by Apollo himself in the *Hymn to Apollo* 514–19." We consider Odysseus' action as a separate motif in chapter 3.

48. Listed are two of the five Iliadic instances of the formula. The other three are 1.468, 1.602, 2.431; 1.468 is again the aftermath of Odysseus' accomplishing the sacrifice to Apollo, perhaps suggesting additional parallels between the two scenes.

49. See Kirk 1990: 278–79 for his and others' views of the alleged problems.

50. This detail is often attacked as a "late addition"; see, e.g., Kirk 1990: 278–79.

51. See Richardson 195, and his quoting Moulton 106: "[T]he vehicle fits no one more than the Priam of book 24."

52. This mismatch is true of the *Iliad* as a whole. According to Frazer 15, 180 Trojans are slain in the poem to 53 Greeks.

53. Kirk 1990: 282: "That *this* is the adapted passage is shown by the inappropriateness of 371 to present circumstances, since they are hardly about to stay awake all night when inside the city walls."

54. Kirk 1990: 287: "[Priam] . . . had naturally left the city to preside over the cremation."

55. Cf. Richardson's (272) remark: "At the beginning of the book [24] we seem to revert to the tone of book 22, with Akhilleus' repeated mutilation of Hektor's body."

56. Cf. Zeus of Odysseus' sacrifices, *Od.* 1.64–67.

57. Zeus also sets in motion the retrieval of Odysseus in the divine councils in *Od.* 1.75–79 and 5.23–42.

58. Lattimore takes it adverbially, without an object, in his translation, "indiscriminately."

59. But compare Pantelia's argument that Helen is capable of bestowing fame like a singer.

CHAPTER 2. *The Overture*

1. See Thalmann 1984: 1–32, on archaic Greek epic's tendency to simultaneously use similarity and antithesis.

2. Cf. how the *Odyssey* proem focuses on the *concluding* elements of that poem's narrative pattern, on which see Louden 1999a: 69–70, 90–94.

3. See also Antenor's speech at 7.348–53; 3.458–59 = 7.350–51.

4. In section IV (lines 314–82) of book 3 Paris will stand for Aineias.

5. The formula also occurs at 5.630, 11.232, 13.604, 16.462, 23.816.

6. In Akhilleus' simile the hunger of the lion is also emphasized by his epithet, σίντης, "ravening" (20.165; cf. 3.25).

7. As W. G. Thalmann reminds me, the only other Iliadic character who wears animal skin is Dolon (10.334). In chapter 4 I argue that he too is a parodic character, a further parallel with Paris.

8. Though at 22.116 the relative pronoun refers to Helen, in each passage Hektor assigns overall responsibility to Paris for having brought her to Troy.

9. But cf. 6.281–83, though this is far more implicit than in 3.87 and 22.115–16.

10. I say more about the parallels between Iris' two scenes in section III.

11. See Richardson's (157) note: "These kinship terms tend to cluster around Helen and Andromakhe."

12. Both are instances of Nagler's (48, 65–66) "attendance motif."

13. See Kirk 1985: 299 on Helen's anxiety here.

14. E.g., Kirk 1985: 279: "There is no special reason why Iris should summon Helen—it is not in accordance with a decision of Zeus or any other god, as is regularly the case elsewhere (e.g. 2.786f.; only at 13.198f. does she act on her own initiative, and then in a completely different way)."

15. See Kirk's (1985) note on 3.245–48.

16. Note particularly Hermes' intervention, and other details, which have led commentators to compare the excursion to a trip to the underworld, as discussed below.

17. See Kirk's (1985: 288) discussion on how it seems odd that Priam would not already know about the duel—i.e., the motif fits more naturally in book 24.

18. See chapter 6 for a fuller discussion of Antenor's role in the *Iliad*. He serves as an example of a moral Trojan, hence his suitability for taking part in the ceremony in book 3.

19. See, e.g., Richardson 308, for a synopsis of Usener's argument.

20. As part of the doubling earlier noted in books 22 and 24, a brief version of this motif also occurs at 22.416–17.

21. Akhilleus makes additional remarks about Priam's power to endure suffering: 24.519: πῶς ἔτλης ἐπὶ νῆας Ἀχαιῶν ἐλθέμεν οἶος; 24.565–6: οὐ γάρ κε τλαίη βροτὸς ἐλθέμεν, οὐδὲ μάλ᾽ ἡβῶν, / ἐς στρατόν.

22. See Reece 19–22, 227–29 for analysis of Akhilleus' hospitable reception of Priam.

23. Perhaps the closest parallel involving μάχαιρα in archaic Greek poetry is Apollo's remark in the *Homeric Hymn to Apollo*, δεξιτερῇ μάλ' ἕκαστος ἔχων ἐν χειρὶ μάχαιραν/σφάζειν αἰεὶ μῆλα· τὰ δ' ἄφθονα πάντα παρέσται (535–36).

24. In book 22 Hektor's neck is cut or slit, but his windpipe is not severed.

25. In chapter 7 we reconsider these passages in connection with the goddess Anat.

26. In chapters 6 and 7 we have further discussion of Hektor as a human sacrifice and offer Near Eastern parallels.

27. See Armstrong for fuller discussion of the *Iliad*'s arming scenes.

28. The arming scene perhaps alludes to the narrative pattern's motif, *5a. Aineias consults with an archer, "Lykaon."* In book 3 Paris functions as a parallel not only to his brother Hektor but also to Aineias, as closely associated with Aphrodite, and as a prominent Trojan warrior who does not die during the course of the poem. For the duel Paris has borrowed a breastplate from his half brother Lykaon (3.333), and the scene thus incorporates the motif of "Aineias" consulting with a Lykaon before he duels with the best of the Akhaians.

29. See Fenik's (1968: 6) brief discussion and Stanley 34.

30. Also part of this chain is 23.821, as discussed in chapter 1, when Diomedes threatens Aias' neck in the funeral games for Patroklos. Diomedes is here again the victorious best of the Akhaians.

31. This loss must look ahead to Hektor's armor being taken, 22.367–68.

32. On pivotal contrafactuals, see again Louden 1993.

33. Note the strong contrast with the divine interventions of Aineias, where Poseidon sets him down at the edge of battle (20.328), or Apollo sets him down in Apollo's temple in the Trojan acropolis (5.446), i.e., suitable places to be set down.

34. Cf. Chaucer's Pandare in his *Troilus and Criseide*.

35. The *Iliad* has only one other occurrence of στίλβω (18.596).

36. See Janko 1992: 201 on the many verbal and formulaic parallels between the two episodes.

37. As such the episode may have inspired Euripides to have his Helen rebel and even disavow Aphrodite; see *Helen* 1097–1104.

38. Cf. 20.294: ὃς τάχα Πηλεΐωνι δαμεὶς Ἄϊδόσδε κάτεισι; 22.40: Πηλείωνι δαμείς· ἐπεὶ ἦ πολὺ φέρτερός ἐστιν; 22.270: ἄφαρ δέ σε Παλλὰς Ἀθήνη/ἔγχει ἐμῷ δαμάᾳ.

39. See Janko's summary note on 14.313–28: "Zeus' solicitation is a hugely distended version of Paris' (3.438–46)—a dismissal of all else in favour of intercourse, because of the burgeoning desire he feels."

40. Among other studies of Milton's close appropriation of structures and syntax from Homeric epic, see Louden 1996c.

41. E.g., Hughes, on 9.1037–45.

CHAPTER 3. *The Middle Sequence*

1. On books 8–17 as composing the second movement of the *Iliad*, see also Schein 1997: 349 and Stanley: sec. III. I analyze books 9–10 in chapter 4, as part of the introductory pattern.

2. Cf. Whitman 163: "[H]is prowess [is marked] by a savagery which is the product of a deep uncertainty and fear."

3. Perhaps the only other episode that vies with book 14 for divine scandal potential is the depiction of Aphrodite and Ares in book 8 of the *Odyssey*. Cf. the *Ate* narrative in *Il*. 19, in which Zeus is deceived by Hera.

4. Petegorsky 178. For more on βίη versus μῆτις as alternatives for taking Troy, see Nagy 1979: 47–49.

5. Homeric epic often employs πλήσσω to depict being struck by a god: 8.12, 455; 15.117; 16.816; *Od*. 12.416.

6. Discussed in chapter 6 as subgenre *12. God panics the army by hurling lightning, reversing the tide of battle.*

7. See Fenik 1968: 220 on how unique Zeus' action is within the *Iliad*. In OT myth, typically an angel of god comes down to cause destruction, rather than Yahweh himself, as at 2 Kings 20:35.

8. Cf. Milton's tendency to have pivotal events occur at noon at *Paradise Lost* 9.739, 4.564.

9. Cf. Kirk 1990: 314: "This is typical of the stops and starts, the aborted enterprises, of this Book."

10. See Fenik 1968: 222 on how unusual Zeus' second intervention is.

11. See Kirk 1990: 312–13 on the criticism and objections these lines have prompted.

12. See Janko's (1992: 147) comment on Hektor's presumption in the book 13 passage.

13. There is no consensus as to what the τέρας is. B. Hainsworth (214) notes that the aegis is called τέρας at 5.742, when Athena holds it. Cf. Fenik 1968: 78.

14. In chapter 5 we consider Agamemnon's association with all three negative figures, Eris, Ate, and the Dream, as a subgenre of myth, *5. God sends the king a deceiving spirit.*

15. See again Armstrong for fuller discussion of the *Iliad*'s arming scenes.

16. See B. Hainsworth 231 for a list of common motifs.

17. See Fenik 1968: 82 and Friedrich 52 ff; the latter further characterizes Agamemnon's exploits as having the gruesome quality the poem usually assigns to second-rank warriors. Cf. B. Hainsworth 212: "Agamemnon's attack has something of the reckless fury of a desperate man"; and 231: "Agamemnon launches a ferocious attack and slays eight Trojans with great brutality."

18. Cf. Apollo commanding Hektor to avoid Akhilleus at a similar stage in his *aristeia* (20.375–78).

19. Diomedes is wounded near the beginning of his *aristeia* (5.98 ff) but recovers quickly.

20. Fenik (1968: 89) compares wounding Agamemnon with the wounding of Odysseus.

21. Antenor is discussed at length in chapter 6.

22. B. Hainsworth 261; see also Edwards's (1991) note on 20.38.

23. Fenik (1968: 91) notes similarities between Odysseus and Diomedes here and at 8.90 ff.

24. The sequence of Asios, a Phrygian, Glaukos, a Lykian, and Hektor, the chief Trojan, also suggests the three contingents around which the best of the Akhaians' *aristeia* is structured, against the leader of the Dardanians (Aineias, motif 5), a great Lykian (Glaukos, Sarpedon, Asteropaios, motif 8), and the leader of the Trojans, Hektor himself (motif 9 and ff).

25. I return to this topic in chapter 5, *1. Siege myths*.

26. See Janko 1992: 47–48. Chapter 5 discusses the friction between Agamemnon and Kalkhas as *3. The king who quarrels with his prophet*.

27. Cf. his additional charges, 13.633–34: ἄνδρεσσι . . . ὑβριστῆσι . . τῶν μένος αἰὲν ἀτάσθαλον.

28. Chapter 6 contains a much fuller discussion of hospitality in the *Iliad*.

29. Janko 1992: 127: "[T]he criticism of his morality is muted but unmistakable." We return to fuller discussion of the episode in chapter 6, *8. Trojan misconduct*, b and c.

30. Milton alludes to Juno in depictions of Satan, *Paradise Lost* 9.1029–45.

31. But see Janko 1992: 171 on a possible derivation of the epithet from θρονόν, "flower."

32. Elsewhere in the *Iliad* only Hades and the Erinus are στυγερός; Dee 2001: 136.

33. See Janko 1992: 184–85 on conjectures as to what kind of garment is meant.

34. This appears to refer to the Trojan Horse. See Louden 1996a: 289 and Haft.

35. Cf. Athena disarming and panicking the suitors with the aegis, *Od.* 22.297 ff.

36. See Janko 1992: 306 on Hektor's recklessness.

37. The motif thus resembles some Germanic folk tales: a mortal wishes for something foolish, which makes his own lot worse than it had been before the wish.

38. The motif is repeated shortly thereafter, 16.210 = 16.275, though with Patroklos now depicted as instilling *menos* in the rest.

39. Janko (1992: 354) and Fenik (1968: 9–10, 191–92) note parallels between the two *aristeiai*.

40. On the implied description of Hektor, see Janko 1992: 362.

41. We explore the third simile at greater length in chapter 6.

42. See also Fenik 1968: 199 on parallels between retreats by Hektor here and in books 11 and 20.

43. But see our earlier discussion of 13.219–329, in which the middle sequence briefly employs motifs associated with Aineias.

44. See Lateiner 2002 for full discussion of the passages.

45. See also 16.766: ὕλην, in a simile applying to both Hektor and Patroklos. For discussion of wood being gathered for the two funerals, see the analysis of motif 20 in chapter 1.

46. Compare Vergil's treatment of this recurring theme in the *Aeneid* (a warrior seen as making a mistake in claiming armor or clothing from a slain foe), first with Euryalus (8.373–74), then Camilla (11.778–82), and finally Turnus himself (10.496–97, 12.941–44).

47. See Janko 1992: 408 (on 16.775–76).

48. See, e.g., Zeus' pronouncement on mortality, 17.446–47, discussed below.

49. Divine wraths in the *Iliad* are discussed at length in chapter 7.

50. We discuss the passage at greater length in chapter 6, *8f. General arrogance and hubris by the Trojans: Hektor.*

51. We offer fuller discussion of parallels between Hektor and Dolon in chapter 6.

52. As earlier noted, in chapter 4 we argue that Phoinix parallels Patroklos as "a companion dear to Akhilleus."

53. On the group of similes as a series, see Edwards 1991: 135: "It is hard not to think this sequence of similes rises to an intentional culmination."

54. Cf. Fenik 1968: 187: "17.593 ff: Z shakes the aegis and routs the Greeks. . . . In only one other place in the *Iliad* does Zeus intervene so directly against the Greeks (8.130)."

CHAPTER 4. *The Introductory Pattern*

1. The other is at 4.220–32, which essentially picks up where the catalog and marshaling scene in book 2 leaves off, after the intrusive book 3 has ended. The scene with Odysseus (4.336–63) replays Odysseus' roles in books 1 and 2, as will be noted below.

2. Cf. Edwards 1991: 141: Book 18 "is perhaps the most striking in the poem for boldness, originality of artistic technique, and the brilliant composition of Akhilleus' speeches."

3. Both his comments to Aias, and earlier, 9.423: ὄφρ᾿ ἄλλην φράζωνται ἐνὶ φρεσὶ μῆτιν ἀμείνω, on which see Petegorsky 177.

4. Commentators have previously noted parallels between the assemblies in books 1 and 19. Edwards (1991: 239) calls attention to discussions by Lohmann (1970: 173–74) and Arend (1933: 117–18).

5. On πλάζω in the *Odyssey* as signifying divine wrath against mortals who offended a god, see Louden 1999a: chap. 4. The verb clearly has this force elsewhere in the *Iliad*, e.g., *Il.* 21.269.

6. E.g., Kirk (1985: 59), who asserts that "Akhilleus' opening remarks to Agamemnon are perfectly unprovocative."

7. For discussion of the repetition, see B. Hainsworth 61–62.

8. Cf. Agamemnon of himself at 2.111.

9. However, his doing so (καὶ οὔ πω λῆγε χόλοιο: 1.224) seems a violation of Athena's command (1.210).

10. Most critics see Nestor as quite ineffectual here. E.g., Taplin 90: "[H]e utterly

fails to heal the dispute because he defers too much to Agamemnon." Also Hogan 42: "[T]he ineffectual mediation of Nestor in Book 1"; cf. 52.

11. For a brief comparison of the two contexts, see B. Hainsworth 66.

12. On bifurcation as a typical technique of Homeric epic, see chapters 1 and 3 on how the initial and middle sequences bifurcate the "best of the Akhaians" into two figures; cf. Louden 1999a: 2, 7, 138, n. 7, 140, n. 30.

13. Apollo's wrath thus anticipates and parallels the wrath of Akhilleus. Cf. Rabel 39: "Apollo . . . serves as the prototype of Achilleus in the formal pattern of strife sketched at the beginning of book 1." See Rabel 37–43 for further discussion of parallels between the wraths of Apollo and Akhilleus.

14. Quoted in Griffin 1995: 51. There is a vast bibliography on this well-known topic, on which see Griffin 51–53. For a survey of earlier work, see Lesky 1967: 103–5, as noted in Nagy 1979: 49. See also Scodel's useful summary of proposed solutions (2002: 162–63). I have confined myself, however, to those pieces directly relevant to my argument.

15. I do not claim that my approach solves all aspects of this notorious problem but do hope to shed new light on many relevant issues.

16. Griffin (1995: 96) notes an additional unexpected parallel between Phoinix and Khryseis: Phoinix is surprisingly with Agamemnon, as book 9 opens, unusual for a man soon to be depicted as having a specially intimate relationship with Akhilleus; Khryseis is unexpectedly captured in Thebe, not in her own city, Khryse.

17. Most of these parallels were noted earlier by Boll and Segal.

18. Partly because of this, Segal argued that some of the duals are used correctly in Eurybates' scene in book 1 but that in book 9, some of the duals refer only to the two heralds.

19. However, the death of Patroklos and Akhilleus' desire for revenge against Hektor are probably more central to Akhilleus' change of heart than anything Odysseus and Agamemnon do.

20. A few additional brief variants of the motif (retrospective instances embedded in character speeches) are noted below.

21. Minchin in a review of Louden 2002 points out that a listening audience could probably not detect such ring composition. However, cf. the ring compositional arrangement of the three sequences in the *Odyssey* (Louden 1999a: 27–28, 133), also a structure probably not perceptible to a listening audience but present in the poem's architectonics nonetheless.

22. Griffin (1995: 96) is one of the few who thinks the Eurybates of book 1 is the same as the one in book 9.

23. The phrase is a slight variation (*kudos* in place of *kleos*) on the formula we identified as defining an *aristeia* in the *Iliad* (motif 4 in chapter 1), occurring at 5.3, 273 and 18.121.

24. Among many who have commented on the topic, Nagy (1996: 138–45) argues that Akhilleus targets Odysseus. Cf. D. F. Wilson 81. Bassi (330–31) takes Akhilleus' comment as referring to Agamemnon. B. Hainsworth (102) suggests Akhilleus aims the remark at *both* Odysseus and Agamemnon, as does Heiden (2002a: 432–

33). Additionally, Akhilleus has a general referent in mind, "anyone who acts this way."

25. Nagy (2003: 53–55) argues for a snub by Akhilleus in his greeting, that his use of some dual forms deliberately excludes Odysseus. In my view it is unlikely that Akhilleus would violate the sacred conventions of hospitality and contravene its tenets in such a way. His initial hospitality to the delegation is exemplary, until, during the speeches, he loses his temper at the mention of Agamemnon.

26. See Reece 224–25 for analysis of the extensive hospitality elements present in the scene.

27. Cf. B. Hainsworth 81: "Diplomatic business in the *Iliad* is conducted by Odysseus alone . . . or by Odysseus and an appropriate or interested party."

28. Cf. Heiden's point (2002: 433) that if Akhilleus here targets Odysseus with his remark, he is not only being inhospitable but hypocritical, since he earlier greeted the delegation dearly.

29. Cf. Scodel 2002: 164: "There is no real evidence that Odysseus and Achilles were traditional enemies—indeed, the epics make them friends."

30. See further discussion, and parallels from OT myth, under subgenre 2 in chapter 5.

31. Nagy (2003: 54–55) and Wilson (83–86) argue that Odysseus has ulterior, personal motives in his speech and that he acts as a trickster, out to "deceive" Akhilleus. Different contexts bring out different sides of characters in myth. Though he can often be said to be a trickster in the *Odyssey,* I do not think Odysseus is a "trickster" when he leads the delegation to restore Khryseis and perform a hekatomb to Apollo, or when he restores order to the assembly in book 2, or anywhere in the *Iliad.* Even in the *Doloneia,* Odysseus acts in close teamwork, there with Diomedes. In book 19 Odysseus will speak forcefully against Akhilleus but without animus or personal agenda (see the motif below, *12. Odysseus succeeds in restoring order in a second, or later Greek assembly, against an Akhilleus figure*). But that episode parallels the book 2 assembly (Thersites) and the *Doloneia,* not the book 9 delegation.

32. Typically, however, commentators have sought to defend the presence of Aias and find fault with Phoinix as a member of the delegation. See B. Hainsworth 81–82.

33. See Kakridis 28, noting that earlier commentators had already made the equation.

34. See Louden 1995 for additional examples and further discussion of this type of wordplay in Homeric epic.

35. But see Scodel 2002: 167–70 for an argument justifying his presence.

36. Cf. Edwards 1991: 271: "The mention of old Phoinix is noteworthy; he rarely appears outside book 9."

37. See D. F. Wilson 1–6 for a recent summary of many of the principal arguments.

38. We note further in this chapter, as earlier in chapter 3, that the middle sequence makes frequent use of proxies.

39. As commentators have pointed out, most recently D. F. Wilson, Agamem-

non's offer also contains within it means of subordinating Akhilleus to Agamemnon, should he accept the gifts.

40. Akhilleus associates Agamemnon with *ate* throughout his speech: μ' ἀπάτησε (9.344), ἐξαπατήσειν (9.371), μ' ἀπάτησε (9.375), in a further parallel to the scene at 1.412.

41. On ὠκύμορος, see Slatkin 36–37.

42. The parallel has been noted by many, e.g., Slatkin (45): "In its implications, this favor from Hephaistos corresponds to the initial one requested of Zeus." There is a difference in that in book 1 her visit to Zeus is delayed until Odysseus finishes the hecatomb to Apollo.

43. See Taplin 15–18 for a chart and discussion of the days and nights into which the *Iliad* sets its plot.

44. Cf. events at Jericho (Josh 6:1–21): Israelites are accompanied by the Ark as Akhilleus is by Athena.

45. A deity's hastening or retarding the course of the sun is a common motif in myth. Cf. Zeus in the myth of the House of Tantalus, and Yahweh in Josh 10:12–13.

46. B. Hainsworth 152: "The opening lines of Book 10 recall the way in which Book 2 is joined to Book 1."

47. For a persuasive defense of the integrity of book 10 with regard to its themes, see Petegorsky 175–254. Cf. Rabel 136, n. 1: "The so-called *Doloneia*, though perhaps originally a separate composition, has been well integrated into the structure of the *Iliad*." See also Stanley 119–28, 164; D. F. Wilson 210, n. 3.

48. B. Hainsworth 185: "The Trojan scene mirrors that before the Achaean camp exactly, except that Hector's call for volunteers elicits only one response."

49. On this complementary opposition between the two Homeric protagonists as highly traditional, see Nagy 1979: 47–49 and Petegorsky 183–222.

50. The episode thus continues Odysseus' thematic association with heralds, as noted above.

51. This scene resembles some in late books of the *Odyssey*, when the suitors ignore the disguised Odysseus' advice, encouraged by Athena to commit further outrageous acts (*Od.* 18.346–47 = 20.284–85).

52. On Odysseus' role in books 2 and 10 as alluding to the Sack of Troy, see Haft.

53. Thalmann 1988: 19, "It is often observed that Thersites' speech is a parody of Achilles' earlier reproaches of Agamemnon . . . Thersites is Achilles' comic double." Cf. Edwards 1991: 254–55 and Hogan 1981: 52–53.

54. The episode thus repeats the pairing of Odysseus and Eurybates in the book 9 delegation, indirectly offering further suggestion that some of the problematic duals refer to these two characters.

55. Kirk 1985: 151: "Odysseus' speech . . . is constructed with great care and even brilliance."

56. I thank Jerise Fogel for acquainting me with these two rhetorical devices.

57. Cf. Rabel 139 (on the *Doloneia*): "This second mission confronts not Achilleus but a lesser figure, who nonetheless resembles him in a number of ways." Cf. Rabel 140.

58. Rabel 139: "The repeated use of the dual form to describe their movements
. . . seems to echo the dual number from book 9." Cf. Rabel 122, n. 19: "I will sug-
gest . . . that the duals in the journey of book 9 serve equally to stress the symmetry
with book 10, where Odysseus and Diomedes journey into the Trojan camp."

59. Edwards 1991: 253, citing J. B. Hainsworth 1966.

60. Edwards 1991: 253: "The communal meal is also an important element in
social harmony, in which Akhilleus is still unwilling to participate." See also Nimis
23–42.

61. His two speeches in the book 19 assembly together function as a counterpart
to his speech in book 2.

62. Edwards 1991: 267: "[Akhilleus] also explicitly accepts that Odysseus has
won in the matter of the meal."

63. Yet another instance of Homeric epic referring to Odysseus in a dual.

64. Except in the book 9 delegation, where he does not make his *own* speech but
conveys Agamemnon's.

65. On the interruptive quality of books 3 and the first half of 4, see again J. B.
Hainsworth 165.

66. Kirk 1985: 376 (on *Il.* 4.422–56): "The correspondence with the first elabo-
rate march-out which culminated in the catalogs in book 2 is especially striking."

67. See again J. B. Hainsworth 162 on the underlying sequence of motifs 12–13.

CHAPTER 5. *Subgenres of Myth in the Iliad I*

Epigraph: West 1966: 31.

1. See the introduction for a definition of *myth* as used in this study.

2. Cf. Janko 1992: 10, 399, 136; B. Hainsworth 29; Morris 1995.

3. See also the Sumerian epic *Enmerkar and the Lord of Aratta* 252–62 (Jacobsen
297). Cf. Janko 1992: 400 (on *Il.* 16.702–6): "Patroklos' lack of a scaling-ladder may
be a heroic exaggeration."

4. Cf. Ezek 21.22, 26.8–9; Jer 6.6; Amos 4.3: breaches in the wall; Amos 4.6;
Ezek 5–7: famine and pestilence; Nah 3; Lam 5.10: famine; etc.

5. Cf. Hektor's remarks at *Il.* 18.288–92.

6. E.g., Kirk 1990: 161: "Agamemnon's rebuke is remarkable . . . for its ruthless-
ness."

7. For fuller discussion of the ban, see especially Niditch 8–10, 20–21, 23, 26,
28–77, 80–84, 86–88, 97, 105, 111, 113, 125, 128, 136–37, 140, 141, 149, 154, and von
Rad 85, 112, 135, 140, 151, 157, 159–60.

8. The ban was also practiced by other Semitic peoples of the time. The Moab-
ites had exactly the same practice, as the Mesha stele reveals (see Smelik 29–50),
slaying all of the Israelites they conquered and dedicating the victims to their god,
Kemosh.

9. On Lam 2:10, cf. especially the depiction of Priam at *Il.* 24.162–65.

10. For further OT passages using lament relevant to the *Iliad*, see also Jer 15:3,
13–14; 18:21–23 as food for birds and beasts: Ezek 29:5; Jer 19:7, 34:20; 1 Sam 17:44.

11. See further discussion of this motif in J. P. Brown 2000: 143–45.

12. The passage is from an account of Sennacherib. Commentators have also argued for Homeric parallels in non-OT depictions of his exploits. See West 1997: 375–76, 378–80.

13. Additional OT instances of the exterminating angel include: Num 14:36–37; 1 Chron 15; cf. Exod 12:23; see also Miller 31 ff, and 119 and Considine 140–41 for further discussion of these and similar scenes in OT myth.

14. As noted here and below, Ahab, Sennacherib, and Saul are largely the same type as Agamemnon. Sennacherib parallels Agamemnon more as a military commander; Ahab and Saul parallel Agamemnon more in his personal relations with others.

15. Cf. how Agamemnon's speech is so effective that even Zeus is persuaded (8.245–46) not to carry the destruction to the level he had intended.

16. I follow Robert Alter's rendering of Hebrew *qubbah* as "alcove" against the *Oxford Study Bible*'s "nuptial tent," which erroneously conveys the notion of marriage between the Israelite and the Midianite woman (Alter, personal communication, June 27, 2003).

17. Cf. his exemplary hospitality to the delegation in book 9 (until *after* he has heard Agamemnon's offer).

18. Friction between a king and a holy man is common in other literature; cf. King Dushyanta's shabby treatment of the holy hermit in the *Shakuntala*, and King Leontes' disparaging of Apollo's oracle, *The Winter's Tale* 3.2.

19. Cf. 1 Sam 19:18–24, with David as Akhilleus, Samuel as Kalkhas, Saul as Agamemnon, as discussed below.

20. West (1997: 349–50) notes a few of these parallels.

21. On *eris* in Greek myth, see Hogan.

22. With regard to having to sacrifice one's own child, the link between Saul and Agamemnon takes us out of the *Iliad*, since Homer never explicitly alludes to the incident. However, the parallel is further evidence that both characters are depicted in the same specific subgenres of myth.

23. Note also that Saul attempts to pin David with his spear (1 Sam 19:10); cf. Akhilleus' awarding Agamemnon the prize for throwing the spear in the games at *Il.* 23.884–95.

24. On the Philistines possibly being Mycenaean Greeks, see Stager 152–69 and Hindson 23, 143, 154, 156.

25. Typologically this equates him with the suitors' failure to heed warnings in the *Odyssey*, and Lot's sons-in-law who ignore apocalyptic warnings in Genesis 19.

26. West (1997: 189–90, 356) briefly notes a few of these parallels.

27. Cf. Vergil associating Allecto with Turnus (*Aen.* 7.412 ff) and Tisiphone with Mezentius (*Aen.* 10.761–62).

28. The three figures are further linked by other formulas and descriptions. Dream and Ate share forms of the same epithet: οὖλος (2.6, 8), οὐλομένη (19.92). Descriptions of Ate as βλάπτουσ᾽ ἀνθρώπους (19.94) and ἣ πάντας ἀᾶται (19.91, 129) are somewhat parallel to Eris being described as πολύστονος.

29. See chapter 7 for further discussion of Athena's special function and parallels in Gilgamesh's relation with Shamash and Aqhat's with Anat.

30. Kuhn; Nagy 1974 and 1979; see also Holland 1993 and Louden 1996a.

31. *Gilgamesh* III iv (Old Babylonian Version), Dalley 144. See also "They shall have established fame for their [future (?)"; *Gilgamesh* IV vi, Dalley: 71.

32. See Niditch 91 ff for further discussion of these and similar scenes.

33. See Niditch's comments (92) on the repeated formula at 2 Sam 21:19 and 1 Chron 11:23.

34. On duels in the OT, see especially de Vaux 122–35, and Niditch 91–94.

35. As noted in chapters 1 and 2, the three duels are all linked, those in *Il.* 7 and 22 being counterparts of each other in the initial and final sequences, while that in book 3 serves an overture function. See Yadin for an argument that the OT myth of Goliath is influenced by its authors' awareness of Homeric epic.

36. Hindson 34 compares Hektor's and Goliath's challenges; cf. West 1997: 214.

37. See Kirk 1990: 22; cf. Kirk 1985: 266: "προμάχιζεν . . . implies going out as a fighter by oneself. . . . So Alexandros was behaving here like a challenger on behalf of the Trojans."

38. Edwards 1987: 73: "Sometimes an expected arming scene is replaced by a kind of surrogate." See also Kirk 1990: 264 on Aias' arming.

39. See McCarter 1985: 287, including his discussion of how the Hebrew text may have become confused.

40. If the root were to be found in Linear B texts, it would probably begin with a q- (cf. gwer (4): βροτος, βιβρωσκω).

41. See Kirk's typical assessment (1990: 230), "a second formal duel, curiously like that of book 3 but without stated or accomplished purpose."

42. Cf. *The Oxford Study Bible* (Suggs et al. 335): "The slaying of Goliath was romanticized in later times as a deed of David himself." On the priority of the Elhanan account, see Yadin. Elsewhere (1 Chron 20:5), Elhanan slays Goliath's brother.

43. Among other inconsistencies, McCarter (1985: 294) notes that David is said to flee to Jerusalem after slaying Goliath (1 Sam 17.54): "A striking anachronism: Jerusalem was not in Israelite hands until the beginning of David's reign (cf. 2 Sam 5:6–9)."

44. De Vaux 125: "*gibbor* . . . a 'hero,' a 'brave.' . . . Under David we find the word used in the plural to denote the group of his most valiant companions, especially the Three and the Thirty, whose names, along with some of their exploits, are reported in 2 Sam 23:8–39. . . . Each of them was a champion and as such would have to give his best in single combat."

45. See McCarter 1984: 86–87 on the general tendency and for further instances of the same phenomenon.

46. De Vaux (126) notes structural/formulaic parallels between accounts of Benaiah's duel and David's with Goliath.

47. Pritchard 589–91, 434–37 has the full Sumerian ("Man and his God") and Akkadian ("Akkadian Observations on Life and the World Order") texts.

48. Cf. Pope xxxii: "The Prologue-Epilogue also presents a number of literary features and motifs which are characteristic of Semitic epic, as known from Akkadian literature and more recently from the Ugaritic texts. These literary features appear as a sort of substratum which may well derive from a very ancient Job epic." Divine councils are discussed in chapter 6 as subgenre 9.

49. Cf. the divine friction between Jupiter and Juno in the *Aeneid*.

50. Cf. Job comparing Yahweh's treatment to an episode of siege warfare, "He made breach after breach in my defences; / like a warrior he rushed on me" (16:14); "His raiders gather in force, / raising their siege-ramps against me / and he regards me as his enemy" (19:12).

51. I regard Elihu of Job 32 as a separate, or later addition. See Pope 241, n. 2, on how the Elihu section differs from the rest of the work; cf. Suggs et al. 539: "Probably a later addition." In both myths the number of participants in the delegation is itself problematic.

52. Eliphaz's comments are also close to Odysseus' criticism of Thersites, *Il.* 2.246–56, which is indirect criticism of Akhilleus, as we argued in chapter 4.

53. Cf. the depiction of Akhilleus in mourning (*Il.* 18.22–27), as again suggesting Job.

CHAPTER 6. *Subgenres of Myth in the Iliad II*

1. See, e.g., Redfield's overly positive study of Hektor.

2. The genre may also be present in the Hittite myth, *The Song of Release* (secs. 42–63 = pp. 75–77 in Hoffner).

3. On theoxeny in Genesis 18–19, see Louden 1999a: 22, 70, 95–99, 132.

4. See Richardson 279 for discussion of the phrase. We discuss the Judgment of Paris at length in chapter 7.

5. The basic outline of the myth also suggests close parallels with the *Aeneid*, 7–12.

6. See Boling's (1975: 276) brief comparison, and Pitt-Rivers 158.

7. See Fenik 1978: 79–81, on Agenor's monologue (21.553–70).

8. According to Apollodorus (*Epit.* 3.29), Antenor prevented the Trojans from killing Odysseus and Menelaos on this embassy (making him the exact opposite of Antimakhos). Apollodorus further states (*Epit.* 5.21) that Odysseus and Menelaos rescued his son, Glaukos, when Troy was being sacked, because of his father's earlier good deed.

9. Von Kamptz 56: "Ἀντήνωρ . . . 'gegen . . . oder 'anstatt, gleichwertig." Cf. Mühlestein 37: "Antenor bedeutet also 'Männern entgegentretend.'"

10. Would these again be goods Paris stole from Menelaos?

11. B. Hainsworth (188) notes only "Hector's ready acquiescence in Dolon's ridiculous demands underlines Trojan arrogance in anticipated victory."

12. For parallels between Elpenor and Leodes within the *Odyssey*, see Louden 1999a: 31–49.

13. Cf. Isa 14:12–14, discussed below, under divine councils.

14. Cf. Edwards 1991: 107: "In the similar couplet at *Od.* 18.130–31 it is mankind's blind hopes, especially of escaping retribution, that makes nothing 'more feeble than man.'"

15. The *Iliad* may allude to this episode in the *Doloneia*, when Odysseus and Diomedes perform a similarly furtive act, aided by Athena.

16. Rabel (92), noting the discrepancy, suggests Hektor's remark is "rhetoric designed to explain his absence without unnecessarily alarming the troops."

17. Cf. her post-Homeric depictions. Gantz (642–43) notes a fragment of the *Lakaina*, apparently by Sophocles, depicts Theano handing over the Palladium to Odysseus and Diomedes. See also Bacchylides 15 (Gantz 595, 610).

18. Cf. Poseidon's association with the verb πλάζω in the *Odyssey* (Louden 1999a: chap. 4). In chapter 7 I consider the phrase again in connection with the goddess Anat.

19. Morris (1995), however, argues that this Near Eastern human sacrifice parallels the death of Astyanax, not Hektor. I would connect the death of Astyanax with another Near Eastern practice, the ban. The slaughter of Astyanax is an instance of the Greeks slaying man, woman, and child, acting as if under the ban, as the Israelites do when they sack cities.

20. Boling 1975: 209: "Human sacrifice in Israel was not condoned. Neither was it unknown. It is presented as a move made in desperation (2 Kings 16:3), or, indeed, as punishment ordered by Yahweh (Ezek 20:25–26, 31). The story of the near sacrifice of Isaac (Gen 22) presupposes the reader's assent to the possibility."

21. Boling (1975: 197) notes the phrase rendered as "intrepid warrior" (*gibbor hayl*) is also used of Gideon (Judg 6:11–12).

22. Cf. also Shakespeare's *Coriolanus*.

23. Agamemnon's sacrifice of Iphigeneia was also to fulfill a vow (Euripides *IT* 21: ηὖξω).

24. On 1 Kings 16:34, see Cogan 423 for DeVries' suggestion that the passage refers to "threshold sacrifices." For additional reference to human sacrifice in OT myth, see Ps 106:37–38.

25. OT myth makes further allusion to human sacrifice in apocalyptic contexts, discussed below as subgenre 13.

26. Chapter 7 will reconsider Athena's involvement with Hektor's death for its relevance to the Ugaritic Anat.

27. Gordon (1967: 54) suggests a parallel in OT myth in David's group sacrifice of Saul's descendants.

28. At 23.174 ἀποδειροτομέω may just refer to the sacrifice of the dogs, but the verb still occurs in the line preceding the account of the sacrifice of the twelve Trojans, juxtaposed with that act.

29. On the parallels, see Louden 1999a: 70–71, 99, 131.

30. See Miller 12ff on the earlier Ugaritic/Canaanite divine councils, and 66–74 on the many depicted in the OT itself.

31. On the sun, see especially Ps 19:4b–6, 148:3, as well as the place-name Bethshamesh, literally "Temple of the Sun."

32. See also Jer 23:18 and Dan 7:10 for additional instances of divine councils in OT myth.

33. See J. Day 54–55 for additional discussion of divine councils in the OT.

34. Cf. Lefkowitz 53: "[U]ltimately they care even more about satisfying their own desires. The exception to this rule is Zeus, who sees that justice is done in the end."

35. Additional parallels between Zeus and Akhilleus are noted below in our discussion of theomachy.

36. Tablet I (Dalley 234).

37. Revelation 12 essentially combines into one episode what are two separate subgenres of myth in Hesiod's *Theogony*, the war between different groups of immortals (the rebel angels / Titanomachy), and the fight with the immortal dragon (Devil/Typhoeus).

38. On ἔρις as a specific subgenre of myth, see chapter 5, *4. The king . . . quarrels with his greatest warrior (or eris)*.

39. At 5.890 Zeus can be said to be angry with Ares.

40. As he does at 8.399–431: Zeus threatens present-time theomachy.

41. A divine parallel in the middle sequence would call for Athena, Poseidon, or Hera to be defeated by Ares or Apollo.

42. Richardson (88) also notes a parallel between 21.403–4 and 7.264–65, Hektor's duel with Aias.

43. West 1997: 487: "This desertion of a city by its gods is an absolutely commonplace motif in Sumerian and Akkadian literature." It is equally common in OT myth; examples are given below.

44. The same motif or subgenre of myth occurs in the Ugaritic myth of *Aqhat*, when the titular hero improperly applies it to the goddess Anat: 4.VI 39–41.

45. See Rabel 40 ff for a comparison between Apollo's wrath against Agamemnon in book 1 and Akhilleus' own wrath against his commander.

46. One of the suitors makes the same type of threat of disfigurement and mutilation to the disguised Odysseus (21.307–8, 18.85–87).

47. Even the New Testament, Revelation 12, has a heavenly divine rebellion, set before the creation of mortals, in which the defeated immortals are cast down to the underworld, the traditional inherited pattern.

48. See West 1997: 296–97. See also Ps 18:7–19; 29:3, 10; 33:6–7; 74:12–17; 77:16–20; 104:2–9.

49. Cf. Job 26:12: "With his strong arm he cleft the sea monster; / he struck down Rahab by his skill."

50. But see Nimis 73–84 for a very different argument.

51. Cf. Cogan 445: "the battle of the gods," and 446: "The competition between YHWH and Baal."

52. Elijah thoroughly soaks the altar before the fire appears, thereby increasing the miracle; cf. Cogan 443.

53. Stager 152–69; cf. Hindson 23, 143, 154, 156.

54. McCarter 1985 109: "[T]he ark as the visible sign of Yahweh's presence func-

tioned in the ideology of Israelite warfare as a battle palladium for the armies of Israel." Cf. McCarter 1985: 106: "That the ark itself was thought of as a cherub throne . . . as well as a battle palladium, is beyond doubt."

55. The ark figures in a further implicit theomachy at Joshua 3–4 when it parts the waters in the river, again a reworking of the ancient myth, Yahweh's defeat of the water dragon, Leviathon or Rahab.

56. In a further possible connection between Dagon, the Philistines, and the Greek culture portrayed in the *Iliad*, E. L. Brown argues that -daon, the second component of the name Poseidaon is the same as Dagon, and that Greeks imported the name from West Semitic culture.

57. Cf. Hera's threat against Ares, πεπληγυῖα (5.763).

58. Among many other such passages, see Josh 10:10–11, 24:12; 1 Sam 2:10, 7.10; Exod 1:15–16; 2 Chron 14:14.

59. For additional passages, see 2 Chron 14:14; Ps 6:10, 44:6, 48:4–7, 64:7–9; Zech 12:4, 14:13; Ezek 38:27; etc.

60. Cf. *Gilgamesh* VI iii–iv. For discussion, see Louden 1999a: 23–25, 70–72, 95–103.

61. I retain ἀπηύρα as it is in the text, and keep its usual meaning. For discussion, see West 1978: 217.

62. See Walsh 101 on the tone of the passage as apocalyptic.

63. Cf. 5.177–78, Aineias' supposition that Diomedes in his *aristeia* is actually a god angry at the Trojans over their offerings. The verb is again *koteo* and hints at a miniature apocalypse.

64. On each of the *Odyssey* passages as concluding their respective sequences in the *Odyssey*, see Louden 1999a: 23–25.

65. Cf. Zeph 1:14–18; Jer 50; Isa 66:15–16; Ps 9:5–6, 21:8; Nah 1:6, 8.

66. On this as the meaning of Hektor's name, see Scully 59 and Louden 1995: 29.

67. Cf. also 22.410–11, as Priam and Hekabe see Hektor's corpse dragged before Troy, "As if all of steep Troy were consumed with fire, from its peak down."

68. I take the term from Milton, *Paradise Lost* 11.818. Milton, in turn, may be translating Gen 6:9. For discussion of the mythical type, see Louden 1990: 115–26, 171–72, and, as operative in the *Odyssey*, Louden 1999a: xvii, 69–70, 96, 98, 132, 157, n. 58.

69. On Telemakhos serving this function in book 1 of the *Odyssey*, see Louden 1999a: xvii, 69–70, 96, 98, 132.

70. The OT myth of Enoch (Gen 5:21–24), an elliptic, germinal story (much as the *Iliad*'s references to a post-Troy Aineias), sparked a later suppletive tradition in which he was fully developed as the survivor of an apocalypse; cf. Milton's depiction at *Paradise Lost* 11.661–711; discussion in Louden 1990: 115–19.

71. Here Yahweh says that even if Noah, Daniel, and Job were to seek to intervene, he would spare them, but no one else. This Daniel, as discussed in chapter 7, is the father of the Ugaritic hero, Aqhat.

72. Commentators have often turned to the conjecture that eighth- or seventh-century aristocrats, claiming descent from Aineias, accounted for his prominence

(see Edwards 1991: 299–300, and P. M. Smith, who persuasively argues against this theory). Nagy (1979: 265–75) conjectures that the episode is a confrontation between separate epic traditions of Aineias and Akhilleus.

73. See Edwards 1991: 316 for a schema of the whole Dardanian lineage.

74. Cf. Yahweh's concern for Solomon, because he is David's son, at 1 Kings 11:34.

75. Thus Lot in this respect parallels Baucis and Philemon, and Telemakhos; see Louden 1999a: 22–23, 25–27, 95–97.

76. In the apocryphal books Enoch's ties with apocalypse are considerably developed: 1 Enoch, 2 Enoch, Wisd of Sol 4:10–14, Eccles 44:16, 49:14; cf. New Testament: Jude 14–15.

77. Cf. Samson's unnamed mother, who plays a much more central role in the myth than does Manoah, her husband (Judg 13:2–24).

78. Janko (1992: 143) notes that the first attestation of Askanios as the son of Aineias is in Hellanicus.

CHAPTER 7. *The Iliad's Divine Economy, the Goddess Anat, and the Homeric Athena*

Epigraph: West 1988: 169.

1. See Louden 2005: 90–94 (on which this discussion is based) for fuller analysis of the epic triangle.

2. Ugaritic in this study refers to essentially the same people that the OT will later call the Canaanites, Homer the Sidonians (*Il.* 6.290–91, 23.743; *Od.* 4.85, 618; 13.285; 15.118, 425), and classical Greeks the Phoenicians. For discussion of problems with the terms Canaanite and Ugaritic, see M. Smith 2001: 14–18.

3. Conversely, I hope this chapter encourages Ugaritic scholars to reexamine Homeric epic and Greek myth for further use as comparanda.

4. Cf. Morris 1992: 79: "The Ugaritic and Phoenician assembly of gods commanding separate functions and domains, offerings and ritual occasions, provides the closest model for the Greek pantheon now attested in Mycenaean tablets."

5. Below I bring the Ugaritic *Aqhat* into the discussion.

6. Also Ellil has a divine wrath at both Gilgamesh and Enkidu in *Gilg.* VII.

7. The divine economy of Christian myth replicates the same essential structure with God as Zeus, Christ as Athena, and Satan as Poseidon.

8. Below I argue that the Ugaritic myth, *Aqhat*, also has the same triangular structure, with two of the equivalent gods, El and Anat.

9. The song of Hephaistos, Aphrodite, and Ares (8.267–367) is as close as the *Odyssey* gets to theomachy.

10. At 18.168: Hera dispatches Iris without Zeus knowing, and during the main theomachy she orders Hephaistos (21.328ff) to attack Xanthos.

11. Ninsun occupies a very similar position in *Gilgamesh*'s divine economy.

12. Eos, as mother to Memnon, serves as a further instance of the same rela-

tionship. Even though Eos and Memnon are not so depicted in our *Iliad,* there is a general consensus that the *Iliad*'s depiction of Thetis with Akhilleus reflects influence of Eos' role with Memnon in other epic. See Slatkin 22–31. On Aineias' special qualities, see chapter 6, *14. The one just man.*

13. But this too finds a parallel in the figure of the goddess mother of the hero: Thetis' suggestion to Akhilleus that he lie with a woman (24.130–31).

14. For full discussion of Homeric epic's depictions of Hephaistos' various creations, see Morris 1992: chap. 1.

15. Cf. Hera's offer to have him make a throne for Hypnos (14.238–40).

16. Du Buisson 51: "Anat et Athena ont des rapports avec le dieu fabricant et forgeron."

17. El, Baal, and Asherah are named frequently in the OT and were all clearly worshiped by the Israelites until Yahwist monotheism finally won out during the captivity in Babylon. Anat is mentioned in place names (Anathoth [Josh 21:18, 1 Kings 2:26, etc.], which may have been a cult center for the goddess, Bethanath [Judg 1.33]), and the hero Shamgar is said to be a son of Anat (Judg 3:31, 5:6).

18. See M. Smith (1994: 8, n. 20) on the meaning of the epithet, *btlt;* and in Parker 165, n. 12: "The word refers to a young woman, married or unmarried, who has not yet given birth."

19. E.g., Mullen 68, n. 110: "Her violent nature is completely unparalleled in the Ugaritic materials."

20. Considine and West (1997) are notable exceptions.

21. Considine makes many other important Homeric/Ugaritic links but not otherwise with Anat/Athena; but cf. 147.

22. For the text, see *Corpus Inscriptionum Semiticarum,* pt. 1, vol. 1, 114–15. On the equation of Anat and Athena, see further discussion at Handy 103.

23. For discussion of the sanctuary, see Gjerstad 626–28; Karageorghis 107–8; and Markoe 170 ff.

24. Cf. Lucian's *De Dea Syria;* Astargatis, perhaps a combination of Asherah and Anat, becomes Decerto.

25. For a more complete overview of Anat, see P. L. Day.

26. On Anat's iconography, see Eaton.

27. The *Cypria* (West 2003: 70–71: argument 2) also attests the tradition that Paris went among the Sidonians before returning to Troy with Helen.

28. E.g., Handy 88: "When a situation arose in which there was no deity to perform a necessary task, El did not step in and do the work, but he did provide a deity to accomplish the task."

29. See Mondi 160 for a brief comparison.

30. See Considine (101, 107) for a broad comparison between how Anat treats El and Athena Zeus.

31. On the typical Homeric wordplay (Odysseus/ὠδύσαο), see Louden 1995: 34–39.

32. Miller 24: "The activities of the god Baal and the goddess Anat, the warrior

deities par excellence in the Ugaritic texts, are intimately related and must be examined together." The precise meaning of Anat as Baal's sister is unknown, given her unspecified mother. Again the *Iliad* may serve as a parallel. Athena and Ares are thought of as siblings, sired by the same father, Zeus, but with different mothers, Metis and Hera.

33. Gordon (1965b: 181) compares this to Athena and Hera restraining Akhilleus (*Il.* 1.194–221). Cf. West 1997: 350.

34. E.g., Kirk 1990: 101: "Moira would surely have prevented such a theological absurdity."

35. In another defeat for Ares, Hephaistos catches and holds him in bonds at *Od.* 8.296–97.

36. Cf. the description of the prophet Melampous at *Od.* 15.232.

37. For discussion of the passage, see M. Smith 1994: 153. In additional parallels, Yamm/Poseidon both have authority over Baal/Ares. Yamm defeats Baal, a humiliating loss for the god. In Greek myth Poseidon thematically exercises legal control over Ares. In the *Odyssey* when Ares is caught in Hephaistos' web, Poseidon will pay his bond (8.344–58). Elsewhere Poseidon holds Ares under indictment for murder (Apollodorus 3.14.2). Anat defeats Yamm, or Ocean. In extra-Homeric Greek myth, Athena defeats Poseidon in the contest to determine which deity would be the tutelary god of Athens (Apollodorus 3.14.1). For discussion of their contest and Poseidon's defeat by Athena, see Cook 1995: 7–8, 129–34, 181–83, 185–86.

38. The closest parallel is Aphrodite and the Graces, but they also have separate existences away from the goddess (e.g., 18.382; cf. 14.267–69).

39. Miller 19. Cf. 20: "Baal was understood to be the leader of an indeterminate host apparently conceived in part as a military force."

40. Cf. Ezek 5:17, 28:23, Yahweh's descriptions of the bloodshed he will send.

41. Miller (47) notes that the passage is "the only occasion in the myths in which a god or gods are engaged in battle with human beings."

42. Translation by M. Smith 1995: 369.

43. Anat is mentioned as nursing a hero in the *Kirta* (2 Cat 1.15 ii 27); cf. P. L. Day 64.

44. Technically only Athena arms, while Hera prepares the horses and chariot, and the goddesses ride jointly to attempt to subvert Zeus' will. For analysis of both passages, see Kirk 1990: 132–36, 330.

45. Cf. O'Brien's (77) comment on "Hera's relentless rage and demonic degeneracy." OT myth may associate Hera's equivalent, Asherah, with human sacrifice, e.g., Mic 5.14: "Asherah, I shall pull up your sacred poles / and demolish your blood-spattered altars."

46. See Louden 1999a: 7, 140, n. 30, as well as our discussions of Diomedes/Aias in chapter 1 and Agamemnon/Patroklos in chapter 3, on one character's qualities bifurcated into two parallel figures.

47. See again Walsh 29, 45, for discussion of Athena's epithets here.

48. Cf. in OT myth Yahweh or an angel striking mortals: Num 14:12; Deut 28:28; 1 Sam 6:19; 1 Kings 14:14; Jer 21:6, 30:14; Ezek 39:3; Isa 37:36, 60:10.

49. Gordon (1965b: 187) briefly notes parallels between Anat's bloody feast and Athena's treatment of the suitors.

50. Earlier scholars have neglected Homeric parallels and compared Aqhat with other Greek myths, e.g., Aktaion (Astour 163–68) and hunting myths in general (Fontenrose).

51. Ugaritic scholars lack a consensus on how to classify the *Aqhat*. I regard it as an epic because it deals with mortals *and* immortals and has a heroic mortal for its title character. The *Baal Cycle*, on the other hand is clearly not an epic as it does not deal with mortals. I would classify it as a hymn, parallel to some of the Psalms, those parts of Hesiod's *Theogony* that focus on Zeus' exploits, and the *Homeric Hymns*.

52. M. Smith 2001: 31: "Some cases, such as the mythic rendering of Anat's murder of Aqhat in 1.18, might seem to counter the notion of the deities as generally benevolent, yet this case represents human disobedience and divine punishment." Cf. Wyatt 1998: 247: "So Aqhat sins by insulting a goddess, whose vengeance is sure and terrible." Considine 89: "Aqhat's reply to . . . the goddess could hardly have been more offensive. He . . . contemptuously rejects her offer . . . and mocks her."

53. Wyatt 1998: 270, n. 90: "Evidently, Aqhat makes his offering to the gods, who came down to participate in the sacrifice, which from their perspective is a feast."

54. Though a few lines are missing, we can tell from Kirta's response that the second option is riches.

55. Cf. Gordon's comparison (1967: 17–18, 45, 50). I return to Paris below.

56. On the temptation myth as deriving from Q, and on Matthew as reflecting the original sequence of the options, see Fitzmyer 507.

57. Although some commentators, since antiquity, have attacked the passage as a later addition, for a defense of its authenticity, see Janko 1992: 27, 169, 175, 185.

58. In a fuller depiction of the Judgment of Paris, the end of book 10 of Apuleius' *Golden Ass*, the naive Lucius fails to realize that he is Paris, has made the same choice for pleasure, and paid a similar price.

59. See chapter 1, motif *10. As a result of the plotting of Apollo and Athene, the best of the Akhaians now encounters Hektor, in a duel to decide the whole war.*

60. As Richardson (126) notes, Athena's argument closely parallels Hera's against letting Sarpedon live (16.440–43).

61. On ἠθεῖος, Richardson (131) notes: "It seems to be used especially when referring to a brother."

62. The line is variously rendered, "You are (my) brother and I am [your] sister" (Hallo); "Come, brother, and I [ ]" (Parker).

63. Cf. Athena's (and Apollo's) taking the form of a vulture to observe Hektor's duel with Aias (7.58–61).

64. Gordon (1965b: 162) compares Aqhat's turning down of Anat's offer of immortality with Odysseus rejecting Kalypso's offer of same (*Od.* 5.209). But neither Gilgamesh nor Odysseus receive his offer of immortality as part of a scene of divine choices. But they can be taken together as instances of a hero responding to a goddess' offer of immortality, with Odysseus as the tactful mortal.

65. I quote Janko (1992: 147) again: "It is fine to call another 'honoured like a

god,' but to refer it to oneself, adding that one would be equal to Athene and Apollo, smacks of presumption." Cf. 13.54, Poseidon's assertion that Hektor "claims to be the son of mighty Zeus."

66. Cf. Kirk 1990: 196: "There is of course no reason why Hektor should not wash his hands."

67. Richardson (130) on *Il.* 22.214–47: "Here begins the first stage in the process of Hektor's fatal deception by Athena. Cf. her deceit of Pandaros (4.86–104), and her role in the second half of the *Odyssey* (especially 13.296–99 and 20.345–72)."

68. However, the *Iliad* earlier asserted that Apollo, κλυτότοξος, had given this bow to Pandaros (2.827).

69. E.g., in the games for Patroklos in book 23 Athena causes Aias Oileus to lose the footrace and fall in manure, taken to allude to her later causing his death. See Louden 1996a: 290; Richardson 202–3, 249.

70. E.g., as at *Od.* 13.291–99, where Athena defines her relationship with Odysseus as based on their mutual talent in cunning strategies.

71. Cf. Stanford liii: "[H]ow arrogantly patronizing Ajax could be towards the goddess."

72. She was going to offer him immortality (Apollodorus III 6, 7)—cf. Anat's offer to Aqhat—but was disgusted when he ate Melanippos' brains.

73. Odysseus and Neoptolemos' interaction with Philoktetes is also reminiscent of Odysseus and Diomedes' interaction with the archer Dolon.

74. Cf. theoxenies, and myths of a choice between a god's offers, both of which are positive or negative.

75. Cf. Boling 1982: 460: "Beth-anath is mentioned in lists of several campaigns by New Kingdom pharaohs." Cf. Kapelrud 10.

76. Hindson 108: "The name 'Shamgar' is definitely not Hebrew and seems to be of Hittite or Hurrian origin. He may also have been a Canaanite himself or of mixed Israelite background." Cf. Boling 1975: 89: "The name is apparently Hurrian, occurring in Nuzi texts."

77. Cf. Boling 1975: 89: "Analogical evidence connecting Anath with the semi-nomads known as Haneans in Mari texts, who on several occasions provide the king of Mari with sizable military contingents, lends support to the identification of Shamgar as a mercenary."

78. Quoted by Eaton (35, n. 114) from Cyrus H. Gordon, *Before the Bible: The Common Background of Greek and Hebrew Civilizations* (London: Collins, 1962), p. 62.

79. Shupak 517–18. Cf. P. L. Day 67, who further notes discussion by Cross suggesting the surname *Bin 'Anat* "is associated with military families."

80. See Bowman 216 and his citing of A. Vincent, *La religion des Judeo-Arameens d'Elephantine* (Paris: Librairie Orientaliste Paul Geuther, 1937); cf. Eaton 34–35; Gordon 1967: 42.

81. P. L. Day 70; cf. Eaton 26; Walls 145–46; and Gray 320, n. 34, on Anat and Rameses II and III.

82. On Athena associated with victory, note her epithets (Dee 2001): ἀγελείη, ληῖτις; associated with protection: ῥυσίπτολις.

83. Cf. McCarter 1985: 443. On Anat's temple at Beth-Shan, see also Craigie 375.

84. See, for instance, the passage immediately following in 2 Kings 23:4, "to remove from the house of the Lord all the objects made for Baal, for Asherah, and for all the host of heaven."

85. Cf. Craigie 377–78.

86. The depiction of Yahweh here (Judg 5:4, 21) is also reminiscent of Ugaritic depictions of Baal as the "Rider on the Clouds"; cf. Johnson.

87. M. Smith (1990: 63) offers a catalog of relevant passages, several of which are discussed below.

88. Apropos of Isa 63:2–3, 6, cf. Joel 3:13: "Wield the knife for the harvest is ripe . . . empty the vats, for they are full to the rim"; such linkages survive into New Testament myth as well, e.g., Rev 19:13. Cf. Lam 1:15: "He marshalled rank on rank against me to crush my warriors. The Lord trod down, like grapes in the winepress, the virgin daughter of Judah"; Jer 46:10.

89. See Miller 110–11 for further discussion.

90. On the Israelites bathing their feet in their enemies' blood, see also Ps 58:10. On Yahweh shattering his enemies' heads, see also Ps 110:5–6.

91. See Smith 1990: 63 for a list of OT passages that display parallels to depictions of Anat.

92. The translation is by Smelik (33).

93. Handy 103: "[I]n one Cypriot inscription of the fourth century B.C.E., the goddess Anat was equated with the Greek goddess Athena. This identification of two goddesses from separate cultures was also attested in Philo of Byblos's texts, where Anat the daughter of El, was conflated with the patron deity of Athens, Athena. n. 33: Philo of Byblos I.10.18, 32."

Glossary

Akhaians/Achaeans: The Greeks, in the *Iliad*, especially Greek warriors.

apocalypse (apocalyptic myth): A god, angry at mortals' disrespect, destroys them in large numbers.

aristeia: A higher than usual level of prowess attained by a warrior, inspired by a god, who is for a time virtually unstoppable on the battlefield.

ate, Ate (ἄτη): Delusion, recklessness; also personified as a goddess.

best of the Akhaians: The hero who can deliver his people, the Greeks, and defeat any opponent in a duel. Akhilleus is the real best of the Akhaians, but Menelaus, Diomedes, Telamonian Aias, Agamemnon, and Patroklos, all serve as temporary substitutes.

bie (βίη): Force, violence, the physical power of a warrior.

bifurcation: A Homeric technique whereby the qualities of one character (e.g., Akhilleus) are split and distributed among two other parallel characters (e.g., Diomedes and Aias).

Dardanians: A people closely related to the Trojans, living in the foothills of Mount Ida, led by Aineias.

divine council: A meeting of the gods, with Zeus presiding, to discuss mortals.

divine economy: The depiction of the gods in a myth.

divine interdiction: A god's command that a mortal not do something.

divine wrath: A god's anger at a mortal.

Doloneia: Book 10 of the *Iliad*, centered on the swift-footed Trojan, Dolon.

duals: Inflected forms of words that refer to two of a kind (neither singular nor plural).

eris (ἔρις): Strife, a bitter quarrel; a type of myth that depicts a bitter quarrel.

executive function: Rule by a god over other gods, Zeus in Greek myth, El in Ugaritic.

hospitality myth: A myth focusing on a guest and host, whose interactions are protected by Zeus Xenios, Zeus the god of guests.

Indo-European: The reconstructed ancient language from which Greek, Latin, Sanskrit, Iranian, and most European languages derive; the people who spoke this language.

khermadion (χερμάδιον) sequence: An action in which a warrior hefts a large boulder and hurls it at another warrior.

Lykians: The third contingent (after the Trojans and Dardanians) fighting on the Trojan side, led by Glaukos or Sarpedon.

menos (μένος): Battle might, power, which a god instills in a warrior to prompt his *aristeia*.

metis (μῆτις): Cunning.

narrative pattern (extended narrative pattern): The lengthy sequence of interconnected type-scenes or motifs that, repeated three times, constitutes the skeletal narrative of the *Iliad*. The principal narrative pattern is books 4–7, 8, 11–17, and 20–24; the introductory narrative pattern (in which Akhilleus appears in all three sequences) is books 1–2, 9–10, and 18–19.

one just man: The survivor of an apocalypse.

overdetermined/overdetermination: When a god and a mortal both share responsibility in making something happen.

pivotal contrafactual: A frequent kind of Homeric syntax taking the form: "and now X would have happened had not Y intervened."

sequence (initial, middle, final): one of the three separate statements of the narrative pattern. Books 1–7 constitute the initial sequence, 8–17 the middle sequence, and 18–24 the final sequence.

teikhoskopia: The view from the wall, the episode in book 3 in which Helen and Priam gaze out on the battlefield.

theomachy (theomachian): Gods' fighting with each other.

theoxeny: A myth in which a god or angel is disguised as a guest to test a host's behavior.

Ugaritic: An ancient West Semitic language, the myths surviving in this language dating from circa 1400 B.C.E., and the people using this language, roughly equivalent to the biblical Canaanites and Greeks' Phoenicians.

Bibliography

Alter, Robert. 1999. *The David Story: A Translation with Commentary of 1 and 2 Samuel*. New York: W. W. Norton.

Anderson, O. 1997. "Diomedes, Aphrodite, and Dione: Background and Function of a Scene in Homer's *Iliad*." *Classica et Mediaevalia* 48: 25–36.

Arend, W. 1933. *Die typischen Scenen bei Homer*. Berlin: Weidmann.

Armstrong, J. 1958. "The Arming Motif in the *Iliad*." *American Journal of Philology* 79: 337–54.

Astour, Michael C. 1965. *Hellenosemitica: An Ethnic and Cultural Study in West Semitic Impact on Mycenaean Greece*. Leiden: E. J. Brill.

Austin, Norman. 1966. "The Function of Digressions in the *Iliad*." *Greek, Roman and Byzantine Studies* 7: 295–312.

———. 1975. *Archery at the Dark of the Moon: Poetic Problems in Homer's* Odyssey. Berkeley: University of California Press.

Barnstone, Willis. 1984. *The Other Bible*. San Francisco: Harper & Row.

Bassi, Karen. 1997. "Orality, Masculinity, and the Greek Epic." *Arethusa* 30: 315–40.

Baumgarten, Albert I. 1981. *The Phoenician History of Philo of Byblos: A Commentary*. Leiden: E. J. Brill.

Beye, Charles Rowan. 1984. "The Epic of *Gilgamesh*, the Bible, and Homer: Some Narrative Parallels." In *Mnemai: Classical Studies in Memory of Karl K. Hulley*, edited by Harold D. Evjen, 7–19. Chico, CA: Scholars Press.

Bierling, Neal. 1992. *Giving Goliath His Due: New Archaeological Light on the Philistines*. Grand Rapids, MI: Baker Book House.

Boardman, John. 1998. *Early Greek Vase Painting*. London: Thames & Hudson.

Boling, Robert G. 1975. *Judges: Introduction, Translation and Commentary*. Anchor Bible. Garden City, NY: Doubleday.

———. 1982. *Joshua: Translation, Notes, and Commentary*. Anchor Bible. Garden City, NY: Doubleday.

Boll, F. 1917–18. "Zur homerischen Presbeia." *Zeitschrift für die deutsch-osterreichischen Gymnasien* 68: 1–7.

———. 1919–20. "Noch einmal zur homerischen Presbeia." *Zeitschrift für die deutsch-osterreichischen Gymnasien* 69: 414–16.

Bowman, Charles Howard, III. 1978. "The Goddess Anatu in the Ancient Near East." Ph.D. diss., Graduate Theological Union, Berkeley, CA.

Brenton, Lancelot C. L. 1851. *The Septuagint with Apocrypha: Greek and English*. Reprint, Peabody, MA: Hendrickson Publishers, 2001.

Brown, Edwin L. 2000. "The Roots of Poseidon in the Levant." Paper presented at the meeting of the Classical Association of the Middle West and South, Knoxville, Tenn., April 8.

Brown, John Pairman. 1995. *Israel and Hellas*. Beihefte zur Zeitschrift für die alttestamentliche Wissenschaft, vol. 231. Berlin: Walter de Gruyter.

———. 2000. *Israel and Hellas*. Vol. 2: *Sacred Institutions with Roman Counterparts*. Beihefte zur Zeitschrift für die alttestamentliche Wissenschaft, vol. 276. Berlin: Walter de Gruyter.

Brug, John F. 1985. *A Literary and Archaeological Study of the Philistines*. BAR International Series 265. Oxford.

Bryce, Trevor R. 1986. *The Lycians in Literary and Epigraphic Sources*. Copenhagen: Museum Tusculanum Press.

Burkert, Walter. 1966. "Greek Tragedy and Sacrificial Ritual." *Greek, Roman and Byzantine Studies* 7: 87–121.

———. 1983a. *Homo Necans: The Anthropology of Ancient Greek Sacrificial Ritual and Myth*. Translated by Peter Bing. Berkeley: University of California.

———. 1983b. "Oriental Myth and Literature in the *Iliad*." In *The Greek Renaissance of the Eighth Century B.C.: Tradition and Innovation*, edited by R. Hägg, 51–56. Proceedings of the Second International Symposium at the Swedish Institute in Athens, June 1–5, 1981. Stockholm: Svenska institutet i Athen.

———. 1985. *Greek Religion*. Translated by J. Raffan. Cambridge, MA: Harvard University Press.

———. 1992. *The Orientalizing Revolution: Near Eastern Influence on Greek Culture in the Early Archaic Age*. Translated by Margaret E. Pinder and Walter Burkert. Cambridge, MA: Harvard University Press.

Carter, Jane B., and Sarah P. Morris, eds. 1995. *The Ages of Homer: A Tribute to Emily Townsend Vermeule*. Austin: University of Texas Press.

Chantraine, P. 1990. *Dictionnaire etymologique de la langue grecque*. Paris: Editions Klincksieck.

Cogan, Mordechai. 2001. *1 Kings: A New Translation with Introduction and Commentary*. Anchor Bible. New York: Doubleday.

Collins, Derek. 1998. *Immortal Armor: The Concept of Alkē in Archaic Greek Poetry*. Lanham, MD: Rowman & Littlefield.

Considine, Patrick. 1969. "The Theme of Divine Wrath in Ancient East Mediterranean Literature." *Studi Micenei ed Egeo-Anatolici* 38, no. 8: 85–159.

Coogan, Michael D. 1998. *The Oxford History of the Biblical World*. New York: Oxford University Press.

Cook, Erwin F. 1995. *The Odyssey in Athens: Myths of Cultural Origins*. Ithaca: Cornell University Press.

———. 2004. "Near Eastern Sources for the Palace of Alkinoos." *American Journal of Archaeology* 108: 43–77.

Corpus Inscriptionum Semiticarum. 1881–1962. *Pars Prima: Inscriptiones Phoenicas Continens*. Paris: Academie des Inscriptions et Belles-Lettres.

Craigie, P. C. 1978. "Deborah and Anat: A Study of Poetic Imagery (Judges 5)." *Zeitschriften für alttestament* 90: 374–81.

Cross, Frank Moore. 1973. *Canaanite Myth and Hebrew Epic: Essays in the History of the Religion of Israel*. Cambridge, MA: Harvard University Press.

Dahood, Mitchell. 1968. *Psalms II:51–100*. Anchor Bible. Garden City, NY: Doubleday.

Dalley, Stephanie. 1991. *Myths from Mesopotamia*. Oxford: Oxford University Press.

Damon, Phillip. 1969. "Myth, Metaphor, and the Epic Tradition." *Orbis Litterarum* 85: 85–100.

Davison, J. A. 1965. "Thucydides, Homer and the 'Achaean Wall.'" *Greek, Roman and Byzantine Studies* 6: 5–28.

Day, John. 1985. *God's Conflict with the Dragon and the Sea: Echoes of a Canaanite Myth in the Old Testament*. Cambridge: Cambridge University Press.

Day, Peggy L. 1995. "Anat." In *Dictionary of Deities and Demons in the Bible*, edited by Karel van der Toorn, Bob Becking, and Pieter W. van der Horst, 61–77. Leiden: E. J. Brill.

Dee, James H. 2000. *Epitheta Hominum apud Homerum: The Epithetic Phrases for the Homeric Heroes: A Repertory of Descriptive Expressions for the Human Characters of the Iliad and the Odyssey*. Hildesheim: Olms-Weidmann.

———. 2001. *Epitheta Deorum apud Homerum: The Epithetic Phrases for the Homeric Gods*. Hildesheim: Olms-Weidmann.

———. 2002. *Epitheta Rerum et Locorum apud Homerum*. Hildesheim: Olms-Weidmann.

de Jong, Irene. 1987. *Narrators and Focalizers: The Presentation of the Story in the Iliad*. Amsterdam: B. R. Gruner Pub.

de Vaux, Roland. 1971. *The Bible and the Ancient Near East*. Garden City, NY: Doubleday.

de Vet, Thérèse. 1996. "The Joint Role of Orality and Literacy in the Composition, Transmission, and Performance of the Homeric Texts: A Comparative View." *Transactions of the American Philological Association* 126: 43–76.

Dothan, Trude. 1982. *The Philistines and Their Material Culture*. New Haven: Yale University Press.

Du Buisson, Robert Du Mesnil. 1973. *Nouvelles études sur les dieux et les myths de Canaan*. Leiden: E. J. Brill.

Due, Casey. 2002. *Homeric Variations on a Lament by Briseis*. Lanham, MD: Rowman & Littlefield.

Eaton, Alfred Wade. 1964. "The Goddess Anat: The History of Her Cult, Her Mythology and Her Iconography." Ph.D. diss., Yale University.

Edwards, Mark W. 1987. *Homer: Poet of the Iliad*. Baltimore: Johns Hopkins University Press.

———. 1991. *The Iliad: A Commentary*. Vol. 5: *Books 17–20*. Cambridge: Cambridge University Press.

Erbse, Hartmut. 1969. *Scholia Graeca in Homeri Iliadem (Scholia Vetera)*. Vol. 1. Berlin: Walter de Gruyter.

Feeney, D. C. 1991. *The Gods in Epic: Poets and Critics of the Classical Tradition*. New York: Oxford University Press.

Fenik, B. C. 1968. *Typical Battle Scenes in the Iliad*. Hermes Einzelschriften 21. Wiesbaden: F. Steiner.

———. 1974. *Studies in the Odyssey*. Hermes Zeitschrift für klassische Philologie Einzelschriften 30. Wiesbaden: Franz Steiner Verlag GMBH.

———, ed. 1978. *Homer: Tradition and Invention*. Leiden: E. J. Brill.

Fineberg, Stephen. 1999. "Blind Rage and Eccentric Vision in *Iliad* 6." *Transactions of the American Philological Association* 129: 13–41.

Fitzmyer, Joseph A. 1981. *The Gospel According to Luke (I–IX): Introduction, Translation and Notes*. Anchor Bible. Garden City, NY: Doubleday.

Foley, John Miles. 1990. *Traditional Oral Epic: The Odyssey, Beowulf, and the Serbo-Croatian Return Song*. Berkeley: University of California Press.

———, ed. 2005. *The Blackwell Companion to Ancient Epic*. Oxford: Blackwell.

Frazer, R. M. 1993. *A Reading of the Iliad*. Lanham, MD: University Press of America.

Friedrich, W. H. 1956. *Verwandung und Tot in der Ilias*. Göttingen: Vandenhoeck und Ruprecht.

Frye, Northrop. 1957. *Anatomy of Criticism: Four Essays*. Reprint, New York: Atheneum, 1966.

Gabel, John B., Charles B. Wheeler, and Anthony D. York. 1996. *The Bible as Literature: An Introduction*. 3rd ed. New York: Oxford University Press.

Gantz, Timothy. 1993. *Early Greek Myth*. Baltimore: Johns Hopkins University Press.

Gjerstad, Einar. 1935. *The Swedish Cyprus Expedition* Vol. 2. Text. Stockholm: Victor Pettersons Bokindustriaktiebolag.

Golden, Leon. 1989. "Διὸς ἀπάτη and the Unity of *Iliad* 14." *Mnemosyne* 42: 1–11.

Gordon, Cyrus H. 1965a. *The Ancient Near East*. New York: W. W. Norton.

———. 1965b. *The Common Background of Greek and Hebrew Civilizations*. New York: W. W. Norton.

———. 1967. *Homer and the Bible*. Ventnor, NJ: Ventnor Publishers. Reprint of *Hebrew Union College Annual* 26 (1955): 43–108.

Gray, John. 1979. "The Blood Bath of the Goddess Anat in the Ras Shamra Texts." *Ugarit-Forschungen* 11: 315–24.

Gresseth, Gerald K. 1975. "The Gilgamesh Epic and Homer." *Classical Journal* 70: 1–18.

Griffin, Jasper. 1980. *Homer on Life and Death*. Oxford: Clarendon Press.

———. 1995. *Iliad IX*. Oxford: Clarendon Press.

Gunn, David. M. 1993. "Saul." In *The Oxford Companion to the Bible*, edited by Bruce M. Metzger and Michael D. Coogan, 679–81. New York: Oxford University Press.

Haft, Adele J. 1990. "'The City-Sacker Odysseus' in *Iliad* 2 and 10." *Transactions of the American Philological Association* 120: 37–56.

Hainsworth, Bryan. 1993. *The Iliad: A Commentary*. Vol. 3: *Books 9–12*. Gen. ed. G. S. Kirk. Cambridge: Cambridge University Press.

Hainsworth, J. B. 1966. "Joining Battle in Homer." *Greece and Rome,* 2nd ser., 13: 158–66.

Hallo, William W. 1997. *The Context of Scripture.* Vol. 1: *Canonical Compositions from the Biblical World.* Leiden: E. J. Brill.

Halperin, David H. 1990. "Heroes and Their Pals." In *One Hundred Years of Homosexuality and Other Essays on Greek Love,* 75–87, 176–79. New York: Routledge.

Handy, Lowell K. 1994. *Among the Host of Heaven: The Syro-Palestinian Pantheon as Bureaucracy.* Winona Lake, MN: Eisenbrauns.

Hard, Robin. 1997. *Apollodorus: The Library of Greek Mythology.* Translated by Robin Hard. Oxford: Oxford University Press.

Heiden, Bruce. 1996. "The Three Movements of the *Iliad.*" *Greek, Roman and Byzantine Studies* 37: 5–22.

———. 1998. "The Placement of 'Book Divisions' in the *Iliad.*" *Journal of Hellenic Studies* 118: 62–81.

———. 2000. "Major Systems of Thematic Resonance in the *Iliad.*" *Symbolae Osloenses* 75: 34–55.

———. 2002a. "Hidden Thoughts, Open Speech: Some Reflections on Discourse Analysis in Recent Homeric Studies." In *Omero Tremila Anni Dopo,* edited by Franco Montari, 431–44. Rome: Edizioni di Storia e Letteratura.

———. 2002b. "Structures of Progression in the Plot of the *Iliad.*" *Arethusa* 35: 237–54.

Hernandez, Pura Nieto. 2002. "Odysseus, Agamemnon and Apollo." *Classical Journal* 97: 319–34.

Heubeck, Alfred. 1988. *A Commentary on Homer's Odyssey.* Vol. 1: *Introduction and Books I–VIII.* Edited by Stephanie West Heubeck and J. B. Hainsworth. Oxford: Oxford University Press.

Hindson, Edward E. 1971. *The Philistines and the Old Testament.* Baker Studies in Biblical Archaeology. Grand Rapids, MI: Baker Book House.

Hoffner, Harry A. 1998. *Hittite Myths.* Atlanta: Scholars Press.

Hogan, James C. 1981. "*Eris* in Homer." *Grazer Beiträge* 10: 21–58.

Holland, Gary. 1993. "The Name of Achilles: A Revised Etymology." *Glotta* 71: 17–27.

Hughes, Merritt Y. 1980. *John Milton: Complete Poems and Major Prose.* Indianapolis: Odyssey Press / Bobbs-Merrill Educational Publishing.

Jacobsen, Thorkild. 1987. *The Harps That Once . . . Sumerian Poetry in Translation.* New Haven: Yale University Press.

Janko, Richard. 1982. *Homer, Hesiod, and the Hymns.* Cambridge: Cambridge University Press.

———. 1992. *The Iliad: A Commentary.* Vol. 4: *Books 13–16.* Gen. ed. G. S. Kirk. Cambridge: Cambridge University Press.

Johnson, Brenda M. 2000. "Deborah, Jael and Canaanite Mythology." Mount Saint Agnes Theological Center for Women. http://msawomen.org/works/deborah.html.

Jones, Allen H. 1975. *Bronze Age Civilization: The Philistines and the Danites.* Washington, DC: Public Affairs Press.

49. *Homeric Researches.* Lund: C. W. K. Gleerup.

———. S. 1995. "Joshua 7: A Reassessment of Israelite Conceptions of Cor-
   ⸲ Punishment." In *The Pitcher Is Broken: Memorial Essays for Gösta W. Ahl-
   m,* edited by Steven W. Holloway and Lowell K. Handy, 315–46. Shef-
   ⸲eld: Sheffield Academic Press.

———. Sa-Moon. 1989. *Divine War in the Old Testament and in the Ancient Near East.*
   Berlin: Walter de Gruyter.

———. ⸲pelrud, A. 1969. *The Violent Goddess: Anat in the Ras Shamra Texts.* Oslo: Universi-
   tetsforlaget.

Karageorghis, Vassos. 1998. *Greek Gods and Heroes in Ancient Cyprus.* Athens: Com-
   merical Bank of Athens.

Keel, Othmar, and Christop Uehlinger. 1998. *Gods, Goddesses, and Images of God in
   Ancient Israel.* Translated by Thomas H. Trapp. Minneapolis: Fortress Press.

Kirk, G. S. 1974. *The Nature of Greek Myths.* Harmondsworth: Penguin Books.

———. 1985. *The Iliad: A Commentary.* Vol. 1: *Books 1–4.* Cambridge: Cambridge
   University Press.

———. 1990. *The Iliad: A Commentary.* Vol. 2: *Books 5–8.* Cambridge: Cambridge
   University Press.

Knox, Ronald, and Joseph Russo. 1989. "Agamemnon's Test: *Iliad* 2.73–73." *Clas-
   sical Antiquity* 8: 351–58.

Krischer, Tilman. 1971. *Formale Konvenionen der homerischen Epik.* Munich: C. H. Beck.

Kuhn, Adalbert. 1853. "Ueber die durch nasale erweiterte verbalstaïmme." *Zeitschrift
   für Vergleichende Sprachforschung* 2: 455–71.

Lang, Mabel. 1989. "Unreal Conditions in Homeric Narrative." *Greek, Roman and
   Byzantine Studies* 30: 5–26.

Lateiner, Donald. 2002. "Pouring Bloody Drops (*Iliad* 16.459): The Grief of Zeus."
   Colby Quarterly 38: 42–61.

Lefkowitz, Mary. 2003. *Greek Gods, Human Lives: What We Can Learn from Myths.* New
   Haven: Yale University Press.

Lesky, Albert. 1967. *Homeros.* Sonderausgaben der Paulyschen Realencyclopädie
   der classischen Altertumswissenschaft. Stuttgart.

Lipinski, Edward. 1995. *Dieux et déesses de l'univers phénicien et punique.* Orientalia lova-
   niensia Analecta 64. Leuven: Uitgeverij Peeters & Departement Oosterse
   Studies.

Lohman, D. 1970. *Die Komposition der Reden in der Ilias.* Berlin: Walter de Gruyter.

Lord, Albert. 2003. *The Singer of Tales.* Cambridge, MA: Harvard University Press.

Louden, Bruce. 1990. "Interactive Narrative Techniques in the *Iliad,* the *Odyssey* and
   Paradise Lost." Ph.D. diss., University of California at Berkeley.

———. 1993. "Pivotal Contrafactuals in Homeric Epic." *Classical Antiquity* 12: 181–
   98.

———. 1995. "Categories of Homeric Wordplay." *Transactions of the American Philo-
   logical Association* 125: 27–46.

———. 1996a. "Epeios, Odysseus, and the Indo-European Metaphor for Poet."
   Journal of Indo-European Studies 24, nos. 3–4: 277–304.

———. 1996b. "A Narrative Technique in *Beowulf* and Homeric Epic." *Oral Tradition* 11: 346–62.

———. 1996c. "Milton and the Appropriation of a Homeric Narrative Technique." *Classical and Modern Literature* 16: 325–40.

———. 1999a. *The Odyssey: Structure, Narration, and Meaning.* Baltimore: Johns Hopkins University Press.

———. 1999b. "Bacchylides 17: Theseus and Indo-Iranian Apam Napat." *Journal of Indo-European Studies* 27, nos. 1–2: 57–78.

———. 2002. "Eurybates, Odysseus, and the Duals in Book 9 of the *Iliad*." *Colby Quarterly* 38: 62–76.

———. 2005. "The Gods in Epic, or the Divine Economy." In *The Blackwell Companion to Ancient Epic,* edited by John Miles Foley, 90–104. Oxford: Blackwell.

Lowenstam, Steven. 1981. *The Death of Patroklos: A Study in Typology.* Beiträge zur Klassischen Philologie 133. Königstein: Verlag Anton Hain.

———. 1993. *The Scepter and the Spear: Studies on Forms of Repetition in the Homeric Poems.* Lanham, MD: Rowman & Littlefield.

MacKenzie, John L. 1968. *Second Isaiah: Introduction, Translation, and Notes.* Anchor Bible. Garden City, NY: Doubleday.

Marinatos, Nanno. 2000. *The Goddess and the Warrior.* London: Routledge.

Markoe, Glenn. 1985. *Phoenician Bronze and Silver Bowls from Cyprus and the Mediterranean.* Berkeley: University of California Press.

Martin, Richard P. 1989. *The Language of Heroes: Speech and Performance in the Iliad.* Ithaca: Cornell University Press.

McCarter, P. Kyle, Jr. 1984. *II Samuel: A New Translation with Introduction, Notes and Commentary.* Anchor Bible. Garden City, NY: Doubleday.

———. 1985. *I Samuel: A New Translation with Introduction, Notes and Commentary.* Anchor Bible. Garden City, NY: Doubleday.

Miller, Patrick D., Jr. 1973. *The Divine Warrior in Early Israel.* Cambridge, MA: Harvard University Press.

Minchin, Elizabeth. 2004. Review of Louden, "Eurybates, Odysseus, and the Duals in Book 9 of the *Iliad*" (2002). *Scholia Reviews* 13. www.classics.und.ac.za/reviews/.

Mondi, Robert. 1990. "Greek Mythic Thought in the Light of the Near East." In *Approaches to Greek Myth,* edited by Lowell Edmunds, 142–98. Baltimore: Johns Hopkins University Press.

Morris, Sarah P. 1992. *Daidalos and the Origins of Greek Art.* Princeton: Princeton University Press.

———. 1995. "The Sacrifice of Astyanax." In *The Ages of Homer: A Tribute to Emily Townsend Vermeule,* edited Jane B. Carter and Sarah P. Morris, 221–45. Austin: University of Texas.

Morrison, James V. 1992a. "Alternatives to the Epic Tradition: Homer's Challenges in the *Iliad*." *Transactions of the American Philological Association* 122: 61–71.

———. 1992b. *Homeric Misdirection: False Predictions in the Iliad.* Ann Arbor: University of Michigan Press.

————. 1994. "Thematic Inversion in the *Iliad:* The Greeks under Siege." *Greek, Roman and Byzantine Studies* 35: 209–27.

Moscati, Sabatino. 2001. *The Face of the Ancient Orient: Near Eastern Civilization in Pre-Classical Times.* Mineola: Dover Publications. Reprint of 1960 edition.

Moulton, Carroll. 1977. *Similes in the Homeric Poems.* Hypomnemata 49. Göttingen: Vanderhoeck and Ruprecht.

Mühlestein, H. 1987. *Homerische Namenstudien.* Beiträge zur klassischen Philologie 183. Frankfurt am Main: Athenäum.

Mullen, E. Theodore, Jr. 1980. *The Divine Council in Canaanite and Early Hebrew Literature.* Chico, CA: Scholars Press.

Nagler, Michael N. 1974. *Spontaneity and Tradition: A Study in the Oral Art of Homer.* Berkeley: University of California Press.

Nagy, Gregory. 1974. *Comparative Studies in Greek and Indic Meter.* Harvard Studies in Comparative Literature 33. Cambridge, MA: Harvard University Press.

————. 1979. *The Best of the Achaeans: Concepts of the Hero in Archaic Greek Poetry.* Baltimore: Johns Hopkins University Press.

————. 1990. *Greek Mythology and Poetics.* Ithaca: Cornell University Press.

————. 1996. *Homeric Questions.* Austin: University of Texas Press.

————. 2003. *Homeric Responses.* Austin: University of Texas Press.

Niditch, Susan. 1993. *War in the Hebrew Bible: A Study in the Ethics of Violence.* New York: Oxford University Press.

Nimis, Stephen A. 1987. *Narrative Semiotics in the Epic Tradition.* Bloomington: Indiana University Press.

O'Brien, Joan V. 1993. *The Transformation of Hera: A Study of Ritual, Hero, and the Goddess in the Iliad.* Lanham, MD: Rowman & Littlefield.

Oldenburg, Ulf. 1969. *The Conflict between El and Ba'al in Canaanite Religion.* Leiden: E. J. Brill.

Owen, E. T. 1949. *The Story of the Iliad.* Reprint, Wauconda, IL: Bolchazy-Carducci, 1989.

Pantelia, Maria C. 2002. "Helen and the Last Song for Hector." *Transactions of the American Philological Association* 132: 21–27.

Parker, Simon B. 1997. *Ugaritic Narrative Poetry.* Atlanta: Scholars Press.

Parks, Ward. 1990. *Verbal Dueling in Heroic Narrative: The Homeric and Old English Traditions.* Princeton: Princeton University Press.

Petegorsky, Dan. 1982. "Context and Evocation: Studies in Early Greek and Sanskrit Poetry." Ph.D. diss., University of California at Berkeley.

Pitt-Rivers, Julian Alfred. 1977. *The Fate of Shechem; or, The Politics of Sex: Essays in the Anthropology of the Mediterranean.* Cambridge: Cambridge University Press.

Pokorny, J. 1994. *Indogermanisches Etymologisches Wörterbuch.* Tübingen: Francke.

Pope, Marvin H. 1973. *Job: Introduction, Translation, and Notes.* Anchor Bible. Garden City, NY: Doubleday.

Powell, Barry B. 1991. *Homer and the Origin of the Greek Alphabet.* New York: Cambridge University Press.

Prendergast, Guy Lushington. 1983. *A Complete Concordance to the Iliad of Homer.* Rev.

and enlarged by Benedetto Marzullo. Darmstadt: Wissenschaftliche Buch-gesellschaft.

Pritchard, James B. 1969. *Ancient Near Eastern Texts Relating to the Old Testament*. 3rd ed. Princeton: Princeton University Press.

Pucci, Pietro. 1987. *Odysseus Polutropos: Intertextual Readings in the Odyssey and the Iliad*. Ithaca: Cornell University Press.

Rabel, Robert J. 1997. *Plot and Point of View in the Iliad*. Ann Arbor: University of Michigan Press.

Redfield, J. M. 1975. *Nature and Culture in the Iliad: The Tragedy of Hector*. Chicago: University of Chicago Press.

Reece, Steve. 1993. *The Stranger's Welcome: Oral Theory and the Aesthetics of the Homeric Hospitality Scene*. Ann Arbor: University of Michigan Press.

Richardson, Nicholas. 1993. *The Iliad: A Commentary*. Vol. 6: *Books 21–24*. Cambridge: Cambridge University Press.

Robinson, J. 1976. *The Second Book of Kings*. Cambridge Bible Commentary on the New English Bible. Cambridge: Cambridge University Press.

Russo, J., Manuel Fernández-Galiano, and Alfred Heubect. 1992. *A Commentary on Homer's Odyssey*. Vol. 3: *Books XVII–XXIV*. Oxford: Oxford University Press.

Schadewalt, W. 1975. *Der Aufbau der Ilias*. Frankfurt.

Schein, Seth L. 1985. *The Mortal Hero: An Introduction to Homer's Iliad*. Berkeley: University of California Press.

———. 1997. "The *Iliad*: Structure and Interpretation." In *A New Companion to Homer*, edited by Ian Morris and Barry Powell, 345–58. Leiden: E. J. Brill.

Scodel, Ruth. 1982. "The Achaean Wall and the Myth of Destruction." *Harvard Studies in Classical Philology* 86: 33–50.

———. 1992. "The Wits of Glaucus." *Transactions of the American Philological Association* 122: 73–84.

———. 2002. *Listening to Homer: Tradition, Narrative, and Audience*. Ann Arbor: University of Michigan Press.

Scully, Stephen. 1990. *Homer and the Sacred City*. Ithaca: Cornell University Press.

Seaford, Richard. 1989. "Homeric and Tragic Sacrifice." *Transactions of the American Philological Association* 119: 87–95.

Segal, Charles. 1968. "The Embassy and the Duals of 9." *Greek, Roman and Byzantine Studies* 9: 101–14.

Shannon, Richard Stoll, III. 1975. *The Arms of Achilles and Homeric Compositional Technique*. Mnemosyne Supplement 36. Leiden: E. J. Brill.

Sheppard, J. T. 1922. *The Pattern of the Iliad*. Reprint, New York: Barnes and Noble, 1969.

Shupak, Nili. 1989. "New Light on Shamgar ben 'Anath." *Biblica* 70: 517–25.

Sinclair, T. A. 1966. *Hesiod: Works and Days*. Hildesheim: Georg Olms Verlagsbuchhandlung.

Slatkin, Laura. 1991. *The Power of Thetis: Allusion and Interpretation in the Iliad*. Berkeley: University of California Press.

Smelik, Klaas A. D. 1991. *Writing from Ancient Israel: A Handbook of Historical and Religious Documents*. Louisville, KY: Westminster/John Knox Press.

Smith, Mark S. 1990. *The Early History of God: Yahweh and the Other Deities in Ancient Israel*. San Francisco: Harper Collins.

———. 1994. *The Ugaritic Baal Cycle*. Vol. 1: *Introduction with Text, Translation and Commentary of KTU 1.1–1.2*. Leiden: E. J. Brill.

———. 1995. "Anat's Warfare Cannibalism and the West Semitic Ban." In *The Pitcher Is Broken: Memorial Essays for Gösta W. Ahlström*, edited by Steven W. Holloway and Lowell K. Handy, 368–86. Sheffield: Sheffield Academic Press.

———. 2001. *The Origins of Biblical Monotheism: Israel's Polytheistic Background and the Ugaritic Texts*. New York: Oxford University Press.

Smith, P. M. 1981. "Aeneidai as Patrons of *Iliad* XX and the Homeric Hymn to Aphrodite." *Harvard Studies in Classical Philology* 85: 17–59.

Stager, Lawrence E. 1998. "Forging an Identity: The Emergence of Ancient Israel." In *The Oxford History of the Biblical World*, edited Michael D. Coogan, 123–75. New York: Oxford University Press.

Stanford, W. B. 1963. *Sophocles: Aias*. Reprint, Bristol: Bristol Classical Press, 1981.

Stanley, Keith. 1993. *The Shield of Homer: Narrative Structure in the Iliad*. Princeton Princeton University Press.

Stawell, Florence Melian. 1909. *Homer and the Iliad: An Essay to Determine the Scope and Character of the Original Poem*. London: J. M. Dent.

Suggs, M. Jack, Katharine Doob Sakenfeld, and James R. Mueller, eds. 1992. *The Oxford Study Bible*. New York: Oxford University Press.

Taplin, Oliver. 1992. *Homeric Soundings: The Shaping of the Iliad*. Oxford: Clarendon Press.

Thalmann, W. G. 1984. *Conventions of Form and Thought in Early Greek Epic Poetry*. Baltimore: Johns Hopkins University Press.

———. 1988. "Thersites: Comedy, Scapegoats, and Heroic Ideology." *Transactions of the American Philological Association* 118: 1–28.

van der Toorn, Karel, Bob Becking, and Pieter W. van der Horst, eds. 1995. *Dictionary of Deities and Demons in the Bible*. Leiden: E. J. Brill.

Van Erp Taalman Kip, A. Maria. 2000. "The Gods of the *Iliad* and the Fate of Troy." *Mnemosyne* 50, no. 4: 385–402.

von Kamptz, Hans. 1982. *Homerische Personennamen*. Göttingen: Vandenhoeck und Ruprecht.

von Rad, Gerhard. 1991. *Holy War in Ancient Israel*. Translated and edited by Marva J. Dawn, introduction by Ben C. Ollenburger. Grand Rapids, MI: William B. Eerdmans.

Wade-Gery, H. T. 1952. *The Poet of the Iliad*. Cambridge: Cambridge University Press.

Walls, Neal H. 1992. *The Goddess Anat in Ugaritic Myth*. Society of Biblical Literature Dissertation Series Number 135. Atlanta: Scholars Press.

Walsh, Thomas R. 2005. *Fighting Words and Feuding Words*. Lanham, MD: Rowman & Littlefield.

Watkins, Calvert. 2000. *The American Heritage Dictionary of Indo-European Roots*. 2nd ed. Boston: Houghton Mifflin.

Webster, T. B. L. 1956–57. "Homer and Eastern Poetry." *Minos* 4: 104–16.

———. 1958. *From Mycenae to Homer*. London: Methuen.

———. 1970. *Philoctetes*. Cambridge.

Weinfeld, M. 1983. "Divine Intervention in War in Ancient Israel and in the Ancient Near East." In *History, Historiography and Interpretation: Studies in Biblical and Cuneiform Literatures*, edited by H. Tadmoor and M. Weinfeld, 121–47. Jerusalem: Magnes Press, Hebrew University.

West, Martin L. 1966. *Hesiod: Theogony*. Oxford.

———. 1978. *Hesiod: Works and Days*. Oxford.

———. 1988. "The Rise of the Greek Epic." *Journal of Hellenic Studies* 108: 151–72.

———. 1997. *The East Face of Helicon: West Asiatic Elements in Greek Poetry and Myth*. Oxford: Clarendon Press.

———. 1998. *Homerus Ilias.*, Vol. 1. Stuttgart: Teubner.

———. 2003. *Greek Epic Fragments*. Cambridge, MA: Harvard University Press.

———. 2004. "West on Rengakos (*BMCR* 2002.11.15) and Nagy (*Gnomon* 75, 2003, 481–501)." *Bryn Mawr Classical Review* 4: 17. ccat.sas.upenn.edu/bmcr/.

Whitman, Cedric H. 1958. *Homer and the Homeric Tradition*. New York: W. W. Norton.

Wilson, Donna F. 2002. *Ransom, Revenge, and Heroic Identity in the Iliad*. Cambridge: Cambridge University Press.

Wilson, John R. 1986. "The *Gilgamesh* Epic and the *Iliad*." *Echos du monde classique/Classical Views* 30, n.s., 5: 25–41.

Wright, David P. 2001. *Ritual in Narrative: The Dynamics of Feasting, Mourning, and Retaliation Rites in the Ugaritic Tale of Aqhat*. Winona Lake, MN: Eisenbrauns.

Wright, G. M., and P. V. Jones. 1997. *Homer: German Scholarship in Translation*. Oxford: Clarendon Press.

Wyatt, Nicolas. 1984. "The Anat Stela from Ugarit and Its Ramifications." *Ugarit Forschungen* 16: 327–37.

———. 1998. *Religious Texts from Ugarit*. Sheffield: Sheffield Academic Press.

Yadin, Azzan. 2004. "Goliath's Armor and Israelite Collective Memory." *Vetus Testamentum* 54, no. 3: 373–95.

Yamagata, Naoko. 1994. *Homeric Morality*. Mnemosyne Supplement 131. Leiden: E. J. Brill.

Zimmerli, Walther. 1983. *Ezekiel 2: A Commentary on the Book of the Prophet Ezekiel Chapters 25–48*. Translated by James D. Martin. Philadelphia: Fortress Press.

Index

divine councils, 6, 106, 169, 179–80,
    207–9
divine interdictions, 103
divine wraths, 110, 114, 117, 170
Dolon, 11, 109, 111, 112, 140–44, 146,
    147, 197–98, 200, 271
Doloneia, 81, 110, 132, 143–44, 147, 271
Dyskolos, 145

Eaton, A., 276, 279, 281
Edwards, M. W., 1, 18, 19, 29, 53, 95,
    108, 122, 136–37, 144, 200, 220,
    237, 238, 253–54, 307n. 14
El, 7, 169, 208, 246, 249–51
Elijah, 8, 12, 19, 158, 168–70, 221–22
Elishah, 8
Enoch, 236–38, 309n. 70, 310n. 76
Enuma Elish, 12, 211, 213, 218
eris, 88, 96, 119, 130, 142, 147, 160–66,
    210, 212, 257
Eumaios, 128, 133
Euphorbos, 108–9
Euripides: *Alcestis*, 184; *Helen*, 296n. 37;
    Ion, 77; *Iphigeneia in Aulis*, 307n. 23
Eurybates, 4, 121–34, 142–43
Eurypylos, 91–92, 102
Eurytos, 273
exterminating angel, 154–55

Fenik, B., 1, 20, 57, 85, 88, 100, 105,
    294n. 45, 299n. 54

Gideon (Jerubaal), 169, 178, 277
Gilgamesh, 7, 170–71, 179, 207–8, 231,
    235, 241, 267, 269, 275, 305n. 31
Glaukos, 4, 28–30, 34, 93–94, 105–6
Goliath, 172–79
Gordon, C. H., 8, 26, 134, 262, 270,
    307n. 27, 312n. 33, 313n. 49

Haft, A., 143, 144, 298n. 34
Hainsworth, B., 88, 90, 122–23, 140,
    144, 150, 199, 232, 272–73, 297n.
    13

Hainsworth, J. B., 146–48
Heiden, B., 291nn. 3–4, 301n. 28
Hekabe (Hecuba), 31–33, 49, 150, 154
Hektor, 2–3, 5, 11, 14, 22, 23, 25, 30–
    52 passim, 53–79 passim, 80–111,
    139–41, 197–200, 228, 242–43,
    274; association with myths of
    human sacrifice, 71–73, 202–7;
    burning of the ships, 84–86, 102,
    198, 259
Helen, 4, 31–32, 52, 54–55, 60–64,
    76–79
Helenos, 31
Helios, 138
Hephaistos, 18, 25, 40, 112, 113, 137–38,
    215–16, 244–45
Hera, 5, 10, 11, 16–17, 21–22, 36, 49,
    80, 81, 84–86, 98–101, 106, 114,
    138, 141, 156, 180, 208, 210–18,
    243–44, 258–59
Herakles, 161, 165, 185, 209, 244,
    272–73, 293n. 20
Hermes, 50, 67, 73, 217
Hesiod
    Theogony: 9; *617,* 212; *705,* 212; *855,*
        224; *868,* 83
    Works and Days: 5–7, 237; *11–46,* 160;
        80, 67; *137–38,* 227; *143–73,* 170;
        240–41, 227; *242–47,* 228–29;
        282–84, 186
Hindson, E., 174, 175, 278, 304n. 24
Homer, *Iliad*
    1: *1.51–53,* 154; *1.54,* 114–15; *1.55–56,*
        155; *1.58,* 115; *1.60–61,* 155; *1.106–7,*
        160; *1.122,* 116; *1.131,* 145; *1.132,* 116;
        1.135–39, 116; *1.169–70,* 116; *1.173–*
        87, 119; *1.194–95,* 109; *1.248–49,*
        119; *1.308–17,* 120, 123; *1.318–48,*
        121; *1.321,* 126; *1.326,* 121; *1.327,*
        127; *1.334–35,* 124, 128; *1.386,* 156;
        1.389–92, 121; *1.397–406,* 213–14;
        1.411–12, 118; *1.417,* 136; *1.495–531,*
        169
    2: *2.184,* 125; *2.214,* 142; *2.337–68,*

A PATRIOT
IN
BERLIN

A PATRIOT
IN
BERLIN

Piers Paul Read

Weidenfeld & Nicolson
LONDON

First published in Great Britain in 1995 by
Weidenfeld and Nicolson
An imprint of The Orion Publishing Group
Orion House, 5 Upper St Martin's Lane, London WC2H 9EA

A CIP catalogue record for this book is available
from the British Library

ISBN 0 297 81729 9

Typeset by Deltatype Ltd, Ellesmere Port, Cheshire

Printed in England by
Clays Ltd, St Ives plc

It has been hard for outsiders to realize that Russian national feeling is a spiritual emotion largely detached from the mundane things of life, that for centuries past Russia has meant for her people much more than just a country to be loved and defended: 'Russia' was more a state of mind, a secular ideal, a sacred idea, an object of almost religious belief – unfathomable by the mind, unmeasurable by the yardstick of rationality.

Tibor Szamuely: The Russian Tradition

PART ONE

1991

30 August

ONE

The neighbour on one side was an old woman living alone. She was deaf and remembered nothing. The house on the other was divided into flats. The owners were questioned when they returned that evening. One, a middle-aged spinster, remembered music, loud choral music, in the early hours of the morning ten days or so before. She had telephoned the police to complain. Some time later the music had stopped and she had fallen asleep.

A cassette remained in the tape deck. None of the team investigating the deaths could decipher the Cyrillic script on the label so Kessler, the senior detective, played the tape for a moment or two – Slavonic church music, undoubtedly the music that had kept the woman awake. He turned up the volume, taking care not to superimpose his fingerprints on any that might be there already.

The sergeant, Dorn, put his hands to his ears. 'Why so loud?'

Kessler said nothing. Instead, he hit the walls of the large living room with his fist. The music must have been played at full volume to have woken the woman next door: the windows had been closed, the walls were thick, and the houses on this stretch of Dubrowstrasse were at least fifty metres apart – large Teutonic villas built at the turn of the century in the heyday of the German empire.

'They go for a million marks, houses like this,' said Dorn, looking around at the large rooms with bare walls. 'And when the government moves here from Bonn, they'll double again. I bet the children of the woman next door can't wait for her to pass on. She's squatting on a fortune . . .'

Why so loud? Kessler stopped the tape and switched off the system. To lose the sound of the shot that killed the man? No. His body lay in the hall at the bottom of the stairs: he must have been killed as they entered. To smother the screams of the woman? Surgical tape had covered her mouth. Stooping over the body tied to the chair, and studying her face through a magnifying glass, Kessler could see traces of the white adhesive above and below the edge of the tape, and on the sticky side, dangling loose on her chin, several small black hairs from her upper lip lay on top of one another, suggesting that it had been removed on several occasions. To let her talk? Or scream?

Kessler stepped back because of the stench. A robust Berliner who had seen many a corpse in his time, he was shaken all the same by the sight of this woman's body. She wore a light cotton dress, but in her writhing the dress had torn, rucked and twisted to uncover most of her body, and the folds were now brittle where the sweat had dried. Sweat had matted the strands of dark hair that had fallen over her face and now seemed glued to her skin. There were black stripes where ropes bound her wrists and ankles, and discoloration where her back and buttocks pressed against the chair. There were patches on the upholstered seat, too, that gave off a pungent odour distinct from that of rotting flesh; but there seemed to be no blood on her body, on the red weals where they had burned her skin, almost certainly with cigarettes, so that it now looked as if she had suffered from smallpox or bubonic plague.

There were shreds of tobacco on the floor. Kessler crouched and picked one up with a pair of tweezers. It was dark and finely cut, probably from a Turkish or a Bulgarian cigarette. He put the

4

shred into a small transparent plastic bag and the bag into his pocket.

The woman's head lolled right back, the open eyes gazing at the ceiling. From the lines and the complexion, Kessler estimated that she was at least forty, but attractive in a swarthy, Levantine way. The face was untouched, but the sight of it disturbed Kessler more than the marks on her skin – particularly the way in which her features were set in an expression of an agony that could all too easily be taken for rapture.

'Did they fuck her?' asked Dorn.

Kessler turned away. 'Tied like that? And with her clothes on?'

'Shall I look in her mouth?'

'Leave that to them.' Kessler nodded towards the team of forensic technicians.

'How did she die?'

Kessler pointed to a small circular bruise on the back of her neck. 'An injection, I'd say. Probably cyanide.'

'To save a bullet?'

'Possibly.'

'Not just cruel but stingy too.'

Kessler was called to the telephone in the hall. The police post at Schlachtensee had received a complaint from a flat on Dubrowstrasse at 3.32 a.m. on the morning of Tuesday 20 August 1991. A patrol car had called at the house in question. A man had come to the door, had apologized and had promised to turn off the music. He had been tall, in his late 30s or early 40s, and had spoken German but the officers had thought that he might be a foreigner, pehaps a Yugoslav or a Russian.

This information helped Kessler establish the approximate time of death for the two corpses: certainly, it smelt about right. It also added weight to his hunch that neither the victims nor the murderers were German. The dead man in the hall had the kind of pudgy face and potato nose that Kessler associated with Slavs; and the woman's eyes and cheekbones, her black hair and sallow skin, suggested a touch of Tartar blood. The tape label was in Russian, and most of the books in the house were printed in Cyrillic script.

Clearly, they had passed themselves off as Germans. The bills for gas and electricity that he found in a drawer were addressed to

5

Hermann Ludwig, and in the same bureau was writing paper, some headed Hermann und Klara Ludwig with the address on Dubrowstrasse. It seemed likely, despite the absence of pictures, that the large rooms on the ground floor had been used as a gallery. There was little furniture, and spotlights pointed at rectangles of discoloration on the bare walls.

Only the kitchen, and one of the bedrooms upstairs, looked lived-in: the double bed was unmade and dirty dishes remained on the draining board of the sink. Kessler, in the kitchen, wrinkled his nose at the new odour of rotting rubbish.

'Phew,' said Dorn at his elbow.

'*Russische Gemütlichkeit*,' said Kessler.

'You think they are Russians?'

'Yes.'

'Mafia?'

'Perhaps.'

'Come back, DDR, all is forgiven'.

Kessler smiled. Like many West Berliners, he looked back with some nostalgia to the days when the wall had made it easy to control crime in their half of the city. As a boy, living in Wilmersdorf, he had watched the US aeroplanes fly supplies to the Tempelhof to break the Russian blockade; and less than two weeks before, when watching the attempted coup in Moscow on the television news, he had felt a twinge of that old *angst*; but by and large, life had been good in the divided city, certainly less complicated for a policeman than it was today with whole quarters of the city inhabited by Turks, Croats, Serbs, Hungarians, Czechs, Poles and Russians – even Vietnamese and Ethiopians – each with their own network of criminals and racketeers.

'What do you think?' he asked Dorn as they returned from the kitchen into the hall.

'Could be theft with trimmings . . .'

'Theft of what?'

'Paintings?'

Kessler looked around. 'And the trimmings?'

'The woman.'

'Why?'

'Why not? A little bit of what you fancy. Particularly if you've got to lose her anyway.'

Kessler looked uncertain. 'A professional thief wants to be in and out as quickly as he can.'

'Usually, yes.'

'He doesn't want to hang around listening to music or torturing women.'

'Unless the thief happens to be a pervert . . .'

'I don't think he did it for fun.'

'Why not?'

'Because every now and then he took the tape from her mouth.'

'To kiss her?' Dorn laughed.

Kessler remained grave. 'To let her speak. To give her a chance to tell them what they wanted to know.'

'And did she?'

Kessler hesitated. He thought of the look on her face. 'Yes, in the end, I think she probably did.'

Dorn shook his head. 'They can be really nasty, these Russian mafiosi.'

'They're certainly learning.'

'Well, so long as they only kill one another,' said Dorn, 'I don't really care.'

PART TWO

1992

September–December

TWO

Nikolai Gerasimov looked down from the office of General Savchenko in the Lubyanka at the bare plinth in the middle of Dzerzhinski Square. Where the statue of Felix Dzerzhinski had once stood, there remained only a stump. Nothing had yet replaced the founding father of the Cheka, the first Soviet secret police.

It was an unusually warm, even sultry, September day. The Lenin Hills were hidden behind the haze over Moscow. There was a move to call them the Sparrow Hills once again. Gerasimov had no view on the matter. He was neutral, even indifferent. Indeed, if anything had surprised him over the past months, it was the discovery of how little he cared when Marx and Lenin had followed Dzerzhinski into the dustbin of history. He had been an enthusiastic member first of the Komsomol and then the Party, but when President Yeltsin had suspended the Party with a stroke of a pen, his only thought had been: Will I lose my job? Will they abolish the KGB?

Both were unnecessary anxieties. Without the Party, the secret police became the only effective means for governing the country;

and Gerasimov had all the necessary qualities for preferment by the new regime. He was young, fit, good-looking, and spoke flawless English and German. His father was a retired army general, his wife the daughter of a physicist. Above all, he had that indifference to ideology, now called 'professionalism', that qualified him as an officer in the new security service of the Russian Federation, and had led to a request for his secondment from Service A for special duties under General Savchenko in the Twelfth Department.

Others had been sacked to placate Yeltsin and the democratic forces. Officers responsible for the nastier measures taken against the dissidents, had gone. So too had those known by Western intelligence agencies as the authors of some of the old KGB's more unsavoury operations; and a number suspected of aiding the KGB commander Kryuchkov in planning the coup.

Gerasimov's superior, General Savchenko, who now came back into his office, was secure. Posing for ten years as the London correspondent of a Moscow magazine, he had picked up some British mannerisms and habits of thought – a certain tolerance of eccentricity and aversion to dogma. He had helped brief Gorbachev before his first visit to London, and when drunk would boast that he had played cupid for Mikhail Sergeyevich and Mrs Thatcher. Now a senior officer on the staff of the Twelfth Department of the First Chief Directorate, one of the few sections which still had offices in the Lubyanka, he was known to be close to Vadim Bakatin, chief of the KGB since the coup.

Savchenko was not uncritical of the actions of the new regime. He had confided to Gerasimov that it had been a mistake to let such dangerous men loose on the world with only a small pension in inflationary times; and now he had been given the task of 'damage limitation' (he had used the English phrase to Gerasimov to describe his role), restructuring or closing networks that the sacked officers had controlled, and doing what he could to recover the large sums in foreign currency that they had been allocated by the KGB to finance their operations abroad.

'Enjoying the view?' he asked as Gerasimov turned away from the window.

'I was wondering who would replace Dzerzhinski on the plinth.'

The general rolled his eyes and sighed, as if to say: 'Don't start on that.' He was a squat, heavy man in a crumpled, shiny suit who, before the coup, had been trying to cut down his smoking to a pack a day. Now he was back to three.

'Save your energy,' he said to Gerasimov. 'Dzerzhinski is dead. We have enough trouble with the living.'

Savchenko threw the fat file that he had brought into the office onto his new desk. Both men sat down, Savchenko behind a battery of telephones on his desk, the most prestigious of them, the one with the hammer-and-sickle emblem which had connected him directly to the Central Committee, now a museum piece. Gerasimov faced him on a comfortable leather chair. The wood of the desk and the furniture matched the yellow beech veneer of the walls. The door to the office was upholstered with purple plastic, as was common in Russia, to preserve privacy by muffling the sound – a pretence in the past, thought Gerasimov, since there had been microphones hidden behind the wooden veneer. And now? The microphones were probably still there, but he doubted whether anyone could be bothered to listen.

'Orlov,' said Savchenko, patting the file on his desk. 'Andrei Orlov. Captain. Did you know him?'

'No.'

Savchenko gave a quick, penetrating look at Gerasimov – not mistrustful so much as thorough. 'Are you sure? He was at the Foreign Intelligence School?'

Gerasimov blushed at having answered so quickly. He thought back to his days at the Yurlovo. There had been a Gennady Orlov in his year, but he could remember no Andrei Orlov. He shook his head. 'I don't remember him.'

'No, well, he is a few years older.' Savchenko opened the file. 'And you never met him here, in the canteen, or socially, with some of your friends?'

'Not that I can recall.'

'There are a number of Orlovs . . . It is a common name.'

'Yes, of course. I know Gennady Orlov . . .'

13

'But not an Andrei?'

'No.'

Savchenko seemed satisfied. He looked down at the contents of the file and scratched the skin beneath the tousled hair on his head. 'This Orlov was one of our best men.' He paused. His breathing was wheezy. 'For most of his career he was with the First Chief Directorate. He did a spell in Africa for the Ninth Department, then in Washington for the First, and then worked in Moscow on the Washington desk. Two years ago, he was seconded to work in the Second Chief Directorate under General Khrulev. Khrulev, as you may know, committed suicide after the coup.'

'I had heard,' said Gerasimov.

'He, too, was one of our best men. A good comrade. Zealous . . . too zealous. A true believer at a time when . . .' Pause. Wheeze. 'At a time when it is prudent to retain a little scepticism . . . about everything and anything.' He looked up at Gerasimov. 'Loyalty to one's country, of course, and to the government of the day, but not to one's own convictions. Not to a cause.'

'I understand.'

'Professionalism . . . professionalism . . .' Savchenko repeated the word as if he was trying to inculcate that quality in himself as much as in Gerasimov.

He lit another cigarette. 'You know, with Kryuchkov in prison, and Khrulev dead, and most of Khrulev's people sacked or in disgrace, it is difficult to pick up the trail of what they were doing just from the files . . .' He paused and wheezed and flicked through the papers.

'Were they involved in ongoing operations?' asked Gerasimov.

Savchenko gave a sigh. 'Not according to the files. About two years ago, Khrulev put Orlov in charge of a particular operation in Germany. Khrulev had at one time served with the Eleventh Department and so had good contacts in Berlin.'

'The operation . . . ?'

'Kryuchkov had told Khrulev to stop the illegal export of icons. It was big business, as you know, but no one had thought much of it; in fact many of our own people packed the odd icon in their suitcase when they went abroad to get hold of some extra currency. It was a perk that went with the job. But Kryuchkov

14

disapproved of it – squandering the national heritage, cheating the state of foreign earnings, that kind of thing. Orlov was considered something of an expert . . .' He pushed the file over to Gerasimov.

Gerasimov looked first at the mugshot of a handsome, clean-shaven man with strong features and plenty of wavy brown hair.

'As you can see,' Savchenko said, 'Orlov's background is unusual. He is the son of Anatoly Orlov.'

'Anatoly Sergeyevich? The painter?'

'Precisely. Brezhnev's favourite artist.'

Gerasimov nodded. He remembered trudging round art galleries as a child, looking up at the enormous canvases painted by Anatoly Orlov portraying triumphant workers with square jaws and grim faces, clutching red banners against a radiant sky.

'They not only had an apartment in Moscow,' Savchenko went on, 'but also a dacha in Zhukovka, a gift from the Central Committee. Anatoly Sergeyevich held the Order of Lenin and any number of state prizes. His paintings are in every gallery in the Soviet Union.' He laughed, and then coughed, and then laughed again. 'They were still there, at any rate, when I last went into the gallery . . . but they may not be there now.'

Gerasimov looked down at the file. 'Andrei Orlov was not a painter?'

'No. But he knew and he cared about art. Khrulev felt that he could trust him, for that and for other reasons that do not appear in the file.'

'What other reasons?'

Savchenko waved his hand. 'He had good connections . . . But that is beside the point. He was an excellent Chekist. At the time of the coup, Orlov was out in the field. He was closing in on a man called Maslyukov in Berlin.'

'An icon smuggler?'

'A smuggler and a receiver. But more than that. An organizer and fixer. Almost a mastermind. In one of the memos, Khrulev estimates that more than half the icons smuggled out of the Soviet Union ended up with Maslyukov in Berlin.'

'Did he find him?'

'Yes. He found him but it was messy. Three of them went in,

Orlov and two others. Either they were expected, or Maslyukov guessed who they were. Maslyukov was killed. His wife . . .' Savchenko continued his train of thought for a moment in the silence. 'They used extreme methods to persuade her to talk. They recovered the icons. Orlov sent back ninety-seven, many of them major works, with a junior officer. His name's in the file.'

'Partovsky?'

'Yes. This Partovsky took a Volkswagen van on the ferry from Travemünde to Tallinn, then drove from Tallinn straight to the Tretyakov Gallery where they remain today. Orlov flew back two weeks later and was sacked.'

'Why? If the operation was a success?'

'Because of Khrulev. He had not only worked for Khrulev but it was thought that he shared Khrulev's point of view. He was offered a job on the security staff of the Tretyakov along with Partovsky. Partovsky accepted. Orlov refused.'

'So what did Orlov do?'

'He disappeared.'

'What do you mean?'

Savchenko frowned. 'What I say. He left the service. No one bothered to find out what he was up to. And now that we want him, he can't be found.'

'Why do we want him?'

Savchenko sighed. 'In reviewing the past operations of General Khrulev, I have come across certain . . . irregularities. Some of his files are missing – not just files like this' – Savchenko nodded at the file in front of Gerasimov – 'but also computer files, erased from the hard disk, and the back-ups removed from Khrulev's safe. Khrulev, you see, was permitted to work on his own. The icon operation, in particular, had to be secret, even within the Lubyanka, because so many of our own people had done business with these Maslyukovs. For this reason, Khrulev may have used agents in Germany who were known only to him. It is the files relating to these agents that have disappeared.'

'Could Khrulev have erased them before he killed himself?'

'It's possible.'

'Or do you think Orlov might have taken them?'

Savchenko shrugged. 'That too is possible.'

'Why would he want them?'

Savchenko lit another cigarette. 'I don't know. That is just what we would like to ask him. And there is something else. There is reason to believe that Orlov may have got hold of the Maslyukovs' money, but he only returned the icons. He may therefore be guilty of appropriating state funds.'

'So he may simply have gone back to the West to live on the Maslyukov's money?'

'If you study the file, you will see why that is unlikely. Orlov was not chosen by Khrulev simply for his talents. They were like-minded. Zealots. They shared the same ideals. And I cannot believe that Orlov has changed simply because of the failure of the coup.'

'So why did he want the money?'

'I don't know, but consider this. Khrulev sent Orlov to Berlin to recover the icons. Just as Orlov is about to pounce on the Maslyukovs, the coup occurs. Khrulev commits suicide. Does Orlov abort the operation? No. He goes ahead feeling, perhaps, that he now bears the responsibility for Khrulev's mission – not just the mission to recover the icons, but the mission in a much wider sense. Indeed, the failure of the coup, followed by the suspension of the Party, must have made it clear to Orlov that if the Party was to survive, it would have to go underground, and that if it was now cut off from the resources of the Soviet government, it would have to raise funds as best it could.'

'But if he got hold of the Maslyukovs' money, why has he now gone back to the West?'

'That is what I want you to find out.'

'Do we know where he is?'

Savchenko shrugged. 'The only thing we know for sure is that he took a night train to Kiev on the twelfth of October of last year. From there it is possible that he flew to Vienna on one of his Western passports, possibly posing as a German microbiologist who had been in Kiev for a convention.'

Gerasimov could not restrain a start of excited anticipation at the thought of a trip to the West. 'Do we know the names on his Western passports?'

'We know the passports he used for the icon operation. But he may have new ones. Orlov had friends in Directorate S. It's quite possible that someone arranged for replacements.'

Gerasimov leafed through the file. 'Who was the third man?'

'A non-commissioned officer, a Chechen called Kastiev. He returned, but not with Partovsky, and was then sacked.'

'And now?'

'He too cannot be found.'

'Was he sacked for his links with Khrulev?'

'No. He was . . .' Savchenko hesitated. 'His methods . . . his speciality, as it were, belonged to an earlier era.'

'Kryuchkov's?'

'More like Beria's. It is regrettable, in my view, that such people should ever have been employed by our state security. We may all have to do unsavoury things from time to time, but the Chechen is the kind of man . . . Well, in my view, he should be either in prison or an asylum, not the KGB.'

'Do you think he's with Orlov?'

Savchenko shrugged. 'Kastiev is cunning, even fanatical, but he speaks no languages. He would not have gone West without Orlov, so if we can find Orlov you will find Kastiev too.'

'What about their wives?'

'Kastiev was not married, and Orlov hasn't lived with his wife for several years.'

'All the same, she might know where he is.'

'Yes. But leave her alone for the moment. Her father is someone who still has powerful friends.'

'So should I pick up his trail in Vienna?' asked Gerasimov, trying not to show his eagerness.

Savchenko shook his head. 'No. At least, not yet. There must be someone in Moscow who knows where Orlov can be found. Read the file. Talk to the people here who knew Orlov. Talk to the officers still in the Lubyanka who served under Khrulev. There is also Partovsky at the Tretyakov and, if you get nowhere with other sources, there is Orlov's father and Orlov's wife. But be tactful. People's respect for our state security is not what it was.'

At six that evening, Gerasimov drove out of the Lubyanka in a beige Samara, his briefcase containing the file on Andrei Orlov on the seat beside him, and at once became caught in the traffic. Before the coup, he might have sped up one of the emergency lanes, confident that if stopped by the militia he could get away with it as an officer in the KGB; but now, in these democratic times, not even the generals in Zils used this privilege. It was prudent to be discreet.

Nor did Gerasimov resent the time spent in his 1989 Samara, a small car with only two doors but one of the only Soviet models with a modern, Western design. He had bought it with all his savings, and a loan from his father, the general; and he had added accessories, a Blaupunkt radio and a radar scanning device, brought back from trips to the West.

He crossed the ring road and continued north on Prospekt Mira towards the Sputnik Park. The engine hiccuped, the car faltered, but then picked up again. Gerasimov cursed the dirty petrol that clogged the carburettor. He would have to ring Georgi. The traffic stopped. He changed into neutral and revved the engine to prevent it dying. He looked at the faces of the other drivers, then at the people on the pavement making towards the Rizakaya metro station. As always, their expressions were gloomy and inscrutable. Two generations of terror had taught them to hide their feelings, and the present political changes were too recent to persuade them to drop their masks now.

Gerasimov looked at his own face in the mirror of the Samara. Did he look different? He was fitter and healthier than most Muscovites: the staff restaurant at the Lubyanka might not be quite as lavish as it was in the days of the KGB, but it still provided a better bill of fare than the average office or factory canteen. He also had regular medical checkups, access to a gym and, before the coup, an annual holiday with his family at the KGB's own holiday complex on the Black Sea. He still had the marks on his face from acne in adolescence, but then so did Harrison Ford, and Gerasimov liked to think that when he stuck out his jaw he bore a close resemblance to the American star.

Gerasimov also had a certain confidence in his bearing: an ordinary Muscovite could sense that he was one of the few who was accustomed to kick the many around. But even the most confident can face frustration, and as the Samara chugged forward, Gerasimov's forehead creased into a frown. He was hungry but was not sure that there would be anything for supper. The conference with Savchenko had gone on longer than expected. The special store in the Lubyanka had been closed when he came out, and the canteen had run out of supplies. He had called his wife to warn her, but her reply – a deep sigh – did not encourage him to hope that she had then gone out to join a queue at a state shop or squander her housekeeping allowance at the free market.

More likely, she would suggest going to some astronomically expensive cooperative restaurant, even if one could be found which would take roubles rather than dollars. And Gerasimov had run out of dollars. Surely some would have to be allocated for this investigation of Orlov? Without a trip to the West it was a tacky assignment. Gerasimov was trained to use his wits against an enemy; now he was being asked to investigate a colleague, and for all Savchenko's talk of professionalism, there was a political whiff about the job – a quiet purge by the democrats of those officers who might suffer from too much nostalgia.

Not that Gerasimov had much sympathy for the likes of Orlov. Gerasimov had first gone to the West in his twenties, and had been stunned by the prosperity, but had somehow been prepared by years of ideological training in school and university, the Komsomol and the Party, to accept that the capitalist countries were richer because they had got off to a good start. It was only when he was sent to Singapore in 1986 to pick up the products of some industrial espionage that he realized that Asian nations, in one generation, had overtaken the Communist nations of the Soviet Union and Eastern Europe. Why, if Socialism was superior, did Russians have to steal secrets from Chinks?

No doubt Gorbachev had reached the same conclusion: Gerasimov had come back to the new policy proclaimed at the 27th Party Congress – *glasnost* and *perestroika*. But two months later came the catastrophe at Chernobyl, and after that things had gone from bad to worse. A leopard can't change its spots. Too many had a vested interest in the *status quo*. Gerasimov had seen the way in which his own superiors had paid lip service to *glasnost* and *perestroika* while working behind the scenes to frustrate them. It was not just that they wanted to hang on to their privileges: it was also the impossibility of envisaging any other way. Free speech? Free elections? The slogans of the imperialists and capitalists they had been trained to fight. A free market? The only entrepreneurs in the Soviet Union were the gangsters the KGB were supposed to prosecute – the currency speculators, icon smugglers and black marketeers. It was like being told to go over to the enemy without a fight.

But when it had come to the crunch during the attempted coup last summer, no one could face the thought of a return to the old days either. Seeing *Vremya*, the nine o'clock news on television, was like watching a newsreel that someone had dug up from the archives of Stalin's days. The old rhetoric and bombast had raised the blood pressure of Gerasimov's father, the general; but the officers of the KGB's Alpha group had refused to storm the White House. The coup had collapsed, Yeltsin had triumphed, and Gerasimov's only thought had been for his job.

Any Muscovite who knew the block of flats on the Ulitsa Akademika Koroleva where Gerasimov now parked the Samara would have understood why. The flat which went with the job was easy to reach from the centre of town, had a fine view over the Sputnik Park and had been built to a far higher standard than that usually found in Soviet dwellings. Some of the apartments were assigned to Western journalists and one of Gerasimov's duties was to keep his eyes and ears open in the lobby and the lift – a small price to pay for two bedrooms, a living room and a kitchen and bathroom with Finnish fittings.

The furniture was Russian: the same glass-fronted bookcase and three-piece suite that could be found in a million other apartments. The large colour TV had been made in Riga, but there was a Panasonic video-recorder brought back from a trip to Frankfurt and a Sansui stereo system from the trip to Singapore. Of the books in the bookcase, some like Jack London's *The Iron Heel* were English-language editions published in Moscow dating from Gerasimov's days as a student in the Institute of International Relations. Others were Russian classics by Anton Chekhov and Maxim Gorky; and there were a few Western best-sellers – by Arthur Haley or Jeffrey Archer – whose tattered covers betrayed how often they had been lent to the Gerasimovs' friends.

Since the advent of the video, neither Gerasimov nor his wife Ylena had done much reading. Thanks to Georgi, they were able to get hold of pirated editions of most Western movies, some of which Ylena watched two or three times. Her job in the library of the All Union Institute of Geology was not challenging: she had persuaded her doctor to certify that she was susceptible to migraines and so often returned in the early afternoon to watch yet again a grainy copy of *Pretty Woman* or *Gone with the Wind*.

She also followed all of the soap operas, both Brazilian or home-grown, and when Gerasimov entered his flat that evening he was greeted not by the smell of cooking but the sound of the TV. He hung up his coat in the closet in the hall, removed his shoes, put his briefcase in the bedroom and then went into the kitchen to confirm that there was nothing either in the fridge or on the stove. That established, he went to the living room to try to disengage his wife's attention from the television and discuss what they should eat that night.

Ylena was curled up on the sofa, a box of biscuits at her side. She looked at Gerasimov for less than a second, to let him know that she knew he was there; then her attention went back to the screen. Gerasimov's spirits sank when he saw that most of the biscuits had been eaten: Ylena was a woman who acted on whim, and she only thought about food if she was hungry.

Like Gerasimov, she was in her early thirties and was still attractive with brown hair, blue eyes and a porcelain pale complexion; but already the soft femininity found in Russian girls had been replaced by a fixed look of dissatisfaction. In the Soviet Union, dreams had faded fast, and if Ylena as the wife of an officer in the KGB had been pampered in relation to other Soviet wives, with the flat, the car and holidays in the Crimea, her life nevertheless fell far short of the glossy luxury she saw on videos from the West, and now, since the coup, had fallen shorter still.

Nor had her privileged status saved her from the wear and tear of married life where the pill was unobtainable, even to the wife of an officer in the KGB, and condoms were so precious that they were washed after use and hung on a line to dry. She had had a baby, Sasha, soon after they had married; after that, four abortions in seven years; then nothing – neither sex nor abortions – until Georgi came up with some pornographic videos, after which came a short-lived revival of their sex lives followed by two more abortions.

Gerasimov suspected that she slept from time to time with some geologist at the institute – probably behind the cupboards containing specimens of rock – or even with her boss, Professor Bloch: someone had recently supplied her with tights and tampons, and he had noticed a box of Roget et Gallet soap in the bathroom. She had told him that her friend Liubov had been given them by a French scientist who visited the botanical institute where she worked. Gerasimov had let it go at that. After all, he had affairs from time to time with typists and translators at the Lubyanka.

They stayed together, or had until then, partly because of Sasha, partly because it served the interests of both. Ylena liked the flat, and the perks that went with Gerasimov's job. Gerasimov knew that apparent stability would help his career, as did his connection with his father-in-law who was in good standing with the Party. Now, of course, the Party had been suspended and even those like Gerasimov who had kept their jobs in the security service of the Russian Federation could no longer count on the perks that had kept Ylena happy. The cursory glance, and the sour look she had on her face when she finally turned off the television, were the punishment meted out to the now not so mighty hunter who had failed to bring home a rabbit for the pot.

'Where's Sasha?'

'With my mother. She had a chicken.'

'Couldn't you have bought a chicken?'

'You said you could get some sausage.'

'I missed it. I was busy.'

She pouted and shrugged. 'It was too late to go out, and anyway, do you know what they cost, now, on the market? Who can afford a chicken except the spivs and profiteers?'

'Your mother . . .'

'She was given it by her friend Natalia. She's been at their dacha.'

'That was kind of her.'

'She's done things for them.'

Gerasimov glanced at the cabinet where he knew there was a bottle of vodka still a third full. He longed for a drink but knew that if he started drinking on an empty stomach, with Ylena in that mood, it might end in a squalid brawl.

To try to placate both his wife and his growling stomach, he gave up all thought of thrift and suggested eating out.

It did not produce the enthusiasm in Ylena that he had expected. She sighed. 'Where?'

'The place on Petrovsky Boulevard.'

'They only take currency.'

'Since when?'

She shrugged. 'Lubov told me. They went there last week.'

'What about the new cooperative near the Kazan station? I was told that they take roubles.'

'They won't let you in unless they know you.'

'I'll show them my service card.'

She laughed – with derision, not merriment. 'Then they'll cut your throat.'

'I'll call Georgi. He'll get us in.'

'Don't call Georgi.'

'Why not?'

She wrinkled her nose.

'I've got to call him anyway about the car.'

She looked away. Gerasimov went to the telephone in the hall. It was only a year since Georgi had had a telephone, but his number had already been added to the list pinned to a board on the wall. Gerasimov dialled the first digits, then stopped and with his left hand disconnected the line. Inexplicably, he suddenly felt that he should collect his thoughts and consider the tone he should adopt in talking to Georgi. He frowned, irritated with himself for hesitating in this way. Georgi, after all, was his creation – a young fixer who in the old days would have been condemned as a workshy parasite, but who in the Brezhnev years became an indispensable bridge between the theory and practice of life in a socialist state.

Gerasimov had first met him outside the block of flats in the grim suburb where he had lived before his promotion: a sly, ingratiating young Armenian who had offered to clean his car. Gerasimov had given him the job for twenty kopeks, and then casually asked if he knew where he could get any windscreen wiper blades: he had forgotten to remove them the night before and they were gone in the morning.

Georgi delivered new blades that evening, and offered replacements for the old Lada's balding tyres. Gerasimov had known that they would be certainly stolen, but he did the deal; and in the years that followed he came to rely upon Georgi not just to maintain his cars, but to provide the mundane things that were not to be found even in the KGB's special stores: washers, bath plugs, fuse wire . . . In return Gerasimov would supply Georgi with Western goods that were surplus to his own requirements: packets of razor blades and Marlboros, bottles of cognac, jars of Nescafé and tins of ham.

By the time Gerasimov and Ylena had moved to the flat on the Ulitsa Akademika Koroleva, Georgi, now in his twenties, had expanded into more complex fixing for a wider clientele including some of the foreign journalists who lived in the same block. Foreign currency, airline tickets, residence permits were available to all those who could pay. Gerasimov remained Georgi's most favoured customer; Georgi had found him the Samara, and would himself fetch and deliver it just to change the oil. In return, Gerasimov protected Georgi from the militia who were always on his tail. He let it be known that Georgi's dealings were of some value to the KGB, and such was the residual fear of that organization that impending charges of illegal currency dealing and black marketeering were dropped.

In the year since the coup, all that had changed. With its boss behind bars, the KGB was demonstrably no longer above and beyond the law. Now it was not Gerasimov's influence but Georgi's bribes and intimidation of potential witnesses that kept the militia off Georgi's back. He could well afford the bribes: his business was booming. He had a team working under him, some looking less like fixers than thugs. He still saw to the Samara, sending someone to fetch it whenever Gerasimov called, but he himself had a two-year-old Mercedes and a three-roomed apartment near the Kremlin.

It was the realization that it was becoming absurd to call this flourishing entrepreneur about the clogged carburettor of his Samara that made Gerasimov hesitate before making his call. He turned towards the living room, as if to consult Ylena, but then remembered that she was against calling Georgi. He looked back at Georgi's number on the board above the telephone. Why was he so nervous? Nothing Georgi had said suggested that he was no longer willing to fix the Samara: in fact he had been exceptionally friendly and unctuous when they last met. Almost certainly, and quite rightly, he still felt indebted for services rendered in the past. Nevertheless, it might be more in keeping with Georgi's new status to mention the clogged carburettor in passing, and ask about the restaurant first.

He dialled the number. His call was answered by Georgi's wife. Gerasimov could hear music and voices in the background. Georgi came to the telephone.

'Georgi.'

'Nikolai. Just one moment.' He shouted to someone to turn the music down.

'We thought of going out tonight to that cooperative near the Kazan station. Do you know if it's any good?'

'Don't touch it.'

'Ah. Where would you suggest?'

'Are you at home?'

'Yes.'

'I'll pick you up in half an hour.'

'If you really . . .'

'Don't worry. I'll be there.'

The Mercedes was driven by one of the bulky bodyguards. Georgi sat in the back; he was without his wife.

'Ylena sends her apologies,' said Gerasimov as he climbed in beside Georgi.

'She's not hungry?' The young man grinned, showing some teeth capped in gold.

Gerasimov shrugged. 'She says she's tired.'

'Never mind.'

The car moved off, the driver barging into the traffic as if the

Mercedes was an official Zil. 'It's good to see you, Nikolai,' said Georgi with a trace of patronage in his tone. 'You've been on my mind. There are many things we could talk about. This is now the land of opportunity, you know, for those who know how to seize it.'

'I dare say.' Gerasimov glanced uneasily at the young man beside him. He had grown plumper in the months since the coup, and wore a dark blue suit. He was balding at the temples, which made him seem as old as Gerasimov when in fact he was not yet thirty. His breath smelt of garlic and tobacco.

'Did you get the videos I sent over?'

'Yes.'

'*Pretty Woman?*'

'Yes.'

'A classic . . . I show it to the girls so that they can learn. Class! Style!'

Gerasimov was not sure what girls he was speaking about: certainly not the friends of Georgi's daughter since the daughter was only two.

'The place I'm taking you to is new. I want to know what you think. I have an interest in it. Fifty per cent.'

Again, Gerasimov smarted at the patronizing tone, but felt relieved nonetheless to think that Georgi would pay the bill.

'There's good money in these cooperatives but they can be a nightmare because you have to ensure your own supplies which means pay-offs right down the line . . .' He stretched out an arm and pointed his finger out of the window. 'I mean right down the line – to Georgia, Armenia, Azerbaijan . . .'

He continued to explain the economics of owning a restaurant as they drove down the Nikitski Boulevard and finally came to a stop in a side street near the Arbat. Georgi went to a door on the ground floor of a nondescript building; it could have been to an office or a flat. He knocked twice. A small hatch cut into the door opened, a pair of eyes looked through. Georgi said his name. The hatch closed, the door opened, and both Georgi and Gerasimov were let in.

The inside of the building had been done up in style. Gerasimov had been to half a dozen of the better cooperatives, and this was on a par with the best. A girl took their coats, and the head waiter, wearing a black tie, led Georgi to a corner table with a civility that was quite unknown in the former Soviet Union. The carpet, the chairs, the tablecloth, the cutlery, were all certainly from abroad.

The restaurant was about half full. The light was dim and there was an air of discretion about the diners, who either kept their eyes down or looked at those at the same table. Gerasimov thought he recognized a senior officer from the Lubyanka but he was with a younger woman so Gerasimov looked away. Almost half the diners had the swarthy look of the Caucasus, and some were greeted by Georgi as he crossed the room.

Almost as soon as they sat down, a carafe of vodka was placed on the table, soon followed by small plates of chopped-up herring, celery, tomato, and a medium-sized jar of caviar. Georgi poured out the vodka. 'To our wives,' he said and they clinked glasses.

'Yes,' said Gerasimov, 'to our wives.'

It was the first of a number of toasts. The first carafe of vodka was soon emptied and, without having to ask, a second appeared. The food took longer; they were given salad but then had to wait a good half-hour for some bortsch. Gerasimov, finding Georgi's conversation irksome, only too readily allowed him to fill his glass. He talked about the past and the future, about business and pleasure, about taking pleasure in business and making a business out of pleasure. What he said was of little interest – increasingly drunken drivel – and it was the tone rather than the content that annoyed Gerasimov, vacillating between unctuousness and condescension, both appealing to Gerasimov for approbation and yet somehow sneering at him for being there, sponging off his former minion.

Both men became drunk. Georgi sent for a bottle of French wine – Gerasimov dared not think what it cost – and then insisted that Gerasimov help him drink it. Three-quarters of an hour after the bortsch, the waiter served them with dry pork chops and some noodles. By now Gerasimov had lost his appetite but he could hardly forgo such a luxury. He forced the food down, listening as he did so to Georgi's increasingly slurred exposition of what he called 'a Russian interpretation of the new world order'.

'You see, Nikolai, my dear friend, we have to understand that there is only one path to take and that is the same path taken by the Americans because Russia is like America – a big, big country – and that is the path we should have taken and would have taken if that swine Lenin and all those Jews hadn't hijacked the country and led us down the road to our present ruin. Decades lost . . . How many decades? Nineteen seventeen, nineteen twenty-seven . . .' He started to count them off on his fingers but became muddled. 'Years. Years and years, wasted, going down the wrong road, but now we're on the right road, but way back, way back . . . We're like America a hundred years ago, and we have to go through the same historical processes as they did . . . with gold rushes and Al Capone . . .'

Gerasimov scarcely listened to what Georgi was saying. This lecture by the little twerp on world history was as pretentious as it was patronizing. What did he know? He had never even graduated from high school, and here he was droning on like a professor. Yet despite his inattention, and the effect of the vodka and wine, Gerasimov remembered his clogged carburettor, and all the time was wondering how he could slip it into the conversation.

'. . . and the Godfather. Did you see the videos of *The Godfather*? Yes? Marlon Brando, Al Pacino. You know, some of the boys think I look a little like Al Pacino?'

'Why not? They say I look like Harrison Ford.'

Georgi laughed. 'Well, I'd say Kevin Costner. Elliott Ness in *The Untouchables*? You must have seen that. I sent it over to Ylena. It was a bit fuzzy but still . . . You should learn from movies like that. The militia, they're corrupt, like the Chicago police. You KGB men, you're the G-men. The Untouchables.'

Gerasimov frowned. Had he seen *The Untouchables*? He could not remember. 'I don't think I saw it.'

'I'll send another copy. And some Dutch porno – fantastic stuff. Women with women! You can't imagine . . .'

Gerasimov forced a grin to establish that he was one of the boys, but at the same time shook his head: 'No, we're not into that at present.'

The waiter put some pink ice cream in front of Gerasimov.

Georgi waved his away, lit a cigarette, and took a long look at Gerasimov through narrowed eyes as he exhaled the smoke towards him across the table. 'Not into *it* . . .' he said, 'or not into *her?*'

While Gerasimov had discussed his defunct sex life with a number of his friends, he had never considered that he was on those kind of terms with Georgi, but having eaten caviar and drunk a good half pint of vodka at Georgi's expense, and faced now with a goblet full of pink ice cream, it seemed churlish not to confide in him, man to man. 'Well, you know how it is . . .'

'Sure,' said Georgi, 'but a man's a man . . .'

'I get by,' said Gerasimov, the roguish grin back on his face.

'And a woman's a woman.'

'Sure.'

'We're friends, aren't we?'

'Of course.'

'So let me give you a bit of advice . . .'

Gerasimov kept a grin on his face and nodded.

'A woman's a little like a car . . .'

At last, thought Gerasimov. The carburettor.

'She needs fuel.'

'Don't we all?'

'The higher the octane, the better she runs.'

'Unless the carburettor . . .'

Georgi raised his hand, frowning at this interruption. 'Wait. Let me finish. She runs better on high octane – pretty clothes, nice restaurants, holidays in the Crimea . . .'

'Sure.'

'Not just Ylena. They're all the same.'

Gerasimov nodded, waiting patiently to return to the carburettor.

'But they also need servicing, Nikolai. Regular servicing, thorough servicing . . .'

'I know.'

'And Ylena hasn't been getting that from you . . .'

'Well, from time to time . . .'

'Nikolai.' Georgi looked at him almost with reproof. 'I know the score. She told me.'

'She told you?'

'You tell me if I'm wrong.'

'You're not wrong, but . . . but when did she tell you?'

Georgi sighed. 'Nikolai, we're friends, aren't we?'

'Of course, but . . .'

'Nikolai, I can't bear to see a good woman go to waste. I've been seeing Ylena . . .'

'You've been seeing . . . You've been *fucking* Ylena?' Gerasimov gripped the side of the table, his knuckles white with the force of his grip.

Georgi sighed and stood up. 'Let's get out into the fresh air.' He sauntered away from the table and signed a chit of some kind at the head waiter's desk.

Gerasimov followed him dumbly. He was dizzy from the drink. They stood side by side, silently, waiting for their coats. Gerasimov could not decide what he should say or what he should do. He could pound Georgi to a pulp. Once out into the street, he *would* pound him into a pulp: his KGB training would more than make up for the extra years; but then who would see to his Samara?

Out on the street, the fresh air increased the dizziness and sense of dislocation. Had Georgi really said that he had been sleeping with Ylena? He gripped the lapel of Georgi's fancy Italian overcoat. 'Are you telling me, just like that, that you've been screwing my wife?'

'Your wife? She's not your wife. She's Ylena, a fantastic woman, Nikolai, getting plump, the way our women do, but really fantastic.' He shook his head in wonderment. 'I mean, how you could let something like that lie fallow?'

Gerasimov drew back his arm to strike Georgi, but before he could bring his fist forward he felt it gripped from behind. He was held by Georgi's driver.

Georgi shook his head in affected sorrow as if Gerasimov had let him down. 'Come on, Nikolai. Don't get so upset. If it wasn't me, it would have been someone else.'

Gerasimov dropped his arm and, released by the driver, staggered a few paces away. He looked up to the top storey of the building on the other side of the street, then higher up to the sky.

31

There were no stars, just dreary cloud coloured by the dim orange light of the street lamps.

Georgi took him by the arm. 'Come on.'

Gerasimov allowed himself to be led back to the Mercedes and slumped into the back seat with Georgi beside him. For a while they sat in silence; then in a flat tone of voice Gerasimov said: 'Send someone to see to the Samara, will you? There's something wrong with the carburettor.'

Georgi looked ahead. 'I'll do that, and more.' He leaned forward and said to the driver: 'Go to the Cosmos.' Then he turned to Gerasimov. 'I dare say you could do with a service, too.'

'What?'

'Let's go see some of my friends.'

Gerasimov closed his eyes, his head resting on the back of his seat. He longed to go to bed but not with Ylena. How could she? With Georgi! With the greasy Armenian errand boy! Why? For the soap? The tights? Was is just Russian women, or did all women barter with their cunts?

The Mercedes drove up a ramp of the Cosmos Hotel. Gerasimov opened his eyes. He looked up at the tall Western-style tower block: still no stars. He climbed out after Georgi. Four or five girls, beautifully dressed and made up, clustered around Georgi. 'Get us in, Georgi, please . . .' Georgi glanced towards the doorman, then turned to two of the girls. 'You're with me.'

As he passed the doorman, Georgi slipped him a roll of dollars. In the immense atrium of the hotel, Gerasimov waited with the driver while Georgi went to the desk. The girls hovered a short way away, their faces straining to give an air of sophistication.

Georgi returned with a key. They all went up in the lift. Georgi gave the key to the driver who gently took Gerasimov's arm and led him along the corridor. Georgi kept the two girls by the lift. Gerasimov looked back and saw them talking. The driver opened the door and led Gerasimov into the suite. 'Look, TV, minibar, bathroom . . .' He showed him round with a certain pride. Then the girls came in, Georgi behind them.

'Have a good time,' Georgi said to Gerasimov.

Gerasimov looked at him with no expression. 'Tell the bitch . . .'

'Forget it. I've got other things to do.'

'The Samara . . .'

'Sure. I won't forget the Samara.'

Georgi left the room with his driver. The girls came back into the room. One pouted. The other giggled. The pouter sidled up to Gerasimov. 'So, sexy, how do you like it?' She loosened his tie and undid a button of his shirt. The giggler was smaller and blonde. 'Both together, or one at a time?' A hand went under his shirt and stroked his skin; another undid the buckle of his belt. 'He's generous, your friend Georgi,' said the pouter. 'You've got both of us all night.'

'So take your time, big boy,' said the blonde, 'take your time.'

He lay back on the bed like a patient in a hospital, and like nurses the girls removed his clothes. They then took off their own, careful not to crease the blouses and skirts, and climbed back onto the bed in their exotic Western underclothes and started kissing and nibbling his skin. Like eager young actresses, they did what they had seen on the videos but inexpertly confused the roles of tooth and tongue. Typical Russian whores, thought Gerasimov as he flinched at the pain. They even get a blow job wrong.

THREE

The young American art historian, Francesca McDermott, had slept little when crossing the Atlantic from Boston to Frankfurt and so dozed off on the connecting flight to Berlin. She awoke only as the plane approached Tegel, now one of the two airports serving Berlin. She looked down out of the window. It was September. The trees of the Spandau Forest were already losing their leaves. The pale sun reflected off the water of the Tegeler See. The plane turned to make its approach: Francesca could make out the Radio Tower and the Olympic Stadium.

Ten years before, when Francesca had last been to Berlin, Tegel had been in the French sector of the city. Now that Germany and Berlin were reunited, there was little sign of occupation by the Western powers beyond the fact that Lufthansa was not yet permitted to fly from Frankfurt to Berlin: the line carrying Francesca was Air France. Everything else about the airport was German, West German – the cleanliness, the efficiency, the brisk courtesy of the airport personnel. Since it was now classified as an internal flight, there was no passport check; but no one curious about Francesca's nationality would have had to see her passport to know that she was a citizen of the United States. She was tall, healthy and handsome, pert Irish features on a body that had been fed steak, not potatoes, and now jogged every morning and played squash at weekends. She walked towards the baggage claim rondel with the assurance of a well-educated, well-dressed and well-paid professional woman from the land of the free; a competitive glint in the eye; an elegance that is composed rather than seductive; and a similar sexual allure – healthy rather than luxuriant, proclaiming that a woman is a woman, not just the plaything of a man.

Ten years before, Francesca McDermott had looked different – not quite a hippie, because she was already a graduate student, but rarely out of jeans, and with the hair, now so well cut at such great cost, then gathered in a ponytail by an elastic band. For this reason, when she came to the gate, the woman she recognized as Sophie Diederich did not recognize her. And that was just as well. Francesca's face betrayed the shock she felt at the sight of Sophie – not simply because Sophie, who was anyway five years older than Francesca, now looked a good ten years older than that, but because in all other ways she was so entirely *un*changed – her hair in greasy wisps, her clothes the same dungarees worn in dissident circles back in the 1980s.

All sorts of reasons for Sophie's wretched appearance passed through Francesca's mind – stress, diet, persecution, not least the month she had spent in prison in the old DDR: but even so, she thought, a woman can make the best of herself or at least appear to try, and a look of sisterly determination crossed Francesca's face as she pushed the baggage trolley towards her friend.

Sophie Diederich, who had not had the advantage of recognizing Francesca in advance, could not hide an expression of slight confusion as she realized that the tall, elegant woman in a beige suit and red silk scarf held at her throat by an antique brooch was the same Francesca that she had known ten years before; and when she did, although her face broke into a smile of unreserved delight, she checked the impulse to hug her as if it might now be somehow inappropriate. Francesca, both more composed and more controlled, pushed the trolley aside and with a cry of

'Sophie, I can't believe it!' embraced and kissed the small woman in dungarees.

They went to the car park where Francesca was again a little taken aback by the sight of Sophie Diederich's car, an East German Wartburg with a two-stroke engine that puttered like an overworked sewing machine as they set off down the motorway towards the Stadtring. Surely the wife of the new Prussian Minister of Culture should be driving a BMW or, at worst, a Volkswagen?

'We'll go down the Ku'damm,' said Sophie cheerfully, 'so you can see how it's all changed . . .'

She drove haphazardly, as if realizing that the shiny Western cars would give her old Wartburg a wide berth. She chattered in German as she drove; Francesca, her German now rusty, sometimes found it hard to follow. 'Dearest Francesca, it is so wonderful that you are here – there is so much to tell you – and you, you are a professor? No, a lecturer . . . but Dr . . . *Dr* McDermott . . . and from that thesis that you were working on here on the Bauhaus, yes?'

'That's right.'

'And it was just like fate when they said we must get an expert from America, perhaps even Francesca McDermott, because then the Americans will be more likely to lend their paintings, and Stefan agreed and so, even, in the end, did the Russian, and it never occurred to me that this was *you*, our Francesca, but then Stefi said it was you and that he had invited you over because now Stefi – you know he's a minister? – he can decide these things, and he has only to flick his fingers and there is the money because all the parties want the New Grouping – that's Stefi's party – to support them in a coalition, and they know that Stefi can influence them one way or another.'

'Is he the leader?'

'You know, the group has no leader. We had too much of leaders before with Ulbricht and Honecker. And it's not a party, as such, only a group, because we had too much, much too much, of the word party . . .'

'I can believe it.'

'But Stefi really is a first among equals. The candlelit vigils – you must have read about them or seen them on the TV? – he was among the first to organize them when it was still dangerous, very dangerous . . . No one imagined – no one even dreamed – that the whole thing would collapse so quickly.'

'It was incredible.'

'Incredible, yes. And if it wasn't for Gorbachev and Shevardnadze there would have been no change from Communism to democracy. The wall would still be standing. And thank God for Yeltsin, too, but he is unfair to Gorbachev, I think . . . At any rate, for us Germans Gorby is a hero, a big hero, but there also had to be little heroes, and Stefi was a little hero . . . He organized the vigils, and he was on the citizen's committee that took control of the Stasi headquarters here in Berlin.'

'With all those files?'

'The files! God help us. Six million of them! They started to burn them, you know, because they thought the Stasi would be back; but then they realised that they were burning the records of the spies themselves – the IMs, the "unofficial collaborators" – but Francesca, if you knew . . . Our friends, our dearest and closest friends in the Evangelical Church, the Peace Now movement, and the Ecological Group – Stasi spies! All along! Spies and provocateurs!'

'I read about it, Sophie. It must have been terrible . . . As bad as anything that went before.'

'In a way it was worse . . . Ah, look, here we are in the Ku'damm. You remember? You had a room near the Savignyplatz, didn't you?'

'Yes. On Schlüterstrasse.'

'It is so nice around there, so lively. And then, we could only imagine it.'

'You haven't moved West?'

'No. God forbid. That's what they expect. A house in Charlottenburg! A Mercedes! But Stefi won't hear of it. We are where we always were. You'll see. Nothing has changed.'

Francesca looked out at the shops and cafés on the Kurfürstendamm – not so very different, now, from what she remembered from ten years before. 'And have you seen your Stasi file?' she asked Sophie, to get back to the subject they had touched on before.

37

'No.'

'Are you going to?'

Sophie sighed. 'Perhaps. I don't know. Stefi's against it.'

'Why?'

'He says the wounds will never heal if we keep reopening them, and that he would rather not know if some of our friends were Stasi spies. He prefers to give them all the benefit of the doubt.'

'I can understand that.'

'You see, when the Wall came down we were all so deliriously happy we could not believe it, but now, only three years later, we see the problems . . .'

The two women in the Wartburg had now passed the Kaiser Wilhelm Memorial Church at the foot of the Kurfürstendamm – its ruins preserved as a memorial to World War II – and now turned towards the Tiergarten. 'There are so many *practical* problems.' Sophie went on. 'The sewers, the electricity . . . Did you know that the grid supplying East Berlin was controlled from Kiev? There are the industrial and economic problems . . . Politically, we are now one country, but economically the two halves of Germany are half a century apart . . . There is also the *moral* problem, the lack in the provinces of the old DDR of any positive values, any values at all . . . Look, here's the Goddess of Victory on top of her column, and there's the Brandenberg Gate.'

Francesca looked out at these landmarks through the windows of the Wartburg. 'But no more checkpoints?'

'No more checkpoints, just traffic jams. There still aren't that many places where you can cross from one half of the city to the other.' She jerked the car forward. 'I'll try by the Invalidenstrasse . . . We can see Unter den Linden some other time.'

'There's no hurry . . .'

'Does that mean you'll stay?'

'I would certainly like to,' said Francesca, 'if it can be arranged.'

'Oh,' said Sophie with a laugh, 'they don't understand anything about contracts or salaries or anything like that. You can ask for anything you like.'

Francesca blushed. She had not so much been thinking of remuneration – her salary on sabbatical would pay the mortgage on her apartment in Boston – but rather of status and authority

. . . But that would come later. Now, while she was alone with Sophie, she wanted to catch up on her personal life.

'Sophie,' she said quietly. 'What happened to Paul?'

'Ah, Paul . . .'

'I mean, not just *to* him, but between you and him, because when I was here . . .'

'We were married. I know.'

'And you seemed so happy . . .'

For the first time since Francesca's arrival, Sophie Diederich appeared almost subdued. 'Paul . . .' she began; then she hesitated and said: 'Poor Paul.' And then added: 'You know, after the Communists were thrown out, he was made mayor of his village?'

'Where's that?'

'North of Berlin. Bechtling. Not far from Dierberg.'

'Does he live there?'

'He is the pastor.'

'Wasn't that kind of quiet, after his position here in Berlin?'

'Of course but, you see, he was ill, very ill. He was in a sanatorium. He simply couldn't cope . . .'

'With what?'

'His work. His position. The expectations people had of him.' She became agitated as she spoke. 'You see, now we are finding out what terrible things they did to men like Paul . . .'

'Who?'

'The Stasi. They had a word – *Zersetzung* . . .'

'Subversion?'

'Obliteration. They planned to undermine, crush, destroy anyone who opposed them in any way, and Paul, beccause he was first the chaplain to the Protestant students, and then a dissident . . .'

'But Stefi was a dissident too.'

'Of course. But Stefi was stronger because he could be humorous about everything whereas Paul was always so earnest. You know, it was enough to worry about the Stasi but he was also always anxious about God and the devil . . .'

'So what happened? Did he have a nervous breakdown?'

'Yes. He really went almost mad, and it was terrible for him but

39

also for me and the children. Thank God Stefi was there . . . He was really wonderful to Paul and to me, when Paul could no longer cope with anything . . . with his work, but also with me and with his family. You see, when he left the sanatorium, he would not come home. He went back to his parents in Bechtling. He would not see me. He would not talk to me. It was then that Stefi took me on.'

'I guess Stefi loved you a little as well?' suggested Francesca.

Sophie brightened up. 'Do you think so? Do you remember that?'

Francesca looked out of the window. 'He was always one for the girls.'

'Yes,' said Sophie sweetly. 'He was one for the girls, and yet he chose me.'

As she said this, they crossed the railway bridge on the Invalidenstrasse and reached the band of raked earth which had been the free-fire zone on the eastern side of the Wall. Once in East Berlin, Francesca was astonished by how little had changed, not just since the reunification of the city, but in the ten years that had passed since she had last been there. The buildings were uniform, drab and poorly maintained – mile upon mile of apartment blocks with only the occasional shop or café.

When they reached Friedrichshain, Sophie turned into the Wedekindstrasse and stopped the car outside the pre-war block of flats that Francesca remembered so vividly from ten years before. Here again, nothing appeared to have changed. The vestibule was dark and shabby, and all at once Francesca felt extraordinarily conspicuous in her Burberry raincoat and beige suit. She was embarrassed by the size of the smart suitcase that Sophie now heaved out of the back of the Wartburg. Francesca tried to take it from her. 'No, no,' Sophie insisted. 'We're used to hard labour.' And, as she lugged it up the two flights of dank stairs, she added: 'There were no deliveries under socialism. We had to carry our furniture, fridge, everything, up these dreadful stairs.'

She opened the door to her flat and went in. Francesca stood on the threshold, remembering the conspiratorial visits she had paid to this same apartment either to attend the readings of the dissidents' unpublished works, or simply to spend an evening with Sophie and Paul. Then, it had been furnished with old pieces of furniture given to Paul by his father, including a piano at which Paul had accompanied Sophie singing Schubert *Lieder*, his earnest features gradually relaxing as the music calmed his mind, his eyes looking gently up at Sophie whose thin little voice had them all enchanted.

Now Paul had gone and the appearance of the apartment had completely changed. Gone were the carpets and rugs, the oil paintings and photographs of Paul's parents and grandparents – everything, in fact, that had given the apartment a flavour of Germany before the war. Now the floors were sanded, and the furniture was Scandinavian in style – a squat white sofa, two beanbags, one black, the other red. In the place of the piano there was a large television, and there were now contemporary prints and paintings on the wall – of a mediocrity, Francesca decided with her professional eye, that could only be found in Eastern Europe.

'My, it's changed, Sophie,' said Francesca as she came in.

Sophie took this as a compliment. 'The hi-fi comes from before reunification, and the records. They were cheap in the DDR.'

'So were the books, I guess,' said Francesca, looking at the shelves which on two of the walls went from floor to ceiling.

'And there was not much else to do but read,' said Sophie.

'Well, they do furnish a room.'

'Cheaper than wallpaper, even if one could get it.'

'And the paintings?'

'That's by Brigitte Schönemann, a friend. That's by a Czech friend, Jaroslav Zermak . . . In fact, they're all by friends.'

Francesca crossed the room to study the paintings – the Schönemann, a drab pastiche of 1960s abstractionism, and the one by the Czech, a daub like a squashed cockroach except that the real thing would have been more impressive.

'Of course, you're an art critic now,' said Sophie.

'Not an art critic, no, an art historian. I know very little about anything outside my field . . .'

'Russian art?'

41

'Experimental Russian Art: 1863 to 1922.' She rattled this off: it had been the title of her thesis.

'Wonderful,' said Sophie.

Francesca turned and smiled. 'Well, it's a happy coincidence if that's what Stefi wants to know about.'

Sophie almost jumped up and down with excitement. 'Listen, we mustn't talk about it now. Wait until Stefi gets back this evening. Now, we'll have some coffee and cake.' She patted her stomach over the dungarees as she made for the kitchen. 'I'm so fat that I don't normally touch them, but in your honour, Francesca . . .'

'And what about me?'

Sophie looked back. 'You're thin as a rake, and anyway, you can afford to get a little fat, you're so tall. Now come into the kitchen while I boil the water and tell me about your life.'

What each woman wanted to know about the other was the state of their affections, but, as Francesca had already discovered, the story of Sophie's divorce from Paul was clearly a painful one to remember; and Francesca, while she had many friends in the United States who were divorced, could not get over a sense of sadness and perplexity that Sophie was now married to the quick-witted and devious Stefi, and not the gentle, heroic Paul. She was therefore quite willing to wait until she and Sophie had re-established the intimacy that had existed ten years before, and be the first to unload the secret details of her life that in any case were not so secret since Francesca had nothing to hide. Her parents were fine, still in Ann Arbor; her father was now retired and they travelled a lot; her brother worked for NASA in Cape Canaveral; her sister was an associate editor on *See the World* magazine in New York City. Francesca herself lectured on Russian art at Boston University: her book on the Russian constructivists had come out two years before and had been well received. She had a nice apartment in Boston with a view of the Charles River which she had shared for a while with a friend who taught at MIT but now lived in alone.

'You aren't married?' asked Sophie.

Francesca laughed – a touch of bravado mixed with the hilarity. 'Not yet. But I have a friend . . .'

'Tell me about him.'

'Well, he's kind of nice and intelligent and amusing and handsome . . .'

'And rich?'

'Rich enough. He's a publisher in New York which is a bore but we get to meet most weekends. Either he flies up or I fly down.'

'How old?'

Francesca nodded, pondering: 'I guess he's getting on for forty.'

Sophie frowned. 'And not married?'

'He's been married. He's got a kid who lives with his ex-wife.'

'But he's divorced?'

'Sure. He's been divorced for five or six years.'

'So why not marry again?'

'He's kind of cautious . . . and so am I.'

'But if you want babies, Francesca . . .'

Again, the brave laugh. 'Sure, the biological clock is ticking away . . .'

'So?'

'So . . . I don't know. I mean, we're talking about it . . . having babies . . . marrying.'

'And?'

'Well, maybe we're getting there, but he's got his job and I've got mine. You know . . .'

Sophie sighed. 'He should catch you while he can.'

'Or should I catch him. In America these days we don't just wait for the men to make up their minds.'

'Then propose to him . . . this, what is he called?'

'Duncan.'

'Propose to Duncan.'

'We've haven't got quite *that* far. I mean, the woman going down on bended knee. But, you know, you both make a mature decision at the right time . . .'

'But what is the right time?'

Francesca laughed. 'When Duncan's analyst says so, I guess.'

Sophie wrinkled her nose and frowned. 'Analysts . . . I hate them.'

'You have them here?'

'Very few. But Paul went to a psychiatrist and he became worse, far worse.'

Sophie filled two cups of coffee and brought two huge slices of cheesecake out of the fridge. The two women sat down at the kitchen table like two happy teenagers – Francesca because her shining skin and healthy hair did indeed make her look several years younger than she was; Sophie because her dishevelled hair, naive manner and trilling, almost yodelling voice – together with the dungarees – gave the impression of an almost determined childishness which only the lines on her face and the grey strands in her hair belied.

Stefan Diederich was due back at seven. Francesca, resting on the sofa in his study which served as the Diederichs' occasional spare room, awaited his return with a certain nervousness. In her unworldly way, Sophie had not realized quite how many clothes were contained in Francesca's huge suitcase, and so had not thought to offer her somewhere to put them. Some had therefore to be left in the suitcase, others were draped over the chair at the desk, and her cosmetics were laid out on the top of a filing cabinet. Francesca regretted, as always, her inability to travel light.

At five, Sophie's two children returned. Francesca could hear their voices amplified by the bare boards of the living room. The voice of the eldest, Martin, had already broken; the high-pitched tones of the daughter, Monica, might have been those of any American fourteen-year-old girl complaining to her mother about something that had gone wrong at school.

Francesca knew that it would be fatal to fall asleep: she would never get over her jet-lag if she did. She got off the sofabed and walked round the room. It was large with high ceilings, the walls lined with books, more books. She had forgotten how erudite and earnest all those dissidents had been – how protected, despite West Berlin television, from the mass culture of the West. Compared with her own small study in Boston, with its bright curtains and English watercolours on the wall, Stefan's study was severely functional, saying little about his character or taste. There were no bowls or vases, no photographs or framed diplomas; simply the books, the papers and a manual typewriter on the desk. The very anonymity of the presiding spirit brought the temptation to look through the papers on the desk, but Francesca McDermott's forthright nature came from a constant good conscience. The temptation was resisted.

She met the children when she emerged from the study to take a shower; this was shortly after six. They were eating in the kitchen, but stood up and greeted her with an old-fashioned formality. Monica, the daughter, even gave a form of curtsey as she shook her hand. Sophie showed her to the bathroom, apologizing for its inadequacy as she looked with some unease at Francesca's fluffy, flowing terry-towel bathrobe. The shower, in fact, was fine. It worked. The water was hot. Francesca had known many worse, particularly in London, but she started to rehearse in her mind the way she would suggest she move to a hotel without hurting Sophie's feelings.

Francesca faced a dilemma after her shower as to what she should wear for supper. Her simplest evening costume would seem offensively elegant. She therefore chose her designer jeans as the nearest thing to Sophie's dungarees, only to find, when she emerged, that Sophie had changed into a dress which, Francesca considered, belonged in a museum of bad taste. It was too late to change back, and Sophie seemed patently relieved that at least Francesca had not changed into a ball gown. She offered her a glass of wine from a half-empty bottle which Francesca had noticed unopened in the kitchen that afternoon.

The wine relaxed them both, and the two old friends were chatting easily on the sofa when they heard the sound of a key in the latch. All at once, Sophie's face tightened; she stood and went towards the door. Stefan entered, his brow creased with a look of mild irritation. He handed his briefcase to Sophie as he kissed her cursorily on the cheek.

Even if she had not been expecting him, Francesca would have recognized Stefan at once: small, alert, hair spare at the front, close-shaven on the neck, greying, now; the face still lean, but with deeper wrinkles around the eyes; the same thin lips and clipped moustache. At first he did not notice her. Then Sophie said quietly: 'Francesca is here,' whereupon Stefan's eyes started to flutter like the noticeboard at an airport, stopping finally at an expression of genial delight.

'Francesca,' he said as he walked forward as if, like Sophie, he was one of her long-lost friends; and, since he was now married to Sophie, Francesca responded in kind, suppressing her misgivings as she kissed him on the cheek.

'My dear Francesca,' Stefan went on, 'this is wonderful . . . and so *right*, so *apposite*, that you should be here, *now*, when you were here, *then* . . .' He went to an armchair and sat down, pointing to the sofa like an executive who was used to having his way. 'You know, there are thousands of people from the West – from the Federal Republic, from Scandinavia, from the Netherlands, from America – who are now claiming to have been with us in those dark days . . . Sophie has probably told you . . . journalists, politicians – when in fact it was quite the contrary; it was the policy of the Federal government to woo Honecker and the others, and to ignore us, even work against us, because we were rocking the boat . . .' He took the glass of wine Sophie held out for him. 'But you came, you befriended us, you took risks, even, I think, with your own government. You really *are* an old friend and, if we can persuade you to join in this project we have in mind, then it will really be a kind of happy ending . . . no, not an ending, but a happy ending to volume one.'

'I'm all ears,' said Francesca, who had sat down on the sofa as she had been told. 'Sophie has given me some tantalizing hints but she wanted to wait for you . . .'

'This is the idea . . . An exhibition, a *major* exhibition, a definitive retrospective, here in Berlin, of forbidden Russian art, the Russian art of the diaspora, the Russian art that kept the Russian spirit alive during the dark days of Stalin and his dogma of socialist realism.'

Francesca grew alert. 'Do you mean all the painters who left Russia and came West?'

'I do.'

'Chagall, Kandinsky . . .'

'Gabo, Pevsner, but also those who stayed behind like Tatlin and El Lissitzky . . . I don't think people have any idea what they were doing at the time of the Russian Revolution – how dynamic their art would have been had it not been obliterated by Stalin's Neanderthal conception of art.'

'Would it be a . . . significant exhibition?' Career considerations reined in the great excitement that had been Francesca's first reaction to Stefan's idea.

'Listen,' said Stefan. 'Thirty-five years ago, in 1958 or 1959, there was a major exhibition in the Haus der Kunst in Munich of *Entartete Kunst* – decadent art – all the paintings that the Nazis had removed from Germany's public galleries because they were considered decadent or were painted by Jews. That is what we want to do here. We want to show the young people of East Germany and Eastern Europe – and that includes Russia, Belarus and Ukraine – just how crude and stupid and philistine the Communists were with their imbecile social realism . . .'

As he was speaking, Francesca's emotions were drawn in two conflicting directions. On the one hand, she was swept up by the undoubted truth in what Stefan said, and the urgency and enthusiasm with which he said it; but on the other, she could not quite shake off the doubts about his sincerity that remained from the impression she had formed of him ten years before. Perhaps it was just because he had once been an actor that he now sounded like an actor speaking his lines. He used the right words, the right cadences, the right expressions, and yet left Francesca with the impression that the role he was playing had been created by another author and that the ideas he expressed were not his own.

Despite this, however, Francesca found herself increasingly excited by the idea of an exhibition of the kind he had described – of Russian art that had flourished in the first years of the Revolution but had then been banned and execrated by the Soviet regime. Her friends in America – Duncan was one of them – believed that the Russians had simply chosen the wrong political and economic system in 1917 as one might choose a dud model of a car, and, as a result, they now felt that all you had to do was change to democracy and free enterprise for all to be well.

Francesca knew that it was all much more complicated than

47

that; that the Russian soul faced two ways – towards the East and the West; and that it had to be coaxed to accept its own liberation by more than trade agreements and hard currency loans. If the Russians could be shown that they were not outsiders knocking at the door of contemporary Western culture, but could claim as their own some of the artists who had created that culture, then it would be far easier for them to become assimilated into the new world order.

There were also, of course, the secondary but powerful considerations of what organizing such a major international exhibition would do for Francesca's career. She needed to know what her role would be but was afraid to appear too pushy. It was better to appear sought-after than seeking.

'When would it be?' she asked, calculating that, with a sabbatical of only a year, it might mean giving up her post at BU.

'Next July,' said Stefan.

'Next July? That's impossible.'

Stefan leaned forward. 'Of course it's impossible. Normally, an exhibition of this size would take two, three, even four years to plan and stage. But we don't have that time, Francesca. History will not wait for us. It must be now or never, and I believe that with the right political backing we can achieve the impossible and put on the exhibition in ten months' time.'

Francesca shook her head. 'We would need a lot of help.'

'My ministry would be at your disposal. The city of Berlin, the Federal government in Bonn, all would help.'

'And I would organize the whole exhibition?'

'You, and Günter Westarp.'

'Who is Günter Westarp?'

'Günter is harmless,' said Sophie without making it clear whether she meant this as a compliment or an insult.

'Günter is the director of the New German Foundation,' said Stefan, 'which will organize the exhibition.'

'Is it a gallery?'

'No. It is simply a cultural foundation, set up here in Berlin. We have yet to decide where to stage the exhibition. It depends, to some extent, on how many galleries are prepared to lend their works.'

'Of course. How about funding?'

'No problem. Our state government has already put up the money to develop the idea. That was within my gift, as it were, and there are a number of private sponsors queueing up to join in. It is a project that will attract much publicity and bring great prestige.'

'And is Günter Westarp an art historian?'

Stefan smiled. 'Of a kind. To be quite honest, Francesca, his appointment was a reward for his work as a dissident in the DDR.'

'Did I meet him here in the old days?'

'No, he was in Leipzig, and suffered badly from the Stasi.'

'He is very sweet,' said Sophie. 'A good man, but not so bright . . .'

'That is why we need you,' said Stefan.

'But aren't there German experts?' asked Francesca.

'Of course. We were given a whole list of them. But I made the case that having you as organizer of the exhibition would reassure the galleries and collectors in America where in fact many of the works of art are to be found.'

Francesca nodded. Certainly, no one in the States would have heard of Günter Westarp or the New German Foundation.

'So? What do you think? Will you do it?'

'I'd certainly like to,' said Francesca.

'What can we do to make up your mind?'

'It's a question of a contract, I guess.'

Sophie glanced uneasily at Stefan.

'We must discuss that with my officials,' said Stefan, 'but I can assure you that we see you as a valuable . . . commodity in, what do you call it? A sellers' market?'

Francesca laughed and said 'great' but felt afraid that she might have given her friends the impression that she was mercenary. She put her arms around Sophie's shoulders and said: 'It's worth much more than money to be back with you in Berlin.'

'Come, let's have supper,' said Sophie.

They walked towards the kitchen; then Stefan stopped. 'Ah. Yes. I had forgotten.' He turned back to Francesca. 'There is, I am afraid, one further condition . . .'

'What's that?'

'We have already taken on a Russian. It was thought . . . well, you can imagine – for all the reasons we have given, it was thought tactful to have an art expert from Moscow to assist you.'

Francesca frowned. 'But are there any experts in Moscow on their experimental art?'

'Apparently, yes. Dr Serotkin. Andrei Serotkin. Do you know of him?'

'No.'

'I have met him. He seems knowledgeable enough.'

'Well, I guess if you can work with him,' said Francesca, 'then so can I.'

FOUR

Shortly after ordering Nikolai Gerasimov to find Andrei Orlov, General Savchenko left Moscow on a tour of inspection of Russian intelligence residences abroad. Every now and then Gerasimov would receive cryptic messages sent via Savchenko's office: from Washington, 'Spoke to Kirsch about our friend. He knew him well. Kirsch is prepared to speak to you when he is next in Moscow.' From Toronto: 'Any progress?'

Gerasimov had made no progress and began to dread Savchenko's return. It was difficult enough to get anything done in Moscow where no one returned calls or kept appointments. Also Gerasimov had been distracted, to say the least, by complications in his personal life, moving out of the flat that he shared with his wife to lead a nomadic existence on the sofas of family and friends.

Gerasimov rehearsed in his mind the arguments he would advance for his lack of success. First, Orlov had had few friends. Second, those that there were had been unwilling to talk to Gerasimov. As Savchenko himself had said, the security service no longer struck terror into those it questioned, least of all officers who outranked Gerasimov. Savchenko would surely accept that the chaotic conditions in the Caucasus made it impossible to trace Kastiev, the Chechen. He might find it more difficult to understand why Gerasimov had not yet got around to interviewing Partovsky, Orlov's adjutant, in the Tretyakov Gallery in Moscow.

Soon after receiving Savchenko's message from Toronto, Gerasimov was called by an officer in Savchenko's office to say that Kirsch had arrived from Washington and would await him in an hour's time. Gerasimov went down to the canteen, bought a cheese roll and a cup of coffee, and took them back to his office where he unearthed the fat file on Andrei Orlov. He quickly brushed up his knowledge of Orlov's background: his father, a celebrated painter; education at Moscow's exclusive School No. 6; top marks in English, German, maths and gymnastics. Were the marks genuine, or had the teachers given a helping hand to the son of an illustrious father?

It seemed clear from the file that Orlov himself had known from an early age how to get on under the system. He had been a team leader in the Pioneers at the age of ten, and Secretary of the Communist Youth Movement, the Komsomol, in his last year at the Institute of International Relations at Moscow University. Tatiana Ivanovna, his future wife, had been a member of the committee and, when Orlov had been made a Party member at the age of twenty-five, Ivan Keminski, Tatiana's father, had been one of the sponsors. Full marks for opportunism. If you must date a fellow student, choose the daughter of a top official in the secretariat of the Central Committee.

Orlov had graduated from the institute with the highest marks of his year. From the KGB's Foreign Intelligence School at Yurlovo, he had gone to Department 12 of the First Chief Directorate. His first work in the field had been under the cover of an interpreter at international conferences both in the Soviet Union and abroad. In 1976, he recruited an Indian physicist at a scientific congress in Kiev. In 1978, he accompanied a group of Russian scientists to the United States, again posing as their interpreter, writing meticulous reports on their contacts with their American colleagues, guarding them against approaches from the CIA.

In 1980, Orlov was transferred to Department 9, and after two years on the Africa desk went with his wife Tatiana to the KGB residence in the Soviet Embassy at Dar es Salaam. Again, a creditable performance: an up-and-coming civil servant in the President's office recruited as agent of influence in his first twelve months. Reports from the residence chief and from the Africa desk in Moscow all praised Orlov to the skies. It was decided that Orlov was wasted on the Africans. He was recalled to Moscow, and after a year on the US desk, Andrei Orlov was sent to Washington under the cover of a cultural attaché in the Soviet Embassy.

The telephone rang on Gerasimov's desk. Kirsch was waiting for him in Savchenko's office. Gerasimov swallowed the cold dregs of his coffee and closed the file. He went up the stairs with the dread feeling in his stomach of a student about to be examined on a subject he has not prepared. He should know more about Kirsch beyond the fact that he had served for a number of years in the Washington residence and was presumably a Jew.

Kirsch was sitting on a chair by a coffee table in the corner of Savchenko's office smoking a cigarette. He was small, dark, with sparse black hair: age, Gerasimov estimated, late fifties or early sixties. He was trim, even dapper, in well-cut Western clothes. As Gerasimov entered, a girl brought in a glass of tea and a plate of biscuits on a small metal tray. She put it down beside Kirsch. Nothing was offered to Gerasimov. Nor did Kirsch get up off his seat.

'You want to know about Orlov?' he asked as Gerasimov sat down on the empty sofa.

'If you could give me some background . . .'

'I understand that he has disappeared?'

'We have not been able to trace him since he flew from Kiev to Vienna over a year ago.'

Kirsch nodded and sipped his tea.

'There has been no sign of him in the United States?'

Kirsch sniffed, derisively. 'If Orlov is up to something, he is unlikely to leave his calling card at Russian embassies around the world.'

'We do not know that he is up to something . . .'

53

Kirsch looked at his watch. 'I am unable to help you in your principal task – that of finding Andrei Orlov. But if you think it would help, I can tell you something about Orlov's tour of duty in Washington.'

'He went there, I believe, in 1988?'

'Yes. In '88 or early '89. He came with his wife, Tatiana, and their young son. They were both an immediate success. They were young and good looking. They became a popular couple on the political and diplomatic circuit. We paid for elegant clothes and subscriptions to country clubs. Both played tennis. Orlov was good at squash. We instructed Tatiana to befriend the women. She joined a reading group organized by a Congressman's wife. She became interested in art, took up sculpture and went to classes once a week. We encouraged them both to present a soft image. They could even be apologetic, if they thought it appropriate, about our involvement in Afghanistan or our record on human rights.'

'That must have gone against the grain . . .'

'For Orlov? Yes. But what you should understand is that he is a man who is unusually adept at concealing his true feelings.' Kirsch took another sip of his tea. 'He could enter into American life with great gusto while at the same time . . .'

Gerasimov waited.

Kirsch put down his glass. 'He gave the Americans the impression that he loved them while I have yet to find anyone who held them in greater contempt.'

Gerasimov took out a notebook and wrote: 'Master of duplicity.'

'Of course, we were all as it were . . . adversarial in our approach. We were still fighting the Cold War. But there were very few of us who had such a visceral dislike of the Americans and the American way of life.'

'Do we know why?' asked Gerasimov. He was genuinely puzzled.

'Why what?'

'Why he hated the Americans so much?'

Kirsch shrugged. 'He was hardly trained to love them. We were all Leninists, after all. The Americans were capitalists, imperialists, exploiters.' Kirsch took out a packet of Marlboro cigarettes. 'But Orlov also saw a cultural dimension . . . You must understand that culturally Orlov was a cut above most of our officers, a result, no doubt, of being the son of a painter.' Kirsch removed a cigarette from the packet. He did not offer one to Gerasimov. 'He had a particular loathing for abstract art – the icons of emptiness, he would call them – and for the great art galleries where these icons were venerated.'

'Yet his wife studied sculpture.'

Kirsch lit his cigarette. 'Yes. That was to become a problem.'

Gerasimov waited for Kirsch to expand on this but he went off at a tangent.

'Orlov was good at his job. It was the time of President Reagan's Star Wars. The American's defence technology was outstripping ours. Moscow told us to get hold of the microchips and computer components that might help us keep up. The pressure was intense. We were reminded that the atomic secrets from Los Alamos had reached the Kremlin within the week. Orlov, through offshore trusts and secret bank accounts, set up bogus companies in the US to get hold of what we wanted and smuggled them out of the country in the baggage of Sandinista sympathizers flying to Nicaragua.'

'If he did so well,' said Gerasimov, 'why was he recalled?'

Kirsch sighed. 'There were two problems. First, his wife. You realize that she was Keminski's daughter? That was a great embarrassment to us in Washington because she began to get serious about her art, and then about religion. Psychologically . . . well, I think she was upset when Orlov on a couple of occasions found himself in a position where he could obtain important information by entering into intimate relationships with certain American women . . . You understand what I mean. He was acting under orders. It goes with the job. And Tatiana Orlova must have known that, but when she lost faith in our system she no longer saw the necessity, and so they became estranged. We knew what was going on from Orlov. But I think he loved his wife, and took it personally . . .'

'Was he recalled because of that?'

'Orlov had one failing. He could be arrogant, and that not only irritated some of the other officers at the Residence who were envious of his success; it also made him enemies in Moscow. On his own initiative, he started writing position papers and sending them back to Keminski who passed them on to the Central Committee. They were highly critical of Soviet policy since the war. In his view, this had exaggerated the military threat posed to the Soviet Union when it was the cultural imperialism of the US that posed the greatest danger to the long-term viability of the Soviet system.'

'Was he wrong?'

'Probably not. But our military-industrial complex had its patrons on the Central Committee, and this was not what they wanted to hear.'

'But with Keminski behind him . . .'

'Keminski's position was made awkward by the conversion of his daughter. Her religiosity was no cover. She had ceased to submit reports.' Kirsch stubbed out his cigarette. 'But that was not the reason for Orlov's recall. As I understand it, these position papers came to the notice of Khrulev just as he was recruiting a team for his icon operation. It was Khrulev who had Orlov recalled.'

Gerasimov doodled on his notebook. What more could he ask Kirsch? 'Could you hazard a guess,' he asked, 'as to what Orlov might be up to now?'

Kirsch shook his head. 'No. In my view, it was a great mistake to have dismissed him. I know that attitudes are changing, but a man like Orlov should be kept busy if only to prevent him from getting up to anything else.'

'Can you think of anyone who might know where he is?'

'Yes. His father-in-law, Ivan Keminski.'

'He has been placed out of bounds.'

'And would not tell you what you wanted to know. What about Tatiana?'

'They are separated.'

'Even so. They have a son.'

'If Keminski will not talk, why should she?'

'Keminski remains a Communist, but if Tatiana is a believer she should sympathize with the reforms. And try the old father.

Andrei was fond of his parents. For all his Bolshevik zeal, he was always a family man.'

A bored looking secretary showed Nikolai Gerasimov to the officer at the Tretyakov Gallery of former KGB Lieutenant Alexander Partovsky. He was young – much younger than Gerasimov had expected – with a shy manner and an intelligent expression. Gerasimov found this disconcerting. It was bad enough to be investigating a fellow officer, but worse to be asking someone to sneak on his last operational commander. He could see that Partovsky was ill at ease – not afraid, as so many were when being questioned by state security, but rather embarrassed, as if the whole exercise was somehow squalid.

'I have been asked to make enquiries about Captain Andrei Orlov.'

'Yes.'

'You knew him well, I think?'

'I was with him in Berlin.'

'Precisely.'

'We recovered more than ninety illegally exported icons.'

'So I understand.'

Partovsky nodded towards the door of his office. 'Some of them are now on show.'

'The operation was successful, then?'

'Yes, thanks to Comrade Orlov.'

'He was competent?'

'More than that.'

'But it was messy . . .'

'How?'

'People were killed.'

'We were expected. It was kill or be killed.'

'What about the woman?'

Partovsky blushed. 'She had information . . .'

'About bank accounts?'

'Yes.'

'She told you?'

'In the end.'

'You persuaded her?'

57

'Yes.'

'You tortured her?'

'I . . .' He stopped. 'Our orders were to use whatever means were necessary.'

Gerasimov made no reply to this but looked down at his notes. 'And then you returned with the icons?'

'By Travemünde. Yes.'

'With *all* the icons?'

There was a slight hesitation. 'All the icons, yes.'

'And the bank accounts?'

'They were left to Orlov.'

'Did she tell you how much they contained?'

'I was not present at her interrogation.'

'Who was there?'

'Comrade Orlov and Comrade Kastiev.'

'The Chechen?'

'Yes.'

'Did Orlov tell you how much money the bank accounts contained?'

'No.'

'There is no record that any of these funds were repatriated.'

Again, a slight hesitation. 'Perhaps Comrade Orlov failed to gain access to the accounts.'

'He flew to Zürich?'

'So I believe.'

'And then returned to Moscow?'

'Yes.'

'Did you see him in Moscow?'

'Yes.'

'Did he tell you whether or not he had gained access to the accounts?'

'No. We did not talk about it.'

'What did you talk about?'

'Our future. The country. The Party. Things had happened while we we. e away.'

'He too was offered a job at the Tretyakov, I believe?'

'They were grateful to us for recovering the icons.'

'But Orlov turned it down?'

58

'Yes.'

'Why?'

Partovsky shrugged. 'It didn't appeal to him.'

'It suggests that he had something else in mind.'

'Perhaps.'

'Did he tell you what that was?'

'Not specifically.'

'In general?'

Partovsky struggled to find the right words. 'He is . . .'

'What?'

'A patriot.'

Gerasimov sniffed. 'What does that mean?'

'He was more concerned for Russia than he was for himself.'

'One can afford to be patriotic with access to bank accounts in Zürich.'

Partovsky looked angry. 'It is inconceivable to me, comrade, that Captain Orlov would have spent state funds on himself.'

'Then how does he live?'

'I don't know. He may have savings.'

'Despite inflation?'

'His father, as you know . . .'

'Yes, I know. The famous painter.'

'He must have money.'

'Perhaps.'

'And the . . .' Partovsky hesitated.

'What?'

'As I understand it, Orlov had friends in the Party.'

'Did you know that he had gone back to the West?'

'I assumed he would.'

'Why?'

'There was some unfinished business.'

'To do with the icons?'

'No.'

'The bank accounts?'

'Possibly. I don't know. He didn't confide in me. He merely asked me . . .'

'What?'

'To go with him.'

Gerasimov became alert. 'He asked you to go with him, to settle some unfinished business, but did not tell you what that business was?'

Partovsky looked unhappy. 'It was understood that I could only be told if I was committed to the general idea . . .'

'Of what?'

'Of saving Russia.'

Gerasimov was genuinely confused. 'So Orlov went back to the West to save Russia?'

'He had some project . . .'

'What was it?'

'I don't know. He didn't tell me. But the icons . . . the operation . . . torturing the woman . . . It affected him.'

'You said that it had nothing to do with the icons.'

'Nothing as such. But the icons were smuggled out of Russia and sold to the West by slime like Maslyukov and even corrupt Chekists' – here Partovsky darted a look at Gerasimov – 'and the way the police in the West knew all about it and did nothing to stop it because the icons were Russian, part of our heritage, our culture . . . To see them traded as commodities, just to decorate the houses of the bourgeoisie in Frankfurt and New York . . .' Partovsky was agitated. 'You must understand, comrade Gerasimov, that Captain Orlov was not only efficient and courageous but he also had great conviction. He believed in what he was doing.'

'And you?'

'I obeyed orders.'

'And when you returned?'

'As you know, I was dismissed from the service and was advised to take this post at the gallery.'

'And you would like to keep it?'

'Of course.'

'Which you would not if it was felt that you were concealing information to the detriment of the state.'

'I have told you all I know,' said Partovsky glumly.

'Why should we believe that?'

Now a slight look of contempt came into Partovsky's eyes.

'You are still in the service, comrade Gerasimov. I am not. Nor is Orlov. But we have all had the same training. If you were Orlov, if you had something in mind, would you let out any information to someone who was not part of the operation?'

Gerasimov did not answer.

'If I had agreed to join him, Orlov would have told me. But I did not.'

Gerasimov saw the sense of what Partovsky was saying. He changed the subject. 'General Khrulev, I think, had his own agents in Germany?'

'So I understand.'

'Did any of them help you recover the icons?'

Again, a slight hesitation. 'There were two cars and a van. I am not sure how Orlov got hold of them.'

'No Germans were with you?'

'No.'

'Only . . .' Gerasimov looked down at his notes. 'You and the Chechen?'

'Yes.'

'What happened to him?'

'To Kastiev? I don't know.'

'And the van?'

Partovsky shrugged. 'The van? I don't know. It was picked up by someone from the Centre and returned to the pool.'

Gerasimov stood up. As he did so, he noticed a look of relief come onto Partovsky's face. Undoubtedly, he had revealed only as much as he felt he had to about Orlov – things he judged that Gerasimov might discover from other sources. Almost certainly he knew more, or at any rate could hazard a guess.

'You must look at the icons,' said Partovsky, leading Gerasimov down the corridor towards the gallery. 'This is the cream of the Tretyakov collection, and the gallery as you know has been recently restored.'

'By Finns, I believe.'

'Superb, don't you think? And our security is state-of-the-art . . .' As he spoke, there was a loud electronic bleep.

They came into the gallery. There, on the walls, were a series of magnificent icons – of Christ, of the Virgin, of St Nicholas, of St

Parascevi, among them the celebrated icon of Our Lady of Kazan, and Andrei Rublev's *Holy Trinity*. A number of visitors were shuffling from painting to painting, watched by lethargic attendants. The only sounds were the hum of the humidifiers and the occasional loud electronic bleep.

'What's wrong with the alarm?' asked Gerasimov, more interested in the Western technology than he was in the icons.

'As you can see,' said Partovsky proudly, 'there is an electronic beam in front of the exhibits which when broken triggers the alarm . . .' There was another bleep. Partovsky looked towards the icon of the Virgin of Kazan. 'But look . . .'

Gerasimov turned. An old peasant woman wearing felt boots and a tight headscarf had knelt down and now bowed forward to kiss the icon, blocking the beam. There was a loud bleep. The attendant yawned.

'Why don't you stop them?' asked Gerasimov.

Partovsky shrugged. 'The equipment is state-of-the-art,' he said, 'but our people, I am afraid, are not.'

FIVE

At the request of the Minister, Stefan Diederich, a flat was found for Francesca McDermott by the Prussian Ministry of Culture in the Hansa Quarter of West Berlin. It was on the fourth floor of a modern block near the Academy of Art with views over the Englischergarten. Francesca was told that her Russian colleague, Dr Serotkin, would be given an apartment in the same block when he returned to Berlin.

Because the telephonic communications were still poor in the eastern half of the city, the office provided for the exhibition's organizers was also in West Berlin, in the same building on the Schöneberger Ufer used by the New German Foundation. It looked out over the canal onto the New National Gallery and, beyond the New State Library, to what remained of the Berlin Wall on the old Potsdammerplatz.

The proximity of this office to Francesca's flat enabled her to establish an agreeable routine. At seven every morning, she would jog in the Englischergarten under the watchful eye of the Goddess of Victory. She ate her usual breakfast of yoghurt, muesli and Lapsang Souchong tea, and then drove to the office in a leased Volkswagen Golf.

From the start, her mood was good; indeed, she had to rein in a sense of exhilaration. Whether it was the celebrated Berlin air, or the challenge of a job that was tailor-made both for her ambitions and her qualifications, Francesca felt charged with an unusual energy and sense of liberation.

In part, she recognized, this came from getting out of the rut of her life in Boston – a pleasant enough life, certainly, with a nice apartment, tenure at BU, and Duncan in New York but one that had changed little since her appointment five years before. Here, in contrast, was both a challenge and a change, but an undemanding change, with everyone appearing to fall over themselves to smooth her path and make things easy. Finding a place to live in a crowded city might have been difficult, but she had to spend only two nights in the Diederichs' flat on the Wedekindstrasse before moving into the flat.

Things were just as well arranged at the office. Günter Westarp, the director of the New German Foundation, was theoretically the co-organizer of the exhibition, but it was clear from the start that the two assistants seconded from the New National Gallery – a young man and a older woman – as well as the two secretaries, all regarded Francesca as the one in charge.

Westarp had some knowledge of the Bauhaus in its Weimar phase: it was his attempt to speak up for modernism that had antagonized the authorities in the DDR. However, he had no academic standing, no natural authority, and Francesca feared that if the director of the Museum of Modern Art in New York or the National Gallery in Washington should ever set eyes on him, the project would be doomed. He was short, almost squat, with a docile yet dogged look on his sagging, fleshy face. His hair was thin and dirty; its greying, greasy strands reached halfway to his shoulders. He always wore jeans – not crisp denim designer jeans like Francesca's but tawdry East-bloc imitations, creased and moulded about his crotch and precariously close to being bell-bottomed. His thick knitted cardigan seemed as greasy as his hair: the only luxuriance was in the large, drooping, Günter Grass moustache upon which, after eating, fragments of food hung like baubles on a Christmas tree.

The other members of the permanent staff scarcely disguised their contempt for their Ossie cousin. Knowing full well that Günter only spoke German, they spoke English in their discussions with Francesca; at times Francesca found herself translating what they had said back into German for the benefit of Günter. Günter appeared quite content with his subordinate role. He sat at his desk in the offices of the New German Foundation on the floor below, signing the letters and memos that were set before him after only a cursory glance. If any question was put to him directly at a meeting of the secretariat or the exhibition committee, he always looked to Francesca to provide an answer; soon, the incoming letters and faxes were passed directly to her.

Francesca's only worry was Serotkin. She understood the necessity of having a Russian work on the project; she could even see some advantage in having a man with good contacts in Moscow as part of the team: they would want many paintings from the public collections in Moscow and St Petersburg, and there was archival material that she would dearly love to bring to Berlin. However, she could not discover why this particular Russian had been chosen, nor find anyone in her field who had heard of him or his work.

Günter Westarp knew nothing about him: he said that Stefan had chosen Serotkin. And Stefan, when Francesca questioned him, said that Serotkin had been put forward by the Ministry of Culture in Moscow. Stefan could hardly say what he was like: he had only met him on two or three occasions. He was apparently dark, middle-aged, taciturn and had a beard. He spoke German well; possibly English as well. He had seemed knowledgeable about art, and enthusiastic about the exhibition.

Francesca had formed an image of Serotkin in her mind. He would be pedantic, donnish, his beard clipped like Lenin's; his manner cautious, occasionally evasive as it was so often in Soviet academics, bullied in their studies by the dogmas of Marx. He would probably be lazy and indecisive, happy to leave the researchers to do the work and Francesca or Günter to carry the can. Indeed, the more she thought about the bumbling professor, the less anxious she became that he would cramp her style. After a couple of weeks, she had almost ceased to think about him, distracted as she was by the momentous task of getting the exhibition off the ground.

The first thing that Francesca and her team had to do was decide on the scope and the name of the exhibition, choose the artists to be represented and discover the whereabouts of their works. They would then have to approach the lenders, a delicate matter that was crucial to the success of the whole enterprise. Francesca knew that many in the United States would be reluctant to allow major paintings by, say, Kandinsky and Chagall to cross the Atlantic. It was therefore essential to approach them in the right way – to appeal to the idealistic impulses of the major lenders like the Museum of Modern Art in New York whose participation was essential if works from lesser collections were to follow.

Francesca told Stefan time and again how important it was that he should seek endorsement for the exhibition at the highest level, if possible from the Federal Ministry of Culture. An approach should be made to the cultural attachés of the different embassies in Bonn and letters to the major lenders would have to be signed by Stefan himself, as the provincial minister, before Francesca made her requests for the loan of specific works of art.

All this was agreed. The New Grouping, in coalition with the Christian Democrats in the Prussian government, could count on the support of the Federal government in Bonn. The Federal government would also provide the usual indemnity in lieu of insurance for the works of art if the arrangements for security were satisfactory.

There was a long discussion by the exhibition committee as to what the title should be. Francesca's thesis had been called simply 'Russian Experimental Art'; but it was argued by the female researcher, Frau Dr Koch, that the art in question was, in retrospect, hardly experimental because the word 'experimental' suggested a trial that might fail. Stefan Diederich thought that the title of the exhibition should be something like: 'The Indomitable Spirit: Russian Art in Exile' or 'The Russian Role in Contemporary Culture'. Other ideas were thrown up by different members of the committee. Why not simply 'Russian Art: 1917–1993'? Francesca said that was too bald and academic. The title must surely contain the message that the exhibition was meant to convey: she therefore preferred Stefan's original suggestion 'The Indomitable Spirit: Russian Art in Exile', and it was on this that the committee agreed.

The next question to be considered was the *scope* of the exhibition. Was it to be huge and comprehensive? Or should it confine itself to a few fine examples of the work of the artists involved? Francesca argued forcefully for the latter: in her view, the impact would be greater if the visitor was not overwhelmed by a large number of works. There was also the danger that the artists with a relatively small output would be lost in the plethora of works by more prolific artists, or might not be seen at all by visitors who gave up from cultural satiety or sheer exhaustion.

In this Francesca was backed by the director of the New National Gallery who also sat on the committee. Günter appeared to agree until he caught the eye of Stefan Diederich; whereupon he brought his contribution to the discussion to an indecisive end as quickly as he could. Stefan's intervention was more decisive in tone but equally confused in content. He suggested that it was not a question they could decide there and then, but should be put on an agenda for the next meeting. Francesca objected that this would hold up the whole enterprise: the letters had to go out to the lenders; a decision had to be made on whether they would need a single site or multiple sites; but the most Stefan would do to meet her objections was to bring forward the date of the committee's next meeting.

Francesca returned from the offices of the Prussian Ministry of Culture where the meeting had been held to her own office on the Schöneberger Ufer in a mood of simmering irritation. It was a wet day. She had missed her morning jog in the Englischergarten. She had drunk regular coffee at the meeting because no decaf was on offer; and though no one had come up with any argument against it, her 'quality over quantity' proposal had been put on hold. It was her first setback and it triggered the release of a number of other pent-up annoyances, most of them imprecise and irrational, like her hatred of the bland antiseptic decor of her office, of Frau Dr Koch's rubber plant, of the eager zeal of the young researcher, Julius Breitenbach, who, as she passed his office, was looking through the 1989–90 catalogue of Sotheby's auction house in London.

Seeing that Francesca had returned from the meeting, Julius rose and followed her into her office. 'Do you know, by any chance,' he asked, 'who bought Kandinsky's *Fugue* in . . .'

'No I don't,' Francesca snapped at him, throwing her folder down on her desk.

Julius blushed and backed away. 'I'm sorry . . .'

'No. Wait.' Francesca frowned. 'Wasn't that in the Guggenheim?'

'Yes. They sold it at auction last year, but I don't know who bought it.'

'You'd better call Sotheby's. It's an important work. We have to have it.'

Julius retreated again, closing her door. Francesca kicked off her damp shoes under the desk. There was a knock on her door. 'Yes?' she said, unable to suppress a note of exasperation. Frau Dr Koch, the older researcher, looked through. 'Dr Serotkin is here,' she said.

'*Here?*'

The Russian stood behind her. Frau Dr Koch stepped aside to let him pass into Francesca's office. Francesca stood to greet him but, feeling the carpet beneath her stockinged feet, realized that she was not wearing her shoes. 'Shit,' she muttered and, before taking more than a glimpse at Serotkin, she crouched down behind her desk to recover them.

'I'm sorry,' she mumbled as she stood up again. 'I lost my shoes.'

The man who stood before her was so unlike the man she had imagined that at first she thought that he could not be Serotkin. Later, when she came to describe him to Sophie Diederich, she used the word 'dashing'. She said it was because he reminded her of the Bulgarian patriot, Insarov, in Turgenev's *On the Eve*. When she mentioned Serotkin to Duncan over the telephone to New York, she avoided using the word 'dashing', only because he might take this to mean attractive, which it did not. To start with, Serotkin had a beard – a black beard matching the thick black hair on his head – and Francesca hated beards. Then his eyes were a murky colour, his face was too long, his cheekbones were too high, his nose was too straight. He was also formal and solemn as he shook hands with her, and she liked men to be friendly and smile.

Francesca realized, of course, that this first encounter could be something of an ordeal for the Russian art historian who, whatever his professional abilities, might be a little intimidated by a more sophisticated colleague from the West. She therefore asked him to sit down and did her best to put him at his ease. She buzzed the secretary to bring some coffee and, rather than sit like a boss at her desk, crossed to the sofa next to the chair chosen by Serotkin.

'Have you come from Moscow?' she asked.

'No,' he replied shortly.

Francesca waited for him to say something further, but he did not. 'I guess we all assumed you were in Moscow or St Petersburg . . .'

'No.'

'But you are *from* Moscow, aren't you?'

'Yes.'

Francesca did not want to give the impression that she was interviewing Serotkin, but she was keen to know the extent of his knowledge and the value of his qualifications. 'Do you teach there,' she asked, 'or are you at a gallery or a museum?'

'I was at the ministry,' he said simply.

'I see.'

'Our system was different to yours. We had experts in different fields working in the ministry.'

'Of course. And you were an expert on this field . . . experimental Russian art?'

'Of course.' His voice was deep, his English flawless. There was no trace of a Russian intonation.

'But you have travelled abroad?' Serotkin was wearing grey flannel trousers and a dark grey herringbone sports jacket, a blue shirt and spotted tie – elegant Western clothes which he carried with a certain ease.

'Yes, I know your country a little. London also. And Germany, of course.' There was a touch of mockery in his eyes as if he was thinking things he was not prepared to say.

'I understand that you speak German?'

'Yes.'

The secretary brought in the coffee. Francesca baulked at more caffeine, but felt that she must drink with Serotkin, as though smoking a pipe of peace. 'While you've been away,' she said, 'we've got off to a fairly smooth start. The only difference, I think, is over the scope of the exhibition.'

'Yes. And the title, I believe.'

'We settled on that. "The Indomitable Spirit: Russian Art in Exile".'

'It is imprecise.'

She frowned. 'How do you mean?'

'Well, this art we are considering was not all created in exile. Some was in Russia.'

'But most of the artists went abroad.'

'Some remained. Malevich. El Lissitzky.'

'Sure. But they were censored and suppressed.'

His eyes flashed. 'Certainly.'

'So even if the painters remained in the Soviet Union, the spirit was forced into exile.'

'Nevertheless, it is imprecise.'

Francesca frowned. She disliked being crossed, particularly on something that had been decided, and she was also irritated that Serotkin was not responding to her friendliness as he should. 'And the scope?' she asked, somewhat sharply.

'It must be . . . comprehensive.'

'I took the view . . .' she began.

'I know. Diederich told me. But I feel that only a comprehensive collection will do justice to the theme.'

'You mean *all* the Kandinskys, *all* the Chagalls?'

'As many as possible.'

'I just don't know if we'll get people to lend, and the transport costs will be enormous . . .'

'Diederich has money for that.'

'And the insurance . . . Some of these paintings are now worth very large sums of money.'

70

Serotkin paused. 'I realize that.'

'We're talking millions of dollars.'

'Of course.'

She stood, went to her desk and picked up her phone. 'Julius, what did that painting by Kandinsky sell for at Sotheby's last year?' She listened. 'Uh-uh . . . uh-uh.' She put down the phone and turned back to Serotkin. 'Kandinsky's *Fugue* went for over twenty million dollars.'

'Yes,' said Serotkin. 'And I believe Chagall's *America*, also from the Guggenheim, was sold for 14,850,000 dollars at the same sale.'

Francesca frowned as she sat down again. Serotkin was clearly better informed than she had supposed. 'So we're talking of *hundreds* of millions of dollars.'

Serotkin appeared unimpressed. 'I understand that in exhibitions of this kind insurance is not a direct expense because the government provides an indemnity.'

'Sure. And it's highly unlikely that the paintings will be burned or stolen. But all the same . . .'

'I think it's for Diederich to worry about things like that,' said Serotkin.

'I agree. But we have to know the scope to draw up our lists . . .'

'Of course. I have, to some extent, with the aid of colleagues, drawn up a list of works in my country.'

'That's fantastic because really we don't know what you have in your collections.'

'No. They were not . . . advertised.' He smiled, and since this was the first smile to have appeared on his face, it lifted Francesca's spirits which, starting low because of the damp day, raised briefly at the first appearance of the 'dashing' Serotkin, had begun to sink again under the impact of his obtuseness on the question of the title and scope of the exhibition.

She took the smile as an invitation to venture a more personal approach. 'It must have been difficult,' she said in a compassionate tone, 'to study experimental and abstract art in the Soviet Union.'

'It was.'

'I guess you weren't encouraged.'
'No.'
'You couldn't teach?'
'No.'
'Or publish?'
'No.'
'Which is why no one has heard of you . . .' It came out baldly; she did not quite mean it that way.

But Serotkin smiled. 'No. Such a field of study was not so very much . . . esteemed under Communism. However, if you have doubts about my abilities . . .'

'Not at all.'
'I could give you the name of colleagues and officials . . .'
'Don't be ridiculous. Would Stefi have invited you if he didn't know you?'

'I trust not.'
'All I meant was how shameful it was that for ideological reasons your studies were suppressed.'

He smiled again. 'Yes. There were suppressed. But now this exhibition gives me an opportunity to realize my life's ambition.'

'Mine too.'

It is often awkward, in an office, to draw lines between professional cooperation and personal involvement. When it came to lunch, for example, which most of them ate in the staff restaurant of the New German Foundation, the two researchers, Frau Dr Koch and Julius Breitenbach, who already kept their distance from Francesca by calling her Dr McDermott, clearly did not consider it appropriate to join her at a table. Her only colleague of the same rank was Günter Westarp who, in the first few weeks, had often accompanied Francesca to the staff restaurant, boring her to death with anecdotes about his days as a dissident in Leipzig, or with obscure items of information to establish his encyclopaedic knowledge of the Bauhaus – encyclopaedic but also indiscriminate: he had gathered facts like a train-spotter who knows the number and type of the locomotives passing through a station but has no interest whatsoever in their destination.

To escape from Westarp, Francesca either brought a sandwich to the office which she ate at her desk, or waited a good half-hour after Günter had left for lunch before herself going down to the restaurant. The Germans all ate early anyway – a heavy meal at midday, or shortly after: if Francesca waited until around quarter to one, she could be reasonably sure of eating some soup or a salad alone with a book or a scholarly review.

The day of Serotkin's return, she followed this tactic only to find that the Russian had done the same thing, and finding themselves side by side at the counter, and at the desk where they paid for their food, they could hardly avoid sitting at the same table.

Held under Serotkin's arm as he carried his tray was a copy of *The Economist*: like Francesca, he had clearly hoped to be able to eat in peace but he put on as brave a face as she did and, after the initial awkwardness, looked at her with almost a twinkle in his eye. 'You don't like German food?'

Francesca glanced down at the salad. 'We aren't used to eating hot food in the middle of the day.'

'We like to eat hot food at midday and in the evening.' He dug into the dish of the day – smoked pork, red cabbage and dumplings.

'But you don't get fat,' she said, glancing at Serotkin's slim figure.

'We don't always get to eat as much as we would like,' he said.

'Are there shortages?' she asked, the compassionate note back in her tone of voice.

'Sure.'

'Do you have a family, Andrei?'

He hesitated. 'Yes.'

'You don't mind my asking?'

'I have a wife and a child,' he said, 'but I am separated from my wife.'

'I guess there's as much divorce in Russia as there is in the United States.'

'We are separated, not divorced.'

She stood corrected. 'Are they in Moscow?'

'Yes.'

'You should have them visit you here in Berlin. I'd like to meet them.'

Serotkin did not respond to this but took another mouthful of food. 'Are you married?' he asked eventually.

'I'm not married but I have a friend. He's divorced.'

He nodded. 'You should be married.'

'Why?'

He shrugged. 'You are a beautiful woman but you are no longer young.'

Francesca was taken aback by this abrupt, double-edged compliment delivered in an offhand manner. 'Marry in haste, repent at leisure,' she said with a slightly forced laugh.

'Is that a proverb?'

'Sort of.'

'But not true.'

'I think it's true enough, if you think of the growing number of divorces.'

'They are not caused by the haste with which people marry, but by their false expectations of what marriage should be.'

'Such as?'

He shrugged. 'Rapture. Fulfilment. Hollywood romance.'

'Is that what you and your wife wanted?'

He frowned. 'No. Our differences were . . . ideological.'

'She was a Communist?'

'No.' He hesitated, as if about to say one thing but, thinking better of it, said another. 'Under our system, there were particular difficulties. It was impossible for a young couple to have their own flat. And women were expected to work. They were expected to work by the government, but they were also expected to look after the home and care for the children . . .'

'By the men,' said Francesca.

'By tradition,' said Serotkin.

'Didn't the tradition change?'

'Traditions will not change if they stem from ineradicable aspects of human nature.'

Francesca's face became a little flushed. She put down her fork. 'But surely no one in Russia believed that it was inherent in

74

human nature that women should work in a factory but also do all the chores in the home?'

'They believed that women should work in the factory because that followed from the principle of equality between the sexes.'

'Of course, but in the home . . .'

'Marx and Lenin never pronounced on who should wash the dishes or iron the clothes.'

'So it was left to the women?'

Serotkin shrugged. 'Of course. That was the tradition.'

'The women shouldn't have put up with it,' said Francesca.

'But it was the women who wanted it that way.'

'*Wanted* it?'

'No Russian woman could love a man who washed dishes or ironed clothes.'

Francesca scowled. 'Then they've sure got a long way to go.'

Serotkin finished his plate of food. 'Does your . . . friend do his own cooking and cleaning?'

'Sure, well, he has a maid, I guess, and we usually eat out because we're both busy.'

'Do you have a maid?'

'Sure . . .'

'A woman?'

'Yes. A Jamaican.'

'Because you're busy?'

'Yes. But that actually doesn't have anything to do with it . . .'

'Of course not.'

Francesca looked up from her yoghurt: she could not tell because of the beard whether or not Serotkin's smile was ironic. 'The fact is,' she said, 'that if Duncan and I were to get married, we should share the chores.'

'And the labour to earn your living?'

'Yes.'

'But . . .' He hesitated, as if considering how far he should go. 'If there is no division of labour within a marriage, if all the labour and all the chores are shared, then what binds the man to the woman or the woman to the man?'

'Well, love . . .'

'And if love goes?'

'Then . . . nothing, I guess.'

'Which puts a heavy burden on love.'

'I don't see how else things could be arranged.'

'In the past, you see, among our Russian peasants, a man could not survive without a woman nor a woman without a man. They remained together because separated they would not survive.'

'And that was *good*?'

His eyes flashed. 'Yes. I think it was good, because it meant that necessity held families together instead of mere . . . whim.'

Francesca found herself growing almost angry. 'So you'd like to see women back in the home?'

Serotkin took a packet of cigarettes out of his pocket and offered one to Francesca. She shook her head, surprised that anyone could imagine she might smoke. 'Have you read the work of Valentin Rasputin?' he asked.

'Rasputin? The monk?'

He frowned, just as a tutor might frown when a student gave a particularly crass answer to one of his questions. 'No. Valentin Rasputin. He is a contemporary writer, a Siberian. Some of his works have been translated.'

'I'm sorry. I don't know them.'

Without asking Francesca whether she minded or not, Serotkin lit his cigarette. 'Rasputin depicts an ideal woman who comes from the Russian tradition. She is not assertive and ambitious – a scientist or a writer or an engineer – but someone warm, stable, affectionate and strong; a mediator, if you like, between the sky and the soil.'

A cloud of heavy blue smoke drifted towards Francesca. It had an unusual, sweet aroma. She fanned her face with her hand. If Serotkin saw this gesture as a complaint, he did nothing to show it.

'It seems to me,' he went on, 'that Western women no longer see themselves as the companions of men, but rather as their competitors, their rivals . . .'

'They just want their due,' said Francesca irritably.

'Their due?'

'Well, their rights.'

Serotkin smiled. 'To what?'

'To equal treatment.'

He nodded. 'In the factory . . .'

'And the office.'

'Yes.'

'And the home.'

He drew smoke into his lungs. 'By equal you mean the same?'

'Sure. Equal means the same.'

'A nut and a bolt may be equal but they are not the same.'

'And is that how you see men and women? As nuts and bolts?'

'More or less.'

'And what if a bolt doesn't want to be a bolt but would rather be a nut?'

'We are what we are.'

'That's fatalistic.'

'Yes.'

'And un-American.'

'I dare say.' He took another drag on his cigarette.

As if by tacit agreement, Francesca McDermott and Andrei Serotkin kept their distance in the days that followed this first encounter after Serotkin's return to Berlin. They met in the office, of course, and Serotkin did indeed prove invaluable in tracing paintings from collections in the former Soviet Union. Francesca's knowledge of Russian was rudimentary; none of the others knew any at all. It was therefore Serotkin who made all the calls that required a Russian speaker and on a Cyrillic typewriter obtained by Julius Breitenbach typed the letters to the lenders.

However, his presence in the office was a mild irritation. It was not so much the recollection of his obnoxious opinions that annoyed her as her own inability to make him out. Serotkin did not fit into any of the predetermined categories that Francesca stored in her mind. She was not someone who allowed her first impressions of a person to become her definitive judgement and, while confident in her ability to judge character, she was not so arrogant as to imagine that her experience of human nature in Wisconsin, Michigan, New England and, to some extent, New York qualified her to assess those from an entirely different culture like Serotkin. She was also always ready to encounter the enigmatic; but to her enigma meant silence and reserve, whereas

Serotkin had been open, almost insolent, in the way he had assaulted her with his offensive views on the position of women. How could anyone, even a Russian, hold such antediluvian views? But then how could anyone in this day and age smoke untipped cigarettes?

She had been thrown, she realized, by her assumption that a Russian academic would be like the kind of European academic she had encountered from time to time. She had been encouraged in this assumption by the quality and good taste of his clothes. She should have been alerted, she saw now, by her very first impression – that quality she had referred to as 'dashing' which she could now neither analyse nor define. Was it only because she had expected a stooping old professor that she had been taken aback by the appearance of a man so fit and slim? He had moved with such confidence around her office, as if used to having his own way with the things and people around him. And there had been the look in his eyes – those murky eyes whose colour she could not remember – that at times encouraged a kind of camaraderie but then betrayed perhaps a sneer, even a trace of cruelty and contempt. Sky and soil! Nuts and bolts! Had he been teasing her over lunch or had he meant what he said?

She soon discovered to her consternation that, when it came to the exhibition, his opposition to her ideas was in earnest. A postponed decision on the scale of the exhibition was on the agenda of the next meeting of the organizing committee which Serotkin attended. Francesca argued as before for a show of limited size on a single site showing only major works by the artists chosen. 'Having looked at the different galleries,' she said, 'I would favour the New National Gallery in West Berlin. It is the only one with the kind of facilities we will require.'

'I disagree,' said Serotkin abruptly. 'It should be a comprehensive retrospective exhibition of the entire body of Russian experimental art.'

The meeting was held in the overheated conference chamber at the Prussian Ministry of Culture. Stefan Diederich was in the chair. He looked down the table to Günter Westarp. 'What do you feel?'

'I think, Herr Minister, that while I appreciate the force behind Dr McDermott's argument which she advanced so eloquently at our last meeting, there is also something to be said, in terms of our political objectives, for thinking on a grander scale.'

'Grand does not always mean large,' said Francesca.

'That is unquestionably true,' said Westarp, glancing nervously around the table at everyone but Andrei Serotkin. 'And from the purely artistic point of view, which is naturally the point of view that one would expect Dr McDermott to take, she is undoubtedly right; but it would hardly help those living in East Berlin and eastern Germany to feel that this was part of their tradition if the exhibition was confined to a gallery in the western half of the city.'

'I concur with this last stated opinion,' said Dr Kemmelkampf, the civil servant in the Ministry of Culture with responsibility for the exhibition. 'There is something to be said for the more comprehensive option simply because it would necessitate the use of sites in the two halves of the city. The symmetry of the two architectural gems from different epochs, Mies van der Rohe's New National Gallery in West Berlin and Schinkel's Old Museum in the east, would itself symbolize the reintegration of the old and the new.'

'What is in the Old Museum at present?' Serotkin asked Diederich.

'Social realists like Strempel and Cremer . . .'

'Paintings of heroic labour by Willi Sitte,' said Günter Westarp, 'and Waldemar Grzimek's statue of a worker on a collective farm.'

'So wouldn't it help to make the point to remove their paintings to make way for works by Kandinsky and Chagall?'

'Most emphatically,' said Diederich.

'But think of the expense and the organization,' said Francesca. 'As it is, we have set ourselves the almost impossible task of organizing a major exhibition in under a year. If we aim to bring to Berlin every work of art by all of the artists on our list . . .'

'As far as finance is concerned,' Stefi interrupted, 'the bigger the better. The foundations to which we look for funding are more likely to be enticed by something grandiose than by something . . . refined.'

'And if the political will is there,' said Kemmelkampf, the civil servant, 'then the organizational means can always be found.'

79

Stefan Diederich turned to Francesca. 'Are you persuaded?'

She shrugged. 'Sure. If that's how you all feel . . .'

The meeting proceeded to consider less controversial matters, and towards four in the afternoon drew to its end.

'Is there any other business?' asked Diederich.

Serotkin raised his hand.

'Dr Serotkin?'

'I was unfortunately absent at the last meeting when this committee reached its decision on the title of the exhibition which was, I believe, "The Indomitable Spirit: Russian Art in Exile".'

'Do you object to the title?' asked Stefan Diederich.

'In my view, it is imprecise, and should be reconsidered.'

Francesca could not withhold a sigh of exasperation. 'We went into it at great length, Dr Serotkin. We have already had stationery printed . . .'

The title is misleading,' said Serotkin, 'since much of the work we are considering was done in Russia. It might make it more difficult – perhaps impossible – to secure loans from Russian museums if we persist with a title of this kind.'

Frowning, Stefan Diederich turned to Günter Westarp. 'Can you remember what other titles we had in mind?'

Günter Westarp nervously tugged at his moustache. ' "The Triumph of the Spirit: the Modern in Russian Art".'

'That was rejected,' said Kemmelkampf, 'because it was thought that it had a resonance with Riefenstahl's film made under the fascists, *The Triumph of the Will*.'

'I have a proposal,' said Serotkin.

'Please . . .' said Diederich.

' "Excursus: the Cosmopolitan in Russian Art".'

There was a silence. Diederich looked up the table. 'Would anyone like to express a view on this proposal?'

'I think it's terrible,' said Francesca.

'Would you care to elaborate?'

'Well, why Excursus?'

'It is a short word,' said Serotkin, 'that seems to encapsulate most aptly what we want to convey.'

Francesca was close to losing her temper. She turned to the chairman, Stefan Diederich. 'With no disrespect, it seems to me that perhaps Dr Serotkin does not understand the precise meaning of obscure words in the English language. Excursus comes from the Latin and means "digression". It is untranslatable into some modern languages. For those who know what it means, it will suggest that the art exhibited is somehow an aberration, and if placed alongside the word "cosmopolitan", it will give the impression that we do not regard it as a genuine manifestation of Russian culture.'

Serotkin smiled at her with the condescension of an adversary in a game who knows he will win. 'It is precisely because "excursus" is a universal and untranslatable word that it will provoke interest in the exhibition.' He stretched out his hands. 'Imagine, in large lettering, on a poster. *Excursus*. It will catch the eye. It also has an affinity with the word "exodus" and as such will be a subtle reference to the exile of so many of the artists who, as latterday children of Israel, escaped from the oppression of the Russian pharaohs into a land flowing with milk and honey . . .'

Francesca frowned: she could not make out whether or not Serotkin was entirely serious. 'I think you mean,' she said, '*like* latterday children of Israel, not *as* latterday children of Israel.'

Serotkin said nothing.

'Unless you meant to refer to the fact that some of the artists were Jews.'

'Presumably not,' said Diederich hastily.

'As to the word "cosmopolitan",' Serotkin went on, opening a Webster's Pocket Dictionary on the table in front of him, 'it is defined here as "belonging to the whole world, not national, local . . .''; but it would also be a pointer to the suppression of such art in that "cosmopolitan" was the term of abuse used for such art by Stalin and the advocates of socialist realism.'

'Just as the word 'degenerate' was used by the Nazis,' said Günter Westarp.

'And the word was used, I seem to remember,' said Dr Kemmelkampf, 'by the exhibition in Munich in 1957.'

'Which in a sense,' said Diederich, 'is the model for our exhibition.'

There was a short silence. Then Dr Kemmelkampf cleared his throat. 'I have to say . . . of course, this is purely a personal opinion . . . that the title proposed by Dr Serotkin does seem more *arresting* than the title we had provisionally chosen.'

'It would certainly look good on a poster,' said Günter Westarp.

'And I think the embedded reference to the show in Munich,' said Stefan Diederich, 'is an important consideration.'

They waited in silence. Francesca looked around the table for allies. The director of the New National Gallery shrugged his shoulders in a gesture of surrender. Frau Dr Koch and Julius Breitenbach, there in an advisory capacity only, avoided meeting her eyes.

'Dr McDermott?' asked Stefan Diederich.

She too shrugged her shoulders in capitulation. 'OK. If that's what you want. Excursus it is.'

SIX

Andrei Orlov's wife Tatiana lived in an old-fashioned block on the Malya Bronnaya, an area favoured by writers and artists. The lift was antique – an ornate cage of the Tsarist era quite unlike the functional tin boxes that carried most Muscovites up to their apartments.

Nikolai Gerasimov pressed the button for the fourth floor with a sceptical look on his face. Despite recent events, he still had faith in progress and therefore doubts about anything old. With a clank, the lift started moving. Gerasimov looked at his watch. It was past four. The boy would be back from school. There was no record of a resident babushka. Tatiana Orlova should be at home.

He rang the bell. A woman came to the door. He first saw the back of her head because, as she opened it, she turned to shout behind her: 'Come, Igor, it's Drusha . . .'

She then turned and saw that it was not the girl Drusha whom she was expecting but a tall, muscular, slightly pockmarked man who, from the look in her eyes that momentarily followed the expression of surprise, knew that she knew who he was, where he came from and why he was there.

'I am Nikolai Stefanovich Gerasimov,' he said politely, still instinctively deferential to the daughter of a man once as powerful as Keminski. 'If it is not inconvenient, I would like to make some enquiries.'

Because she knew, she did not ask what the enquiries were about but stepped aside to let him in. 'A friend of my son's is coming to play,' she said in a matter-of-fact manner, her eyes avoiding Gerasimov's by looking at the ground.

'This won't take long.' He started to remove his shoes but with a wave Tatiana Orlova told him to keep them on. 'There's clay all over the floor,' she said as she closed the door and led Gerasimov down the corridor. As he passed the kitchen Gerasimov glimpsed a young boy writing at the table.

They came into a large room – immense, for a private apartment – that clearly served as her living room and studio, and probably her bedroom too: there was a single bed behind a screen in the corner. In the centre of the room, about five feet from the window, a tripod stood on a square of linoleum, and on top of the tripod on a square board a lump the size of a human head, swathed in a cloth like a turban. From the marks on the linoleum, Gerasimov assumed that this was a lump of clay, covered to retain the moisture. Against the wall, on a shelf, there were some finished works – abstract shapes with no resemblance to any natural form.

Tatiana Orlova invited Gerasimov to sit down on the sofa that divided the area used as a studio from the rest of the room. She herself sat on a wooden chair, crossed her legs and leaned forward – the posture of someone ready to listen. She was wearing blue workman's overalls, smudged with the marks of clay. She was tall and could have been beautiful if she had not been so thin. With more flesh on her bones, her nose would not have been so angular, her cheekbones so protruding, her bosom so flat. The leanness of her face made her eyes seem large – certainly in contrast to the slits of Ylena's piggy eyes. In the sunlight from the window, Gerasimov saw grey strands in her black hair.

'Well?' She looked up, impatient to get things under way.

'I am from the state security service of the Russian Federation.'

'Yes.' She waved her hand as if to say: 'Dispense with the formalities.'

'You will doubtless be familiar with . . .'

'Yes.'

'Your husband, Andrei Anatolyevich Orlov, as you know, worked for the former Committee for State Security.'

'Yes.'

'And we are now trying to make contact with some of the former employees to, as it were, tie up loose ends.'

Gerasimov found, to his irritation, that he was speaking with a certain nervousness without understanding why. Was it because of her connections? Or because she seemed so indifferent to his presence in her flat?

'I have had no contact with my husband,' she said. 'So far as I know, he is not in Moscow.'

'He is in the West.'

She neither acknowledged that she knew this or that the information caused her any surprise.

'Did you know this?'

'What?'

'That he was in the West?'

She hesitated 'I did not know it, but I assumed it.'

'Why?'

'He has not been to see Igor.'

'Normally, he would come to see his son?'

'Yes.'

'How often?'

She shrugged. 'When he's in Moscow, once or twice a week.'

'Did he say, when he last came, when he would come again?'

'He said he would be gone for a time . . .'

'Did he say for how long?'

'No.'

'Or why?'

'No.'

'Did he give you no clue at all as to why he was going to the West?'

'Perhaps to look for work?' She said this coolly, looking Gerasimov straight in the eye. 'After all, he lost his job.'

'He was offered a post at the Tretyakov.'

'That was given to one of his men.'

'You knew that?'

'He told me.'

'He could have had a job there if he had wanted it.'

'Not one suited to his talents.'

'Your husband was, I think, a convinced Communist.'

'Not only my husband . . .'

'No.'

'And . . .' She hesitated. 'It was more complicated than that.'

'You must forgive me if I appear to be intruding on a private matter, Tatiana Ivanovna, but I understand that your separation from your husband was caused by ideological differences?'

She smiled again, a sour, sad smile. 'Are you married?'

'Yes.'

'Sometimes ideology is an excuse for other things.'

'But there was no other woman and no other man.'

'Oh, but there was.'

Gerasimov looked perplexed. 'That was not our understanding.'

'The other man was Jesus Christ.' She said this evenly.

'I see. And the other woman?'

'Mother Russia.'

She spoke with no trace of irony, and it struck Gerasimov that perhaps her impressive, incurious manner was the mask of someone who was mad – that the insanity of believers, like the insanity of dissidents, was not, after all, a contrivance of the Fifth Chief Directorate. In the present circumstances, however, he was more likely to achieve his objective if he treated Tatiana Orlova as if she was sane.

'You became a believer?' he said.

'Yes.'

'And he did not?'

'He believed,' she said, 'but not in God.'

'In Russia?'

'Not just in Russia. The Union.'

'He was therefore against the plans of Mikhail Sergeyevich Gorbachev for a new treaty between the republics?'

'Yes.'

'And so was in favour of the coup?'

86

'He was not in the Soviet Union during the coup.'

'And if he had been?'

She looked at him coldly. 'Your guess is as good as mine.'

'He remained a Communist?'

'So far as I know, he has not torn up his Party card.'

'But he believed . . .'

'In what?'

'In Marxism and Leninism.'

She hesitated. 'It is some time since I discussed such things with him . . .'

'And then?'

'Then? He believed in Marxism and Leninism, yes, but only, I think, as a means to an end.'

'What do you mean?'

'He would say . . ' She stopped. 'Is this relevant?'

'It might be.'

'He would say that a nation must share a belief, whether or not it was true.'

'Then why not become a Christian like you?'

'Because religion is the opium of the people.' She smiled. 'He thought Christianity was too gentle . . .'

'While Communism was strong?'

'Yes.'

'Our people no longer seem to share his point of view.'

Again, she smiled. 'They have turned to worship the Golden Calf.'

Gerasimov looked puzzled. 'What golden calf?'

'When Moses was up in the mountain receiving the Ten Commandments, the people of Israel turned away from God and started to worship a golden calf.'

Gerasimov nodded. 'Do you think,' he said, 'that in view of recent political developments, your husband might have felt authorized to retain state funds?'

'Again, you ask me to speculate.'

'It is my duty.'

She sighed. 'Would he feel authorized? By whom?'

'General Khrulev, for example.'

'I was told that Khrulev was dead.'

'Then certain figures in the parliament – Rutskoi, for example, or Khasbulatov?'

'I don't know.'

'Or even, perhaps, by himself?'

'You mean, would he steal state funds like everyone else?' She laughed. 'No, comrade. Whatever else he may be, Andrei is not a thief.'

The doorbell rang. Tatiana Orlova got to her feet. 'That must be Drusha. Will you excuse me a moment?'

Her courtesy annoyed Gerasimov. After she had left the room, he stood to look around. The room lacked any of the luxuries that Gerasimov would esteem – a colour television, a video recorder, a compact disc player – but had an old oak wardrobe, a table covered with a silk cloth, a huge old samovar: all things from before the Revolution, antiques like her beliefs. 'Privileged bitch,' he said to himself, 'pretending she never fucks or farts.'

He looked behind the screen at her narrow single bed. Georgi's words came back to him: 'Women need servicing, regular servicing, thorough servicing'; but it looked as if there was no one to service this dried out, stuck-up, would-be nun.

He could hear children's voices from the corridor. A single woman with one child in an apartment this size! Perhaps he should offer to move in with her. He would fuck some colour back into her cheeks.

A brave idea. When Tatiana returned, Gerasimov saw that her first glance – a wistful glance – went not to the Russian Harrison Ford but to the turbaned lump of clay. Then, impassively, she looked over to where Gerasimov was standing by the bookcase next to her bed and asked: 'Are there any further questions?'

He was on official business. He must be correct. 'Can you think of anyone else . . . a friend, perhaps, who might know where he has gone?'

She did not sit down. 'You probably know about his friends better than I do.'

'He had no girlfriend?'

'What does it say in his file?'

'Nothing.'

'Is that so difficult to understand?'

88

He could see that she regretted putting the question, even before he answered, because it enabled him to say, as he did: 'Not now that I have met you, Tatiana Ivanovna . . .'

The compliment was unwelcome. 'The children . . .' she began.

'Yes, I am going.' He walked towards the door. 'I would be grateful if you would tell me if you hear from him.'

She said nothing.

As he walked past the kitchen, he glanced in and saw that the boy now sat at the table with a girl of twelve or thirteen. Tatiana made no move to introduce them. Gerasimov moved on down the corridor. 'A fine boy,' he said. 'His father must be proud of him.'

Again, she did not answer. Gerasimov sensed that she was impatient to get him out of the house. 'Remember, a telephone call or a postcard,' he said as she opened the door.

'You will know,' she said, leaving it uncertain as to whether he would know from her or by intercepting her mail and her calls; and then without bothering to say goodbye she closed the door.

Gerasimov was angry. At first he did not know why he was angry —whether it was at the condescension of Orlov's wife or because of the frustrating lack of results of his investigations: probably both. It was quite apparent that both Partovsky and Tatiana were holding something back. Both were too well acquainted with the methods of the former KGB to try to conceal what Gerasimov might discover from other sources; both had appeared to give straight answers to his questions, but neither had cared to confide or to speculate. Both had seen him as an adversary; both in their own way were aiding and abetting the absent Orlov by their minimal cooperation.

Partovsky, he could understand. No one likes to turn in a fellow officer, particularly a former commander whom one has admired. Gerasimov would have sympathized with Tatiana, too, if she had still been Orlov's wife. No woman can be expected to betray the man she loves. But they were separated and ideologically opposed. Tatiana should welcome the defeat of the coup, the death of Khrulev and the sacking of hard-line officers like Orlov from the new security service of the Russian Federation. She should have seen Gerasimov as her protector – a knight in shining armour. Instead, she had treated him as a vulgar interloper who had no business poking his nose into her life.

'Privileged bitch,' he said for the second time, as if the coarse words spoken into the cold air of the dusk could somehow wipe the impassive expression from her face. He was angry not just with her but also with himself – for having fancied her, for having paid her a compliment, knowing quite well that it would be thrown back in his face. The overalls had angered him; her art, like her religion, was the kind of pretension that only the élite could afford.

Gerasimov returned to the Lubyanka and spent what remained of the day planning the evening ahead. He had been sleeping for the last fortnight on his sister's sofa, but sensed that he had already outstayed his welcome. He remained determined not to return to Ylena. He wanted her to suffer. In the end he would move back into their flat on the Ulitsa Akademika Koroleva, but he would first have to get over the rage he still felt at the thought of Ylena with Georgi and that night at the Cosmos Hotel.

Gerasimov was running short of old friends to land on. The patience of most of them had worn thin. The last resort would appear to be Klaudia, an old girlfriend whom he saw from time to time. She would certainly give him a bed for the night unless someone else happened to be in it, but she lived right out in Prazskaya and he could not turn up empty-handed. It would mean sacrificing the bottle of vodka locked in the bottom drawer of his desk: a high price to pay for a night either on Klaudia's sofa or in Klaudia's bed.

He could stay in a hotel, but that would be tricky. It would not be easy to find a room. It would be recorded by the militia and so would find its way into his file, giving an impression of 'domestic instability' that might affect his future career. In the end, Klaudia seemed the most satisfactory solution. He called her. Her drowsy voice answer·d the telephone. She said he could come but warned him that she had nothing to eat.

Gerasimov scrounged some ham and a tin of pilchards from the Lubyanka canteen and, since there was no petrol in the Samara, set off for the suburbs on the metro, changing at Prazskaya onto a bus. He reached Klaudia's flat by nine. It was quite clear that she had made no effort to tidy up or improve her own appearance. As always, it was hard for Gerasimov to recognize the bright-eyed blonde he had screwed when she was eighteen in the fat slut of thirty-five with her unbrushed hair and worn slippers.

He was not offended: the great advantage of Klaudia was that though she gave nothing she expected nothing in return. He went through the routine pretence of being pleased to see her. She looked indifferent until he gave her the bottle of vodka, at which point she perked up. He brought out the ham and the tin of pilchards. She had some bread. They ate and they drank. Klaudia started on a long, plaintive story about how she had been done down by her supervisor in the typing pool at Radio Moscow where she worked. Gerasimov tried to listen but he longed to sleep. His mind wandered. He filled their glasses. He was getting drunk. Klaudia started shaking her finger at him. He tried to focus once again on what she was saying. It was the old story that they should have married; that it was because of him that her husband had walked out on her; he was so jealous; just because she was seeing . . . and so on. He had heard it all before. Like the bottle of vodka, it was the price he had to pay for a night's board and lodging.

And Klaudia, as always, was thrown in. By the time they had finished the bottle, the vodka had produced illusions of desire. They staggered from the kitchen into Klaudia's bedroom and fell onto her bed. Gerasimov went to work, too drunk to feel much pleasure, simply doing what had to be done. And as he groped her flabby body, he began to imagine that she was Ylena. His grunts became angry, his thrusts became blows. Then he thought of the lanky, stuck-up sculptress and became angrier still, yanking back strands of Klaudia's hair which, being mistaken as a sign of passion, only heightened her excitement until, after a few more brutal thrusts, Gerasimov slumped onto her in a stupor, spent and steeped in self-disgust.

SEVEN

That evening, while Nikolai Gerasimov found solace with Klaudia Spizenko, typist in the pool at Radio Moscow, Tatiana Orlova changed out of her overalls into a dress, left her son Igor with Drusha, the thirteen year old daughter of her neighbour, and walked up to the Tverskoi Boulevard where she caught a bus.

She got off the bus after it had crossed the Kalinin Bridge over the Moscow River where the huge Hotel Ukraine faces the White House, the parliament of the Russian Federation. Barbed wire entanglements, tanks and barricades still remained as relics of Yeltsin's defiant resistance against the coup the year before.

Next to the Hotel Ukraine, there was a second skyscraper of the Stalinist era with a grandiose entrance and pale grey walls. As she walked towards it in the dusk, Tatiana shuddered. Since she had learned that so many millions had died in the gulags at the time this block had been built, she had always imagined that the bricks had been made with their ground-up bones.

Tatiana was admitted by the concierge who kept watch on the door. 'Are they there, Katerina Petrovna?' she asked.

'So far as I know.' The grim-faced woman did not smile, but her tone was familiar, even friendly.

Tatiana took the lift to the ninth floor and, as she came out onto the landing, took a key from her bag. With the key, she let herself into an apartment.

'Hello,' she shouted as she closed the door.

'Tania?' came the voice of an older woman.

'Mother?'

'We're in the kitchen.'

Tatiana's mother had no need to say this, for although it was a large flat with big rooms, some facing across the river to the White House, Tatiana's childhood had been spent in that kitchen. It was there that her mother had felt at ease.

Her parents were eating – her mother standing at the stove, her father sitting at the table. The mother embraced her: the father, gruffly but with evident pleasure, patted the seat beside him on the bench that ran along the wall.

Tatiana sat down where he had suggested – her thin body slipping easily in between the bench and the table. Her mother, a small, broad woman with a round face and grey hair combed back into a bun, put a bowl of soup and a spoon in front of her daughter. Tatiana glanced at it, then smiled up at her mother, thanked her, picked up the spoon but, instead of dipping it into the soup, turned to her father and asked: 'Where is Andrei?'

Ivan Keminski frowned. He was a man of around sixty with dark features, a grave look and the same high cheekbones and pointed nose as his daughter.

'You know,' he said. 'He went West.'

'They were asking about him.'

'Who?'

'Someone from the Lubyanka.'

'What did you tell him?'

'That I didn't know where he was or what he was doing.'

'Which is true.'

'Yes. But if they are suspicious, then . . .'

'What?'

'I am afraid.'

'For Andrei?'

She blushed. 'Not just for Andrei. Also for you.'

Her father laughed, but as he did so Tatiana glanced at her mother and saw that she, too, was anxious.

'I know that you and he have something planned,' she said.

'A joint venture, that is all.'

'What kind of joint venture?'

'Nothing. Just a bank.'

'A *bank*? The last two Marxists in Russia are starting a *bank*?'

'Not starting a bank, no. Just opening a branch of a Western bank.'

'But Father . . .'

'They have suspended the Party. There is no more Central Committee. No more secretariat. I am out of a job. Andrei too.'

'But a bank . . .'

He frowned again. 'What would you want me to do? Sell apples from the dacha in the market?'

'No.' She shook her head. She knew – she saw, she could not avoid it – how terribly the recent events had upset her father who had given his life to the Communist cause. Since her conversion to Christianity, she had often argued with him and, being young and quick-witted, she had sometimes got the better of him; but in those days he had always had his position to sustain him as a leading idealogue at the centre of influence of one of the two great powers of the world. Now, since the coup and the suspension of the Party, it had become impossible to argue against him without appearing to gloat over the downfall of the Soviet state.

'Why not a bank?' asked Tatiana's mother, still standing at the stove. 'We have plenty of room in the apartment. All you need is a telephone and a typewriter and a fax – that's a bank!' She said this with childlike enthusiasm, but it was unconvincing. She still had a worried look on her face.

'But what do you know about banking, Father?' Tatiana asked.

'You don't need to know much. There are banks in the West which want to invest in Russia. They need people with contacts. I have contacts. That is my capital, my contacts.'

'And what do they bring?'

'The money. Currency.'

'And what has Andrei to do with it?'

'Well, precisely, he is in Europe to arrange things. To set it up.'

Tatiana looked uncertain. It sounded plausible, and would have been plausible had the idea been put forward by two other men.

'Is there no more to it than that?' she asked.

'What more should there be?'

'Andrei served under General Khrulev and General Khrulev was involved in politics up to his neck.'

'Maybe. Perhaps that's why they want to question Andrei. But the coup failed. Khrulev is dead. We now have to change our ideas to survive.'

Tatiana put down her spoon. The soup was untouched. 'I know you love Andrei,' she said to her father, 'and that you were sorry when we separated . . .'

Keminski shrugged. 'What's done is done.'

'I know that perhaps you think it was my fault, that becoming a believer made it impossible for Andrei . . .'

'No man wants to be married to a nun.'

Tatiana blushed. 'I wasn't a nun, Father. I was always, well, a wife.'

'Don't talk of these things,' the mother muttered.

Tatiana looked up. 'I am afraid, Mother. I am afraid not just for him but of what he might do. And I blame myself, because a man with a family will think twice before he does anything dangerous.'

'But there is nothing dangerous about a bank,' said Ivan Keminski.

She turned on her father. 'Whatever you may say, Father, you will not persuade me that Andrei has now become a bourgeois businessman. I know him. I know him better than anyone. He is a believer, a true believer, a Soviet patriot, a Bolshevik dreamer, and I fear he will stop at nothing to make those dreams come true.'

'An idealist,' said Ivan Keminski, 'not a dreamer, as any Chekist worthy of the name should be.'

The telephone rang. Ivan Keminski left the room to answer it. Tatiana was relieved. When her father became bombastic, she knew that the time had come to change the subject.

'Ah, Nogin, at last . . .' Her father's voice boomed from the hallway. 'I've been trying to get through to you for several days

. . . Did you get the message? My nephew, yes . . . in Jena. I'd be most grateful . . . Bored, I think . . . Without currency, they can hardly afford to breathe. Yes. That would be kind . . . Here? Don't ask. Terrible. To think we fought for this . . . Courage, my old friend . . . Courage of a different kind.'

Keminski came back into the kitchen. Tatiana rose to go. 'Is Piotr in Germany?'

'No, in Saratov. Why?'

'Then who is your nephew in Germany?'

For a moment, the old man looked confused. 'What nephew in Germany?'

'I thought you just said, on the telephone, that you had a nephew in Jena?'

'Ah yes. It's Piotr. Of course it's Piotr. I only have one nephew, after all. He's going there, briefly, on some business or other and I told him to look up my old friend Nogin. He's still stationed there. You won't remember Nogin. We were in the army together. Back in 1945 our tanks ran neck to neck in the race from Stalingrad to Berlin. Brave soldier. Good comrade. He got there first. And now, I dare say, he'll be one of the last to leave.'

EIGHT

Colonel Yevgeni Mikhailovich Nogin, Ivan Keminski's old comrade-in-arms, commanded the Soviet base at Waldheim, fifty miles north of Berlin. His most pressing duty during the short, dark days that winter was finding something for his men to do. There was no reason now to train for a war with NATO. They knew they were to return to Russia when, if ever, somewhere was built for them to live. What reason was there to get up in the morning, let alone turn up on parade? The most Nogin could hope to get out of his men was an hour or two each morning spent servicing the tanks before they were loaded onto trains at the Tucheim sidings on the first stage of their journey back to the scrapheaps in Russia.

By mid-afternoon, most of Colonel Nogin's men were tipsy. By sunset, they were dead drunk. If they had no vodka, wine or cognac, they stole pure alcohol from the dispensary or even antifreeze from the workshops. Since Colonel Nogin himself was not immune from this national weakness, he was usually flushed when the time came to eat dinner with his fellow officers in the mess. Not only was his face red in patches; one or two buttons on his tunic were often left undone. Most of his subordinates were in the same condition.

Only Captain Sinyanski was always sober. At one time, Colonel Nogin had been afraid of Sinyanksi who was known to report back to the Third Directorate of the KGB. At the time of the coup, Sinyanski had become agitated – plotting, so Nogin suspected, to arrest and incarcerate those officers whom he considered ideologically unsound. After the collapse of the coup, and the subsequent restructuring of the KGB as the security service of the Russian Federation, Sinyanski had become dejected. He was now a toothless tiger. Nogin no longer feared him. He even came to like him. Sinyanksi was more intelligent and so better company than most of the other officers, and Nogin shared many of Sinyanski's feelings, particularly his anger at the way Gorbachev and Shevardnadze had surrendered Germany without a fight.

Although it was now stranded in the middle of hostile territory by the receding tide of Soviet power, the garrison at Waldheim was little affected by the collapse of the Communist government in the DDR. There were no more May Day parades in the nearby town of Tucheim where girls with blonde pigtails from the Freie Deutsche Jugend would present their 'fraternal liberators from fascism' with bunches of flowers. But nor were his men stoned by the local inhabitants when they went to Tucheim on leave as Nogin had once feared.

It was not until December that Nogin heard from Piotr Perfilyev, Keminski's nephew in Jena. He immediately invited him to stay at the base for the weekend. They were glad to see some fresh faces and were hardly short of space. In due course, Perfilyev turned up at Tucheim on the train. Nogin sent a junior officer, Lieutenant Vorotnikov, to meet him.

Perfilyev was brought straight to Nogin's house. He wore civilian clothes and told Nogin that he was working in Jena as an engineer. Perfiliev was a tall bearded man well into his thirties, perhaps even forty, who bore no resemblance either to his uncle, Ivan Keminski, or his mother, Keminski's sister, whom Nogin had met in Moscow after the war.

Perfilyev produced as a gift for the garrison six bottles of Stolichnaya vodka. The five that found their way to the officers' mess ensured a warm welcome for the visitor who was placed next to Nogin at dinner. Perfilyev's health was the first of many toasts that were proposed in the course of the evening.

As they became drunk, the officers lost their inhibitions and an argument started up between Sinyanski and the young lieutenant, Vorotnikov, about the slander in a new guide to the former concentration camp at Sachsenhausen, situated between Waldheim and Berlin.

'If it's true, it's true,' said Vorotnikov. 'Hitler built Sachsenhausen. Stalin made use of it after the war. Think of what he did to the kulaks in Ukraine. The one was as bad as the other . . .'

'Untrue,' shouted Sinyanski. 'Certainly, Stalin did what had to be done because he faced desperate odds. People died, I grant you that. Perhaps innocent people were killed. But the end justified the means. Without collectivization there would have been no industrialization, and without industrialization, there would have been no tanks to fight the fascists at Stalingrad and Kursk. Where would those swines in the West be now if our fathers and grandfathers hadn't laid down their lives in the Great Patriotic War? The concentration camps would still be in business and there wouldn't be a Jew left alive!'

'That's as may be, Alexander Sergeyevich,' another junior officer broke in, 'but you can't build the future on the courage and heroism of past generations. It won't build our economy. It won't buy food.'

'Lenin and Stalin imposed Communism,' shouted another, 'and Communism doesn't work.'

'Who says it doesn't work?' countered Sinyanski. 'No country on earth has achieved so much in so short a space of time. In 1918 we were a bankrupt nation of muzhiks. In 1945 we were a major world power.'

'And now we're a bankrupt nation of muzhiks once again,' said Lieutenant Vorotnikov.

'Only because so-called reformers have bartered the achievements of three generations for a loan from the World Bank.'

'They had no choice . . .'

A number of voices now clamoured to be heard, but since no one could rise above the other, and since most were now too drunk to sustain a cogent argument of any kind, they all eventually petered out; whereupon Nogin, from curiosity as well as politeness, turned to Perfilyev, who until that point had remained silent. 'Have you a view of the current situation, comrade? You know better than we do what's in store for us when we get home.'

'I sympathize with our friend here,' said the visitor, nodding towards Sinyanski, 'but I am afraid that we have to acknowledge that we have been outmanoeuvred by the enemy.'

'Outmanoeuvred?' asked Nogin, hoping that the conversation was moving on to military matters that he could better understand.

'Outwitted is perhaps a better word,' said Perfilyev.

'How do you mean?'

'It was a mistake to spend all our resources on defence, and on prestige projects like the space programme or foreign aid. We should have invested in the quality of life . . .'

'I agree,' said Nogin. 'To think of all those roubles going to Cuba and Nicaragua and Ethiopia, when our own people were going short.'

'What Marx and Lenin promised, after all,' Perfiliev went on, 'was not wealth but justice, a society in which each gave according to his ability and each received according to his needs.'

'But after seventy-five years of socialism,' said Vorotnikov, 'there are still millions who do not receive according to their needs.'

'Yes,' went up a cry. 'What about our housing?'

'We are impoverished,' said Perfilyev, 'precisely because we concentrated our resources on preparing for a war that would never be fought. If they had been used instead on public welfare, then we could have shown the world the superiority of our socialist way of life.'

'But the Americans and Germans would still be richer,' said a Major Ivashenko, Nogin's second-in-command, 'and they would enjoy liberties that were not permitted under our Soviet system.'

'Liberties?' asked Perfilyev who, though he had drunk little, was now flushed. 'I have lived in America, comrade, and I can tell you that their so-called liberty is just the cant of their corrupt intelligentsia. In reality, it is the most intolerant and unequal society the world has ever seen. You can become rich, true, but once you are rich you are imprisoned in your suburban villas behind chain fences while drug-crazed hoodlums prowl the streets, hunting and pillaging and murdering their own kind. That is what liberty means in America, comrades – to exploit if you can, and rob if you cannot.'

'I get the impression,' said Nogin, 'that you did not warm to the Americans?'

'Warm to them? No. I loathed them. They are a nation of mongrels, the descendants of all the miscreants, malcontents and traitors who abandoned their native lands in the old world – sectarians like the Puritans and Quakers, greedy English colonists, slave-owners who preached liberty as an excuse to turn against their king; the runts in the litter of every slum in every minor nation from Latvia to Sicily, from Ireland to Greece. What is the driving spirit of every colonial culture? Greed! To hell with the people. Every man for himself. From the conquistadores in Mexico to the cattle barons in the Wild West – exploit the soil, enslave the people! And if they will not work as slaves? Herd them into reservations and let them die!'

As he was speaking, Perfilyev's eyes had widened, and their expression had grown intense. His deep voice, rising in pitch as he proceeded, held the attention of his intoxicated audience. Sinyanski looked at him with evident satisfaction. Nogin, too, could not suppress a sense of exhilaration to hear the old enemy attacked in this way. Even the young lieutenant, Vorotknikov, appeared impressed by the fervour of Perfilyev, if not by the substance of what he said.

Only the adjutant, Major Ivashenko, retained his scepticism. 'You may be right,' he said, 'but if our people now reject socialism, what can we do but follow their example?'

'It will be fatal to try,' said Perfilyev. 'Socialism suits the temperament of our people: they were always averse to capitalism of any kind. They resisted Stolypin's reforms after 1905. They will resist Yeltsin's now. Unless, of course, the so-called reforms are forced upon us by the Americans and the World Bank. Then, comrades, you have only to look south over the border to see what the future holds. Look at Turkey, a once great empire reduced to the condition of a third-rate power, its people transported to Germany to provide cheap labour for Krupp and Thyssen on the Ruhr.'

'There are Russian workers,' said Ivashenko, 'who would be only to happy to work for Krupp and Thyssen . . .'

'Of course,' said Perfilyev, an angry look now in his eyes. 'Because they are enticed by the thought of riches, and imagine that the higher their standard of living, the happier they will be. But there are some things that matter more than money, Comrade Major. Justice. Dignity. Honour. We may have been poor under Brezhnev. There may even have been cases of corruption. But what comparable country was better off? Thailand, where a quarter of a million children work in brothels? India, perhaps, where children are mutilated to make more effective beggars on the street? Or Mexico, its people admitted over the Rio Grande to work as helots in cities with the sacred names of Los Angeles and San Francisco, now the Sodom and Gomorrah of the modern world?'

It was late. The bottles were empty. The officers were sobering up, their moods sinking from joviality into melancholy. The future seemed grim. Even those like Ivanshenko who did not agree with Perfilyev found it hard to contradict him, above all because here was a rare Russian who appeared to have seen something of the world.

'So what's to be done?' asked Nogin, accepting a cigarette offered by Perfilyev.

'Another coup!' said Sinyanski. 'And next time, no scruples!'

'Things must get worse before they get better,' said Perfilyev. 'But when the moment comes . . .' He clenched his fist, as if catching and then crushing a mosquito hovering in the air.

'And in the meantime?' asked Nogin.

'We should learn from the Germans,' said Perfilyev. 'After World War One, they were only permitted an army of a hundred thousand men. They therefore made officers serve as NCOs, and

NCOs serve as privates. That way, they kept the nucleus of an army ten times the size.'

'But can the Americans dictate the size of the Russian army?' asked Nogin. 'Has it come to that?'

'It is not so much the army that has to be prepared,' said Perfilyev. 'It is the Party.'

'Ah.'

'Why do you think Yeltsin suspended it, straight after the coup, with the stroke of a pen? Because the Americans, who helped him to defeat the coup, knew that without the Party the Soviet Union was ungovernable and would fall apart.'

'But now that the Party has no state to support it, how can it survive?' asked Sinyanski, also accepting a cigarette offered to him by Perfilyev.

'It will go underground once again,' said Perfilyev, 'as it did before the Revolution.' He struck a match and lit first Nogin's cigarette, then Sinyanski's, then his own.

Nogin inhaled and then sighed as he blew out the smoke. 'I don't pretend, comrade, that I was ever a good student of Marx or Lenin, and I joined the Party because it seemed the thing to do. But there's no doubt in my mind that it was the Party, as you say, that held the Union together and so was the guarantee of the greatness of Russia. Without the Party, well, it's as you say, and quite evident for anyone to see. We're going down to God knows what depths of poverty, chaos and degradation . . .'

'It's worse than you think,' said Perfilyev darkly.

'Worse?'

'Take the job our team is doing, here in Jena. Our ministry of Medium Machine Building had some top-secret projects with our German comrades, first-rate military research. We've been told to dismantle the equipment so that it can be sent back to Moscow, but I happen to know that some of Yeltsin's people in the Defence Ministry mean to sell it to the Americans . . .'

'Impossible!'

'You can't imagine what it's like back in Moscow, Comrade Colonel. Anyone will do anything for dollars.'

'Can't you denounce them?'

'To whom? Everyone is getting a cut.'

'Then stop them!'

'How?'

'I . . . you could . . . couldn't you destroy the equipment? That would surely be better than letting it fall into the hands of the Americans.'

Perfilyev pondered. 'Where? In Germany, now, we are watched . . .'

'Bring it here.'

'Here?'

'To the base. Why not?'

'It is bulky . . .'

'We have plenty of space.' Nogin turned to Sinyanski. 'Don't we have space enough, comrade?'

'Of course. The hangars, where the tanks used to be.'

'And to destroy it?' asked Perfilyev.

'Burn it. We have some gasoline. Or we can use it for target practice for the tanks. The one thing we're not short of is shells.'

PART THREE

1993

January–May

NINE

In the first months of 1993, Francesca McDermott worked harder than she had ever worked before. The challenge she faced was not so much how to make the Excursus exhibition a triumph, but how to save it from becoming a fiasco.

From the first, Francesca had been warned by friends and colleagues in the United States that she had bitten off more than she could chew. A major exhibition could not be arranged in less than a year. At first, she had reassured herself that the back-up provided by the Germans for a show on the limited scale she envisaged could be mounted by the following July. By the time the decision had been made to make Excursus a mammoth, two-site exhibition, it was too late for Francesca to pull out.

Even then, she did not believe they would be lent all the works they had requested. However, Excursus had been endorsed at the highest political level. It aroused enthusiasm wherever it was mentioned. Pledges of backing were pressed upon the organizing committee by banks, conglomerates and foundations. In December, the Museum of Modern Art in New York agreed to lend all the works of art that had been requested. By January, it had become clear that where MOMA had led, every major national gallery was now eager to follow. Directors and private collectors wrote from all over the world offering works that Francesca had not known existed.

Many of the practical arrangements were handled by Dr Kemmelkampf and his civil servants in the Prussian Ministry of Culture; however, it became quite clear to Francesca that they had little experience in mounting exhibitions of this kind. The timetable presented particular problems. Günter confided in Francesca that a fierce dispute had broken out between the ministry and the gallery directors. The latter had already had to cancel the exhibitions they had planned for July and the first half of August. Those that went before had also to be curtailed to make way for Excursus, provoking considerable ill-feeling in members of the museum staffs who had been working on these projects for several years.

The differences had come to a head, according to Günter, over the issue of where the Excursus works of art should be stored upon arrival in Berlin. Normally, they would be sent straight to the gallery with the best facilities, in this case the New National Gallery; but because of its commitment to a major retrospective, it had not the space to handle even a part of the Excursus works of art.

'But surely there is space in one of those galleries or museums in East Berlin,' said Francesca, discussing the question with Günter one morning in his office.

'Of course there is space,' said Günter, 'but the facilities are too primitive to satisfy the lenders or, for that matter, the people in Bonn.'

'What does the ministry propose?'

'The ideal solution would be a secure warehouse where the paintings could be held until the moment came to hang them.'

'Does such a warehouse exist?'

'Of course. There is one in Tegel.'

'Then why don't we use it?'

Günter shrugged. 'You may well ask. It is all to do with budgets and precedents. Exclusive use of the warehouse would be expensive. Kemmelkampf has told Stefi that if the galleries are given this facility on this occasion, they will regard it as their right in the future.'

'But surely they realize that Excursus is exceptional?'

'Of course. But you must know about such bureaucratic wrangles. We are now in a position where everyone knows that an outside warehouse is the only solution, but no one feels able to suggest it.'

'Why don't you suggest it?'

'I have suggested it. I have even offered to pay for it through an additional grant from the New German Foundation. But still Kemmelkampf is worried by this question of precedent.'

'To hell with Kemmelkampf,' said Francesca. 'I'll tell him that the lenders will pull out unless the paintings go to that warehouse.'

'Perhaps you should look at it first.'

'Do I need to?'

'I would feel more confident. We are not as experienced as you are about this kind of thing.'

They drove out to Tegel the next day in Francesca's Golf. It was only a short way up the Stadtring, but it took them some time to find the warehouse belonging to Omni Zartfracht Gmbh (Omni Fragile Freight Co.). The manager of the company's Berlin office was there to show them round.

Francesca was enormously relieved. The warehouse was ideal. It was newly built behind a chain and barbed-wire fence with state-of-the-art temperature and humidity controls and the security of a Fort Knox. It was large enough to store all the works of art if they could stipulate exclusive use until the exhibition was over. Günter, too, seemed impressed.

At the next meeting of the organizing committee, Francesca proposed storing the works as they arrived at the OZF ware-house. There followed the anticipated argument by Kemmelkampf about the precedent, which seemed of less interest to the gallery directors than Francesca had been led to suppose. Francesca argued forcefully that the American lenders would insist upon the very highest standards. Günter pointed out that it would certainly be expensive but if the committee felt there was no other solution, then the money could be found. Dr Kemmelkampf hoped that the company would make an allowance for the prestigious publicity they would gain if a contract was agreed. Stefi said that the Federal government would have to be satisfied as to the competence of the company and measures taken to protect the works of art. Francesca agreed. 'But I imagine that all concerned would feel as I did that we are extraordinarily fortunate to have something like this on offer at such short notice.'

Only Dr Serotkin made an objection: he said the Soviet galleries would find it irregular to entrust works of art from public collections to a private company.

'Perhaps only because there are no private companies in Russia,' said Francesca tartly.

'I defer to your superior experience,' said Serotkin with one of his ironic smiles.

'Are there any other objections?' asked Stefan Diederich. There was none. 'Then I suggest that it be minuted that at the suggestion Dr McDermott the committee authorizes Herr Westarp and Dr Kemmelkampf to enter into negotiations with the Omni Zartfracht company for the use of their warehouse in Tegel.'

With no dissenting voice, the motion was carried.

After this satisfactory solution to the problem of storage, Francesca's chief task became the preparation of the catalogue – a major document that would not only survive for years after the end of the exhibition, but would also carry Francesca's name and her achievement all over the world.

It was the catalogue that obsessed her. Every now and then, she would have to have lunch with some visiting cultural dignitary – a museum director from Paris, a cultural attaché from Tokyo – and although she behaved properly on such occasions, her mind never left her office where, with Frau Dr Koch, she was assembling illustrations and information for the catalogue from the different galleries and collectors.

It was a tormenting task. The major galleries, by and large, were able to provide Francesca with what she wanted; but even they often had no suitable photographs of the paintings they planned to send, and only a hazy idea of who had owned their paintings before them. Some private collectors were entirely ignorant of the provenance. Francesca made calls and sent faxes to such far-off places as Nagasaki and Bogotá. Her own and Frau Dr Koch's research into the history of the paintings was frequently frustrated by the professional envy of scholars and experts. Some had to be flattered into cooperation and asked to contribute to the catalogue, but then would fail to send their copy.

A large number of works were in galleries in the former Soviet Union. For these, Francesca was at the mercy of Andrei Serotkin. When Stefi Diederich had first told her that he was to be a member of the organizing committee, she had accepted him with some reluctance; later, she had come to see the advantage of enlisting someone with contacts in Russia; and finally she had had to acknowledge to Stefi that Serotkin was indispensable, having got the agreement from the Tretyakov in Moscow and the Russian Gallery in St Petersburg for the loan of all the works she had requested, including Tatlin's *The Sailor*, Goncharova's *The Cyclist* and Popova's *Italian Still-Life*.

By February, however, Francesca began to wonder whether or not she could rely on Serotkin's assurances. She had only his word for the galleries' consent, usually based on no more than a telephone call, occasionally backed up by an indecipherable fax. When she asked him for letters from the galleries concerned, confirming their consent, Serotkin would laugh without saying what his laugh denoted. She would send him memos, asking, say, if colour slides were available from the Tretyakov of Malevich's *Dynamic Suspension*, and, getting no answer, she would go to his office and ask if there was any news about the slides.

'Ah, that . . .'

'We've got beautiful slides of the early Maleviches from the Stedelijk, and his *Yellow Quadrilateral on White*. It would be a pity if we couldn't illustrate any of those in Russian collections.'

'It's not so simple. In Moscow, good colour reproduction is not always possible.'

'If it can't be done, Andrei, it can't be done. But we have to know.'

To compound Francesca's frustration, Serotkin would absent

himself every now and then, sometimes for as long as a week. He never said where he was going, or when he would return. Francesca suggested to the committee that they take on another Russian-speaking researcher, but this was vetoed by Günter Westarp on the dubious grounds of cost. She therefore had to wait for answers to her queries until Serotkin chose to come back.

She complained about Serotkin's absences to Stefi. Stefi said he suspected that Serotkin had a mistress whom he visited from time to time. Sophie said he probably got drunk 'like Yeltsin. All Russians do.' Their explanations only added to Francesca's irritation. It was intolerable that Serotkin should leave his post without a good cause. On occasions, upon his return, she asked him where he had been but he would always make an evasive reply such as: 'Ah, well, you know, we Russians are not used to hard work'; or he would say in German, 'Geschäft ist Geschäft' (business is business), without explaining what his business was.

Julius Breitenbach, who overheard this exchange, confided to Francesca that most Russians in Germany went in for a little import-export on the side, and it was perhaps to some enterprise such as this that Serotkin had referred. 'They have so little money,' said Julius. 'Quite possibly he is investing his stipend in fax machines or video recorders and is shipping them back to Moscow.'

Francesca found this explanation degrading but she could not be sure that it was not true. Part of the irritation caused by his unexplained absences was that it added to the mystery of Serotkin. She had never had any reason to revise her first impressions that he was 'dashing', even handsome; earnest, yet with a twinkle in his eye. She noticed that the secretaries, Dora and Gertie, and even Frau Dr Koch, became downcast whenever he was absent and perked up whenever he returned.

After almost six months in the same office, Francesca still could not make him out. Was he intelligent? He spoke English and German with a remarkable fluency, but his knowledge of Russian Experimental Art was merely adequate for someone who was supposed to be an expert in the field. Was he amusing? It was hard to tell. After the first discussion in the canteen about the position of women, their only exchanges had been about Excursus. He was always courteous and correct, but at times his politeness seemed almost *ironic*. At the meetings of the organizing committee, he always spoke with a certain wit, and he often smiled when Francesca spoke, but she had the impression that he was amused by who she was rather than by what she said.

Of course, it was Francesca herself who had drawn the line of demarcation between their professional and private lives, and she had been relieved that Serotkin had respected her decision, limiting their contacts to the office and their exchanges to matters concerning the exhibition. But as the months passed, it began to irk her that Serotkin made no attempt to question the rules she had laid down. She became curious, not just about his absences but about what he did at weekends or during his spare time. It even occurred to Francesca that since they were both alone in Berlin, it might make sense to go to a play or a movie together, but it was difficult to think of an unobtrusive way to change the pattern she had established.

Francesca hinted to Sophie that she and Stefi might ask them over one evening, but Sophie said that Stefi hated Russians, and preferred to see as little of Serotkin as he could. It was therefore up to Francesca to get across to Serotkin that, so far as she was concerned, the time had come to change the rules; but whenever she made up her mind to say something to him, she backed down at the last moment, finding that she was unwilling to risk the embarrassment of his turning her down. She was humiliated by the memory of how she had thought Rasputin the writer was Rasputin the monk; in fact, to try to make up for that gaffe on some future occasion, she had found a book by Valentin Rasputin and had read a number of his stories. However, conversation with Serotkin in the Excursus office never turned towards literature from art, and Francesca was on the point of abandoning the idea of getting better acquainted when fate intervened in an unexpected way.

Francesca McDermott and Andrei Serotkin lived in the same block of flats. They rarely met in the lobby: Francesca did not even know on which floor Serotkin had his flat. Each morning, Francesca went jogging in the Englischergarten and she knew that Serotkin did too. She had seen him from the window of her living room, and estimated that he rose half an hour before she did, and so had usually done his round before she set out.

In December it had become too dark for a single woman to venture safely out into the park. Francesca had given up her jogging. However, she missed the exercise and when she could went to a gym to work out. At the beginning of February, when the mornings grew lighter, Francesca resumed her jogging and on one or two occasions passed Serotkin either in the lobby or in the Englischergarten. Both exchanged a curt 'good morning', Serotkin sweating, Francesca bleary-eyed. Francesca preferred to avoid these early-morning encounters. She was hardly looking her best.

One morning in March, Francesca was doing her round of the Englischergarten wearing her charcoal-grey tracksuit when she was joined by three men wearing trainers, jeans and grubby sweatshirts. From their appearance, she judged them to be Turks. This in itself did not alarm her: she had been told that, after Istanbul and Ankara, Berlin had a larger Turkish population than any other city in the world. The three men had as much right as she did to jog in the Englischergarten and it was only paranoia induced by comparison with New York's Central Park that aroused alarm at the sight of their dark skin.

After a few minutes, however, the three men crowded around her, one on each side, one behind and as they ran, they tried to engage her in conversation. '*Guten morgen, Fräulein. Schönes Wetter, was?*' As she ran along the path, puffing somewhat (she was still out of condition after the winter break), Francesca asked them to leave her alone. '*Bitte, lass mich in Ruhe.*' She also looked around to see if there was anyone to whom she could look for help. There was not. Finally, she stopped, gasping for breath, and told them with as much authority as she could muster to fuck off.

The tallest and oldest of the three – a man of about thirty – now looked around, and he too saw that there was no one else in sight. He moved even closer to Francesca. '*Aber, warum so unfreundlich?*' he asked with a leer.

Francesca was now alarmed and tried to dodge past him, but the Turk grabbed her by the sleeve of her track suit. The two others leaped forward, gripped Francesca by her arms and, while the first covered her mouth, dragged her off the path and behind some shrubs and trees. She was pulled back onto the ground. The first man took his hand off her mouth but, before she could shout, he covered it with his own mouth, climbing onto her while unzipping his jeans.

Francesca struggled, and for a moment managed to kick him off, but the two other men still held her arms and the first, picking himself up, his jeans around his knees, hissed in Turkish to the other two, one of whom then took hold of both her wrists while the other grabbed a leg. Francesca was able to shout, but she was unable to get up off the ground. And while the second Turk held onto her left leg, the first tugged at her tracksuit bottom and pants and eventually removed them. Then he came upon her, the wobbling pink point of his penis protruding from a black fuzz at his groin. Francesca, stifled by the smell, still struggled beneath his heavy body. She felt his hand move like a wedge between her legs, and begin to prise them open . . . And then a hand pulled him off her by the roots of his hair and she saw, towering above her, Serotkin.

Hobbled by his jeans, the first Turk could do little to prevent Serotkin throwing him aside but, while the third still held Francesca, the second let go of her leg, took a knife out of his pocket, flicked open the blade and went for Serotkin. Serotkin, only now turning back from the first Turk, dodged the lunge of the second, then caught him with a kick in the stomach that sent him gasping to the ground.

Now the third let go of Francesca and, while she scrambled to get her right leg back into her pants and tracksuit bottom, threw himself at Serotkin; but once again, Serotkin, with a certain ease, stepped aside and struck the Turk on the back of the neck with a blow of such force that it left him lying motionless on the gravel path.

The first Turk, who had by now fastened his jeans and buckled his belt, saw what had happened to his companions and turned to run away, but before he could escape, Serotkin first kicked him in the groin, then landed a blow on his chest that made him stagger, choke, and finally fall beside his companion on the ground.

Despite her shock and humiliation, Francesca had the

115

composure to feel astonished that this Russian art historian should dispatch her three assailants with such ease. Indeed, from the expression on his face, it even seemed as if he took a certain pleasure in the escapade; and though he now came to help her to her feet, asking if she was all right, there was nonetheless the same hint of irony as if even this atrocity had its amusing side.

'Shall I go for the police?' he asked.

'No, don't leave me.' Involuntarily, she clutched his arm.

'Very well.'

She started to walk towards the path and only after a few steps realized that her feet were bare. 'I've lost my trainers,' she said.

They turned back. One of the Turks looked up but, seeing Serotkin, closed his eyes and lay still. Serotkin found Francesca's trainers and held her steady while she put them back on her feet.

'Like the first time,' he said.

'What?'

'Don't you remember? No shoes.'

She laughed and then she wept, sobbing without constraint as they walked back to their block of flats, an arm of Serotkin's around her shoulder, one of hers around his waist. And even as she cried, Francesca thought that tears were funny things because, mingled with the shock of what she had just endured, was a certain joy that he had remembered that she had been barefoot when they first met.

Serotkin accompanied Francesca back to her flat. She called the police. When two uniformed officers arrived, both made a statement, Serotkin's more than modest about his heroic role. He then went up to his own flat to take a shower and change. When he returned, half an hour later, Francesca too had bathed and changed. She insisted on going to work, and accepted Serotkin's offer to drive her to the Excursus office in his Opel. At times she trembled: she had no appetite for breakfast, undoubtedly because of the shock, and when she got to her desk she found it difficult to concentrate on her work.

In the middle of the morning, two plainclothes detectives from the Berlin police came to make some further enquiries, and to ask

Francesca and Serotkin to sign the statements they had made that morning. 'You're a lucky woman,' the detective sergeant said to Francesca, 'to have had this particular guy come along.'

Francesca agreed. The detective looked up at Serotkin. 'You must be trained in unarmed combat?'

Serotkin shrugged. 'In the army, you know . . . We all did our national service.'

The detective looked down at the statement. 'Sure. But even so . . .'

The policemen left. Serotkin went back to his office. Francesca telephoned Sophie to tell her what had happened. Sophie immediately insisted on driving over from the Wedekindstrasse and taking Francesca out to lunch. They went to the restaurant on the top of the Ka De We department store, and Sophie's sympathy was overwhelming and sincere; but as Francesca listened to her chatter about how dangerous Berlin had become, especially for women, and how the police were often quite lackadaisical when investigating cases of rape because they were men and could not imagine what it felt like to be a woman, and in fact often seemed to regard all single women as fair game . . . even as she listened to this burbling stream of ideas that she could not but recognize as her own, Francesca found that she was thinking of Andrei Serotkin and wishing that he, not Sophie, was sitting opposite, eating his pork and red cabbage, and exhaling the smoke of his dark, untipped cigarettes.

Sophie departed, after eliciting a promise from Francesca that, if she would not come and stay with her in the flat on the Wedekindstrasse, she would at least let Stefi pick her up and bring her to supper. As the afternoon wore on, however, Francesca felt less and less like an evening with the Diederichs. At half past four, she called Sophie and cried off. She said she was tired and wanted to go back to her flat to sleep. She then left her office and went down the corridor to Serotkin's. It was empty. Tears came into her eyes. She crossed the corridor and looked in on Frau Dr Koch. 'Has Dr Serotkin left?'

'Perhaps. I don't know. I haven't seen him.'

Francesca turned and, as she did so, saw Serotkin go into his office. She went to the door. 'Andrei . . .'

117

He looked up.

'I was wondering if, by any chance, you were free this evening?'

He smiled. 'Have you work for me to do?'

She blushed. 'Not work, no. I thought that perhaps, well, you might like to have dinner?'

'Ah.' He hesitated and a troubled look came onto his face. Then he appeared to come to a decision and said: 'Yes. I would like that very much.'

Francesca told herself that hers was only a friendly gesture towards a man who had saved her from a fate worse than death. She told herself that it only made sense to take the opportunity presented by the day's events to pursue her grumbling curiosity about Serotkin. She told herself that since she could not face work or solitude or Stefi Diederich, it only made sense to seek the company of a colleague who knew what had happened and so would make allowances for her fragile state: she told herself everything except that she was already more than half in love with Andrei Serotkin.

Francesca persisted in this self-delusion back in her flat, as she got ready to go out. Serotkin, who had brought her to the office, also drove her home. They had agreed to meet in the lobby at eight. Francesca therefore had a couple of hours to soak in a bath, then, swathed in her towel, to lie on her bed. She considered calling Duncan in New York but decided against it because he would still be in his office and it would be awkward for him to express sympathy in front of others. She could call him later, when she got back from dinner with Serotkin; and as her inward focus moved from the gentle American in New York to the violent Russian in Berlin, she felt an involuntary spasm of crude desire.

She jumped off the bed as if she had been touched by something more tangible than a message from her brain, went back to the bathroom, unwrapped the towel, and for a moment looked at her naked body in the full-length mirror on the wall. Serotkin had seen part of that naked body but this knowledge, rather than inspiring shame or embarrassment, induced a sense of vulnerability that only increased the feeling of bodily longing.

She went back into her bedroom, straightened the bed cover, put away her discarded clothes, then sat down at the dressing table and, with meticulous care and precision, put mascara on her eyelashes and shadow around her eyes. She dressed, choosing an outfit that was both sober and alluring – her best underclothes, bottle-green tights, a black skirt and a green cashmere sweater that matched the tights. Around her neck she put a string of black pearls, given to her by a former boyfriend, a banker in New York. She brushed her thick blonde hair, nodding it back from time to time, and picked off a stray strand that dropped onto the sweater. Finally, she put on a pair of simple black leather shoes, and sprayed some Amarige on the inside of her wrists and around her neck.

Serotkin was waiting in the lobby. He too had changed his clothes – grey trousers, a navy-blue blazer, a light blue shirt and striped tie. He smiled when he saw Francesca, a smile that seemed somehow melancholy, and led her out to his car.

'Where shall we go?' she asked.

'I thought you would benefit from a change of scenery,' he said.

Francesca was quite happy to let Serotkin make the decisions. They drove in silence, around Ernst Reuter Platz, past the Charlottenburg Palace, onto the Stadtring and then the Avus, leaving at the exit leading onto the Potsdammer Chaussee. Serotkin then doubled back into the Grünewald, turned up a track and stopped the car outside a restaurant in the middle of the woods.

'Have you been here before?' he asked.

She shook her head. 'No.'

'It's nice in summer, of course, when you can sit out on the terrace.'

They went up the steps into the restaurant. The head waiter led them to a table by a window from which they could see the sun setting over the water of the Wannsee.

'This is lovely,' said Francesca.

'It may help you to feel that you are out of the city, at least for a while.'

'Thanks.' She wanted to bask in his solicitude but could not decide whether he was being considerate because he cared for her

119

or merely because he felt obliged by the circumstances to do the right thing.

'You must try and forget about this morning,' he said.

'There would be more to try and forget if it wasn't for you.'

'It was nothing.' He picked up the menu. They chose what they wanted to eat and drink.

'You have the proverb, I think,' said Serotkin. ' "Every cloud has a silver lining." '

'Yes.'

'I think the silver lining to this morning's cloud might be to oblige you to work less hard. It is not good for you.'

'The work has to be done.'

'You can delegate some of it to others.'

'I'm not good at that.'

'It is part of the art of leadership.'

'I guess I'm not much of a leader.'

'Oh, but you are.'

'Unattractive in a woman?'

'In an attractive woman, everything becomes attractive. That is the danger.'

'The danger?'

He hesitated, then turned with apparent relief to the waiter who had come to their table with a glass of Schnaps and a bottle of wine. The food followed, and all the while Francesca was considering how she could return to that danger Andrei had mentioned without appearing to fish for a compliment. 'Do you think,' she asked, 'that there are big differences in the nationalities? I mean, in the way we feel and the way we think?'

'Yes. There are big differences.'

'Do you think they matter?'

'In what way?'

'Well, in art or love or international negotiations?'

'In international negotiations, clearly, each country employs experts who are specialists in the way the other party feels and thinks. That suggests they think that it matters.'

'In art, then.'

'There are specialists, too.'

'But the eye is universal. You can appreciate a painting by an American and I can appreciate a painting by a Russian.'

'Perhaps.'

'You don't think so?'

'Your thesis, I think, was to *explain* Russian experimental art. Therefore, you too are a specialist, and must have been drawn to the subject by some curiosity, and curiosity implies something unknown.'

'I don't think that it was the national differences that interested me. After all, a painter like Malevich, whose father worked in a sugar factory in Kiev, is about as deep-rooted in his ethnic culture as you can get, but his artistic influences were blatantly international.'

'May I take notes, Frau Doktor?'

Francesca blushed. 'I'm sorry. You know all that already.'

'If it was not because the painters were Russians, then what led you to choose that theme?'

'Well . . .' She hesitated, then shot a furtive smile across the table. 'You will be horrified to hear that I was led into it from a course I took in Women's Studies. I had meant to write a thesis on women painters which was hardly original – in fact, in American faculties it's well-trodden ground. But in doing the preliminary research, I came across Natalia Goncharova, Liubov Popova, Olga Rosanova and Alexandra Exter. They gave me the idea.'

'They were talented.'

'Thank you!' The gentle tone of Francesca's ironic rejoinder was a measure of how far her attitude towards Andrei Serotkin had changed.

'But they were not innovators. They merely imitated what was in fashion.'

'So did the men.'

'Precisely.' There was a flash in his eyes. 'They followed the fashions set in Paris. They had lost touch with their own people.'

Francesca was puzzled. 'They *thought* they were in touch with the people. After the Revolution, they took agit-prop trains around Russia, carrying books and films and painting to the peasants and workers.'

'They were taking their idea of art to the people, not letting the people's idea of art come to them.'

'And didn't the people benefit?'

Serotkin was about to answer, but then seemed to think better of what he had intended to say. 'We are talking shop,' he said.

'I'm sorry.'

'I would like to know more about Francesca McDermott the woman, and less about Dr McDermott the art historian.'

'What would you like to know?'

'Where you were born. What family you have.'

She gave him a brief curriculum vitae, describing her childhood and the different members of her family, now scattered around the United States.

'None of you still lives in Wisconsin?'

'I think Susan might go back there. I guess it depends on who she marries.'

'And you? Does it depend on who you marry?'

She looked away. 'I like the east coast.'

'So you should marry someone from New York.'

'Perhaps. Or Boston.'

'A publisher, perhaps?'

She looked at him across the table. 'Hey, have you been doing some background research?'

Serotkin laughed. 'Diederich mentioned that there was some-one . . . But I don't want to pry into your private life. Tell me about your career.'

'There's not much to tell. I went to high school in Madison and then Ann Arbor, and then to Harvard.'

'That can't have been easy.'

'It's easier if your father is a college professor.'

'Influence?'

'No. Home tuition.'

'What did you major in?'

'German. But I also took a course in Russian and the History of Art.'

'And Women's Studies.'

'Yes. And ʾfter Harvard I spent a year in Berlin.'

'That was where you met Diederich?'

'I met Stefi through Sophie who was then married to Paul Meissner. I was living in West Berlin, doing research on the

122

Bauhaus. A magazine in New York asked me to write a piece on an East Berlin painter – I can't even remember his name. He was part of a group of dissidents around Paul and Sophie.'

'Diederich was part of the group?'

'He was on the fringe. I remember him, but not well. Paul was the leader. He was a wonderful person. Brave and gentle and charismatic and incredibly kind to me.'

'Were you in love with him?'

Francesca laughed. 'God, no. Paul was an Evangelical pastor and married to Sophie. They had two kids. He was chaplain to the students at the university and so the Stasi gave him a really tough time. He was harassed in every imaginable way and his own church gave him only lukewarm support. It was crazy to let me visit them so often: it was really compromising, in those days, to be seen with a foreigner, particularly an American. But I got hooked on the atmosphere in that flat. They were so brave and cheerful and kind of . . . pure. I never knew anything like it, either before or since.'

Serotkin was silent.

'Then my year came to an end. I went back to the United States. And later I heard that Paul had had a severe nervous breakdown. The marriage broke up. Sophie married Stefi.' She shrugged. 'And here we are.'

Serotkin's expression had become sombre. 'It was a cardinal error of the regime to fail to appreciate the cultural value of religious belief.'

Francesca was puzzled. 'Are you religious, Andrei?' she asked.

'No. I am an atheist. And you?'

'My grandparents were Irish Catholics, but my parents didn't practise and I wasn't even baptized.'

'So you are an atheist?'

'More of an agnostic, I guess. I don't know how you can know.'

'I am an atheist,' Serotkin said again, 'because if a God was even a possibility . . .' He stopped.

'Then what?'

'Then men and women would not be free. They would be his playthings, his children, his slaves.'

By now, they were eating their dessert – Francesca a crême brulée that she only allowed herself as consolation for her earlier ordeal. She was feeling a little woozy: she had noticed Serotkin, after his initial glass of Schnaps, had left her to drink most of the wine. She tried to pull herself together enough to steer the conversation away from the gloomy subjects of religion and politics to something more appropriate to a date with a handsome man.

'Now tell me about you,' she said to Serotkin.

'You already know most of what there is to know.'

'I know you're an art historian who works for the Ministry of Culture in Moscow; that you have got a son and that you're separated from your wife.'

'That's about it.'

'What about your parents?'

'My father was a soldier. He fought in World War Two.'

'And you were in the army?'

'Yes. It's obligatory.'

'Which is where you learned unarmed combat?'

'I was in a parachute regiment.'

'And you've kept yourself in shape.'

He shrugged. 'Once you learn these things, you never forget them.'

'Like riding a bicycle.'

'Yes.'

'And . . .' She wanted to ask if he had a girlfriend but did not quite dare. 'And are you happy?' she asked.

He darted a look at her, almost of anger. 'There is not much to be happy about in Russia just now.'

'Is it really true that people are starving?'

'Not starving, no. But they have trouble finding food.'

'Your parents?'

'Even my parents.'

'And your wife?'

'She is younger. It is worst for the old.'

Francesca shook her head. 'It's unbelievable. A superpower that can't even feed its own people. I'm surprised they don't string up all the Communists on the nearest lamp posts.'

'It is not . . .' he started, then bit back his words. 'There are not enough lamp posts.'

'I guess there aren't. But all the same, it must make you mad.'

'It does.'

'And want to do something about it.'

'Yes.'

'And here you are, stuck in Berlin, with a hysterical American. Poor Andrei.'

'You are not hysterical. I am impressed by how calm you have been.'

'I might have been less calm if it had actually happened.'

'Yes.'

'So if I'm calm, it's thanks to you.'

'Anyone would have done it.'

'So you keep saying. But I'm not so sure.'

'You have such assaults in America, I believe.'

'Sure. Nowhere's safe.'

'It will not serve the feminists' cause if, once again, women need men for their protection.'

'There's always mace.'

'Mace?'

'You know. Canisters of gas that you keep in your purse. They're sometimes more effective than men.'

'But you don't need it.'

'Why not?'

'Because you have your friend.'

'Duncan? Sure. But he's in New York and I'm in Boston and anyway . . .'

'What?'

'He's not quite the type to go in for macho heroics.'

'Which may be the reason why you love him. A new man for the new woman.'

'Do I love him?'

Serotkin looked embarrassed. 'I'm sorry. I assumed . . .'

'Sure. Well, I guess I did love him, at least I thought I loved him, but real love would survive a long separation, wouldn't it?'

'I'm not an expert on love.'

'You must know something about it.'

'Yes. Real love would survive a long separation.'

'It wouldn't depend on time or place?'

'No.'

'Or nationality?'

'No.'

'So, since I no longer feel it, I guess I never really loved Duncan.'

'It is over?'

'Yes.'

As she said this, Francesca did not feel that she was betraying Duncan or misleading Serotkin. Quite the contrary: it was only as she spoke that she realized that what she was saying had been true. It was over. Neither she nor Duncan had as yet admitted it, either to themselves or to one another: there had been calls twice a week – dreary, affectionate, long-drawn-out conversations over the transatlantic lines – with each exchanging bits of news that were of little interest to the other, and expressing encouragement and affection that was no more than routine. There was, perhaps, a trace of deception in the way she now suggested to Andrei that she had been free of any kind of commitment over the past four months, but it seemed no different to the kind of deception that resulted from applying mascara to her eyelashes or dabbing on Amarige to make her body smell nice. She did not want to give the impression that men drove bumper to bumper into her heart or into her bed.

'And you?' she asked Serotkin: it seemed that she had the right to ask him now.

'I am not in love,' he said.

'I'm sorry.'

'Why?'

'Wouldn't you like to be in love?'

'I have been very busy.'

'We've all been busy.'

'Not just with the exhibition. There are other things.'

'Your mysterious absences . . . Stefi thought you must have a mistress.'

Serotkin shook his head. 'No.'

'So where do you go?'

'I visit colleagues.'

'In Germany?'

'Yes. And Switzerland. After all, when Excursus is over, you will go back to America, but my future is not assured.'

'Won't you have your job at the Ministry?'

'It was a Party job. The Party is now suspended.'

'I'm sorry.' She thought for a moment. 'I'm sure, if you wanted to, particularly if Excursus is a success, you could get some sort of teaching post in America.'

'Perhaps.'

'Unless you prefer import–export.'

Serotkin looked puzzled.

Francesca laughed. 'Julius thought you were running some kind of business on the side shipping fax machines and video recorders back to Russia.'

He frowned. 'Some of us are reduced to that.'

'He wasn't serious,' she said quietly.

Serotkin looked sorrowfully into her eyes, as if rebuking her for saying something that was not true.

She blushed. '*I* didn't think it was true.'

'Thank you.' He did not seem grateful.

'But I had my suspicions about the mistress.'

'That is more plausible,' he said acidly. 'Americans regard love as a form of recreation.'

Francesca recoiled at the bitter tone with which he said this. 'That's a little unfair.'

'Is it?'

'How much experience do you have of Americans in love?'

'I am judging from the cinema.'

'Movies are more about sex than love.'

'Sex, then, is a recreation. The hero and heroine go to bed together before the end of the first reel.'

Francesca looked down, afraid that what he said might be true. 'Happiness is so often elusive. Americans want to snatch it while they can in case they wake up the next morning and find it gone.'

'Happiness lies in more than a satisfactory one-night stand.'

'Sure. It lies in love.'

'Yes, in love. But not just in sexual love.'

'What other love is there?' It was a stupid question, and she regretted asking it before the words were out of her mouth.

'There is love of one's parents and one's children . . .'

'Of course.'

'And one's country.'

'I know.'

'I have never known anyone die for a woman,' said Serotkin, 'but I have known several who have been happy to die for their country.'

'And kill for their country,' said Francesca.

'Of course,' said Serotkin. 'If you are prepared to die, you must be prepared to kill. To kill, and worse . . .'

They said nothing as they drove back through the Grunewald. It was not a hostile silence; quite the contrary, Francesca felt that the intimacy between that had been fortuitously forced upon them that morning had been confirmed by the evening spent together. However, it was an intimacy of a kind that she had never previously encountered, and that therefore left her somewhat baffled. In the United States, after a date, the traffic signals usually shone green or red or perhaps amber. With Andrei, it was as if there was some technical malfunction. All the lights were flashing on and off at the same time. Using a cruder but well- worn metaphor, Francesca felt as if she had hooked a fish as she had intended, but had then been dragged off balance into the water as the fish tried to escape downstream. Andrei was drawn to her: she could tell from the way he behaved in her presence; but for some reason she could not fathom, he was doing his utmost to resist her attraction, considerate at one moment, almost angry at another. Why would a man who wanted a woman deliver a diatribe against sex on the first date? They were both adult and uncommitted; both alone in a foreign city. They had known one another for six months. Why should what seemed proper to her seem depraved to him?

Francesca thought that when it came to the point Andrei's actions would belie his words. She so longed for him to embrace her that she almost wished for a return of the morning's assault to give her the excuse once again to sob on his shoulder. He smoked in the car, his strong, untipped cigarettes, and as he exhaled she took a certain pleasure in drawing into her lungs the same smoke that had been in the deepest recesses of his body. This intimacy was better than none. She would rather he had laid his hand on her leg, the leg he had seen naked that morning. But he did not even stretch out and take hold of her hand. Why? Was he being high-minded? Did he desire her but feel that it would be wrong to take advantage of her vulnerable condition? She felt now that she had loved him for much longer than she had supposed, just as she now realized that her affair with Duncan had ended some time ago; but while she could present this second revelation as a retrospective truth, and would tell Duncan in due course, she could hardly confess to the first until Serotkin had owned up to his own feelings for her. Then she could draw in the line and lift him out in a net.

Even as they stopped the car in the park beneath their building, she thought it might happen that night; that their yearning would be too strong to allow either of them to go to their separate flats. She thought of the conventional tactic of asking him up for a drink or a cup of coffee, but after what he had said about Hollywood morals, it seemed impossible. They reached the lobby. They entered the lift together. Serotkin pushed first the button for the fourth floor, then the button for the ninth. Francesca stood close to him and, when the door opened, turned her face towards his.

Serotkin clasped her hand. 'Goodnight.'

'Goodnight.' She turned to go, then remembered that she should at least be polite. 'Thank you, Andrei.'

He smiled. 'I thank you.'

'You should have let me pay my share.'

'Please. I am a Russian.' The automatic door started to close; his foot went forward to stop it. 'By the way, do you play squash?'

'Yes.'

'Shall we play a game together?'

'I'd like that.'

'It will be safer than jogging.'

He removed his foot. The door closed. Francesca went to her flat. She was embarrassed to remember how she had straightened the bedspread. She sat down on the bed and called Duncan. She did not tell him about the assault but said as kindly as she could that their relationship was over. Duncan listened, and said little in reply, but his few words were enough to get across that he not only agreed but was also relieved that she had come to this decision.

TEN

The investigation into the murders in the Dubrowstrasse had made little progress by the spring of 1993, despite the efforts of the detectives Kessler and Dorn. Other cases had intervened, some of which remained unsolved, but it was only when it came to the Maslyukovs that Kessler, who for twenty years had said that he knew everything that went on in West Berlin 'before it happened', for the first time in his life felt at a loss. He had established what he had suspected from the first – that the couple were Russians, a married couple, Grigori and Vera Maslyukov, nominally art dealers, in practice receivers of stolen goods: a 'fence' between those who smuggled icons out of Russia and the more reputable dealers and collectors in the West.

Kessler's contacts in the Russian underworld in Berlin told him that Maslyukov was a KGB agent; but in Kessler's experience, every Russian émigré regarded every other Russian émigré as a KGB agent. Their suspicions meant nothing at all. The idea that Maslyukov had been an active agent, or even a 'sleeper', seemed far-fetched.

More probably, Kessler's first supposition was correct: the

Maslyukovs were casualties in a war between different factions of Berlin's Russian mafia. The icons had gone, undoubtedly stolen by whoever had killed Maslyukov and had tortured his wife. That hardly pointed to the CIA or the West German *Bundesamt für Verfassungsschutz* (Office for the Protection of the Constitution), the BfV.

Kessler's best hope lay in a tip-off from among the Russians living in Berlin. But so much had changed since the breach of the Wall. Illegal immigrants were flooding into the city. New gangs had taken over from the old ones. There had been gun battles in the streets of Kreuzberg: Russians had been shot dead in a restaurant on the Kurfürstendamm. He asked for names but his usual informants knew nothing about the new networks of Georgians and Azerbaijanis, and were clearly too prudent to ask.

Dusting down the furniture in the Dubrowstrasse had produced no fingerprints. The murderers had worn gloves. The shreds of tobacco on the floor by the feet of the tortured woman were almost the only clue. Analysis showed that they were from Bulgarian cigarettes made for the Soviet market – BTs. Before the fall of the Communists, they had been sold in East Berlin: now, they were hard to find. Dorn had spoken to scores of tobacconists, finding a few who still stocked them; he had even identified a number of regular buyers, but none had the profile of a killer or a thief. If the murderer lived in Berlin, they had yet to find him, and as month followed month with no progress, Kessler fell back on a second hypothesis: the cigarettes had not been purchased in Berlin at all, but had been brought by the murderers from the Soviet Union itself.

It then became a matter of checking arrivals and departures at East Berlin's Schönfeld airport, and border crossings at Franfurton-Oder, both by road and rail – a tedious task that used manpower and time. Kessler's superior, Kommissar Rohrbeck, became irritated. He could hardly deny him resources – a murder was a murder; but like Dorn he could not summon up much outrage about the death of a couple of Russian crooks.

Nor could Kessler. Indeed, the more he learned about the Maslyukovs, the less he liked them. Their files showed how little they paid the smugglers and how much they charged their Western clients. The mark-up on the icons was several thousand per cent. It was also clear that their declared income, upon which they paid their taxes, was a small fraction of their profits. Their account at the Berliner Bank had only DM32,000. The rest of their assets were probably in Liechtenstein or Switzerland. There were references on the hard disk of their Nixdorf computer to the existence of such accounts, but no files or documents that identified them were found.

However, it was not the tax evasion that led Kessler to dislike the Maslyukovs but the image he formed from the evidence of those who had had dealings with them; not their friends, because they did not seem to have had any friends, but other dealers, in particular a middle-aged German woman, Katerina von Duse, who had a gallery off the Kurfürstendamm. 'I tell you,' she told Kessler in an almost hysterical voice, 'these Maslyukovs were the very lowest sort, quite pitiless. I am not at all surprised that they have been killed.'

'Why do you say that?' Kessler had asked.

'A young couple – Russians, clearly . . . they spoke very little German – came into the gallery about six months ago and offered me an icon – a beautiful St Nicholas, early sixteenth-century. It was wrapped in a cloth and carried in a briefcase. They had some kind of bill of sale from the Patriarchate in Moscow, almost certainly a forgery, but all the same I made them an offer. I cannot remember exactly what it was. Say ten thousand marks. Not a bad offer, but all the same I could see what was going through their minds. They were astonished that it was worth so much, but just because I had offered them more than they had imagined, they now thought that perhaps it was worth more, so they said they would think about it and went away. I heard nothing for a week, but then the girl came in alone and asked if the offer was still open. I said it was but she looked frightened. She said that the boy had gone to Maslyukov who had offered them only a thousand marks. She said she would come back with the icon that afternoon, but she never returned, and ten days later Maslyukov offered me the same icon . . . for thirty thousand marks.'

'Did you buy it?'

'No. It was overpriced.'

'The young couple never returned?'

'No.'

'Perhaps Maslyukov put up his price.'

'No. He frightened them. That was his style. So many had no proper visas or bills of sale, and if threats did not work . . .'

'What then?'

'I don't know. There were stories.'

'Of what?'

'Accidents. Maslyukov had some very unsavoury friends.'

'A charming profession!'

She frowned. 'Are there no corrupt policemen?'

Kessler laughed. 'So I am told. But tell me: did you ever come across Maslyukov's wife?'

Katerina von Duse wrinkled her nose. 'Once or twice. A dreadful woman.'

'Why?'

'Worse than her husband. Grasping. Also vulgar.'

'Would she have known details of the business?'

'Certainly. She was cleverer than he was. An Armenian, I think, or a Jew.'

'Could they have been killed by a rival dealer?'

'He had no rival,' she said. 'Not in Berlin, at any rate. Those that there were had disappeared.'

Even before he heard this opinion from Katerina von Duse, Kessler had come to dislike Vera Maslyukov. The image of her fat, putrid corpse had lodged in his mind. The set of her features in death, the features twisted in that horrible caricature of sexual ecstasy, still disturbed him. She had been tied up, tortured and then killed. He should feel sympathy, pity, outrage: instead, he only remembered the hair from her moustache, some on the tape, some still on her upper lip. The pungent aroma that still lingered in his nostrils made Kessler imagine that she had somehow wallowed in her agony just as she had wallowed in pleasurable sensations; that she was primitive, indulgent, a grotesque blob of flesh around her own nerve endings. He loathed the victim but still had to find the man who had killed her. That was his job.

Kessler's obsession with Vera Maslyukov distracted him from a close scrutiny of her husband's corpse. It was only when he seemed to have reached a dead end with the tape that had gagged her, and the shreds of tobacco on the floor, that Kessler returned to the report from the forensic experts on Grigori Maslyukov.

His body had been found at the bottom of the stairs, five or six metres from the front door. His hand held the butt of a revolver on the inside pocket of his jacket. No bullet had been fired. Presumably they had shot him because he was reaching for his gun. His revolver was a Smith and Wesson; the bullet extracted from his body was from a Beretta. Both were common weapons. The specialists had been unable to make much of the markings from the bullet that had gone through Maslyukov's heart. Only one comment in their report attracted Kessler's attention. 'The subject was killed by a single bullet entering the heart, a remarkably accurate shot from a short-barrelled weapon of this kind, if fired across the hallway from the front door.'

Remarkably accurate. Anything remarkable was unusual and anything unusual was a clue. If the revolver itself was not significant, the use of it was; because it was far harder than people supposed from watching television to bring down a man with a single shot, unless it is from point-blank range. From the position of Maslyukov's body, the trajectory of the bullet suggested that he had been shot from the direction of the door. Had the killer entered with his weapon drawn? Or had he beaten Maslyukov to the draw? Either way, he had had no time to take careful aim yet had fired a single shot that went straight to the heart.

So what? Kessler had the plan of the hallway spread out before him with the position of Maslyukov's body marked in ink and the probable path of the bullet a black dotted line. Had Maslyukov recognized his assailant? Who had let him in? Had they had a key? Or had Vera opened the door? All in all, it suggested a more accomplished operation than one would expect from Russian mafiosi.

Dorn came into Kessler's office. 'We've got nowhere,' he said. 'It's a waste of time.'

'Have you looked into people *leaving* for the Soviet Union the day after the crime?'

'Yes. From Schönfeld, nothing. Or nothing convincing. There were direct flights from Frankfurt to Moscow and Kiev.

But if they were taking the icons with them, they could hardly have packed them all into suitcases ˙ . . .'

'No.'

'They are more likely to have left them in Munich or Frankfurt or even here in Berlin.'

'Or Switzerland. Or Liechtenstein.'

Dorn shook his head. 'We're wasting our time, chief. What's the point of checking all these entries and exits? It won't be Russians from Russia who topped them, and if it was, they would hardly fly in and out like a trade delegation . . .'

'No.'

'Can we drop it, then?'

'Yes.'

Dorn turned to go but Kessler held him back. 'What about this?' He tapped his pencil on the dotted line showing the trajectory of the bullet.

'What about it?'

'One shot. Straight to the heart.'

'Luck?'

'Or skill.'

'They don't have skill, these gangsters. That's why they use Uzis or sawn-off shotguns.'

'Precisely.'

Dorn looked puzzled. 'So what do we conclude from that?'

'That he was a good shot, a very good shot.'

'Experienced?'

'Trained.'

'Ex-army?'

'Not with a Beretta.'

'Then what? Intelligence?'

'More likely.'

'Ours or theirs?'

'Could be either.'

'Any noise from the BfV?'

'No. But then we haven't enquired.'

'It's a long shot.'

'Yes.' Kessler looked down at the plan. 'Precisely. A long shot. Let's see where it takes us.'

136

There were channels for liaison between the West Berlin police and West Germany's 'Office for the Protection of the Constitution', the BfV, but Kessler chose not to use them. They were slow. It would mean briefing his superiors on the progress of his investigation which in itself would be awkward since there was none. He had also found that the local BfV people were reluctant to put things on the record. Requests went to Cologne; authorization was arbitrary. Kessler always ended up with a fraction of what he wanted to know.

He also knew that the BfV still had their hands full dealing with the disbanded East German secret police, the Stasi. His request would go into an in-tray and might not be considered for weeks. He therefore said nothing to his superiors but telephoned a contact called Grohmann and arranged to meet him that evening in a bar in Wilmersdorf.

Grohmann was hardly a friend. Kessler felt no particular fondness for him or anyone else in the BfV. The paymasters of the BfV were the Christian Democrats in Bonn, and reflex anti-Communism made it suspicious of the West Berlin police whose leftist sympathies dated from the days of the Weimar Republic. Kessler was hardly soft on Communism, and he appreciated that West Berlin had been sustained by the subventions from the Federal Republic; all the same, he felt no great affection for the government in Bonn.

But just as Berlin had needed Bonn, so Bonn had needed Berlin, not just as a showcase for capitalism and democracy but also as a centre for its operations to the East. They might treat the city police as auxiliaries but they needed those auxiliaries all the same; and if Kessler now wanted some help from Grohmann, he was only calling in favours he had done for Grohmann outside official channels in the past.

Grohmann was ordinary in appearance – medium height, glasses, brown trousers, a green blouson. He might have been a maths teacher on his day off, or perhaps the company secretary of a small firm. He looked at his watch when Kessler came in, even though Kessler was on time, and after a curt nod of greeting asked him what he wanted to drink.

Kessler ordered a beer. Grohmann paid – not from generosity, Kessler suspected, but to be able to leave without waiting for the barman to return.

'Maslyukov,' said Kessler.

Grohmann sipped his beer. 'Grigori Maslyukov?'

'Yes.'

'The art dealer. I remember reading about it.'

'In the papers or in a memo?'

'In the papers.'

'He was murdered. So was his wife.'

'So I read.'

'They tortured her first.'

'I didn't read that.' Grohmann peered into his glass as if looking for a fly in his beer.

'We didn't put it out.'

'Why was she tortured?'

'We don't know. In fact, we know very little. We need help.'

'As it happens,' said Grohmann, 'when I read about Maslyukov, I checked to see if we had him on our files.'

'And did you?'

'Yes.'

'And?'

Grohmann put down his glass. 'Nothing much. He came West in 1982, was given asylum, imported icons, made a fortune . . .'

'An entrepreneur?'

'Yes.'

'Not an agent?'

Grohmann shrugged. 'If he was, he wasn't active. They may have been saving him for something.'

'Any reason to think that?'

'No. I think he was probably what he seemed to be.'

'So no reason for anyone *here* to kill him?'

'Here?'

'Any of you people, or the Americans.'

'Certainly not us . . .'

'The Americans?'

'I doubt it.'

Kessler glanced at Grohmann, trying to assess whether or not he meant what he said. 'Whoever killed him was a good shot.'

'What weapon?'

'A Beretta.'

'Ah.'

'What?'

'Much favoured by the KGB.'

'Could it have been them?'

'Possibly . . .'

'Why?'

'Because of the icons. They may have come to reclaim them and have met with . . . resistance.'

'If they were stolen, why not go through Interpol?'

'Official channels? No. Too corrupt in Russia. Too slow in Brussels. And anyway, it would be difficult to prove that they were stolen.'

'So they send a team to recover the icons, are recognized or ambushed, and shoot Maslyukov before he shoots them?'

'That's possible.'

'Why torture the wife?'

He shrugged. 'To find where other icons were hidden, perhaps. Or the numbers of bank accounts.'

'Have you any idea who might have led such a team?'

Grohmann scratched his chin. 'In the past, the KGB did some of the smuggling of icons. It was a perk that went with foreign travel. So if they mounted an operation to get them back, it would have to be insulated or else Maslyukov's former customers would tip him off.'

'Which means?'

'That it wouldn't have been done through the usual KGB personnel. It would have been a special operation, mounted directly from Moscow.'

'So the chances of identifying the killer would be small?'

'I can make enquiries but . . .'

'What?'

'Even if we identify the killer, it's unlikely that he could be extradited.'

'Unless Yeltsin wanted to establish his law-abiding credentials.'

'In which case it might make sense to play the game strictly according to the rules and ask Interpol for help from the Russian police.'

'Would they give it?'

Grohmann shrugged. 'They'll send someone, certainly, because Interpol pays. Whether he helps or hinders is another matter.' Grohmann drank down the rest of his beer. 'But you're going to a lot of trouble. Does it matter that much who killed the Maslyukovs after all this time?'

'It matters,' said Kessler, 'not because of the Maslyukovs, but to get the message across that Berlin is not going to become like the Chicago of Al Capone.'

ELEVEN

On the day General Savchenko was due back in Moscow, Nikolai Gerasimov drove out to Zhukovska to visit the celebrated painter, Anatoly Sergeyevich Orlov. He used a Volga from the Lubyanka car pool; his Samara was once again in the hands of Georgi Nazayan. Ease of access to Georgi's mechanic was one of the reasons why Nikolai had returned to live with his wife in the flat on the Ulitsa Akademika Koroleva. He had neither forgiven nor forgotten, but had grown tired of sleeping on sofas, wearing dirty shirts and travelling by bus.

Gerasimov took some time to find the dacha. The straight roads cut through the pine forest all looked alike. Each house was set back behind a fence in its own hectare of land. Some had no numbers. They were all large by Soviet standards, most built in the 1950s with three or four bedrooms, given by the Party to those considered to have made an outstanding contribution to their country in science or the arts. Rostropovich had lived there. So had the physicist Sakharov until he had been turned into a dissident by his second wife, Ylena Bonner. Gerasimov's lip curled at the thought of Sakharov. Times had changed but not

Gerasimov's instinctual distaste for those who had betrayed the Soviet cause.

He finally found Orlov's villa, and parked the Volga outside the gate. A drive led from the gate to a garage and the back door of the house. There was a lawn in front of the house – a small clearing in the forest. The grass was uncut and was half covered by damp, dead leaves. The doors to the garage had moss growing between the planks of wood. They did not appear to have been opened for years. Gerasimov looked up and saw a large north-facing window that he took to be that of old Orlov's studio. Some slates were missing from the gable. Ferns grew out of the gutter. More moss had grown where there was damp on the walls.

Gerasimov knocked on the door. There was silence. He had telephoned; he was expected; but so strong was the impression that the house was empty that, had it not been for the window of the studio, he might have decided that he had come to the wrong place. He knocked again and, after waiting and listening for a further few minutes, he heard a shuffling of slippered feet.

The door opened. A tall woman, between sixty and seventy years old, invited him in. Like Tatiana Orlova, she did not ask who he was or why he was there.

Gerasimov stepped into a pantry. Muddy boots stood on the floor. Empty vases stood in a low sink.

'Natasha Petrovna?'

'Yes. Come this way.'

She led him through from the pantry into a dark hallway, and from there into a living room that was scarcely lighter: it looked out onto the garden but the garden itself was enclosed by pine trees, their shade welcome in summer, no doubt, but on a cloudy day in April shrouding the house in gloom.

'If you will wait,' she said, 'I will tell my husband that you are here.'

Gerasimov remained standing. From the look of the furniture it seemed that little had been changed since the house was built in the late 1950s. The chairs were made of varnished wood, with upholstered backs and seats. The same veneer had been used for the dining table and for the glass-fronted bookcases that ran along the wall. There was a grand piano at one end of the room and, displayed on a sideboard like birthday cards, stood leather folders containing certificates from different Soviet institutions – the Academy of Sciences, the Central Committee – commending Anatoly Orlov for his services to the arts. On one, Gerasimov saw the signature of Stalin; on another, Khrushchev's; on a third, that of Leonid Brezhnev. There was an Order of the Red Banner, an Order of Lenin, all the honours that could be bestowed on a favoured artist; and when he looked up at the pictures hanging on the walls, Gerasimov could see that several had been painted by Orlov, some of them portraits, early works before he had evolved the distinctive style so familiar to every Soviet child – faces of workers set in the heroic, proletarian mould with square jaw, grim look, clenched fist, unyielding eye.

Over the mantel there was a portrait of Lenin, again one of the kind that had hung in galleries in every major city of the former Soviet Union. It was on a smaller scale, of course, which made it unsuitable for a public collection. There was even a twinkle in the Soviet leader's eye.

'That is an early work.'

Gerasimov turned. Behind him stood an old man wearing a dressing gown. Beneath the dressing gown he wore loose trousers, a shirt and a badly knotted tie. On his head was a tasselled fez.

'It is entitled *Lenin Amused*, and was thought unsuitable for public exhibition. Prophets are not supposed to have a sense of humour.'

Gerasimov, for all his professional training, could not suppress a look of astonishment at the old man's costume.

'Ah. I see that you're amused, too. Well, it's cold in my studio, damned cold, so I have to wear a hat and a fur hat's too heavy and a peaked cap cuts out the light.'

'I am sorry to disturb you, Anatoly Sergeyevich,' said Gerasimov, assuming the kind of deferential posture he thought appropriate in the presence of a man who, however eccentric his appearance might be, remained one of the most celebrated painters in the Soviet Union.

'Don't worry,' said Anatoly Orlov, still referring to Gerasimov's astonished expression. 'People are always puzzled

143

when they meet me. They expect me to look like one of the heroic figures in my paintings. They're not puzzled by my wife, of course. She looks the part. She was the model for some of those heroines holding the red flag. You met her, didn't you? Of course you did. She let you in. Monumental! A strong woman. A good woman, a good wife, a good mother, a good citizen. And now she's angry.'

'Angry?'

'With events. The counter-revolution.'

'I see.'

'She thinks you've been sent to spy on us . . .'

'Only to ask . . .'

'We've nothing to hide. We're Bolsheviks. We've always been Bolsheviks, and if that drunkard Yeltsin wants to drag me off to prison, or throw me out on the streets, I'll be proud to go.' He clenched his fist and raised it to the level of his shoulder. 'They can suspend the Party with the stroke of a pen, but they can't suspend the Bolshevik spirit in the Orlovs, the spirit that made this country great, that sent a shiver down the spine of every damned capitalist and imperialist west of Brest and east of Vladivostok!'

'Comrade Orlov . . .' Gerasimov began.

'Comrade? Are you ironic? Am I your comrade? Or are you a lackey of the pusillanimous Gorbachev and the drunkard Yeltsin? Reformers! Democrats! Ha! Traitors, more like, out to sell Russia to the Jews in America and make us serfs of the World Bank.'

He spoke in a declamatory style, as if addressing a crowd, striding to and fro, his dressing gown swirling round his ankles. 'So what do you want to know? What am I painting? Not Yeltsin's ugly mug, that's for sure. Not the sly Asiatic eyes of that Siberian opportunist, no! I'm painting . . . Come, I'll show you.' And quite suddenly he turned and took the far larger Gerasimov by the arm, led him from the room, back across the hallway and up the stairs.

'What do you know about art?' he asked Gerasimov.

'I have . . .'

'Not much. I know.' He said this kindly. 'We had such a huge task – to educate the masses – that what we taught had to be rudimentary, yes . . .' He paused on the landing to catch his breath, looked into Gerasimov's eyes and repeated the word: 'Rudimentary. And, of course, art had to serve the cause . . .' They continued up the stairs. 'There was no room for fancy theorizing, none of your "art for art's sake" ' – he spoke these words with derision – 'which gave all those flowery pictures by the Impressionists which now sell for millions in the West – all mirrors of their decadence. The mad Van Gogh – there, to elevate the distortions of a lunatic and call that art! And Renoir. Pornography. "I paint with my penis." He admitted it. He never pretended otherwise.'

They had come to a door at the end of a corridor on the first floor. Anatoly Sergeyevich Orlov paused; he still held Gerasimov by the arm. 'And in Russia? A few pathetic imitations, always running after the latest Western fad. Just like now. But that wasn't our authentic tradition. Have you read Chernyshevsky? "The true function of art is to explain life . . ." And the Wanderers put that thought into action. Repin, Surikov – they knew what they were doing. The Moscow school. But then Vrubel came from Petersburg and the rot set in. Bloody foreigners, charlatans who jumped on the band-wagon, just like now. Experimental art. Abstract art. Cubism. The Suprematists, Constructivists – rubbish, all rubbish. And they thought *they* were the revolutionaries! Ha! They were the frauds. Cunning Yids who bamboozled the critics and even for a time the Party. But they were never Bolsheviks. Never. They didn't care a damn about the people. They despised the workers and poured scorn on anyone who scratched their heads in front of their paintings and asked what their scribblings were all about. Tatlin? Bits of wood. El Lissitzky? Squares and circles. Chagall? Yiddish kitsch. Kandinsky? Disintegration! Disintegration of form. Disintegration of meaning. Doodles. Ravings. The icons of nihilism. The delirium of a drunk!'

He opened the door and led Gerasimov into his studio – a huge room with the high window that Gerasimov had seen from outside, a patch of brown on the white ceiling beneath the missing slates. It faced north, making the room even darker than the living room below. 'Damn cold, eh?' said Orlov. 'We can't get anyone to deliver coal for the stove. And no light bulbs. I paint in the dark. Dim light. Dim eyes. But colour in the painting, what?'

And there was colour – a bright red in the flag held aloft by an armed worker as he stormed the gates of the Winter Palace. '*Lest We Forget*. That's what I've called it. Lest we forget!' And suddenly the old man fell silent, brooding over his painting.

To Gerasimov it was familiar: he had seen dozens like it in different art galleries as a child. The storming of the Winter Palace had been one of the subjects he preferred: better, certainly, than the realistic depictions of workers surpassing their quotas in steel mills or on collective farms. 'It's very fine,' he said lamely.

'But no one will buy it,' said Anatoly Orlov, quieter now, his brow creased in a frown. 'Look.' He turned and pointed to a stack of canvases in the corner of the studio. 'They've started to return them. Some just arrived. Others have a covering note. "We've no room in our storerooms, Anatoly Sergeyevich, and yours are no longer the kind of pictures the public enjoy." That from Perm. And from Lvov, no paintings, but a letter. "If you would like your works returned, kindly forward the cost of transporting them. Otherwise, they will be destroyed." '

'I am sorry,' said Gerasimov with a certain sincerity.

'The question is this,' said the old man. 'Is art to lead or is it to follow? Is it to teach? Can it help but teach? And if it teaches, what does it teach? The earliest paintings – the buffalo in the caves at Lascaux. Were they there for decoration? No. The statues of the Greeks? The expression of an ideal. The Bayeux tapestry? A celebration of victory in war. And our Russian art, Comrade Chekist? Our venerated icons? Were they there simply to decorate the churches? Or were they the embodiment of the people's faith? When the icon of the Virgin of Smolensk was paraded in front of the troops before the Battle of Borodino, was it just to show the soldiers a pretty picture? Or was it an invocation to a higher power, the power of the Mother of God which it portrayed? We are a nation, Comrade Chekist, to whom the icon was also the idea. And now . . .' He turned to look at the stack of his rejected paintings. 'Now there is no more art in Russia, because the Russians have lost faith in the idea.'

There was a moment of silence. If Anatoly Orlov had any further thoughts, he did not choose to share them with Nikolai Gerasimov. Eventually, Gerasimov cleared his throat and said:

'Anatoly Sergeyevich, it is my duty to ask you whether you know where we can get hold of your son, Andrei Anatolyevich.'

The old man snapped out of his reverie. 'Andrei? No. I don't know where he's gone.'

'He has left the country . . .'

'I'm not surprised.'

'As you know, he is no longer . . .'

'They got rid of their best man.'

'There were . . .'

'Afraid of him, I dare say. I'm not surprised.'

'There were changes in the personnel.'

'It always happens when there's a shake-up. The dregs float to the top.'

It occurred to Gerasimov to point out that the October Revolution had been just such a shake-up but he did not want to set Anatoly Orlov going on another tirade. 'His abilities were respected,' he began.

'Nonsense. He was sacked because he still believed.'

'It was thought that officers who could not adapt to the new conditions . . .'

'Who wouldn't be lackeys of the West . . .'

Gerasimov was becoming irritated. For all the old man's distinction, he could not permit him to waste his time. 'There are loose ends,' he said. 'We have to find him.'

'Then find him.'

'We had hoped you would help.'

Anatoly Orlov now seemed to feel that time was passing to no avail. He led Gerasimov out of the studio, down the passage towards the stairs. 'He has gone to the West. He had business there. A joint venture, I believe. Import. Export. How should I know? You sacked him. He had to live. To use his talents. He can speak five languages. Did you know that? He could pass for a German or an American or a Frenchman. You trained him well.'

'Has he contacted you?'

'No.'

'Have you an address or a number?'

'No.'

'Has he called you?'

'No. He was a Chekist, remember? We never expect to hear from him when he's away on an operation . . .'

'You said he was on business.'

The old man looked confused, as if he might have said something to compromise his son. 'We haven't heard from him,' he said. 'I don't know what he's doing. He would never tell me, anyway. I'm a painter, not a politician.'

They had reached the landing halfway down the stairs. 'So he did talk to politicians?'

'I didn't say that.'

'If he had talked to politicians, who might they be?'

'Who said he talked to politicians? Damn it, there were no politicians in the Soviet Union before Mikhail Sergeyevich had those damned elections in 'eighty-nine. Elections! A beauty contest among weasels!'

Gerasimov did not want to engage in a debate about *glasnost* and *perestroika*. 'I would greatly appreciate it, Anatoly Sergeyevich, if you would let us know if by any chance your son should contact you.'

'Humph.' The painter reached the hall where his wife Natasha Petrovna was waiting for them. She looked fleetingly at her husband, an anxious look in her eye, then turned to Gerasimov with no expression.

'I was just saying to Anatoly Sergeyevich,' said Gerasimov, 'that we are most anxious to get hold of your son Andrei.'

She nodded.

'If he should call you . . .'

'Of course.' She led him towards the pantry and the back door.

Gerasimov turned to take his leave of the painter. 'Thank you for receiving me, Anatoly Sergeyevich . . .'

The old man laughed. 'It was no favour. I have time on my hands.'

'The light bulbs,' Natasha Petrovna whispered to Gerasimov as she opened the back door. 'The large ones, for the studio lamps. They are so hard to find.'

'I will see what I can do,' said Gerasimov.

She nodded, not to thank him, but merely to acknowledge that she had heard what he said.

'These are difficult times,' said Gerasimov.

'Indeed.' For a moment she watched as Gerasimov walked back down the damp drive towards the gate. Then she closed the door.

Back at the Lubyanka Centre, Gerasimov was told that General Savchenko had returned and wished to see him at once in his office. He was ushered straight in. The general sat at his desk, leafing through the thin report that Gerasimov had prepared for his return.

'I realize,' he said sharply, before Gerasimov could open his mouth, 'that you may have had other duties, and that this investigation which I entrusted to you posed particular problems . . . I realize too that I may have given the impression that there was no particular urgency in the matter. Nevertheless, it astonishes me that . . .' He stopped, flicked though a few more pages, then went on: 'No. Nothing astonishes me. But it surprises me, Comrade Lieutenant, that in . . . what is it, now? . . . eight months . . . you have accomplished so little.'

Gerasimov cleared his throat. 'As you say, Comrade General, there have been particular problems associated with this case. First of all, because of the secrecy of the icon operation, very few officers had any contact with Orlov in the period preceding his disappearance . . .'

He waited to see if this excuse impressed Savchenko.

'And?' asked the general.

'Well, you yourself imposed limitations. For example, I am quite sure that Orlov's father-in-law, Ivan Keminski . . .'

'You saw the daughter?' Savchenko interrupted.

'Yes.'

'Unforthcoming?'

'She said she knew nothing.'

'And Orlov's father?'

'I saw him this morning. The same.'

'Keminski,' said Savchenko, rummaging through another pile of papers on his desk, 'has apparently just registered as the agent of a private Swiss bank.'

'That could well be something to do with Orlov.'

'I know.'

'Can I go and see Keminski?'

Savchenko hesitated. 'Better not. He still has friends who . . . It's all very delicate. If we tread on the wrong toes, we could be ordered to leave Orlov alone.'

'So how should I proceed?'

Savchenko considered for a moment, tapping his nicotine-stained teeth with the end of a pencil. 'Although I had hoped you would have done better than this,' he said eventually, tapping Gerasimov's report with the pencil, 'I have to concede that the enquiries I made on my travels also proved fruitless. You talked to Kirsch?'

'Yes. He provided some useful background.'

'But nothing more. I know. No one in our Western residences had seen or heard of Orlov. It is quite possible, of course, that some may have done so but were unwilling to admit it. A large number of those still in the service are unsympathetic to the reform programme. They do not think that it will succeed, and fully expect that in a year's time we may see Rutskoi or Khasbulatov in the Kremlin instead of Yeltsin.'

'I do not see what more we can do unless Orlov himself breaks cover . . .'

'We have got nowhere with people,' said Savchenko, lighting a cigarette, 'but there may be something we can learn from *things*.'

'Things?'

'First of all, there are the passports. Orlov must have some false identity, and the papers to support that identity must come from Moscow.' The cigarette dangled from Savchenko's lips as he once again rummaged through the papers on his desk. He found what he was looking for, glanced at it, and then pushed it over the desk to Gerasimov. 'There is a protégé of Khrulev's . . .'

Gerasimov looked down at the memo. 'Peshkov . . .'

'Peshkov, yes. He was apparently placed in Section Six by Khrulev, and handled the documentation for the icon operation. I suggest you visit him at home. Lean on him. Threaten him, if you like . . .'

'On whose authority?'

'Mine. And you can mention the chief, Bakatin. He's as keen as anyone to find Orlov.'

'Very well.' Gerasimov half rose to go but Savchenko had not finished with him.

'And then there's the van,' said the general, exhaling the smoke of his cigarette.

'The van?'

'It struck me, when I was in Germany, that the Volkswagen transporter used by the young officer . . . I forgot his name . . .'

'Partovsky.'

'Yes. Partovsky. That transporter which he used to bring the icons back to Russia is the only material link to Orlov's operation in Berlin. Orlov may have bought it, or some associate may have bought it for him. Perhaps Orlov still has links with that associate. Certainly, it is worth looking at the van to see if it provides some kind of lead that you have failed to get from people.'

The white Volkswagen transporter had disappeared. It was reported in the log of the Centre's transport office that it had been collected from the Tretyakov two weeks after Partovsky's return. A driver called Akinviev had brought it to the Lubyanka, but it had then been moved on to the central depot on the outskirts of Moscow by a driver whose scrawled signature appeared to read 'M. Gorbachev'.

Nikolai Gerasimov drove out to the depot in the Volga that afternoon. He looked through the logbook with the duty officer to make sure that there was no record that the transporter had arrived. The duty officer readily admitted that it had almost certainly been sold by one of the drivers. 'We have no M. Gorbachev on our list, Comrade Captain, not even Mikhail Sergeyevich, even though he's out of a job.'

'We have to find it,' said Gerasimov, not smiling at the officer's joke. 'It's not just a question of the theft. It's an operational matter.'

'Try the militia,' said the transport officer. 'They know the people who handle stolen goods.'

A counsel of despair. No one in the militia would want to help the former KGB, particularly not Gerasimov who had so frequently stymied their moves against Georgi. But the very thought of Georgi gave Gerasimov an idea, and so, instead of returning to the Lubyanka Centre, he drove back into Moscow on the Prospekt Mira and stopped off at his flat on the Ulitsa Akademika Koroleva.

Ylena was watching a video. She looked miserably at Gerasimov. He did not greet her but went straight to the bedroom to take off his clothes, then to the bathroom to take a shower. As he passed through the lobby on his way to the bathroom, Ylena shouted: 'The Samara's ready.' He made no reply. He took his shower and then, with a towel round his waist, went to the door of the sitting room and said: 'Is it here?'

'No. He said to call when you wanted it.'

'Tell him I want it now.'

'You tell him.'

He looked at her with an expression of menace in his eyes.

She sniffed. 'I don't want to talk to him.'

'Call your fucking lover. Tell him to bring the car.'

He heard her sniffing as he went back to the bedroom, and then a click as she picked up the telephone. 'And tell Georgi I want to talk to him,' he shouted. The sniffs became sobs. 'Tell him it's business – nothing personal. Tell him, what's a fat slut between friends?'

The sob became a yowl, but slipped back to a sniff as she delivered his message over the telephone. She then went back to the television while Gerasimov, in fresh clothes, lay on the bed, reading while he waited.

Georgi came with his heavies. It was the first time the two men had met since the night out that had ended at the Cosmos Hotel, and so quite possibly Georgi feared that Gerasimov had planned some revenge. But Gerasimov, greeting him at the entrance to the block, was all charm. 'Georgi . . . It's been a long time. And I never thanked you for the great time I had with your girls, better, I should think, than you've ever had with that fat slut of mine.'

Georgi darted an uneasy look, trying to guess whether or not rage lay behind this male bravado, but Gerasimov was too well trained to betray his real feelings to an Armenian spiv. He put his arm round Georgi's shoulder and gave a genial smile. 'Do you want to come up?' he asked.

'I have things to do,' said Georgi. 'The Samara's clean. She's humming like a bird.'

'I'm grateful. But now I have another favour to ask you.'

'Fire away.'

'A Volkswagen van.'

'You want a van?'

'A specific van. A white Volkswagen transporter that dis-appeared in September 1991 on its way from the Lubyanka Centre to the transport department depot.'

'Stolen?'

'Sold. A private deal by one of our drivers . . .'

Georgi narrowed his eyes. 'You want the man?'

'No. Not the man. The transporter. And not to keep. Just to look. It's a lead in an investigation. I can't say more.'

Georgi looked uncertain. 'It's a long time ago.'

'I know. But there can't have been many vans like that from the Lubyanka.'

'I can ask around . . .'

'That's all I ask. From our end, these days, everything's a pale shade of grey. But you, from your end – well, quite honestly, Georgi – when a police state falls to pieces, it's over to people like you.'

Again Georgi narrowed his eyes. Was this a compliment or an insult? But Gerasimov kept up his genial façade. 'It would be a *big* favour,' he said. 'I mean, not just to me but to the people above me. They'd owe you one.'

Georgi nodded. 'And you don't want it back?'

'No. Just a look.'

'At the Lubyanka?' He looked uneasy.

'No. Here will do.'

Georgi walked back towards his Mercedes. 'I'll do what I can.'

Gerasimov now drove back to the Lubyanka.

'Did you find the van?' asked the dispatch officer.

'No. Let's look at the log again.' Gerasimov followed the duty officer to his desk. 'M. Gorbachev. Who's the joker?'

The officer shrugged. 'I don't know.'

'Who was on duty that shift?'

'I was.'

'Aren't you meant to check that the drivers sign their names?'

'In theory, of course . . .'

'And you can't remember who took the van?'

The man now began to look uneasy. 'Offhand, no. So many vehicles come and go . . .'

'But not brand-new German vans.'

'If I could remember the bastard, I swear . . .'

'Swear all you like. It still looks bad.'

The man now began to look afraid. 'What can I do?'

'Do you want my advice?'

'Yes.'

'Report it stolen. That's what they said at the depot. Call the militia. Let them find it.'

The young officer put his hand on the telephone. 'Right away, comrade. Now I have been informed that it never reached the depot, I'll report it stolen.'

It was now dark, and time to pay a visit to Peshkov, the man in the second division of Directorate S of the First Chief Directorate, the KGB's counterfeiters, the best in the world – purveyors of everything from United States passports to British birth certificates, German *Ausweise*, French share certificates – anything and everything required for operations abroad.

Gerasimov decided not to call on Peshkov in his offce. The visit might come to the attention of Orlov's friends in the Second Chief Directorate. It would be equally compromising if Gerasimov were to go to his home in a conspicuously official car like the Volga. He therefore took a bus back to the Ulitsa Akademika Koroleva to pick up the Samara.

The car purred down the Prospekt Mira towards the centre of Moscow. Georgi's mechanic had serviced the car well, as well as Georgi had serviced his wife. This thought, that would once have made Nikolai grind his teeth, now produced only a sardonic smile.

Gerasimov knew the block where Peshkov lived: it had been built to house Directorate S personnel. With the air of a friend who was paying a visit, Gerasimov showed his service card to the concierge and took the lift to the fourth floor.

Peshkov's wife came to the door. With the same nonchalance, Gerasimov said: 'Trouble at the office' and walked through the door.

'Grigori,' she shouted.

Peshkov was eating his supper off a low table in the living room while watching TV. Two children came out ahead of him. The elder, a girl, stood staring at Gerasimov; the younger, a boy of eight or so, dangled from the exercise bars on one of the walls of the hall.

Peshkov came out of the living room, frowning and wiping his mouth. With a nod of his head he sent his wife into the kitchen. The children followed. He gestured to Gerasimov, who had taken off his shoes, to follow him into the living room where he turned down the sound on the TV.

'I'm sorry to interrupt you at home,' said Gerasimov.

'Never mind,' said Peshkov. He was only forty – Gerasimov knew this from his file – but being bald looked older. Perhaps he was ill.

'I've been ordered to make certain internal enquiries . . .'

'By?'

'General Savchenko, but it has been authorized by Bakatin.'

Peshkov nodded. 'Go ahead.'

'Khrulev.'

'What about him?'

'He ran his own outfit within the Second Chief Directorate.'

'Yes.'

'The last operation was insulated . . .'

Peshkov was looking at the television. Was he bored by what Gerasimov was saying? Or trying to hide the fact that he was scared?

'It was insulated,' Gerasimov went on, 'because it was an operation to recover icons and some of our own people had been selling them in the West.'

'We are never told about operations,' said Peshkov.

'But you knew that this one was for Khrulev's eyes only?'

'Yes.'

'Captain Orlov was your liaison . . .'

Peshkov said nothing.

'Not even your department head knew.'

'No.'

'You answered to Khrulev.'

'Yes.'

'And now's Khrulev's dead.'

'So I hear.'

'So who ordered you to provide new passports for Orlov?'

Peshkov did not move. With his eyes still on the television, he picked up a slice of bread from his plate.

'Orlov left the service,' said Gerasimov. 'He's now in the West. We have reason to believe that you provided the passports. We want to know the names.'

Peshkov took a bite out of the slice of bread and chewed it slowly in his mouth. 'Orlov has left the service?' he asked.

'Yes. You must have known that.'

'To provide documents for an ex-officer would be a serious offence,' said Peshkov.

'Yes,' said Gerasimov.

'Why would one do it?'

'You tell me.'

'I would if I knew.'

It was clear that Peshkov was not going to admit to what he had done. 'Listen,' said Gerasimov, leaning forward, resting his elbows on his knees. 'No one is interested in prosecuting anyone who through misplaced loyalty, or even for a dollar or two, gives a little help to a friend. No one's interested in knowing who's a progressive and who's a hard-liner in your department because, quite frankly, as long as you do your job, no one cares. What interests us is a list of names, nationalities, passport numbers, on my desk, or sent through the post. No questions asked. No one told.'

'And if not?'

'The Cold War is over, comrade. There are ten times too many people doing our job. Some are going to have to go and, to be quite honest, there aren't that many opportunities for someone in your line of work.'

Gerasimov left his card on the table, then put on his shoes and let himself out, leaving Peshkov in front of the television while his wife and children cowered in the kitchen. He was hungry, but he was also tired – too tired to eat out or go back to any bed but his own. He drove back to the Ulitsa Akademika Koroleva.

There was a smell of cooking in the flat. In the kitchen, the table was set for two. A fat round candle stood between the salt cellar and the pepper pot. Hearing him enter, Ylena shuffled out of the bedroom. Both her lips and her eyes were red – the lips from lipstick, the eyes from tears.

'Expecting company?' Gerasimov asked sarcastically.

She sniffed, shuffled into the kitchen and lit the candle.

Gerasimov shook his head, incredulous that after ten years of marriage he could still be surprised at the depths of his wife's vulgarity and sentimentality. A reconciliation dinner! He washed his face and hands in the bathroom before going to shut himself in the bedroom, but he was waylaid by the smell of bortsch, and his appetite got the better of his resolve. He sat down at the table. Ylena ladled the soup into his plate, then sat, her plate empty, sniffing soulfully and looking pathetically into his eyes.

The telephone rang. She went to answer it. 'Yes, yes, yes.' She came back into the kitchen. 'He thinks he's found your van. He'll bring it round tomorrow night.'

Gerasimov left for work at the Lubyanka at seven the next morning. Before going to his office, he had a word with Melnik, the transport officer. When he got to his desk he found a letter. His name was handwritten. There was no stamp. Inside was a sheet of paper with a list of names, numbers and nationalities – the passports forged for Orlov by Peshkov, one American, one German, one Swiss, one French and one Soviet.

Gerasimov went to see Savchenko. 'This list of passports, Comrade General.'

'Well done.' Savchenko took the list and studied it. 'Why a Soviet passport, I wonder?'

'I asked myself the same question.'

'Did Peshkov have any ideas?'

'Peshkov admitted to nothing. This list is off the record.'

Savchenko nodded. 'So we have no way of knowing whether

our friend Orlov is travelling around Europe as the American Edward Burton, the German Hans Lauch, the Swiss Franz Grauber or the Frenchman Marcel Jeanneret?'

'No. Presumably in Germany he will be a German, and to get at the bank accounts in Zürich he will be Grauber, the Swiss.'

'And the Russian, Serotkin?'

'To return to Moscow incognito.'

Savchenko nodded. 'Do we know if photographs had already been affixed to the passports?'

'No.'

'Almost certainly not. Orlov will have changed his appearance.'

'So even with the names and the passport numbers he won't be easy to find.'

'Unless . . .' Savchenko leaned forward and took a piece of paper from the top of the pile on his desk. By its shiny surface, and smudged Latin lettering, Gerasimov judged that it was a letter from the West that had been faxed and refaxed a number of times. 'There has been a request through Interpol for our assistance in the case of the murders of the Maslyukovs in Berlin.'

Gerasimov frowned. 'How will we respond?'

'How indeed?' Savchenko sat back in his chair. 'The usual thing is to send some dumb ox from the militia who speaks no German and would act more as a hindrance than a help. But in this case . . .'

'Tell them about Orlov?'

'Who was acting on our orders? No. That would be most . . . damaging to our relations with the Federal Republic. But if we sent you to Berlin, and if you could gain access to their database, then you should be able to find Orlov before they do.'

'And when I do?'

'Find out what he's up to.'

'And if he won't tell me?'

'Bring him home.'

'And if he won't come home?'

'Insist. Point out the danger he runs of being prosecuted for the Maslyukovs' murder, and the harm it would do to Russia's credibility as a civilized nation.'

'And if he *still* won't come home?'

'*Then eliminate him.* If Orlov was to fall into the hands of the Germans, there might be a public trial. Think of the harm that would do to the reputation of the Russian Federation. If there is the slightest risk, you must do your duty and eliminate him. However admirable his services may have been in the past, he cannot be allowed to compromise the future.' And, as if to illustrate the point, Savchenko drove the butt of his cigarette into the base of the glass ashtray with a savagery unexpected in such a portly, amiable man.

Once the decision was made, and the order given, the different departments of the new security service of the Russian Federation went to work with all the efficiency of the old soviet KGB. There was a minor dispute as to whether the Deutschmarks required should be charged to the department of the militia that dealt with Interpol or the foreign currency account of Directorate S. It was quickly resolved and Gerasimov was told that he would leave for Berlin on his own passport in two days' time.

All he needed, now, was any evidence he could glean from the Volkswagen transporter. He telephoned Partovsky at the Tretyakov Gallery to say that his presence would be required that evening, and at six went to fetch him in the Samara. Partovsky looked uneasy as he climbed into the car next to Gerasimov, and Gerasimov's high spirits made him more nervous still. 'It may be difficult for me to say for sure . . .' he began.

'There must have been some documents,' said Gerasimov, 'to get you onto the ferry.'

'Yes, of course. The logbook, the insurance, that kind of thing.'

'What happened to them?'

'They were left in the van.'

They reached the Ulitsa Akademika Koroleva. Gerasimov parked the Samara by his block. Partovsky accompanied him up to the apartment. Again, there was a smell of cooking: Ylena was keeping up the blitz on his baser instincts, doubtless with Georgi providing the sausage and the wine. She looked disconcerted when Partovsky came in behind her husband, and, like Partovsky, regarded Gerasimov's high spirits with suspicion.

Gerasimov introduced Partovsky. 'He's here to identify the van.'

The two men took off their coats and shoes and went through to the living room.

'Some vodka?' asked Gerasimov.

'No, I . . .'

'Come on.' Gerasimov went to the glass fronted cupboard, took out a half-full bottle and two glasses. 'After all,' he said, 'we've found the Volkswagen. That's something to celebrate.'

Ylena came in. 'Will you eat with us?' she asked Partovsky.

'No, thank you. My wife . . .'

'Of course he'll eat with us,' said Gerasimov. 'Who knows when Georgi will turn up.' He turned to Partovsky. 'Call your wife. Tell her you'll be late.'

'Very well. If you insist.' Partovsky acquiesced but made no move to telephone his home.

Gerasimov raised his glass. 'To Comrade Orlov, wherever he may be.'

'To Orlov,' said Partovsky, also raising his glass, and then adding with a touch of defiance. 'To Andrei Orlov, a brave man.'

They emptied their glasses. Gerasimov refilled them. 'And to our wives.'

'To our wives.'

'As faithful as the day is long.'

Ylena sniffed. 'It's ready,' she said.

'Then let's eat.'

They went through to the kitchen. A third place had been set by Ylena, the candle taken away.

'I have a wife who can not only cook,' said Gerasimov, 'but who to get hold of the food will do what has to be done.'

'You're a lucky man,' said Partovsky.

'Lucky indeed,' said Gerasimov.

Ylena served up the bortsch. They ate, silent except for the occasional slurp.

'We have a son,' Gerasimov said eventually, 'but I rarely see him.'

'He's with my mother,' said Ylena to Partovsky.

'The Russian babushka,' said Gerasimov. 'What would we do without her?'

'Do you have a child?' Ylena asked Partovsky.

'Yes. A daughter.'

'How nice.'

For a moment, Gerasimov was almost touched by the wistful, childlike look on his wife's face. But it was too late for pity. The doorbell rang.

Ylena went to answer it, then returned to the kitchen. 'It's Georgi. He'll wait downstairs.'

Gerasimov looked at his watch. 'Excellent.' He turned to Partovsky. 'Would you like some more?'

'No, thank you. I've had enough.'

'Would you like some coffee?'

'No, thank you.'

'Another time.'

The two men put on their coats and shoes. Ylena hovered in the kitchen. Partovsky followed Gerasimov out of the flat and down the landing to the lift.

'All we need to know,' said Gerasimov, 'is whether or not this is the van you brought from Germany to Tallinn.'

'I understand.'

'The question of how it disappeared need not concern you.'

Partovsky nodded.

There was a Dutch journalist with a Russian photographer in the lift. Gerasimov and Partovsky stood in silence side by side as it descended to the ground floor.

Georgi was waiting in the lobby. Two of his men were outside the door. He narrowed his eyes at Partovsky. 'Who's this?'

'He brought the van to Russia. He can tell us if it's the right one.'

'Is it his?'

'Is it yours?' asked Gerasimov, smiling.

'No,' said Partovsky. 'It isn't mine.'

They went out to the parking lot. A white VW van was parked next to Georgi's Mercedes. It had Soviet licence plates.

'It wasn't easy to find,' said Georgi, his little eyes flitting to and fro between Gerasimov and Partovsky as if trying to discover why Gerasimov should be in such a bumptious mood.

They reached the van. A third thug sat at the wheel of the Mercedes. Georgi slid back the door of the van. 'Was it a diesel?' he asked Partovsky.

'Yes.'

Gerasimov looked in the glove compartment. It was empty. 'No documents,' he said.

Georgi laughed. 'Not likely.'

Gerasimov pulled the lever that opened the bonnet, then went round to the front of the van. The plates with the engine and chassis numbers had been chiselled off. 'No numbers,' he said to Partovsky.

'I never noted them anyway,' said Partovsky. 'But it's the van, all right.'

'How can you tell?'

'Come and look.'

Gerasimov walked round to the back of the van. Beyond the car park he could see four men in a Lada peering in their direction.

'Those scratches, on the inside. I remember them because the van was more or less new.'

'Anything else?'

'There are two empty Fanta cans under the seat and some sandwich wrapping. Those were mine.'

'They file off the numbers,' said Gerasimov, 'but don't take the trouble to clean it out.'

'And the name of the garage,' said Partovsky. 'I remember that. On the back window. Look. Autohaus Bedaur, Leipzig. There can't be two white VW diesel vans in Moscow from the same garage in Leipzig.'

'So you'd swear to it?'

'Yes. This is the van.'

Georgi had been following their examination of the Volkswagen. He now turned away to find himself facing two plainclothes detectives from the militia.

'We have reason to believe,' said the first, 'that you are in possession of stolen state property.'

Georgi darted a look over their shoulders: his three men were already handcuffed to uniformed policemen. He turned to Gerasimov. 'Tell them.'

Gerasimov shrugged. 'You're asking too much, I'm afraid.' He turned to the detective and shook his head. 'Inflation. The prices people ask, and for stolen goods!'

With a roar Georgi lunged at Gerasimov, but before he could reach him he was seized by the two detectives, handcuffed and led away. The older detective said nothing but merely nodded to Gerasimov before turning to follow his men.

Gerasimov took Partovsky by the arm. 'Thank you, comrade. You have been a great help. The militia have been after that scoundrel for years. It's been hard to get evidence against him but this, I should say – state property, after all – should put him away for quite a while.'

TWELVE

Francesca McDermott, who had been a junior squash champion in Madison, Wisconsin, and a member of the women's team at Harvard, anticipated that her skill might make up for a man's natural advantages when playing Andrei Serotkin. So it proved in the first couple of games. He was good but she was better, or so she thought.

In the third game, her presuppositions were shaken by a defeat. Francesca was puzzled. She could not quite make out what had gone wrong. Perhaps unconsciously she had been unwilling to humiliate the man she loved by winning three games in a row. She tried harder in the fourth game and won. She tried equally hard in the fifth game and was beaten. It was only then that she realized that Serotkin far outclassed her. He had been playing with her like a cat with a mouse, letting her win only when he chose to do so.

'My God, Andrei,' she said, panting, 'this just isn't fair. You must have played in the Soviet team.'

'No.'

'So where did you learn to play like that?'

'There were courts at the ministry. And in Washington, of course.'

'You were at Washington? You never told me that.'

His expression did not change. 'Briefly, in the embassy. I stood in for the cultural attaché.'

'No wonder your English is so good.'

Francesca thought no more of it. As Stefi had once pointed out, Russians had learned the hard way the importance of keeping themselves to themselves. She knew she was only going to get to know Serotkin little by little, and she did not want to jeopardize these friendly meetings by appearing too inquisitive.

Francesca also recognized that a measure of mystery was a necessary ingredient in love, and she was in love: there was no question about that. When Andrei Serotkin entered the room, her heart lifted; when he left it, her heart sank for the few moments it took to conjure him up once again in her imagination. That they were not lovers did not dishearten her while the exhibition brought them together every day, and while she felt confident that his feelings, although undeclared, were nevertheless engaged.

The games of squash were the proof. Andrei had suggested them, and he seemed to enjoy the opportunity they provided to compete with Francesca and win. She had known competitive men before, and she had known some who had appreciated her ability to give them a good run for their money. All sports bind players together with the mixed strands of rivalry and friendship. With Andrei, however, the games seemed to be more than a game, and the objective was not just to win. It was as if he felt challenged by her in ways that possibly he did not fully understand, and that he must establish not just that he could beat her, but that he could tease her and manipulate her – physically in the squash court, intellectually in the office.

Francesca always rose to the bait. Her mind was out of kilter with her emotions and, though ready to surrender her body should he choose to take it, she was not prepared to defer to his judgement when they disagreed on art.

Serotkin had defeated her in the early days on the scope of and the title of the exhibition. Now they joined battle on the question of 'texts'. At an earlier meeting, Frau Dr Koch had proposed that blown-up photographs should be displayed alongside the paintings, either portraits of the artists or pictures of places pertinent to the exhibition such as the church at Abramtsevo or Tatlin's model for a monument to the Third International.

Francesca had argued against this on the grounds that the place for photographs of this kind was in the catalogue, not on the walls. Rival images among the exhibits would dissipate the impact of the art. The committee had agreed. Defeated on this issue, Frau Dr Koch regrouped and mounted a new offensive on the question of displaying excerpts from the manifestos of the different artistic schools – the Futurists, the Constructivists, the Suprematists – as well as quotations from the writings of Kandinsky. Here again, Francesca argued, large placards would distract from the paintings: they would make visitors feel that they were there to learn rather than enjoy. The gallery directors and Dr Kemmelkampf agreed; Stefan Diederich had no view; Günter Westarp was undecided. It seemed that the texts would go the same way as the photographs when Andrei Serotkin raised his hand.

'Dr Serotkin?' asked Stefan Diederich.

'I should like to ask Dr McDermott whether she is confident that, without texts of the kind proposed by Frau Dr Koch, those who look at the works of art will understand what their creators had set out to achieve?'

'I believe they explain themselves,' said Francesca.

'I was thinking, for example,' said Serotkin, 'Of Larionov's "Rayonnist" Manifesto of 1914.' He looked down at a book open on the table in front of him.

We declare that the genius of our days to be: trousers, jackets, shoes, tramways, buses, aeroplanes, railways, magnificent ships . . . We deny that individuality has any value in a work of art . . . Hail nationalism! We go hand in hand with house painters.

'Or there is Kandinsky's *Concerning the Spiritual in Art*, the bible of the modern movement. Don't you feel that we should at least display some quotations from that?'

'I am not sure,' said Francesca.

166

'Perhaps we could use the opening. "Every work of art is the child of its time: often it is the mother of our emotions." '

'Isn't that a truism,' asked Julius Breitenbach, 'and so comes across as somewhat banal?'

Andrei Serotkin turned to Francesca. 'Perhaps Dr McDermott could tell us whether or not it is banal.'

Francesca cleared her throat. 'I think that Kandinsky's writing is very interesting, but more as an adjunct to his art than in itself. To display excerpts like that would only tend to confuse people . . .'

'Because they are too stupid to understand them?' asked Serotkin.

'Not necessarily.'

'Or because the writings themselves are nonsense?'

'Because, as I said, the writings are not really theories as such, but more the expression of the kind of ideas that inspired Kandinsky; not so much the philosophy of art or aesthetics, more like the prose poems he was writing at the time.'

'Ah yes,' said Serotkin. 'The prose poems.' He read from the book.

A circle is always something
Sometimes even a great deal.
Sometimes – seldom – too much.
Just as a rhinoceros is sometimes too much.
Sometimes it sits in compact violet – the circle.
The circle the white circle.
And becomes indisputably smaller. And smaller still.

'Perhaps this,' suggested Serotkin, 'should be exhibited on a board?'

Francesca frowned. Was Andrei sincere in what he said, or was he mocking Kandinsky? 'We have put some of his poems in the catalogue,' she said. 'I should have thought that was enough.'

'And speaking for us Ossies,' said Günter Westarp, 'I think we have had quite enough of slogans pinned up on walls. Let's just have the paintings with some labels and have done with it.'

Serotkin raised his hands in a gesture of capitulation. 'Very well. My suggestions are withdrawn.'

On the following Wednesday, Francesca and Andrei Serotkin played squash after work and then went to a nearby café for a drink.

'You know, Andrei,' said Francesca, 'I sometimes think you have a mischievous side to your character.'

'Mischievous? How?'

'At Monday's meeting. Were you serious about putting those texts on the walls?'

'Were they serious when they wrote them?'

'Probably . . . But that doesn't mean that they should be taken seriously. In my experience, artistic talent and intellectual rigour rarely go together.'

'Yet artists have ideas, and if their works of art are really the mother of our emotions then they have influence too.'

'I should have thought the influence was largely subliminal and imprecise.'

'That had not been the view of those who have used art to promote their interests.'

'Like?'

'The dominant classes throughout history, in particular the clergy and the bourgeoisie.'

'That theory denigrates the genius of the artists,' said Francesca.

'Not their genius, no. Their integrity, perhaps, but even then . . . An artist had to live.'

'And what interest is promoted today through modern paintings?' asked Francesca. 'What are they meant to do to our emotions?'

Serotkin's eyes darted a quick look of anger, even contempt, towards Francesca but when he spoke he chose his words with care. 'The argument would go, I think, that with the collapse of Communism, and the worldwide triumph of pluralism, capitalism and democracy, we see not just the end of history but also the end of art.'

'From where I sit, there's never been more interest in art.'

'Of course. Art is revered as never before. It has replaced religion. In Western Europe, and above all in the United States, the great art galleries are the temples where people come to revere the icons of their age. But what are these icons? The squiggles of Jackson Pollock, the daubs of De Kooning or the monochrome canvases of Rothko. When you look at contemporary American paintings, you marvel not at the skills of the artist, not at the beauty of what he has depicted – because in essence he has depicted nothing – but at the fact that these empty canvases are sold for millions of dollars. It is this that gives them their status as icons of the new religion. They could have been painted by anyone – even by machines. They bear no trace of the human hand, let alone the human mind or the human eye. When you revere a work of abstract art, you are worshipping capitalism in its purest form: added value for added value's sake!'

'Is this what *you* believe?' asked Francesca.

'These were the ideas that were put forward by some of the people in the ministry in Moscow.'

'And what did they say about contemporary realists whose paintings also go for millions of dollars – Francis Bacon, say, or Lucian Freud?'

'My colleagues would argue that if these are the mothers of the emotions of the Western world, then no wonder it is so diseased, degenerate and depraved.'

'Artists cannot look at the world through rose-tinted spectacles.'

'Of course not. But when Grünewald portrays the cruelty of the crucifixion, or Goya the horrors of war, the works are protests against what they portray, and there is the implicit promise of redemption. The paintings of Bacon and Freud hold no such promise. They are the icons of despair.'

'It almost sounds as if you agree with your colleagues.'

Serotkin smiled. 'If I did, would I be here?'

Francesca, who went on to have supper with the Diederichs, told them what Serotkin had said about modern art. 'And at the end of it all, I still can't make out what Andrei himself actually believes.'

'He may not believe anything,' said Stefi.

'But it's his speciality, isn't it?'

'You have to understand the way things worked under the Soviet system. Most of them only wanted to find a well-paid sinecure, and then keep their heads down. Serotkin would never have been allowed to specialize in experimental art if he had actually believed in it. That would have made him a dissident on cultural matters. He most certainly would not have been given a post in the Ministry of Culture. He probably drifted into the job because it gave him the chance of occasional foreign travel.'

'Yes. He said he'd lived in Washington for a time.'

'Did he? I didn't know.'

'Apparently he stood in for the cultural attaché.'

Stefi shrugged. 'There you are. A second-rank cultural bureaucrat.'

'I think he's worried,' said Francesca, 'that there may not be a job for him when he goes back.'

'I dare say.'

'Couldn't you find him something here? He really is very knowledgeable and he speaks both German and English so well.'

'Wouldn't you rather he got a job in America?' asked Sophie with a smirk.

Francesca blushed. 'I was only thinking that if there was some way we could help him . . .'

'I get the impression,' said Stefi, 'that Dr Serotkin is quite capable of looking after himself.'

'And sometimes others,' said Sophie. 'Even damsels in distress.'

Again, Francesca blushed. 'He certainly did me a good turn, so I'd like to do one for him in return.'

Sophie giggled. 'The easiest way would be to marry him. Then he could get an American passport.'

'He hasn't proposed,' said Francesca.

'I'm sure he will,' said Sophie. 'You work together. You play squash together. You live in the same block.'

'But we don't live together,' said Francesca emphatically. 'I've never been into his apartment.'

'But he's been to yours.'

'Only once, after the attack, to call the police.'

Stefi frowned. 'I would advise you,' he said, 'not to get romantically involved with Serotkin.'

'You would say that,' said Sophie, 'but it's only because you hate Russians. But he wasn't reponsible for the DDR, and Francesca isn't an Ossie, so there's no reason why she should feel the same.'

'Russians are deceptive,' said Stefi. 'They look like Europeans, but under the skin they are Asians, as cruel as Mongols and as contemptuous of women as the Turks.'

'I have always found Andrei very considerate,' said Francesca.

Stefan shrugged. 'You are grown up, Francesca. You can make your own judgements. But I advise you to be cautious.'

'And where would we be if we had been cautious?' asked Sophie. 'You take a risk when you fall in love.'

Later that evening, Stefi told Francesca in confidence that Bonn had let it be known that the President of Germany, Richard von Weizsäcker, might be willing to come to Berlin to open the Excursus exhibition on 1 July. It was a tentative offer because the President realized that the exhibition's organizers might not want a political leader, or, if they did, might prefer an East German, or even a prominent Russian dissident. Stefan asked her to think about it, and perhaps discuss it in the strictest confidence with Andrei Serotkin and Günter Westarp.

When Francesca saw Günter in the office the next morning, he took her aside and lobbied against the idea. It would be insulting for Gustav Kiepert, the Minister President of Prussia, who had been asked to open the exhibition six months before. 'It's typical of the Wessies. When they think something is going to be successful, they want to take it over and make out that the idea was theirs all along.'

Francesca could see why Günter should think this, and she pretended to agree, but she was somehow irritated that he could not shake off his Ossie inferiority complex and rise to the occasion. From where she stood, it could do no harm to her reputation if her name was associated with an exhibition opened by the President of a major nation, rather than by the Minister President of a minor province. Who in the United States had heard of Kiepert? She was sure that Andrei would feel the same, or that she could persuade him to feel the same, and she waited impatiently for him to arrive at the office.

He did not come. She grew fretful and, late in the morning, went to the secretaries' office and casually asked if anyone knew what had happened to Dr Serotkin.

'Oh yes,' said Gertie. 'He called in sick.'

'You might have told me,' said Francesca.

'I'm sorry. There was no meeting so I thought . . .'

'Did he say what was wrong?'

'Influenza.'

'Have you his home number?'

Gertie flicked through the cards on a Roladex and jotted down the number.

'And his address.'

'He's in the same block as you, Frau Doktor.'

'I know. But what's the number of his apartment?'

Gertie could not help giving Dora a quick smirk before writing down the address. 'There,' she said, handing the piece of paper to Francesca. 'And I've put down the post code too!'

Francesca went back to her office. She picked up the telephone to call Andrei but then thought better of it. He might be sleeping. He might also decline an offer of a sick call, but he could hardly turn her away if she looked in on him on her way home.

It felt odd to Francesca to go up in the lift beyond the fourth floor and find herself on the landing of the ninth floor where everything was replicated – the colour of the walls, the pattern of the carpet – yet was in some intangible sense different. Serotkin's apartment, like hers, was in the north-west corner of the building. She straightened her clothes, brushed back her hair, pursed her lips to bring up the colour, then rang the bell at his door.

There was silence. Her briefcase weighed heavily on her arm. She waited, doing her best to keep the casual 'I just thought I'd look in' look on her face. She rang again. Again there was silence. Perhaps he was asleep, drugged with a sleeping pill. Or perhaps he was not there, his illness a pretext for another of his mysterious trips out of town. She rang for a third and last time. As she did so, she imagined she heard a shuffle behind the door, and the spyhole seemed to darken.

There was another shuffle, then the sound of muffled voices. Curious but also embarrassed, she was about to leave when suddenly the door opened. She said 'Hi, I was just . . .' but then stopped. The man who faced her was not Serotkin. He had black hair and dark skin like an Arab or perhaps a Turk. His face had no expression. He neither smiled nor frowned nor seemed surprised that she was there.

'I'm sorry,' she said. 'I thought this was Dr Serotkin's apartment.'

The man stepped back, no words but only the movement indicating that she was to come in. She walked into the hallway, of the same dimensions as her own, and then – following a silent gesture from the man – went into the living room. Again it was the same as her own with a kitchen at one end and a fireplace at the other. The same furniture was upholstered in a different colour and was arranged in a different way, but what immediately struck Francesca was the magnificent icon of Christ above the fireplace, its severe eyes watching her, almost rebuking her, as she stepped forward to take a closer look.

She knew little about icons, beyond the influence they were said to have had on artists like Goncharova, Tatlin and Kandinsky. However, this one was patently old, probably sixteeth- or seventeeth-century, and was almost certainly Russian, not Balkan or Greek. To judge from the sombre expression, it was probably of Christ as the universal judge. How on earth, she wondered, did Andrei Serotkin get hold of a work like this that normally you would only find in a church or a museum?

'*The Saviour* from Pskov.'

She turned. Serotkin stood behind her; the other man was nowhere to be seen. Serotkin was wearing pyjamas and a dressing gown. His face was pale. From its expression, she could not tell whether or not he was pleased by her visit.

'What do you think?' He nodded at the icon.

'It's wonderful.'

'I find it a source of solace. It instils a mood of great calm, but it is also inspiring.'

'A mother to emotions?'

'Precisely.'

'Is it yours?'

'It is on loan. A little corner of Russia while I am here in Berlin.'

'You're very lucky.'

'Yes.' As he said this, Serotkin started to cough.

This reminded Francesca of the pretext for her visit. 'I'm sorry to burst in on you like this. I was told that you were ill and I wondered if I could do anything to help.'

Serotkin smiled and pointed towards a chair. 'That is kind.' Francesca sat down. 'As you can see, a friend from Moscow happens to be passing through Berlin. He is able to get me a few things . . .' Serotkin did not sit down but went to a cupboard. 'Would you like a drink?'

'No. Really. I just thought . . . I mean, have you seen a doctor?'

'No. I am not so ill. I shall be better tomorrow.'

'You should have called me.'

'I had my friend.'

'Am I not your friend?'

He took out a bottle of vodka and two small glasses. 'I hope so.' He sat down and placed the glasses on the same low coffee table that Francesca had in her flat. 'You must have a drink, to keep me company.'

'Sure.'

'Russians believe that vodka is the best cure for all diseases.' He laughed, then coughed, then laughed again. He handed her a glass filled with vodka, then took one into his own hand. 'Your health . . . and mine!'

They touched glasses.

'Is your friend staying with you?' asked Francesca.

'No,' He turned towards the door. 'You should be introduced to him, except he has gone out for some aspirin. He is an interesting fellow, a native Chechen, but unfortunately he speaks little English or German.'

'What does he do?'

'He is a scientist, a biologist.'

'And what is he doing here?' Francesca could not help feeling a certain antipathy towards the Chechen.

'A conference of some kind.'

'Well, if he's busy, I can always come up and make you some supper.'

'Thank you, but I can manage.'

She frowned. 'It would be a favour to me, Andrei. I would like a chance to try and repay you for what you did for me.'

'I did not regard that as part of a transaction.'

Francesca blushed. 'No. Of course not. I didn't mean that.'

He appeared to relent. 'Come tomorrow, then. By then my friend will have gone.'

Francesca awoke with a start at three in the morning with the idea in her head that Andrei Serotkin was gay. Had she dreamed it? The more she thought about it, the more it seemed to make sense of his behaviour – his narcissistic fitness, his strange absences, above all his failure to respond to her advances. Clearly, the Chechen was his boyfriend. She had sensed his antagonism when she entered his flat: he must have realized that she was a rival, and for the same reason she had taken an instant dislike to him. At the time, she had put this down to his being an Arab; not, of course, that there was anything wrong with being an Arab or, for that matter, gay; but in love and war . . .

These thoughts prevented Francesca from going back to sleep. How could she have been so stupid as not to have realized it? Clearly, Russian gays were not as open as American gays: because homosexuality had been frowned on in the old Soviet Union, Russian gays had to be particularly discreet. Was it this that had broken up his marriage? It would explain why he had never bothered to get divorced. It would also explain his choice of profession. Gays were common in the art world.

At around six, Francesca fell asleep. At seven her alarm went off. She rose feeling awful, mixed her yoghurt and muesli and boiled the kettle to make her Lapsang Souchong tea. She felt depressed. She assumed at first that this was because she had slept badly, but then remembered the idea that had woken her during the night.

In the cold light of dawn, she was less sure. Andrei had withstood her advances, true, but she was quite certain that he found her attractive. A woman can always tell, either by the way a man looks at her or by the way he *avoids* looking at her, or by the way he only looks at her when he thinks she is not looking at him. Francesca also had to admit that neither Andrei nor the Chechen had any of the characteristics of a gay; nor did the clothes either had been wearing show the kind of fastidiousness that Francesca had observed in her gay friends. The Chechen had been wearing scruffy jeans and a nylon blouson, and Andrei, although his clothes were elegant enough, had let them get rumpled, and he never bothered to brush off the ash that fell from his strong cigarettes.

Of course, not all gays were neat and dapper, and perhaps the Chechen was a passing fancy, a bit of 'rough trade'. The issue remained open in Francesca's mind as she drove to work, and grumbled on in the back of her mind throughout the day.

The proofs of the catalogue were in. Francesca wondered if she could get Serotkin to check the Russian entries while he was still ill. She made a number of calls to Milan and Paris about the dispatch of some of the paintings. At twelve she had lunch with Stefan Diederich and the cultural attaché from the US embassy in Bonn to discuss the possibility of taking Excursus to New York. She told Stefi that Serotkin was ill, and asked if he knew anything about his Chechen friend. For a moment, Stefi seemed confused: a morsel of poached salmon remained poised on the end of his fork between his plate and his mouth. Then he said: 'A Chechen? No. What is a Chechen?' which permitted the US attaché, who had served in Moscow, to deliver an impromptu lecture on the different nationalities found in the Caucasus and around the Caspian Sea.

After lunch, Francesca drove out to the Omni Zartfracht warehouse in Tegel with Günter Westarp, Julius Breitenbach and Frau Dr Koch to supervise the unpacking of the first paintings. Such was the security, they were refused entry. They had to wait for an official to arrive from the ministry to get them in. Even after they had been admitted, and stood admiring El Lissitzky's celebrated *Proun* from the Yale Art Gallery in New Haven, they were watched by the special security guards – young men in beige uniforms, black belts and leather gloves.

Leaving Julius Breitenbach in charge of the unpacking, Francesca returned to the Excursus office with Günter Westarp and Frau Dr Koch. A number of calls and faxes had already arrived from the east coast of the United States, and at six o'clock the traffic started with the west coast and the southern hemisphere. It was seven before Francesca got back to her flat, and eight before she went up to Serotkin's, carrying two plastic bags containing the ingredients of a light supper.

Serotkin opened the door. He was still in his dressing gown but looked much better. At her insistence, he retreated to his bedroom while Francesca went into the kitchen. She put the bags down on the counter that divided it from the living room. From the wall above the fireplace, the eyes of Christ the Saviour looked severely at what she was doing, as if discerning the ulterior motives for her mission of mercy.

Francesca unpacked the bags, taking out a carton of milk, a tin of pheasant broth, a packet of chicken breasts, some string beans. She frowned as she realized that the director of the Los Angeles Museum of Modern Art might try to call her at home, and wondered whether or not she should telephone his office and leave Serotkin's number. But it could wait. Of more interest to her at that moment were the contents of Andrei's kitchen cupboards: a few tins, a few jars, packets of tea, coffee and rice.

When supper was ready, Francesca went to the door of Serotkin's bedroom. It was ajar. She knocked gently. He asked her in. He lay on the bed – the same kind of bed as there was in her flat below – propped up against some pillows. A book, in Russian, lay open on the bedclothes.

'Shall I bring you a tray?' she asked.

He shook his head. 'No. I shall come to the table.'

Francesca went back to the kitchen. Serotkin followed in his dressing gown and slippers. He sat down where she had laid a place on the dining table in the living room. Francesca served up the pheasant broth. 'What would you like to drink?' she asked. 'Some vodka?'

'Why not? Yesterday's dose did me some good.'

'You don't think some milk would do better?'

177

'Milk? Yes. The national drink of the Americans, after Coca Cola.'

She filled a glass from the carton and placed it on the table. 'We went out to the warehouse this afternoon,' she said, 'and unpacked the first painting.'

'Wonderful.'

'Their security's tight as hell. At first, they wouldn't let us in.'

'Better too strict than too lax.'

'I guess so.' She started her soup. 'And the proofs of the catalogue are in.'

'At last.'

'We've got to turn them around in three weeks.'

'Have you brought them? I can do them in bed.'

'It might tire you.'

'I feel much better. I shall return to work tomorrow.'

Francesca wanted to ask Andrei about his friend the Chechen but she held back. It might seem nosy. Instead, she asked: 'What have you been reading?'

'Dostoyevsky.'

'*The Brothers Karamazov?*'

'*Crime and Punishment.*'

'I haven't read that one.'

'The hero, Raskolnikov, is a murderer.'

'You mean the anti-hero.'

'No. He is the hero. That is what makes it an interesting novel. At the beginning of the book, Raskolnikov murders an old woman for her money yet retains the reader's sympathy throughout.'

Francesca frowned. 'How can you sympathize with a murderer?'

'He acts from the highest motives. He feels that he is destined to do great things for humanity, like Napoleon. But he lacks the means – the development money, as we would call it today. The only way he can see to raise it is by killing the dreadful old crone – a pawnbroker. He dares himself to do it, not just to get the money, but to prove to himself that he is a man of destiny by overcoming the inhibitions of conventional morality.'

'But that's not right, is it? That all great men are above morality?'

'I would say so, yes.'

'We would have impeached President Nixon.'

'Perhaps Nixon was not a great man.'

She laughed. 'There's no perhaps about it.'

'But Abraham Lincoln . . .'

'He was great.'

'Only because history went his way. Imagine how you would judge him now if the South had won the Civil War.'

'Isn't that kind of cynical?'

'To the victor goes the spoils, including the luxury of deciding what is right and what is wrong.'

'You mean, there's no objective morality?'

Serotkin hesitated. 'Dostoyevsky believed that there could only be an objective morality if there was a God to define it.'

'And you?'

'I don't believe in God.'

'I wish you'd finish your soup,' said Francesca.

Serotkin smiled. 'Women are fortunate. Instinct serves as conscience, and all reasoning is made superfluous by intuition.'

Francesca frowned. 'Is this Dostoyevsky speaking or Andrei Serotkin?'

'Perhaps just Mother Russia.'

'Dostoyevsky at least had the excuse that he lived in the nineteenth century . . .'

'Whereas I should know better because I live in a more enlightened age?'

'Yes.'

'The age of Auschwitz and Hiroshima . . .'

'You can hardly blame them on feminism.'

'They are part of the same phenomenon.'

'What is that?'

'The rejection of Christian order that followed the rejection of Christian faith.'

'Serotkin or Dostoyevsky?'

'Dostoyevsky.'

'Does Serotkin agree with Dostoyevsky?'

'Up to a point.'

'What point, if he doesn't believe in God?' She was speaking from the kitchen where she was taking the chicken breasts out of the oven.

' "Man does not live by bread alone".'

'So let him eat chicken.' Francesca put a loaded plate in front of Serotkin.

He did as she told him, but Francesca sensed that thoughts continued to ricochet around his brain. He seemed agitated, even feverish, and showed little interest as she prattled on about what had happened in the office during the day. When she told him that they had unpacked El Lissitzky's *Proun* from Yale, he frowned and said: 'In the end, I think, we will have most of the modern Russian paintings in American collections.'

'Yes.'

He thought for a moment, then said: 'There is an interesting character in *Crime and Punishment* called Svidrigailov. At the end, he has to choose between shooting himself and going to America. To Dostoyevsky, I think, they amounted to the same thing.'

'And what does he do?'

'He shoots himself.'

Serotkin ate only half of his chicken, and turned down Francesca's offer of fruit or yoghurt. He said he would like some coffee, and she said that she would bring it through to him in his bedroom once she had cleared away the dishes. He went back to his room. Francesca cleared the table, put the dishes in the dishwasher and put on the kettle to make coffee. While waiting for it to boil, she went to the bathroom. It was the same as her own. There were spots of dried soapsuds on the mirrored door of the cabinet above the basin. She wondered whether anyone came in to clean for Serotkin or whether he cleaned his flat for himself. She wiped off the dried soapsuds with a damp tissue, then opened the cabinet in which in her bathroom she kept shampoo, foundation cream, cleansing lotion and her contraceptive pills. Serotkin had only a bottle of Odol mouthwash, shaving cream in a pressurized can, a phial of aspirins and a square bottle labelled *Polyman Color. Tönungs Shampoo. Natur Schwartz*. It was black hairdye. So the philosophizing Andrei was not so high-minded after all!

It was a sign of how much Francesca was in love with Andrei

Serotkin that she found this touch of vanity endearing. Little by little, the veil was being lifted from the inscrutable Russian to reveal him to be a man as vulnerable and fallible as any other who caught flu and worried about looking old.

She went back to the kitchen, made the coffee from the packet of decaf she had brought up from her flat, and took the pot with two cups on a tray into his room. He lay on his bed, propped up against pillows, reading. She put the tray on the dressing table, filled the cups, handed one to Serotkin, drew up a chair and sat down next to the bed.

Now that she knew, his hair did seem a little too good to be true. The beard, too. Of course, he was silly. He would be just as attactive, perhaps even more attractive, if a few of his hairs were grey. It would add *gravitas*. She could just imagine an amphi-theatre of enthralled students at BU.

'What are you reading?' she asked.

'Poems by Mayakovsky.'

'Would you read one out loud?'

Serotkin started to recite but from memory, the book un-opened in his hand, his voice suddenly both dramatic and melodic as the words in his native Russian tumbled out in his deep base voice.

> 'Does the eye of the eagle fade?
> Shall we stare back to the old?
> Proletarian fingers
> Grip tighter
> the throat of the world:
> Chests out! Shoulders straight!
> Stick to the sky red flags adrift!
> Who's marching there with the right?
> Left!
> Left!
> Left!'

'I guess you prefer that to Kandinsky's poem?' said Francesca.

'It was written around the same time,' said Serotkin.

'But Mayakovsky killed himself,' said Francesca.

'Yes. Like Svidrigailov. Whereas Kandinsky went to America, like Solzhenitsyn.'

'I think I would have been happy, if I had been Mayakovsky, to know that sixty years later people were still reciting my poems.'

'Even though his poems no longer give birth to emotions?'

'There are emotions other than Bolshevik zeal.'

'Of course.

> How fearful, in and out of season
> to pine away from passion's thirst,
> to burn – and then by force of reason
> to stem the bloodstream's wild outburst . . .'

As he recited Pushkin's verse the daylight faded but neither Francesca nor Serotkin moved to switch on the electric light. Serotkin gazed at Francesca as if Eugene Onegin's words to Tatiana were addressed to her, while Francesca kept her eyes fixed on the open neck of Serotkin's pyjamas. The triangular patch of skin, pale-coloured in the gloom, seemed to make him vulnerable, like the patch of skin on Achilles' heel. Just as he had glimpsed her nakedness in the Englischergarten, so she now felt that she was glimpsing his, and she felt an urge to lean forward and lay her hand on his chest with a protective caress.

He began to recite, again from memory, a poem by Yevgeny Yevtushenko.

> 'My beloved will arrive at last,
> and fold me in her arms.
> She will notice the least change in me,
> and understand all my apprehensions.
> Out of the black rain, the infernal gloom,
> having forgotten to shut the taxi door,
> she'll dash up the rickety steps,
> all flushed with joy and longing.
> Drenched, she'll burst in without knocking,
> and clasp my head in her hand;
> and from a chair her blue fur coat
> will slip blissfully to the floor . . .'

Both were now silent. Francesca could not tell in the dusk whether Andrei's eyes were open or closed. She got silently to her feet, stepped closer to the bed and looked down. His eyes were open. He took her hand. She sat down on the bed and with the hand that was free obeyed the urge to touch his skin beneath his neck. With her finger and thumb she could feel the strong lines of his collarbone, and beneath it feel the pulse of his blood. She held her hand there for a moment, then she felt his hand come round her shoulder and draw her down.

'Andrei . . .' she whispered. She meant to say 'you are ill, you are weak' but it was she who felt weak while his arm felt strong. They kissed. Her hand moved further over the warm skin beneath his pyjamas. Is it true, she wondered, that with women intuition and conscience are one and the same thing? Then he held her more tightly and she wondered no more.

PART FOUR

1993

May–June

THIRTEEN

The principal objective of Nikolai Gerasimov when he arrived in Berlin was to spin out his assignment for the maximum length of time. His expenses were paid under an arrangement with Interpol by the city government of West Berlin: the *per diem* allowance in Deutschmarks, if he stayed long enough, should buy him a fax machine, a stero system or even a second-hand Mercedes.

Pursuit of this strategy was made easier by Gerasimov's instructions from General Savchenko to play the plodding officer from the militia, and on no account let it be known that he was an officer in the security service of the Russian Federation or that the Maslyukovs had been killed by a team from the KGB. Gerasimov's mission was to find Orlov, not to help the Germans find Orlov; and when he did, either bring him back to Moscow or if necessary stub him out like Savchenko's cigarette.

Gerasimov was met at Schönfeld airport by two men who introduced themselves as Inspector Kessler of the Berlin police and Herr Grohmann from the international police liaison department of the Federal German Ministry of the Interior. They drove him to a two-star hotel in a small street off the Hohenzollerndamm, and waited in the lobby while he took his suitcase to his room. They then drove him to the headquarters of the criminal police on Gothaerstrasse in Schöneberg. There, in his office, Inspector Kessler described the murder, showed Gerasimov photographs of the scene of the crime, and produced a thick file of papers – transcripts of interviews, analysis of forensic evidence, lists of exits and entries from Schönfeld and Tegel. Good, Gerasimov thought to himself. It will take me a while to wade through this lot.

Gerasimov's own initial contribution was small. Following the plan worked out by Savchenko, and outlined to him by the general himself who had accompanied him to the airport, Gerasimov told Kessler that it was the view of the Russian militia that the Maslyukovs had almost certainly been killed by a rival group of smugglers and racketeers. 'We have been on their trail for some time. Their chief is a man we call Ivan the Terrible. Ruthless . . .'

'And cruel,' said Kessler, pointing to the photograph of Vera Maslyukov.

'What are those marks on her body?' asked Gerasimov.

'Cigarette burns. She was tortured.'

'Typical, I am afraid, of this Ivan the Terrible.'

'Do you have any idea who he is?' asked Grohmann. As he spoke, a younger man came into the office who was introduced as Sergeant Dorn.

'We are fairly sure he is an Armenian called Georgi Nazayan. But you must realize, gentlemen, that the Soviet Union . . . that is, the former Societ Union . . . is no longer as well policed as it once was. We used to know everything that happened almost before it happened, but now, among other Western imports, we have a crime wave . . .'

'Clearly,' said the younger detective, 'there was little crime in a country when half the people were in the police.'

'I have one or two leads I should like to discuss with you,' said Gerasimov, ignoring Dorn's jibe. 'And doubtless, you have things you would like to discuss with me.'

'We have to confess,' said Kessler, 'that we have made almost no progress. We are fairly sure that the Maslyukovs' icons were stolen, and we have reason to believe that one of the assailants smoked Bulgarian cigarettes.'

'That would be enough for Hercule Poirot,' said Gerasimov who had recently seen the video of *Death on the Nile*, 'but I realize that real life is rarely as straightforward as it appears in the books of Agatha Christie.'

'Perhaps you would like to look through the file,' said Grohmann, 'to see if anything there links up with your own investigation.'

'Of course.'

'Could you do that overnight?'

'Ah . . . I am afraid I am slow at reading German. Perhaps you could give me twenty-four hours?'

'As you like.'

'It's some time since the murders,' said Dorn. 'A day or two more won't make much difference.'

'And perhaps we could see your file?' asked Kessler.

'Can you read Russian?' asked Gerasimov.

'We have people who do,' said Grohmann.

'Then I shall send for it from Moscow.'

'You brought no copy with you?'

'I am afraid our copier was *kaputt*. But it can be easily arranged.'

'Good.'

'It may take a day or two.'

'Of course.'

'Perhaps even a week.'

'We understand.'

'But in the meantime, there is this . . .' Gerasimov patted the file that he had been given. 'And, if you will allow me a certain freedom of action, there are one or two leads I might follow up on my own.'

Kessler looked at Grohmann. 'Of course,' said Grohmann. 'The old Cold War suspicions are a thing of the past. You have your visa. Go where you like. And if you need help of any kind, just let us know.'

Gerasimov found German women the most attractive in the world. There was something about their long limbs and serious

189

faces that drove him to a high pitch of erotic excitement. Their coldness, their matter-of-fact manner, their sensible approach to life, their disdain for the silliness of the English or the flirtatiousness of the French, made it all the more exhilarating when things got under way, their bodies rising and falling like pistons on some precision-made machine from Krupp. What a contrast to the lazy, dumpy, squat, inept sluts in Russia.

Back in his room at the hotel, Gerasimov dumped Kessler's file on top of the television, took a shower, changed his clothes, went down to the hotel restaurant and, while he was eating, planned his strategy for the night.

The choice was between doing a tour of the bars and nightclubs in the hope of finding a *Mädchen* who would appreciate his rugged good looks, or squandering a chunk of the Deutschmarks had been handed over to him by Kessler on a tall, no nonsense German whore. It was some time since he had been West: he was not sure what he would have to pay. And since it was his aim to save his allowance, Gerasimov decided to try the bars and nightclubs first.

He walked up the Kurfürstendamm, then down to the area around the Zoo station. It was too seedy. Everyone seemed either an Arab or a Turk. Where would the German girls go who were out for a good time? He walked west on the Kantstrasse, then turned left into Savignyplatz. This was more like it: innumerable little restaurants and *Stuben* with young people spilling out onto the street.

He came to a bar, Der Riesige Liliputaner – the Giant Midget. Berlin humour. Gerasimov went down the steps into a cellar. It was dark – he had to stoop to avoid hitting his head on the low ceiling – and almost empty. A couple sat in the corner, two men at the bar. Gerasimov turned and went out. Further down the same street, he went into a crowded café, sat down at a table and ordered a beer. He looked at the menu: alfalfa salads, nut cutlets, cottage cheese on sourdough rye. It was for vegans and vegetarians: no wonder the waitress had looked surprised when he ordered a beer.

Gerasimov studied the people. They all seemed young, and although they gabbled away in German, none of the girls had the blonde, blue-eyed, long-legged look he was after. Perhaps they no longer existed – the Prussian look smothered by the dark-haired, dark eyed dwarves from Saxony and Bavaria.

Gerasimov finished his beer, paid the waitress and went back into the street. Perhaps he should try the bars at the grander hotels – the Hilton or the Kempinski. But there any woman on her own would probably be a whore and would cost him a fortune. He still hoped he could get what he wanted for the price of a few drinks but, as he stalked the pavements, crossing the Kurfürstendamm and the Lietzenburgerstrasse, and turning right into Pariserstrasse, Gerasimov's confidence began to wane. The brightly lit shop windows displayed elegant clothes at prices which terrified him. He could not help converting the price tags into roubles which showed that whole year's salary would hardly buy him a pair of shoes.

The cars, too, seemed larger and shinier than he remembered: Mercedes, Audis and BMWs were crammed up against the kerbs of every street, or clustered at every interchange, their drivers slim, suave women or well-groomed men. What have I got to offer them? he asked himself glumly. All the women are much richer than I am. They would have to be perverse to want to sleep with a penniless muzhik.

It was one of Gerasimov's strengths that these moments of self-doubt did not last long. He not only had a confident personality, but he had been trained to work upon the assumption that every problem had a solution. His mind began to turn towards possible ways of making money beyond reselling an imported stereo system or video recorder. Clearly, Orlov was onto some scam. He had probably pocketed the Maslyukovs' money and was setting up some racket of his own. He might like a partner: certainly, until he found him, Gerasimov should keep an open mind.

He was beginning to feel tired. He had been on the move since he left Moscow that morning where the time was two hours ahead. He took out his Falkplan of Berlin, and fumbled with its folded pages by the light of a shop window to find where he was and plan a route back to his hotel. It was not far. He put the map back into his pocket and walked north along Uhlandstrasse. Within a block of his hotel, his eye caught the sign of a bar called

Whisky-a-go-go. A Scotch would help him sleep. He went into the bar – plush, carpeted and filled for once with adults, not the young.

Gerasimov sat down on a stool at the bar and ordered a J & B. Next to him sat a couple, a man of around fifty with close-cropped hair, the woman with long henna-dyed hair, perhaps in her mid-thirties. It was hard to tell in the subdued light. They were talking in German but the man spoke it badly. Gerasimov thought he must be a Swede or a Finn. They were making some arrangement to meet the next day and, having made it, the man slapped DM100 onto the bar, shook hands with the woman and left.

She turned back to face the bar and called the barman to give her another drink. He seemed to know her: he gave her a long look that Gerasimov could not quite interpret.

Commiseration? For a moment, Gerasimov simply sat studying the bottles ranged against the wall. He fancied the woman but could not decide how to proceed. She seemed respectable. She was elegantly dressed. She was probably a businesswoman, in Berlin for a meeting with customers from abroad. Gerasimov had to be cautious. Better not admit to being a Russian. He would say he was Canadian. His English was good enough and, in his experience, no one had a preconception of what a Canadian was like.

Gerasimov turned to the woman and said, in deliberately faulty German: 'Are you from Berlin?'

She gave him a long look of appraisal before she answered: 'Yes.'

'I just flew in today.'

She took out a cigarette and allowed Gerasimov to light it. She took a drag and, as she blew out the smoke, asked: 'From where?'

'Regina, Saskatchewan.'

She frowned. 'Is that in America?'

'Canada.'

'You are Canadian?'

'That's right.'

'I am afraid I speak little English.' She said this in English.

'My German isn't too bad.'

She gave another appraising look from under her eyelashes. 'Are you a businessman?'

'Yes. Pharmaceuticals.'

She nodded and took another drag on her cigarette.'

'And you?'

'Fashion.'

'You're a model?'

She shook her head. 'No. I choose designs for foreign buyers.'

'Was that one of your clients?'

She blew out the smoke. 'More or less.'

'Can I buy you a drink?'

She looked down at her glass which was still half filled with wine. 'In a moment, perhaps.'

This was not going to be easy. 'I haven't been in Berlin for a number of years . . . It seems to have changed.'

'Yes. The Wall came down, you know.' She almost smiled.

'I read about that.'

'But even before, it was full of foreigners – Turks, blacks, and now the gypsies from Romania.' She wrinkled her nose.

'That can't be easy to take for someone born in Berlin.'

'To be cosmopolitan is one thing. To become a refugee camp is another.'

'Sure.'

She finished her glass of wine. Gerasimov bought her another and started to tell her about the company he worked for in Regina. At an appropriate lull in the conversation he introduced himself. 'You don't even know my name. Nick Turner.'

She nodded and said: 'Nick. My name is Inge.'

'Inge. Well, I am glad to meet you.' He shook her by the hand. Gerasimov was warming to his role as a Canadian businessman: the challenge dissipated his fatigue.

They talked further – about his business, about her business, about their private lives. She was unmarried. He was divorced with two difficult adolescent children. Eventually, Inge looked at her watch and said: 'I suppose I should be going.'

'OK. Me too.' He called the barman and asked for the bill. Again, the barman glanced at Inge – a fleeting, familiar look, hard to interpret. Without presenting an account, he asked Gerasimov for DM100. Gerasimov swallowed but paid up: if he wanted the woman, he could not seem to be mean.

'Can I drop you off at your hotel?' Inge asked.

'That would be kind.'

She led him to a shiny blue Audi 80. Gerasimov got in beside her. 'The Trebizond. Do you know where that is?'

'It's only a block away.'

'Is it? I'm sorry. I'm kind of lost. I guess I could have walked.'

Inge said nothing but turned to see if she could drive out into the stream of traffic. 'The Trebizond is not very elegant,' she said.

'It's pretty basic,' said Gerasimov. 'It was booked by the German company, and I guess they were feeling stingy.'

'The Germans are stingy,' said Inge, swinging her car out into the street.

When they reached the hotel, she drew up by the kerb fifty yards or so from the door.

'Would you like a nightcap?' asked Gerasimov.

She gave him another cool look. 'Why not?'

Gerasimov could hardly believe his good fortune. They went into the lobby. She waited by the lift while he fetched his key from the desk.

They were alone in the lift as it went up to the tenth floor. In the harsh fluorescent light Gerasimov noticed a faint line of speckled grey at the roots of her hair. He adjusted upwards his estimate of her age.

In his room he went to the minibar. 'What would you like?'

'Later, perhaps.'

He turned back. Inge came towards him, raised her arm and loosened his tie. 'Five hundred marks. OK?'

Gerasimov swallowed and opened his mouth but did not speak.

Inge pulled his tie away from his neck and started to undo the top buttons of his shirt. 'It's usually more,' she said.

He nodded.

'If you would give it to me now, it would make me more relaxed.

Gerasimov reached into the inside pocket of his jacket, took out the grubby envelope containing a month's expenses and counted out the banknotes.

She took the money and handed Gerasimov a condom in exchange. 'You won't be disappointed.'

She was as good as her word. She did not have blue eyes, blonde hair or long legs, and her breasts and skin had the slackness of a woman well over forty, but her underclothes were clean and lacy, and she smelt superb. Deftly, she slipped off her own clothes and helped Gerasimov out of his, and when they started to make love, her movements and murmurings persuaded him that she was transported against her will. Her eyes became bleary, her murmuring became groans, her groans gasps, until finally involuntary cries came for her mouth – yes, yes, yes, *ja, ja, ja*; or was it – he could not believe it – not *ja, ja, ja* but *da, da, da!* With a grunt, he collapsed. She eased out from under his body and went to the bathroom.

'You're Russian?' he shouted in Russian.

'*Konechno*. Sure.'

Gerasimov groaned and hid his face in the pillow.

Chastened by the fiasco of the night before, Gerasimov spent the next morning reading through Inspector Kessler's file. As he proceeded through its many pages, he felt a certain patriotic pride at the way Orlov and his team had frustrated the pedantic investigators of the German police. There were no footprints or fingerprints, only the bullet that had killed Grigori Maslyukov and the fragments of tobacco from the cigarettes that might have been used to burn his wife.

The bullet had come from a Beretta and they must know that Berettas were sometimes used by the KGB. But they were a common enough weapon: if it was just that that had led them to invite Gerasimov to Berlin, then Inspector Kessler and his friends were clutching at straws.

The cigarette burns surprised him. Orlov was trained for any eventuality but torture seemed uncharacteristic. The woman must have known something that he was determined to find out. Orlov smoked – it was in his file – probably BTs when he could get them: but then so did several million others from the former Soviet Union, not to mention Bulgaria itself and other neighbouring countries. Gerasimov did not know about Partovsky, or Kastiev, the Chechen. Partovsky seemed even less likely than Orlov to have stubbed cigarettes out on the wretched woman. It was proably the Chechen: those savages from the Caucasus thought nothing about that kind of thing.

The papers from the file were spread out over Gerasimov's unmade bed. The whore's scent lingered on the sheets to remind him of his humiliation. He wished now that he had made her give the money back but she might have made a fuss, brought in some pimp, caused a rumpus in the hotel that would get back to Kessler who might complain to Interpol so that eventually it would come to Savchenko's ears which would mean demotion, possibly dismissal – certainly the end to assignments abroad.

The bitch. With some relish, Gerasimov began to visualize stubbing cigarettes out on her flaccid skin: more than the pretence that she was German, he resented the cool way she had led him to believe that she was going to give him a free ride. All the same, even if she was not worth DM500, she had learned some tricks of the trade in Berlin: she was in a different class to the bumpkins in the Cosmos Hotel in Moscow.

Gerasimov went back to the files. The junior detective, Dorn, had checked the coming and going from Schönfeld airport, but they must know that no trained agent from the First Chief Directorate would fly in from Moscow on a Russian passport, murder the Maslyukovs and then fly out again the next day. Orlov had almost certainly travelled as the German Hans Lauch and would now be in Switzerland as Franz Grauber, France as Marcel Jeanneret or even the United States as Edward Burton. The best way to trace him would be through hotel registers, apartment rentals or car-hire companies. There might also be bank accounts in any of these names. The bulk of the Maslyukovs' money, if he had retrieved it, would be in a secret numbered account, but he would have to have established some facility for his everyday requirements.

The names would have to wait. If he gave them now to the Berlin police, they might find Orlov within a week or at any rate before he did, and Savchenko's orders were most emphatic. On no account was Orlov to be allowed to talk to the German police. Gerasimov must find him and if necessary kill him, and the best way to do that was through the Volkswagen dealer in Leipzig. But that, too, could wait.

That night, Gerasimov went to the movies – *Terminator II*. He turned in early and was ready in the lobby of his hotel at eight the next morning when Inspector Kessler came to fetch him and take him out to Zehlendorf to visit the scene of the crime.

'Were you able to read the file?' asked Kessler.

'Of course.'

'What do you think?'

'Your investigations have been most thorough.'

'Could it be the work of this man you call Ivan the Terrible?'

Gerasimov shrugged. 'As you know, there are no real clues to point in any particular direction.'

'There is the tobacco . . .'

'Yes. Bulgarian tobacco. A favourite smoke in the Soviet Union. But also in Bulgaria, Romania, Hungary . . .'

'Of course.'

'It seems extraordinary,' said Gerasimov, 'that if large numbers of icons were stolen, they have not reappeared in the art market.'

'Agreed,' said Kessler. 'That's why we think it's not a simple burglary.'

'I see that the Maslyukovs had foreign bank accounts?'

'We assume so. Numbered bank accounts in Liechtenstein and Switzerland.'

'Is there no way to discover whether anyone has used them since the murder?'

'We don't even know the numbers or where they are.'

'And could anyone, knowing the numbers, make withdrawals?'

'With a certain type of numbered account, yes.'

'To obtain the numbers was perhaps the reason for torturing the Maslyukov woman?'

'Yes.' Kessler paused, then said bluntly: 'The job was so expert that some have suggested an intelligence angle.'

'Ah.'

'Perhaps Maslyukov was a conduit for funding secret operations?'

'For the CIA?' asked Gerasimov innocently.

'Or perhaps some Soviet organization?'

'The KGB?'

'Is it possible?'

'I gather some of their people have been involved in icon smuggling . . .'

'And they use Berettas.'

'Yes. But then so does James Bond.'

Kessler grunted. 'You heard nothing in Moscow?'

'The KGB never did confide in the militia and now, as you may know, there is no KGB. However, the influence of the Lubyanka is still there, and I would not have been sent here if the KGB had anything to hide.'

'I see.'

'It seems more likely, in my opinion, if this really has the hallmark of an intelligence operation, that it is the work of some former officers in the Stasi who have been obliged by their reduced circumstances to turn to crime.'

Kessler scratched his cheek. 'We thought of that. The hypothesis was rejected.'

'Why?'

'The ex-Stasi agents are under surveillance.'

'All one hundred thousand of them?'

'The important ones. Anyway, there's no evidence to suggest it.'

They arrived at the house in the Dubrowstrasse where the Maslyukovs had been killed. The house was empty. Kessler opened the front door. 'It was only rented by the Maslyukovs,' he said. 'The owners have tried to let it but until now . . .' He sniffed the musty air. 'It still smells of murder.'

They did a tour of the house. Kessler pointed out to Gerasimov where Grigori Maslyukov's body had been found, and where Vera Maslyukov had been tied to the chair. The chair had been removed to the police laboratories; so had the tape deck and cassettes. The two men went to the kitchen, then to the bedroom. 'Their correspondence?' asked Gerasimov.

'At the lab . . . what there was of it.'

'Some of it in Russian?'

'Yes.'

'It might be useful if I looked through the letters.' Another timewaster.

'Very well.'

They came down the stairs. 'It's a pity,' said Gerasimov, 'that we weren't informed earlier.'

'Applications through Interpol take time.'

'Of course. And I don't wish to suggest that our technical expertise is equal to yours. However, trails are more difficult to follow when they are cold.'

'I agree.'

'Our friend, Ivan the Terrible – '

Kessler frowned. 'You think it might have been him?'

'It's certainly a theory worth pursuing.'

'We shall see what we can do when we get your file on Ivan the Terrible from Moscow.'

'Of course. And in the meantime I might pursue some enquiries among the Russians living here in Berlin. You never know. They may be willing to tell things to a compatriot that they would not say to the German police.'

Kessler left Gerasimov at the police laboratories to look through the Maslyukovs' correspondence, then drove back to his office in Schöneberg where he summoned Dorn.

'The Russian tart. What did she say?'

'That he claimed to be a Canadian called Turner and thought she was German. She said she charged him two hundred DM but she had five hundred in a roll in her purse. I tell you, chief, if that man's KGB, then no wonder the Soviet Union went down the drain.'

'Are you sure she isn't a contact?'

'For the clap?'

'For the KGB.'

Dorn shrugged. 'Ask your friend in the BfV. From where I stand, she's a shop assistant who moonlights as a part-time whore.'

'Odd that he should choose a Russian.'

'Berlin's crawling with them.'

'All the same . . .'

'He spent yesterday in his bedroom. The maid said that there were papers spread out all over the bed. In the evening he went to see Schwarzenegger . . .'

'Did he meet anyone in the cinema?'

'No. Unless he slipped a note to the person sitting next to him. Our man was three rows behind.'

'So he may be just what he seems?'

'What do the BfV say?'

'Leave him on a long leash. Go on with surveillance but keep it discreet.'

Dorn left. Kessler called Grohmann. 'So far, he's behaving as if he's just what he says he is, a plodder from the Moscow militia.'

Grohmann did not reply.

'Are you there?'

'Yes. I'm thinking.'

'We keep an eye on him, right?'

'Yes. But he mustn't know. If the Maslyukov murders were one of their operations, he'll do what he can to throw dust in our eyes. Or simply obstruct by inaction . . .'

'That seems to be his tactic so far.'

'What about this Ivan the Terrible?'

'Nothing on our files. But then there are new groups from Russia arriving all the time.'

'We've nothing to lose by leaving him to his own devices if that's what he wants. Check on everyone he goes to visit. If there is an Ivan the Terrible, he may find him. If it was a KGB operation, he may expose it by trying to cover up the trail.'

'I don't have the men for twenty-four surveillance,' said Kessler.

Grohmann hestiated, then said: 'I'll see if I can arrange some help.'

FOURTEEN

It quickly became known in the Excursus office that Dr McDermott and Dr Serotkin were now more than colleagues and friends. Francesca tried to act normally in Andrei's presence, but inevitably gave herself away – not to the men like Günter Westarp or Julius Breitenbach, or even to that dedicated academic, Frau Dr Koch; but Dora and Gertie, the two secretaries, were quick to note her changed manner and passed on their discovery to the incredulous Julius with whom they were on gossiping terms.

The first person to get confirmation of the suspicions that she had harboured for some time was Sophie Diederich. She realized at once that there could be no other explanation for Francesca's metamorphosis in so short a space of time from a brisk, ambitious academic to a gentle, dreamy, cosy girlfriend who, instead of rabbiting on about Kandinsky and Malevich, brought every conversation back to Serotkin.

'So you are more than just good friends?' Sophie said to Francesca one day when they met for lunch.

'Can you be more than good friends?' asked Francesca with a sly smile.

'Yes, of course you can. Stefi and I were friends, and then we were more than friends. We were lovers.'

'Isn't it better to be friends first, and then lovers?'

'I suppose so. Unless he is also a friend of your husband's.'

'I haven't got a husband.'

'So?' Sophie waited.

Francesca nodded. 'Yes.'

'You're lovers?'

'Mmm.'

'You're crazy.'

'I know.'

'He only wants an American passport,' Sophie blurted out.

Francesca looked offended. 'That hasn't come up.'

'So what does he want?'

'Me, I guess.'

'Don't believe it.'

'Thanks!'

'I don't mean that you aren't attractive but . . .'

'What?'

'Stefi mistrusts him.'

'He's certainly mysterious.'

'If . . . if he fancied you,' said Sophie, 'then why did he wait for so long?'

'I was the one who waited.'

'What made you change your mind?'

Francesca sighed as she considered. 'I don't know. *Le coeur a ses raisons que la raison ne connaît point*, I guess.'

'I don't understand French.'

'That's Pascal. The heart has its reasons that reason cannot comprehend.'

'I admit that he's handsome,' said Sophie reluctantly.

'Dashing,' said Francesca.

'And he did save you from those Turks . . .'

'That must be it,' said Francesca, laughing. 'I just melted before his machismo except . . .'

'What?'

'He was the one who took the melting. I had to hit him when he was down.'

202

'*You* seduced *him*?'

'It's always the woman who decides.'

'So what happened?'

'He was sick, in bed. I . . . ministered to his needs.'

'When he was *sick*?'

Francesca smiled as she remembered. 'He was getting better.'

'Even so.'

'Kill or cure.'

Sophie shook her head. 'But what do you know about him?'

'Next to nothing. But I like that. In America, men give you their life story on the first date and, by and large, never talk about anything except themselves. Unless they feel they have to give you a turn to get you into bed.'

'So what does the professor talk about when you are alone together? Kandinsky?'

'Yes. Kandinsky. And his own ideas about life and history, Russia, women. He recites poetry. He has a phenomenal memory. He can quote whole chunks of writers like Dostoyevsky. Again, in America, art historians only talk about art.'

'So you love him for his mind?'

'His body's not so bad.'

'Francesca!'

Francesca's expression became serious. '*You* should understand, Sophie, because there's something mysterious about Stefi, too.'

'Of course. And the trouble with Paul was that he was so honest and transparent that you always knew what he would think and what he would say.'

'So you got bored.'

Sophie shrugged. 'Yes. I did.'

'Love only lasts if there is mystery.'

'And will yours last?'

'I hope so.'

'Will you marry him?'

'He hasn't proposed.'

'He will.'

Francesca frowned. 'I'm not so sure. He seems decisive, but

203

inside there are areas where he's really confused. I mean, here he is, an expert on modern art, yet I get the impression from some of the things he says that he actually hates it. He loves me, but hates America: he seems to agree with Dostoyevsky that there's not much to choose between emigrating to America and committing suicide. He loves Russia. He hates the suffering of the Russian people. But he's ambiguous about the reforms . . .'

'He doesn't like Gorby?'

'No.'

'He'd like to rebuild the Berlin Wall?'

Francesca laughed. 'No. I'm sure he wouldn't go as far as that. He just loves Russia and its traditions and its values, and I guess he's afraid they'll now get swamped as it opens up to the Western world.'

'Shall I tell you something interesting?' said Sophie. 'That is just what Paul used to say about the DDR.'

'Would he say that now?'

'I don't know. We only talk about arrangements for the children. But a friend said she had heard him preach at Bechtling, and he was warning his congregation of Ossies against the fleshpots of the West!'

Andrei Serotkin now slept in Francesca's flat. He kept a pair of pyjamas in the cupboard in her bedroom and a toothbrush in her bathroom. The Odol and the Polyman Color remained in his flat on the ninth floor.

After sleeping alone for so long, Francesca found it difficult to get used to sharing her bed with a man. Andrei did not snore, and he had the decency not to smoke in bed, but he slept fitfully: often, she would wake up at three or four in the morning and see in the dim light that came through the blinds from the street lamps that he was lying on his back, his arms clasped behind his neck, staring at the ceiling.

Sometimes, if she snuggled up to him, a strong arm would come down around her shoulders; but there were occasions when he would rebuff her, turning away to face the wall. She could not fathom his moods. At times he was boyish and cheerful, at others sombre, almost grim. Frequently he would tease her, with evident affection, but on occasions he would become moody and silent, behaving as if he loathed her. He had dreams from which he awoke grinding his teeth, and even in the midst of making love a look of hatred would come onto his face and a physical ferocity replace the gentleness that had inspired his earlier caresses.

After one or two solicitous enquiries about his insomnia and bad dreams had been rebuffed, Francesca came to appreciate once again the truth of what Stefi had said about Russians: they had learned to keep themselves to themselves. Unlike most of her American friends, Andrei disliked analysing his feelings or discussing the past. He made a number of depreciating remarks about the debilitating effect of psychoanalysis: introspection, he seemed to think, was unworthy of a man.

Whenever Francesca touched on his marriage, she found Andrei reluctant to discuss it. He would not even tell her the name of his wife. 'You are now the only woman in my life.'

'But before you met me . . '

'Love is eternal, and eternity has no before or after.'

He was equally reticent about his family. She sensed that he was fond of his parents, of his sister and of his son, but she gained no impression of the kind of life he led in Moscow, a subject that particularly interested her since it was a life she might come to share. She made some oblique references to this – the future – but found that here too he was unwilling to be drawn, even into conjecture. She saw only too clearly that their time in Berlin would soom come to an end and, while she had no wish to test a bond so freshly formed, she could not bear to imagine that they would simply go their separate ways.

Although they were able to spend their nights together, the days were hectic and were often spent apart. Then there came a lull before the storm – a moment when the catalogue had gone to press and the works had all arrived in the warehouse in Tegel, but there was a week still to go before the hanging could start. That Sunday was one of the first in the past six months when Francesca had not gone into the office or worked at home. Both she and Andrei therefore had the luxury of lying in bed until ten; making an American breakfast with English muffins and bacon and egg; reading *Die Zeit* and *Welt am Sonntag* and *Time* magazine while listening to a compact disc of *Tosca*.

It was one of the first hot days of June, when the sunshine seemed to insist upon an excursion of some kind – to Charlottenburg, Potsdam, Köpenick or the Grosser Mügelsee. However, they lingered so long over breakfast that it was twelve before they were dressed. They therefore decided simply to take the S Bahn to the Friedrichstrasse station, and from there walk to the Museum Island. In the Pergamon Museum they studied the superb displays of classical antiquities – the gate of Ishtar from Babylon, the Sumerian temples, the great Pergamon altar itself, all brought to Berlin by German archaeologists in the nineteenth century. Later, as they walked back down Unter den Linden towards the Brandenburg Gate, Serotkin spoke to Francesca about the rise and fall of empires and the fickleness of destiny. She only half listened. She was happy simply to be leaning on his arm.

They passed the Brandenburg Gate, crossing the great swathe of no-man's-land where the Wall had once stood.

'I guess that in terms of world history,' said Francesca, 'the Berlin Wall will hardly rate a mention.'

'Not, certainly, if you compare it with the Great Wall of China.'

'Unless to compare and contrast: a wall in China to keep the barbarians out, a wall in Germany to keep them in.'

'You are confident that history will see the Communists as barbarians?'

'Isn't shooting people who want to emigrate barbaric?'

'Two hundred people were shot trying to escape from East Berlin over a quarter of a century. In Detroit, the same number are shot in a week. Add to that the number who die as a result of drugs, and one is entitled to wonder what is meant by civilization.'

'People cannot be civilized if they are not free.'

Serotkin looked at her with amused condescension. 'The Roman Empire was a military dictatorship. The barbarians were democratic.'

Francesca was getting out of her depth. 'Let's not argue,' she said, clinging more tightly to his arm.

They were now walking down the long boulevard leading from the Brandenburg Gate to the column surmounted by the Goddess of Victory. The whole area was redolent with history. To their right, through the trees of the Tiergarten, they could see the Reichstag, burned down at the time of the Nazis, now rebuilt. A little later they came to the Soviet Memorial, a stone monument flanked by two tanks and two cannon from World War II, and dominated by a huge bronze statue of a Soviet soldier, a rifle with fixed bayonet slung over his neck.

Here Serotkin stopped amid the cluster of tourists and looked up impassively at the two live Soviet soldiers who remained guarding this monument to their country's triumph.

'I didn't realize,' said Francesca, 'that there are still Soviet soldiers in Germany.'

'Some have left but others must wait until homes have been built for them in Russia.'

'And what will the Germans do with this memorial when they go?'

'Demolish it,' said Serotkin grimly.

'Or move it to the Pergamon Museum,' said Francesca. 'After all, it's the nearest thing to a Soviet altar.'

'No, they will demolish it,' said Serotkin again. 'They will not want a constant reminder in the middle of their capital city of who it was who freed them from Hitler.'

'Wasn't it kind of a joint effort?'

'Yes. American money and Russian blood.'

'There were the British . . .'

'Marooned in Britain.'

'And the French.'

'Defeated.'

'The Americans, then.'

'Neutral, until Hitler declared war on *them*.'

'It was Stalin who made a pact with Hilter.'

'He had no choice.'

Francesca did not want to get into an argument about the past, nor, it seemed to her, did Andrei. She could tell from the movement of his jaw under the skin, as he clenched and unclenched his teeth, that he was biting back words – not words directed at her but some dispute that was going on in his own mind.

She took his arm, a gesture that was meant to signify that she loved him whatever their differences of opinion. He did not shake her off but turned and looked at her with an expression bordering on contempt. 'Tell me, Francesca, since you know so much about history. When have Russian soldiers marched through the Brandenburg Gate?'

'At the end of the war, I guess.'

'And before that?'

She shook her head. 'I don't know.'

'Chasing Napoleon, on his retreat from Moscow.'

'I thought he was defeated by the British at the Battle of Waterloo?'

'Finally, yes. Wellington dealt with an ad hoc army, assembled in a hundred days. But it was the Russians who defeated his *Grand Army* in 1812. Just as with Hitler, we are employed by the West Europeans to dispose of their tyrants.'

'While unable to get rid of your own.'

Serotkin frowned. 'We disposed of the Tsars.'

'But Stalin died of natural causes.'

'Under Stalin,' said Serotkin, 'we were admired by many and feared by all. Now that we are democrats, Russia is universally despised.'

'At times,' said Francesca, 'you sound as if you wished that Stalin was still around.'

Serotkin hesitated. 'Stalin was ruthless, but any government is ruthless when it comes to its nation's vital interests.'

'He was more than ruthless,' said Francesca. 'He was cruel.'

'For cruel necessities you sometimes need cruel men,' said Serotkin. 'It used to be thought that the Russians could only be governed by terror.'

'But not now . . .'

'We shall see.'

'*You're* not governed by terror, are you?'

He paused, then said: 'It is always preferable to be governed by love, but sometimes one has to choose between two different loves.'

'Maybe you think you have to choose when in fact you can have both.'

He turned towards her and once again looked into her eyes, but this time his expression was sad. 'I think you know, Francesca, how much I love my country. When . . . all this is over, I shall have to go back.'

'Would you like company?'

He hesitated.

Francesca blushed. 'I'm sorry. I didn't mean to put you on the spot.'

'What about your job? Your tenure?'

As a reply, she simply squeezed his arm.

'Francesca . . .' He hesitated again, as if searching for the right words. 'Francesca, there are things about me . . . things that I have done and things that I must do. You don't know me. I am not what I seem.'

Thinking of the hairdye, Francesca smiled. 'Didn't you say that a woman's conscience is her intuition? Well, when I'm with you I feel it's right, and when I'm not, I feel it's wrong.'

'There are other things than love.' As he said this, he sounded uncertain.

'A month ago, I would have agreed.'

'The exhibition, the paintings . . .'

'Who wants art when you can have life?'

Serotkin turned and looked at Francesca as if to see whether or not she was sincere in what she said. 'If you had to choose,' he asked, 'between me and all those paintings in the exhibition, one or the other – not to *have*, but to *exist* – which would it be?'

She did not hesitate. 'You.'

He looked away as if this was not the answer he wanted. For some time he stood silently staring up at the bronze soldier towering above the memorial. 'Valentin Rasputin once wrote: *Truth is remembering. He who has no memory has no life.*' He turned back to face Francesca. 'There are things in our past, you see, that no Russian can forget, and the memory leads him to a certain course of action. But in time that action also becomes a memory, just as our being here will become a memory.'

He turned to walk on, took a few paces, then stopped and once

209

again looked directly into her eyes. 'In a month's time,' he said, 'on the fourteenth of July, Bastille Day, I shall come back to this Soviet altar, and if you are here, I shall ask the same question, and if your answer is the same, then I promise you that we shall remain together for the rest of our lives.'

FIFTEEN

After two weeks in Berlin, Nikolai Gerasimov could no longer postpone his trip to Leipzig. It was clear that Inspector Kessler was beginning to wonder whether or not to cut his losses and send him back to Moscow; and General Savchenko, to whom he spoke from time to time on a secure line from the former Soviet Embassy, now the Russian consulate, on Unter den Linden, was also impatient. Gerasimov's excuse – that the Germans were keeping him busy – was beginning to wear thin.

Kessler appeared happy to let him conduct investigations on his own: indeed, he encouraged him to do so. When Gerasimov told him that he was going to Leipzig, Kessler informed the city's police and provided him with a letter 'to whom it may concern' asking for full cooperation. A room was reserved in a hotel, a first class ticket provided by Kessler's office, and Gerasimov was met at Leipzig's palatial railway station by a plainclothes detective from the city's police.

Leipzig depressed Gerasimov. He remembered, from his study of German literature at the Institute of International Relations in Moscow, that the city had been described by Goethe in his *Faust* as 'a little Paris'. Now, after nearly fifty years of socialism, it was more like a large Nizhni Novgorod or Dnieperpetrovsk. Many of the older edifices still showed traces of the war: some bombed out blocks had not been rebuilt, others had the pockmarks left by Soviet shells. The postwar buildings were mostly tawdry and shabby, as yet untouched by the transfusion of hard currency from the West.

The young Leipzig detective who met Gerasimov at the station had clearly been moulded by the old regime. Inadvertently, he addressed Gerasimov as 'comrade' and drove him with some pride to a modern tower-block hotel. Gerasimov recognized it at once as a Soviet-style Hilton. They waited for more than a quarter of an hour in the scrum around the reception desk as a sullen girl slowly searched for their booking among scraps of paper scattered over the broken-down computer. Gerasimov felt at home.

After handing Gerasimov his card and promising any assistance should it be required, the Leipzig detective clicked his heels and departed. By now it was mid-afternoon. Not wanting to stay in Leipzig any longer than he had to, Gerasimov left his suitcase in his room, returned to the lobby and bought a map of the city from the hotel shop. If he was watched it would look as if he meant to do some sightseeing before settling down to work.

Gerasimov did not even look round to see if he was followed as he walked to the centre of the old city: he took it for granted that he was under surveillance. He looked at the Old Town Hall and the old Commercial Exchange; he went into the Church of St Thomas and, on coming out again, paused to look at the statue of the church's former organist, Johann Sebastian Bach.

Opposite the church was a café. He went in, sat down and ordered a cup of coffee and a slice of strudel. One of the tourists by the statue of Bach looked round every now and then to make sure he was still there. Gerasimov paid for the coffee and the strudel and, when the tourist's attention was distracted, went into the kitchen of the café and, without a word of explanation, out through the back.

He climbed onto the first tram that came along. It took him along the Martin Luther Ring and Harkorstrasse. He got off at the Fine Art Museum, and there waited on the traffic island in the middle of the road. No car had stopped when he got off the tram, nor did one alter direction when Gerasimov got on the next tram travelling in the opposite direction. As it approached the centre, he got off again by the New Town Hall, hailed a taxi and asked the driver to take him to the corner of Goldschmidt and Nürnbergerstrasse, a block away from the showroom of the Volkswagen dealer, G. Bedauer.

Again, no car was hovering as Gerasimov paid for the taxi. To be doubly sure, he walked round the block, stopped at a shop window. He was not being followed. He reached the forecourt of the Autohaus Bedauer just as a rubicund, fifty-year-old man was closing up.

'Good evening. Herr Bedauer?'

The man turned. 'Yes? How can I help you?'

He was not a local: Gerasimov could tell from the accent. He was probably a Wessie come to give his country cousins a lesson in free enterprise.

'I am sorry to have come so late in the day,' said Gerasimov in a slangy western German. 'And I'm not even here to buy a car.'

'Never mind, never mind. We are here to serve. That is what the people here will not understand.' He opened the door to the showroom, invited Gerasimov to enter, and then led him between two shiny new Golfs to his office at the back.

As the two men sat down, Herr Bedauer behind his desk, Gerasimov handed him the letter from Berlin's chief of police. 'I'm working on a special investigation,' he said. 'All in confidence, of course.'

The dealer read the letter, then handed it back to Gerasimov. 'Always happy to help the forces of law and order.'

'We are interested in a white Volkswagen van sold by you a little under two years ago, probably in July, possibly June '91.'

'It can't have been before July.'

'Why not?'

'Because that's when I started in business. My first sales were in July '91.' Herr Bedauer stood and went to the filing cabinet behind his desk. 'Have you the registration?'

'Unfortunately not.'

'Chassis number? Engine number?'

213

'No.'

'There will be more than one,' said Bedauer. 'When the Ossies got their Deutschmark, they went crazy. I sold everything Wolfsburg sent me.' He thumbed through the files. 'If my secretary was still here, she would know where to look . . . Commercial vehicles . . . here we are. July 1991, you say?'

'Yes.'

Bedauer took out a file and sat down at his desk. He went through the papers. 'We sold twenty-two vans that July.'

'How many were white?'

'Wait a moment.' Bedauer went through the file once again, removing some of the papers. 'Here we are. Eight white vans.'

'Now, do you happen to know if any of them are still in Leipzig?'

'Most, I should imagine.'

'The van that interests us is not in Leipzig.'

'Stolen, eh?'

'Used for an illegal purpose. So if you could remove, for example, those vans that have been serviced here over the past years or so.'

Bedauer looked through the seven invoices. 'Grützner . . . that's still in Leipzig. So is Dunklebeck. He's opened up a building supply business. Doing well. And Kuhn, the flower shop. I see that almost every day. But these five. I don't know. I'd have to check the service department but the garage is closed.'

'Could you do it in the morning?'

'Of course.'

'And if, in the meantime, you could give me the names and addresses of the five . . .'

'Now?'

'I would be grateful.'

Bedauer took out a pen and started to write, slowly and methodically, on a pad. 'Telephone numbers?'

'If possible.'

'They will be on Dieter's Roladex.'

'Dieter?'

'Our sales manager.' Bedauer stood and went to a desk out in the showroom. He returned a few minutes later and handed the list to Gerasimov. 'If you leave a number,' he said, 'I'll call you tomorrow when I've had a look at the service records.'

'I'll be out and about,' said Gerasimov. 'I'll call you, if I may.'

'Give me a little time.'

'Around eleven?'

'Fine.'

Gerasimov took a tram back to the centre of Leipzig. He watched the news on television in his hotel room, then went out again to have supper in the restaurant beneath the Old Town Hall, Auerbach's Cellar. This too brought back memories of his study of Goethe's *Faust*: however, Gerasimov did not choose it for its literary connotations. It was, he thought, the kind of place a tourist would choose, which might persuade his shadow that, after they had lost him that afternoon, he had disappeared into an art gallery or a museum.

Gerasimov also wanted to find a place where he could talk to someone unobserved. The trouble with Leipzig, or any of the other cities in East Germany, or Eastern Europe for that matter, was the homogeneity of the population. Under the Communists, it had been almost as difficult to enter East Germany as to leave it. As a result, there was no national or racial diversity in the population of Leipzig. All the people you saw in the shops or the streets had the same white faces. In a local Gaststätte, Gerasimov would have stood out in the crowd, just as Faust and Mephistopheles had in Auerbach's Cellar in Goethe's poem:

Those two travellers coming from afar,
Their foreign fashion tells you what they are . . .

Gerasimov could still remember the lines. Now, as he ate roast pig's knuckle, he observed, as he had suspected, that the very celebrity of Auerbach's Cellar had drawn in foreign tourists and visiting businessmen, so that no stranger was any more noticeable than any other.

While Gerasimov was eating and drinking, he concentrated on his food or his beer. It was important to savour the taste so that he could take back memories to Moscow. Between courses, he opened a copy of *Der Spiegel*, sometimes reading the magazine, sometimes studying the list of names, addresses and telephone numbers that he had been given by Bedauer.

Two of them were commercial enterprises, three private individuals. Rather than wait for Bedauer to look at the service records, Gerasimov could try telephoning the private buyers that evening on the pretext that he was looking for a second-hand van. The chances were good that this would reveal whether or not the van was still in Leipzig. The danger here was that the buyer who was Orlov's associate might not only lie; he would also be alerted by the enquiry and then warn Orlov that someone was on his trail. There seemed no alternative but to see each person face to face.

Gerasimov rose early the next morning and took a tram out to the St Alexis Church on Philipp-Rosenthalstrasse, built to commemorate the 22,000 Russian soldiers who had died fighting Napoleon in the Battle of Leipzig. Gerasimov was more interested in German launderers than Russian glory. He walked past the premises of St Alexis Wäscherei, one of the two commercial premises on the list. He did not care whether or not he was being followed by the Leipzig police: one could not know what he was doing from the cursory way he glanced into the yard behind the laundry and saw bags of dirty linen being unloaded from a white Volkswagen van.

Mentally, Gerasimov crossed that name off his list. He walked on for half a mile or so, then caught a tram to a stop a short distance from 52 Giesenstrasse, the second address on his list. This was a painter and decorator, and Gerasimov expected to find a small shop. Instead, it was a large block of flats: clearly the man worked from home. Gerasimov went into the block. The lift was new: an illuminated number showed that it was now on the seventh floor. If Gerasimov waited, anyone following would know to which floor he had gone. Wearily, he started up the stairs.

On the thirteenth floor, he came to the flat. He rang the bell. As he waited, he heard the screaming of a child. A bedraggled woman came to the door, a sniffing one-year-old clasped to her hip.

'Is Herr Thiele there by any chance?'

'He's out on a job.'

'Ah, I was wondering . . .'

'He'll be in this evening.'

'I have his address but not his number.'

'OK. Hold on.'

The woman went back into the flat, leaving the door ajar. Gerasimov waited. She returned with a card.

'I can't remember who gave me his name . . .' Gerasimov began.

The child wiped its nose with the back of its hand. The mother looked restless. 'He put an ad in the paper . . .'

'Or could I have seen his name on the side of his van?'

'Perhaps.'

'A white one? A Volkwagen?'

'That's right.'

'That must have been it.' He put the card in his pocket. 'Many thanks. I'll give him a call.'

It was now eleven. Gerasimov called Bedauer from a public box. 'Yes,' said Bedauer. 'I've been through the records. St Alexis Wäscherei have their van serviced here regularly. Rolf Rosegger . . . you can cross him off. Apparently he traded in the van for a Suzuki jeep three months ago. He's a friend of one of my lads. The painter hasn't had his van serviced here: they think he may service it himself. No one knows about Dieter Bleicher or Manfred Kraus. Neither have been here since they bought the van.'

After thanking Herr Bedauer, Gerasimov put down the telephone, irritated that he had been told largely what he knew already. The laundry and the painter had been crossed off the list. Rosegger was a possibility; the trade-in could be a ruse; but if he was a friend of one of Bedauer's young mechanics he was unlikely to have worked for Orlov. That left only two: Bleicher and Kraus.

Bleicher's address was out on the road to Torgau and Dresden, the furthest from the centre of Leipzig. Gersimov decided to tackle him first: he could call on Kraus on the way back to his hotel. He took another tram, changing several times on the way. It was almost one before he reached Bleicher's address. It turned out to be that of a bookshop. It was closed for lunch. There was no sign of a Volkswagen van.

Gerasimov settled down in a Gaststätte with a glass of beer and a plate of sausage, sauerkraut and roast potatoes. At two, he walked back to the small square in the centre of the suburb, looking into one or two shop windows before returning to Bleicher's bookshop. He sauntered past the entrance, then stopped, as if something in the window had caught his eye. In point of fact, there was little on display to tempt anyone: it appeared to have been, and perhaps remained, a state owned shop selling dusty titles from the days of the DDR.

A young woman sat on a tall stool behind the counter, tying up bundles of books with old fashioned paper and string. She had dark untidy hair and steel-rimmed glasses.

'Is Herr Bleicher here?' asked Gerasimov.

The woman looked up. 'One moment.' She continued with her work and only when the knot was tied, and the loose ends of string trimmed with scissors, did her attention return to Gerasimov.

'You want to see Herr Bleicher?'

'Yes.'

'What about?'

'A private matter.'

The woman frowned, got off her stool and went through to a room at the back of the shop. A moment later she returned, followed by a small, balding man.

'Yes?' he asked.

'I represent Allied Insurance,' said Gerasimov.

'And?'

'A white Volkswagen van was involved in an accident . . .'

'That is nothing to do with us,' said Herr Bleicher. 'It was stolen.'

'Ah. When was that?'

'When was it Lisle?' The older man turned to the young woman who was sitting once again on her stool.

'October or November.'

'Did you report it to the police?'

'Of course.'

'And your insurance company?'

'Yes.'

'And did you replace it with another Volkswagen van?'

'No. With a Ford. But what has that got to do with the accident?'

Gerasimov's mind was working quickly. The theft could well have been a way to cover up the fact that the van had been given to Orlov, but they would hardly have waited to report it until October or November. 'Nothing as such,' he said. 'It has nothing as such to do with the accident, but in insurance we are always interested in whether or not claims are settled . . .'

'Interested! I should say so. They knocked twenty per cent off the price for wear and tear when the van was almost brand new.'

'Your policy was not new for old?'

'Who knows what it was! All that damn small print. If you ask me, we were better off before when we didn't have to worry about that sort of thing.'

'Indeed,' said Gerasimov. 'My superior, Khrulev, would agree.' He studied the man's face for any recognition of the name Khrulev. There was none.

'Insurances, taxes,' muttered Bleicher. 'A fat lot of good that's done us, eh, Lisle? No one wants to read books any more. They're all watching TV and videos.'

'So you can't help me with the van?' asked Gerasimov.

'Help you? I thought you were meant to help us.'

'Try our company next time.'

'Allied, you said? Give me your card.'

'Alas, I've run out. Business is so good.'

'For you, perhaps.'

'You don't know where the van is at present?'

'Oh, of course. The thief sent me his name and address!'

'I'm sorry. A silly question.'

'Ask the police. I filed a complaint. But they'll never find out who stole it. They never do, now. They're too busy fighting the skinheads. What a mess, what a mess.'

Gerasimov, more or less satisfied by now that the bookseller was not the man he wanted, began to move towards the door. 'I'm sorry to have taken up your time.'

219

'You don't want to buy a book? Something by Lenin, perhaps? We are selling his collected works at half price. Or Engels, or Marx, or Ulbricht? They'll be collectors' items in a year or two.'

'Thank you, no. Perhaps some other time.' Gerasimov fled out into the street.

Gerasimov's hopes now rested on Manfred Kraus, hopes not just of finding Orlov but of getting back to the fleshpots of West Berlin. The day, starting cloudy, had now cleared. The late afternoon sun shone on the dilapidated buildings and colourless shops passed by the tram that took Gerasimov back towards the centre of Leipzig. In Russia he found such shabbiness tolerable because it was familiar, and the familiar was even lovable, like an old pair of slippers: but here, in Germany, it somehow seemed like a mirror held up to the face of the eternally slothful Slav. Gerasimov imagined a reproachful voice saying: 'The Romans left roads, the British railways. What will remain from the Russian Empire?'

This line of thought brought on in Gerasimov one of his occasional fits of depression. East Germany had always seemed the showpiece of the eastern bloc, ahead in every way of the Soviet Union. The shabbiness of socialist Leipzig appeared to Gerasimov the very best he could hope for from the future. If he played his cards well, he could hang onto his job, and perhaps put some icing on the cake of his basic pay and conditions by doing favours here and there, or by using trips abroad to import some Western electronic goods; but Gerasimov knew that he would never have the vision or the determination to cut loose and stay in the West as Orlov had done. It was not that he had much to go back to in Moscow: the slut, Ylena; a son whom he rarely saw; and possibily some kind of revenge from Georgi's gangster friends. But to succeed in the West, he knew, you had to be the type to get yourself out of bed in the morning; actually to work in your office rather than simply pass the time of day; to have ideas and follow them through, instead of waiting for orders and then carrying them out with only a semblance of zeal. Gerasimov could comprehend the concept of professionalism –

being good at one's job as an end in itself – but initiative was another matter. It was not the sort of thing a Russian had in his bones.

As he pursued Orlov, Gerasimov grew increasingly convinced that his quarry must have foreign blood. It was not like a Russian to sustain a covert scam over so long a period of time. After the Revolution the émigrés had mostly settled passively in the big cities of Western Europe and America, working as waiters and taxi-drivers, or, if they were lucky and had an aristocratic name, marrying an indigenous heiress. The only Russians to have made their fortunes were the Russian Jews. Perhaps Orlov has some Jewish blood, or German blood, like Lenin.

Gerasimov changed trams at the railway station on the Platz der Republik. Avoiding surveillance was almost second nature to him, which in itself, had he thought about it, might have told any surveillant that he was not what he seemed. But the chances were that Kessler suspected it already. That did not matter. What was important was to find Orlov before they did. He got off the second tram on the Petersteinweg, a block from his destination, which he then approached on foot by a circuitous route. Turning a street corner, he waited once again in front of a shop window to make sure he was not followed. Reassured, he walked on down the street of tall nineteenth-century apartments, their walls still black from the soot blown from the factories since the time of the Kaiser.

Even before he reached it, something caught his eye – a glint of gold that was the only colour in the otherwise gloomy street. When he reached it, he found that it was a small brass plaque that had caught the reflection of the setting sun. On the plaque, in black lettering, was written: *Manfred Kraus, Private Investigator*.

The entrance to the office was through a door that led directly off the street. There was a bell. Gerasimov pushed it.

'Yes?' A woman's voice.

'To see Herr Kraus.'

There was a short silence, then: 'Have you an appointment?'

'Unfortunately, no.'

Another silence. 'What is it about?'

'A personal matter.'

'Your name?'

'Kessler.'

'One moment.'

Gerasimov waited. Then came a buzzing, and the door clicked open. Gerasimov walked up some steps and came to a second door just as it was opened by a small, frumpish, middle-aged woman. She nodded, stood back to let him enter and, pointing to a faded blue sofa, asked him to wait.

Gerasimov did as he was told. The woman went back to her seat behind the desk, and continued to type on a heavy manual typewriter. When she had finished, she put the letter into a folder and then stood to put the carbon copy in one of the brown filing cabinets behind her desk. Gerasimov noticed that the drawer ran easily, and with a rumble, as if it was empty. It seemed likely that if Kraus was a private detective he had not been in business for long.

The furniture in the office was familiar to Gerasimov. The desk and the cupboards had the same beech veneer found in the offices of every state enterprise from the River Elbe to the Sea of Japan. The green plastic telephone had an old-fashioned dial, and the heavy plastic intercom with black cloth over the speaker might have been a radio from World War II.

There was a click and from the speaker came a man's voice. 'Please ask Herr Kessler to come in.'

The frumpish secretary got to her feet, beckoned to Gerasimov and went to open the door to the inner office. Gerasimov smiled to thank her; she did not smile back.

A tall man, aged over fifty and wearing a suit, rose reluctantly from behind the desk. He did not offer to shake hands but, as the secretary closed the door behind him, pointed to a chair, saying: 'Please sit down.' The impression he gave was of a busy doctor seeing a tiresome patient at the end of a difficult day. The pedantic, mildly irascible expression on his otherwise unexceptional features, together with his neatly trimmed grey-flecked hair and rimless spectacles, led Gerasimov to promote him from a general practitioner to a hospital consultant; or, had one passed him in the street, one might also have taken him for a company director or a senior civil servant. The only anomaly that

Gerasimov noticed was an underlying nervousness that contradicted his authoritative manner which in turn seemed inappropriate in this two-roomed office in a back street of Leipzig.

'How can I help you, Herr Kessler?' Kraus asked.

'I was wondering,' said Gerasimov, 'whether you could undertake some investigative work on behalf of a client?'

Kraus had a ballpoint pen poised over a pad. 'You are . . .'

'Acting for this client.'

'A company?'

'Yes.'

'Named?'

'Khrulev.'

Kraus hesitated for a second too long before noting down and repeating the name Khrulev. 'And what is the nature of the investigation?'

'We wish to find a vehicle . . .'

Kraus frowned. 'Perhaps the police . . .'

'A white Volkswagen van, purchased here in Leipzig in July 1991.'

In the fading light of the afternoon, it was difficult for Gerasimov to see the expression on Kraus's face.

'More important,' said Gerasimov, 'there is also a man . . .'

Kraus held up his hand. Gerasimov stopped.

'Ah yes, I remember,' said Kraus. 'You wrote to me about it. Let me find your letter.' He scrawled on the pad, then turned it to face Gerasimov. *Don't talk here.* 'Here we are. Yes. Your client, if I am not mistaken, owns a Bulgarian import–export agency which formerly bought shoes from a factory in Weissenfels . . .'

'Correct,' said Gerasimov, writing on the pad: *Auerbach's Cellar, 19.00.* He turned it to face Kraus.

'After the change from Mark to Deutschmark, the shoes became too expensive for the Bulgarian market, but their quality not sufficiently high for the Western market. As a result the factory closed down . . .' Kraus scrawled on the pad: *This is madness. I am watched.* He turned it back to face Gerasimov and pointed to the outer office.

'So far as I remember,' he went on, 'your client offered a Volkswagen van to pay for the residual stock and while the management took possession of the Volkswagen they were

223

unable to deliver the shoes because in the meantime the factory had been taken over by the Treuhand organization.'

'Quite correct,' said Gerasimov, pushing the pad back to Kraus, having merely underlined his original message: *Auerbach's Cellar. 19.00.*

Kraus shrugged. 'Very well. We will see what we can do.'

'I would be most grateful.'

'I shall make some calls. We can talk later.'

'Many thanks.'

Both men stood up. 'By the way,' said Kraus. 'I had heard that your managing director was . . . not well.'

'That is true. Herr Khrulev is indisposed. But the new management is still most interested in the business in hand.'

'Of course.'

Kraus escorted Gerasimov to the door of the outer office. The secretary remained at her desk.

'Thank you for calling.'

'Thank you for receiving me without an appointment.'

'I am the one who has been remiss.'

'I look forward to hearing from you.'

'Good day.'

'Good day.'

The young Leipzig detective greeted Gerasimov in the lobby of his hotel. 'Good evening, Herr Inspector. I just called on the offchance that there was something you would like me to do.'

'Thank you, no.'

'Inspector Kessler telephoned to ask whether you had made any progress . . .'

'Disappointing. It has been disappointing. One or two leads, but they have led nowhere. In fact, there is nothing more I can do in Leipzig. I shall return to Berlin in the morning.'

'Would you like me to make a reservation?'

'That would be kind. A mid-morning train.'

'And this evening? Can I offer you our hospitality?'

'Thank you, no. I must read the material provided by Inspector Kessler. I'll grab something to eat in the hotel or in the town.'

'Very well.' The young man bowed and clicked his heels. 'I shall come in the morning with your reservation.'

'Many thanks.'

Back in his room, Gerasimov took off his jacket and shoes and lay on his bed. What line should he take with Kraus? Clearly, he had been one of Khrulev's agents and had provided the van for Orlov. What else had he done for Orlov? What had been his cover at the time? The shiny new plaque and the empty drawers of the filing cabinet suggested that he had not been a private detective for long. Nor did he look like a man who had spent his life on petty investigations. His manner was too imperious: he was a man who was used to command.

An executive? Not under socialism. An army officer? Too cunning. The speed with which he had concocted the story about the shoes in Weissenfels had impressed Gerasimov. Here was a man accustomed to thinking on his feet. And why was he watched? And by whom? If his cover was blown as a Soviet agent, then he would not have been afraid to mention Khrulev. It seemed more likely that he had worked for the Stasi under East Germany's Communist regime.

That was it! Kraus must have been an Eleventh Department agent within the Stasi, probably recruited by Khrulev, and answerable to Khrulev alone. To recover the icons, Khrulev could not trust ordinary KGB channels: too many agents had done business with Maslyukov. The team had been Orlov, Partovsky and the Chechen with Kraus providing support in the field. By then the Stasi had been disbanded: Kraus, starting up as a private investigator, would have been under some kind of surveillance. But even if Kraus had been an officer in the Stasi, there had been so many Stasi operatives that it was unlikely that a close watch would have been kept on him. Probably it was left to the secretary to make reports to the BfV. He could understand now why Kraus had been afraid to talk. It was one thing to have been in the Stasi, quite another to have spied for the KGB.

What approach should Gerasimov employ? Quite possibly Kraus had held a commission in the old KGB with a higher rank, no doubt, than Gerasimov's. Was he still committed, or keen to end that chapter of his life? Had he helped Orlov in obedience to an order from Khrulev? If so, would he be prepared to take orders from the new security service of the Russian Federation? Or was he a hard liner who still shared Khrulev's Communist zeal? Would Gerasimov have to blackmail him with the threat of exposure? Or simply rely on the man's Prussian sense of duty? With Khrulev dead, Savchenko was now in command.

As Gerasimov had predicted, most of his fellow guests in Auerbach's Cellar were tourists or businessmen from outside Saxony – some from western Germany, others from further afield. There was a group of Italians and an American couple with two bored adolescent children.

Gerasimov chose a table between the Italians and the Americans. Promptly at seven, Kraus came down the steps in the restaurant, looked around as if looking for a spare table, came up to Gerasimov and said: 'Do you mind if I sit here?'

'Please . . .'

Kraus sat down and studied the menu. 'If we are watched,' he said softly, 'we will fool no one.'

Gerasimov nodded, and leaned forward as if to introduce himself. 'Whoever watches you may not know me, and whoever watches me may not know you.'

Kraus nodded. 'We can only hope so.'

The waiter came. 'Together or separate?' he asked.

'Separate,' said Kraus.

They sat in silence until the waiter had returned with two glasses of beer. Then, as if they were indeed two solitary businessmen, Gerasimov began talking, at one point opening his copy of *Time* magazine to point to an article, as if it had something to say about the issue under discussion. 'There are changes in Moscow,' he said to Kraus as he did so.

'So I read.'

'Khrulev is dead.'

'Yes.'

'His place has been taken by General Savchenko.'

Kraus said nothing.

'You are to answer to him.'

This last remark was a gamble but it seemed to pay off. 'You must explain to the general,' said Kraus, 'that my position is precarious. Mielke is under arrest. Wolf's position is also insecure. Either of them could expose me to improve their own position. They are prosecuting officers who gave orders to shoot fugitives trying to escape over the Wall. And my links with the Dzerzhinski brigade are already known.'

'But they have not prosecuted you?'

'No. By and large, Stasi officers are being left to their own devices. No pension, of course, even though they honoured the Nazis' pension commitments after the war . . .'

'Scandalous.'

'But there are still the files in the Ruschestrasse. There is no knowing what they may find there.'

'It will take them years to sort through those . . .'

'I know. And my links with Moscow will not appear in those files. Only Mielke knew, and perhaps Wolf. But General Savchenko should understand that there is little I can do now for Moscow, and really the risk I run in performing an auxiliary logistical role is out of all proportion to the value of the service . . .'

'I understand.'

'Khrulev offered me a post in Moscow but I have a wife and children here in Germany. Moving to Leipzig from Berlin was bad enough for them. They certainly do not want to move to Moscow. But if I remain here, it is imperative that contacts be kept to a minimum, if they are not terminated altogether. For if the BfV ever discover the connection with the Lubyanka, then they could put me under great pressure. A charge of treason is not unknown – as a means of persuasion, you understand, to tell all I know. That is why a meeting like this is so dangerous to everyone concerned.'

Ah, thought Gerasimov: he is trying to put a little pressure on me to leave him alone. 'I am here for two reasons,' he said. 'The first is to reassure you that your past services are not forgotten, and will not be forgotten, by the new security service of the Russian Federation.'

'It would be better . . .'

Gerasimov raised his hand. 'Let me finish. Your past services are not forgotten but any future participation is a matter for you to decide.'

A look of great relief came onto Kraus's face. 'It would be infinitely preferable for me simply to be left alone.'

'Of course. That is what we supposed. And that brings me to the second point. The help you gave to Comrade Orlov two years ago was much appreciated but his more recent demands were quite unauthorized.'

Kraus turned pale. 'Unauthorized? He told me that he was acting under orders.'

'Whose orders?'

'Khrulev's.'

'Khrulev is dead.'

'I know that now. But not then.'

'No one will hold you responsible,' said Gerasimov slowly, 'if you can help us to limit the damage.'

'The damage?'

'Where is Orlov?'

'I don't know.'

'What is he doing?'

'I don't know.'

'What did he want from you?'

'Names.'

'Whose names?'

'Names of men, former officers and men in the Dzerzhinski brigade whom he could recruit for an operation . . .'

'What operation?'

'He didn't say.'

'Did you give him such names?'

'Yes. Two names. An officer and an under-officer.'

'How did you choose them?'

'For their commitment, their zeal, and their loyalty to the Soviet cause. It was my job at the Ruschestrasse to know who was ideologically sound.'

'Did you contact them?'

'No.'

'Did he?'

'I believe so.'

'Why?'

'I was called by one for confirmation.'

'Of what?'

'His credentials.'

'From where?'

'Bautzen.'

'What did he want them for?'

'I don't know.'

Gerasimov frowned. 'He must have given you some idea of what he had in mind.'

Kraus looked perplexed. 'It was not customary to ask questions. I simply obeyed orders.'

'If they were orders.'

'Two months before, he had been sent by Khrulev. I assumed that Khrulev had sent him again.'

'Two men . . ,' Gerasimov repeated. 'What on earth could he want with two men?'

'I believe two was only the start. He intended to call upon the two to recruit more.'

'Up to how many?'

'Twenty or thirty. I am not sure.'

'Did he propose to pay them?'

'I don't know. He appeared to have ample funds at his disposal, but the quality he looked for was not venality, it was commitment. He realized that there were still some who remained dedicated to the Communist cause.'

'You could presumably furnish me with the names of the two men?'

Kraus hesitated. 'I have destroyed the file. It was too dangerous for me to keep it.'

'Can't you remember them?'

'The two names. Not the addresses.' He took out a notepad and started to write them down.

'He told you nothing about the operation, or about who was involved.'

'I assumed that it was the same team as before.'

'Partovsky? The Chechen?'

'I never knew their names.'

'Anyone else?'

Again, Kraus hesitated. 'He was in touch with someone with the code name Chameleon.'

'Who is Chameleon?'

'An unofficial collaborator of our state security, who also worked for Khrulev, but not one under my control.'

'Do you know his real identity?'

'No I don't. But I got the impression from Orlov that it was someone now in a position of some influence.'

'But surely his cover is blown?'

'No.'

'His file?'

'It has gone.'

'Who saw to that?'

'According to Orlov, Chameleon saw to that himself.'

'A clever fellow.'

'Not clever enough. Orlov could prove that he had been controlled by Khrulev, so Chameleon had no choice but to cooperate.'

'Orlov blackmailed him?'

Kraus shrugged. 'In effect.'

'And you don't know his name.'

'No.'

The two men had finished with their food. Kraus's was mostly uneaten.

'Another beer?' asked Gerasimov. 'A dessert? Coffee?'

'I had better go,' said Kraus. 'My wife will be expecting me. I told her only that I was working late.'

Gerasimov called the waiter to pay the bill. 'If any of the opposition should ask you about Orlov, say nothing.'

'And if they ask me about you?'

'I was after the consignment of shoes from Weissenfels. They might even believe it.'

The two men rose to go. 'When you saw Orlov, that second time. Had his appearance changed?'

'No. I don't think so. A little unkempt, perhaps.'

'What do you mean?'

'My daughter tells me it is now the fashion.'

'What?'

'The unshaven look. Designer stubble, I believe it is called.'

SIXTEEN

As the day approached for his great patriotic gesture, Colonel Nogin grew increasingly ill at ease. Keminski's nephew, Perfilyev, had been back to the base at Waldheim on three or four occasions. Nogin had been delighted to see him, not least because he always arrived with a case of vodka but, five months on from their first meeting, he did not feel that he knew Perfilyev any better or that he could altogether trust him. Perfilyev was intelligent, amusing and a good listener – a quality of value to a bored veteran of the Great Patriotic War; but, while Nogin had told Perfilyev everything there was to know about Nogin, Perfilyev had given away very little about himself. He was also one of those men who make others feel that it is somehow improprer to enquire, so Nogin did not feel he could ask Perfilyev, for example, how he got hold of the Deutschmarks to buy the vodka, or the chocolates and other delicacies that he always brought for the officers' wives.

Nogin knew well enough that everyone involved in the dismantling of the Soviet military machine in East Germany was making out of it what he could, from the private soldier who sold his cap to the nuclear engineer who hawked plutonium from the boot of a car; and so it would not have surprised Nogin if he had learned that Perfilyev, despite his denunciation of the corrupt reformers, should have some Deutschmarks earning business on the side. Such contradictions had always been part of the Soviet way of life, and if Perfilyev had put to Nogin some modest scheme for selling surplus weapons systems to the third-world countries, or tanks for scrap, as a way of bolstering Nogin's pension when he finally retired, Nogin would have been happier than he was with his promise to destroy highly secret equipment from Jena.

Nogin recognized, of course, that there was a world of difference between selling weapons to Arabs or Africans to kill one another, and selling sophisticated systems to the potential enemies of Russia. For this reason, Nogin did not intend to go back on his promise to place the base at Perfilyev's disposal, even though he could reasonably argue that he had been drunk when the promise was made. But the whole plan made him feel uneasy. If schemes to raise currency were uncovered, the currency could be used to escape the consequences. Where the rewards were purely political, noble motives would not save one from the Lefortovo prison.

There were other reasons for his unease. The first was that the scale of the thing was greater than he had been led to expect. Perfilyev now talked of several vanloads of equipment arriving on a single night. The second was the sense Nogin had gained, for no particular reason, that it would be less dangerous now to proceed than to change his mind. He had always known that engineers working for the Ministry of Medium Machine Building might be more than they seemed, but the mystery surrounding Perfilyev had taken on an element of menace. He did not give the impression of being a man who would take kindly to being thwarted.

The third was the realization that there were others in Jena besides Perfilyev who were involved. On the last two occasions that he had come to Waldheim, Perfilyev had been accompanied by a Chechen. As a rule, Nogin disliked Chechens along with Azeris, Armenians, Georgians and Jews. He had to tolerate them:

many of his troops now came from the Muslim republics of the Russian Federation; but he never trusted them. Behind the shifty expression in their narrow Asiatic eyes lay centuries of resentment at Russian rule.

Nogin realized that Perfilyev might have had to bring the Chechen into the conspiracy because it would be dangerous to leave him out. Perfilyev introduced him as a friend and fellow engineer, working on the same project in Jena. To Nogin, he did not look like an engineer, nor did the two men behave as if they were friends.

Nogin had left the detailed arrangements for the operation to Captain Sinyanski: it had occurred to him that if the whole thing blew up in their faces, Sinyanski would make a suitable scapegoat because of his earlier links with the KGB. Nogin could argue that he had cooperated at the request of Sinyanski who had led him to believe that the operation had been authorized by the security service of the Russian Federation.

It became apparent, however, that Sinyanski was thinking along the same lines. After the last visit of Perfilyev and the Chechen, Sinyanski came late to report to Nogin that Perfilyev had changed his instructions: the machinery was not to be destroyed on arrival, but was to be hidden in the empty hangars pending Perfilyev's further instructions. Sinyanski pointed out to Nogin that this increased the risk: ashes could be scattered but what was hidden could later be found. He insisted that Nogin decide whether or not to go ahead with these new arrangements.

Nogin reached for his telephone, but then remembered that he had neither an address nor a number for Perfilyev. Should he call Keminski in Moscow? It seemed too risky. He told Sinyanski they would have to wait until Perfilyev returned.

Sinyanski now raised another odd aspect of the whole thing, already noticed by Nogin – the apparent disharmony between Perfilyev and his Chechen friend. On their last visit they had stayed with Sinyanski: he was not married, and had two spare rooms. After the two visitors had supposedly retired to their respective rooms for the night, Sinynaski had overheard an acrimonious exchange in Perfilyev's bedroom. He had picked up only scraps of their conversation, and from them gained the impression that they had been quarelling about some woman.

Nogin laughed, and felt relieved. The best of friends could quarrel about a woman. But Sinyanski went on to add some other words that he had picked out through the wall of his bedroom: 'CIA . . . jeopardy . . . if necessary . . . the whole enterprise . . .' spoken by the Chechen, interspersed with Perfilyev's mollifying 'of course, of course'.

'And there is something else,' said Sinyanski. 'When they were arguing, the Chechen addressed Perfilyev not as Piotr Petrovich but as Andrei Anatolyevich which leads me to suspect that quite possibly he is not the man you suppose.'

Nogin remonstrated. Sinyanski must have misheard. Perfilyev had been sent to him by Keminski, Nogin's comrade-in-arms during the war. But the more he heard, the less he liked it, and he started to chide Sinyanski for getting them involved. Sinyanski reminded his commander, politely, that it was he who had introduced Perfilyev, and who had agreed to destroy the equipment on the base, at which Nogin exploded, blaming all the misery and misfortune of his country on the machinations and skulduggery of Chekists and Jews. But before Sinyanksi left, he had calmed down. The two men were in this together, and neither saw any alternative but to see it through.

PART FIVE

1993

June–July

SEVENTEEN

Only four days before the hanging of the Excursus exhibition was due to start, Andrei Serotkin told Francesca that he had to fly back to Moscow. His father had suffered a stroke. This was not a catastrophe so far as the exhibition was concerned: he had never shown much interest in the hanging. It was sad for Francesca but she did not complain. She knew that Serotkin was close to his father, and could see that he was anxious. He promised to return to Berlin as soon as he could, almost certainly for the official opening in the Old Gallery by President von Weizsäcker, and quite definitely for their assignation on Bastille Day, 14 July.

For the rest of that week, Francesca was kept busy at the office. There were no other crises. The invitations had gone out for the reception following the exhibition given by the city of Berlin, and for the more exclusive lunch at the New National Gallery the next day. All the works of art were ready in the OZF warehouse for distribution to the two galleries on the following Monday morning. The first finished copies of the catalogue came into the office on the Friday morning. They looked superb.

It was only when Francesca awoke that Saturday morning that

she started to pine for Serotkin. If she had had a photograph of him, she would have been able to gaze at it; as it was, she had only his toothbrush and pyjamas to remind her that he was not a figment of her imagination. She lay on her bed, musing about him, tantalized as always by the residual mystery in the man she should by now know so well. She recalled her first impression, that he had been 'dashing', reminding her of the Bulgarian patriot, Insarov, in Turgenev's novel, *On the Eve*. She went into her living room, took the book from the shelf and started to reread it. She laughed when she came to the passage where one of the characters, Bersenyev, comes to see the heroine, Elena, saying: 'Fancy, our Insarov has disappeared.'

'Disappeared?' said Elena.
'He has disappeared. The day before yesterday he went off somewhere and nothing has been seen of him since.'
'He did not tell you where he was going?'
'No.'

That could well have been an exchange between Günther Westarp and Francesca. She also smiled when she reached the scene where on a picnic a drunken German who pesters the ladies is thrown by Insarov into the river. A prophetic passage, thought Francesca, if you set the scene in Berlin's Englischergarten and replace the German with three Turks.

She read on and was struck by other similarities that made her feel her love for Serotkin had in some strange fashion followed the same pattern as Elena's love for Insarov. Serotkin was as mysterious as Insarov, and had the same sense of dedication to a greater purpose, even if it was not clear to Francesca what that purpose was. When Insarov tells Elena that he must go and fight for his country's independence, she volunteers to go with him. When Insarov falls ill, Elena goes to visit him and, when he is still weak, they make love just as she and Serotkin had done.

It was extraordinary, now that she reread the novel, how many similarities there were between the fictional and the real lives. But then she frowned. How did it end? Stopping, briefly, to make herself some lunch (a prawn salad with low-cal mayonnaise, a slice of Vollkornbrot, a glass of skimmed milk and an apple), she raced through the pages: on the broad lagoon which separates Venice from the narrow strip of accumulated sea sand called the Lido, Elena and Insarov lie in a gondola. In Insarov there is a cruel change.

> He had grown thin, old, pale and bent: he was constantly coughing a short dry cough, and his sunken eyes shone with a strange brilliance.

Consumption, thought Francesca, munching her apple, the AIDS of the day. They go to the opera in Venice. Insarov grows weaker.

> 'It's all over . . . I'm dying. Goodbye, my poor girl, goodbye, my country . . .'

Elena sends for the doctor. The doctor comes. 'Signora, the foreign gentleman is dead.'

Francesca shuddered. That was not how *her* story would end. Soon they would return to the Soviet Memorial and make a commitment to one another for life. Then either she would go back to Russia with Andrei, or he would change his mind about leaving his country in the lurch and go back to America with her. The first solution was the more romantic; the second, the more practical. Francesca was not sure what she would do in Moscow, or how they would live on a salary paid in roubles. Nor did she like the sound of Russian obstetrics: she took it for granted that Andrei would want a child.

Knowing that Andrei Serotkin was away, Sophie Diederich invited Francesca to supper that Saturday evening, a small private celebration for the authors of Excursus now that the donkey work was done. 'Everyone said it was impossible,' said Sophie. 'But we did it. And it would be nice to have one last quiet evening together – just you and Günter and Stefi and me – before all the public celebrations begin.'

Francesca felt a little sad that Serotkin's name was not included in this inner circle, but she had to concede that it had no right to be there. She also acknowledged that, if it had not been for Stefi and

241

Sophie, she would not have been chosen to organize Excursus; and if she had not been chosen to organize Excursus, she would not have met Andrei Serotkin. For that, she owed the Diederichs at least one last tedious evening at their flat in the Wedekindstrasse.

Francesca felt mildly ashamed that she now found the Diederichs a bore and, as she drove across Berlin that evening, she tried to analyse why it was so. Undoubtedly, Serotkin was part of the reason: the bright light that shines from one's lover always makes others seem dim. Stefi could be witty, and undoubtedly had a lively mind, but Francesca still found him insubstantial and unconvincing. She realized that politicians were inevitably insincere, but Stefi gave the impression that he was untrustworthy through and through. It was partly this that had led to Francesca's growing exasperation with dear, sweet and slightly stupid Sophie: how could she love so uncritically a patent *shyster*, particularly when she had been married to a man like Paul?

Perhaps, in a way, Paul had been to blame. His very nobility had encouraged in Sophie the kind of hero-worship that came naturally to the traditional German wife. When Paul had had his nervous breakdown, showing that he had weaknesses too, Sophie had simply transferred her loyalties to the understudy waiting in the wings.

The memory of Paul gave Francesca a twinge of guilt. She thought of him, she realized, as if he was either dead or locked up in a lunatic asylum when in fact he was living as an Evangelical pastor at Bechtling, a village only an hour or two's drive from Berlin. Why had she not been to see him? She had been too busy. And when the work had eased up, there had been Andrei. At the back of her mind, there was a niggling prick of conscience which told her that if Paul had been in a position to further her career, she would certainly have found time to pay him a visit. Now, with the hanging starting on Monday, followed two weeks later by the opening of the exhibition, and God knew what thereafter, Francesca wondered whether she would ever get to see him unless she drove out to Bechtling the next day.

Stefi was drunk. This surprised Francesca because she had never seen him drunk before. Sophie tried to cover it up as soon as Francesca arrived by whispering that her husband was 'in a filthy mood'; but it was quite apparent from Stefi's bloodshot eyes and his slightly slurred speech, as well as the glass of vodka held in his hand.

'So, the American,' he said as soon as he saw Francesca, bowing with an ironic flourish. 'So elegant, as always, as befits a princess from the triumphant superpower . . .'

Francesca frowned. She had, in fact, dressed down (black trousers, a blue shirt) and, if her wardrobe lacked the versatility to plumb the depths reached by Günter Westarp who sat despondently on the sofa, it was hardly the costume of a princess.

She decided to rise above the irony, and try to make her mood match his. 'Forget the super*power*, Stefi. Let's drink to the super*man*, Stefan Diederich, who has done what everyone said could not be done – planning and staging a major exhibition in under a year.'

'Thank you.' He bowed again, then reached over to the sideboard where he kept his drink. 'You will drink vodka, yes? We are all drinking vodka here.'

'I'd rather have a glass of white wine.'

'So, you have a taste for Russians but not for Russian drink.'

'Stefi!' said Sophie.

Francesca laughed. 'Funnily enough, Andrei doesn't drink that much.'

'Most dangerous,' said Stefi. 'A Russian who doesn't drink.' He handed Francesca a glass of white wine.

'Why?'

'A symptom of megalomania.'

'I don't get it.'

Stefi refilled his glass with vodka. 'A man who conquers his own weaknesses thinks he can conquer the world. Look at Lenin, Stalin, Gandhi . . .'

'Gandhi was hardly a conqueror.'

'On the contrary. He thought he could conquer the forces of evil, like the megalomaniac of all megalomaniacs, Christ.'

'Phooey,' said Sophie. 'You're just trying to justify getting drunk.'

'What was it Caesar said? "Let me have men about me that are fat; sleek-headed men and such as sleep o'nights." Does he sleep o'nights, Francesca?'

'Stefan!' shouted Sophie again. 'You go too far?'

'He sleeps very well, thank you,' said Francesca.

'But he is not fat.'

'No. As a matter of fact, he is exceptionally fit.'

'*Exceptionally* fit! Have you never paused to wonder why?'

'I guess he feels better that way.'

'And can dispose of Turkish rapists just like that.' Stefi gave an impression of a kung fu fighter, spilling the vodka he held in his hand.

'It certainly came in useful.'

'"Would he were fatter,"' said Stefi.

'Why?'

'"Such men as he be never at heart's ease, while they behold a greater than themselves, and therefore are they very dangerous."'

Francesca frowned. She knew that Stefi disliked Russians in general, and Serotkin in particular, but that was no reason to badmouth him in her presence. 'I don't think that Andrei's dangerous,' she said.

'Why should he be dangerous?' asked Sophie.

Stefi turned to Westarp. 'Why should he be dangerous Günter? Tell us.'

Günter looked mournfully at Stefan Diederich. 'You tell me, Stefi. You always know best.'

This jibe seemed to annoy Stefan. 'Know best? How can one know best? We either know, or we don't know, and what we know often turns out to be lies. First it is socialism and the dictatorship of proletariat; then it is capitalism and democracy. What can we do, Günter, but be picked up and blown hither and thither by the strongest gust of wind?'

Günter did not answer.

'Gloomy riddles,' said Sophie. 'We are meant to be celebrating, and all we get are these gloomy riddles. Well, let's eat, and see if some food won't improve our morale.'

Sopies's veal fricassee and potato dumplings had a sobering effect on her husband, and improved the mood of Günter Westarp. Over strudel and coffee, Günter even made a short speech saying that 'whatever the outcome', he felt privileged to have been associated with Excursus, in particular to have worked alongside Francesca McDermott. Her example had taught him how professionalism and hard work could be combined with courtesy and charm. He raised his glass to her – the Diederichs followed – and drank to Francesca.

Feeling a heel for the horrible things she had thought about Günter, Francesca replied to the toast, saying how working on Excursus had changed the course of her life, not just professionally, but also from a human point of view (giggles from Sophie). Stefan had taught her how an artistic phenomenon could be turned into a political message that would enlighten and inspire the nations of Eastern Europe, dispossessed by Communism of their culture and tradition; and Günter had shown how the indomitable spirit of a single man could survive decades of intellectual oppression in one of the most efficient totalitarian states known to history. The lights had seemed to go out behind the Iron Curtain, but small flickering flames had remained alight in men and women like Stefi, Sophie and Günter Westarp; and only a small flame was needed to reignite the spiritual conflagration represented by the works of art now in the Excursus exhibition – the greatest collection of modern Russian painting that the world had ever seen.

It was overdone, and Francesca's images had got a little out of hand, but it led Sophie to clap her hands and Günter to mumble, 'Thank you, thank you,' as a big tear ran down his cheeks into the brush of his Günter Grass moustache.

For a moment, Stefi remained silent, his head bowed, his eyes staring down at the table. Then he looked up. 'Excellent,' he said. 'You must make such a speech at the opening of Excursus. When I am in Bonn, I shall make sure that you are included in the programme. *Spiritual conflagration.* I like that. Von Weizsäcker will like it too.'

At nine the next morning, Francesca set out in her Golf to visit

Paul Meissner. She had not told Sophie nor forewarned Paul: since it was a Sunday, she felt reasonably certain that she would find the pastor at Bechtling. The traffic was light. She quickly reached Neuruppin, and then drove north to Dierberg where she turned off onto a side road that led through beautiful forests and past numerous small lakes. A second turn took her out of the forests into vast pastures with large herds of cows.

The brick church at Bechtling was visible a mile or two away, its pointed black spire like a witch's hat. When Francesca reached the village, she felt saddened that a man who had held such promise should now live in such an obscure parish, ministering to the needs of peasants from the local collective farm. She stopped her car in the village square, embarrassed that it should seem so conspicuous beside two shabby Trabants and a rusty Skoda. There was no one in sight to ask for directions to the house of the pastor. The single shop was closed. There was no café or *Gaststätte*. She looked at her watch: it was twenty to eleven. The pastor was probably in his church.

When Francesca opened its huge creaking door, a dozen people in the congregation all turned to look at the intruder. Francesca almost fled, but in the pulpit above the row of gnarled faces she saw one that she knew of old. Paul was preaching. Seeing her, he stopped in mid-sentence and said: 'Please come in.' He smiled. He had recognized her. Francesca sat down in the back pew and Paul continued his sermon.

Francesca could not concentrate on what he was saying: she was too shaken by the change in his appearance. He had aged – twice the number of years that had passed since she had last seen him. Yet despite his lined face and his grey hair, she saw how much the boy she had seen at the Diederichs looked like him, and realized how hard it must have been for him to have been separated from his children.

Paul was preaching about love and forgiveness – a predictable homily, perhaps, but a controversial message in a once Communist country where the victims were now the victors. It was up to God to punish the wicked for their sins, he said. It was Christ, not man, who was to judge the living and the dead. Vengeance is mine, says the Lord. I will repay.

The sermon ended. Paul came down from the pulpit and went to the altar. Francesca, who had only entered a church for the odd funeral or wedding, did not know when to kneel or sit or stand; but neither, it seemed, did most of the congregation, and since she sat at the back, her confusion was hardly noticed.

At the end of the service, they sang a hymn. Again, few of those present appeared to know either the music or the words. There was no organ, and the only voice that saw them through was that of the pastor himself, far stronger than his enfeebled appearance would lead one to suppose.

The hymn over, the villagers shuffled out of the church, glancing slyly at Francesca as they passed her. Paul Meissner had left the altar, and Francesca thought that perhaps she should go round to the back of the church to intercept him as he left; but as she rose from her seat, Paul came out of the sacristy dressed not in the robes of a pastor but wearing grey trousers, a shirt and a jersey. When he reached her, he smiled. 'Come,' he said, putting his arm around her to lead her out of the church.

He closed the door with a large key, then set off from the church towards the village, Francesca walking beside him. 'I had hoped to see you,' he said. 'I had heard that you were in Berlin.'

'I have been arranging an exhibition.'

'Yes. Excursus. I look forward to it.'

'It was thanks to Sophie . . .'

'And Stefi. I know.'

'I'd wanted to see you, but we became so busy . . .'

He smiled. 'Of course. That doesn't matter. For God, a day is the same as a year and a year the same as a day. So long as you remembered me . . .'

'How could I forget?'

'*You* could forget, I am sure. There must have been so many other things going on in your life.'

'Nothing like that year in Berlin.'

'You saw us at our best. After you left . . .' He laughed. 'Not *because* you left, but *after* you left, we were not quite so heroic.'

'You fell ill.'

'Is that what you heard?'

'Yes. You had a nervous breakdown.'

Paul nodded. 'I suppose you could call it that.'

They came to a low, one-storey house, indistinguishable from any of the other houses in the village. Paul led Francesca into the narrow hallway. There was the smell of cooking.

'I don't want to impose myself,' said Francesca.

'My mother will be expecting you,' he said. 'She will have seen you in the church.'

They walked down the short hallway to the kitchen. A frail old woman stood at the stove, a look of suffering and distinction on her thin, pale face.

'Mother,' said Paul Meissner. 'This is my American friend from ten years ago, Francesca McDermott.'

Frau Meissner wiped her hands on her apron and then reached forward to greet Francesca. 'Paul has often spoken about you,' she said.

'I am so sorry to surpise you like this.'

'We are delighted. Our life is mostly rather quiet.'

'I didn't mean to turn up for lunch.'

'It is an old tradition,' said Paul, 'to cook enough for an unexpected guest.'

He turned and led Francesca back into the small living room of the little house. At once, Francesca recognized some of the furniture and pictures from the flat in the Wedekindstrasse ten years before.

'Do the children visit you?' asked Francesca.

'Yes. From time to time. They find Bechtling a little dull.'

'It must have been hard to lose them.'

'Of course. But in the DDR, given who I was, I could not hope to win custody.'

'And you were not well.'

Paul hesitated. 'I was not perhaps quite so ill as we thought at the time.'

'Sophie said that you were in the clinic.'

'Yes. That is certainly true. But we have now discovered that some clinics in the DDR were not there to help their patients get well.'

Francesca looked puzzled. 'I read something about harassment . . .'

'The Stasi had a way of dealing with dissidents which they called *Zersetzung*. It was a programme for the annihilation of anyone who opposed the regime. They preferred not to arrest us or imprison us: that earned them bad publicity and produced martyrs. They preferred to wear us down with petty privations, and above all to demoralize us so that we would lose faith in ourselves. We know this now, because we have had access to their files.'

'Have you seen your file?' asked Francesca.

'I will come to that in a minute.' Paul had always had a slightly pedagogic manner, like a university teacher in a seminar. 'At the time, we had no idea of how thoroughly we were being manipulated by the Stasi. Every now and then, I would be called in for questioning, and threatened with prosecution for speaking out against the state. They were particularly enraged because of my success with students, but it was difficult for them to pin anything on me because, as you will remember, I was always careful not to speak out against the state. I always insisted that we must render unto Ceasar the things that are Caesar's, reserving for God only the things that belong to God.'

'Sure.'

'But they were clever at twisting what I had said to make it sound seditious. What was demoralizing for me was not the number of times that I would be called in for questioning, but the discovery under interrogation that they were so well informed about what I had said. I began to feel paranoid, imagining that there were radio transmitters in my living room, my bathroom, even under our bed. The alternative – that it was not secret microphones but our closest friends who were relaying everything that we said to the Stasi – seemed too dreadful to contemplate. We were also on our guard against disinformation. We knew that the Stasi would do what they could to sow distrust in our group. It was therefore essential, to preserve our sanity, to be open with one another within our inner circle of friends. We sustained one another by holding prayer meetings and readings – reciting poems and stories that could not be published; by finding work for those who lost their jobs because of their political opinions. But all the same, the pressure was sometimes intolerable. I was not given much support by my bishop. His secretary was of the opinion that we should avoid all open criticism of the regime. It now emerges, from the files, the he was a Stasi IM – *Inoffizielle Mitarbeiter*, unofficial collaborator – reporting back after each meeting everything I or the bishop had said.

'Inevitably, the strain took its toll on our marriage. You will remember how Sophie was in those days – cheerful, brave, very loyal, but not at heart . . .' Paul groped to find the right word. 'Not so much interested in intellectual or spiritual ideas. She sometimes felt, I know, that I put my conscience before my wife and family, that life would be so much easier if I would only compromise with the regime.

'As you can imagine, the fear that there were radio transmitters under our bed, and perhaps cameras hidden behind holes in the walls, poisoned the physical expression of our conjugal love. I must also recognize, in view of what happened, that Sophie was always more appreciative than I was of the carnal side of our married life – something for which I, not she, was to blame. My anxiety led to long periods of abstinence which, St Paul warns us, permits the devil to do his work. Frustration made Sophie irritable, and her irritability made me anxious. I felt that she did not support me in my work. Persuading young people to put God before the state, to prefer confirmation in the Evangelical church to the Communists' pagan ceremony, the *Jugendweihe*, was setting them off on a path that would entail great suffering. It was an awesome responsibility. My nerves suffered. I slept badly, and started to have persistent headaches. Sophie urged me to go to a doctor, a particular doctor, recommended by one of our closest friends.

'I believed, of course, that one should try and bear suffering as Christ bore His cross on the path to Cavalry, but in the end I was persuaded. I went to see the doctor – a Dr Friedemann – who recommended a course of pills. These made me feel worse. On top of the headaches came long periods of black depression. My inner doubts grew about my work. To my friends – you will remember – I was something of a hero, and in West Germany stories were written about me as a dissident leader and a champion of democracy. This gave ammunition to the Stasi. Time and again

I was brought in for questioning and threatened with prosecution and imprisonment in Hohenschönhausen or Bautzen. Time and again my bishop warned me to take care. The irony, of course – and you may remember this, too – was that in my homilies to the students I preached as vigorously against Western materialism as against Marxist materialism. I was emphatic in my criticism of the greed and injustice that sustain the market economies of the West. That enraged the Stasi for whom only Communism could be permitted to hold the moral high ground; it also irritated visiting West Germans, and Sophie too. I would never accept gifts from Western visitors such as cigarettes or toilet water. Sophie accepted my decision; she accepted everything I said; but she was got down by my depressions, and started to suggest that perhaps they had a psychological cause. So did Dr Friedemann. He had read Freud and Jung, which was unusual in the DDR, and thought that perhaps I lived in the shadow of my father, that I drove myself too hard to win his approval, or perhaps to do better than he had done to win my mother's love. To me this was nonsense, but Sophie thought that there might be something in it, and so did our friend, that closest friend, the one who had recommended Dr Friedemann. They urged me to trust Friedemann, and so when he suggested that I go for treatment to a clinic, I agreed.

'There, dear Francesca, there . . .' Paul stopped. His face, which until then had held the benign expression of a patient teacher, became twisted for a moment as if the memory rekindled some kind of terror. 'There, I was given a course of injections, supposedly part of a therapy which . . .' He shook his head. 'I cannot describe the effect of those drugs on my mind. When I slept, I had grotesque nightmares; when I awoke, they continued, and if anything became worse. I was pursued, I was tormented; all my anxieties grew out of all proportion. I began to fear that there were microphones hidden in my pillows and mattress, and so took a knife and cut them to shreds. They put me in a straitjacket and tied me to the bed. I raved. I was deranged. But all the while I kept a kernel of sanity, not by thinking of liberty or democracy or of the Church or even of God, but by remembering Sophie and the children. It was for them that I was determined to pull through.

'The course of injections came to an end. The nightmares ceased. I became calm. Whatever fears remained, I kept to myself. All I wanted was to go home. In time, they agreed. A date was fixed. They said that Sophie had been informed, and had arranged for a friend from Leipzig to come and fetch me in his car. He came. He drove me back into Berlin and carried my small overnight bag up the stairs to our flat. He had a key – many of our friends had a key. We went in. It seemed to be empty. The door to our bedroom was ajar. I pushed it open. On our bed was a naked couple making love, Sophie and our closest friend.'

'Stefi?'

'Yes. Stefan Diederich.'

'And the man who brought you to the house?'

'The friend from Leipzig? Günter Westarp.'

Francesca was silent. She could think of nothing to say. The story he had told, and told with such conviction and apparent pain, was not only horrifying in itself but quite as terrible in its implications. 'But does that mean that Sophie was working for the Stasi?'

'Sophie? No. She was weak but innocent.'

'But Stefan? And Günter?'

'I don't know.'

'In your file . . .'

'My file has not been found. Nor has a file been found as yet for Stefan or Günter, even though the three of us were prominent dissidents.'

'Why not?'

'It seems that someone removed them in good time.'

'But who? And why?'

'When the regime collapsed, gangs of skinheads broke into the Stasi headquarters on the Ruschestrasse. A committee was formed by the dissidents to take charge. One of their first resolutions was to destroy the files. They said the Soviets would intervene and the Stasi return. Later, of course, they realized that they were destroying the evidence against the Stasi.'

'Stefan was on that committee?'

'A leading member.'

'So he could have destroyed the files?'

252

'Mine, Sophie's, Günter's, his own.'

'Is there no reference to him in any of the files that have been found?'

'Investigators are going through them now. Dr Friedemann's file has been found. He was working for the Stasi. So was the director of the clinic. In several files, there are references to an unofficial collaborator among the dissidents code-named Chameleon. It is possible that this is Stefan.'

'But . . . has no one exposed him?'

'There is no proof.'

'Surely the West Germans suspect?'

'I am sure. But they are in a difficult position. Stefi is an elected member of the regional assembly. He is a leader of the New Grouping upon which the Christian Democrat government depends. There is also a growing resentment among the East Germans against the highhanded behaviour of the officials from Bonn. And a feeling, which I share, that it is best for us all to forgive and forget.'

'To forgive? After what you went through? Can you bring yourself to do that?'

'Me? No. But for God, nothing is impossible. I love my children. I must think of their future, not my past.'

'But a future with a Stasi spy as their stepfather, and a minister in the regional government?'

'As a stepfather, he has not done badly, and as a minister of culture he can do no harm.'

EIGHTEEN

Francesca drove back to Berlin with her mind in some confusion. Could what Paul had said be true? Or was he creating a myth in his mind to explain Sophie's leaving him for Stefan? Paul himself had said that he had no proof, yet the more Francesca thought about Stefan Diederich, the more plausible Paul's story became. There had always been something shifty about Stefi and Sophie was as gullible as a goose.

Before she had left Bechtling, Paul had asked Francesca not to tell Sophie what he had said. It would only make her unhappy and destroy the stability of his children's home.

'But you,' Francesca had said. 'How can you bear to see them flourishing in that way?'

'God rewards us for our suffering,' said Paul, 'in a way it is sometimes difficult for others to understand.'

Francesca was not a Christian, but she could see that from a Christian perspective it might jeopardize Paul's terminal bonus in the next world if he was now to seek revenge. However, she had to consider the implications of what she had learned for the here and now. If both Stefan Diederich and Günter Westarp had been unofficial collaborators for the Stasi, what bearing had this on their decision to put on a major exhibition of Russian experimental art? Francesca remembered her first meeting with Stefi nine months before when he had talked with such enthusiasm about the cultural rehabilitation of Eastern Europe after almost half a century of Communist rule. Had it been bogus or sincere?

When Francesca had put the question to Paul Meissner, he had come up with no satisfactory answer. Perhaps Stefi had had a genuine change of heart and wished to atone for his past wrongdoing. Or perhaps he had thought an exhibition like Excursus would help cover his tracks. It seemed to Francesca, as she drove through Neuruppin, that there must be more to it than that. Paul's judgement was distorted by compassion. She needed the advice of someone she could trust. But who was there? Only Andrei, and he was in Moscow. Francesca cursed herself for not getting a telephone number from him before he left.

There remained Sophie. Whatever doubts she might have had about Stefi, Francesca was convinced that Sophie was straight. She was naive, and perhaps had cultivated her naiveté to avoid resolving painful contradictions or facing up to disagreeable truths; but if she knew more than she let on, it would be more than she let on to herself. She had to talk to Sophie and, remembering that Stefi had flown to Bonn, Francesca decided to look in on the flat in the Wedekindstrasse on her way home.

When she saw Francesca at her door, Sophie kissed her without embracing her because her hands were covered with flour. 'I'm making pastry,' she said, leading Francesca into the kitchen where her two children were eating their supper. 'I always cook when Stefi's away so that I can spend more time with him when he returns.'

Once the children left the table, Francesca helped Sophie clear up. Then Sophie opened a bottle of wine and, while filling two glasses, asked Francesca how she had spent her day. For a moment Francesca hesitated, then she told Sophie that she had been to see Paul.

Sophie turned to Francesca. 'Paul . . .' she repeated in an almost reproachful tone of voice. 'How was poor Paul?'

255

'He was . . . fine. I mean, as well as can be expected.'

'You should have told me that you were going to see him.'

'I went on impulse, and anyway, I thought that you wouldn't want me to go.'

Sophie said nothing.

'But I had to go, Sophie. He was also my friend, after all, and once we start hanging there just won't be time.'

'What did he say?' she asked.

'Nothing special.'

'About me . . .?' Her brow wrinkled as if she was preparing herself to rebut some terrible slur.

'He was very nice about you, Sophie. He seemed to me to be extraordinarily . . . understanding.'

'Yes.' She said this as if it was not necessarily a good thing to be.

'He is a good man,' said Francesca.

'Yes, but he is not the only good man.'

'Of course not.'

'Stefi is a good man, too.'

'I dare say.'

Sophie's face went a shade pinker. 'He thinks of others, does kindnesses that no one knows. He got Günter his job . . .'

'I know.'

'And he insisted that you should be the one to organize the exhibition when everyone said it should be a German.'

'I appreciate that, Sophie.'

'And only today, before he left, he said that if anyone asked, I was to say that the Excursus exhibition had been your idea.'

'My idea?'

'Yes. Because he is now sure it will be a success and he wants all the credit to go to you.'

Francesca was dumbfounded. She sat, silent and frowning, trying to work out what might be going on in Stefan Diederich's mind. 'Sophie,' she said eventually, 'are you sure . . . are you absolutely sure . . .?' Her voice petered out.

'Yes, I am sure. He is a good man. He was always our friend and when he saw how terrible things were for me, he . . . he . . .'

'He made love to you.'

'Yes.'

'And you let him?'

'Yes.'

'Even though Paul was still your husband?'

Sophie's face was now flushed, either from emotion or from the wine. 'He was not my husband, not really. How could he be my husband or anyone's husband when he was so ill, so depressed?'

'Didn't you ever suspect, Sophie, that it was the Stasi who made him ill?'

Sophie appeared confused. 'Now, yes, because we know that the doctor was an unofficial collaborator, it is possible that they made him worse, but he was always so gloomy and spiritual, worrying about God and Hell, and never any fun . . .' She started to sniff.

'He was serious,' said Francesca, 'but he wasn't always gloomy.'

'Stefi was fun.'

'Yes, but . . .' It was too late to turn back. 'Paul told me that what finally broke him – what pushed him over the edge – was coming back from the clinic to find you in bed with Stefi.'

Sophie looked stunned. 'That is a lie,' she said, her sniffs turning to sobs.

'Paul said that he was brought back by Günter just at the moment . . .'

'Oh God, oh God,' moaned Sophie. 'That can't be true, it can't. Why do you tell me this? It can't be true.'

'Sophie . . .' Francesca tried to remain composed. 'I am only telling you what Paul told me.'

'He is lying. He must be lying. He is so jealous. He has never forgiven me. He makes up such stories just to punish us . . . And now, you too, you say these terrible things about Stefi who has been so good to you . . .'

Francesca was a little taken aback to find that *she* was the one in the dock. 'I am sorry, Sophie. Perhaps I should have kept quiet. But, well . . .'

'You don't like Stefi. You never did. So now you spread these lies about him . . .'

'It's not that I don't like him, Sophie. It's just that I don't . . .

257

Well, if what Paul said was true, then there would be some serious implications . . .'

'Implications? What do you mean, implications?'

'Well, possibilities.'

'I know what you mean. You think that Stefi worked for the Stasi. Of course. It's so easy to say that, isn't it, because his file is missing so he can never disprove it. Other people say it, I know, behind his back because they are envious because he is a minister and they are nothing, nothing . . . But if Stefi was an IM, then why did he marry me? Was he ordered to do it? Is that what you mean? Are you suggesting that for ten years I have been making love to a man who does not love me? Do you think that a woman cannot tell? I tell you, Francesca, that Stefi has loved me in a way that Paul never did for all his talk about holy matrimony. Paul did not love my body as Stefi loves my body and certainly, *certainly*, he never loved my soul.'

Francesca left the flat on the Wedekindstrasse as soon as she reasonably could, and if she and Sophie did not part enemies, they hardly parted friends. Francesca's disclosures had served no purpose. All they had established was that Sophie still loved Stefi, and that Sophie was still a fool.

All at once, in the dark dusk of East Berlin, Francesca felt frightened and far from home, surrounded by Germans, none of whom she could trust. She wished that Andrei had been in Berlin, if only to tell her that her anxiety was absurd. It was quite possible, after all, that Stefan had had nothing to do with the Stasi; that Paul's suspicions were, as Sophie had suggested, a way of demeaning his rival in his own mind.

But if Stefi *had* worked for the Stasi, why should he want to put on an exhibition of experimental Russian art? And why should he want Sophie to say that it had been Francesca's idea? Sophie assumed that it was to give her friend all the credit, but if anything went wrong she would also be there to take the blame.

The realization that she had been instrumental in bringing such an unique collection to Berlin at Stefi's instigation filled Francesca with unease. Many of the world's finest modern paintings were now sitting in the warehouse in Tegel. Who had recommended the warehouse to the committee? She had, at Günter's suggestion. She had checked the security; it had seemed superb, but she had known nothing about the company that owned it, or about the staff that were employed to guard the works of art. Who reassured them about Omni Zartfracht? She could not remember. Either one of Stefi's officials or Günter Westarp who, according to Paul, had also collaborated with the Stasi.

The brighter street lights and shop windows told Francesca that she was now in West Berlin. She was still making for her flat in the Hansa Quarter, but she now realized that she could not possibly just go home. She must pass on her anxieties, but to whom? The police? The American consul? What could she tell them? That she did not trust the provincial Minister of Culture? They would think she was crazy.

Andrei was the only person who would listen without laughing and then either reassure her or know exactly what should be done. But without Andrei she had to do something herself, and the only thing she could think of was to drive on to Tegel and make sure that the paintings were safe. She was well enough known by the Omni Zartfracht people; she could say that she had come to make some last minute checks before the hanging started the next day.

She drove down the Hardenbergstrasse, joined the Stadtring at Charlottenburg and a short time later reached Tegel. It was now dark, and outside the centre of the city there were few lamps and no shop windows to light up the streets. Francesca was tense and exhausted. She took a wrong turn and lost her way. She had to stop the car, take out her Falkplan and read the street sign to take a bearing. She found where she was and memorized the route to the warehouse. A light blinked on her fuel gauge; she was almost out of gas. She had never been to the warehouse at night and could not see any familiar landmarks in the dark. Then suddenly she saw the line of lights illuminating the fenced perimeter and came at last to the gate.

Francesca stopped her car and got out to ring the buzzer to announce her presence to the guard, but before she pressed it she saw that one of the gates was open. The gap was not wide, perhaps five or six inches, but it was nevertheless odd. She looked down to the warehouse. Its doors were closed. There were no vehicles outside the office, but a light came from the window. She knew that normally at least three security guards were on duty all through the night. She feared they were all drinking coffee or playing cards.

She pressed the buzzer and waited. There was no answer. She tried again. There was still no answer. She went back to her car, switched off the motor, then walked through the open gate and down the fifty yard tarmac drive to the office door. She knocked, waited and heard nothing. She turned the handle. The door opened. She went in.

The lights were on in the anteroom but there was no one there. Francesca shouted 'hello'. There was no answer. She went through to the office. Here too the lights were on but the room was empty. Assuming that the guards were doing their rounds in the warehouse itself, Francesca went through to the space where the paintings were kept. This was in darkness but she knew where to find the switches and turned on the lights.

It was empty. The works of art had gone. Francesca fell back, trembling, only saving herself from falling by taking hold of the edge of the table upon which the paintings had been examined after being unpacked. Her first thought was that they had been stolen; her second, that this was impossible, that they had been taken in advance to the museums or perhaps moved to a different area of the warehouse. She recovered enough to stand without the support of the table. She walked forward towards the racks at the back of the warehouse. It was dark. She did not know where to find the switches for the lights. She peered into the gloom. Slowly, her eyes adjusted to the poor light. She could see back to the bare wall. There was nothing. The warehouse was empty. All the pictures and sculptures had gone.

She was about to turn away and run to the office when her eyes made out the face of a man standing in the shadow of one of the racks. He was so still that for a moment she thought he must be a statue or a tailor's dummy. But the eyes moved; they were watching her, like those of a lizard waiting for the best moment to seize and swallow its prey. As she stepped back, he came forward and she recognized the dark features of the man who had been with Andrei when he was sick.

Her first impulse was to turn and run; her second, to behave as if nothing unusual had happened. 'Hi,' she said. 'Aren't you Andrei's friend?'

He said nothing and Francesca remembered Andrei saying that he spoke little of anything but Chechen and Russian.

'The paintings,' she said, gesturing towards the empty spaces. 'They seem to be gone.'

Again he did not answer, but pointed towards the entrance to the office.

Francesca turned and walked as he had instructed. He followed close behind. They went into the empty office. 'Is Andrei around?' she asked.

He pointed to a chair. 'Sit,' he said in English.

Francesca glanced towards the telephone but thought it prudent, while his eyes were on her, to sit down. The Chechen moved behind her. She thought it would suggest alarm and therefore suspicion if she looked to see what he was doing. She heard a crack, and the light dimmed. She turned to see him approaching with flex from a lamp. She leaped to her feet and ran towards the door, but he was there before she was. She backed away. He came forward, no words coming from his mouth and no expression on his face. She came up against a desk and looked towards the window but before she could move further he was upon her. He grabbed her and turned her savagely to face away from him, her arm behind her back.

She felt the wire encircle her wrist. She struck out with her free hand but could not reach him. A moment later, he took hold of that hand too, pulled her back to the chair and pushed her down. She was forced to lean forward as he lifted her arms over the back of the chair and secured them. Then, with a second strand of flex, he bound her ankles to the feet of the chair.

She shrieked for help. He stood and slapped her face. She closed her eyes and was silent; when she opened them again, he had gone. She turned her head as best she could to see if he was standing behind her, then, sensing that she was alone in the office, shouted again. He came back through the door from the warehouse, sauntered across to where she was sitting and slapped her again. In his hand was a reel of packaging tape which he now stuck over her mouth and wound around her face.

Francesca sat, half suffocating as she inhaled air through her narrow nostrils. The Chechen sauntered back to lean his body against a desk and light a cigarette. He watched her. She became calmer and breathed more easily. Slowly, rational thoughts supplanted instinctive terror. If this was Andrei's friend, then perhaps Andrei would appear. But time passed and Andrei did not appear, and all the while the Chechen watched her, his body propped against the desk, smoking untipped cigarettes. His eyes still had no expression, but their glance had a direction, studying her neck and her breasts and her legs. She felt fear and then, oddly, a certain shame, as if she had somehow invited his lingering looks.

She heard a car. So did the Chechen. He looked towards the door and at the same time took out a gun. They heard the catch of the entrance to the anteroom. He held the gun ready. The inner door opened. Francesca turned her head and saw Andrei. She started to cry. Tears ran down her cheeks as she waited for him to cut her loose and take her in his arms.

Andrei Serotkin glanced at the Chechen, then at Francesca. Neither man spoke. The Chechen's arm went down but he did not put away his gun. The two men started talking in Russian, words Francesca could only half understand. The Chechen seemed angry, Andrei uneasy. At one point, with an unpleasant leer, the Chechen took the lit cigarette from his mouth with his left hand and offered it to Andrei. Andrei frowned, looked at his watch and shook his head. His right hand went to the inner pocket of his jacket. For a moment Francesca thought that he was going to take out a gun. Instead, he removed a small black case. He turned his back to Francesca, put the case on the desk. When she could see his hands again, one was holding a syringe.

He crossed to where she sat and looked down into her imploring eyes. 'This will send you to sleep,' he said in English, his tone indifferent.

She shook her head and tried to speak. He held the syringe up to the light to make sure no air was left in the needle. 'I am sorry it had to come to this,' he said quietly, 'but as I tried to explain a number of times, no individual can be allowed to frustrate the destiny of a nation.' He moved behind her. 'Don't you remember? That afternoon in front of the memorial . . .' She felt a sharp pain in the muscle of her neck and at once began to feel drowsy. 'If you remember, you will understand why things have to end in this way.' He came round to face her once again and looked down into her eyes. '*Truth is remembering*' he whispered. '*He who has no memory has no life.*' Her muscles grew weak. Her head slumped forward; her eyelids closed. '*Truth is remembering. . .*' She felt his hand raise her chin. With a great effort she opened her eyes and looked into his. It seemed, in Francesca's last moment of consciousness, that Andrei Serotkin smiled.

NINETEEN

Inspector Kessler, because he ate too much on a Sunday, always felt dyspeptic and therefore irritable on a Monday morning. His mood was made worse on the morning of Monday, 21 June by the report he found on his desk from the Leipzig police describing their failure to trace the movements of the Russian, Gerasimov, whenever he left his hotel. It read as if they were proud that one of their former masters could outwit them with such ease. It was particularly humiliating for Kessler because a second report from the BfV passed on by Grohmann described succinctly every move Gerasimov had made from the visit to Bedauer, the Volkswagen dealer, to his dinner in Auerbach's Cellar with the private detective Manfred Kraus, formerly *Generaloberst* Franz Riesler of the state security in the DDR.

Clearly, Gerasimov was not a policeman: they had realized that from the start. It was natural enough that he would use old contacts in the Stasi. But what was the relevance of Riesler? Why had he bought the Volkswagen van two weeks before the murder of the Maslyukovs? If the KGB had been responsible, why would Gerasimov need to find this out? Even the BfV had been unable to eavesdrop on the two men's conversation in Auerbach's Cellar, but the secretary had overheard what had been said at the office. From this, it appeared that Gerasimov was less interested in the murderer of the Maslyukovs than in the barter of a Volkswagen van for a consignment of shoes! Certainly Grohmann had drawn this conclusion, appending an acid note to the report to the effect that in his view Gerasimov was not an undercover agent but an undercover blackmarketeer.

Kessler looked at his watch. A meeting was scheduled with Grohmann and Gerasimov at ten. It was in the BfV report that Gerasimov on his return to Leipzig had gone straight to the Soviet consulate on Unter den Linden. If he did not come up with anything interesting that morning, Kessler would suggest that the time had come for him to return to Moscow.

Kessler left his office to go down the corridor to get a plastic cup of coffee from the machine. He usually waited until mid-morning, but it was a Monday, and he would need his wits about him to deal with Grohmann as much as Gerasimov.

Dorn passed him in the corridor. 'Know anything about those paintings, chief?'

'What paintings?'

'You know. The big exhibition of Russian rubbish they got planned.'

'I saw something about it.'

'Apparently, they're lost.'

Kessler went back into his office. He looked through the report once again. Could it be that Gerasimov himself was part of the group within the KGB that was involved in the import and export of both icons and shoes? In which case, Gerasimov had probably been sent to do what he could to obstruct them. And they were paying his expenses!

A junior officer, a girl, looked through the door of Kessler's office. 'Did you get the message?'

'What message?'

'They called while you were getting coffee. You're wanted urgently upstairs.'

Kessler glanced at his watch. 'If Herr Grohmann and the Russian turn up, ask them to wait.'

'Understood.'

Kessler swallowed what remained of his coffee, went back down the corridor and up a single flight of stairs to the office of Berlin's chief of the criminal police, Kommissar Edgar Rohrbeck. From the look on his superior's ashen face, Kessler assumed that he too suffered from dyspepsia on a Monday morning. Then he saw that three of his senior colleagues had been called in and he realized that something serious must be going on.

'Gentlemen,' said the Kommissar. 'We have had a call from the New German Foundation to say that the paintings for the Excursus exhibition have disappeared.'

There was a baffled silence from the assembled officers. 'Disappeared from where?' asked Kessler.

'The exhibition is due to open in two weeks' time. The hanging of the paintings was due to start today. In the meantime, the paintings and sculptures had been stored in a new warehouse at Tegel belonging to Omni Zartfracht. Omni Zartfracht were due to start delivering the paintings to the galleries at eight o'clock this morning. When they failed to arrive, the organizers called OZF. There was no reply. Two of the organizers drove to Tegel to see what had gone wrong. They found the warehouse deserted, the paintings gone.'

'It must be a joke,' said one of Kessler's colleagues, Inspector Allerding.

'Or they've just been taken to the wrong location,' said another, Inspector Hasenclever.

'Or they're stuck in the traffic,' said Kessler.

'Unfortunately,' said the Kommissar, 'none of these hypotheses can be true. There was never any intention to move all the works of art in a single day. Moreover, several vans were seen on Sunday at the OZF warehouse. None of these vans is there today.'

'Isn't there an office for OZF?'

'The telephone does not answer. Officers have been sent to investigate.'

'But they can hardly have been stolen,' said Allerding.

'I fear we must work on that assumption,' said the Kommissar, Rohrbeck.

'But you can't fence world-famous paintings like that.'

'No. But you can threaten to destroy them.'

'Are they insured?'

'They are covered by an indemnity by the Federal government.'

'For how much?'

'I don't know, precisely. But their total value may be as much as a billion marks.'

The four officers looked stunned.

'But no government would pay a ransom,' said Hasenclever.

'That remains to be seen,' said Kommissar Rohrbeck. 'Our job is to make sure that it does not have to make that choice. I want you all to drop what you're doing until we find the paintings. I shall take overall command.' He turned to Kessler. 'What are you working on?'

'The Maslyukov case.'

'Drop it. You've wasted too much time on that already. Get out to Tegel. There were over three hundred works of art. They cannot have disappeared without trace.'

Kessler ran down to his office, two steps at a time. Grohmann was waiting. 'Listen,' said Kessler, 'there's been some gigantic heist, so the Maslyukov case will have to wait.'

'But Gerasimov is coming.'

'Do me a favour. Deal with him.'

Grohmann frowned. 'I can't do that. This is a police matter, not a question of national security.'

'He went to see a *Generaloberst* from the Stasi. That puts it on your plate.'

Grohmann hesitated. 'I shall have to take advice.' He turned to go but, just as he did so, Dorn ushered Gerasimov into Kessler's office.

Gerasimov had a look of great self-importance, like a magician about to produce a white rabbit from under his hat. 'Good morning, gentlemen,' he said.

Kessler looked past Gerasimov to Dorn. 'Are you ready to move?'

Dorn looked surprised. 'When you are.'

Kessler turned back to Gerasimov. 'I'm afraid something has

come up. My boss has taken me off the case. Temporarily, I hope. Herr Grohmann will explain . . .'

Grohmann gave an exasperated splutter. 'This is impossible!'

'But I have the names,' said Gerasimov. 'The names and passport numbers of Ivan the Terrible.'

'Good, good,' said Kessler. 'Give them to Herr Grohmann.' And, after shaking the Russian by the hand, he pushed past him and out through the door.

Dorn switched on the siren as he weaved through the traffic round the Innsbruckerplatz, up the Stadtring and then the Schumacher-damm to Tegel. They were at the Omni Zartfracht warehouse only fifteen minutes after leaving police headquarters. Four patrol cars were already there, their lights still flashing. The large doors to the warehouse were closed. Two uniformed policemen stood guard. Inside, in an anteroom, three others waited, their bulky leather jackets cramming the small space.

'Outside,' said Kessler.

He went through to the inner office to find a uniformed sergeant and three men. Kessler knew the sergeant. 'Who are these?' he asked.

'The art people,' said the sergeant.

'Günter Westarp,' said the first, an older, bedraggled figure, from his appearance clearly an Ossie.

'Julius Breitenbach,' said a younger man. He looked not only pale, but likely to vomit at any moment.

'Dr Kemmelkampf, from the Ministry of Culture,' said a third, a tall, thin-faced figure, like a schoolteacher, the eldest of the three.

'Who was first on the scene?' asked Kessler.

The young man raised his hand. 'I came here with Herr Westarp from the New National Gallery. We were expecting the works of art . . . we telephoned . . .'

'How did you get in?'

'The gate was closed but not locked.'

'The office.'

'The same.'

'There was no one here?'

'No.'

'How did you discover that the paintings had gone?'

'We looked,' said Günter Westarp. 'We had been here many times before. You see, they had to be sorted and arranged so that they could be moved out quickly when the moment came . . .'

'Quickly, yes,' said Kessler with some sarcasm. He turned to Dr Kemmelkampf. 'Have you been in touch with the company?'

'Yes, that is to say, they have only a small office here in Berlin.'

'And?'

'Apparently, it is closed. We are trying now to make contact with the head office in Zürich.'

'Looks like a long firm,' said Dorn.

'Please?' asked Dr Kemmelkampf.

'A phantom company,' said Kessler.

'Impossible,' said Dr Kemmelkampf.

'You chose the company?'

'Yes. That is, the ministry . . .'

'You *knew* the company?'

'This warehouse was newly constructed, purpose-built. We were most fortunate in that . . . The large number of works of art . . . There was nowhere else suitable . . .'

'Was the company known to you?'

'Known? Well, not personally, because that was not the responsibility of my department.'

'Who chose it?'

'Who? I am not sure. I would have to look at my papers. But certainly, the ministry endorsed it. We all thought . . . it seemed so convenient. Everything was so rushed, you understand . . .'

Kessler looked around the office. It was unusually tidy: nothing seemed out of place. He turned to the sergeant. 'Has anything been touched?'

'Nothing. Except the letter.'

'What letter.'

Günter Westarp stepped forward. 'There was a letter, on the desk, addressed to me.'

'You opened it?'

'Yes. I thought . . .'

'What did it say?'

'It was a business letter, saying that we would be told how we could recover the paintings.'

'Signed?'

'Raskolnikov.'

'Code name,' said Dorn, 'so when we get the ransom demand, we'll know it's for real.'

'Do you know anyone called Raskolnikov?' Kessler asked Günter Westarp.

Westarp shook his head. 'No.'

'It's the name of the hero in a novel by Dostoyevsky,' said Julius Breitenbach.

'Which novel?' asked Kessler.

'*Crime and Punishment.*'

'So our thief has a sense of humour,' said Kessler, reading the letter typed on a plain sheet of white paper.

> Dear Dr Westarp. In respect to the paintings we have removed from the warehouse, kindly await instructions as to how they might be returned.

The name 'R. R. Raskolnikov' had also been typed, not written. He turned to Dorn. 'Check it for prints.'

'Some hope.'

Kessler again looked round the office. Dorn was right. He could tell at a glance that it had been wiped clean. He opened a filing cabinet. The waybills were neatly placed in their files. They were unlikely to give any clues as to where the works of art had gone. Their best hope was for some tip-off from the underworld, but the complexity and the audacity of this heist – the planning and the money that must have been required to set it up – made it unlikely that it was the work of ordinary thieves.

'Chief . . .' Dorn called Kessler from across the room. Kessler went to join him. 'Something odd here. Two lamps with no flex . . .' He pointed to where they lay on the floor.

'Why odd?'

'Well, when everything else is so orderly . . .'

Kessler turned back to the civil servant. 'Dr Kemmelkampf. I would be grateful if you would return to your ministry and assemble all those who had anything to do with this exhibition.'

'Certainly, except . . .'

'What?'

'The minister is in Bonn. I dare say he will return when he hears. It was a project in which he took a personal interest.'

'Then we shall have to wait until he comes back, but in the meantime, I should like to talk to anyone else involved.' He turned to Günter Westarp and Julius Breitenbach. 'I would like you to do the same. Return to your office in the New National Gallery.'

'It is at the New German Foundation on the Schöneberger Ufer.'

'Go to the Schöneberger Ufer, then. Assemble your staff, the entire staff. Everyone who has had anything to do with the Excursus exhibition. I shall be along later in the morning to question them.'

'There is one problem,' said Günter Westarp.

'Yes?'

'The Russian member of our staff, Dr Serotkin, is absent. He is in Moscow. And we have been unable to locate another, Dr McDermott.'

'Who is he?'

'A woman. An American. She was expected at the New National Gallery but did not turn up. We telephoned her flat but there was no reply.'

Kessler turned to Dorn. 'Call headquarters. Ask them to try and locate this Dr McDermott. And tell them that the fingerprint boys can move in. Not that I expect they'll find much. Whoever is behind this certainly knew what they were doing.'

On his own territory in the Prussian Ministry of Culture, Dr Kemmelkampf had regained his incisive, bureaucratic manner. He showed Kessler and Dorn into his office before going into the conference room where four other officials were waiting. 'We have informed the minister,' he said. 'He has cancelled all his appointments in Bonn and is returning at once to Berlin. He suggests that the matter should be kept out of the news for as long as possible. The Federal ministry feels the same. If the lenders become aware that their works have disappeared, it will do incalculable damage to our cultural relations with other nations. Excursus had the personal endorsement of the Federal Chancellor. It was to have been opened by President von Weizsäcker himself. Everything has to be done to ensure that the paintings are recovered before it becomes known that they have been stolen.'

'I don't control the press,' said Kessler. 'And we were not asked to ensure the security of the paintings.'

'Of course.'

'The thieves have a twelve-hour start. The works could be anywhere in Germany. They may even have left Germany. Checks are being made on the frontiers but, as you know, controls over EC borders are now loose.'

'I understand.'

'The most likely way of recovering the paintings is by finding out who stole them, either from a tip-off or by investigation. Our job is the investigation. Technical experts are examining the warehouse but, to be honest, I don't expect them to find many clues. In my experience, cases that involve fraudulent companies have one thing in common: someone on the inside who puts the business their way. So our best bet is to follow the trail back from the owners of OZF.'

Kemmelkampf looked uncomfortable. 'My colleague, Dr Giesenfels, has tried to contact their head office in Zürich, but apparently . . .' His voice tailed off. 'He had better speak to you himself. Come . . .'

The three men passed through to a conference room where three other civil servants sat at a table, as if waiting for the start of a departmental meeting.

Prompted by his chief, Dr Giesenfels, a small, bald, bespectacled man, delivered his report in a high-pitched voice. 'We have had considerable correspondence with Omni Zartfracht,' he began, peering into a folder open on the table in front of him. 'The invoices were always sent by the Berlin office and were paid into an account at the Berliner Bank. We also had correspondence with their head office in Zürich, and many calls. But this morning, there was no reply from the Zürich number. I talked to the management of the building, and I was told that no one had come to the office this morning.'

Kessler shook his head, an outward sign of his incredulity. 'If I may say so, gentlemen, it seems incredible to me that you should entrust paintings of such value to an unknown company.'

'Unknown?' said Kemmelkampf. 'It was new but it was not unknown.'

'Whose idea was it,' asked Kessler, 'that OZF should be employed to store the works of art?'

'Yes, well . . .' Dr Giesenfels looked down at his file. 'You must understand, Herr Inspector, that because of political considerations, the exhibition had to be organized in a very short period of time. Normally, an exhibition of this size would take three, four, even five years from start to finish. Excursus had to be arranged in less than one. The galleries had already made arrangements for the summer. We had to cancel three exhibitions, and curtail six others. This left a minimum amount of time for the hanging of the exhibitions, and of course storing so many paintings was also a problem, so it was suggested that they be assembled at an outside location . . .'

'Suggested by whom?'

'I am not sure. By Dr Westarp, I believe.'

'And who chose OZF?'

'Again, I cannot be sure. But a preliminary examination of the minutes of the Excursus committee indicate that the recommendation of OZF came from Dr McDermott.'

As they drove from the offices of the Prussian Ministry of Culture to the Schöneberger Ufer, Kessler and Dorn heard from headquarters that the Swiss police had been to the OZF headquarters in Zürich. It was a single room with a telephone and was now empty. They were looking at the register of companies and at OZF's bank accounts and would report back as soon as they had any useful information.

'They'll find nothing,' said Dorn. 'False names, false documents, numbered bank accounts.'

At the Excursus office, the exhibition organizers were waiting in the conference room for the arrival of the police. It was quite clear to Kessler that some of them were in a state of shock. The two secretaries had been weeping and, at the sight of the

273

detectives, both burst into tears once again. The young man, Breitenbach, still looked nauseous, Westarp like a dog that has been whipped and fears it is about to be whipped again. An older woman, introduced as Frau Dr Koch, had her face set rigid in an expression of self-righteous indignation, as if the world had finally reached the sad state she had so often predicted.

At Kessler's suggestion – their sobs and sniffs were distracting – the two secretaries were sent back to their desks. The four who remained then sat down with the two detectives – Kessler taking the chair at the head of the table.

'Is this the entire staff of the Excursus exhibition?' Kessler asked Westarp.

'Yes. Apart from the Minister, Dr Serotkin and Dr McDermott.'

'Still no word from Dr McDermott?'

'No.'

'The Minister is on his way back from Bonn?'

'Yes.'

'And Serotkin is in Moscow?'

'Yes.'

'When did he leave?'

'Four days ago.'

'Why did he leave?'

'For personal reasons,' said Westarp.

'Do you know what these were?' asked Kessler.

'His father had suffered a stroke.'

'And when is he due to return?'

'It is hoped for the opening on the sixth of July.'

'I should like you to tell us, from the beginning, of your contacts with the freight and storage company, Omni Zartfracht,' said Kessler.

'Of course,' said Westarp. 'You see, we were faced with a difficult situation because of pre-existing schedules in the different museums . . .'

'That I know. But why OZF?'

'They offered us just the facilities we wanted – an air-conditioned, climatically controlled warehouse near Tegel, custom-made to handle works of art.'

'Who suggested OZF?'

'I can't remember. I imagine it was the ministry.'

'Dr Kemmelkampf has told us that it was first mentioned here.'

Westarp looked confused. 'Here?'

'At a meeting of the organizing committee, by Dr McDermott.'

'That is possible,' said Günter Westarp. 'I cannot remember who first made the suggestion.'

'You will appreciate,' said Kessler dryly, 'that it is a matter of some importance.'

'Yes, of course. But it was some months ago.'

'For your information, it now seems that Omni Zartfracht was a bogus company set up simply for the theft of the paintings.'

The four around the table were silent. Then Frau Dr Koch suddenly blurted out: 'It's too valuable.'

'I beg your pardon?' said Kessler.

'Art. It is now too valuable. Too expensive. People no longer think of it in terms of the spirit, only in terms of cash.'

'But they cannot sell the paintings,' said Julius Breitenbach. 'They are too well known.'

'It is more likely that they will demand a ransom,' said Kessler.

'And if the ransom is not paid?'

'Destroy the paintings.'

'I cannot believe that,' said Julius Breitenbach. 'In that warehouse were all the best Kandinskys, the best Chagalls, the best Maleviches, El Lissitzkys, Gabos, Pevsners – all that exists in the world of modern Russian art in the twentieth century. It would not be a criminal but a madman who would bring himself to do that.'

Gertie, one of the secretaries, came into the room to say there there was a call for Inspector Kessler from police headquarters. Kessler nodded to Dorn to take it.

'Which of you here,' asked Kessler, 'had contacts with the staff of OZF?'

'The ministry dealt with the contractual side,' said Günter Westarp. 'I talked from time to time with the director of the Berlin office. We all went down to the warehouse from time to time to examine the works of art before we signed for them.'

'Who did you deal with?'

'The warehouse director, Herr Taub.'

'And the younger one, Mishi,' said Julius Breitenbach.

'They were very tight on security,' said Westarp. 'Do you remember the first time? They wouldn't let us in.'

'Were they Germans?' asked Kessler.

'Yes.'

'East or West?'

'Ossies.'

'Accents?'

'Saxon, I would say.'

'Leipzig?'

Breitenbach shrugged. 'Somewhere down there.'

Kessler turned to Westarp. 'What would you say?'

'About what?'

'The accents?'

Westarp looked confused. 'They were, yes, Saxon perhaps. From Halle, perhaps, or Leipzig. But they were not all the same.'

'How many were there?'

'It varied. Half a dozen or so.'

'Would you recognize them again?'

'Taub, certainly.'

'And Mishi,' said Julius Breitenbach. 'I had quite a few chats with him.'

'Can you think of anything unusual about them?'

Günter Westarp shook his head. 'No.'

'They were very good at their job,' said Frau Dr Koch. 'Very efficient.'

'Disciplined,' said Julius Breitenbach. 'Taub gave an order and it was done.'

'They really did not seem like criminals,' said Frau Dr Koch. 'Those that I saw were so young, and so earnest.'

'I agree,' said Westarp.

Dorn came back into the conference room and handed a note to Kessler. Kessler glanced at it, then looked up. 'I am afraid appearances can be deceptive. A call to the Chancellery in Bonn from Raskolnikov has said that all the paintings will be destroyed at midnight tonight unless a ransom is paid of one hundred million dollars.'

Back at police headquarters on the Gothaerstrasse, Kessler was called into conference by Kommissar Rohrbeck together with the two other inspectors, Allerding and Hasenclever. Kessler reported on what he had found at Tegel, and on his preliminary interrogation of the ministry and Excursus staff.

'Any leads?' asked Rohrbeck.

'Not to speak of. From the description of the OZF people, it's possible that some may have come from the Leipzig area. But that's little more than a hunch.'

'We've alerted the police of the different *Länder*,' said Allerding, 'as well as Interpol and the French, Swiss, Italian and Austrian police. There are several reports of vans leaving Berlin on Sunday night, but they come from all different exits to the city. None report a convoy. But we have strict instructions not to say what's been stolen. If Bonn decide to pay, they don't want it known in advance.'

'But it'll leak out,' said Kessler.

'It won't matter, after the event. But no one wants to argue about it beforehand. If it's got to be done, it's got to be done.'

'What about the American?' asked Kessler.

'We've searched her flat, checked airline departures and her picture's been circulated to our men on the street. No sign of her as yet.'

'The FBI?'

'Bonn doesn't want them to know what's going on.'

'What about the Ministry of Culture?'

'We've run the names of the civil servants and the Excursus staff through the database,' said Hasenclever, 'and we're keeping them all under surveillance. We're now working on the staff of the New German Foundation. The database hasn't told us much. The Minister, several of the civil servants, and that man Westarp, are Ossies so we don't have their records. The young man, Breitenbach, was a student activist, and got pulled in on a number of demonstrations, but there's no suspicion of any links with the Red Brigades, and he seems to have been quiet for the last five

277

years. The Russian, Serotkin, was the witness in an attempted rape in the Englischergarten three months ago. He dealt with three Turks who had attacked his American colleague Dr McDermott. And that's about it.'

'I've had the Chancellor's office on the telephone,' said Rohrbeck. 'It has been decided that it is pre-eminently in the national interest to get those paintings back.'

'Then they'd better pay,' said Kessler.

'A hundred million dollars?' said Allerding.

'The indemnity will cost them more.'

'But the precedent,' said Hasenclever.

'Of course,' said Rohrbeck. 'The Chancellor's office is mindful of that. But against the precedent you have to balance not just the cost of the indemnity, but the dreadful damage to Germany's reputation that would result from the destruction of a unique collection of this kind. Our relations with both Russia and the United States would be seriously affected, not to mention the nations of the other lenders. Thus, the decision has been taken to pay the ransom if this is thought to be the only way to get the paintings back. The deadline is midnight tonight.'

Back in his office, Kessler received a call from Inspector Noske, the officer in charge of the fingerprint team. As Kessler had suspected, everything was clean. 'Incredible discipline,' said Noske, 'incredible. They seem to have worn gloves the whole time, or wiped everything down before they left. And methodical. The way the waybills were filed, cross-referenced . . . Why take so much trouble with things you're going to nick?'

Method. Efficiency. Discipline. None of this sounded to Kessler like the work of even the most experienced thieves.

'What about those lamps without their flex?' he asked Noske.

'Someone just ripped it off but we haven't found it and there are no prints.'

'Is there *nothing* else unusual?'

'The only odd thing we've found,' said Noske, 'since they were otherwise so tidy, were some cigarette butts on the floor by one of the desks. Dark tobacco. Untipped cigarettes.'

★

As he replaced the telephone on its cradle, Kessler's eye fell on his open diary and the entry: '10.00 Gerasimov'. A pang of remorse made him call Grohmann.

'Grohmann?'

Silence.

'It's Kessler. I'm sorry.'

A further sulky silence. Then: 'I understand. I heard about the paintings. But don't expect me to take on this case for you. We are not the criminal police.'

'I know. It can wait.'

'Never again do I want to see Gerasimov.'

'Did you talk to him?'

'Briefly.'

'And?'

'He was angry at being stood up.'

'Understandably.'

'He said he had made a major breakthrough. He had the names being used by this Ivan the Terrible – names and passport numbers. Apparently, he speaks five languages fluently and is a master of disguise.'

Kessler laughed. 'He learned this while bartering for shoes in Leipzig?'

'Or he was given the names over the phone from Moscow. I've left the list on your desk.'

'What do we do with him now?'

'That's your affair.'

'Send him back to Moscow . . .'

'Or give him more money to spend on whores. But not BfV money. It has nothing to do with intelligence. I lent a hand and was left holding the baby. Now I'm off the case. It's over. *Schluss. Fertig.* Goodbye.'

Grohmann slammed down the telephone; Kessler replaced his more gently on its receiver.

'Grohmann?' asked Dorn.

'Yes.'

'Pissed off?'

'Yes. He's had enough of our Russian friend.'

'I don't blame him.'

279

'Apparently he's come up with some names and passport numbers for Ivan the Terrible. The list's in the in-tray.' He nodded down to the shallow wire basket on the right-hand corner of his desk.

The telephone rang. Kessler picked it up.

Dorn leaned forward to take Gerasimov's list out of the in-tray.

Kessler slammed down the telephone. 'Diederich's back. Come on.'

'The list?'

'It'll wait.'

Kessler and Dorn were met by Dr Kemmelkampf at the door of the office in East Berlin where they had been earlier that day. They were shown straight into the Minister's office. Before Kessler could open his mouth, Stefan Diederich went on the offensive.

'So, gentlemen. This is a fine kettle of fish. I have had calls from the Chancellor's office in Bonn every half hour asking for a progress report, and so far I have not been able to say anything. Tell me, please, what am I to say next time they call?'

Kessler, flabbergasted by this audacious greeting, stuttered and spluttered: 'I . . . we . . . there have been . . . we have . . . investigations, naturally . . . but there are no real leads.'

Stefan Diederich gave a snort of exasperation. 'You must forgive me, Sergeant . . .'

'Inspector,' said Dorn.

'Inspector. I'm so sorry. You will forgive me if I express a certain disillusion. As you know, I was until recently a citizen of the German Democratic Republic. There were many unpleasant aspects to life in that totalitarian state, but it would have been inconceivable for a collection of some of the greatest art the world has ever produced to simply disappear overnight . . .'

'Herr Minister . . .' Kessler began.

'I am sorry. I realize that you are not the one to whom I should address my complaint. You are merely a humble inspector, and you?' He turned to Dorn.

'Detective sergeant.'

'Detective sergeant. Excellent. Well, neither a detective

280

sergeant nor even an inspector can be held responsible for the abysmal failure of the Berlin police to protect a unique collection of this kind. However, you are here, as I understand it, to clear up the mess . . .'

'To investigate . . .'

'Yes. To investigate and, I hope, to find – because if the paintings are not found, then we are all in the soup, gentlemen: all, from the Chancellor of Germany down to the humblest police inspector and detective sergeant.'

'So far as I know,' said Kessler, 'the Berlin police were never asked to ensure the security of the paintings.'

'Ah,' said Diederich. 'So we have to *ask* for our property to be protected? It is not an automatic right?'

'Of course it is a right,' said Kessler, 'but in particular cases . . .'

'Yes, yes. I understand. And, undoubtedly, an enquiry will discover that since the reunification of Germany, the theoretic unity but actual diversity of administrative powers in the eastern part of Germany can partly be blamed for this fiasco. The very fact that the exhibition was being organized by the government of a former province of East Germany yet had its offices in West Berlin meant that certain areas of competence fell, as it were, between two stools. Actions to be taken by one or other of the different authorities were in fact taken by none. This is an accident of history, and from a historical perspective, the hundred million dollars – if indeed, it is paid – will be added to the total cost of the reunification of our country and, as a percentage of the whole, will be seen to be very small indeed. We have, naturally, already instituted such an enquiry and if any of *my* officials are held to be responsible, then, of course, disciplinary procedures will be taken against them. But this will only be done in some months' time and it is unlikely to placate, say, the Museum of Modern Art in New York or the Musée d'Art Moderne in Paris, not to mention the Tretyakov in Moscow and the Russian Museum in St Petersburg. I tell you, gentlemen, my thinking and that of the Chancellor are at one on this question. The loss or destruction of the works of art is *unthinkable*. Everything must be done to recover them.'

'Certain features have started to emerge,' said Kessler.

'Features? Do you mean clues?'

'Not clues, no. But clearly the robbery was planned over a long period of time.'

'Clearly.'

'The company, Omni Zartfracht, was bogus, set up simply to assemble the paintings.'

'So Kemmelkampf told me. Unbelievable.'

'It is therefore important to know who chose OZF.'

'Not important. Essential.'

'Essential, then.'

'Kemmelkampf has already been through the correspondence and minutes and says that the idea came from the Excursus committee.'

'Yes. Apparently it was suggested by Dr McDermott.'

'Who, I understand, has disappeared.'

'Presumably the ministry checked the company's credentials?'

'Here we may have been remiss,' said Diederich. 'Kemmelkampf left it to a subordinate, Dr Giesenfels, who now tells us that he thought Dr Westarp had taken it in hand. I have to say, Inspector, that this is my responsibility as minister and I would not want to duck it, but for various reasons that I am sure *you* appreciate – the Chancellor's office and the ministry in Bonn are less conscious of local conditions here in Berlin – but for various reasons it was important to give certain posts in the ministry to people from the former DDR who were not only inexperienced when it came to mounting an international exhibition of this magnitude but who, in particular, knew little or nothing about vetting companies with headquarters in Switzerland. As I understand it, the OZF people here in Berlin were efficient and cooperative. They saw no reason to look into the Swiss parent company. I have to say, and this is not meant to be in any way a criticism of Dr McDermott, but my officials were somewhat *dazzled* by this handsome art historian from the United States, and so worked on the assumption that she knew what she was doing when she recommended this company, Omni Zartfracht.'

Kessler nodded. 'What about Dr Serotkin?'

'What about him?'

'He has apparently gone back to Moscow.'

'Yes. His father is ill. He hopes to return for the opening.'

'How did be become involved in the exhibition?'

'It was thought necessary to have a Russian to ensure Soviet cooperation. Many of the works, you understand, were in Russian galleries.'

'Did you choose him?'

'No. We were advised that if you ask for one man, they are certain to send another. And to be blunt, we did not really care who came, so long as he could arrange for the loan of the paintings. We made a request through the usual channels. They sent Serotkin.'

'Did you know him?'

'No. But I know the type, only too well. An apparatchik. He knows very little about modern art.'

'But since the coup . . .'

'At that level of bureaucracy, nothing has changed.'

'Could we get hold of him if required?'

'Of course. Kemmelkampf has the number of the ministry in Moscow.'

'And he became involved *after* you decided to hold the exhibition?'

'Yes.'

'And had nothing to do with the choice of OZF?'

'No.'

Again, Kessler paused. His notebook was open on the table in front of him but the page was blank. 'Can you tell me when it was, precisely, that you decided to put on the exhibition?'

The minister looked embarrassed. 'It was last summer but – this is awkward, but, you will understand, politics is politics – although I have been credited with the idea, and I have not sought to disown that credit, the very germ of the idea was not, in fact, mine.'

'Whose was it, then?'

'Dr Westarp will confirm this, and my wife, that the first mention of a comprehensive, all-embracing exhibition of modern Russian art came at a dinner in our flat last summer from Dr McDermott who was a friend from ten years before, and who in the meantime had made this field her speciality.'

'*She* suggested Excursus?'

'It was a brilliant idea. We jumped at it. Dr Westarp and I. It was just what was needed – politically, culturally, in every way. But things are serious now, so we must keep scrupulously to the truth, and the truth is that Dr McDermott suggested the exhibition with herself as the chief organizer. It was only for that reason, in fact, that we insisted that she be given the job. There were many Germans better qualified but, since it was her idea, it seemed only just.'

It was now past four in the afternoon and the two detectives, who had had no lunch, stopped off on their way back to police headquarters at a stall for a quick *currywurst* and a glass of beer.

'It all points to the American,' said Dorn.

Kessler chewed his sausage without answering.

'Although . . .' Dorn hesitated.

'What?'

'A woman? I mean, I know that these American women are a new breed, but all the same . . .'

'She won't have been on her own. She'd be working for someone else. You need big money to set up a long firm like OZF.'

'Who's behind her, then? The mafia?'

Kessler finished his sausage and wiped the ketchup off his fingers with a paper napkin. 'I don't know. She might have a boyfriend, or she may have been blackmailed. But I'm not entirely convinced it is her. I feel that we're being nudged in that direction.'

'Don't you believe the minister?'

Kessler hesitated. 'Do you?'

'I don't trust any politicians. They always sound false.' Dorn finished his sausage.

'What's curious about Diederich,' said Kessler, turning to go, 'is that he's only been a politician since the fall of the Wall.'

Dorn hesitated. 'I'm still famished, chief. Mind if I buy another?'

'Better bring it back to the office.'

Dorn ordered another *currywurst* and, while it was being prepared and put in a bag, drained his glass of beer.

At five, the three inspectors were called up to report to Kommissar Rohrbeck. 'Time's running out,' said Rohrbeck.

'Still nothing from the frontier police, the state forces or Interpol,' said Allerding.

'The Swiss have come back on the OZF company,' said Kessler. 'Bogus names for the directors. Current account fed from a secret numbered account.'

'Can we freeze it?' asked Allerding.

'It would be a waste of time,' said Rohrbeck. 'Raskolnikov has faxed the numbers of different accounts for the ransom to the Chancellor's office in Bonn, and the OZF account isn't on it.'

'Are those accounts in Zürich?' asked Kessler.

'In Zürich, Luxembourg, Jersey, the Cayman Islands – all over.'

Rohrbeck turned to Hasenclever. 'What about the American, Dr McDermott?'

'We've checked up on her so far as we can,' said Hasenclever, 'without telling the FBI what's going on. She's cleaner than clean. No known criminal connections. They have her flagged only for the year she spent here in Berlin.'

'Her background?' asked Kessler.

'Father a professor of some sort.'

'No Italian family connections?'

Hasenclever shook his head. 'Not that we know of.'

'Why do you ask?' asked Rohrbeck.

'Diederich says that it was Dr McDermott who first came up with the idea of the Excursus exhibition.'

'I thought it was him.'

'He took the credit . . .'

'But doesn't want the blame.'

'He says Westarp and his wife will confirm it. McDermott's also on record as first suggesting the OZF warehouse.'

'We found nothing incriminating in her flat,' said Allerding.

'What about the Russian?' asked Kessler.

'We're trying to locate him,' said Hasenclever. 'No luck so far.'

The Kommissar waved them away. 'I won't keep you. Press on.'

Kessler returned to his office. Dorn was waiting by his desk. 'Did you know that our Dr McDermott was screwing the Russian, Serotkin?' he asked Kessler.

'Where did you hear that?'

'That bloke Breitenbach just called to tell me. Said he thought it might be relevant. They lived in the same block near the Englischergarten. Apparently he spent most nights in her flat.'

Kessler frowned. 'Did they know each other before?'

'Apparently not. It was an office romance or perhaps a pay-off for saving her from the Turks.'

'They never met before they came to Berlin? We're sure of that?'

'According to Breitenbach, no one knew Serotkin. He was just sent here by the Russians. The American initially took a dislike to him. They avoided one another for the first six months.'

'Slow fuse.'

'Or calculation.'

Kessler was seated at his desk, tapping the point of his pencil on his open notebook. Dorn, leaning against the desk itself, took his second *currywurst* out of its bag. 'Do you mind?'

'Go ahead.'

'We've got to find the Yank,' said Dorn with his mouth full. 'She's our only lead.'

'But even if we find her,' said Kessler, 'what evidence have we got against her? The exhibition was her idea? So what? It was a good idea. Even the Federal government thought so. She *suggested* OZF, but she was in no position to insist on it, and she certainly wasn't responsible for checking it out. The thieves planned this thing in such detail it's unlikely that they would build a warehouse on the assumption that the ministry would take up her idea.'

'Sure.' Dorn took another mouthful of sausage and roll.

'We've got to get the FBI to go deeper into her background.'

'Then the Yanks will cotton on.'

'There must be someone who can do it off the record.'

'Not before midnight tonight.'

Dorn put the last piece of *currywurst* into his mouth and licked the ketchup off his fingers. 'Got a tissue, chief?'

Kessler looked in the second drawer of his desk. The box of tissues was empty. 'No. Use some scrap.'

Dorn picked up a piece of paper lying next to the in-tray on Kessler's desk. 'This OK?'

'What is it?'

Dorn squinted down at a row of names and numbers. 'A list.'

'What list?'

'Burton, Lauch, Grauber . . . It's the names used by Ivan the Terrible.'

'Put it back in the basket. Use this.' Kessler tore the top sheet out of his spiral notebook and handed it to Dorn. But Dorn did not take it. He was staring at the list. Then he put it on the desk in front of Kessler. 'Look at this, chief. The last name. It's the same as the Russian on the Excursus committee, Andrei Serotkin.'

Kessler snatched the list. 'Shit,' he said. Then: 'Where's Gerasimov?'

'I don't know.'

'Call Grohmann . . . no, call Gerasimov's hotel. And get a picture of Serotkin from the Excursus people or the visa office.'

Inspector Hasenclever looked through the door. 'The boss says you're to get back to Tegel. They've found the American.'

'Where?'

'Trussed up in the boot of her car parked in a sidestreet near the warehouse.'

'Dead or alive?'

'Alive, but unconscious. They're bringing her round now.'

TWENTY

On their way from the Gothaerstrasse to Tegel, Kessler and Dorn picked up Nikolai Gerasimov from the Trebizond Hotel. Seated in the back of the car next to Dorn, he was told about the theft of the paintings.

'Ah,' said Gerasimov. 'That was what all the fuss was about this morning.'

'Do you think that Ivan the Terrible is the art historian, Serotkin?'

'Have you a photograph?'

Kessler showed Gerasimov the picture of a bearded man that had been faxed from the personnel department of the New German Foundation.'

'Possibly. Yes. I should say so. Orlov with a beard.'

'Orlov? Who is Orlov?'

Gerasimov looked confused. 'Because of the seriousness of the situation, I feel you should know that the real name of Ivan the Terrible is Andrei Orlov. He was responsible for the theft of the icons and the murder of the Maslyukovs, and although now a major criminal, he was at one time a member of a certain security agency of the former Soviet Union . . .'

'The KGB?'

'In a word, yes. The KGB. Of course, he was dismissed.'

'When?'

'Some time ago.'

'Because he was a thief?'

'More or less.'

'But he still has the training and the contacts?' asked Dorn.

'Certainly,' said Gerasimov. 'He was one of our best men.'

'If we had known this sooner,' said Kessler, 'the robbery might not have taken place.'

'It is only now,' said Gerasimov, 'that we have learned of what names he was using on his false documents. If you had listened to me yesterday – '

'Does he know that you know?' Kessler interrupted.

'Possibly not.'

'But possibly yes?'

'You have to understand, Inspector, that things in my country are somewhat confused at the present time.'

'I understand that. But does that mean that this man Orlov may be getting some back-up from the present security service of the Russian Federation?'

'Officially, no. Quite the contrary.'

'But unofficially?'

'Unofficially, of course. There are a number of people – a large number of people – in my country who are unhappy with the reforms. Unhappy, also, to have no power, no privileges and no currency.'

'Would he would have links with agents here in Germany?'

'Yes.'

'With former Stasi officers?'

'Undoubtedly.'

The method, the discipline – suddenly an understanding of what had happened began to take shape in Kessler's mind. 'Is it possible,' he said to Gerasimov, 'that someone in the Ministry of Culture in Moscow intercepted the request of the Excursus committee and sent Orlov posing as Serotkin to Berlin?'

'Quite possible, yes. It is also possible that no request was ever received in Moscow.'

'Can you look into that tomorrow?'

'Of course.'

'If there was no request to Moscow,' said Dorn, 'that would point a finger at the provincial ministry here in Berlin.'

'Yes,' said Kessler.

'What about Dr McDermott?' said Dorn.

Kessler turned to Gerasimov. 'Would this man Orlov be capable of seducing a woman to involve her in his scheme?'

'Of course. That would have formed part of his training.'

'He would be that cold-blooded?'

'Come on, chief,' said Dorn. 'Stubbing out cigarettes on a woman – that's cold-blooded. Fucking a good-looking Yank – that's a piece of cake.'

Rolf Becker, a detective constable, had brought a styrofoam cup of coffee for Francesca McDermott; sitting in an armchair in the office, she held it between her hands. Her blonde hair was dishevelled, her white shirt grubby, her green skirt creased. Encircling her wrists and ankles were stripes of blue bruises and broken flesh.

Kessler went up to her. 'Dr McDermott?'

She looked up. 'Yes?'

'I am Inspector Kessler of the Berlin criminal police.'

She showed no interest.

Kessler drew up a chair and sat facing her. 'I am sorry for what has happened. We have sent for a doctor.'

'I don't need a doctor.'

'Do you feel able to answer some questions?'

She looked up. 'What has happened?'

'The works of art have been stolen.'

She shook her head. 'I hoped it had been a dream but . . .' She looked down at her wrists.

'There has been a demand for a ransom of one hundred million dollars. If it is not paid, they may be destroyed.'

A look of alarm came into her eyes. 'Will it be paid?'

'I don't know. It is not for me to decide. My job is to find the paintings.'

She nodded.

'Do you know where they are?'

She shook her head. 'No.'

'Do you know who has taken them?'

She stared ahead into the middle distance. 'No.'

'Can you tell me what happened last night?'

She opened her mouth to speak but no words came out.

'Why did you come to the warehouse?'

'I was afraid . . .'

'Of what?'

'I don't know . . . that something would happen to the works of art.'

'Why?'

'Because Paul had said . . .' Her voice petered out.

'What?'

'He told me that he thought Stefi had worked for the Stasi.'

'Stefan Diederich? The minister?'

'Yes.'

'Who is Paul?'

'Paul Meissner. He was married to Sophie Diederich . . . before. He said that Stefi and Günter . . .' She waved her hand as if she had not the energy to go on.

'So you came here to the warehouse?'

'Yes.'

'What did you find?'

'No one. Nothing. The gate was open. The paintings had gone.'

'Why didn't you call the police?'

'I was going to . . .'

'What stopped you?'

'A man.'

'Serotkin?'

She looked away to avoid his eyes. 'Another man. He took me and tied me to that chair.' She pointed but did not look.

'Who was this man?'

'I don't know.'

'Was he a German?'

She shook her head. 'No. An Arab or a Turk.'

'And then?'

'He stood there watching me, smoking, and then . . .' Her face fell into her hands. She started sobbing.

Kessler rose to comfort her. As he put his hand on her shoulder, he noticed a red spot on her neck. 'Did you feel a pain in your neck?'

'Yes. He had a syringe. I thought I was going to die.'

Dark tobacco. Untipped cigarettes. And, as on Vera Maslyukov, the mark of a needle. 'Yes,' said Kessler. 'What is odd is that you are alive.'

'Was I poisoned?'

'I don't think so. A strong sedative, that was all.' He beckoned to Dorn. 'Where is the doctor?'

'I don't need a doctor,' said Francesca again.

'Are you sure?'

'Yes. I'm fine.'

Kessler started towards the telephone, then turned back to Francesca McDermott. 'Are you sure that you had never seen the man before?'

This time, she looked straight into his eyes. 'Quite sure.'

Kessler called Kommissar Rohrbeck from the warehouse director's office. 'It's Serotkin and possibly Diederich too.'

'The minister?'

'Some sort of scam by former Stasi and rogue KGB.'

'Can we prove it?'

'Not yet. But it's all falling into place.'

'We've put a call out for Serotkin.'

'We'll never find him. Our only hope is Diederich.'

'Very well. Put it to him. See what he says. But if you put a foot wrong, we may both lose our jobs.'

Kessler called the Prussian Ministry of Culture and was told that the minister had gone home. He turned to Francesca McDermott.

'How are you feeling?'

'OK.'

'If you feel up to it, I'd like you to accompany us to the Diederichs.'

She hesitated. 'Very well.'

★

Dorn sat in the front next to the driver, Kessler in the back between Gerasimov and Francesca McDermott. The car pushed through the traffic, its lights flashing, its siren loud.

Kessler turned to Francesca. 'What can you tell me about Andrei Serotkin?'

'He was my colleague on the Excursus committee.'

'Did you know him before?'

'No.'

'You met him only when you came to Berlin?'

'Yes.'

'Who introduced you?'

'I was told by Herr Diederich that he would be working on the exhibition. I met him when he came to the office.'

'I believe you lived in the same building?'

'Yes. We were both found flats by the Ministry of Culture.'

'Would you describe Dr Serotkin as a friend?'

'Yes.'

'Anything more?'

'Yes. We were lovers.'

'Would it surprise you, Dr McDermott,' asked Kessler, 'to learn that Andrei Serotkin is not the professor's real name?'

She thought for a moment, then answered: 'No, it would not surprise me.'

'Why not?'

'There was always something mysterious about him.'

'Part of his attraction, perhaps?'

'Perhaps.'

Kessler reached into an inside pocket of his jacket and took out a photograph.

Francesca glanced at Kessler, and in a tone of casual curiosity asked: 'If he was not called Andrei Serotkin, what is his real name?'

'Orlov,' said Gerasimov. 'Andrei Anatolyevich Orlov.'

'So he was always Andrei.'

'Yes, but that may be the only thing that Orlov and Serotkin had in common. He was not an art historian . . .'

'I guessed as much,' said Francesca.

'He was a criminal . . .'

She turned away.

'Known by the Russian police as Ivan the Terrible.'

'Why that name?'

Kessler handed her the black and white photograph. It was of the corpse of Vera Maslyukov. 'In 1991, a Russian couple, dealers in icons, were murdered here in Berlin. The husband, Grigori Maslyukov, was shot dead. The wife, Vera was tortured by being burned with cigarettes before she was killed by an injection of potassium cyanide into her neck. We have good reason to believe that this was done by Orlov, alias Andrei Serotkin.'

Francesca's face, already pale, turned white. 'That's impossible,' she whispered.

'I am afraid that there is now little doubt.'

Francesca was silent.

'Dr McDermott,' said Kessler. 'Before we go any further, there is one important question I must ask you, a question which perhaps only you can answer. You knew this Andrei Orlov. You knew him better than anyone else here in Berlin. From what you know of him, do you think it possible that, if the ransom is not paid, he will actually destroy the works of art of the Excursus exhibition?'

Francesca did not hesitate. 'Yes, yes he will.'

'And if the ransom *is* paid, will he return them?'

For a moment she did not reply. She was thinking, concentrating, remembering. Then she said: 'Yes. Yes, I think he will.'

'You are less certain?'

'No, I am certain.'

Kessler leaned forward to speak to Dorn. 'Radio the Kommissar. Tell them of Dr McDermott's answer.' He then turned back to Francesca. 'You are so sure, I presume, because he informed you of his intention?'

'Yes . . . That is to say, no, but he said things which, looking back, now make it clear.'

'That he meant to steal the paintings?'

'Or destroy them.'

'And you were to help him do this?'

'Help him? No.'

'It was your expert knowledge that enabled Serotkin to assemble

294

such valuable works of art; your reputation that reassured lenders in the United States, and where they led others followed. You recommended the fine art warehouse at Tegel owned by the fraudulent company, OZF, and you were present in the warehouse at the time they were stolen.'

Francesca nodded. 'I can see how it looks, but I never thought . . . I never realized . . .'

'That they were being assembled simply to be stolen?'

'How could I know that?'

'But we have been told, Frau Doktor, that you are the one who first suggested a major exhibition of modern art.'

'Me? No. I was asked to help organize it. That was all.'

'Then who first suggested it?'

'So far as I know, it was Stefan Diederich. The Excursus exhibition was his idea.'

The two detectives who had been tailing Stefan Diederich were waiting in their car on the Wedekindstrasse opposite the entrance to the Diederichs' flat. They reported that the children had left with an older woman that afternoon, and that the minister had only just returned.

Kessler, Dorn, Gerasimov and Francesca McDermott walked up the two flights of stairs and rang the bell at the Diederichs' door. It was opened by Stefan Diederich. He looked mildly surprised, almost annoyed, to find visitors at that hour in his home. 'Ah, Inspector! You have found Dr McDermott. Did she tell you that you would find the stolen paintings on the walls of my flat?' He beckoned them in and led them down the corridor to the living room. 'I am afraid that at this rate you are hardly going to save the state one hundred million dollars.'

Sophie Diederich got up from the sofa as they entered. Her face was wet and red from tears. Seeing Francesca, she crossed the room and, sobbing, fell into her arms. 'Stefi has just told me. The paintings have gone.'

'We have made more progress than you might suppose,' said Kessler to Stefan Diederich.

'You have found the paintings?'

'No. But we have found the thief.'

'Who is he?'

'Serotkin.'

'Serotkin? The Russian?' He laughed. 'Surely not.'

'His real name is Orlov. We believe he was responsible for the Maslyukov murders.'

Diederich frowned. 'I remember. Murder, I believe, and torture . . .'

'We have been after him for some time,' said Gerasimov.

Diederich turned. 'And who are you?'

'Gerasimov. Moscow militia.'

'Another Russian! I might have known. Well, you must forgive me, Herr Gerasimov, if what I say appears implicitly to denigrate your nation, but from my own long experience of Russians it seems unlikely that a Russian could single-handedly accomplish a crime which' – Stefan Diederich looked at his watch – 'in a few hours' time will earn a place in *The Guinness Book of Records*.'

'We know he had accomplices,' said Kessler.

'Good. Who were they?'

'That is what we were hoping to elicit from Dr McDermott . . .'

'Do you think *she* was an accomplice?'

'Don't you?'

'Have I ever suggested any such thing?'

'Clearly, if the same person suggested the exhibition and the OZF warehouse, that person becomes the prime suspect, at least as an accomplice.'

'Clearly.'

'You told us earlier today that the idea of the exhibition was first put to you by Dr McDermott.'

'As I recall . . .'

'It was not my idea, Stefi,' said Francesca. 'It was either Günter's or it was yours.'

Diederich looked puzzled. 'No, Francesca. You came to us, don't you remember? You came to supper here and suggested an exhibition of modern Russian art . . .'

'That's not true, Stefi.'

'That's certainly how I remember it, and Günter confirms it. Don't you remember? He was here too. And of course Sophie was here. You remember, don't you, Sophie? It was Francesca's idea.'

Stefan Diederich turned to look at his wife, but Sophie did not meet his eyes. She was now sitting like a sack on the sofa, her head slumped over her bosom. There were damp patches where her tears had fallen on the front of her dungarees.

'Sophie,' Diederich repeated slowly like a teacher talking to a child. 'Tell them what you remember. Francesca came to us, after ten years, to tell us that she was now a specialist in Russian experimental art, and that it would be wonderful if I could use my influence as the regional Minister of Culture to put on an exhibition that she could organize . . .'

Now Sophie looked up. 'What . . . did . . . you do to . . . Paul?' she asked between her sobs.

Diederich faltered, for the first time uncertain. 'To Paul? What has Paul to do with this?'

'To destroy him . . . that was why you said you loved me. You were under orders . . . and Günter brought him . . . and he saw . . . and he fled . . . and I did not even know . . .'

'Sophie! What are you saying? Have you seen Paul? What has he told you?'

'I saw Paul,' said Francesca. 'He told me. You worked for the Stasi. You seduced Sophie as part of their campaign . . .'

'But this is absurd,' said Stefan, turning to the three other visitors as if to appeal to them. But again he faltered. The actor had forgotten his lines.

'The important point at the moment,' said Kessler to Sophie, 'is to establish precisely who first had the idea for the Excursus exhibition.'

Sophie sniffed. 'It was him. It was Stefi, not Francesca. He invited her over. It was all his idea.'

A look of shock, and then of pain, came onto the face of Stefan Diederich. 'Sophie! How can you lie like that? I am your husband.'

'Paul was my husband,' shouted Sophie, 'and I helped to destroy him, and you cannot say that anyone lies because you do not know truth from falsehood, Stefi, you don't, you don't . . .'

'Sophie . . .' He spoke hoarsely, and looked at her with an expression of genuine anguish.

She faced away and suddenly Stefan Diederich appeared to pull himself together. He turned to Kessler and said: 'Her mind has clearly been poisoned against me by Dr McDermott. You have only to talk to Westarp. I shall call him and tell him to come over. He will confirm everything I have said.' Stefan Diederich went towards his study.

'I should like to ask some further questions,' said Kessler.

'Of course. Let me just call Westarp. I won't be a moment.' Stefan Diederich went into his study.

Kessler turned to Francesca. 'Dr McDermott. You will appreciate the urgency of the situation we are in. You know Orlov better than anyone else in Berlin. Can you remember anything . . . anything at all that he might have said at any time at all that would suggest where he has taken the paintings?'

Francesca pondered, then shook her head. 'No.'

'Did he give you an address or a telephone number where he could be contacted in Moscow?'

'No.'

'And before he left,' said Kessler, watching Francesca closely, 'did you make any arrangement to meet with or speak to Orlov again?'

Francesca hesitated. She looked at the photograph of Vera Maslyukov which she still held in her hand. She opened her mouth to answer; but before she did, the sound of a shot came from the study.

Dorn ran to the door and looked in. 'Shit.' He looked back at Kessler. 'Better call an ambulance, chief. The minister's blown a hole through his head.'

Half an hour before midnight, a conference call from the office of the Federal Chancellor in Bonn was put through to Kommissar Rohrbeck in Berlin. Present were Inspectors Hasenclever, Allerding and Kessler, and two men from the BfV, one of them Grohmann. First Rohrbeck spoke. He reported that the stolen works of art had not been found. It was now clear that the robbery had been planned and executed by a Russian called Andrei Orlov, posing as an art historian, Andrei Serotkin. He had suborned former members of the Stasi to assist him, among them the Prussian Minister of Culture Stefan Diederich.

'Diederich is dead?' The speaker had not introduced himself but the voice was unmistakably that of the Chancellor himself.

'Yes. He committed suicide.'

'It seems unbelievable that I was not warned that Diederich might be a traitor.'

Grohmann leaned forward. 'It was known that he might have collaborated with the Stasi but nothing could be proved. His file had disappeared from the Ruschestrasse.'

'And no one suspected that he had been working for the KGB?'

'No.'

'What about the other two – Westarp and Riesler?'

'They are in custody,' said Rohrbeck, 'and have been questioned. It is difficult to make out how much either knew of what Orlov planned to do. It is our judgement that neither knows the whereabouts of the stolen works of art.'

'And what do we know about Orlov?'

'Formerly an officer in the KGB,' said Grohmann, 'apparently dismissed after the coup. His father-in-law, Ivan Keminski, was at one time a top official in the Secretariat of the Central Committee. It is possible that the robbery is to raise funds for the Party now that it is no longer paid for by the state.'

A jumble of voices now came from the console as the Chancellor and his advisors conferred. Then, 'Kommissar Rohrbeck?'

'Herr Bundeskanzler?'

'Our decision rests on your answer to three questions. The first: can you recover the paintings before midnight tonight without paying the ransom?'

Rohrbeck did not hesitate. 'No.'

'The second: is it your view that if the ransom is not paid, the works of art will be destroyed?'

Rohrbeck looked at Kessler. Kessler nodded. Rohrbeck said: 'Yes.'

'The third question: is it your view that, if the ransom *is* paid, the works of art will be returned?'

This time Kessler looked less certain, but again he nodded.

'We think so, yes,' said Rohrbeck.

Once again, the sound of a subdued discussion came from the console. Then, 'Herr Kommissar Rohrbeck?'

'Yes.'

'The view taken here is that we have no choice. We shall instruct the Bundesbank to pay the ransom. But no word of this must ever reach the outside world.'

'Understood,' said Rohrbeck. Then he added, 'I am sorry.'

'You did your best. But please remain on hand. We will inform you' as soon as there is any word from Raskolnikov.'

The five men waited in the Kommissar's office: not all of them were needed, but none wanted to go home. Hasenclever went off to telephone Frankfurt from his office, dragging a police specialist on banking fraud out of his bed to question him on whether money paid into numbered bank accounts could be traced and subsequently recovered. The answers he received brought him back to Rohrbeck's office in a pessimistic frame of mind.

At dawn, Kessler made one of many trips down to the coffee machine on the floor below, returning with five cups on a tray. At seven, the new shift arrived; at eight thirty, the clerical workers, and at nine the first trolley with fresh coffee and buns. By then Grohmann and Allerding were both sleeping, slumped on their chairs.

Every now and then Rohrbeck's telephone would ring, or other officers would look through the door to bring different matters to the Kommissar's attention. Rohrbeck curtly dismissed them and gave orders that only a call from the Chancellery was to be put through.

At twenty to ten, the telephone rang. Rohrbeck snatched it up, then switched on the speaker. It was Bonn. Raskolnikov had made contact. A fax stated that five vans containing the Excurcus works of art were parked in the railway sidings at Tucheim, fifty miles north of Berlin.

TWENTY-ONE

The postponement of the opening of the Excursus exhibition meant that neither President von Weizsäcker nor the American ambassador was able to attend. The reason given was the technical difficulties of hanging so many works of art in so short a space of time. There were some rumours of more serious complications, and even a story in the Berlin *Morgenpost* linking the delay to the bankruptcy of the Omni Zartfracht company, ending with a speculation that some of the paintings had been mislaid for a short period of time.

This was immediately denied by the Excursus organizing committee and the Prussian Ministry of Culture, but it gave rise all the same to enquiries from other papers, and Francesca McDermott had to take some difficult calls from museum directors around the world. At one point, MOMA in New York requested the immediate return of their works, a demand that was only withdrawn after reassurances from the American Embassy in Bonn.

Despite the absence of the President of Germany and the Ambassador of the United States, the opening of the Excursus exhibition was a glittering occasion. The official ceremony, for political reasons, was in East Berlin, under the cupola in Schinkel's Old Museum. The Christian Democrat Minister President of the provincial government made a moving speech about the tragic death of his Minister of Culture, Stefan Diederich, killed when confronting an intruder in his flat. It enabled him to make several political points at the expense of the Social Democrats, and call for a change in Germany's liberal asylum laws that had led to an unprecedented influx of criminals posing as refugees.

Sophie Diederich was not present: she was in a clinic recovering from the shock of her husband's violent death. Dr Kemmelkampf had been summoned to Bonn. Dr Serotkin had been unable to get back from Moscow, and Günter Westarp was also absent, thought to be suffering from some kind of nervous exhaustion caused by the stress of mounting such a major exhibition. As a result, Francesca McDermott became the sole representative of the organizing committee and as such joint hostess with the Minister President's wife at the reception given after the official opening at the Old Museum on 13 July, and at the rather more exclusive lunch the next day at the New National Gallery in West Berlin for lenders, curators and diplomats. Only the French cultural attaché was unable to attend because it was his country's national holiday, the anniversary of the storming of the Bastille.

Despite all the horrors to which she had been subjected the week before, Francesca rose to the occasion. The show was stupendous: to see the work of so many great artists assembled from all over the world, to 'bathe in the form and colour of their inspired vision' (words from her introduction to the catalogue), and to receive, at the same time, the effusive praise of the world's most distinguished curators and critics who, a year before, would not have known her name; and (though this was only a minor consideration) to be able to wear for the first time some of the more elegant clothes that she had brought from Boston – all this was a good antidote to the discovery that her lover, Andrei Serotkin, was a murderer and her friend Stefan Diederich a Stasi spy.

Kessler, Dorn and the Russian detective, Gerasimov, were all present at the opening of Excursus at the Old Museum, and also at the lunch at the New National Gallery the next day. After the earlier débâcle which had cost the German exchequer one hundred million dollars, the governments at both national and provincial level had insisted upon unprecedented levels of security. The three detectives were wearing suits; they mingled with the guests. The two Germans, to Francesca, were unmistakably policemen: no one could possibly suppose that they had anything to do with art. Both looked uncomfortable in these surroundings and so Francesca went to talk to them in an attempt to put them at their ease.

'Well, Inspector,' she said to Kessler. 'What do you think of the exhibition?'

Kessler looked embarrassed. 'I was never one for modern art.'

'If I had a hundred million dollars . . .' began Dorn.

'You don't,' said Kessler, 'and you won't even have a job if you don't keep quiet.'

Francesca, who had been questioned half a dozen times by Kessler while hanging the Excursus exhibition, had become fond of the middle-aged Berlin inspector and his sergeant, Dorn. She knew that they knew, or at least suspected, that she could have told them more about Orlov, alias Serotkin, and she felt grateful that they showed no rancour. She had followed their investigation, and knew what little progress they had made. No prints had been found on the vans found at Tucheim; no admissions gained from Westarp or Riesler, or from suspects among former members of the Stasi's Dzherzhinksi brigade; and no word from Interpol about any Burton, Lauch, Grauber, Jeanneret or Serotkin.

'Any news from Russia?' Francesca now asked Kessler.

'They deny the existence of Serotkin.'

'And Orlov?'

'They say the evidence is insufficient to extradite him. A number of witnesses attest that he never left Moscow.'

'Do you still think that the paintings were hidden in a Russian base?'

'Yes. Almost certainly at Waldheim, a kilometre from Tucheim. But the Russians have refused us access and its senior officers have been sent home.'

'But not the detective,' said Francesca, nodding towards Gerasimov on the other side of the room.

'No, he's still here. He'll hang on until his allowance runs out.'

To Francesca, Nikolai Gerasimov seemed even more out of place than the two German policemen. She had taken against him from the first moment she had seen him in Kessler's car. He had thick, fleshy lips and a pockmarked face but clearly thought he was irresistible to women. On the pretext that he was protecting the security of the works of art from Russian collections, he had loitered round the galleries during the hanging, his eyes always on Francesca, never on the paintings. He followed her wherever she went, and one evening even had the audacity to ask her out to dinner. Francesca had said she was much too busy. 'Perhaps after the opening?' he had asked, to which she had replied with all the disdain she could muster: 'Perhaps.'

She should have said no. The possibility of a date some time in the future had encouraged him to pester her. He had followed her from gallery to gallery, watching her every movement with lecherous eyes, popping up at odd moments to offer to lift a painting, move a ladder or drive her home in his hired car. Francesca recognized that the revulsion she felt towards Gerasimov might have had something to do with her confused feelings about that other Russian, Andrei Serotkin. Gerasimov's vulgarity made her wonder whether she had not been mistaken about the nobility of Serotkin. Was it possible that he had only seduced her to involve her in his plot? That seemed unlikely because she had always thought that it was she who had seduced him. But it was possible, as Sophie had suggested, that Andrei had hired the Turks to pretend to rape her, simply so that he could present himself in an heroic role. 'How convenient, when you think of it,' she had said to Francesca, 'that he happened to be running past at the time! I tell you, Francesca, if he was once in the KGB, then he would be capable of anything. They are trained to seduce American women!'

Sophie had said this the morning after Stefi's suicide when she was still in a state of shock, and might have been unconsciously looking for a scapegoat upon which to vent her mixture of grief and rage. Francesca was there, in her kitchen, in the flat on the

Wedekindstrasse, and it was Francesca who had been the bringer of the bad news that had set off the chain of events ending in Stefi's death.

When Stefi had asked her to back up his lie about who had first suggested the exhibition, Sophie had impetuously told the truth. Why? Because she had realized, on the spur of the moment, that if he could lie so easily about something as big as that, then he could have lied about everything else; and suddenly the whole mystery of why Paul had never come home from the clinic was solved. The monstrous thought that all Stefi's loving words and gestures over the past decade had been simply to comply with a Stasi controller's command made her want to kill him, and at that moment, in front of Kessler, telling the truth was an easy and obvious way to take revenge. Stefi's eyes – the look of real anguish that had appeared as though through two holes in his mask – had confounded her. Perhaps he *had* loved her after all? She had been about to rise and follow him into his study when she had heard the shot. Now she would never know.

It was for this reason, a perfectly understandable reason, that over breakfast the next morning Sophie had not only told this story, but had done her best to persuade Francesca that Andrei Serotkin, too, had been insincere. 'It was the system. There were so many lies, and lies within lies, that it was quite impossible for any of them to be sincere.'

Francesca had agreed. It seemed prudent to seem to accept that she had been used. But, from the moment she had regained consciousness in the OZF warehouse, her swollen wrists and ankles in great pain, her body aching in every joint, the memory foremost in her mind was not the dead look in the eyes of the Chechen, but Andrei Orlov's smile.

She had realized at once that if she was still living it was because Andrei had spared her life, and intuitively she understood all that this implied. He had spared her because he loved her, and because he loved her he would spare the paintings too. That was why she had been able to assure Kessler that Orlov would keep his side of the bargain.

Truth is remembering. He who has no memory has no life. Why had he said this? What was she to remember? Their words at the

305

memorial. But what had they said? He had asked her to choose between him and the paintings. She had chosen him. He had said they would return there on Bastille Day and, if her answer was the same, would never be parted again.

Today was Bastille Day. Would he keep the assignation? Reason told her that he would not. He was now one of the world's most wanted men. With one hundred million dollars, and a safe haven in Russia, it was unlikly that he would linger in Western Europe, let alone return to Berlin. But her intuition argued otherwise.

It was only a short walk from the New National Gallery to the Soviet Memorial. Smiling, Francesca excused herself from the group of admiring dignitaries, critics and curators that surrounded her and made for the ladies' cloakroom. She went down the flight of stairs, past the bookshop and restaurant, through to the administrative office and out to the car park by the back door.

She did not hurry. She walked between the Philharmonia Hall and the New State Library, garish modern yellow buildings that lay between the gallery and the Tiergarten, the second built close to what remained of the Wall. She crossed into the Tiergarten, and took the path that led to the Soviet Memorial. Her mind was calm and reflective as if she was indeed going to the memorial to honour the Russian dead. It was warm. Young people lay on the grass in the shade of the silver-barked birch trees. Would he be there, she wondered, or was he now in Russia sitting beneath the branches of just such birch trees as these?

She came to the wide boulevard leading from the Brandenburg Gate to the Goddess of Victory. On the other side was the war memorial; beyond that, shrouded by trees, the Reichstag. Francesca waited for a break in the traffic, then crossed the road. A cluster of Scandinavian tourists were looking up at the tanks and the cannon and the great bronze statue of a Soviet soldier.

Francesca stood there, quite still, remembering what Andrei had asked her a month before, and the answer she had given with no inkling of what the question involved. Now, as she put the question again, in the full knowledge of what he had done, and suspecting that at the outset he had been planning the destruction of all the works of art, she realized that the answer she would give would be the same. Life, her life, did mean more to her than all that dead art, and even if Andrei was a murderer, a torturer and a thief, she was committed to him for better, for worse. He was a man who loved his country and was tormented by its fall from power. He had done terrible things: the image of the tortured woman remained imprinted in Francesca's mind; but for her sake, he had spared the works of art. If she was given the chance, she had no doubt, the savage Muscovite could be tamed and ennobled by her love.

From the group of tourists behind her, someone stepped forward and in a quiet voice said her name. 'Francesca.'

She turned but at first did not recognize the bespectacled man.

'I did not know if you would remember,' he said.

Now she saw who it was.

'Or that you would come if you did.'

She smiled. Tears came into her eyes. She longed to embrace him but dared not.

'Are you all right?' he asked.

'I'm fine.'

'It was terrible, I realize, but it was the only way. The other man . . .'

Smiling, she interrupted him. 'So it is grey, after all.'

'What is grey?'

'Your hair.'   .

'No, it's brown. He took off the rimless glasses as if to show her what he was really like. 'But it could be black again, if you like, and I could grow another beard.'

'I like you . . .' She raised her hand and touched his cheek. 'I like you any how.'

Her gesture, and words so softly spoken, led him to blush and then look at her with an expression of both gratitude and relief. 'We cannot be long,' he said. 'You may have been followed and I would not want them to think – '

She shook her head. 'I slipped away.'

He looked over her shoulder into the crowd. 'Even so . . .' He turned, and together they walked a few paces in the direction of the Goddess of Victory. 'I came back to explain – '

'You don't have to.'

'I love Russia.'

'I know.'

'I felt that it was the only way.'

She hesitated, then asked: 'Was it your idea, to torture that poor woman, or were you ordered to do it?'

'I was ordered to do what had to be done to recover the money.'

'Was it *you* who did it?'

'No. It was the Chechen. But I told him to do it, and I was there.'

'Did you mean to destroy the paintings?'

A flash of hatred came from his eyes. 'Yes. That was to be for my personal satisfaction.' The memory passed. He smiled. 'But then there was you. You loved the paintings and I . . . well, I loved you.'

By way of reply, Francesca moved up against him and covertly took hold of his hand.

'I have little to offer you, Francesca. Here in the West, I shall always be a fugitive. Even in Russia, my future will depend upon how history unfolds. I shall be poor: all the money has gone to the cause. It is a wretched prospect when compared to the life that awaits you back in Boston.'

'No life awaits me back in Boston. You are now my life.'

'Francesca.' The sound of her name was a cry of joy.

'Can we live by Lake Baikal,' she asked, 'like a couple in one of Rasputin's stories?'

'Of course.'

'In a wooden house surrounded by birch trees?'

'Protected from the outside world by the vastness of the forests and the infinity of the skies.'

She heard a sound from somewhere behind him like that of a ball hitting a bat. As she looked over his shoulder to see what had caused it, he moved forward and for an instant Francesca thought that he was taking her into his arms; but his arms remained limp and his eyes turned to look up at the sky. His mouth opened. A gurgle came from his throat. He began to fall. She held him up. Over his shoulder, she saw the other Russian, Gerasimov. In his hand was a revolver. On his face was a grin. He came closer, poked his gun into the nape of Andrei Orlov's neck, fired a second shot, stepped back, and ran off towards the Russian consulate on the other side of the Brandenburg Gate.

ACKNOWLEDGEMENTS

For the background to this novel, I should like to acknowledge my debt to *The Great Experiment: Russian Art, 1863–1922* by Camilla Gray (Thames and Hudson, 1962) and *KGB Today. The Hidden Hand* by John Barron (Hodder & Stoughton, 1984). Passages from Ivan Turgenev's *On the Eve* (William Heinemann, 1895) were translated by Constance Garnett and are reprinted by permission of A. P. Watt Ltd on behalf of The Executors of the Estate of Constance Garnett. The poem 'My Beloved Will Arrive At Last', translated by George Reavy. is from *Desire to Desire* by Yevgeny Yevtushenko, Copyright © 1976 by Doubleday, a division of Bantam Doubleday Dell Publishing Group, Inc., and is reprinted by permission of Doubleday, a division of Bantam Doubleday Dell Publishing Group, Inc. Extracts from Goethe's *Faust Part One* (Penguin Classics, 1949), translaed by Philip Wayne, are Copyright © the Estate of Philip Wayne, 1949, and are reprinted by permission of Penguin Books. The translations of Mayakovsky's poem 'Left March' is by Herbert Marshall in *Mayakovsky and his Poetry* (The Pilot Press, 1942); of Alexander Pushkin's *Eugene Onegin* by Charles Johnson (privately printed,